The Illustrated
Encyclopedia of
MILITARY
VEHICLES

The Illustrated Encyclopedia of MILITARY VEHICLES

IAN V. HOGG AND JOHN WEEKS

Quantum
Books

A QUANTUM BOOK

This book is produced by
Quantum Publishing Ltd.
6 Blundell Street
London N7 9BH

Copyright © MCMLXXX
Quarto Publishing Limited.

This edition printed 2003

ISBN 1-86160-731-8

QUMEMLV

Printed in Singapore by
Star Standard Industries Pte. Ltd.

PHOTOGRAPHIC CREDITS

The publishers are extremely grateful to Peter
Chamberlain and Christopher Foss for providing so
many of the photographs used in this book. They
would also like to thank Michael Taylor; Trevor
Wood; John Watney; Jon Moore; G. A. Usher;
MacClancy Press Ltd; Mary Evans Picture Library;
The Mansell Collection; The Imperial War
Museum; Bovington Tank Museum; Editions
Robert Laffont, Paris; Soldier Magazine; The
Ministry of Defence; The Central Office of
Information; The US Army; The British Museum
Photographic Library; Ian Hogg; John Weeks.
USA Official; Establishment Cinematographique
des Armes, Paris; Photo Research Agency.

CONTENTS

Below F. R. Simms demonstrates his Quadricycle Maxim Gun Carrier at Roehampton in 1898. *Top right* The traction engine of Fowler's Armoured Road Train sent to South Africa in 1902. *Bottom right* A contemporary drawing of the Boydell engine with its 'footed wheel'.

THE EARLY YEARS

IN THE 1890s, military transportation was still largely dependent upon the horse, and the vocabulary of stores of any army was replete with such descriptions as 'Wheels, Second Class, "C" No. 35', or 'Whips, Driving', or 'Carts, Forage', or 'Wagons Bread and Meat' or even 'Traces Harness, Machine Gun Nearside'. Nevertheless, mechanical traction was beginning to make itself felt in military circles, a wedge which had been slowly making its way into position for almost 50 years and which was to be hammered home with dramatic speed in the first two decades of the coming century.

During the Crimean War the difficulty of hauling supplies through the mud-wallows which passed as roads in the theatre of war led the British War Office to purchase a steam traction engine and send it out to the Crimea. The engine selected was a Boydell, using a peculiar 'footed wheel' which had performed well on ploughland in agricultural use and was expected to overcome the mud problem. The footed wheel was a wheel which had large, flat wooden blocks pivoted to its circumference, and these blocks distributed the weight of the wheel over a greater area of ground and prevented the engine from sinking in soft going. Whilst reasonably successful on farmland, it proved rather less adequate in the liquid mud of the Crimea; while the engine itself was able to proceed, the train of wagons it was supposed to draw was not provided with the footed wheel and thus sank up to the axles and proved too much of a burden for the engine to move. While this problem was being debated the campaign came to an end and the Boydell engine was shipped back to England and disposed of.

In 1858 the Royal Artillery obtained a Bray steam engine, an eight-tonner, which they tested as a possible gun-towing machine. Various tests were carried out, towing as many as three 68-pounder guns plus a number of wagons, and the testing committee reported that 'when more perfectly constructed the engine may be suitable for use in India' and that 'the engine should be employed in the Royal Arsenal in order to gain useful experience for improved construction of such engines'.

The Franco-Prussian War of 1870 brought home to Europeans (Americans had already learned the lesson during the Civil War) that railways had become a vital factor in modern military strategy

and that mobility of an army could be vastly enhanced by intelligent use of them. The German Army's triumphant advance had been facilitated by their ability to mobilize rapidly and concentrate troops by means of railway lines, and the French defence had been equally aided by the movement of bodies of troops by rail. When the German Army flowed across northern France towards Paris, the supply trains began to feel the strain once the advance moved away from convenient railways, and the Siege of Paris was conditioned by the problem of supplying the siege batteries with ammunition all the way from Germany by means of convoys of horsed wagons. The German Army bought two Fowler steam ploughing engines in England and sent them to the supply columns in France; they were not the ideal machines for the task, being of 20 tons weight and burdened with their ploughing attachments, but they performed some useful work. One notable feat was the removal of a railway engine and tender from Nanteuil to Trilport to avoid a blown-up tunnel and an uncompleted bridge, and thus place some motive power on to an engine-less length of railway line. More usually the engines were used to draw trains of wagons on the roads, loaded with ammunition, forage and other stores, from railheads to field distribution points.

The Germans' success with these vehicles seems to have been the incentive which led other armies to look at mechanical traction. In 1873 the Italians began buying steam road engines, and within three years they had 60 in use; but in 1883 they abandoned them entirely, claiming that they were too complicated, demanding too highly skilled men, who were not readily available in the Army, and were too much of a repair burden. In

TECHNOLOGY AHEAD OF ITS TIME

The fifteenth century was as much preoccupied with warfare as our own, and its greatest creative genius did not hesitate to turn his inventiveness to the technology of destruction. The siege, the defence of city or castle, provided the typical military problems. Here, Leonardo devised strategies such as diverting rivers, to defend Venice, or flood Pisa. His speculations went well outside conventional bounds. The flails of the scythed car *below* are turned by a system of gears. The armoured car *bottom* was well ahead of its time. Driven by hand or horse it had a covering of heavy wooden beams and a gap at the top for firing.

Top left Davidson-Duryea three-wheeled car with Colt machine-gun. *Bottom* Davidson's Steam Car of 1900 with its crew of cadets.

1875 the French bought two Aveling engines from England and began experiments in towing artillery. In 1876 the Russians bought an Aveling and a Fowler and found them so good that they bought ten more – make unspecified – and put them to good use in the Russo-Turkish War of 1878, among other things using them to bring up the siege artillery in front of Plevna.

From then on the use of steam engines proliferated throughout Europe and it would be repetitious to detail all the trials and demonstrations recorded in military journals of the period. The first major use in war came with the British Army in South Africa in 1899; 15 engines were sent out for traction purposes, followed shortly by two ploughing engines complete with ploughs, intended to be used for the rapid throwing up of breastworks. This latter task was one which always went

THE GUN MEETS THE PETROL ENGINE

When the French manufacturers of steam carriages De Dion and Bouton began to experiment with petrol engines Simms followed their progress with interest. In 1899 they produced an engine-driven quadricycle which Simms felt had potential for conversion to military purposes. He welded a tripod to the forward section of the frame so that a Maxim machine-gun could be mounted. Ammunition for the gun was held in a tray beneath the tripod.

The photograph below probably pulled in the crowds but in practice the manoeuvrability of the vehicle must have left a lot to be desired.

Simms Quadricycle without and with Maxim Gun.

down well at demonstrations, but there seems to be no record of it ever being done in earnest; when breastworks are needed, it is not usually possible (or advisable) to wait for a steam engine to make its leisurely way to the position.

But before the South African War had

begun there were signs that the steam traction engine might have a rival. The internal combustion engine had made an appearance and in 1896 the French Army had used some Jourdan 'oil motor engines' in the annual manoeuvres. In 1898 the Austrian Army employed motor tractors to tow artillery in hilly country during their annual exercises, and in the same year Mr. F. R. Simms, a well-known English motoring enthusiast, brought about the first combination of the petrol engine and military firepower when he demonstrated his Simms Quadricycle at Roehampton (see box above).

The Simms machine was widely publicized and appears to have spurred others on to design 'war cars' of one sort or another. Later in 1898 Major R. P. Davidson, commandant of the Northwestern Military and Naval Academy at Lake Geneva, Wisconsin (not, in spite of its title, an official establishment but one of many private 'military' schools commonplace at that time in the USA) designed a three-wheeled car which was built by the Charles P. Duryea Company of Peoria. This vehicle mounted an M1895 Colt 'Potato-Digger' machine gun

Left Simms' War Car of 1902 showing the shaped protective plating and two Maxim guns. *Upper right* The Charron Girardot et Voight armoured gun carrier of 1900 with the gun in open barbette. *Lower right* The Erhardt anti-balloon gun of 1909. *Bottom right* The Charron Girardot et Voight armoured car built for the Russian Army.

over the front wheels in a similar manner to Simms' design, but it was large enough to accommodate a three-man machine gun crew in addition to the driver. The gun could be operated while the vehicle was moving and, on arrival at its destination, the crew could dismount with the gun and go into action while the car returned to cover. The Davidson idea of divorcing the firepower task from the transportation function produced a more practical idea – or would have done had the vehicle been more reliable. Contemporary accounts suggest that Davidson and his cadets spent more time mending the car than driving it, and in the following year he had it rebuilt into a four-wheeler, which proved more reliable. He then designed a steam-powered car along the same lines and had two of these built in the Academy workshop in 1900, using them for some years thereafter in cadet manoeuvres. But no official interest was roused.

In 1900 also, a steam car was built in Russia; little is known of it except that it was built by an engineer named Lutski to the orders of the Imperial Artillery

Commission, and it is probable that it was primarily intended as a gun tractor. In any event, trials showed that, like most steam vehicles, it was overweight and underpowered, and the experiment was abandoned.

By this time the automobile was no longer a curiosity, especially in France, and the French Army were probably the first to adopt motor cars for transportation of staff officers. Fired by this military interest, Charron Girardot et Voight, makers of the successful CGV racing cars, constructed an armoured gun carrier by placing an armoured barbette or tonneau at the rear of a touring car chassis and providing it with a Hotchkiss machine gun. Two men manned the gun, a driver controlled the vehicle and an officer supervised. The Army bought the car and, after using it in the 1901 exercises, sent it to Morocco, where it vanished into obscurity.

The early years of the century saw the motor vehicle adopted in increasing numbers as a commercial carrier as motor lorries increased in numbers and armies slowly began to purchase them. They were

not cheap, however, and the prospect of financing a full-scale re-equipping with motor trucks could not be contemplated. For many years, though, there had been a variety of subsidy schemes, whereby horse owners promised to furnish horses to the army in the event of mobilization in return for an annual retainer, and this system was extended to motor vehicles. The Germans appear to have originated this, introducing a system under which commercial operators of trucks could receive a grant of £150 to assist in the purchase of the vehicle, followed by an annual subsidy of £60 per annum for four years. The condition was that if, during the subsidy period, the army mobilized, then the truck was taken for military use. If no mobilization occurred, then the operator was in pocket and, presumably, receptive to the suggestion that he might buy another on the same terms. By the beginning of 1914 the German Army had 825 such subsidized trucks available to it and, together with wholly-owned military trucks, could provide five transport columns each of 10 vehicles for each of the 25 regular Army

Corps. (*Jahrbuch für Deutsche Armee und Marine,* February 1914.) In the same month the *Kriegstechnische Zeitschrift* announced that there were 3,213 motor tractors of 10–40hp and 513 of over 40hp available to be requisitioned in Germany in the event of war, and a 1913 census showed 7,700 heavy trucks and 50,000 cars and light trucks in use in Germany.

Unfortunately, few of these vehicles were of much use away from a surfaced road; the narrow high-pressure tyres of the day were useless on soft ground. This was highlighted by a 1913 report that the Italian Army had adapted a motor tractor for their new 15cm howitzer, but only for road movement; a team of horses accompanied the howitzer and took over the haulage once the road was left behind.

While the commercial vehicle had been gaining ground, one or two suggestions had appeared for more specifically military designs and, particularly, designs incorporating armour protection. As early as 1896 a Mr. E. J. Pennington proposed a war car which was to use a four-wheeled chassis surmounted by a 'bathtub' armoured body above which stood two shielded Maxim guns on pedestal mounts. This idea got no further than the drawing board, but in 1902 F. R. Simms appeared once again with a vehicle resembling the Pennington design, having the same 'bathtub' superstructure open at the top with guns on pedestal mountings. Five men operated this vehicle; one in the centre drove it, two manned a Maxim one-pounder 'pom-pom' at one end of the body, and two others each manned a Maxim machine gun at the other end. Pro-

tected by 6.3mm (¼-in) armour, Simms' War Car weighed 6½ tons, was 8.5m (28ft) long and could move at 14km/hr (9mph). But in spite of demonstrating the car at various motor shows in 1902-3, Simms could raise no interest in the design and he eventually scrapped it.

The Russian Army, having had no success with Engineer Lutski, now called upon the French firm of Charron Girardot et Voight to inspect its armoured gun carrier, but turned it down. The Russian General Staff then laid down a brief specification, indicating what they thought was desirable, passed it to Charron Girardot et Voight, and asked for 36 armoured cars to be made. The resulting vehicle might be said to be the prototype of all the armoured cars which followed; it was a four-wheeled boxy

structure of armour plate surmounted by a revolving turret on the roof in which was mounted a Maxim machine gun, its water-jacket protected by an armoured trough. Steel channel-section girders were strapped along the sides, from where they could be quickly removed and thrown across a ditch to allow the vehicle to pass across. Weighing just over three tons and driven by a 30bhp engine, the Charron was a practical vehicle; the first was delivered to Russia in 1904 and was used for riot control in St. Petersburg, but for some unknown reason the Russians now repudiated the contract and refused to take more. The second car, already built, was bought by the French Army, and no further cars were made.

Probably stimulated by reports of the Charron car, the Austro-Daimler company began looking at armoured car design in late 1903. Their design was of the same general form, a high-set bonnet concealing the engine, with a square cab for the driver and a box body with revolving turret on top, mounting a Skoda machine gun. The driver could see through slits in the armour or, when conditions allowed, could elevate his seat so as to raise his head through a hatch on the cab top, allowing him all-round vision. The Austro-Daimler weighed some 3½ tons, could move at 45km/hr (28mph), and was used by the Imperial Army in the 1905 and 1906 manoeuvres with some success, though no more were bought.

During the next few years one or two other armoured car designs appeared, all of which followed the Charron design. But at this same time a new problem was presenting itself to the military – the heavier-than-air machine and the airship. Both these had reached a point in their development where they were being contemplated for military use, primarily as reconnaissance machines, and the question of air defence arose. The question had, in fact, arisen before; in 1870 the French used balloons to escape from besieged Paris and the German Army had produced a number of 25mm rifles mounted on light carts, the idea being that several equipages were dispersed around the perimeter of Paris and as soon as a balloon was seen ascending the guns turned out like a fire brigade and rushed to intercept its flight. The same principle was now applied using motor vehicles. In 1909, at

the Frankfurt International Exhibition, the two major gunmakers of Germany, Krupp and the Rheinische Metalwaren und Maschinenfabrik (who later adopted the shorter form Rheinmetall by which they are still known), both showed 'motor balloon guns'. In the Krupp design a 75mm gun was mounted on the rear of a 50hp truck, capable of a speed of 45km/hr (28mph). Krupp's greatest problem was to reduce the recoil blow on the chassis when the gun was fired, and this was done by an ingenious system known as differential recoil. Briefly, what happened was that the gun was pulled back against its recoil springs, held back, and loaded; it was then released, to run forward in its mounting, propelled by the spring. A fraction of a second before it reached the fully-forward position, the gun was fired, so that the recoil force had first to arrest the moving mass, then reverse it. This reduced the recoil blow to about one-quarter of its normal force, bringing it within the capability of the chassis to sustain it.

The Rheinmetall design was a 50mm gun mounted in a turret on an armoured car. A contemporary report described it as follows: 'To protect the car, its equipment and gun detachment from hostile fire it is armoured throughout, including the wheels, with 3mm of nickel steel. The entrance, the peep-hole for the driver, and the embrasures in the sides can all be closed and the forward part of the car shut down. The gun with its armoured turret can be revolved on a turntable, and the embrasures are provided with shutters.' There was some debate as to the virtue of armour in this context; it seemed unlikely that the gun would be under fire from the balloon or airship at which it was firing, and there seemed little likelihood of it operating so far forward as to come under fire. An alternative reason advanced was that the addition of the armour was simply there to add weight and make the vehicle more sturdy to absorb the recoil of the 5cm gun without having to indulge in Krupp's differential recoil solution.

Whatever the truth of the matter,

THE INVENTORS

The main enthusiasm of Mr. F. R. Simms *top left* was motoring, but this led him to the first combination of petrol engine and military firepower. He may have inspired Davidson *top right* to design his three-wheeled car mounting a detachable machine-gun. It was Swinton *bottom left* who saw the need for armoured tracked vehicles, and it was his persuasion which worked on responsible bodies such as the Landships Committee. Wilson *bottom right* designed the transmission for early tanks. His improved versions were on all British WWII tanks.

Rheinmetall also displayed a half-armoured car mounting the same 5cm gun. This resembled an ordinary touring car with the gun mounted on a pedestal behind the driver. This reduced the weight by a considerable amount, though without requiring any modification to the recoil system. Strictly speaking these vehicles represent the earliest attempts at self-propelled guns rather than armoured cars, but they were of considerable interest at the time and they demonstrated that it was possible to mount something heavier than a machine gun on to a motor chassis and get away with it.

But for all the clever designs, the sol-diers were highly resistant. In 1905 the US Chief of Staff General Miles proposed converting five cavalry regiments to armoured cars, a suggestion which upset the horsemen and caused such violent opposition that it was eventually abandoned. Having just upset the Ordnance Department by suggesting that their sea-coast gun carriage designs were obsolete by European standards, Miles had thus alienated about half the US Army, and after that he was more careful in the ideas he advanced. At much the same time the Russian Army had used some motor cars in manoeuvres, and the complaint was heard that the 'noise and smell were intolerable' and that horses refused to pass the vehicles.

The most telling point in favour of the horse was, of course, that the motor vehicle was still only useful on a surfaced road, and by the end of the first decade of the century this disadvantage was sufficiently marked to cause a number of inventors to look into ways of making the motor into a cross-country vehicle. It will be recalled that the Boydell engine used in the Crimean War had a footed wheel, which spread the weight on soft ground, though not well enough, and there had been a number of improvements and variations on that theme. In 1886 the Applegarth tractor had been patented, a steam tractor which used an endless track around its wheel and which extended forward to an idler out of contact with the ground. One advantage of this design was that it allowed the machine to clamber across uneven ground. A more practical design was the Batter tractor of 1888, patented in the USA. This used endless tracks in long contact with the ground, and was driven by two steam engines, one driving each track.

In 1908 the Hornsby company of Grantham developed a tracked tractor in which an oil engine drove a sprocket which propelled an endless track, giving excellent cross-country performance. Hornsby's demonstrated this at the Royal Review in 1908, and in the following year they entered the machine in a War Office trial for cross-country tractors, which it won handsomely, collecting the first prize of £1,000 plus a bonus of £180 for 'general excellence'. But that was as far as it went, and no orders came in to Hornsby's factory. In the end, in order to

Below The Hornsby-Ackroyd tractor of 1907 which successfully competed in the War Office trials but did not win any military orders.

recoup some of their development costs, Hornsby's sold their patented track system to an American company, the Holt Tractor Company of Stockton, California. In the Western states of America there was plenty of scope for the caterpillar tractor (as it had come to be known) and within a short time Holt's were busy producing 70hp and 45hp tractors for sale throughout the USA and then in Europe.

In 1911 a young Austrian officer, Lieutenant Gunther Burstyn, saw a Holt tractor at work; he was already familiar with armoured cars and their limitations, and he saw in the Holt track a method of overcoming the armoured car's cross-country problem. He set about designing a suitable vehicle, and in October 1911 submitted drawings to the Austro-Hungarian War Department.

After three months' deliberation, they returned the drawings; a clever idea, they said, and the young officer was to be commended upon his ingenuity. Would he, perhaps, be kind enough to build one so that the idea could be tested? At his own expense, of course. Not having that kind of money, Burstyn could not build one, nor could he interest a commercial manufacturer in the idea; he sent his drawings to the German War Department, which turned the idea down. He then tried to patent it, but this was refused on the grounds that the vehicle was driven by a petrol engine and this method of propulsion had already been patented, while the rest of his design was too impractical to be worth patenting. Disillusioned, Burstyn abandoned his design; he later turned up with another brilliant idea, a short-barrelled muzzle-loading mortar which could be used to fire small bombs out of trenches. They didn't think much of that one either.

At much the same time, across the world, a young Australian civil engineer, L. A. de Mole, was faced with the problem of moving heavy loads across rough country, and he designed a tracked vehicle for the task. Having done so, he was struck by the possibility of military applications of the design and sent drawings to the War Office in London in 1912. They were returned, with a letter stating that the War Office was not interested in experimenting with 'chain rail machines'. De Mole's design was of considerable interest, since he suggested steering it by 'bowing' the tracks; the suspension wheels were mounted on pivoted sub-assemblies at each end of the tracks, while the whole assembly had sufficient play to allow the pivoting unit to pull the track round into a bend, round which the vehicle would steer. It was several years before this idea appeared again.

Below An early tank, painted in disruptive camouflage and stowing the unditching beam and rails on the roof. *Right* Lanchester armoured cars in Belgium, 1915.

THE
FIRST WORLD WAR

IN SPITE OF SEVERAL INVENTORS attempting to interest various military authorities in different types of cross-country machines, when war broke out in 1914 the armies involved had little to show except a scattering of commercial trucks and motor cars and a handful of prototype armoured cars, most of which were, by that time, somewhat elderly. The first few months of war called for little revision of this situation; the horsed troops performed as they had always done and mobility appeared satisfactory. The motor vehicle made some impact in the famous 'Taxis of the Marne' incident, when the Paris taxis were commandeered to rush troops out to stem the German advance on the city, but this, obviously, was an unusual event; had more notice been given, then the poilus would have marched in the traditional and normal fashion – and probably would have arrived too tired to fight. But at the end of 1914, when the 'race to the sea' was run and the trench lines ran from the Channel to the Alps, things began to take on a different hue.

Upon the outbreak of war, of course, the various subsidy schemes had been called due; this brought about 1,000 trucks into the British Army, probably twice that number to the French and an estimated 30,000 vehicles of all kinds to the German Army, though this figure was made up of subsidy vehicles and outright

impressment. Once the war settled into a siege operation these trucks began to demonstrate the advantages of mechanical over horsed traction, and all the combatant armies began increasing their holdings as fast as they could. For Germany and Austria this meant building, while Britain and France not only built but were also able to purchase from America. Not only the numbers but also the types of vehicle expanded beyond pre-war comprehension; most armies had, in the hope of standardization, classified vehicles into broad groups – passenger cars, light trucks (to 1½ ton) and heavy trucks (3 ton). But this neat division was soon shattered by, firstly, the influx of civilian vehicles, which did not fit neatly into these groups, and secondly the sudden demand for specialized vehicles – petrol tankers, ambulances, gun carriages, gun tractors, field kitchens, mobile dental surgeries, searchlight carriers, workshop trucks and innumerable others – of which some were variations on existing vehicles while others were new from the wheels up.

While the soft-skinned vehicles began to proliferate, there was also a rise in the armoured car field. The first armoured cars to see action were a number of Minerva and SAVA touring cars, which Belgian officers had sheathed in boiler-plate, mounted Maxim guns, and used to hold up the advance of the German

cavalry units with some success. Late in August 1914 a Royal Naval Air Service squadron was sent to Ostend in order to assist the operations of the Naval Brigade, and with it went 18 assorted motor cars, primarily intended to go out and rescue aviators who had to make forced landings. Some of these landings were uncomfortably close to the enemy, and after one or two incidents where the cars came under fire from forward German troops, two of the cars were given boiler-plate protection. In September Mr. Winston Churchill authorized the provision of a hundred cars fitted with machine guns, and, after some experiments with boiler plate armouring on the spot, it was decided to build proper armoured bodies on to the chassis in Britain. Rolls-Royce, Lanchester, Talbot and Delaunay-Belleville car chassis were obtained and a more-or-less standard form of body devised. The bonnet and driver's compartment were protected by steel plate, and a revolving turret carrying a Maxim gun was mounted on the roof. The rear section of the chassis was left as a flat-bed truck so that loads could be carried. In addition to these, a number of Seabrook trucks were armoured and fitted with obsolescent three-pounder Hotchkiss guns from naval stocks and with Maxim machine guns; the intention here

was that these trucks, with a crew of nine or ten men, could be rushed out to give support to the armoured cars when opposition became too great for a single car.

Whilst satisfactory, these cars had a short life in their intended role, since once the war settled down to its static phase their opportunities for action became less and less. Eventually the armoured car squadrons were withdrawn from France and sent to other theatres, where they could be of more use – two went to Gallipoli but were of little use there, others went to German South West Africa, Mesopotamia, and one even to Russia and Lapland.

As the trench lines proliferated and barbed wire grew thickly between them,

and as the machine gun began to dominate the front line, several people began to ponder the problem of breaking through this formidable obstacle, and inevitably they began to think about mechanical methods of doing it.

Leaving aside the numerous inventors who suggested shields on wheels, modified steam-rollers and similar devices simply to push down the wire, the first man to put a foot on the right track was Lieutenant-Colonel (later Major-General Sir) Ernest Swinton of the Royal Engineers. Swinton was a professional soldier who had fought in South Africa, edited the official *History of the Russo-Japanese War*, served as secretary of the Committee of Imperial Defence and written several books (one of which, *The Defence of Duffer's Drift*, became a minor classic and the standard textbook on small-unit tactics for the next 50 years). At the outbreak of war he had been sent to France as the official war correspondent; the army of 1914 was not keen to have ordinary civilian reporters wandering around in the combat zone and asking awkward questions, so Swinton, under the alias of 'Eyewitness', provided all the newspapers with material. (This system lasted until the middle of 1915, after which reporters were authorized and Swinton moved to other duties.) On 19 October 1914, Swinton was returning to England for a conference and, *en route,* was pondering the problem of enabling troops to advance in the face of wire and machine guns. What was required, he concludes, was 'a power-driven, bullet-proof, armed engine capable of destroying machine guns, of crossing country and trenches, of breaking through entanglements and of climbing earthworks'. And while thinking about this, he remembered a letter he had received in July, before war broke out, from a South African engineer called Marriott, drawing his attention to the Holt tractor and suggesting that such a tracked vehicle might have applications for military transport. At the time Swinton had passed the idea to the Transportation Department in the War Office and thought no more about it, but he now saw that the tracked tractor offered a basis for the cross-country vehicle which he envisaged.

Upon arriving in London Swinton put his idea to Sir Maurice Hankey, then Sec-

Facing page, above The Holt tractor, as used for towing artillery, 1915. *Facing page, below* One example of the many types of improvised armoured cars used in Belgium in 1914/15. *Below* French 'Artillerie d'Assault' in action near Soissons, July 1918.

retary of the Committee of Imperial Defence. Hankey saw merit in the idea and suggested Swinton should put the proposition to Lord Kitchener, then Secretary of State for War. Kitchener, however, was too busy to see Swinton, who returned to France, but a few days later Hankey saw Kitchener and broached Swinton's idea. Predictably, Kitchener would have none of it.

Hankey now turned in another direction; in addition to his post with the Committee of Imperial Defence, he was secretary to the War Council, and his terms of reference there gave him the duty to place before the council and the Prime Minister

any matters which he felt to be of importance to the war effort.

Accordingly, over Christmas 1914 Hankey wrote a memorandum for the Prime Minister, Mr. Asquith. After expounding on conditions in France and the problems facing the army, he went on to suggest 'numbers of large heavy rollers, themselves bullet-proof, propelled from behind by motor-engines geared very low, the driving wheel fitted with caterpillar driving gear to grip the ground, the driver's seat armoured, and with a Maxim gun fitted...' Mr. Asquith circulated Hankey's paper among the War Council; one of the members was the First Lord of the

Admiralty, Mr. Winston Churchill, a gentleman who was always anxious to keep the Royal Navy in the forefront of developments and contributing to the war effort in any conceivable way.

Churchill had already been giving this matter some thought and had instigated some investigations into trench-crossing devices; fired by Hankey's paper he produced a memorandum of his own, expounding and expanding on Hankey, and he followed this up by setting up an Admiralty Landships Committee to investigate the problem and prepare designs of vehicle. This committee proposed numerous devices and tested others

THE MOTORCYCLE AT WAR

The 1914/18 War gave a great impetus to the motorcycle. It was used for despatch-carrying (*top left* a BSA in German East Africa), as a machine-gun carrier (*top right* the 24th Motor M.G. Battalion, June 1918; *below* the Vickers-Clyno machine-gun combination) and female auxiliaries ferried staff officers (*bottom*) in motorcycle combinations.

over the next six months or so. Meanwhile Swinton, in France and quite unaware of the Landships Committee's existence or activities, refined his original idea and sent another memorandum, complete with specifications of a possible machine and some ideas on how to use it, to Sir John French, C-in-C of the British Army in France. Sir John forwarded it to the War Office, where it appears to have finally stimulated some sort of response; a week later, at the end of June 1915, the War Office sent a representative to sit on the Landships Committee.

Shortly after this Swinton returned from France to take up an appointment as Secretary of the Dardanelles Committee of the War Cabinet, a post which gave him sufficient authority to ask questions wherever he liked, and he soon discovered that not only was there the Landships Committee but several other minor agencies all beavering away at the same problem. Late in August 1915, having obtained the backing of the Prime Minister, Swinton managed to get all these people into the same room together to discuss what they were doing and how they were going about it. As a result, it was agreed that since the Admiralty appeared to have the best-working organization, they could continue to develop the machine, but that the War Office would say what the specification should be and the Ministry of Munitions would give any assistance needed in the supply of material and equipment and, once the design was perfected, take over the production. One advantage of this system was that for the first time the people concerned with the design of the vehicle were given some facts and figures about what sort of obstacles the machine would have to overcome.

Bottom left A Whippet tank, photographed behind the German lines at Morcourt in 1918. *Top* Little Willie as it is today, in the Tank Museum, Bovington. *Bottom* Little Willie as it was, undergoing its early trials in 1916.

At this time some experimental work was being done at the Lincoln factory of William Foster & Sons, a firm of agricultural engineers well known for their tractors. Foster's director, Sir William Tritton, working with Lieutenant Wilson, a naval armoured car expert, had moved away from the various devices the Landships Committee had called for and his firm had designed a machine of their own, known variously as the Wilson, the Tritton or the Lincoln No. 1 machine. This was little more than a steel box mounted upon a lengthened Holt tractor track unit. It was proposed to fit it with a rotating turret on top, but this was felt to add too much complication to the construction and the idea was dropped. Eventually, on 10 September 1915, the Tritton machine was tried out, but the results were

inauspicious; the track had a poor grip, tended to come off its guide wheels, and, due to its position, gave little obstacle-crossing performance. The track and its suspension were entirely redesigned and the new version, known as Little Willie, ran successfully in December 1915.

In order to meet the War Office requirement that the machine should be able to climb a 1.2m (4ft) parapet and cross a 2.4m (8ft) trench, Wilson set about redesigning the layout of the track. One of the earliest ideas to come before the Landships Committee had been a Big Wheel Machine, which was to use wheels of 12m (40ft) diameter so as to overcome obstacles – a figure arrived at by careful mathematical analysis of German trench parapet widths. Such a device was hopelessly impractical, but Wilson fastened on to the 12m (40ft) wheel and reasoned that if he shaped the front of the vehicle's hull to approximate to a segment of such a wheel, and then ran the track around it, he would arrive at a 'wheel' of the requisite diameter without actually being encumbered by the rest of it. And in this fashion the shape of the first armoured fighting tracked vehicle was arrived at.

The first tank – though that name had not yet been coined in this context – took shape as a rhomboidal steel casing with sponsons on each side, armed with ex-naval six-pounder guns, and with ports through which another five machine guns could be fired by the crew. The machine was propelled by a Daimler engine, sitting in the centre of the one and only compartment, driving via a two-speed-and-reverse gearbox to a large differential, from which cross-shafts ran to the sides of the tank to sliding pinion gears giving another two-speed range. From here the drive went by heavy chains to the track driving sprockets at the rear of the tank. The driver sat high in the front, controlling the tank by means of a throttle, with a gear lever controlling the primary gearbox; two 'gearsmen' operated the secondary two-speed gears on the cross-shaft, acting on hand signals from the driver. As might be imagined, to co-ordinate a successful gear

change was a matter demanding considerable practice and no small amount of luck.

The first of these machines was called the Centipede, Foster's registered trade name for their agricultural tractors; this was all very well for restricted use among those 'in the know', but in the interest of secrecy some innocuous cover name was needed. Several expedient tales had already been told to the factory hands engaged in making the machine: the mechanical components were said to be for a Demonstration and Instructional Chassis for some unspecified military driving school, while the hull plating was said to be for 'special water carriers for use in Mesopotamia'. This latter explanation led to the workforce referring to it as 'that tank thing'. This must have stayed in the mind of Colonel Swinton as, on Christmas Eve 1915, he sat with a companion, Lieut.-Colonel Dally Jones, to draw up a report on the progress of Centipede. One

of the questions under review was the matter of a cover name, and after considering and rejecting several suggestions they finally settled on the word tank to describe the new machine. It is extremely doubtful if either of them ever contemplated the repercussions of their decision and the extent to which the word would enter the language of the world.

On 12 January 1916, the first tank moved under its own power; on 28 January it arrived, under conditions of great secrecy, at Hatfield in Hertfordshire, was unloaded under cover of darkness and driven under heavy escort to Hatfield Park, where it was to be demonstrated to various high-ranking figures in military and political circles. On 29 January it made a preliminary canter around a course of obstacles, constructed to give as realistic a picture of front line conditions as possible, and on 2 February the official unveiling took place, when

THE MOTHERS OF THEM ALL

The original British tanks, showing their evolution and improvement in the war years. *Below* The original Mark I, with tail steering gear. *Below left* The Mark II 'Female' with machine-gun in place of 6-pounder in the sponson. *Below right* A Mark IV from the rear quarter. *Top right* A Mark V showing the

improved type of sponson with 6-pounder and machine-gun. *Centre right* The Mark VIII 'Liberty' tank, built by Britain and the USA. *Bottom right* The supply tank Mark IX which could carry reserve troops and stores to accompany an attack.

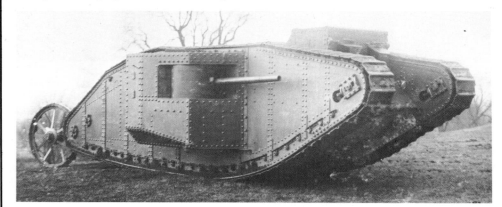

Below left A Renault FT17 tank in Bovington
Museum.
Below right Holt tractors towing 8 inch
howitzers in France, 1918.
Bottom The American six-ton tank M1918,
based on the Renault FT design.

Mother, as the tank came to be called, performed in the hands of Chief Petty Officer
Hill of the Royal Naval Air Service, the
first man in history to be known as a tank
driver. The display, witnessed by Lloyd
George, Minister of Munitions, General
Sir William Robertson, Chief of the Imperial General Staff, Lord Kitchener and
other luminaries, was a success and eight
days later the first order was given for the
construction of tanks for military use.

We have dwelt at some length on the
genesis of the first tank, since it was a most
significant step in the development of
military transport, but it should be pointed
out that similar developments were taking
place in other countries at much the same
time. In France there were many suggestions for armoured rollers and similar
devices and, as in Britain, the impetus
came from consideration of the Holt
tractor. The Schneider company were
agents for the Holt, selling their tractors to
the French Army as gun-towing vehicles,
and in June 1915 they began contemplating adding armour and weapons to
turn the Holt into a fighting machine. The

result was demonstrated in December
1915, and in the same month, quite
independently, a Colonel Estienne,
having seen some Holt tractors towing
guns, wrote to General Joffre suggesting a
Holt-based armoured vehicle. On Joffre's
authority, Estienne visited the Renault
company with his ideas, but Louis Renault
was reluctant to get involved. Estienne
then went to Schneider, discovered that
they were already working on the lines he
proposed, and Estienne, together with
Brillie, the Schneider engineer, drew up a
detailed design based on Brillie's mechanical knowledge and Estienne's knowledge
of what the vehicle might be called upon to

do. The result was the Schneider CA tank,
which went into production in late September 1916.

Unfortunately Estienne had upset
several people by his short-cut approach
via General Joffre; the official *Service
Technical d'Automobile* felt that their
function had been usurped, and that they

had, therefore, better get ahead and
develop an official design to put Estienne
in his place. This resulted in the Saint
Chamond tank, which was far from as
successful as its designers hoped. In the
end, the French became somewhat disillusioned with heavy tanks and opted
instead to go for light, fast, two-man tanks
which would 'swarm' over the battlefield
in the spirit of '*attaque à l'outrance*', a
policy which resulted in the Renault FT.

The German Army was surprised and
shaken by the appearance of the first
tanks, but they were reluctant to consider
adopting such devices themselves; the first
British use of tanks, in unsuitable ground,
led to large numbers being bogged down
in mud, and this led the Germans to the
opinion that they were of little practical
value once the novelty had worn off. They
were as slow as the British and French to
see that success with tanks was a question
of applying them in substantial force on
suitable terrain. There was also the stated
policy of the German High Command that
they would 'not fight a battle of *matériel*'
but would rely upon superior manpower
to crush the enemy. This opinion was
eventually overturned and the German
Army began the development of tank
designs of their own, but it was left so late
that no more than a handful had been
made before the Armistice, and the major
part of German tank strength was made
up of captured Allied machines.

Below A Schneider-Citroën-Kegresse half-track car of 1923, armed with a 37mm gun. *Facing page* The French 75mm 'Auto-Cannon', an anti-aircraft gun on a De Dion Bouton chassis.

THE
INTER WAR YEARS

THERE IS A NATURAL TENDENCY to regard the tank as being the primary mechanical innovation of the World War I, which of course it was; but this should not be allowed to conceal the enormous increase in the number of more mundane mechanically propelled vehicles which the armies adopted. As well as normal cargo-carrying trucks, used for providing every sort of supply to the front, there were increasing numbers of specialized vehicles making their appearance. The gradual rise of air power led to the emergence of the anti-aircraft gun, and, doubtless influenced by the same considerations as had led to the designs seen in Frankfurt in 1909, the idea of mounting anti-aircraft guns on to motor chassis so as to provide a highly mobile defensive force capable of rapid redeployment was one which was widely used. The French mounted their ubiquitous 75mm M1897 field gun into a high-angle mounting and placed this on the rear of a De Dion Bouton chassis to produce the Auto-cannon, while Britain followed suit and placed its 3in gun on to Thorneycroft

and Peerless three-ton motor trucks. These, of course, were supplemented by trucks mounting searchlights and sound-locating equipment. The rise in the amount of complicated armament – and in the quantity of motor vehicles – led to the design of special workshop vehicles, equipped with power tools, which could be brought close to the forward areas to cope with light repairs and maintenance. In order to move field artillery more quickly, the French developed the 'portée' system, in which a 75mm gun and its limber could be run on to the back of a four-tonne truck and rapidly driven to a new location. Taking this idea a stage further, the Schneider company began mounting heavier weapons, up to a 28cm howitzer, on to Holt-type tracked chassis, thus developing the first tracked self-propelled guns.

One drawback which still remained, however, was the inability of most wheeled vehicles to move once they left a made-up road surface, particularly in the glutinous mud which inevitably makes its

appearance close to the front line. The Russians, with a lesser proportion of hard roads than any other combatant, found this particularly restrictive, and their armoured cars were greatly hampered in their tactics. One solution was advanced by Adolphe Kegresse, a French engineer employed as the superintendent of the Czar's personal fleet of automobiles, who removed the standard rear axle, moved it forward, added a second rear axle and wheels, and then ran a flexible rubber track around both sets of wheels to turn the vehicle into a half-track. After trying the idea on some cars, it was applied to a number of Austin armoured cars with considerable success. It has been suggested, and there seems some merit in the idea, that Kegresse took his inspiration from a number of American Lombard half-track tractors, which the Russians purchased in 1916 for use as artillery prime movers. The Lombard had been invented in 1901 by Alvin Lombard of Waterville, Maine, and his original model was steam-powered and used for hauling logs out of the New England woods.

When the Revolution took place in Russia, Kegresse, doubtless because of his place of employment, wisely took to his heels and returned to France, and after the war he patented various aspects of his half-track idea and interested a number of manufacturers in it, as a result of which it was one of the most important automotive aspects of the 1920s. A convoy of Citroën-Kegresse half-tracks made a famous expedition across the Sahara, over terrain which no wheeled vehicle of the day could have traversed, and military circles began to take considerable interest. In Britain

the Crossley Motor Company, which had supplied large quantities of trucks and cars to the military forces during the war, began to develop Kegresse's patents under licence, while the Burford Company also took out a licence. A similar device was developed by the Roadless Traction Company, but in their track unit the original axle of the vehicle was retained, fitted with a driving wheel, and the track unit was laid out forward of the rear axle; one advantage claimed for the Roadless system was that the track unit had a degree of lateral freedom which made steering the vehicle a great deal easier. An interesting variation was the Morris-Martel-Roadless, in which the Roadless track unit went at the front of the vehicle and the steered wheels at the back. Eventually a number of these half-track vehicles were adopted; the British used a Morris-Roadless in India for gun towing, and the French adopted a Citroën-Kegresse for the same task. Other French half-tracks included armoured cars, engineer vehicles, bridge layers, troop carriers and recovery vehicles.

Facing page top The original Austin-Patilov Russian armoured car, converted to a half-track by Kegresse. *Facing page bottom* The British 3 inch AA gun on a Peerless lorry mounting. Numbers of these survived until World War II. *Below* The Crossley-Kegresse infantry carrier adopted by the British Army. *Top left* Martel's one-man tankette prototype. *Middle left* The Citroën-Kegresse of 1923. *Bottom left* The Austin twin-turret armoured car as supplied to Russia in 1915/16. These were later converted by Kegresse.

This latter tabulation tends to indicate the development of specialized military vehicles in their own right, outside the normal run of commercial production, and this, of course, was becoming more and more necessary. Commercial vehicles could be utilized for simple road transport, but when it came to the various specialized tasks of a modern army, there were few commercial equivalents, and armies were being driven to designing their own and, in some cases, even building prototypes to place before manufacturers.

Whether the manufacturers would respond was a different matter; automobile-makers exist to produce profits for their shareholders, and it was increasingly obvious during the 1920s that this, could be done by settling on an easily made design and producing it in volume. Items such as half a dozen bridge carriers, two recovery trucks or a tank transporter had to be largely hand-made, away from the production line, and they absorbed more money than they produced. Nevertheless, there were sufficient manufacturers with a sense of patriotic feeling who were prepared to allow their commercial production to subsidize a proportion of their military designing; they had to, since the military – in any country in the 1920s – were starved of money.

The years between the wars, then, were years in which much fundamental research was done but which produced little mass production of specialized military vehicles. But sufficient vehicles were made, in short production runs or in ones and twos, to indicate success or failure of an idea, after which it was laid away and some new line of approach pursued. Some of the ideas were more spectacular than others, but they all contributed something.

One idea which was to have far-reaching effects, was the machine-gun carrier, and it originated in Britain. It seems to have been born out of a confusion of tactical and economic theory, and whilst the economics may have been sensible the tactical side now shows itself to have been weak and muddled. World War I had left the British Army well prepared mentally to fight the campaign of 1919, indeed in 1939 that was what it set out to do, and though there was the firm belief that there would be no more wars in Europe, there was at the same time the deeply rooted instinct that if it came then everyone would dive back into their trenches again. The machine-gun carrier was originally intended to do as its name suggests, carry a machine gun, and it was to

carry it across bullet-swept ground whilst protecting its crew from harm. Sensible enough, you might imagine, but totally at variance with the experiences of 1917 and the mud of Passchendaele, where any such vehicle would have been bogged down. However, small vehicles are cheap and there was also the cavalry-like concept of small individual armoured vehicles dashing about the battlefield, and this had its attractions for the theorists.

The first ideas were for one-man tanks. Actually they were not tanks at all, but poorly protected carriers, and the prototype was built by Major Gifford Martel at his own expense using commercial components. The War Office was sufficiently interested to give an order for four to Morris Motors, and the trials of these quickly showed up the deficiencies of the one-man idea. Meanwhile John Carden and a Mr. Loyd built a similar vehicle, but quickly moved to a two-man crew with a fully tracked suspension. The War Office liked these better and tried them in the Mechanized Force Tests of 1928-9. This was enough for Vickers, who bought out Carden-Loyd and marketed the little carriers themselves, pointing out to their customers that the British Army was using them. The development continued and the suspension was greatly improved, though it was never capable of carrying heavy loads nor of travelling at high

speeds. It was recognizable by the fact that the roadwheels were small rollers pinned to an external frame outside the hull and carrying the idler wheel at the rear. These little carriers weighed about three tons and could be enlarged into light tanks with little extra effort, though they suffered from track problems for years after their inception.

The sale of the Carden-Loyds and their subsequent effect on tank design was quite extraordinary. They were sold all over the world. Russia took several and developed the T-27 and others from them. Italy built the CV-33 and then tried to expand the principle into a medium tank and a self-

propelled gun, whereupon it failed. Poland took several and produced the TK-3. Czechoslovakia followed the idea for their MU-124 and France built the UE carriers, all with the Carden-Loyd basis. By the mid-1930s there were many countries who owed the genesis of their armoured force to the purchase of a batch of Carden-Loyd carriers, and even Germany took the general idea when designing the PzKpfw I.

Among the more spectacular products of the inter-war period were the Christie tank designs. J. Walter Christie was an American engineer who had gone into the automobile business in its early days and

who, during World War I, was operating the Front Drive Motor Company. Drawn by the possibility of mounting guns on vehicles, he designed a number of self-propelled mountings which were greeted with some approval by the US Army; but in spite of them encouraging him to continue in this line, in 1918 he dropped artillery and decided to design a tank. This, had the Army but known it, was to be symptomatic of their relationship with Christie until he died in 1944; no sooner had they accepted an idea than Christie was off after some other notion, leaving them the task of perfecting the abandoned design.

Christie's 1919 tank used a very simple design of suspension and incorporated Christie's prime novelty – the track could be removed, whereupon the vehicle could be driven on roads on its wheels. This gave it greater speed and manoeuvrability, and it also saved wear and tear on the tracks, a particularly vulnerable feature of tank design at that time and, to some degree, ever since. The US Army bought this machine and made some tests with it, after which they sent it back to Christie and asked him to make a few changes to bring it closer to the Army's conception of what a tank ought to be. This Christie did, somewhat grudgingly, but further tests

with the army showed that it spent more time being repaired than it did being run, and the Army lost interest in it. Christie went ahead on his own, and designed an amphibious tank, one or two of which were bought by the US Marine Corps, and then applied himself to developing a suspension system which would permit high speeds to be attained across country.

In 1928 he offered the US Army a new design in which the tank was carried on a set of large rubber-tyred roadwheels, which touched the track at top and bottom. These were slung on pivoting arms and sprung by large coil springs mounted vertically in the double-skinned hull side, a system which allowed enormous deflection to accommodate rough terrain. As before, it could run with or without its track, and it was propelled by an enormous V–12 aero-engine giving 338hp, which gave the tank the phenomenal speed of 113km/hr (70mph) on wheels (better than many automobiles could manage) or 64km/hr (40mph) on its tracks. Viewed as a tank it was something of an anti-climax, since it was unarmed, though provided with a dummy gun, and the armour was nowhere more than 12mm (½in) thick. But as a spectacular cross-country machine, it enchanted everyone who saw it; the US Army bought five, the Russians bought two, and the Polish Army ordered another two. Christie formed a

Top An Italian Fiat M28 demonstrating its agility. *Centre* The Fiat 2000 was the first Italian attempt at a heavy tank. *Bottom* The German Panzer Kampfwagen I which saw its first combat in Spain.

new company, the US Wheel and Track-layer Corporation, and all appeared to be going well. The Poles cancelled their order and the US Army bought them instead, but shortly after this the US Ordnance Department fell out again with Christie over contractual terms, and thereafter Christie was by-passed, another company being given orders to build tanks based on the Christie design. A contributory factor is said to have been the fact that the Ordnance Department were less than enchanted at having paid Christie some $800,000 over the previous 12 years without ever receiving a tank which worked properly.

But for all his prickliness and eccentricity, Walter Christie will always be remembered for the suspension system he designed. It was first taken up in quantity by the Soviets, who based their BT series of tanks on it, and later by the British, who based their Cruiser tanks on it. Today it can be found, in modified form, on tanks of every nation.

The Americans were, however, reluctant to embrace the Christie suspension because it was expensive, and in the early 1930s money was everything. Instead, the Rock Island Arsenal persevered in a design of a cheaper form of suspension, known as the volute-spring type. A volute spring can best be described as a ribbon of steel coiled up, and then the inner end thrust out so as to form a tapering coil spring. It acts like a coil spring, but the thickness of the ribbon gives it the degree of stiffness necessary to support the weight of an armoured vehicle. Rock Island perfected this system to such good effect that when World War II came along

and money flowed more or less freely, they elected to stay with it rather than go back to the Christie system; for the tanks of the time it was perfectly adequate, and it was not until after 1943, when performance had increased considerably, that they felt it was worth contemplating the Christie system again.

Less spectacular, but equally vital, was the steady development in most countries of four-wheel-drive vehicles for military use. During World War I a number of four-wheel-drive vehicles were in use. The idea of all-wheel drive had been put forward early in the century as a method of obtaining adequate traction, though not necessarily for cross-country

work; there were plenty of roads in those days which were of such poor quality that all-wheel drive was advantageous. Such vehicles as the American FWD, Jeffery, Duplex and Avery were in commercial use prior to 1914 and hundreds were sold to Britain and France once the war began. There they demonstrated their ability to operate off roads, and when the war was over the armies were reluctant to lose this ability. Unfortunately, the 1920s saw improvements in roads to the extent that the all-wheel-drive truck as a commercial proposition almost died out, and so military designers had to work on their own designs. Another factor leading to military design was that commercial all-wheel-drive vehicles, while capable of off-road working, were not really intended for the rough going which military vehicles were called upon to face, and thus the suspension systems were unable to cope with the extreme deflections demanded; only purpose-built military designs offered all the performance which military men wanted.

By the end of the 1920s the design and manufacture of military vehicles had spread around the world, away from its 'traditional' homes, and nowhere was this more notable than in Soviet Russia. Motor vehicles, and particularly the tank, had caught the Soviet imagination – they were forward-looking and technological, and the Soviets were sure that together with aviation and poison gas they were the key to future warfare. Moreover these three fields of development were new ones and there was little 'traditional' background upon which to draw; therefore the Soviets, with application, could be on an equal footing with older nations, everyone being at more or less the same level of competence – and those who worked hardest would come off best.

There was some degree of truth in this theory, but immediately after the Revolution the Soviet nation was in no condition to contemplate research into military science, and it was not until 1928, when the First Five-Year Plan was announced, that any serious work could begin. The First Plan centred on heavy industry and armament production facilities, and part of the target was that, by 1934, the Red Army would have three mechanized brigades, 30 mixed tank battalions, four reserve heavy tank battalions, 13 mechanized

cavalry regiments, and an armoured car company in each infantry division, a grand total of something like 3,500 combat vehicles, plus, of course, the necessary 'soft' vehicles to back all this up. In fact the plan worked so well that by 1933 the Red Army had almost 7,000 tanks alone.

The next stage was the Second Five-Year Plan, which was aimed at completing the entire mechanization of the army. By the end of this plan period (1938) there were over 30 factories producing tanks, armoured cars, trucks and self-propelled guns. One of the lesser problems arising

from this vast expansion was the somewhat basic one of providing drivers for all these vehicles; trained drivers were scarce among the annual intake of conscripts and a massive instructional programme had to be launched by para-military training organizations.

CREATIONS OF CHRISTIE

Top left The Medium T4 Convertible tank. *Top right* Walter Christie (standing) with his M1932 tank. *Below* The Christie T3 demonstrates its facility for travelling on either wheels or tracks. Such adaptability was not destined to become the rule.

A notable feature of Soviet vehicle development was that very few specialist military trucks appeared. The standard truck was the GAZ–AA, which was, in fact, the Ford Model AA 1½-ton commercial truck. The Soviets acquired machinery from the German Ford plant in Cologne in the early 1930s and with Ford assistance the GAZ factory at Gorki was built in 1932. The resulting truck was produced by the tens of thousands and applied to almost every military use, even though it lacked four-wheel drive or any other visible military embellishment. Some were converted to half-track form, and a small number of more specialized vehicles, with all-wheel drive, were developed in smaller factories, but the GAZ–AA was to remain a familiar sight in Russian military formations until after World War II.

One field in which the Soviets did excel was in the provision of fully-tracked tractors for artillery. In view of the terrain problems and the Russian climate, this made a great deal of sense, and factories that produced tracked tractors for agricultural purposes found it easy to make slight modifications and produce similar vehicles for the Army. As well as having the virtue of efficiency, another advantage of these tractors was that since they were basically agricultural vehicles, the annual intake of conscripts produced a reasonable number of men who were familiar with them on the farm and who could be converted into artillery drivers with little additional training. Tractors such as the Stalin and Komsomol were little more than truck bodies carried on full-track suspensions, while others such as the Stalinets were purely haulers, closely resembling heavy farm tractors. A further interesting development of these tracked designs was the adaptation of the suspension unit to towed artillery weapons in place of the normal wheels; a free-rolling track unit gave excellent flotation in mud and snow conditions and matched the ability of the tracked tractor to cross difficult country.

The other nation making great advances in the 1930s was, of course, Germany; but although it is generally believed that the German Army was in the forefront of mechanization, as shown by the renowned Panzer divisions, the fact is that they were a good deal less advanced in

Left The Russian tractor factory at Chelyabinsk: it was a simple matter to convert such plant to tank production. *Below right* An Italian CV33 tank at Bovington. *Bottom* The archetypal German half-track, the 'Mittlerer Zugkraftwagen 8-tonne' of 1935.

basic mechanization of the Army than most other countries. So far behind were they, in fact, that the majority of their field artillery went to war in 1939 behind horse teams.

Where the Germans erred was in trying to over-organize. Where other nations were content to specify a general type of vehicle and let manufacturers come up with their own interpretation, the German Army began by specifying standard chassis for cars and trucks. These were luxurious specifications, to say the least; the car chassis, in three sizes, featured such advanced (and expensive) features as permanent four-wheel drive with limited-slip differentials, independent suspension on all wheels, auxiliary low gears for cross-country work, and two spare wheels mounted on stub axles amidships, where they acted to prevent the car 'bellying' on rough ground. Needless to say, this ideal specification, while producing a splendid vehicle, was not conducive to quantity production, and as a result civilian vehicles of all types were gradually brought into service. This caused complications because of the variety of designs being bought, and before the war a rationalization programme, under Colonel von Schell, was instituted. Each manufacturer was limited to a single basic vehicle of his own design, produced in both two-wheel- and four-wheel-drive models. This brought some sense into military procurement, but even so it would have been better to have had the manufacturers concentrate on one or two vehicles in each class irrespective of who designed them. This, in fact, did take place during the war,

when the standard Opel truck was produced by several factories.

One of the hallmarks of the German Army was the heavy half-tracked towing vehicle used by artillery, and these were developed in a range of sizes and in large numbers. Work on half-tracks began in the 1920s under the hands of several private companies, and in 1926 an extensive trial was carried out to determine the design of artillery tractors. The Army then called for designs of light, medium and heavy tractors and development of these was done by Bussing-NAG, JA Maffei AG and Daimler-Benz, acting under

military guidance. Prototypes were ready by 1932. In 1934 development of lighter types was begun by Borgward and Demag. Eventually design settled down to a pattern using torsion-bar suspension of overlapping wheels in the track unit and models of from one- to eight-ton capacity were produced.

The German Army, like the Soviet, started the inter-war period with the advantage of having no tanks at all; the provisions of the Versailles Treaty denuded them of what few tanks they had owned, and prevented any overt development of fighting vehicles. But behind the scenes a great deal of basic research went on, and in the late 1920s a clandestine testing facility and tank school was operated in Russia with the connivance of the Soviet Army. Experimental chassis were sent to this testing ground and tank commanders and crews were trained in basic tactics and mechanical skills. The principal manufacturers in Germany were given contracts to develop tank chassis under the guise of 'agricultural tractors', and the outcome of these was, firstly, a medium tank known as the 'Neubaufahrzeug' or New Model Vehicle, a 23-tonner with multiple turrets. But since this line of development appeared to proceed too slowly, and since some tanks – any tanks– were needed for training, a design of light tank was pushed forward in 1933. This became the Panzerkampfwagen I and was primarily intended as a cheap training device, though many of them survived to go to war in 1939. This was followed by the PzKpfw II, III and IV models, which formed the basis of the German Panzer divisions by the outbreak of war in 1939.

British development during the between-wars years was hampered by lack of finance and much of the early tank work was done by Vickers, working to specifications laid down by the War Office. This led to light and medium types being taken into service, though never in adequate numbers, and it also led to Vickers building up a sizeable export trade in designs not far removed from those issued to British service. Many of these Vickers models served to start other countries on their tank-development programmes; Russia and Japan both purchased Vickers tanks in the 1920s and, after testing and studying them, went on to develop their own ideas, having saved a great deal of time and

money by escaping the initial stages of design.

Britain also made some notable steps in the development of supporting specialist vehicles, though again the shortage of money prevented many of these being adopted in large numbers. A self-propelled gun, known as the Birch Gun, appeared in 1927, using an 18-pounder field piece mounted in a revolving turret. It was then redesigned to carry the gun in an open barbette, which allowed it to function as an anti-aircraft gun with some success. But due to disputes over the tactical handling of armour, as well as the lack of cash, this line of development petered out and the guns were scrapped in the early 1930s.

The Royal Artillery appear to have been rather less resistant to the idea of mechanization than most other horsed units, and several artillery tractors were produced. Notable among these was the Hathi (Hindustani for elephant), which was first made by a military unit by cannibalizing parts of some captured German four-wheel-drive tractors. It proved to be successful, and commercial models were later made by Thorneycroft in 4 × 4 and 6 × 6 versions. This line of development

eventually led to the 4 × 4 Guy Quad Ant, which was to become the standard field artillery tractor throughout World War II. It might be said here that there was a certain amount of opposition to the idea of developing a specialized gun tractor for field artillery use; the line of counter-argument was that such vehicles were useless for anything else, being unsuited to load-carrying since they consisted entirely of crew space and ammunition lockers. Their opponents would have preferred the artillery to use standard cargo trucks as

towing vehicles, so that once the guns were emplaced the trucks could be used for other tasks. But the artillery, in their wisdom, knew that once trucks are removed for other tasks they prove exceedingly difficult to recall when the guns require shifting, and they managed to retain their 'quads' until well after World War II.

In spite of America's wide-scale adoption of the automobile, the US Army moved slowly on the road to mechanization. This was due to the same two brakes which were to be found in other countries – lack of money and a powerful cavalry clique in the higher echelons of military decision-making. Another drawback was peculiarly American, in that when the United States Army was reconstituted by the 1920 National Defence Act, the war-time Tank Corps was disbanded and tanks were allocated to infantry; as a result, tank design tended to be tied to what the infantry thought a tank should do, which was largely walk alongside the infantryman and protect him. On the other hand, when some of the more forward-looking elements of the cavalry wanted to experiment with armoured vehicles, they were hamstrung by the 'tanks = infantry'

edict, an impasse which was eventually resolved by the fiction of calling all cavalry vehicles 'combat cars', irrespective of whether they ran on wheels or tracks. In many cases the infantry's tank and the cavalry's combat car were identical.

A little-known facet of American military vehicle development was that represented by a quasi-official body known as the Army Ordnance Association. This had been formed after 1918 as 'an organization of American citizens pledged to industrial preparedness for war' and which endeavoured 'to keep alive an interest in and knowledge of the design, production and maintenance of munitions...' Many of its members were in responsible industrial posts, and there was thus an interchange of information between the military and industry. The association also brought the Society of Automotive Engineers into contact with the Ordnance Department, another extremely valuable piece of cross-fertilization. As a result of these contacts and interchanges, industry was constantly aware of what the Army needed, while the Army were kept informed of fresh industrial developments. True, the Army still had little money with which to pursue its

chosen paths, but in many cases manufacturers were able to overlook this and, with their own development funds, help the army to at least a pilot model or prototype. In this way such things as heavy multi-wheel-drive trucks, armoured cars, half-track vehicles and artillery tractors of various patterns were tested; while few were ever carried beyond a single model, they nevertheless gave the Army valuable data

With few exceptions, American tank (and combat car) design was in the hands of the US Ordnance Department, and most of the work was carried out at their Rock Island Arsenal. Few American manufacturers seemed interested in developing tanks – probably because they felt there was little market demand for them – and, in any case, the Ordnance Department were a trifle wary of outside designers after the experiences with Walter Christie. Apart from Christie himself, only the Marmon-Herrington company engaged in tank design and they were largely concerned with producing light armoured vehicles for sale to South American countries; in addition to this, though, they were able to build occasional vehicles to Ordnance specification, as did Cunningham from time to time.

Below The Soviet SU-100 self-propelled gun, an excellent assault gun and tank destroyer in 1944/5. *Facing page* A Crossley-Chevrolet armoured car of the type used in the Western Desert campaign 1940/1.

THE SECOND WORLD WAR

AFTER THE OUTBREAK OF WAR in 1939, and with the spectre of the (apparently) highly mechanized German Panzer divisions in front of them, the various nations of the world, who were either engaged in the war or looking on, all began to overhaul their mechanization programmes with the utmost rapidity. Tanks and armoured cars had to be produced, and with them the trucks and tractors to keep the rest of the army on the move in what promised to be a mobile war. The totalitarian nations began in a strong position, having been able to build up their tank forces and ancillaries before the war, while the democracies were in their usual starting condition, starved of equipment. In the long run, the advantages reversed themselves, in that the countries with vast stocks of tanks tended to hang on to what they had and continue to use them long after they should have been replaced, confident in the belief that the superiority they enjoyed at the commencement of the war would see them through to the end. On the other hand, the countries with little equipment at the start were able to hang on with what they had while designers and

manufacturers got to work on fresh models, so that towards the mid-point of the war there was a qualitative over-hauling of the other side. This, in its turn, led to another burst of activity, and design, especially of tanks, turned into a leapfrog progression, first one side and then the other gaining the upper hand.

The reason for all this was, of course, that tank design had proceeded more or less in a vacuum for 20 years; very few people had any firm ideas on how tanks ought to be handled in war and, therefore, how tank design should be specified, and the few who did have ideas were generally out of agreement between themselves. The 'small wars' such as the Spanish Civil War, the Italian invasion of Abyssinia and the Japanese activities in Manchuria and China had been productive of some very conflicting lessons and really left no one the wiser. It was not until after the Polish campaign of 1939 that reliable conclusions could be drawn, conclusions which were largely reinforced by the events in France during the summer of 1940.

The first thing to become apparent was that the light tank, beloved in pre-war

days for its cheapness, was of no use at all on a modern battlefield, since it could not survive against either larger tanks or anti-tank weapons. The British, quick off the mark for once, abandoned them forthwith (except as driver-training vehicles), but the Americans and Germans kept them in service for some time; the former because light tanks were all they had at the manufacturing stage, and the latter because abandoning light tanks would have halved their armoured strength at one stroke. Both, therefore, had to hold on to their tanks until they could find something heavier with which to replace them, and in the end the Americans, because their light tanks were heavier and stronger than anyone else's, kept theirs in use until 1945.

The second thing to become apparent was that the whole design ethos of the tank required examination; the tank was a combination of three things, mobility, firepower and protection, and in pre-war days most designers had put mobility first, protection second and firepower last. Events in France showed that henceforth the three qualities had to be at least evenly divided or had to have more accent on protection and firepower, since mobility alone was not enough, as the demise of the light tank proved. The epitome of this was the brief action at Arras in 1940, when the Germans came up against the British

Matilda II tank; this was, for its day, exceedingly heavily armoured, and the normal German anti-tank and tank weapons made no impression on it. Only the last-minute deployment of a troop of 88mm anti-aircraft guns as anti-tank weapons saved the day for the Germans. From this, and from later experiments upon captured Matildas, they deduced that more armour and better guns were the priorities. The British, however, over-

looked the conclusions to be drawn from Arras for some time, and continued to stress mobility, so that when armoured warfare was resumed in the western desert in 1941-2 the German tanks outgunned the British by a considerable margin. The other defect in British tanks at this time was a certain lack of mechanical reliability, due to the lack of a coherent design policy in pre-war days; instead of concentrating on a basic design and bringing it to

Facing page top A Soviet T-26 light tank is blessed before going into action in Spain, 1938. *Facing page centre* A British Matilda MkIII infantry tank. *Facing page bottom* A Matilda MkII at Bovington Museum. *Below* A Soviet T-34 Medium tank with 76mm gun and, behind, an SU-100 assault gun.

perfection, the British, blown hither and yon by constantly changing tactical policies, had abandoned a line of research to chase after another, without perfecting any of them.

The only people who had been able to afford the luxury of chasing innumerable designs had been the Soviets, who, with their massive mechanization programme, had the money and facilities to pursue several avenues of approach. As a result,

by 1939 they had a wide variety of tanks in service, most of which were obsolescent, but at least they had a firm idea of what was required. A high-powered diesel engine had been developed and perfected over five years by the Kharkov Locomotive Works; a high-velocity 76mm gun was also perfected; and experience in Spain and Manchuria (in border incidents with the Japanese) had shown that riveted armour was dangerous to the occupants of

the tank and that welded armour had now to be used. Furthermore the armour had to be sloped so as to deflect projectiles instead of presenting a face at right-angles to the shot's trajectory. With all these things in mind the Soviet designers sat down and produced the T–34 medium tank, one of the outstanding designs of history. Production began in May 1940 and because the design was sound from the outset it continued in production throughout the war, a total of 39,698 being built. In similar vein a heavy tank was designed and put into production as the 'Klim Voroshilov'; this was less successful than the T–34, but several thousand were built and it formed the starting point for development, which led to more formidable heavy tanks later in the war.

When the Germans attacked Russia in June 1941 it is doubtful whether the Soviets had as many as a thousand of their two new designs in service, and these were scattered across Russia in 'penny packets'. As a result, the German advance was countered by older designs, and the Panzers shot these out of the way without very much trouble. But within two weeks of the start of the campaign there were reports which presaged trouble; the first came from a unit of Von Manstein's 56th Corps, who reported that an enormous and apparently shot-proof Russian tank of unknown design had suddenly appeared astride a supply route and had, for several hours, stood off every German attempt to dislodge it. Attempts to bring an 88mm

gun into action had been beaten off by the tank's powerful gun, and eventually a major diversion had to be staged to draw the tank into an ambush, where the '88' could destroy it. This was the German's introduction to the KV tank. Shortly after this the 17th Panzer Division reported a 'strange and low-slung tank of formidable appearance' which had emerged from some woods close to the Dniepr river and, with German shot bouncing from its armour, had ploughed a nine-mile swathe of destruction through the German lines until it was stopped by a medium artillery gun which it had inadvertently missed. That was the first appearance of the T–34.

Once the invasion had begun, the

Facing page, left A Soviet KVII heavy tank.
Facing page bottom A Sherman flail tank
clearing mines in Normandy, 1944. *Across
centre* The American 'Aunt Jemima' mine-
clearing roller, in use with the 6th US Army in
1945. *Below* A Sherman Crab, stowing the flail
apparatus. *Lower left* Front view of a Matilda
Scorpion in action. *Lower right* A Sherman
Crab at work.

Soviets, with admirable single-minded-
ness, abandoned plans for all other tanks
except the KV and T-34 and set about
building them as hard as they could. This
plan was all but ruined by the fact that the
German advance had overrun the tank
arsenals in Kharkov, Zhdanov and Kirov;
but as the German advance neared these
plants every scrap of machinery which
could be got out was loaded on to railway
trains and rushed east to Chelyabinsk.
Here the evacuated factories were
amalgamated to form a huge combine
called 'Tankograd', and within two
months new KVs were in production.
Another group of evacuated factories
became the 'Uralmashzavod' (Ural

machinery factory) at Nizhni Tagil, and
set about turning out T-34s. By 1943
there were 43 factories across Russia
doing nothing but turn out KV and T-34
tanks, and it has been said, with some
truth, that by 1944 the Russians could
make tanks faster than the Germans could
destroy them.

In similar fashion, enormous factories
were set up to produce trucks. The ZIS
factory in Moscow was relocated in the
Urals and went on turning out standard
three-ton 4 × 2 cargo trucks, 2½-ton 4 × 4
trucks and minor variations on these two
basic designs for use as engineer vehicles,
searchlight trucks and similar specialist
types. The GAZ factory was also relo-

cated and produced cars, trucks and
ambulances. But the weight of Soviet
effort went on tanks and fighting vehicles,
to the extent that over 400,000 trucks
were shipped from the USA under the
Lend-Lease scheme to keep the Red
Army mobile.

That the Americans could afford to
supply such a vast number of vehicles is
testimony to their mass-production expertise in the automotive field and also testimony to the Ordnance Department's
policy of standardizing certain basic types
of vehicle early in the war and then simply
allowing the manufacturers to turn them
out as fast as they could go. As indicated
above, much of the pre-war period had

been occupied in determining the basic parameters of different types of vehicle, so that by 1939-40 the Ordnance Department were in a position to be able to lay down specifications and know that they would work. As a result, the USA undoubtedly became the 'Arsenal of Democracy' in the motor vehicle field, with over 3,000,000 military transport vehicles, 88,410 tanks, 41,170 half-tracks, 82,000 tractors and several thousand other specialist vehicles.

The two American vehicles that were probably more widely distributed and best known of all were the Jeep and the Deuce-and-a-half or Jimmy. A total of 639,245 Jeeps were built, while almost a million Jimmy trucks were made, and there are quite a few of both types still in use around the world. The Jeep – more properly the 'Truck, ¼-ton, 4 × 4 Command & Reconnaissance' – arose from an Ordnance demand in 1940 for a light car to pull the 37mm anti-tank gun and carry its

crew. The first vehicle to appear was designed by the American Bantam Company, and this was followed by designs from the Willys and Ford companies. The specification called for the vehicle to weigh no more than 600kg (1,300lb), but the Willys company ignored this since they considered it to be ill-founded, leading to an underpowered and understrength result. They were quite right, and the revised specification increased the weight limit to 975kg (2,150lb). The Willys design, having the most powerful engine, was accepted, becoming the Model MA, while the same vehicle, built by Ford, became the Model GPW, from which arose the name Jeep.

The Deuce-and-a-half was the 2½-ton 6 × 6 cargo truck produced by the General Motors Corporation (GMC – hence Jimmy) from 1941 onwards. The size was considered to be the heaviest truck which could be mass-produced, and the demand was so great that Studebaker and Interna-

tional Harvester were also engaged in manufacturing to the same design. As well as the basic cargo model, there were innumerable variations based on the same chassis.

When tank production was first mooted in 1939 the Ordnance Department turned to the heavy engineering industry, considering that they would have the required expertise in handling heavy casting and large assemblies. As a result the first tank contracts went to firms such as the American Locomotive Company, the Lima Locomotive Company and the Baldwin Locomotive Company, and it is to their credit that they met their targets and produced the tanks on time. But in June 1940, William S. Knudsen, President of General Motors, suggested that the automobile industry had more experience at mass-production and ought to be called in. Since by this time the locomotive companies were working at full stretch and there was still an expansion in tank

Facing page A Jeep ferries a surrender party up to the leading tank of the US 4th Armored Division in Germany, 1945. *Below left* An American Light tank M2 in 1939. *Below right* A Marmon-Herrington Light tank used by the US Army in the Aleutian Islands, 1942. *Bottom* An M3 General Grant Medium tank at Bovington Museum.

production envisaged, the Army agreed and Knudsen contacted K. T. Keller, President of the Chrysler Corporation, to ask if Chrysler would take on the task of setting up a complete tank factory and running it for the Government. After examining the drawings of the proposed tank, Chrysler produced their plans for a 21 million dollar arsenal in Detroit; building began in September, and in April 1941 the arsenal turned out its first tank.

The tank they turned out, however, was not the tank they had contracted to make; a great deal had happened in those seven months.

At the start of 1940 the Americans had a light tank entering production and a medium tank on the drawing board; the latter, the M2A1, was completed in May, almost on the day that the German advance through France and Belgium began. In June the National Munitions Program was introduced, which called for, among other things, 1,741 medium tanks to be produced in the next 18 months. It was this which led to the idea of the Detroit Arsenal, and the drawings upon which the Chrysler engineers based their plans were those of the M2A1 medium tank. But while the Chrysler men were poring over these, the Army, after studying reports of the fighting in Europe, came to the conclusion that the 37mm gun of the M2A1 was insufficient and that the medium tank had to have a 75mm gun. While the Ordnance Department agreed in principle, they had to point out that the turret of the M2A1 was too small for a 75mm gun; an entirely new turret would be required, of a size never before attempted in America, and, of course, the hull would have to be altered to suit. While they were happy to go ahead and

design a suitable tank, this would take time, and meanwhile here were Chrysler with 21 million dollars and a contract for a thousand tanks. The solution to this impasse was to make a minimal redesign of the M2A1: to put a 75mm gun into a sponson on one side of the hull, shift the turret over slightly, and retain the 37mm gun in the turret. This would require the minimum amount of redesign and would provide the army with an interim tank. The idea was accepted and became the M3 medium tank; the contract with Chrysler was torn up in favour of an identical contract for 1,000 M3s. Chrysler now had the immense problem of having to design their factory piecemeal as they received drawings of the latest modifications, and

the final drawings were not received until March 1941, three weeks before the first pilot model of the M3 was completed.

The new design with the 75mm gun in the turret turned out to be the famous M4 medium, more commonly known as the Sherman tank, the tank which became, in effect, the Allied standard tank for the rest of the war, since it became the backbone of both American and British armoured units. The Americans were fond of saying that they would 'Win the War with the Sherman', the aim being to fasten on a sound design, modify it as little as possible and turn it out in overwhelming numbers, very much as the Soviets did with their T–34. Unfortunately, the Sherman wasn't a T–34. Had the war ended a year sooner, the Sherman would have lived up to its promoters' hopes, but by the time the Sherman came into full combat use, in 1944–5, the design was four years old and the 75mm gun, which had looked so formidable in 1940, was outclassed by German guns and outmatched by German armour.

To the credit of the Ordnance Department, they had foreseen this and as early as 1940 they had begun work on a heavy tank armed with a 3in gun. This became the M6, an excellent vehicle in many respects and one which would have served well in Europe given a few up-dating modifications. But for reasons never satisfactorily explained the higher echelons of the US Army turned it down and effectively stifled the production of any sort of heavy tank until late in 1944, when it was belatedly realized that a heavy tank was desperately needed in Europe. Since the Ordnance Department had quietly continued to develop a heavy design throughout the war, they were able to produce a suitable tank design off the shelf, but it took time to get into production and the US heavy tank did not appear on the battlefield until the last few weeks of the war and then in insufficient numbers.

One factor contributing to the peculiarly short-sighted attitude over heavy tanks was the American dictum that tanks as such were 'exploitation' vehicles, intended to carry the advance through the enemy defensive line; their job was not, however, to fight other tanks; that was supposed to be left to tank destroyers, specialized armour which fell into the self-propelled gun class. Many and varied, weird and wonderful were the tank destroyers which proliferated in 1940–2 in America; everything from redundant anti-aircraft guns on crawler tractors (with no room for gun crew or ammunition) via obsolete 'French 75' field-pieces on minimal wheeled chassis to 105mm howitzers inserted into armoured cars. Eventually some sanity prevailed and the standardized tank destroyer became the M10, a 3in anti-tank gun in an open-topped turret on a Sherman chassis. This had to be given a more powerful gun before it was really effective, and with that it performed as well as could be asked; but there was always a tendency for the crews to try and use the vehicle as a tank, while there were never enough tank destroyers to take the burden of tank fighting away from the plain tanks entirely. It was not until the war was over that the Americans finally recognized that tanks had to be able to deal with anything which crossed their path and that the artificial demarcation between tanks and tank destroyers had to go.

In September 1939 the British Army mustered some 85,000 motor vehicles, but of that total no fewer than 21,500 were motorcycles and over 26,000 of the vehicles were impressed civilian cars, trucks and motorcycles. Much of this

Below Maintenance time on an M4 Sherman. This vehicle's suspension and tracks in particular required frequent adjustment.

strength was left behind in France in 1940, and as a result the British motor industry worked overtime to make up the deficit and provide the wheels which the army needed. In general, the designs produced were all pre-war in origin and they served well enough. Specialized vehicles were developed on the standard types of chassis, notably in the ¾-ton and three-ton ranges, while most of the heavier cargo trucks were no more than lightly disguised civilian patterns. It was not until 1943, when production had more or less caught up with demand, that manufacturers and military design establishments began to produce new ideas, though all too often some of these were merely copies of foreign design; there were, for example, several attempts to produce a vehicle comparable to the Jeep, there were copies of the American Dodge ¾-ton weapons carrier, and copies of the German Krauss-Maffei ¾-tracked gun tractor. On the other hand some of the projects were eminently practical, or would have been had they started in 1938 instead of 1943, so that they could have been brought to fruition in time to be of some use. One such idea was the Octolat, an eight-wheeled cargo carrier-cum-artillery tractor capable of crossing the most formidable terrain; the war ended before this idea could be perfected, but it is probable that it formed the inspiration for, and some of the background to, the later Stalwart multi-wheel cargo carrier.

In the design and development of tanks, Britain's record makes pitiful reading; the 1946 Report of the Select Committee for National Expenditure was forthright enough to say that 'no tank produced in 1943 was worthy of action, while those manufactured earlier were inferior, both technically and tactically, to German tanks'. The reasons for this are involved and cannot be fully explored here, for it would take up too much space. In broad terms, it can be said that the failure to produce a decent tank stemmed from a combination of lack of guidance from the General Staff and the various branches of the Army as to precisely what was required; the lack of a powerful production engine and the reluctance of the British motor industry to develop one; and political interference, which led to the breaking up of the system of design and development shortly before the war in order to construct a new Minstry of Supply. As a result of this latter move, tank design went into the hands of a largely civilian committee, which regarded the tank as being primarily an automotive device and which gave little consideration to its fighting aspects, resulting in designs which were under-gunned for most of the war. The sudden rush into rearmament in the late 1930s, coupled with the simultaneous reorganization of the whole procedure for design and production, led to a number of hastily conceived designs which, in ser-vice, proved to be mechanically unreli-able. Of one design it has to be written: 'After 70 miles the gearbox gave out and by the end of December [six weeks later] forty-seven mechanical failures had been reported, while the steering brakes had a life of only 127 miles. By April...their performance was being reckoned in miles per transmission...' Yet because nothing better was available, this design had to be made to work, became the Crusader tank, and over 6,000 were built. Five years later, in the desert war, it was still unreli-able.

In desperation (or so it seems in retro-spect) the Tank Board welcomed any design which appeared to promise suc-cess; the Covenanter appeared, designed by a railway engineer, and proved no more reliable than the Crusader, while its crews detested it because the designer, for reasons which he doubtless felt were good, put the radiator inside the fighting compartment 'where it accomplished the dual role of cooling the engine and roasting the crew'. Even worse was the TOG, designed by a team of men who had been responsible for the tanks of World War I and who, it seemed, had learned nothing since.

Part of the trouble seems to have arisen due to the artificial demarcation of British tanks into light, cruiser and Infantry types; the light were supposed to reconnoitre, the cruiser to swoop about the battlefield to disrupt enemy communications, raid headquarters and perform such deeds as had been the prerogative of cavalry raids in days gone by, while the infantry tank was heavily armoured and ponderous to suit its role of accompanying the infan-tryman at walking pace across No Man's Land. This theory led designers into some fearful blind alleys, but worst of all was its

Facing page, top A British Crusader tank, mainstay of the British Army until the arival of the General Lee. *Facing page, bottom* The 17-pounder Archer self-propelled gun, with a General Patton in the background. *Below left* A Churchill Mk VI preserved at Bovington. *Below right* The TOG Mark 24 with 17-pounder gun. *Bottom* A Cromwell IV of 1944.

effect on gun policy; the logic ran thus: a light tank is to reconnoitre, therefore it does not need a powerful gun; the cruiser is for raiding, therefore it does not need a powerful gun; the infantry tank will be impervious, therefore it does not need a powerful gun. Although the gun designers saw the fallacies of this, they were unable to persuade the tank designers to make turrets large enough to take powerful weapons, with the result that British tanks were armed with the two-pounder (40mm) gun long after the Germans had gone to 50mm and even 75mm and the Americans had settled on 75mm as being the minimum feasible size.

In tank design generally, the turning point came when the Germans began to be confronted with growing numbers of Soviet T–34 and KV tanks. These were all but impervious to most German weapons except at suicidally short ranges, and it became imperative for the Germans to overhaul both their tanks and their anti-tank armament. Strangely, tank design in Germany had virtually stood still since 1939, largely because of a misguided belief that the war would be over so quickly that there would not be time to develop and produce fresh designs. Consequently, when in 1942 the German Army began making agitated noises, it took time to get the machinery of design and development turning over. Indeed,

the first response was the suggestion that the Germans should simply make a carbon copy of the T–34, but this, being impractical for many manufacturing reasons, was turned down. The final result was the design of the Panther and Tiger tanks, two formidable vehicles both in the scale of their protection and in their armament, the former having a high-velocity 75mm gun and the latter a tank version of the

celebrated 88mm anti-aircraft gun. But in spite of the best efforts of the designers, the German engineering industry was in no shape to perform prodigies of production, and the total number of Tiger and Panther tanks turned out before the war ended was less than 7,000.

By making the qualitative leap-frog, however, the Panther and Tiger designs spurred the various Allies to overhaul their own designs and, in their turn, make the next leap-frog move. The Soviets, relying greatly on the speed and agility of the T–34 and overwhelming production, left the tank more or less as it was, but concentrated on improving the armament, going up to an 85mm gun. In the KV series they were less happy, since it had not proved quite as good as they had hoped, and a complete redesign was done to produce the Josef Stalin, with ample protection and a devastating 122mm gun. The British, in a masterpiece of improvisation, managed to shoe-horn their 17-pounder gun into a Sherman turret to develop the Firefly tank and began design of the Comet, which was to carry a derated 17-pounder. The Americans, finally convinced that the 75mm gun was no longer master of all it met, tried a number of expedients before settling on a 76mm gun as their main tank armament. This gave about 50 percent better performance than the 75mm, but was still not enough to cope with Panther or Tiger at fighting ranges and, to boot, kicked up such a fearful blast and cloud of dust as to preclude the chance of a quick second shot. The British suggested adopting their idea of mounting the 17-pounder gun, while the Armored Force asked for a 90mm gun derived from an anti-aircraft gun, but neither suggestion appeared acceptable to the Ordnance Department and it took a great deal of

Far left An action sequence showing the tank/infantry team in action in Russia, 1942. *Centre* A PzKpfw IV with short 75mm gun. *Below* A PzKpfw IV in Russia, 1942. *Lower left* A King Tiger with Porsche turret. *Lower right* A Tiger I of 1942. Both these tigers are caged at Bovington.

struggle to get them to change their ideas; finally they adopted the 90mm gun in their heavy tank, but they left the Sherman perilously undergunned to the last.

The armoured car, that earliest of armoured vehicles, had a mixed reception during the war years. As a fighting vehicle, it came into the same category as the light tank and suffered from the same basic defect – it could no longer survive in the face of tanks or anti-tank guns. But as a reconnaissance vehicle, seeking information about enemy dispositions and evading combat where possible, it still performed a valuable function, particularly during the desert war of 1941–2. Britain therefore developed some good armoured cars and America began to follow suit. But once the war left the wide open spaces of the desert and moved on to the European mainland, the armoured car proved less serviceable, since it was all too

easily ambushed in close or built-up country. From 1943, therefore, the demand for armoured cars was reduced, though they were still used until the war ended. In 1940–1 an immense number of armoured car designs appeared in the USA, largely because they offered a quick and easy solution to the problem of putting a protected gun on wheels, but far too many of them were hopelessly impractical. For example, there was the Baker Jumping Car which had the wheels carried on powerful springs and which, it was claimed, could jump over 1.20m (4ft) obstacles; there was the Trackless Tank, an eight-wheeled monster armed with only a 37mm gun, though it was later improved by putting a 3in gun on to it. In general, there seemed to be confusion in the minds of the designers; they were not quite sure whether they were producing armoured cars or self-propelled guns.

Eventually a special board of review, the Palmer Board, sat during the winter of 1942–3, reviewed all the designs on offer and threw most of them out. One useful decision of this board was that nothing over seven tons in weight could be contemplated as an armoured car.

The major automotive growth area of the war period was the self-propelled gun. This was virtually ignored before the war and the first move was a request from the German Panzer troops, in 1938, for an assault gun, a tracked and armoured vehicle carrying a heavier gun than that commonly found on tanks and capable of accompanying assaulting infantry so as to deal with any strongpoint or obstacles which held them up. What evolved from this was a tank chassis with a superstructure raised slightly above the hull level and roofed over, with a 75mm infantry gun mounted firing forward and with limited traverse. The vehicle had no turret, and this alone made it a cheaper and easier vehicle to produce than the comparable tank. It was followed by several variant designs, adapting miscellaneous chassis to the same task or improving the gun power by the use of bigger calibres – the Germans found that captured tanks were a

fruitful source of chassis for these weapons. From this design they moved to developing tank destroyers along similar lines, making them more massively armoured and with more powerful guns, a line of development which culminated in the Ferdinand or Elefant mounting a powerful 88mm gun. This vehicle showed up the basic drawback of tank destroyers of this type; whilst it was a formidable weapon which could demolish anything within the traversing range of its gun, it was virtually defenceless and blind outside that arc, and it proved all too easy for infantry tank-hunters to creep up on the 'blind' side and destroy the Elefant with hand-placed charges.

While the Germans (and Russians, too, who copied the idea) relied upon close-range assault guns, the British and Americans regarded self-propelled artillery from an entirely different point of view. Their main demand was to equip the standard support artillery so that it could keep up with the speed of an armoured advance, deploy rapidly and pull out of position equally rapidly. Towed artillery, particularly in medium calibres (about 155mm), was slow across country and took time to go into and come out of

action. The first serious move in this direction was the British development of Bishop, a Valentine tank chassis upon which was placed a large steel box mounting a 25-pounder field gun. Due to the construction of the armoured box, the gun could only elevate to 15°, which restricted its fighting range to 5,850m (6,400yds) instead of the normal 12,225m (13,400yds) of the field gun. One hundred of these were built in late 1941 and were used in North Africa, but apart from imparting some useful instruction on the tactical handling of self-propelled guns, they were not particularly impressive.

In November 1941 the Americans mounted their 105mm howitzer, their

standard field piece, on to a modified M3 Grant tank chassis; the superstructure was open-topped and built up at the sides into an armoured enclosure, and through the front plate of this the howitzer protruded. Alongside the howitzer was a round pulpit-like structure which mounted an anti-aircraft machine gun, and it was the appearance of this which led the British troops to christen it Priest, conforming to the ecclesiastical tradition begun with Bishop. This, the Howitzer Motor Carriage M7, was used by the British in the desert and in Italy and by the Americans in all theatres and proved to be a most successful vehicle. In British service it was only disliked because it demanded a spe-

cial supply of ammunition, since 105mm was not a British calibre, and the British asked for a similar conversion but mounting the 25-pounder gun. The Americans produced a prototype which resembled the M7, but somewhat marred the effect by pointing out that, of course, American production facilities could not be utilized to make a machine which the Americans themselves would not use. So the idea was taken across the border to Canada, where a factory had been set up to produce the Ram tank, more or less a Canadian version of the M3; this had turned out less successfully than expected, largely because of the British insistence on undergunning it, and so the facilities were turned over to making a self-propelled gun out of the chassis and mounting the 25-pounder on it. This became Sexton, which served with the British Army until the 1950s and is still serving the Portuguese and other armies.

While putting the divisional field piece on tracks satisfied the British at the time, it didn't satisfy the Americans, and they next turned to the problem of moving their medium artillery. The M12 gun was the result of this, and it broke new ground by simply being a mobile platform for the

gun – there was no armour or protection for the crew. This made sense, since no one in his right mind was going to dash into the thick of battle with a 155mm medium gun; it was an indirect-fire weapon pure and simple, and putting it on tracks simply improved its mobility and speed of response by several orders of magnitude. An innovation on this chassis was the use of a bulldozer-like blade at the rear end which, dropped so as to dig into the ground, took the shock of firing from the suspension. The only defect of the whole equipment was that it had been designed around an obsolete weapon, the 155mm M1918 gun, stocks of which were rapidly running out. So a fresh design was begun using the new M1 gun and basing it on the chassis of the M4 Sherman tank; parallel with this was a sister design using the 8in howitzer on the same chassis. Both these entered service shortly before the war ended and continued to serve for many years in both British and American armies.

The American designers, having got the bit firmly between their teeth, then went on to develop self-propelled carriages for the 240mm howitzer and the 8in long-range gun; five of the former and two of

the latter were built, intended for shipment to the Pacific for use in the forthcoming invasion of Japan, but the end of the war arrived before they had been approved for service and they were all scrapped shortly afterwards

One last category of vehicle which must be mentioned in connection with World War II is that of amphibians. Strategic demands dictated that much of the major action of the war, from the Allies' point of view, had to take place after landing on a hostile beach, and it was too much to expect that it would be possible to land all the many types of vehicles dryshod. Therefore a certain proportion had to be designed to swim ashore so as to provide the landing troops with immediate support and supplies. Moreover, once ashore there would be rivers to cross where no bridges existed. Some desultory work on amphibians had been done before the war, but it was the prospect of making landings on remote islands in the Pacific and on the shores of Europe which concentrated the designers' minds from about 1941 onward.

The US Marines had been investigating the techniques of beach landings throughout the 1920s and 1930s, and in 1924 they had tried two Christie amphibious tanks off Puerto Rico, though without much success. In 1932, however, a retired engineer named Roebling began developing a vehicle intended for rescue work in the Florida Everglades, and he eventually developed an aluminium-bodied tracked vehicle which could cross land on its tracks and also paddle itself through the water. Roebling's Alligator was featured in the press, and in 1940 the Marine Corps ordered three. After tests, they decided that this was the vehicle for which they had been searching and

ordered another 200, calling them their LVT–1 (Landing Vehicle Tracked 1). It was followed by LVT–2, and then by a much improved design, LVT–3, which had a stern ramp through which stores and men, even a Jeep, could be loaded. The next step, dictated by combat conditions, was to add armour and finally to fit some LVTs with tank turrets so that they could act as support weapons. Some 18,000 of the various LVT models were eventually made, and their contribution to the war in the Pacific theatre was immeasurable.

In addition to their use in the Pacific, LVTs were also seen in the European theatre, notably in northern Italy and in the inundated areas of the Low Countries. In these conditions, as in the sheltered lagoons of tropical islands, they were quite adequate, but when it came to crossing the English Channel, the LVT was outclassed and some other ideas had to be canvassed. A certain number of LVTs might be carried by larger ships and launched off shore, but the greatest problem was going to be actually fighting ashore, a task which needed massive firepower and immediate support. Somehow tanks had to be swum ashore, since it was unlikely that the heavy tank landing craft would be able to get close enough to the beach to allow the

tanks to simply wade through shallow water.

The prospect of trying to make 20 or 30 tons of tank float was a daunting one, but the answer lay in artificially increasing its displacement to make it buoyant. This was done by Nicholas Straussler, an engineer who had been involved in armoured car design before the war and who now developed the DD (Duplex Drive) tank This was an ordinary tank – a Sherman, for example – with a collapsible canvas screen attached all round the hull. This could be raised by applying compressed air to 36 tubular rubber pillars, and, once raised, it could be secured by steel struts. This gave the tank floating capability, and water propulsion was provided by two propellers, driven through the motion of the tracks and rear idler wheels, which could be lowered into position and then retracted when the tank arrived on shore. Once ashore, the steel struts were unlocked by a hydraulic system and the compressed air was released from the pillars so that the screen collapsed and the tank's gun had a clear field of fire. DD tanks were made in both Britain and the USA and were used with success in the D-Day landings and, after that, in the crossings of the Rhine and Elbe.

Below The British FV439 armoured personnel carrier mounting a 120mm Wombat anti-tank gun. *Facing page, top* American T114 armoured personnel carrier with experimental cannon. *Facing page, bottom* British FV439, a specialised conversion of the standard APC for use as a radio communications centre.

THE POST-WAR YEARS

AFTER THE WAR ENDED the immediate reaction on the part of Britain and America was to disband their immense forces and return to normal as soon as possible, and in that sort of atmosphere little thought was given to future developments. But within a very short time it became apparent that things were never going to 'get back to normal' and military preparedness was something which was going to have to continue indefinitely. The British had, at last, produced a serviceable tank in the Centurion, just as the war was ending, and this was continually improved and developed in the post war years. The Soviets had produced their Josef Stalin III at the Berlin victory parade, and the heavy sloped armour and massive gun on this tank gave rise to questions of parity and

led to work in Britain and the USA on a new generation of tanks with comparable armament.

So far as soft-skinned vehicles went, so many had been produced during the war that most countries were living on their fat for several years, and American surplus

vehicles both soft and armoured were distributed throughout the world with a lavish hand. The French Army were almost entirely re-equipped with American vehicles for several years, as were the Italians, and many nations who had played no part in the war were only too happy refitting their forces with Allied cast-offs. The Korean War was fought almost entirely with the same types of vehicle which had seen service in 1944-5, but that conflict served notice that these designs were reaching the end of their useful lives. Even where the vehicles still filled their designated role, they had been out of production for years, their manufacturers had turned back to other things, and spare parts were becoming increasingly expensive and difficult to obtain. It was time to start designing afresh.

One major lesson which emerged from the World War I was that infantry accompanying armour needed the protection of armour themselves. The Germans had

begun this by producing armoured half-track vehicles for their Panzer Grenadier regiments; in France and Germany, Canadian units had taken redundant self-propelled guns, stripped out the armament and turned them into armoured troop carriers, a fashion which spread rapidly through the Allied armies and served to find a useful employment for tanks when they were replaced by improved models. In the post-war years the development of APCs (Armoured Personnel Carriers) became a high priority, particularly in the light of nuclear warfare, when troops would need protection from fall-out and similar phenomena as well as from conventional weapon fire. The British Saracen was an early entrant in this field, its development having been pushed forward in order that it could be employed in Malaya; this was a six-wheeled vehicle which performed well over most sorts of terrain. The Americans, on the other hand, elected for a tracked solution and developed a number of car-

Inset, left Soviet missile carriers parading in Red Square. *Inset right* The Soviet FROG missile on wheeled carrier/launcher vehicle. *Main picture* Soviet multiple rocket launchers on parade.

This page, top German 'Leopard II A V' Main
Battle Tank; *centre* the Swedish 'S' tank;
bottom left The Soviet T-72 MBT; *bottom right*
the US Army's XM-1 'Abrams' MBT. *Facing
page, top* American M109 self-propelled
155mm howitzer; *centre* American M110 self-
propelled 175mm gun; *bottom left* French
AMX 13; *bottom right* American M42 self-
propelled AA gun with twin 40mm Bofors guns.

riers before settling on the aluminium-
armoured M113. This led the British to try
a tracked solution, producing the Trojan
series. The Soviets began with wheels,
turning out a variety of formidable vehicles, and then began looking at tracks.
But by that time the role of the APC had
come into question; was it merely an
armoured taxi-cab to take the troops to
the scene of battle and drop them there, or
was it to be built so that the occupants
could actually fight from the vehicle? The
latter point of view began to prevail in the
1960s and APCs began to sprout small
turrets with heavy machine guns or small-
calibre cannon, while ports in the passenger compartments allowed the
occupants to fire their personal weapons
while the vehicle was on the move.

The inevitable escalation followed, with
different countries trying to outdo each
other in the degree of protection or
effectiveness of armament carried on their
APCs, until the Soviets made the decisive
step in 1967 by introducing a completely
new class of vehicle, which has since come
to be called the MICV or Mechanized

Infantry Combat Vehicle. The Soviet BMP–1 resembles a long low tank, with a midships turret carrying a 73mm gun with, above it, a launch rail for an anti-tank guided missile. But within the rear section of the hull is a passenger compartment in which eight fully-equipped infantrymen can ride, provided with their own periscopes and firing ports along the side of the hull. The vehicle is, in addition, fully amphibious. Thus it can taxi its passengers to any part of the battlefield, and can also fight very convincingly if it has to, since the armament is capable of coping with main battle tanks or virtually any other obstacle which might be met. At the present time an equivalent vehicle, the XM723, is under test with the US Army; this carries nine men in addition to the crew and will probably be armed with a 25mm cannon and two anti-tank guided missiles.

Tank development since the war has, in general, been a matter of steady development along fairly conventional lines, with the accent being placed on better armament and more sophisticated fire-control

Top left Lightweight Land-Rover with winter camouflage in Norway. *Centre left* British Bedford 3-tonne truck, Northern Norway. *Bottom left* The Volvo over-snow articulated vehicle.

equipment, which will ensure a high first-round-hit probability. During the war the idea of gun stabilization was pioneered; this meant using attitude sensors and mechanical gearing to ensure that once the gun was laid on to the target, it remained at the correct elevation irrespective of how the tank rocked or pitched beneath it. After the war this system was improved and was enhanced by the addition of stabilization in azimuth, so that once the gun was correctly laid and the stabilizer switched in, the barrel remained pointed at the target no matter how the tank pitched or turned. With the advent of micro-electronics it has been possible to develop small, robust computers which can be fitted inside the turret and linked to rangefinders, wind direction and speed analysers, velocity analysers, and the gun sight so as to make all the corrections necessary to compensate for meteorological conditions, target speed and angle, and ammunition characteristics and displace the gunner's aiming point accordingly, practically guaranteeing a hit. Add to this the development of infra-red night-vision equipment, image-intensifying sights, lasers and similar equipment, and it can be appreciated that

Below Stalwart, the British Army cross-country load-carrier. *Upper right* The French AMX-30 tank recovery vehicle. *Lower right* The Chrysler XR 311 reconnaissance car, currently undergoing evaluation

the turret of a modern tank is very full indeed.

Nevertheless, there has been room for some deviations from the general run of conventional design. When gas turbine engines appeared they were tried in tanks, though so far there have been few service applications. One such application is in the Swedish S–Tank, which broke new ground in many ways. The most notable feature of this vehicle was that the gun was fixed to the hull so that it was incapable of being elevated or traversed. To point the gun at the target, the whole tank is aligned, by raising or lowering the suspension to give elevation, and swivelling the tank on its tracks to give direction. This, of course, demands a high degree of precision in control. The advantage is that rigidly mounting the gun permits an automatic loading mechanism to be attached to the breech, which does away with the need to carry a man to load the gun. The crew is thus reduced to three men, the commander, the radioman and the driver, who, since he controls the tank, also becomes the gunner. Another advantage is that doing away with the turret allows the whole tank to be much lower and thus more easily concealed. The

Facing page, top US Army tactical missile on M133 carrier. *Facing page, lower left* A Shillelagh missile is launched from the 152mm gun/launcher of an M551 Sheridan tank.

Below British Swing fire missiles are launched from Striker carriers. *Lower left* A Roland ground-to-air missile carrier on AMX chassis. *Lower right* The French Thomson-CSF Crotale missile carrier.

focuses the blast and bores a hole through the armour to allow blast and flame to pass into the tank; squash-head deposits a poultice of explosive on the outside of the tank and detonates it, driving a shock wave into the plate which detaches a portion of the inner face as a missile within the tank. Chobham Armour defeats these three by using the interlining; it upsets the path of a shot, smothers the penetrating jet of the hollow charge and muffles the detonating wave from squash-head. Chobham Armour has, so far, only been used on Shir Iran variations of the British Chieftain tanks and on the developing American XM–1 Abrams tank.

Soft-skinned vehicles have undergone few changes; the Jeep is still with us, though in somewhat modified form, while the Deuce-and-a-half has become the Eager Beaver, again a modification from the wartime design, but one which still betrays its ancestry. Multi-wheel, specialist high-mobility load carriers capable of keeping up with fast armoured formations are in limited use, while the Soviets have developed a wide range of specialized military trucks, in contrast to their wartime reliance on a basically civilian model. The current fashion is towards high mobility, light weight to permit air transport and engines which can operate on whatever fuel, from aviation spirit to diesel oils, that can be found.

Indeed, the same parameters can be distinguished in every facet of the military vehicle field of the present day. Only the totalitarian states can afford to be lavish with their equipment; the democracies are constantly revising their designs to keep within ever-shrinking budgets and to bestow the utmost mobility and firepower on their small but highly trained armies. As exemplified by the S-tank, if skilful design and mechanical ingenuity can save one man from a tank crew then the money spent on the design becomes worthwhile. The next few years will probably see more and more automation in combat vehicles, with automatic loaders and even more complex fire-control systems. The 1920s saw the rash of two-man tanks abandoned because the driver had his hands full and the commander had far too much to do; there is every indication that we are slowly returning to the two-man tank, now that the silicon chip and the servomotor can be harnessed into doing the routine work.

disadvantage is that the gun cannot be fired while the tank is moving, and this is sufficient to condemn it in the eyes of several military critics.

For many years protection has simply meant the usual tank armour of either homogeneous or face-hardened steel. Since the war, however, it has been obvious that to gain more protection by simply adding more thickness of plate is self-defeating since the weight of the vehicle rapidly increases to the point where mobility suffers. Much work has been done on the development of aluminium armour, but this is only feasible on lightweight vehicles such as MICVs, APCs and tanks intended for carriage by air, and

metallurgical considerations have argued against its use for major types of tank. In the middle 1970s the British Fighting Vehicle Experimental Establishment at Chobham announced a new system of protection called Chobham Armour. Full details of this have not been made public, but it is generally understood to be a form of laminated steel plate with ceramic interlining. This, it is claimed, defends the tank against the three methods of attack currently in use, the armour-piercing shot, the hollow charge and the squash-head shell. AP shot pierces by virtue of its kinetic energy, smashing its way through the plate; hollow charge uses a shaped charge of explosives, which, in effect,

The Valentine tank took its name from the day
its design was submitted to the War Office –
Valentine's Day, 1938. It is seen here entering
Tripoli on 26 January 1943. It was obsolete as
a fighting vehicle by 1944 but formed the basis
for a number of specialist vehicles.

TANKS

ARGENTINA

TAM–3 MEDIUM TANK 1980–

The TAM–3 is an Argentine design for a medium tank which will replace the ageing M4 Shermans (qv) still in the Argentinian Army. The first models have been built under licence in Germany, but full production will be undertaken in Argentina. The TAM–3 uses the German Marder (qv) chassis, modified to take a three-man turret mounting a 105mm gun, developed from the French one fitted to AMX–13 (qv). The gun is stabilized and the turret is low and well sloped. Protection has yielded to weight in order to allow the tank free movement over the Argentine road bridges. At a later date it is intended to build an armoured personnel carrier on the same chassis, so that there is compatibility of components throughout the armoured force.

Length: 6.44m (21ft 11in). *Width:* 3.25m (10ft 7in). *Height:* 2.40m (7ft 10in). *Weight:* 29,500kg (65,020lb). *Crew:* 4. *Power:* one MTU MB 833 Ea–500, 6-cyl., water-cooled, diesel, 600bhp at 2,200rpm. *Armament:* one 105mm gun; two 7.62mm machine guns, one coaxially mounted, one on turret. *Armour:* not known. *Speed:* 75km/hr (46mph). *Range:* 600km (372 miles). *Maker:* in production, at Argentine State Factories in Rio Tercero and Buenos Aires.

TAM-3 Medium Tank

AUSTRALIA

SENTINEL CRUISER TANK 1942–1943

In May 1940 the Australian Government, appreciating that supply of tanks from Britain would be difficult, decided to design and produce an Australian cruiser tank. Considering that at that time Australia had very little heavy

engineering plant and had not even manufactured a motor car, this was an ambitious programme. To begin with an engineer was sent to the United States to study tank production methods, and a design expert was sent from England.

In November 1940 the specification for the AC1 – Australian Cruiser 1 – was set forth; it

Sentinel Cruiser Tank

was to be of 16–20 tons weight, mount a 2-pdr. gun, have a speed of 48km/hr (30mph) and an armour basis of 50mm. It was decided to adapt the mechanical layout of the American M3 (qv) to British ideas on hull and turret design. Engines had to be imported, and it was at first hoped to adopt an American diesel, but when the estimated weight of the tank had crept up to 25 tons owing to an increase in armour protection, a triple layout of Cadillac car engines was adopted. Both hull and turret were to be cast as single units, something never previously attempted.

Difficulties connected with the cutting of gears for the transmission led to a simpler design, known as AC2, being mooted in June 1941, but this was found to have its own drawbacks. The AC1 gearbox was redesigned to suit

Ram II Cruiser Tank

the gear-cutting machinery available in Australia, the AC2 was dropped, and work went ahead on AC1. In January 1942 the first three pilots were built, and in August 1942 the first production models of the Sentinel – as the AC1 was now known – were delivered.

Not surprisingly, some design weaknesses showed up once the tanks began to be used, and production was restricted to only 66 tanks. It was hoped to improve the armament by fitting the new 6-pdr. gun, but supplies of this weapon were desperately needed in the Middle East and none could be spared for Australia. The next steps, therefore, were a redesign to do away with the small mechanical weaknesses which had shown up, and an increase in the firepower by fitting the 25-pdr. field gun into the turret. This was the AC3, and it was successfully tested in July 1942. A decision was taken to put it into production once the initial order for the AC1 was finished. A further step was taken with the development of the AC4 which mounted the 17-pdr. gun in the turret; this model was, of course, larger and heavier than the AC1, but it was never taken past the pilot stage, though plans were laid for producing over 700 AC3 and AC4

By the middle of 1943, however, the threat of Japanese invasion had passed, supplies of American tanks were beginning to flow into the country, and what mechanical facilities were available were needed to maintain these new tanks. Production plans for the Sentinel were therefore cancelled in July 1943, those tanks which had been produced being used solely for training.

Length: 6.32m (20ft 9in). *Width:* 2.76m (9ft 1in). *Height:* 2.55m (8ft 5in). *Weight:* 28,450kg (62,720lb). *Crew:* 5. *Power:* three Cadillac '75', V-8, petrol, total 330bhp at 3,050rpm. *Armament:* one 2-pdr. gun; two .303 Vickers machine guns. *Armour:* 25–65mm. *Speed:* 48km/hr (30mph). *Range:* 320km (200 miles). *Maker:* New South Wales Railway Co., Chullora.

CANADA

RAM CRUISER TANK *1942–1945*
In 1940 the Canadian Government was looking for a suitable tank design to put into production in order to supply Canadian

armoured formations. At much the same time, the British Government had arranged for the supply, from America, of numbers of M3 medium tanks (*qv*). The M3, as it stood, was not satisfactory in British eyes, and the Americans agreed to put a somewhat different turret on to the British order. The result, however, was still unsatisfactory to the British. As a result, the British Tank Commission and the Canadian Government put forward a joint plan to build the American M3 in Canada, but modify it to meet British standards well beyond the point the Americans were willing to go, and use it as an interim tank until American production of the M4 (*qv*) got under way.

The modification consisted firstly of removing the side sponson of the M3 and its 75mm gun, and then fitting a low-silhouette turret mounting the British 6-pdr. gun. Unfortunately this idea ran into opposition from some quarters, since it was declared that the Ram (as the new tank was to be called) was a cruiser, and all cruiser tanks were armed with 2-pdrs. So the first 50 Ram tanks carried 2-pdr. guns in their turret, but the designers had the forethought to build the turret with a completely removable front plate, so that subsequent improvement of the armament would simply be a matter of unbolting the plate and bolting on a new one.

The 2-pdr.-equipped tanks became the Ram 1 and as soon as sanity had prevailed and permission had been given to use the 6-pdr., the Ram 2 with a 6-pdr. gun began to appear. A total of 1,899 Ram 2s were built before production ceased in the summer of 1943.

One design feature of the Ram not found on its M3 forerunner was a small independent machine-gun turret at the left front of the hull, an idea carried over from the British cruiser tank designs. Like the British, the Canadians found that these small turrets soon filled up with fumes when the gun was fired. The turret was removed after the first 100 Ram 2s had been made; the hull contour was modified and a ball-mounted machine gun fitted.

Large numbers of Ram 2 were shipped to Britain to equip the Canadian Armoured Divisions in training there, but since the 6-pdr. was obsolescent, all Rams were withdrawn in 1944 and the units re-equipped with M4 Sherman tanks for the invasion of Europe. As a gun tank, therefore, the Ram never saw action, but

it was widely used in combat in variant models, notably as a command tank for artillery units, and, with its turret removed, as a Kangaroo armoured personnel carrier (*qv*).

Ram 2 *Length:* 5.79m (19ft 0in). *Width:* 2.76m (9ft 1in). *Height:* 2.66m (8ft 9in). *Weight:* 29,485kg (62,800lb). *Crew:* 5. *Power:* Continental R975C1, 9-cyl., radial, petrol, 400bhp at 2,400rpm. *Armament:* one 6-pdr. gun; three .30 Browning machine guns. *Armour:* 13–76mm. *Speed:* 38km/hr (24mph). *Range:* 200km (125 miles). *Maker:* Montreal Locomotive Works, Montreal.

CZECHOSLOVAKIA

LT–35 LIGHT TANK *1936–1943*
The LT–35 was developed by Skoda in the early 1930s, using some of the experience gained in Czechoslovakia from the use of Carden–Loyd carriers (*qv*) over the previous ten years. It went into production in 1936 and

LT-35 Light Tank

entered service the following year, but was taken over by the Germans in 1938 and hardly saw any worthwhile service with the Czechoslovakian Army. In the Wehrmacht it was called the PzKpfw 35(t) and was used in the invasion of France and Russia with some success, although by 1942 it was well out of date and was then relegated to artillery tractor. Production continued under German control in Czechoslovakia until 1941, and perhaps longer. The hull and turret were of riveted and bolted plate with a two-man turret. The main armament was a Czech 37.2mm gun with a coaxial machine gun and one machine gun in the hull front. Vision was not very good and the commander usually travelled with his head clear of the turret roof. Another drawback was that the transmission and steering were rather complex, which led the Germans to modify it. Hungary and Romania built versions of it under licence and used them until 1945.

Length: 4.90m (16ft 1in). *Width:* 2.15m (7ft

0in). *Height:* 2.22m (7ft 3in). *Weight:* 10,500kg (23,148lb). *Crew:* 4. *Power:* Skoda, 6-cyl., in-line, water-cooled, petrol, 120bhp at 1,800rpm. *Armament:* one 37.2mm gun; two 7.92mm machine guns. *Armour:* 12–35mm. *Speed:* 40km/hr (25mph). *Range:* 193km (120 miles). *Maker:* Skoda, Pilsen.

LT–38 LIGHT TANK *1938–1945*
When Czechoslovakia bought the licence to build the Carden–Loyd series of tankettes and carriers (*qv*), the Prague machine-tool works of CKD made them. Using this experience, they produced their own light tank in 1933 and marketed it as the LT–34. It was exported to at least half a dozen countries in various forms and was little more than a Carden–Loyd with a turret. From the LT–34 the firm developed a larger and more satisfactory tank which was entered for a Czech Army trial in 1937. It was adopted and was also sold to six or seven other

LT-38 Light Tank

countries. It was known in Czechoslovakia as the LT–38, but was also called the TNHS, and in Sweden it became the Strv m/41 (*qv*). The Germans took it over for their own army and production continued until 1942. It was used in

the invasion of France and some may have gone to Russia. It was adapted for use as a self-propelled gun and anti-aircraft mount.

The original tank mounted a Skoda 37.2mm gun and coaxial machine gun in the turret, together with a hull gun. The construction was by bolted and riveted plate which was not particularly strong, but the suspension was good and it had reasonable agility. By the standards of the day the engine was quite powerful, and this was one reason why the vehicle could be adapted to so many different roles.

Length: 4.30m (14ft 11in). *Width:* 2.13m (7ft 0in). *Height:* 2.34m (7ft 7in). *Weight:* 9,700kg (21,385lb). *Crew:* 4. *Power:* 6-cyl., in-line, water-cooled, petrol, 150bhp at 2,600rpm. *Armament:* one 37.2mm gun; two 7.92mm machine guns. *Armour:* 8–30mm. *Speed:* 42km/hr (26mph). *Range:* 200km (125 miles). *Maker:* Ceskomoravska Kolben Danek, Prague.

FRANCE

AMX–13 LIGHT TANK *1951–*
In 1946 the French Army decided to re-equip itself entirely with French vehicles and guns. One of the 1946 specifications called for a light

AMX-13 Light Tank with 90mm gun

tank capable of being air transported and carrying a large gun. The first prototype appeared in 1949 and production started in earnest in 1954. Tank production stopped in 1964 but hulls and components for the many variants continued. More than 4,500 vehicles have been built and the AMX–13 design is one of the most successful armoured vehicles of the post-war years. It has been adopted all over the world in more than 25 countries.

The dominating feature of the design, stemming from the need to be an efficient destroyer of tanks, is the unusual oscillating turret and large gun with an automatic loader. The top half of the turret is pivoted on the trunnions and it moves in elevation with the gun. This allows the use of an automatic loader in the turret bustle, and so there is no need for a loader in the crew. The automatic loader has twin revolving magazines, each holding six

rounds, so the gunner can fire 12 rounds at high speed, but once the magazines are empty the crew must dismount and refill them from outside and this places a restraint on the use of the vehicle in a pitched battle. The oscillating turret also restricts the depression of the gun to some extent, which means that more of the hull must be exposed when firing from behind a crest. The armour, though well sloped, is not thick. The small size of the vehicle restricts the height of the crew men to 1.72m (5ft 8in). The powerful engine and good suspension make for mobility and the AMX has a good cross-country performance. The armament has been increased since the first versions, and the stan-

dard gun is now a 90mm. The AMX–13 can also carry anti-tank missiles, and the many variants use the hull for self-propelled guns, anti-aircraft guns, and infantry carriers.

Length (hull only): 4.57m (15ft). *Width:* 2.50m (8ft 2in). *Height:* 2.34m (7ft 7in). *Weight:* 15,000kg (33,069lb). *Crew:* 3. *Power:* SOFAM, 8-cyl., horizontally opposed, water-cooled, petrol, 270bhp at 3,200rpm. *Armament:* one 75mm gun; one 7.5mm machine gun coaxially mounted or one 90mm gun; one 7.62 machine gun. *Armour:* 10–40mm. *Speed:* 60km/hr (37mph). *Range:* 350km (218 miles). *Maker:* Atelier de Construction, Roanne; Creusot-Loire, Chalon-sur-Saône.

AMX-13 Light Tank with HOT anti-tank missiles

AMX-30 Main Battle Tank

AMX-32 Main Battle Tank

AMX–30 MAIN BATTLE TANK *1964–*

The AMX–30 was originally intended to be a joint venture with Germany, each country designing its own tank and the two being evaluated so that both took the better one. In the end this co-operative scheme broke down and the Germans went ahead with their tank, the Leopard I (*qv*), and the French developed the AMX–30. It entered service in 1967 and since then it is estimated that over 2,000 have been made, many of them for service in other countries. The AMX–30 is built of cast armour and mounts a powerful 105mm gun of French design. The driver is the only crewman in the hull, the other three being in the turret. The gunner has a separate heavy machine gun or cannon which can be elevated independently as an anti-aircraft gun, and the 105mm fires an unusual hollow-charge shell in which the explosive filling is contained in a separate liner which is mounted on ball bearings and so does not rotate with the driving band. This complicated arrangement is to ensure that the jet from the explosive does not deteriorate by spinning. The engine and transmission are at the back and can be removed as a unit in one hour by the armoured recovery version using its crane. There are several variants based on the hull, including one which carries the Pluton tactical nuclear rocket and another carrying the CROTALE anti-aircraft system. Another version is armed with the Roland SAM system and there are special variations of the tank itself for operation in different climates. For instance, for Saudi Arabia there are large engine air filters, but no NBC protection.

Length (excluding gun): 6.64m (21ft 8in). *Width:* 3.10m (10ft 2in). *Height:* 2.85m (9ft 4in). *Weight:* 36,000kg (79,366lb). *Crew:* 4.

Power: Hispano-Suiza 110, 12-cyl., horizontally-opposed, water-cooled, multi-fuel, 700bhp at 2,400rpm, built in France by Saviem. *Armament:* one 105mm gun; one 12.7mm machine gun or 20mm cannon mounted coaxially; one 7.62mm machine gun. *Armour:* classified, but estimated to be at least 50mm maximum. *Speed:* 65km/hr (40mph). *Range:* 650km (400 miles). *Maker:* Atelier de Construction, Roanne.

AMX-32 MAIN BATTLE TANK *1979-*

The AMX-32 is the latest French tank to be announced. It was shown to the public for the first time at the Satory Armament Exhibition in June 1979 and represents the current thinking in France as to the shape and size of the main battle tank of the 1980's. It is an updated AMX–30 (*qv*) with greatly improved firepower and better protection, yet total weight is not greatly increased. The turret is new and is designed to accommodate a new 120mm smoothbore gun. It is claimed that this large and formidable weapon is significantly more powerful than the 105mm gun in the AMX–30, yet it can be fitted into a 105mm mounting so that tanks such as AMX–30 can be up-gunned without needing to change turrets. However, the AMX-32 turret is both larger and better equipped than any previous French ones, and it has full stabilization with a laser rangefinder coupled to a COTAC integrated fire-control system. Integral with this sighting system is a night-firing sight which permits the gunner to fire on the move in almost total darkness and at the same time

Char 2C Heavy Tank

gives the commander a separate viewer with the same level of performance. The hull and suspension are basically that of the AMX-30, with thicker armour on the four plates and anti-bazooka skirting over the tracks. Secondary armament is a coaxially-mounted 20mm cannon, with a 7.62mm machine gun mounted externally on the cupola. The power unit is the same as for the AMX-30, with an improved hydraulic torque converter in the transmission. So far only one or two of these tanks have been built, but it may be assumed that they will be accepted by the French Army and also offered for export.

Length: 6.59m (21ft 7in). *Width:* 3.24m (10ft 7in). *Height:* 2.96m (9ft 8in). *Weight:* 38,000kg (83,752lb). *Power:* Hispano-Suiza 110, 12-cyl., horizontally-opposed, water-cooled, multi-fuel, 700bhp at 2,400rpm. Built in France by Saviem. *Armament:* 1 × 105mm or 120mm smoothbore gun; 1 × 20mm automatic cannon; 1 × 7.62mm machine gun. *Armour:* classified. *Speed:* 65km/hr (40mph). *Range:* 520km (323 miles). *Maker:* Atelier de Construction, Roanne.

ARL 44 Heavy Tank

ARL 44 HEAVY TANK *1946–1953*
The great limitation of the Char B1 (*qv*) was the mounting of the 75mm gun in the hull, and, as early as 1938, design studies were put in

hand for a tank with a turret-mounted 75mm gun. The war stopped further work but immediately afterwards it was continued and the first version appeared in 1946, a great triumph for French industry. The ARL 44 used the tracks and suspension of the Char B1, but almost every other item changed. The hull was wider and lower, with a new engine and transmission. The turret was built by Schneider and was large enough to have three men in it and carried the long-barrelled 90mm gun. The front glacis plate sloped in much the same way as the German Panther (*qv*) and behind it were the driver and co-driver, the latter not having a hull machine gun as was popular with other tanks at that time. The original order was for 300 ARLs, but only 60 were made and they were not very successful.

Length: 10.54m (34ft 6in). *Width:* 3.41m (11ft 2in). *Height:* 3.23m (10ft 6in). *Weight:* 48,000kg (105,820lb). *Crew:* 5. *Power:* Maybach HL 230 P45, V-12, water-cooled, petrol, 700bhp at 3,000rpm. *Armament:* one 90mm gun; one 7.5mm machine gun coaxially mounted; one 7.5mm machine gun anti-aircraft mounting on turret. *Speed:* 37km/hr (23mph). *Range:* 150km (93 miles). *Makers:* Renault Frères in conjunction with La Compagnie des Forges et Acieries de la Marine et d'Homecourt, St. Chamond; turret by Schneider-Creusot, Le Creusot.

CHAR 2C HEAVY TANK *1918–1940*
The French Army was very concerned with the need for weight and firepower to overcome the fixed defences of the World War I trenches. The Char series of heavy tanks were meant as breakthrough battering rams and they were made very long so that they could cross wide gaps. They were also narrow, which made it difficult for them to manoeuvre other than in a straight line. They were massive machines, and mounted their main armament of a 75mm gun in a fully rotating turret. There was a secondary machine-gun turret on the rear of the hull and three other machine guns in ball mountings on the sides and front. The all-round tracks and poor suspension only allowed a slow top speed,

but it was better than most others of the time and, had the original order for 300 been built in time, they might have made a difference to the closing stages of the war. In the end only 10 were completed, in 1919, and they were still in service in 1940. They were never used in action, as the Luftwaffe bombed the train taking them to the front.

Length: 10.30m (33ft 8in). *Width:* 2.95m (9ft 8in). *Height:* 4.02m (13ft 2in). *Weight:* 70,000kg (154,320lb). *Crew:* 12. *Power:* Maybach, 6-cyl., in-line, water-cooled, petrol, 260bhp. *Armament:* one 75mm gun; four 8mm machine guns. *Armour:* 6–45mm. *Speed:* 12km/hr (8mph). *Range:* 160km (100 miles). *Maker:* Forges et Chantiers de la Mediterranée, La Seyne, Toulon.

CHAR B1 bis HEAVY TANK *1930–1945*
On the outbreak of war in 1939 the Char B1 bis was considered the most powerful tank in the French Army and one of the more formidable armoured vehicles then in service anywhere in the world. It originated from a design study of 1921 and the first experimental vehicles were on test in 1929. From these came the Char B1 which was made slowly from 1930, but in 1935, when only 35 were completed, the Char B1 bis was started. This was even heavier, but had a more powerful engine and carried the same hull-mounted 75mm short gun. The turret was the same as on the D2, mounting an effective 47mm gun, but having only the commander to load and fire it. The hull of the B1 bis was made by a few cast components bolted on to a frame; it was expensive and time-consuming to make and demanded skilled maintenance. The fighting compartment was in the front and the driver was the key man in the crew since he aimed and laid the 75mm gun with his driving controls, and fired it. A loader loaded it for him. He too was busy since he had to keep the turret stocked. The fourth man operated the radio and fired the hull gun. There was sufficient room in the engine compartment for a small gangway alongside the engine and more ammunition was stowed at the back. The engine was based on an aircraft design and the

Char B1 bis Heavy Tank

suspension owed much to the original Holt tractors. All in all, the Char B1 bis was a self-propelled 75mm gun with an anti-tank gun in the turret, and though its armour was more than enough for the 50mm guns of the Germans in 1940, it was rarely able to use its 75mm gun effectively against other tanks. It failed to live up to its promise in 1940, but the Germans used it in numbers on the Russian Front as an SP gun or flamethrower. About 365 were built in all.

Length: 6.52m (21ft 5in). *Width:* 2.50m (8ft 2in). *Height:* 2.79m (9ft 2in). *Weight:* 32,000kg (70,548lb). *Crew:* 4. *Power:* Renault, 6-cyl., in-line, water-cooled, petrol, 307bhp at 1,900rpm. *Armament:* one 75mm gun; one 47mm gun; two7.5mm machine guns. *Armour:* 20–60mm. *Speed:* 28km/hr (17mph). *Range:* 150km (93 miles). *Maker:* Renault Frères, Billancourt.

CHAR D2 MEDIUM *1938–1940*
The Char D2 was the outcome of a development of the Renault light tank (*qv*) and it started with the D1. The D1 of 1930 was a 12-ton tank with a three-man crew mounting a 37mm gun and a coaxial machine gun in the turret and a hull gun fired by the radio operator. The one-man turret was a mistake, as also was the light armour, but after a short production run the D2 was introduced, with thicker armour and a 47mm gun. The weight

Char D1 Medium Tank

increased, but a more powerful engine gave it a reasonable speed and in 1934 50 were ordered. In 1938 a further 50 were required and were delivered just before the German invasion. The D2 had a modern Puteaux cast APX 1 turret, which was also fitted to the Char B1. An aerial base was fitted as standard and stowage bins were mounted above the track guards. The D2 was used for the trials of the concept of the mechanized division, the DLM (Division Legère Mécanique), which was based on the cavalry idea of extended reconnaissance and avoidance of a pitched battle. It was a theory that collapsed with the German invasion.

Length: 5.05m (16ft 6in). *Width:* 2.17m (7ft 2in). *Height:* 2.64m (8ft 7in). *Weight:* 20,000kg (44,080lb). *Crew:* 3. *Power:* Renault, 6-cyl., in-line, water-cooled, petrol, 150bhp.

Char D2 Medium Tank

Armament: one 47mm gun; two 8mm machine guns. *Armour:* 6–40mm. *Speed:* 22km/hr (13mph). *Range:* 130km (80 miles). *Maker:* Renault Frères, Billancourt.

FCM 36 LIGHT TANK *1936–1940*
The FCM was built to the same specification as the much more numerous Renault R–35 (*qv*), but differed from it in most respects. It was built up from welded plate, all of which was sloped as far as possible to increase the ballistic protection, and in this respect it was advanced for its time. The suspension was covered by angled skirting plates and the suspension itself was the same as on the Char B1 (*qv*). The turret was originally to be the same cast type as on the R–35, but the later versions had an unusual octagonal built-up turret with sloping sides which ran up to form the cupola. Despite the slope of the armour it did not stand up to attack, probably due to the welding techniques of the day, and the plates tended to come apart at the seams. An order for 100 was given in 1936 and they were completed in 1939.

Length: 4.46m (14ft 7in). *Width:* 2.13m (6ft 11in). *Height:* 2.33m (7ft 7in). *Weight:* 12,800kg (23,803lb). *Crew:* 2. *Power:* Berliet MDP, 4-cyl., in-line, water-cooled, diesel, 90bhp at 2,600rpm. *Armament:* one 37mm gun (1918 model); one 8mm machine gun co-

FCM 36 Light Tank

axially mounted. *Armour:* 40mm maximum. *Speed:* 24km/hr (15mph). *Range:* 225km (140 miles). *Maker:* Forges et Chantiers de la Mediterranée, Vincennes.

HOTCHKISS H–35 AND H–39 LIGHT TANKS *1936–1942*
An extraordinary feature of the French Army in the 1930s was the variety of tanks which they accepted, all built to the same, or roughly the same, specification. The two Hotchkiss light tanks were the result of the same requirement which produced the Renault R–35 (*qv*), and

Hotchkiss H-39 Light Tanks

indeed they were fitted with the same cast APX turret. The H–35 had the same armament too, a 37mm 1918 model short-barrelled gun with a single machine gun beside it on a coaxial mount. The hull was made up from cast sections welded together and mounted on a frame with rolled plates underneath, and there was also an escape hatch in the floor, an unusual feature at that time. The engine was in the rear compartment, driving forward to a differential in the nose. The driver sat on the right with the gearbox beside him. As with the other light tanks in the French Army at that time, a light skid could be fitted to the tail to improve the ability of the vehicle's gap crossing. The suspension was similar to that of the R–35, though the roadwheels were in groups of two, with the 'scissors' springing between them and rather restricting movement. The H–39 was a later version with thicker armour and a more powerful engine, and it continued to be built until the war stopped the factory. The Germans took over the entire Hotchkiss tank force, which in 1939 was about 821 tanks, and used them to supplement their own formations. A few were sent straight to Russia in 1941, but the majority were converted into ammunition or weapon carriers or even self-propelled guns. Some survived the war and went to Israel where they soldiered on for a few more years before being replaced by more suitable ex-World War II vehicles.

H–39 *Length:* 4.22m (13ft 10in). *Width:* 1.85m (6ft 1in). *Height:* 2.14m (6ft 7in).

Weight: 12,000kg (26,456lb). *Crew:* 2. *Power:* Hotchkiss, 6-cyl., in-line, water-cooled, petrol, 120bhp at 2,800rpm. *Armament:* one 37mm gun; one 7.5mm machine gun. *Armour:* 12–40mm. *Speed:* 36km/hr (23mph). *Range:* 150km (93 miles). *Maker:* Hotchkiss et Cie, Levallois-Perret.

Renault AMR 33 Light Tank *above*
Hotchkiss H-35 Light Tank *below*

RENAULT AMR–33 LIGHT TANK
1934–1940

The French Army did much work in developing light tanks in the years between the wars, and the cavalry was particularly active in promoting the idea of using light tanks for reconnaissance. In 1931 a requirement was drawn up for a light reconnaissance tank, an armoured car and a small support tank. The AMR–33 was the Renault design for the light tank. Once again it only had a crew of two and the armament was insufficient for anything more than a brush with an infantry patrol, but it was taken into service in 1934 and remained as one of the standard vehicles of the cavalry until the collapse in 1940. The engine was at the front and drove the tracks by a front sprocket. The suspension of four roadwheels was unusual, though it used the popular Renault idea of horizontal springs worked by bell cranks. Altogether about 200 were built.

Length: 3.53m (11ft 6in). *Width:* 1.61m (5ft 3in). *Height:* 1.72m (5ft 8in). *Weight:* 5,000kg (11,023lb). *Crew:* 2. *Power:* Renault, 4-cyl., in-line, water-cooled, petrol, 85bhp. *Armament:* one 7.5mm machine gun. *Armour:* 6–13mm. *Speed:* 55km/hr (37mph). *Range:* 140km (87 miles). *Maker:* Renault Frères, Billancourt.

RENAULT FT–17 LIGHT TANK
1917–1940

The little Renault tank was the second to be taken into service with the French Army. It was designed in late 1916, but the first production models did not come off the line until a year later and it was the middle of 1918 before there were any substantial numbers of them. At that time the orders were for 3,500 and in the end most of them were delivered. Although a Renault design, production of the tank was sub-contracted to several other firms. Essentially it was a small narrow armoured box with a driver in front, a fighting compartment in the centre and an engine at the rear. The commander was also the gunner and he had a turret with a 360° traverse, the first such turret to be on a tank in service. The armour was thin and the offensive armament only one machine gun, but later versions had a 37mm Puteaux light gun. A signals version had no turret, but carried three men and a wireless set. After the war the Renault was used in the French colonies and was exported all over the world. It was built in the United States by the Ford Motor Company. In France more than 1,600 were still in service in 1940 and were taken over by the Germans for internal security duties.

Length (including unditching tail): 5.02m (16ft 5in). *Width:* 1.74m (5ft 9in). *Height:* 2.14m (6ft 7in). *Weight:* 7,000kg (15,432lb). *Crew:* 2. *Power:* Renault, 4-cyl., in-line, petrol, water-cooled, 35bhp at 1,500rpm. *Armament:* one 8mm machine gun or one 37mm gun. *Armour:* 6–22m. *Speed:* 7.7km/hr (4.7mph). *Range:* 35km (22miles). *Maker:* Renault Frères, Billancourt; Berliet, Bourg; Delauney Belville, St. Denis; SOMUA, St. Ouen; Ford in United States under licence.

RENAULT R–35 LIGHT TANK *1936–1944*

The specification for the R–35 arose from the manoeuvres of 1932–3 when the French infantry decided that they needed another, more heavily armoured, light support tank. They ultimately chose the Renault R–35, which became the most numerous light tank in the French Army by 1939, when there were roughly 2000 of them. It was of the usual French layout with a two-man crew, a small turret, restricted range, but in this case quite good armour. The construction was of cast sections bolted together, with flat plates forming

Renault R-35 Light Tank

the floor. The engine was at the back, behind a fireproof bulkhead, driving forward to a gearbox beside the driver. The commander had a short-barrelled, 1918 model, 37mm gun and a coaxial machine gun; his vision was rather limited by poor episcopes, so that he usually sat on his open hatch door and looked over the top of the turret. The suspension owed much to the parallel work done by Renault on the cavalry light tanks, and used the same bell crank and horizontal-spring layout. In action in 1940 the R–35 never got a chance to show its ability and most of them were taken over by the Wehrmacht and put to use in Russia. In 1942, when they were obviously outclassed as fighting tanks, they were used as munition carriers and some were given a 47mm Czech gun on a top-heavy superstructure and employed until 1944 as anti-tank guns.

Length: 4.20m (13ft 10in). *Width:* 1.85m (6ft 1in). *Height:* 2.40m (7ft 9in). *Weight:* 10,000kg (22,046lb). *Crew:* 2. *Power:* Renault, 4-cyl., in-line, water-cooled, petrol, 82bhp at 2,200rpm. *Armament:* one 37mm gun; one

Renault R-35 Light Tank

Saint Chamond Assault Tank

7.5mm machine gun. *Armour:* 6–45mm. *Speed:* 20km/hr (12.5mph). *Range:* 140km (87 miles). *Maker:* Renault Frères, Billancourt.

SAINT CHAMOND ASSAULT TANK *1917–1918*

The Saint Chamond was designed by the French Army, using a Holt Tractor as the basic hull and suspension and fitting a long armoured box over it. The motive power came from a Panhard petrol engine driving a dynamo and providing electricity to an electric motor at each track. The armament was impressive, but the long overhang of the hull meant that it quickly became stuck when crossing trenches and the complicated transmission was unreliable. The idea was abandoned when 400 had been built.

Length: 8.68m (28ft 6in). *Width:* 2.66m (8ft 9in). *Height:* 2.36m (7ft 9in). *Weight:* 22,000kg (48,501lb). *Crew:* 8. *Power:* Panhard, 4-cyl., in-line, water-cooled, petrol, 90bhp. *Armament:* one 75mm gun; four 8mm machine guns. *Armour:* 6–17mm. *Speed:* 8km/hr (5mph). *Range:* 60km (37 miles). *Maker:* La Compagnie des Forges et Acieries de la Marine et d'Homecourt, St. Chamond.

SCHNEIDER ASSAULT TANK *1917–1919*

The Schneider first appeared in 1917 and it could be said to be an American Holt tractor chassis with an armoured box on the top. The box was boat-shaped at the nose and flat at the back and there was a little overhang, though not enough to prevent trench crossing. A

Schneider Assault Tank

short-barrelled 75mm gun was mounted in a sponson on the right front, and there was a machine gun in a ball mounting on each side. The Schneiders were first used in action at Chemin des Dames in April 1917 and the losses reached almost 40 per cent, mainly from

petrol tank explosions. Later the armour was increased and the tank continued to serve until the end of the war. Over 400 were built, but some were made into supply carriers.

Length: 6.32m (20ft 9in). *Width:* 2.05m (6ft 9in). *Height:* 2.34m (7ft 7in). *Weight:* 14,600kg (32,187lb). *Crew:* 6. *Power:* Schneider, 4-cyl., in-line, water-cooled, petrol, 55bhp. *Armament:* one 75mm howitzer; two 8mm machine guns. *Armour:* 6–11.5mm. *Speed:* 7.5km/hr (4.6mph). *Range:* 48km (30 miles). *Maker:* Schneider–Creusot SA, Le Creusot.

SOMUA S–35 MEDIUM TANK *1936–1943*

The SOMUA S–35 was designed as a result of a cavalry requirement for a support tank, but it was quickly adopted as the standard medium tank of the French Army. It had good armour, using large cast components bolted together, good mobility, using a powerful engine and adequate suspension, and in theory the firepower was sufficient also. Its main drawback was that it had a one-man turret, with the commander doing all the fighting as well as being divorced from his crew. He was thus unable to give his full attention to either gun-

SOMUA S-35 Medium Tank

nery or commanding. Despite this drawback the S–35 gave a good account of itself in 1940 and it was undoubtedly the best French tank of the war. The Germans were impressed and took it into service, using a few on the Russian front. When the war started an improved version was in the final stages of design. This would have had a more powerful engine and better suspension, but the one-man turret remained. A few were built, but the Germans did not continue the idea. The S–35 hull was divided into a rear engine compartment, with the transmission alongside the engine, and a crew compartment in front. The radio operator sat beside the driver, and had no other task than his radio. Once again, the view of all three crew members was limited by poor optics and restricted vision slits.

Length: 5.50m (17ft 11in). *Width:* 2.10m (6ft 11in). *Height:* 2.70m (8ft 10in). *Weight:* 20,048kg (44,200lb). *Crew:* 3. *Power:* SOMUA, V-8, water-cooled, petrol, 190bhp at 2,000rpm. *Armament:* one 47mm gun; one 7.5mm machine gun. *Armour:* 55mm maximum. *Speed:* 37km/hr (23mph). *Range:* 257km (80 miles). *Maker:* SOMUA, St. Ouen.

GERMANY

A7V COMBAT TANK *1918*

The difficulties experienced by British tanks in operating over shell-torn mud in the Somme led the Germans to discount them as a worth-while weapon for quite a long time, but eventually a special department for tank development was set up, the 'Allegemeine Kriegsdepartement 7, Abteilung Verkehrswesen', and from this title came the designation of the tank which was eventually designed. It adopted the Holt chassis virtually as it was and put an armoured hull on top of it. The tank was armed with a captured Russian 57mm gun in the front plate and six or seven Maxim machine guns poking from ports around the body. The interior was one large compartment containing the engine, guns and crew, a total of 18 men. The commander was provided with a small cupola raised above the hull, but his only communication with the crew was by shouting over the noise of the engine. Although it pioneered the use of sprung suspension, its cross-country performance was poor due to it being under-powered and having insufficient ground clearance. One hundred of these tanks were ordered, but only about 30 were built due to shortages of material. They were first used in March 1918 and made little contribution to the German war effort.

Length: 7.34m (24ft 1in). *Width:* 3.06m (10ft 0½in). *Height:* 3.30m (10ft 10in). *Weight:* 29,900kg (65,920lb). *Crew:* 18. *Power:* two Daimler-Benz, 4-cyl., petrol, each 100bhp at 1,600rpm. *Armament:* one 57mm gun; six or seven 7.92mm Maxim machine guns. *Armour:* 15–30mm. *Speed:* 13km/hr (8mph). *Range:* 40km (25 miles). *Maker:* Daimler, Marienfelde.

Maus Super Heavy Tank

E–100 HEAVY TANK *1943–1945*

When the Maus tank project (*qv*) was begun by Dr. Porsche, the Army Weapons Office decided to start their own heavy tank project in opposition, aiming at a slightly more practical vehicle. This became the E–100 design, but it

E100 Heavy Tank

proceeded very slowly. In 1944 all super-heavy tank development was stopped, but a small force of workers continued assembling the E–100 prototype in a remote factory until the war ended. The chassis was almost completed in 1945, but the turret was never finished. It had been intended to arm the tank with a 15cm or possibly a 17cm gun. The general design was more or less a scaled-up Panther tank (*qv*).

Length: 10.27m (33ft 8in). *Width:* 4.48m (14ft 8in). *Height:* 3.29m (10ft 9in). *Weight:* 140,000kg (137 tons). *Crew:* 5. *Power:* Maybach, V–12, water-cooled, petrol, 23,095cc, 800bhp at 3,000rpm. *Armament:* one 15cm or 17cm gun. *Armour:* 40–240mm. *Speed* (estimated): 40km/hr (25mph). *Range* (estimated): 120km (75 miles). *Maker:* Adler-werke, Frankfurt-am-Main.

MAUS SUPER-HEAVY TANK *1943–1945*

In June 1942 Dr. Ferdinand Porsche, then head of the German Tank Commission, was instructed by Hitler to develop a tank capable of mounting a 12.8cm or 15cm gun in a revolving turret. Code-named Mammut (Mammoth) the idea was ridiculed by the military authorities, but the design was pushed ahead in the face of considerable difficulties. The enormous weight of 188 tonnes was the principal problem, and the original torsion-bar suspension had to be abandoned in favour of a Skoda-designed volute-spring type in order to take the weight. The intended air-cooled engine never materialized and a modified Mercedes-Benz aircraft engine was pressed into service for the first prototype and a diesel engine for the second. The first prototype was tested in June 1944; the second began tests in September, but the engine blew up and the trial was never completed. An order for 150 models was cancelled and the prototypes were destroyed in the face of the Soviet advance.

Length: 7.00m (22ft 11½in). *Width:* 3.40m (11ft 2in). *Height:* 3.58m (11ft 9in). *Weight:* 188,000kg (185 tons). *Crew:* 6. *Power:* Mercedes-Benz, V–12, water-cooled, petrol, 1,080bhp at 2,400rpm. *Armament:* one 12.8cm L/55 gun; one 75mm L/36 gun co-axially mounted; one 20mm cannon. *Armour:* 40–350mm. *Speed:* 20km/hr (12.5mph). *Range:* 185km (115 miles). *Maker:* Alkett, Berlin.

A7V Combat Tank

PANTHER MEDIUM TANK 1942–1947

The Panther tank originated with a hurried demand for a 30-ton medium tank capable of meeting the Soviet T–34 (qv) and beating it. It was developed by the Maschinenfabrik Augsburg-Nürnberg and incorporated sloped armour and a 75mm gun twice as long (and thus more powerful) than that of the PzKpfw IV (qv). On Hitler's orders it was fitted with an even longer gun, and went into production in November 1942. Weighing 45 tons it was somewhat heavy for a medium tank but, with its powerful gun, thick armour and a good turn of speed, it proved to be an excellent design. Its hurried development, however, led to some teething troubles; of the first 300 made, those which survived their first battle had to go back to the factory for extensive modification. But after this setback it went on to become probably the best German tank of the war, superior to the Soviet T–34 in every respect. About 5,500 were built, a poor figure compared with the T–34 or M4 Sherman (qv) indicative of the German failure to mobilize its full potential.

Length: 6.85m (22ft 6in). *Width:* 3.30m (10ft 10in). *Height:* 2.94m (9ft 8in). *Weight:* 44,800kg (98,767lb). *Crew:* 5. *Power:* Maybach, V–12, water-cooled, petrol, 23,095cc, 700bhp at 3,000rpm. *Armament:* one 75mm L/70 gun; two 7.92mm machine guns. *Armour:* 20–120mm. *Speed:* 46km/hr (29mph). *Range:* 180km (110 miles). *Maker:* Daimler-Benz, Berlin.

PANZERKAMPFWAGEN I (PzKpfw I) LIGHT TANK 1934–1945

The PzKpfw I was an interim vehicle intended for rapid building and the training of the new armoured formations that were raised when the German Army openly rearmed from 1933 onwards. It was a small two-man tank very much in the style of the time, and like so many of its contemporaries, it shows evidence of deriving its layout from the Carden-Loyd carriers (qv), although it went one better and had a rotating turret. Driver and commander shared the same compartment, the driver on the left and the commander in the small turret on the right. The transmission train ran along the centre of the floor to a differential which drove the front sprockets. The engine was originally a Krupp flat-four, but after 500 were built the 1B model was introduced with a larger engine, a slightly longer hull, an extra roadwheel and better performance. Nearly 2,000 of the 1B

PzKpfw I Light Tank

were made and both types were tried out in the Spanish Civil War where they were found to be inadequate against any form of anti-tank gun. However, there were not enough heavier tanks in 1939 and the 1A and 1B had to fight in Poland and France. A few were even taken to Russia in 1941, but the remaining chassis were quickly taken out of front-line service and used for other purposes, such as carrying light anti-tank guns. About 200 were converted into small command vehicles with a three-man crew and two radios.

Length: 4.01m (13ft 3in). *Width:* 2.10m (6ft 9in). *Height:* 1.72m (5ft 8in). *Weight:* 5,400kg (11,905lb). *Crew:* 2. *Power:* Krupp M305, 4-cyl., horizontally-opposed, air-cooled, petrol, 60bhp at 2,500rpm. PzKpfw 1B: Maybach, 6-

PzKpfw IB Light Tank

PzKpfw II Light Tank

cyl., water-cooled, petrol, 100bhp at 2,300 rpm. *Armament:* two 7.92mm machine guns in turret. *Armour:* 7–13mm. *Speed:* 37km/hr (23mph). *Range:* 200km (125 miles). *Maker:* Henschel Werke, Leipzig.

PANZERKAMPFWAGEN II (PzKpfw II) LIGHT TANK *1936–1943*
The new German Army of the early 1930s was intended to have medium tanks with good guns, but these soon showed themselves to be a long time in coming and it was decided to build another interim tank together with the PzKpfw

I (*qv*). The PzKpfw II was called for in 1935 and the first ones were in being in 1936. It was another light tank with a three-man crew and armed with a 20mm gun. Throughout the life of the tank there were almost continuous improvements to the original design, most of them directed towards more power from the engine and thicker armour. More than 1,000 took part in the Polish Campaign of 1939 and in France in 1940 the PzKpfw II was the backbone of the armoured formations. As late as 1942 there were still over 800 on the establishment, though by that time they were well out-

dated for front line use. The main virtue of the tank was that it was relatively cheap to make, but it suffered from a small turret, and there was thus no possibility of increasing the size of

the main gun. Vision was poor and space for the crew cramped. The suspension was adequate and mobility quite good, though the tracks were narrow.

Length: 4.75m (15ft 7in). *Width:* 2.13m (7ft 0in). *Height:* 1.98m (6ft 6in). *Weight:* 7,305kg (16,105lb). *Crew:* 3. *Power:* Maybach TR, 6-cyl., water-cooled, petrol, 6,000cc, 120bhp at 2,600rpm. *Armament:* one 20mm KwK 38 automatic gun; one 7.92mm machine gun co-axially mounted. *Armour:* 10–30mm. *Speed:* 35km/hr (22mph). *Range:* 192km (120 miles). *Maker:* MAN, Nuremberg.

PzKpfw II Light Tank

PANZERKAMPFWAGEN III (PzKpfw III) MEDIUM TANK 1939–1945

The PzKpfw III was one of the two tanks specifically designed for the new armoured formations of the Wehrmacht and it was based on the experience gained with the two small interim designs. The idea was that there should be two main types of tank in battle, an anti-tank tank, armed with a high-velocity armour-piercing gun, and a support tank armed with a larger gun firing HE shell against targets other than vehicles. The PzKpfw III was to be the first type and when, it first appeared it was armed with a not very adequate version of the infantry 37mm anti-tank gun. However, it did have a large turret ring which enabled larger guns to be fitted later. There was a good deal of

development during the prototype stage and the version which came into production was the Ausf. E. Subsequent models went to Ausf. N, the alterations being mostly concerned with extra armour, wider tracks and more engine power. Production was well advanced in 1939 and nearly 100 IIIs were involved in Poland. About 350 invaded France in the next year; 1,500 were in service in 1941 and 2,600 were built during 1942. The tank was well laid out and there was adequate room for each crewman. The commander had a good view from his cupola, and the driver had an excellent 10-speed gearbox to transfer the power to the front drive sprockets. The suspension was by transverse torsion bars and the cross-country performance good, but this was not enough, for

the armour was too thin for most of the Allied guns and the 37mm could not penetrate either the Matilda (qv) or the T–34 (qv). Later versions were given a 50mm gun and the last models, for Russia, carried a 75mm gun.

Ausf. E *Length:* 5.48m (17ft 8in). *Width:* 2.92m (9ft 6in). *Height:* 2.46m (8ft). *Weight:* 19,400kg (42,770lb). *Crew:* 5. *Power:* Maybach HL 120 TRM, V–12, water-cooled, petrol, 11,867cc, 300bhp at 3,000rpm. *Armament:* one 50mm KwK 39 short-barrelled gun; one 7.92mm machine gun coaxially mounted; one 7.92mm machine gun in hull. *Armour:* 30–90mm. *Speed:* 40km/hr (25mph). *Range:* 175km (109 miles). *Maker:* production was spread among many firms; original design by Daimler-Benz, Berlin.

PANZERKAMPFWAGEN IV (PzKpfw IV) MEDIUM TANK *1939–1945*

The PzKpfw IV was to be the second standard tank of the armoured battalions. One of the four companies was to be entirely equipped with it and would give the close support needed by the three companies of PzKpfw III anti-tank tanks (*qv*). The IV was therefore a similar design, though with a bigger turret and a short-barrelled 75mm gun. It soon proved itself in the Polish campaign and again in France. Production got under way slowly as it was originally intended that fewer would be needed than the IIIs. When it was seen to be successful and capable of standing up to the best of the Allied and Soviet vehicles, there was an urgent call for more, which was only met with difficulty. In the end, about 9,000 IVs were built between 1939 and 1945 and it was the only German tank to be in continuous production throughout the war. The design was laid down

PzKpfw IV Medium Tank

in 1934 and proved to be outstanding. The hull was made up of welded plates with a large bolted superstructure on top carrying the turret ring. The turret was also welded and well sloped. It held three crew members and was big enough to permit the mounting of larger guns, though with modifications to the mantlet. The engine was the well-tried Maybach which also powered the III. The suspension used four twin bogies on each side and four return rollers, a sure recognition feature. Continuous improvements were made to the armour and the gun. A long-barrelled 75mm, the KwK 40, was installed in the Ausf. F and G versions and the IV now took on the task of the III, namely that of fighting the opposing tanks. It continued to do this until the end of the war, and for two years it was the only German tank capable of holding its own with the T–34 (*qv*) and any of the Allied models. PzKpfw IVs which were returned to workshops for repair were mod-

TIGER HEAVY TANK *1942–1945*

The German Army had called for a heavy tank as early as 1937, but the call was ignored until the invasion of Russia brought the T–34 (*qv*) against the Panzers. This led to a hurried revival of the demand, and two prototypes were produced, one by Porsche and one by Henschel. The Henschel, being the simpler design, was accepted and went into production in August 1942. At the time of its introduction, and for some time afterwards, the Tiger was the most formidable tank in the world and it retained its reputation until the end of the war. The main armament was the powerful 88mm gun, which could defeat 100mm of armour at 1,000m (3,280ft) range, while the Tiger's frontal armour was impervious to any Allied gun except at suicidally short ranges. Due to its weight, however, the engine had to be geared down and thus the performance suffered, and it

as possible to out-manoeuvre a Tiger with some skill. A notable defect was that unless the engine was running, the turret could only be traversed by hand, which put the tank at a disadvantage when caught from a flank. In spite of these faults, though, the Tiger built up a formidable reputation; one instance is recorded of a single Tiger holding off an entire Allied division, killing 25 tanks before it was finally stalked and defeated. However, only 1,354 were built before August 1944.

Length: 8.22m (27ft 0in). *Width:* 3.73m (12ft 3in). *Height:* 2.84m (9ft 4in). *Weight:* 55,000kg (121,255lb). *Crew:* 5. *Power:* Maybach, V–12, water-cooled, petrol, 23,095cc, 700bhp at 3,000rpm. *Armament:* one 88mm L/56 gun; two 7.92mm machine guns. *Armour:* 26–110mm. *Speed:* 38km/hr (24mph). *Range:* 100km (60 miles). *Maker:* Henschel GmbH, Kassel.

ified to the latest standard and the whole fleet was progressively up-dated as the new versions were brought out.

Ausf. F2 *Length:* 5.40m (17ft 9in). *Width:* 2.86m (9ft 5in). *Height:* 2.65m (8ft 9in). *Weight:* 23,200kg (51,146lb). *Crew:* 5. *Power:* Maybach HL 120 TRM, V–12, water-cooled, petrol, 11,867cc, 300bhp at 3,000rpm. *Armament:* one 75mm KwK 40 (L/43) gun; one 7.92mm machine gun coaxially mounted; one 7.92mm machine gun in hull. *Armour:* 10–50mm. *Speed:* 40km/hr (25mph). *Range:* 209km (130 miles). *Makers:* Krupp-Grusonwerke AG, Magdeburg; later production at Steyr-Daimler-Puch AG, St. Valentin.

KING TIGER II, MAIN BATTLE TANK
1944–1947
No sooner had the Tiger tank (*qv*) gone into service than a fresh design was demanded, mounting the more powerful 88mm L/71 gun, a weapon capable of penetrating 185mm of armour at 2,000m (6,416ft) range. The design was to use sloped armour, in the manner of the Panther (*qv*), and, as before, both Porsche and Henschel were asked for prototypes. Porsche were so confident of the order that they began making turrets, but the Henschel design was selected and thus the first production models appeared with Porsche turrets. So far as gun power and protection went, the King Tiger was the best tank of the war, but it paid for this in its lack of performance and lack of reliability due to the engine and transmission being over-stressed. Nevertheless, when properly handled, the King Tiger dominated the battlefield and was practically indestructible. It replaced the Tiger I in production in August 1944 and 485 were built before the war ended.

Length: 7.23m (23ft 9in). *Width:* 3.73m (12ft 3in). *Height:* 3.07m (10ft 1in). *Weight:* 69,400kg (153,000lb). *Crew:* 5. *Power:* Maybach, V–12, water-cooled, petrol, 23,095cc, 700bhp at 3,000rpm. *Armament:* one 88mm L/71 gun; two 7.92mm machine guns. *Armour:* 40–185mm. *Speed:* 35km/hr (21mph). *Range:* 170km (105 miles). *Maker:* Henschel & Sohn GmbH, Kassel.

Royal or King Tiger Tank

LEOPARD I MAIN BATTLE TANK
1965–

When the German Army was reformed in 1955 its first tanks were American M47s (*qv*) and M48s (*qv*). A co-operation programme was then mounted with the French to develop a new battle tank. Like most of these international programmes nothing came of this idea, and Germany went ahead with her own design. Two consortia of companies were organized and each produced a prototype. After several years of tests, a design was selected for produc-

tion in 1963, and the first service tank appeared in 1965. Since then almost 6,000 tanks and tank-derived specialist vehicles have been built, and the Leopard I is undoubtedly the most successful post-war tank, having been adopted by several other countries.

The Leopard I is of conventional layout with the driver in front, three men in the turret, and the engine and transmission at the rear. Main armament is the British 105mm L7 gun.

Since the original Leopard I there have been several improvements incorporated in the

design; the turret is now of spaced cast armour, the gun is fully stabilized, night-vision equipment is fitted and improved tracks are used.

Length: 7.08m (23ft 3in). *Width:* 3.25m (10ft 8in). *Height:* 2.64m (8ft 8in). *Weight:* 40,000kg (88,185lb). *Crew:* 4. *Power:* Mercedes-Benz, V–10, multi-fuel, super-charged, 37,400cc, 830bhp at 2,200rpm. *Armament:* one 105mm L7 gun; two 7.62mm machine guns. *Armour:* 10–70mm. *Speed:* 65km/hr (40mph). *Range:* 600km (375 miles). *Maker:* Krauss-Maffei, Munich.

LEOPARD II MAIN BATTLE TANK *1977–*

In 1963 the United States and German governments agreed to co-operate in producing a main battle tank for the 1970s – MBT70 (*qv* XM–1). After seven years of escalating costs and in the face of severe differences of opinion upon various features of the design, the co-operation was ended and the Germans set about developing a fresh design of their own. The experience gained during the MBT70 phase was drawn on, and within four years 17 prototypes of the new tank, named Leopard II, had been built and were under test. The latest improvements were incorporated as they became available, and production tanks are expected to enter service with German Army units in 1979.

The Leopard II is undoubtedly the most advanced tank presently in production or ser-

Leopard II Tank

vice. The hull and massive turret are made from Chobham laminated armour; the main armament is a new 120mm smoothbore gun developed by Rheinmetall. The engine, an improved version of that used in Leopard I (*qv*), is capable of providing all the necessary power to give the tank incomparable mobility and, as a bonus, can be removed and replaced by a new engine in 19 minutes flat, a remarkable example of maintenance design. Fire con-

Leopard II A V

Merkava Main Battle Tank

trol is by electronic computer, allied to a stereoscopic rangefinder and full stabilization of the gun.

In 1976 a Leopard II AV (AV meaning Austere Version) was developed in the hope of interesting the US Army and possibly providing a NATO standard tank. This used a new and more 'squared-off' turret with laser rangefinder, new fire-control systems, improved engine auxiliaries, increased fuel capacity and other modifications. However, the US Army decided upon the XM–1 tank, and there seems little chance of wider adoption of the AV.
Length: 7.45m (24ft 5in). *Width:* 3.54m (1ft 7in). *Height:* 2.45m (8ft 0in). *Weight:* 54,500kg (120,150lb). *Crew:* 4. *Power:* MTU MB873, V–12, multi-fuel, turbocharged, 39,800cc, 1,500bhp at 2,600rpm. *Armament:* one 120mm smoothbore gun; two 7.62mm machine guns. *Armour:* not disclosed. *Speed:* 68km/hr (42mph). *Range:* not disclosed. *Maker:* Krauss-Maffei AG, Munich.

ISRAEL

MERKAVA MAIN BATTLE TANK *1978–*
The Merkava represents the latest thinking in tank design, suitably modified for the peculiar needs of Israel. The Merkava is in fact a defensive tank, meant for fighting from prepared positions, and for this reason much emphasis is placed on protection. The engine and transmission are in the front and the turret is narrow and low. The crew have a large compartment at the rear which is suitable for resting or for carrying men and ammunition if necessary. There is a large stock of ammunition for the main gun, and the present power/weight ratio is quite low, indicating that the designers did not envisage a need for rapid movement or agility. The turret has a mantlet that will allow

a larger gun to be fitted at a later date, and a more powerful engine can be accommodated easily. So far the only models that exist of this tank are pre-production versions, but full production has probably already begun.
Length: not known. *Width:* not known. *Height:* not known. *Weight:* 56,000kg (123,424lb). *Crew:* 4. *Power:* Teledyne Continental AVDS 1790–5A, 12-cyl., air-cooled, diesel, 900bhp at 2,400rpm. *Armament:* one 105mm gun; two 7.62mm machine guns, one coaxially mounted, one on turret. *Armour:* classified, but heavily sloped and likely to be spaced. *Speed:* 50km/hr (31mph). *Range:* not known. *Maker:* Israeli Military Industries, Haifa.

ITALY

CV 33 TANKETTE *1933–1943*
The Italian Army bought a number of Carden-Loyd tankettes (*qv*) in 1929 and also obtained a licence to manufacture them. From these they developed their own versions and in 1933 brought out the Carro Veloce 33 which was an improved Carden-Loyd. It was a very light two-man vehicle with both men sitting side-by-side. The engine was at the back, driving forward to a differential in the nose and front drive sprockets. The commander had one machine gun with limited traverse and elevation, but there was a Series 2 in 1935 which mounted a 37mm gun. The early hulls were made by a mixture of riveting and welding, but a later modification used bolted construction and fitted a single 13mm Breda heavy machine gun. An even later series in 1938 had modified suspension and there were many variants, including, incredibly, a self-propelled gun. There were large export orders for the tankette and it was used in the Spanish Civil War, where

its limitations were well shown up. Lack of money prevented its being replaced and it served the Italian Army through the first campaigns in the Western Desert, but it was an easy target for anti-tank rifles and was virtually useless by then.
Length: 3.18m (10ft 5in). *Width:* 1.43m (4ft 7in). *Height:* 2.13m (7ft 0in). *Weight:* 3,450kg

CV33 Light Assault Tank

(12,125lb). *Crew:* 2. *Power:* SPA CV3, 4-cyl., in-line, water-cooled, petrol, 43bhp at 2,400rpm. *Armament:* one 6.5mm machine gun or two 6.5mm machine guns or one 13mm heavy machine gun. *Speed:* 42km/hr (26mph). *Range:* 125km (78 miles). *Maker:* Fiat/Ansaldo, Turin.

FIAT 2000 HEAVY TANK *1919–1934*
The Fiat 2000 was a World War I tank of advanced design and concept. As such it would have been a success on the Western Front, but the first vehicles did not appear until late 1918, although the design started in 1916. More followed in 1920, though it seems unlikely that there were ever more than six or seven altogether. The hull was a large armoured box with the tracks running half way up the sides. The fighting compartment overhung the tracks and a smooth sheet of armour covered the

suspension. Inside, most of the transmission was under the floor, which allowed the crew considerable freedom to move. The driver sat alone in the front with a machine-gun position either side of him. There were three guns to each side, covering all approaches, and a 65mm gun in an all-round traversable turret on the roof. It was a formidable vehicle for its day, and had reasonable cross-country ability. It survived into the 1930s.

Length: 7.40m (24ft 3in). *Width:* 3.10m (10ft 2in). *Height:* 3.81m (12ft 6in). *Weight:* 40,000kg (88,185lb). *Crew:* 10. *Power:* Fiat A 12, 6-cyl., in-line, water-cooled, petrol, 240bhp. *Armament:* one 65mm gun; seven 6.5mm machine guns. *Armour:* 15–20mm. *Speed:* 6km/hr (3.7mph). *Range:* 75km (47 miles). *Maker:* Fiat, Turin.

FIAT 3000 LIGHT TANK *1923–1943*
Italy was provided with a Renault FT–17 light tank (*qv*) in 1918 and started to design a variant using Italian components and factory methods. The first model did not appear until 1920 and production was not under way until 1923. The Fiat was both lighter and faster than the original French Renault and it mounted twin machine guns in the turret. Later, in 1929, one machine gun was replaced by a 37mm gun which did much to improve the striking power of the tank and at the same time a new engine was fitted and better suspension. A few models

Fiat 2000 Heavy Tank

Fiat 3000 Light Tank

were fitted with a radio and a trial was made with fitting a self-propelled howitzer, but this was not continued. For at least 10 years the Fiat was the only tank in any numbers in the Italian Army and it remained in service until as late as 1943, by which time it was hopelessly outdated and incapable of surviving on the battlefield.

Length: 3.58m (11ft 9in). *Width:* 1.66m (5ft 5in). *Height:* 2.20m (7ft 0in). *Weight:* 5,500kg (12,125lb). *Crew:* 2. *Power:* Fiat, 4-cyl., in-line, water-cooled, petrol; 50bhp at 1,700rpm; later models had 65bhp engines. *Armament:* two 6.5mm machine guns or one 37mm gun; one 6.5mm machine gun. *Armour:* 6–16mm. *Speed:* 24km/hr (15mph). *Range:* 95km (59 miles). *Makers:* Fiat, Turin assisted by Ansaldo and Breda, Milan.

L6/40 LIGHT TANK *1941–1953*
The L6/40 was developed from the light tanks and tankettes produced by Fiat/Ansaldo in the early 1930s and was intended to replace the CV 33 (*qv*). The first prototype appeared in 1936, armed with either two machine guns or one machine gun and a 37mm gun, mounted in a small turret. The Italian Army ordered 280, but the production vehicles had a 20mm gun and a coaxial machine gun. The chassis was a modified CV 33 with a more powerful engine and markedly improved suspension. The hull was built up from flat plates bolted and riveted and little attention was paid to sloping the armour. Production did not begin until 1939 and it was not available in significant numbers until 1942. By then it was well out-of-date and a contingent which was sent to Russia did not return. Most of the L6/40s were employed in North Africa, and some were held in reserve in Italy. There was a flamethrower version with 200ls (44 gal) of fuel carried in a drum on the back, and the 20mm gun replaced by the projector. A variant using the same chassis was the L40 self-propelled anti-tank gun. This had a

L6/40 Light Tank

fixed turret closely resembling that on the CV 33 and mounted a 47mm gun with no overhead cover. It was hoped to mount all anti-tank guns on these chassis, but production never caught up and most of those converted were sent to Russia.

Length: 3.81m (12ft 5in). *Width:* 1.95m (6ft 4in). *Height:* 2.00m (6ft 8in). *Weight:* 6,800kg (14,991lb). *Crew:* 2. *Power:* SPA 18D, 4-cyl., in-line, water-cooled, petrol, 70bhp. *Armament:* one 20mm Breda; one 8mm machine gun coaxially mounted. *Armour:* 6–30mm. *Speed:* 42km/hr (26mph). *Range:* 200km (124 miles). *Maker:* Fiat/Ansaldo, Turin.

M13/40 Medium Tank

M13/40 MEDIUM TANK *1941–1944*
The M13/40 was directly derived from the M11/39 which was introduced in 1937. The M11/39 relied heavily on the preceding tankettes for its hull shape and suspension, but there was a small turret with two machine guns above the crew compartment. A gunner sat alongside the driver, just as in the CV 33, and

operated a 37mm gun which could only fire to the front. As with all hull guns this was soon found to be an inadequate mounting and in 1939 the tank was redesigned and became the M13/40, entering service in 1940. The hull was slightly enlarged, and strengthened. Thicker armour was fitted, together with a more pow-

M14/41 Medium Tank

erful engine; the crew compartment was made bigger and on it was mounted a larger turret with room for two men, a 47mm gun and a co-axial machine gun. Although it was still lacking in many respects, and even when it was introduced it was close to being out of date, the

M11/39 Medium Tank

M13/40 became the main Italian battle tank and, with its successor the M14/41, fought throughout the war. In the desert campaigns the M13/40 was found to be prone to break-downs because its engine was not provided with filters for sand. It had a low power-to-weight ratio which gave it a poor cross-country performance, and its armour plates tended to split at the bolted seams when struck by shot. Despite all this it was as good as many of the British tanks in 1941 and captured specimens were pressed into service. The M14/41 was

Type 2 Amphibious Tank

given a more powerful engine with proper desert filters and was mechanically more reliable, but little else was changed. Despite their classification as medium tanks all this family were light enough to be moved on large flat-bed lorries for long marches. Eight hundred of the M13/40 were built, and over 1,000 of the M14/41. Both types were out of service use by 1944.

M13/40 *Length:* 4.92m (16ft 2in). *Width:* 2.20m (7ft 3in). *Height:* 2.40m (7ft 10in). *Weight:* 14,000kg (30,865lb). *Crew:* 4. *Power:* SPA 8 TM40, V–8, water-cooled, diesel, 125bhp (M14/41, 145bhp). *Armament:* one 47mm gun in turret; one 8mm machine gun coaxially mounted; two 8mm machine guns in hull. *Armour:* 14–40mm. *Speed:* 32km/hr (20mph). *Range:* 200km (125 miles). *Maker:* Ansaldo–Fossati, Turin.

JAPAN

TYPE 2 AMPHIBIOUS TANK *1942–1945*
Probably due to their involvement in Manchuria, where roads and bridges were few, the Japanese began experimenting with amphibious tanks in the late 1920s. Several experimental designs were developed but not put into production, and then in 1940 the Japanese Navy took over the development, since it was decided that such tanks would be

part of the equipment of the Marine Corps. The resulting Type 2 appeared in 1942. It was more or less a Type 95 light (*qv*) tank with the addition of buoyancy chambers and with the hull built up and sealed against the entry of water. The two buoyancy chambers would be released from inside the tank. Propulsion in the water was by twin propellers driven from a power take-off and steering was by two rudders.

The Type 2 was largely used for Marine amphibious landings, being launched from landing craft some distance from the shore so as to solve the reef-crossing problem. Once ashore the buoyancy chambers were jettisoned and the tank fought as a normal land vehicle.

Length (with buoyancy): 7.41m (24ft 4in). *Length* (without buoyancy): 4.87m (15ft 10in). *Width:* 2.79m (9ft 2in). *Height:* 2.33m (7ft 8in). *Weight* (with buoyancy): 11,255kg (24,915lb). *Weight* (without buoyancy): 9,570kg (21,100lb). *Crew:* 3. *Power:* Mitsubishi, 6-cyl., air-cooled, diesel, 14,355cc, 110bhp at 1,400rpm. *Armament:* one 37mm gun; two 7.7mm machine guns. *Armour:* 6–12mm. *Speed* (land): 40km/hr (25mph). *Speed* (water): 10km/hr (6mph). *Range* (land): 200km (125 miles). *Range* (water): 150km (93 miles). *Makers:* Japanese Naval Arsenals.

TYPE 61 MAIN BATTLE TANK *1962–*
When the Japanese Self-Defence Force was constituted in the 1950s, its first tanks were from American sources. These were not entirely satisfactory because the average Japanese soldier is slighter of stature than the average American; moreover, these tanks exceeded the Japanese railway loading gauge. In 1954, therefore, design of a Japanese tank began, resulting in the Type 61, first issued in 1962. Its design was influenced by that of the

Type 61 Main Battle Tank

American M47 (*qv*) and it does resemble that tank in many respects, although it is more compact. As with their previous tanks, the Japanese have chosen to use a diesel engine instead of petrol, and the main armament is a Japanese-built 90mm gun based on the American type used in the M47/48 series (*qv*). Suspension is by torsion bars, using six road-wheels on each side, and particular attention has been paid to ease of maintenance. Some 500 were built, and the Type 61 is expected to remain in first-line service for some years yet.

Length: 6.29m (20ft 8in). *Width:* 2.94m (9ft 8in). *Height:* 3.14m (10ft 4in). *Weight:* 35,000kg (77,160lb). *Crew:* 4. *Power:* Mitsubishi, V–12, air-cooled, turbocharged, diesel, 600bhp at 2,100rpm. *Armament:* one 90mm gun; one .30 machine gun; one .50 machine gun. *Armour:* 15–64mm. *Speed:* 45km/hr (28mph). *Range:* 200km (125 miles). *Maker:* Mitsubishi Heavy Industries.

Type 74 Main Battle Tank

Type 89A Medium Tank

TYPE 74 MAIN BATTLE TANK *1973–*
In 1964 the Japanese Army, appreciating that the Type 61 (*qv*) would not serve indefinitely, began development of a new tank for the 1980s. After testing several prototypes the design was settled and the Type 74 went into production in 1973 at a newly-built tank factory. The layout is conventional, and the turret is exceptionally well shaped to deflect shot. Main armament is the British 105mm L7 gun, licence-built in Japan. The suspension is of a hydro-pneumatic type which permits the driver to adjust the vehicle's ground clearance in accordance with the terrain to be covered and also allows the attitude of the tank to be altered to assist in laying the turret gun from a hull-down position. A sophisticated electronic fire-control system, employing a laser range-finder, ballistic computer and full gun stabilization is fitted. Infra-red night-vision equipment is standard and the tank carries a snorkel allowing it to ford rivers to a depth of 3m (9ft 10in). The Type 74 is one of the most advanced tanks presently in service anywhere.

Length: 6.85m (22ft 6in). *Width:* 3.17m (10ft 5in). *Height:* 2.69m (8ft 10in). *Weight:* 38,000kg (83,775lb). *Crew:* 4. *Power:* Mitsubishi, V–10, turbocharged, air-cooled, diesel, 21,500cc, 720bhp at 2,200rpm. *Armament:* one 105mm gun; one 7.62mm machine gun; one .50 machine gun. *Armour:* not disclosed. *Speed:* 60km/hr (37mph). *Range:* 500km (310 miles). *Makers:* Mitsubishi Heavy Industries.

TYPE 89 MEDIUM TANK *1934–1945*
The Type 89 medium tank was developed in the late 1920s after a series of tests with foreign designs, notably a Vickers Medium C (*qv*). The first models, known as the 89A, used a petrol engine, but experience in Manchuria led the Japanese to develop an air-cooled diesel engine. This went into use in 1934 and the tank was then known as the 89B. Both models were used in China and in the Philippines during the early part of World War II.

The 89 was of conventional layout, with driver and hull gunner at the front, a two-man turret, and the engine and transmission at the rear. It was one of the last tanks to carry an

Type 95 Light Tank

extended girder tail unit to assist in crossing trenches, an idea copied from the French Renault FT–17 (*qv*).

Length: 4.29m (14ft 1in). *Width:* 2.13m (7ft 0in). *Height:* 2.18m (7ft 2in). *Weight:* 11,500kg (25,353lb). *Crew:* 4. *Power:* Mitsubishi, 6-cyl, diesel, 120bhp at 1,800rpm. *Armament:* one 57mm gun; two 6.5mm machine guns. *Armour:* 10–17mm. *Speed:* 28km/hr (17mph). *Range:* 160km (100 miles). *Maker:* Mitsubishi Heavy Industries.

TYPE 94 TANKETTE *1934–1945*
The Type 94 was one of the class known as tankettes, ultra-light vehicles for reconnaissance and carrying supplies to forward troops under fire. Developed in 1934 it owed a great deal to the British Carden–Loyd machine-gun carriers (*qv*) which had been bought by Japan in the late 1920s. It mounted a turret carrying a single machine gun and was unusual in having a door in the rear of the hull for loading and unloading stores. Though moderately nimble, this tank tended to shed its tracks if driven too fast.

Length: 3.07m (10ft 1in). *Width:* 1.62m (5ft 4in). *Height:* 1.62m (5ft 4in). *Weight:* 3,400kg (7,496lb). *Crew:* 2. *Armament:* one 6.5mm machine gun. *Armour:* 4–12mm. *Speed:* 40km/hr (25mph). *Range:* 200km (130 miles). *Maker:* Tokyo Gas & Electric Co.

TYPE 95 LIGHT TANK *1935–1945*
Development of this tank began in 1934. After the prototypes had been tested in action in China and Manchuria, it went into production in 1935. The type number is derived from the last two digits of the Japanese calendar year 2595. It was a three-man design, the driver and hull machine gunner sitting at the front, and the commander occupying the turret where he had to fire the 37mm gun, command the tank

and also fire the rear-mounted machine gun when required.

About 1,250 were built and the design was considerably modified during the war; the gun was improved to a 47mm model, while some tanks were fitted with a 57mm gun to become the Type 3 (1943) model. In the following year numbers had their turrets removed and replaced by turrets of the Type 97 tank (*qv*) with a 47mm gun to become the Type 4. In spite of these changes the Type 95 and its variants were obsolescent before the war broke out and were no match for Allied tanks or antitank guns.

Length: 4.36m (14ft 4in). *Width:* 2.05m (6ft 9in). *Height:* 2.18m (7ft 2in). *Weight:* 7,400kg (16,315lb). *Crew:* 3. *Power:* Mitsubishi NVD 6120, 6-cyl., air-cooled, diesel, 120bhp at 1,800rpm. *Armament:* one 37mm gun; two 7.7mm machine guns. *Armour:* 6–12mm.

Speed: 45km/hr (28mph). *Range:* 250km (155 miles). *Maker:* Mitsubishi Heavy Industries.

Type 97 Medium Tank

TYPE 97 MEDIUM TANK *1937–1945*

In 1936 the current Type 89 medium (*qv*) was beginning to become out-dated and a fresh design was sought; two competing designs were tested and the Mitsubishi Chi-Ha model was selected for production as the Type 97. Probably the best Japanese tank design of the period, it was conventional in layout, with driver and hull gunner at the front and a two-man crew in the turret. The engine was at the rear, driving via a long propeller shaft to the gearbox and final drive at the front. Suspension was by six roadwheels at each side, paired in three bogies. The main armament, a 57mm gun, was unusual in having vertical trunnions, in addition to the usual horizontal trunnions, which allowed the gun to be traversed 5° in either direction independently of the movement of the turret, a system which allowed very precise aiming without having to move the

Type 94 Tankette

turret mass through small angles.

Length: 5.51m (18ft 1in). *Width:* 2.33m (7ft 8in). *Height:* 2.23m (7ft 4in). *Weight:* 15,000kg (33,070lb). *Crew:* 4. *Power:* Mitsubishi, V–12, air-cooled, diesel, 170bhp at 2,000rpm. *Armament:* one 57mm gun; two 7.7mm machine guns. *Armour:* 8–25mm. *Speed:* 38km/hr (25mph). *Range:* 210km (130 miles). *Maker:* Mitsubishi Heavy Industries.

TYPE 97 TANKETTE *1937–1945*
The Type 97 was the last tankette to be adopted by the Japanese Army. It was taken into service in 1937 to replace the unreliable Type 94 (*qv*). It had a riveted hull of good ballistic shape with the driver in the front, and a turret mounting a 37mm gun and occupied by the commander/gunner. Engine and transmission were at the rear, thus abandoning the rear-door stores-carrying concept of the earlier tankette. However, experience showed that cargo carrying was still desirable and a number were built without turrets, with the engine moved forward to leave a fully-enclosed cargo space at the rear end. The Type 97 tankette remained in service throughout the war with the Japanese Army.

Length: 3.68m (12ft 1in). *Width:* 1.80m (5ft 11in). *Height:* 1.77m (5ft 10in). *Weight:* 4,750kg (10,470lb). *Crew:* 2. *Power:* Ikega, 4-cyl., air-cooled, diesel, 65bhp at 2,300rpm. *Armament:* one 37mm gun. *Armour:* 6–12mm. *Speed:* 42km/hr (26mph). *Range:* 250km (155 miles). *Makers:* Tokyo Gas & Electric Co.

POLAND

TK–3 TANKETTE *1932–1940*
The TK–3 was yet another little armoured vehicle inspired by the Carden–Loyd carrier (*qv*). Poland bought a Mark IV Carden–Loyd in 1929 and from it produced their own version in 1932. Three hundred were built before it was realized that for modern war something better was needed and the TK3 was developed with a

Type 97 Tankette

different engine, better suspension, and thicker armour. Three hundred and ninety were built, but it was obvious by 1938 that both types were outdated and attempts were made to improve their firepower by fitting a 20mm gun. This did not get very far before the Germans invaded and the entire tank force was swept away by the Panzer advance. The few tankettes which remained after the invasion was over were impounded by the Germans for use as carriers and light artillery tractors. A few were used for internal security duties in Poland.

Length: 2.65m (8ft 6in). *Width:* 1.55m (5ft 10in). *Height:* 1.35m (4ft 4in). *Weight:* 2,500kg (5,511lb). *Crew:* 2. *Power:* Ford Model A, 4-cyl., water-cooled, petrol, 3,200cc, 40bhp at 2,300rpm. *Armament:* one 7.92mm machine gun. *Armour:* 8mm. *Speed:* 45km/hr (28mph). *Range:* 201km (125 miles). *Maker:* State Engineering Works.

7TP LIGHT TANK *1934–1939*
The 7TP was a development of the Vickers six-ton tank (*qv*), 50 of which were bought by Poland in 1931–2. The first model of the 7TP

7TP Light Tank

had the distinctive Vickers twin-turret, but this was soon discarded in favour of a Swedish single turret armed with a Bofors 37mm gun and about 160 of this type were built before difficulties arose over the supply of turrets. There followed a number of experiments with improved 7TPs and a Christie-type tank, but these came to nothing, and when the Germans invaded in 1939 there were only the obsolete 7TPs and the TK–3s (*qv*) to oppose them. It seems that few 7TPs survived and there are no records of them being taken into service with the Wehrmacht.

Length: 4.60m (15ft 1in). *Width:* 2.41m (7ft 11in). *Height:* 2.16m (7ft). *Weight:* 11,000kg (24,250lb). *Crew:* 3. *Power:* Saurer, 4-cyl., water-cooled, diesel, 110bhp at 2,000rpm. *Armament:* one Bofors 37mm gun; one 7.92mm machine gun coaxially mounted. *Armour:* 8–40mm. *Speed:* 32km/hr (20mph). *Range:* 160km (100 miles). *Maker:* State Engineering Works.

TK-3 Tankette

SOVIET UNION

BT–7 FAST TANK 1935–1945

The BT tanks derived their name from the initials of the words 'Bystrochodya Tank' (Fast Tank) and the original specification of 1931 called for a tank capable of operating well behind enemy lines in an independent role, very much as the cavalry saw themselves doing. Speed and range were essential for this, and Russia bought one of the American Christie chassis (qv) to form the basis of the design. The resulting tank was the BT–7, a tank with the typical Christie pointed hull and four large Christie roadwheels on each side. It could run on its wheels or its tracks, and when on wheels

BT-7 Fast Tank

the tracks were stowed on the track guards, power went to the rear roadwheel, and the front roadwheel was steered. However, this was found to be of little value in war and was never used. The turret was taken from the T–26 (qv) and mounted the 45mm anti-tank gun and the command versions carried a radio with a rail aerial running round the turret. For fire support to the fast-moving tank units a version was built with a short 76.2mm gun in a modified T–28 (qv) turret, and there were several other variants with turrets taken from different tanks. The BT–7 proved itself to be capable of a good deal of modification and later versions were fitted with diesel engines and heavily sloped armour. The importance of the BT–7 and its variants is that it formed the basis for the T–34 series (qv) and so laid the foundations for the Soviet victories in 1944–5. As a fighting tank itself the BT–7 was out-

classed early on in the war and those that survived the first battles became bridgelayers, smokelayers and similar specialized vehicles.

Length: 5.66m (18ft 7in). *Width:* 2.29m (7ft 6in). *Height:* 2.42m (7ft 11in). *Weight:* 13,900kg (30,644lb). *Crew:* 3. *Power:* Model M17T, V–12, water-cooled, petrol, 500bhp at 1,650rpm. *Armament:* one 45mm M1935 gun; one 7.62mm Degtyarev machine gun coaxially mounted. *Armour:* 10–22mm. *Speed:* 73km/hr (46mph). *Range:* 430km (270 miles). *Maker:* Kharkov Locomotive Works.

IS–3 HEAVY TANK 1943–1970

By mid-1942 it became imperative for the Soviets to develop a heavy tank with greater speed and manoeuvrability which was capable of combating the German 88mm gun. The best answer seemed to be an improved KV (qv), but

IS-3 Heavy Tank

the final version was well removed from the original KV. The suspension was lowered to allow a large flat turret to overhang the tracks.

The hull was sloped in all directions and the hull gunner was removed to improve the shape of the glacis plate. A 100mm gun was fitted, but by mid-1944, when the design was finalized, a 122mm version of the artillery gun was installed, albeit with little ammunition. This was the IS–2 (Josef Stalin 2). From this evolved the IS–3 which was revolutionary in every sense. Designed in 1944 by Kotin, it had fully sloped armour and a glacis plate in the form of a shallow inverted 'V' for better shot deflection. The turret was a shallow dome mounting a high-velocity 122mm gun. It was the most powerful and advanced tank of its time and it astonished Western observers when it first appeared in the Berlin Victory Parade in 1945. Despite its protection and large gun the IS–3 weighed no more than the German Panther (qv) and was just about as agile. All of this was achieved at the expense of internal storage and crew comfort, but this was accepted and the tank remained in service in a number of variants until the 1970s. It was used in the Warsaw Pact countries, but the only other customer was Egypt who took about 50 in 1956.

Length: 6.81m (22ft 4in). *Width:* 3.44m (10ft 6in). *Height:* 2.93m (8ft 11in). *Weight:* 46,250kg (101,963lb). *Crew:* 4. *Power:* Model V–2 IS, V–12, water-cooled, diesel, 39,000cc, 520bhp at 2,000rpm. *Armament:* one 122mm D-25 L/43 gun; one 7.62mm machine gun co-axially mounted; one 12.7mm machine gun on anti-aircraft mount on turret. *Armour:* 19–132mm. *Speed:* 37km/hr (23mph). *Range:* 150km (94 miles). *Maker:* almost certainly the factories in Tankograd Chelyabinsk-Kirov.

KS Light Tank

KS LIGHT TANK 1921–1941

The KS was really a French Renault FT–17 (qv) copied and built without the benefit of licence, but its production was in every way a remarkable achievement for a country torn by civil war and with no indigenous automobile industry. A Renault captured from the White Russians was 'reverse engineered' by the Krasny Sormovo Machine Building Plant and the Russian version was rolled out inside six months. Only a small number was finally completed, but most of them displayed a feature that was to become the hallmark of Soviet tank design, they had a larger gun than the original.

This was a short-barrelled 37mm with a coaxial machine gun. No other Renault version carried such armament in the turret, and perhaps with reason since there was only one man to handle them. Although these tanks stayed in service until 1941 they had by then long since been restricted to training duties only.

Length: 4.00m (13ft 1in). *Width:* 1.75m (5ft 9in). *Height:* 2.25m (7ft 5in). *Weight:* 5,800kg (15,432lb). *Crew:* 2. *Power:* Fiat, 4-cyl., in-line, air-cooled, petrol, 33.5bhp at 1,500rpm. *Armament:* one 37mm gun; one 7.62mm machine gun coaxially mounted. *Armour:* 8–16mm. *Speed:* 8.5km/hr (5.3mph). *Range:* 60km (37.5 miles). *Makers:* Krasny Sormovo Machine Building Plant; armour rolled by Izhorskiy Factory, Petrograd; engine from ZIS Plant.

KV I Heavy Tank

KV-1 HEAVY TANK *1940–1945*
The KV series arose from the need to have a heavy tank to batter through fixed defences, and in 1939 Soviet Russia was the only country in the world to have such a tank in production. The KV (Klim Voroshilov) was designed in 1938 to replace the T–35 (*qv*) with its many turrets. Gun design had improved to the point where the 76.2mm gun could fire both HE and armour-piercing shell, and so there was no longer any need for more than one turret, the main gun could do all the tasks needed. This allowed a smaller and better protected vehicle to be produced, and the crew was reduced by half. Armour was as thick as possible, the engine was the proven diesel from the BT–7 (*qv*), uprated to 600bhp, and the multi-wheeled suspension with torsion-bar springing came from the experimental T–100 tanks where it had proved to be reliable. The first models of the KV–1 were sent to Finland in early 1940 to break through the Mannerheim Line, and they did well. The tank was ordered into production and when the Germans invaded there were just over 600 of them. Six months later 1,300 had been built and by 1945 over 13,000 had been turned out. There was continual development: thicker armour was added and some of the welded components were cast in one piece. In 1943 the tank was

up-gunned by fitting the 85mm M1944 gun and a new turret, which was also adopted by the T–34 (*qv*). The KV–2 was the same chassis fitted with a monstrous box-like turret

KV II Heavy Tank

mounting the D–10 152mm howitzer; this was so heavy that the power traverse could not work properly except on a level surface. Although it did well against the Mannerheim Line in 1940 the KV–2 failed against German high-velocity guns and it was soon outclassed. All the KV series were replaced by the IS tanks (*qv*) in the late stages of the war. A severe handicap throughout the service life of this tank was a frail and unreliable transmission which often failed in battle.

Length: 6.27m (20ft 7in). *Width:* 3.10m (10ft 2in). *Height:* 2.16m (7ft 11in). *Weight:* 47,500kg (104,719lb). *Crew:* 5. *Power:* Model V–2–K, V–12, water-cooled, diesel, 39,000cc, 600bhp at 2,000rpm. *Armament:* one 76.2mm M1939 gun; after 1943, one 85mm M1944 gun

and three 7.62mm machine guns (one coaxially mounted, one in a ball mount in the back of the turret, one in the hull). *Armour:* 40–77mm. *Speed:* 35km/hr (22mph). *Range:* 250km (156 miles). *Makers:* Kirov Factory, Leningrad, Chelyabinsk Tractor Factory.

MS LIGHT TANK *1928–1942*
The deficiencies of the KS Renault light tank (*qv*) were soon shown up in service and a specification was drawn up in 1924 for an improved model. The first model was ready in late 1927 and required some further modifications, but the final version was put into serial production in 1928 and 960 were built in the next three years. It was a decided improvement over the Renault, although it still only had a two-man crew. The suspension was better, utilizing vertical coil springs acting on twin bogies, and the wheels themselves had rubber tyres. In order to reduce weight and length of the hull the engine and transmission were in one unit and were placed across the hull at the rear, a most advanced idea that brought its own troubles in maintenance. There were several variants, including one with a larger turret, but the tank went out of first-line service in 1932 and was relegated to the reserve until the last one disappeared in 1942. It was also known as the T–18. In 1941 the last type of T–18 was finally modified to carry a 47mm gun, but this was insufficient to cope with the Panzers.

Length: 3.50m (11ft 6in). *Width:* 1.76m (5ft 9in). *Height:* 2.12m (6ft 11in). *Weight:* 5,500kg (12,125lb). *Crew:* 2. *Power:* modified Fiat, 3-cyl., air-cooled, petrol, 35bhp. *Armament:* one 37mm Hotchkiss gun; one 7.62mm

MS Light Tank

T27 Tankette

machine gun coaxially mounted. *Armour:* 8–16mm. *Speed:* 16.5km/hr (10.3mph). *Range:* 60km (37.5 miles). *Maker:* Bolshevik Factory, Leningrad.

PT–76 LIGHT AMPHIBIOUS TANK *1952–*
The PT–76 is an interesting example of the way in which the Soviets have clung to the idea of the value of light tanks for reconnaissance duties. It is a considerable advance on the pre-war tanks, with their light armour and inadequate guns, and the PT–76 is heavily armed. In the squat, two-man turret there is a 76mm gun which is a direct descendant of the one originally fitted on the T–34 medium tank (*qv*). The armour is well sloped, and the glacis plate is particularly effective. It can swim without any

PT-76 Light Amphibious Tank

preparation and carries a snorkel tube on the back of the turret and trim plate on the nose. Propulsion is by water jets in the back of the hull. The engine is powerful and there is adequate performance under all conditions. The chassis has been used for an entire family of variants and the tank and many variants have been exported to more than twenty communist countries. It has been most successful, though some which appeared in Vietnam were quickly destroyed either by US armour or by hand-held rocket launchers.
Length: 6.94m (22ft 8in). *Width:* 3.16m (10ft 4in). *Height:* 2.22m (7ft 2in). *Weight:* 14,000kg (30,865lb). *Crew:* 3. *Power:* Model V–6, 6-cyl., water-cooled, diesel, 240bhp at 1,800rpm. *Armament:* one 76.2mm gun D–56T; one 7.62mm machine gun. *Armour:* 11–14mm. *Speed:* 44km/hr (27.5mph). *Range:* 260km (162 miles). *Maker:* State Tank Arsenal, Volgograd.

T–10 HEAVY TANK *1957–*
The T–10 is a development of the IS–3 (*qv*) and can also be looked upon as the IS–10. The main differences from the IS are a longer hull, an extra roadwheel in the suspension, a later model of gun with a bore evacuator, a larger turret, improved internal stowage, a more powerful engine and better armour. In general terms the performance is unchanged and the

range of the internal fuel tanks is still restricted. More recently a T–10M has appeared with an even longer gun fitted with a complicated multi-baffle muzzle brake and night-vision aids, as well as a 14.7mm machine gun on the turret. It has a snorkel and NBC protection. These tanks are used in separate battalions to provide fire support for the mediums, but they would also be the spearhead of any armoured breakthrough, relying on their armour to defeat any anti-tank weapons and their massive firepower to destroy the opposition. T–10s, and 10Ms are in service throughout the Warsaw Pact countries and in Syria and Egypt.
Length: 7.41m (24ft 4in). *Width:* 3.56m (11ft 8in). *Height:* 2.43m (8ft 0in). *Weight:* 52,000kg (114,640lb). *Crew:* 4. *Power:* one V–2–IS, V–12, water-cooled, diesel, 39,000cc, 700bhp at 2,000rpm. *Armament:* one 122mm improved L/43 gun; one 12.7mm machine gun coaxially mounted; one 14.7mm KPV machine gun anti-aircraft mount on turret. *Armour:* 20–250mm. *Speed:* 42km/hr (26mph). *Range:*

T26 Light Tanks

250km (155 miles). *Maker:* probably the same as the IS–3.

T–26 LIGHT TANKS *1932–1945*
The T–26 series of light tanks was one of the more numerous and more successful designs of pre-war tanks in Russia. In fact it was not a native design and was directly derived from the Vickers six-ton model (*qv*) which the Red Army bought in 1930. By 1931 the factory production lines were laid down and mass-production began in 1932, a subtle and unprofitable compliment to the Vickers Design Department. There were many variants on the T–26; the early ones had the twin turrets of the Vickers originals, but later ones

had several different types of turret and armament. All tanks made after 1933 had a single large turret with either a 37mm or a 45mm gun, or in some cases a flamethrower. There were command vehicles fitted with radio and lighter armament and several variants for artillery towing, bridge laying and similar specialized tasks. After 1938 all hulls were welded instead of the previous riveting. Production ceased in 1939 but it continued in use until 1945, though not in first-line service after 1943.
Length: 4.62m (15ft 2in). *Width:* 2.44m (8ft). *Height:* 2.08m (6ft 10in). *Weight:* 8,000kg (17,637lb). *Crew:* 3. *Power:* T–26, 4-cyl., air-cooled, petrol, 91bhp at 2,200rpm. *Armament:* two 7.62mm Vickers machine guns or two 7.62 Degtyarev machine guns or one 37mm gun and one 7.62mm machine gun or one 45mm gun and one 7.62mm machine gun or one flamethrower and one 7.62mm machine gun and other combinations. *Armour:* 6–25mm. *Speed:* 28km/hr (17.5mph). *Range:* 225km (140 miles). *Makers:* Bolshevik and Kirov factories, Leningrad, and others.

T–27 TANKETTE *1931–1941*
The T–27 was another pirated design from Vickers. Soviet Russia bought a number of the Carden–Loyd Mark VI carriers (*qv*) and decided to build a Russian version. This turned

out to be virtually identical, and as a result it was not much more use. Production started in 1931 and by 1933 there were about 2,500 of them and they became one of the most numerous armoured vehicles in the Red Army for the first part of the 1930s. They were used on all exercises and in some small internal security operations. The cavalry tried them as light reconnaissance vehicles and they had the same task in infantry divisions. Unfortunately the deficiencies of the type precluded their full employment, one severe drawback being the poor armour, another the cramped crew compartment which necessitated recruiting small men as drivers. After 1933 they were used for training and towing light artillery pieces, in which roles they were still working when the Germans invaded. Despite these failings, the T–27 served to introduce the concept of armoured warfare to the Red Army at a very low cost in machines, and it also pointed out the pitfalls of the tankette idea.

Length: 2.62m (8ft 6in). *Width:* 1.83m (6ft). *Height:* 1.44m (4ft 9in). *Weight:* 2,700kg (5,952lb). *Crew:* 2. *Power:* GAZ-AA, 4-cyl., water-cooled, petrol (modified Ford Model A), 40bhp at 2,200rpm. *Armament:* one 7.62mm machine gun. *Armour:* 4–10mm. *Speed:* 42km/hr (26mph). *Range:* 120km (75 miles). *Maker:* Bolshevik Factory, Leningrad; Ordzhonikidzi Factory, Moscow.

T–28 Medium Tank

T–28 MEDIUM TANK *1933–1941*

In the great surge of tank designing which occurred in Russia in the early 1930s a suitable medium was required. Taking a Vickers A6 (*qv*) as a basis, the Kirov Plant developed the T–28 by 1933. It was an advanced vehicle for its day, with three turrets; a main turret carrying a short-barrelled 76.2mm gun and co-axial machine gun and two more machine guns in small sub-turrets on the front of the hull. There was adequate power and all tanks carried two-way radio. The suspension was the Vickers-type vertical plunger with twin bogies and all the rollers and springs were protected by an armoured skirt. It was a bulky vehicle with many flat faces on the armour, but it was quite fast and reasonably agile. In the 1939 Winter War with Finland the armour was

T–34 MEDIUM TANK *1940–*

The T–34 is one of the outstanding tanks of this century and it was a major weapon in the defeat of the German Army in 1945. Design started in 1936 using the BT–7 (*qv*) as a basis, but enlarging the hull, lengthening the suspension by inserting an extra roadwheel, and sloping all aspects of the armour. The gun was the high-velocity 76.2mm, an innovation for a medium tank. The turret was low, and well sloped, while the gun was mounted near to the roof where it was somewhat limited in depres-

sion. The two men inside the turret were very cramped. Later versions fitted a cast turret with better protection and more room, and throughout the life of the tank there were continual improvements. In 1943 the D–5T 85mm anti-aircraft gun was fitted and again the turret was enlarged, this time a modified one was taken from the KV–85 tank. The T–34/85 was one of the most powerful tanks in existence when it appeared, and the Soviet system of mass production could flood the battlefields with them. In 1944 11,000 were built. The

suspension was excellent and gave little trouble. The wide tracks were carefully designed for travel over snow and the spring mud; for extra range drums of fuel were strapped on the rear decking. The diesel engine proved to be reliable and resistant to fire, while the welded hull stood up well to hits from enemy guns. The tank has continued in service throughout the Communist world since 1945, though in the Soviet Union it was phased out in favour of the T–54 (*qv*) in the mid-1950s.

Length: 6.19m (20ft 4in). *Width:* 2.92m (9ft 7in). *Height:* 2.39m (7ft 10in). *Weight:* 32,000kg (70,547lb). *Crew:* 5. *Power:* one Model V–2–34, V–12, water-cooled, diesel, 38,800cc, 500bhp at 1,800rpm. *Armament:* one 76.2mm Model 1939 L–11 gun (from 1943, one 85mm D–5T gun); two 7.62mm Degtyarev machine guns (one coaxially mounted, one in hull). *Armour:* 18–60mm. *Speed:* 50km/hr (31mph). *Range:* 300km (186 miles). *Makers:* originally, Komintern Factory, Kharkov; mass-production in many plants after pilot models passed.

found to be inadequate and extra plates were welded on to the glacis and turret faces, but this was still insufficient protection and the T–28s were easy targets for the German PzKpfw III (*qv*) and IV (*qv*). In the first tank battles of 1941 almost the entire fleet of T–28s was wiped out, leaving the infantry defenceless.

Length: 7.44m (24ft 5in). *Width:* 2.86m (9ft 3in). *Height:* 2.86m (9ft 3in). *Weight:* 28,000kg rising to 32,000kg in the late models (61,729lb–70,547lb). *Crew:* 6. *Power:* M–17L, V–12, water-cooled, petrol, 500bhp at 1,400rpm. *Armament:* one 76.2mm gun; three 7.62mm machine guns. *Armour:* 20–80mm. *Speed:* 37km/hr (23mph). *Range:* 220km (140 miles). *Maker:* Kirov Tank Plant, Leningrad.

T-35 Heavy Tank

T–35 HEAVY TANK *1933–1939*
The T–35 was a typical breakthrough tank of the late 1920s when warfare was still seen in terms of trench lines and massive setpiece assaults with infantry. At that time the only opponent of the tank was the field gun, and it was thought that massive tanks with plenty of firepower could roll over the enemy trenches and crush everything in their way. The T–35 was a product of that thinking and it followed the general lines of the British A–1 Independent (*qv*). The big central turret mounted a short 76.2mm gun and a coaxial machine gun. There were four smaller turrets grouped around the main one. Two mounted a 37mm gun and a machine gun in each, the other two had one machine gun. There was also a hull-mounted machine gun alongside the driver. To man this multitude of guns 11 men were required, including the driver, and the size of the hull and superstructure was such that it could never be adequately armoured. About 60 of these vehicles were built, there being several variants with minor alterations to the armament and layout, but soon after they came into service infantry anti-tank guns improved to the point where these slow monsters were too vulnerable for their proper role. They were tried out in the Winter War against Finland and some were still in service at the Battle of Moscow in late 1941. One or two were tried as self-propelled artillery mountings.

Length: 9.72m (31ft 10in). *Width:* 3.23m (10ft 6in). *Height:* 3.44m (11ft 3in). *Weight:* 50,000kg (110,200lb). *Crew:* 11. *Power:* one Model M–17T, V–12, water-cooled, petrol,

T-40 Light Amphibious Tank

39,000cc, 500bhp at 2,200rpm. *Armament:* one 76.2mm short gun; six 7.62mm Degtyarev machine guns. *Armour:* 10–30mm. *Speed:* 30km/hr (19mph). *Range:* 150km (94 miles). *Maker:* not known.

T-37 LIGHT AMPHIBIOUS TANKS
1934–1942
The T-37 was a direct copy from the Vickers Carden–Loyd amphibious tank, eight of which were bought in 1930. Some minor changes were made and after two experimental models the T-37 appeared in 1933. The main difference from the Carden–Loyd was in the suspension, which had been taken from the Horst-

T-37 Light Amphibious Tank

mann design and was better for the conditions in Russia. The turret was moved to the right side of the hull, but the remaining details were almost the same as those of the original series made in Vickers. About 1,200 were built between 1933 and 1936 and improvements of various kinds were brought in throughout the programme. The later models had thicker armour and were too heavy to float, but all the remainder were capable of swimming. In 1935 some T-37s were airlifted by slinging them between the undercarriage legs of TB-3 bom-

bers, and some T-27s (*qv*) were carried in the same way; in the invasion of northern Romania in 1940 several T-37s were flown in this way.

In 1936 the T-38 was brought in as a replacement for the T-37. The differences were not great externally, but there was a better engine, transmission and track layout which improved performance and reliability. Both types suffered from an inadequate armament and a two-man crew. A small propeller provided the water propulsion, but the amphibious ability does not seem to have been used much. Both types fought in the Winter War of 1939–40 and in the early stages of the 1941 invasion.

T-37 *Length:* 3.75m (12ft 4in). *Width:* 2.06m (6ft 7in). *Height:* 1.82m (5ft 11in). *Weight:* 3,200kg (7,055lb). *Crew:* 2. *Power:* GAZ–AA, 4-cyl., water-cooled, petrol, 40bhp at 3,000rpm. *Armament:* one 7.62mm machine gun. *Armour:* 4–9mm. *Speed:* 35km/hr (22mph). *Range:* 185km (116 miles). *Makers:* Ordzhonikidzi Factory and others.

T-40 LIGHT AMPHIBIOUS TANK
1941–1946
The T-40 was the successor to the T-37 (*qv*) and T-38 (*qv*). It was taken into service in the reconnaissance units of the cavalry and armoured forces in 1941. It was a completely new design from its predecessors, using torsion-bar springing, welded and sloped armour and a sloped turret. However, traces of the earlier models still remained. The engine and turret were off-set, the crew was still only two, and the armament was only machine guns. Water propulsion was by a propeller and rudders. The last models were given a 20mm gun to improve their striking power, but even so they must have been easy prey for the German tanks and armoured cars. Many of these small amphibious tanks were used for frontier patrolling along the eastern border with China.

Length: 4.43m (13ft 6in). *Width:* 2.51m (7ft 8in). *Height:* 2.12m (6ft 6in). *Weight:* 5,590kg (12,342lb). *Crew:* 2. *Power:* GAZ-202, 6-cyl., water-cooled, petrol, 85bhp at 3,600rpm. *Armament:* one 12.7mm machine gun and one 7.62mm machine gun coaxially mounted or one 20mm machine gun and one 7.62mm machine gun coaxially mounted. *Armour:* 6–13mm. *Speed:* 45km/hr (28mph). *Range:* 350km (220 miles). *Maker:* probably the Ordzhonikidzi Factory.

T-54/55 MAIN BATTLE TANKS *1947–*
The T-54 is an improved T-34 (*qv*), with a longer hull, a larger turret, more slope on the armour and also thicker armour, and a more powerful gun. It was derived from the T-44, itself an improvement on the T-34 (*qv*), and the first T-54 prototype was on trial in 1947. It is an impressively powerful vehicle and shows much skill in the design. It has been taken into service in at least 35 countries, not all of them in the Communist Bloc, and it is built under licence in China and several of the Warsaw

T-38 Amphibious Tank

T-55 Main Battle Tank

Pact countries. The hull is an all-welded steel monocoque and the turret is a large single casting with the cupolas and hatches welded on. The suspension is the same Christie-type as on the T–34, with a gap between the first two roadwheels to take up the extra hull length. Springing is by torsion bars. The engine is fitted transversely at the back of the hull, together with the transmission, and the drive goes to the rear sprocket. There is a snorkel for deep

T-54 Main Battle Tank

fording and the tank only needs about 15 minutes preparation for water crossings.

In 1960 the T–55 appeared. This has more power in the engine, more space for ammunition stowage and a stabilizer for the main gun. In 1963 this was followed by the T–55A, the main difference being that the hull-mounted machine gun was taken out. Both types have

been used in the Arab–Israeli wars, in Vietnam, Algeria, Angola and the fighting in Somalia. There are many variants of both models, and different countries refer to their versions by different type numbers, but the main characteristics of all of them are the same. The only criticism of the T–54 series is that the turret is restricting for the crew and limits the depression of the gun, the internal stowage of ammunition is also limited, and fuel has to be carried in external drums when extra range is needed.

Length: 6.45m (21ft 2in). *Width:* 3.27m (10ft 9in). *Height:* 2.40m (7ft 10in). *Weight:* 36,000kg (79,370lb). *Crew:* 4. *Power:* Model V–54, V–12, water-cooled, diesel, 39,000cc, 520bhp at 2,000rpm. *Armament:* one 100mm D–10T gun; one 7.62mm machine gun mounted coaxially; one 7.62mm machine gun mounted in hull; one 12.7mm machine gun on anti-aircraft mount on turret. *Armour:* 20–170mm. *Speed:* 48km/hr (30mph). *Range:* 400km (249 miles). *Makers:* various Soviet State Tank Factories and licensed countries.

T–60 LIGHT TANK *1941–1945*
The T–60 was a replacement for the T–40 amphibious tank (*qv*), and it followed hard on its heels. The Winter War and the German invasion showed up the main deficiencies of the light amphibians, not the least being the fact that the value of being able to swim was almost entirely offset by the light armour needed for flotation. The T–60 therefore abandoned the swimming idea and was entirely land

based. The frontal armour was thicker and a 20mm gun was fitted as standard. However, the general layout of the amphibians remained and the turret was on the left of the hull with the engine beside it, allowing the overall size to be remarkably small. There was one variant, the T–60A, which had thicker armour and different roadwheels. When the T–60s were outclassed in the fighting, the chassis was used for artillery towing and also as a mobile mounting for rocket launchers.

Length: 4.29m (14ft 1in). *Width:* 2.46m (8ft 1in). *Height:* 1.89m (6ft 2in). *Weight:* 5,150kg (11,345lb). *Crew:* 2. *Power:* GAZ–202, 6-cyl., water-cooled, petrol, 70bhp at 2,800rpm. *Armament:* one 20mm machine gun; one 7.62mm machine gun. *Armour:* 7–20mm. *Speed:* 45km/hr (28mph). *Range:* 615km (382 miles). *Maker:* State Tank Factories.

T-60 Light Tank

T–62 MAIN BATTLE TANK 1963–

The T–62 is the current main battle tank of the Warsaw Pact forces, though it will soon be replaced by the T–72 (qv). It entered service with the Soviet Army in 1963 and is a direct successor of the T–54/55 (qv). The external differences are not immediately obvious, but the hull is slightly larger, there is a new turret mounting a new gun and the power of the engine has been increased. Performance remains roughly the same. The larger hull allows the armour to slope a little more and a larger turret to be fitted. This turret is more rounded than on the T–54 and gives more protection. The gun is a smoothbore of 115mm bore, firing fin-stabilized ammunition at the rather slow rate of four or five rounds per minute. There is a stabilizer to allow firing on the move, full NBC protection and night-vision equipment for gunner and driver. A snorkel is carried as standard and there are arrangements for laying a smoke screen by injecting fuel into the exhaust. Since 1965 the tank has been built in very large numbers.

It has been used by Egypt, Syria, Libya and the Warsaw Pact.

Length: 6.71m (22ft 0in). *Width:* 3.35m (11ft 0in). *Height:* 2.40m (7ft 10in). *Weight:* 36,500kg (80,468lb). *Crew:* 4. *Power:* one Model V–2–62, V–12, water-cooled, diesel, 39,000cc, 700bhp at 2,200rpm. *Armament:* one 115mm U–5TS gun; one 7.62mm machine gun coaxially mounted; one 12.7mm DShK machine gun anti-aircraft mounting on turret. *Armour:* 20–170mm. *Speed:* 50km/hr (31mph). *Range:* 500km (310 miles).

T-62 Main Battle Tank

T–70 LIGHT TANK 1942–1947

The T–70 was the last of the two-man light tanks to be introduced in the Russian Army. The reason for retaining such ineffective vehicles so late in the war was that the main factories for building heavy tanks had been destroyed by the Germans, and until they could be started again in the Urals even a light tank was better than none at all. At least a light tank could give some fire support to the hard-pressed infantry battalions and for about a year, until the mediums began to come out of the new factories, these inadequate little tanks plugged the gap. The T–70 was mass-produced by one of the largest automobile plants in the USSR, and it did not interfere with the tank factories' output. It was up-armoured in mid-1943, but by the end of that year it was being replaced and the chassis were converted to

T-70 Light Tank

light self-propelled gun mountings or for use as tractors and carriers.

Length: 4.66m (15ft 3in). *Width:* 2.52m (7ft 8in). *Height:* 2.10m (6ft 9in). *Weight:* 9,950kg (21,958lb). *Crew:* 2. *Power:* two ZIS–202 6-cyl., water-cooled, petrol, each engine developing 70bhp at 2,800rpm. *Armament:* one 45mm gun; one 7.62mm machine gun co-axially mounted. *Armour:* 10–60mm. *Speed:* 50km/hr (32mph). *Range:* 450km (279 miles). *Maker:* Gorki Automobile Factory.

T–72 MAIN BATTLE TANK *1975–*

The T–72 is the successor to the T–62 (*qv*) and a derivative, the T–64, which was apparently not made in large numbers and may only have been an experimental interim vehicle. The T–72 is a larger vehicle than the T–62, though it still follows the same general shape and layout. There is an extra roadwheel in the

T–72 Main Battle Tank

suspension to accommodate a longer hull and the engine has either been considerably up-rated, or changed altogether. The crew has been reduced to three and an automatic loader installed for the gun. This gun is a high-velocity 122mm smoothbore firing the now fashionable fin-stabilized projectiles from a fully stabilized mounting. It is believed to have a battle range of at least 2,000m (6,561ft) though the rate of fire and quantity of ammunition carried may both be low. There is a laser rangefinder and a small ballistic computer for laying the gun and it may use a combustible cartridge. The armour is even more sloped than on the T–62 and the glacis plate is extremely tough. The new suspension has improved the performance and increased the speed on all surfaces and there is full night-vision equipment so that the vehicle can move and fight as well by night as by day. It is coming into service with the Soviet Army as we go to press.

Length: 7.43m (24ft 4in). *Width:* 3.07m (10ft 10in). *Height:* 2.46m (8ft 1in). *Weight:* 40,000kg (88,000lb). *Crew:* 3. *Power:* type unknown, estimated to be water-cooled diesel, 1,000bhp. *Armament:* one 122mm smooth-bore gun; one 7.62mm machine gun coaxially

mounted; one 12.7mm machine gun anti-aircraft mounting on turret. *Armour:* not known, but likely to be an increase on T–62. *Speed:* 60km/hr (37.5mph). *Range:* 500km (310 miles). *Maker:* not known.

SPAIN

LIGERO TIPO A–4 LIGHT TANK *1933–1936*

The Tipo A–4 was one of the family of light tanks produced in Spain under the general name of 'Carro de Combate Trubia', and they were all directly derived from the Renault FT–17 (*qv*). The Trubia designs had covered track frames, full mud-guards, a high bow to the hull and a conical turret. There are several interesting features on these tanks and details are now very scarce, but it seems as if the crew

was more than two men since there were several machine guns in ball mountings. A later version added a single machine gun in the glacis plate for the driver to use, and all of the Trubia series carried a roller in front to assist in climbing obstacles. It is doubted whether any of them survived the Civil War.

Length: 5.18m (17ft 1in). *Width:* 1.81m (5ft 11in). *Height:* 2.38m (7ft 10in). *Weight* (estimated): 10,000kg (22,048lb). *Crew:* 2 or 3. *Power:* not known. *Armament:* three or four 7.92mm machine guns. *Maker:* not known.

VERDEJA LIGHT TANK *1938–1940*

The Verdeja tanks were interesting vehicles which never advanced very far in production. They suffered from the economic decline in the aftermath of the Civil War and were shelved just when they had shown their potential. For their day they were as good as any elsewhere in Europe. The hull was low and flat with the engine in the front protected by a long sloping glacis. The first model had a turret from a German Panzer I (*qv*) modified to take a Russian 45mm gun. The next version had a Spanish conical turret with the same gun but a mantlet that enabled it to elevate to 75°, for what pur-

Verdeja Light Tank

pose is not clear, but it may have been intended for use as an anti-aircraft gun. A third version reverted to machine gun armament, including one in the hull for the driver.

Length: 5.07m (16ft 8in). *Width:* 2.13m (7ft 0in). *Height:* 1.72m (5ft 9in). *Armament:* see above.

SWEDEN

INFANTERIKANONVAGN 91 (Ikv–91) TANK DESTROYER *1970–*

The Ikv–91 was designed from a specification calling for a light vehicle of good mobility to provide an effective anti-tank defence for the infantry battalions. The resulting vehicle is an interesting version of a self-propelled gun in which the gun is in a fully-rotating turret. The

Ikv-91 Tank Destroyer

gun is a Bofors 90mm similar to that in the AMX–13 (*qv*). It is a low-pressure system so as to reduce the trunnion pull, and it is laid and corrected with the aid of a computer. The projectiles are fin-stabilized and the chief anti-armour shell is an advanced HEAT type. The gun is not stabilized, so that for accurate shooting the vehicle needs to be stationary. The hull is large and thinly armoured, the glacis plate being proof against 20mm only. This large hull allows a good stock of ammunition to be carried and the vehicle can swim with no more preparation than the raising of the trim vane and the engine pipe extensions. The engine is a commercial model and it is powerful enough to give a good power-weight ratio and battlefield agility to this fairly large hull. The Ikv–91 would not be used as an ordinary tank in battle, but would fight from concealed hull-down positions, using its speed to avoid confrontations with heavier armour.

Length: 6.41m (21ft 1in). *Width:* 3.00m (9ft 10in). *Height:* 2.35m (7ft 8in). *Weight:* 15,500kg (34,100lb). *Crew:* 4. *Power:* one Volvo–Penta Model TD 120, 6-cyl., turbocharged, diesel, 300bhp at 2,200rpm. *Armament:* one Bofors KV 90 S 73 90mm Low Pressure gun; one 7.62mm machine gun coaxially mounted; one 7.62mm machine gun externally on turret. *Armour:* classified; glacis plate will withstand 20mm projectiles. *Speed:* 69km/hr (43mph). *Range:* 550km (342 miles). *Maker:* Hägglunds and Soner AB, Örnsköldsvik.

Strv. m/42 Light Tank

Strv. m/40 Light Tank

Strv m/40 LIGHT TANK 1941–1953

The Strv m/40 was developed from a series of light armoured vehicles built by the Landsverk firm in the mid-1930s and which were native designs, though they may have owed a good deal to existing vehicles in other countries. The first successful tank from Landsverk was the

m/38, a small number of which were bought by the Swedish Army. This weighed 8,500kg (18,734lb) and from it was developed the m/40 which was the first tank to be built in quantity for the Swedish Army. It was fairly conventional in design, with a built-up hull using riveting and welding to join the plates. The driver was in the front of the hull with the transmission beside him and there was a low two-man turret mounting a 37mm gun and two coaxial machine guns. The turret shape was advanced for its time and bore a resemblance to some of the German types. The engine compartment was behind a fire bulkhead at the rear. Cross-country performance and reliability were generally good, though it must be remembered that these tanks were only ever used on exercises and never in action. The 37mm gun was quickly outdated, but was not replaced, and the vehicle remained in service long after it was obsolete elsewhere. A few were sold to Dominica in the 1950s for use as

internal security vehicles.

Length: 4.9m (16ft 1in). *Width:* 2.1m (6ft 11in). *Height:* 2.10m (6ft 11in). *Weight:* 9,500kg (20,944lb). *Crew:* 3. *Power:* Scania–Vabis, 6-cyl., in-line, water-cooled, petrol, 142bhp. *Armament:* one 37mm gun; two 8mm machine guns coaxially mounted. *Speed:* 48km/hr (30mph). *Range:* 200km (124 miles). *Maker:* Landsverk AB, Landskrona.

Strv m/41 LIGHT TANK 1942–1955

The Strv m/41 is the Czechoslovakian LT–38 (*qv*) built under licence in Sweden and fitted with a more powerful Swedish engine. These tanks were obviously a good investment for Sweden, since they continued to serve until the 1950s and were then totally rebuilt and their components used in making the Pbv 301 armoured personnel carrier, the first tracked carrier to be built for the Swedish Army. There were two versions of the m/41, the second one having a more powerful 160hp engine, but otherwise being unchanged. A few chassis were converted into self-propelled 105mm guns, but this does not seem to have been pursued–perhaps the gun was too heavy for the light chassis. A total of 240 was built.

Length: 4.57m (15ft 0in). *Width:* 2.13m (7ft 0in). *Height:* 2.37m (7ft 8in). *Weight:* 10,500kg (23,148lb). *Crew:* 3. *Power:* Scania–Vabis, 6-cyl., in-line, water-cooled, petrol, 145bhp. *Armament:* one 37mm gun; one 8mm machine gun coaxially mounted; one 8mm machine gun in hull. *Armour:* 25mm maximum. *Speed:* 45km/hr (26mph). *Range:* 200km (125 miles). *Maker:* Scania–Vabis, Södertälje.

Strv m/42 LIGHT TANK 1942–1957

The Strv m/42 was developed from the m/40, which was a native Swedish design and not a licence-built foreigner. The hull and chassis of the m/40 were lengthened by adding two more roadwheels and on to this enlarged hull a new

Strv. m/41 Light Tank

turret was fitted. It had a small overhang at the back and a larger mantlet projecting forward so that there was room for a 75mm gun. This was a substantial step forward in armament and it allowed the armoured formations a much better punch, though it was only a low-velocity gun and within two years it was out-of-date when compared to the tanks used by the Axis and the Allies. A distinction of the turret was that it carried two spare roadwheels on the back, one on either side. In 1956 these tanks were rebuilt and fitted with a larger turret and a high-velocity 75mm gun, bringing their specification more up-to-date, and they were then known as the Strv 74. There were two types of 74, the H and the L and they differed in the quantity of ammunition stowed and the type of gearbox fitted. These continued in service until the early 1970s, an active life which has probably only been excelled by the M4 Sherman (*qv*).

Length: 4.90m (16ft 1in). *Width:* 2.20m (7ft 4in). *Height:* 1.61m (5ft 3in). *Weight:* 22,500kg (49,590lb). *Crew:* 4. *Power:* Scania–Vabis. *Speed:* 45km/hr (26mph). *Range:* 200km (125 miles). *Maker:* Landsverk AB, Landskrona.

Strv S 103 MAIN BATTLE TANK *1966–*

The S 103 is unique among present-day tanks in that it has a crew of three and no turret. The design originated in 1956 and the first vehicles entered service ten years later. The intention behind the unusual design was to reduce the overall height, and thus make it easier to conceal in battle; to simplify the manufacture by having no turret with its complicated rotating mechanism and power linkages; and to reduce the numbers of trained men by having a crew of three and fitting an automatic loader. The tank bristles with other novelties. There are two engines, a diesel for normal running and a Belgian-built gas turbine as a 'boost' for rough going. The driver is also the gunner. The commander is also the gunner for the anti-aircraft machine gun, and the radio operator sits facing backwards: he can drive the tank in reverse.

The gun is laid by the driver pointing the entire vehicle at the target and the suspension is hydro-pneumatic with a large degree of vertical movement, so that the whole tank can be canted up or down to give the desired elevation to the gun. There are very fine servo motors to make the final movements for aiming, but it does mean that the engine has to run all the time the tank is in action in order to provide the power. It is also a little slower than a conventional turret. Despite the advantages of the idea, it is probably not cheaper to build than any other tank and it is noticeable that no other country has bought any. There are rumours that the next Swedish tank will have a turret, but at least the S has been a brave experiment.

Length (without gun): 8.42m (27ft 7in). *Width:* 3.62m (11ft 10in). *Height:* 2.50m (8ft 3in). *Weight:* 39,000kg (85,980lb). *Crew:* 3. *Power:* Rolls-Royce K60, multi-fuel, 240bhp at 3,650rpm, Boeing 553 gas-turbine, 490bhp at 38,000rpm. *Armament:* one 105mm gun; three 7.62mm machine guns. *Armour:* classified information. *Speed:* 50km/hr (31mph). *Range:* 390km (242 miles). *Maker:* Bofors A B, Sweden.

SWITZERLAND

Pz 61 AND 68 MAIN BATTLE TANKS
1971–
Until the late 1950s Switzerland had no indigenous tank manufacturing plant and relied on foreign purchases for its fleet. However, in the 1950s the Federal Engineering Works set about designing its own tank. After some experiment the Pz 61 went into service and 150 were built. This was an interesting vehicle, probably owing much to the Centurion (*qv*) in its general design, and using the same gun. The hull was largely cast, as was the turret, and both were well sloped. The suspension was unusual in that the roadwheels were sprung by means of Belleville washers, a system that has not been used for large numbers of tanks before, though some World War II German designs had it. The engine is an imported German unit with a

Swiss transmission married to it driving a rear sprocket. The Pz 68 is an improved version with a fully stabilized gun and various minor alterations to the engine and transmission as well as a better NBC outfit. Both Pz 61 and 68 are used as variants, the two most frequent being the recovery and bridgelaying versions. The tank is a good example of a modern, well-made design, but it is rather high in its silhouette and its range is short.

Length: 6.94m (22ft 8in). *Width:* 3.14m (10ft 4in). *Height:* 2.75m (9ft 0in). *Weight:* 39,700kg (87,523lb). *Crew:* 4. *Power:* one MTU MB 837, 8-cyl., diesel, 704bhp at 2,200rpm. *Armament:* one 105mm L7 gun; one 7.5mm machine gun coaxially mounted; one 7.5mm machine gun anti-aircraft mounting on turret. *Armour:* 20–60mm. *Speed:* 55km/hr (34mph). *Range:* 300km (186 miles). *Maker:* Federal Engineering Works, Thun.

UNITED KINGDOM

BLACK PRINCE INFANTRY TANK *1945–*
In September 1941 the British General Staff asked the Tank Board to develop fresh designs of both cruiser and infantry tanks, mounting the heaviest and highest-velocity guns possible. At that time the 17-pdr. (3in) anti-tank gun was well forward in its development, and the obvious solution was to graft this gun into the existing Churchill tank (*qv*). Unfortunately, though, the Churchill turret was not wide enough to accept the larger gun, and increasing the tank's size was precluded by an old regulation that all tanks had to fit within the railway loading gauge limits. A tentative solution was reached by mounting a redundant 3in anti-aircraft gun into the front plate of the Churchill, but this was not a success.

In 1943 the width limit was rescinded, in recognition of the fact that tanks were frequently carried by road, and the Vauxhall Motor Company was asked to produce a redesigned Churchill, wider, heavier and carrying the 17-pdr. gun in the turret. This was designated A43 or Black Prince, and was to be an interim design to hold the ring until the projected A41 Centurion (*qv*) was ready. In the event, both designs reached pilot stage at the same time, just as the war ended in Europe in 1945. Six pilot models of Black Prince were made, but the project was then abandoned.

In essence, Black Prince was no more than an enlarged Churchill, having precisely the same general configuration, but with more room and a turret capable of taking the 17-pdr. Mark 5 gun. Due to its parentage, it would doubtless have performed well enough and would have had few teething troubles, but in comparison to the Centurion it was obsolete before it started.

Length: 8.81m (28ft 11in). *Width:* 3.44m (11ft 4in). *Height:* 2.74m (9ft 0in). *Weight:* 50,800kg (112,000lb). *Crew:* 5. *Power:* Bedford, horizontally-opposed, 12-cyl., petrol, 21,241cc, 350bhp at 2,200rpm. *Armament:* one 17-pdr. Mark 5 gun; two 7.92mm Besa machine guns. *Armour:* 18–88mm. *Speed:* 18km/hr (12mph). *Range:* 120km (75 miles). *Maker:* Vauxhall Motors Ltd., Luton, Beds.

Panzer 68 Main Battle Tank

Black Prince

Carden-Loyd One-man Tank

CARDEN–LOYD TANK DESIGNS
1925–1930

Mr. (later Sir) John Carden was an engineer who, in the late 1920s, was running a garage in London owned by a Mr. Loyd. Carden had designed and produced a popular cycle-car and then designed a light tracked vehicle with the intention of enhancing the mobility of infantry. In 1925 the prototype was demonstrated; little more than a light steel box supported on tracks, propelled by a 23hp engine and carrying one man and a machine gun. This was followed by a Mark 1 version which did little more than add a three-sided steel shield around the occupant.

At that time there was considerable interest in vehicles which could move on tracks across country but on wheels on roads, so as to save

Carden-Loyd Two-man Tank

wear on the tracks. The Carden–Loyd Mark 1* followed this trend and was a Mark 1 body carried on two large roadwheels, one at each side, with a small third wheel at the rear for steering. Within this layout was the track assembly, and the wheels could be raised so as to bring the tracks into contact with the ground when required. Powered by a Ford Model T engine, the Mark 1* could reach 48km/hr (30mph) on its wheels or 24km/hr (15mph) on tracks.

In 1926, the wheel-and-track idea began to fade, and Carden–Loyd produced the two-man tankette which carried a driver and machine-gunner side by side and which had a tracked suspension carried on rubber-tyred bogies.

Late in 1926 the War Office ordered eight wheel-and-track machines, and the tankette was suitably modified, using the same type of suspension arrangement as on the Mark 1*. Known as the Mark 5 it carried a Vickers machine gun and was built of 9mm armour plate. These vehicles were used during the life of the Experimental Mechanized Force formed in 1927.

As a result of the Mechanized Force trials in 1927–8 it was decided that an infantry machine-gun carrier was needed. In 1928 Vickers–Armstrong bought out the Carden–Loyd company, John Carden going to Vickers as a designer, and under this new management a fresh design, the Mark 6, was developed. This had improved suspension, additional armour and more stowage space. This proved to be a very successful design and was widely exported, while numbers were built under licence abroad. Several countries took the Carden–Loyd Mark 6 as their starting point in developing their own designs, and thus it became the inspiration for such vehicles as the Italian CV 33 (qv), the French UE, and the Soviet T27 (qv) among many others.

So far as the British Army was concerned, the Carden–Loyd failed to make the grade as a

light tank, but it formed the start of a long line of infantry tracked carriers of varying pattern which served in increasing numbers until after World War II.

CAVALIER CRUISER TANK 1941–1945

In January 1941 the War Office issued a demand for a new cruiser tank in the 24-ton class, armed with the 6-pdr. gun and with 7.6cm (3in) of frontal armour. The first approach was made to Nuffield Mechanization & Aero, Ltd., and their design given the title A24, Cruiser Mark 7, or Cavalier. To save time, the engine and many other components of the existing Crusader tank (qv) were taken as a basis. The hull and turret were severely rectangular, and a Christie-type suspension was fitted. Six pilot models were ordered, and the first of these appeared in January 1942.

Such was the urgency of the situation, however, that an initial production order for 500 was given in June 1941, long before the first pilot model had been seen or tested, a calculated gamble aimed at reducing the time between design and production. Unfortunately, the gamble failed; when the production tanks appeared they were found to have fallen heir to most of the mechanical troubles which had plagued the Crusader, due to the retention of the engine and drive units. Consequently the Cavalier was never used in action, being restricted to use as a training tank. In 1943 numbers were converted into armoured recovery vehicles and others into armoured artillery command posts for use with self-propelled field regiments, and in these roles the Cavalier continued to serve until the end of World War II.

Length: 6.35m (20ft 10in). *Width:* 2.88m (9ft 6in). *Height:* 2.44m (8ft 0in). *Weight:* 26,925kg (59,360lb). *Crew:* 5. *Power:* Nuffield Liberty, V–12, petrol, 27,000cc, 410bhp at 1,500rpm. *Armament:* one 6-pdr. gun; two 7.92mm Besa machine guns. *Armour:* 20–76mm. *Speed:* 38km/hr (24mph). *Range:* 300km (185 miles). *Maker:* Nuffield Mechanization & Aero, Ltd., Oxford.

Cavalier Cruiser Mark VII

CENTAUR CRUISER TANK *1942–1948*

The Centaur tank, or A27 Cruiser Mark 7, was developed by Leyland Motors Ltd. in response to the same basic specification which had produced the Cavalier (*qv*). The principal feature was the use of a new engine; Leyland had previously suggested converting the Rolls-Royce Merlin aircraft engine to use as a tank engine, calling the result the Meteor. Unfortunately, at that time (early in 1941), Rolls-Royce had no aircraft engines to spare for conversion to tank use, so that Leyland were told to go ahead with their design, but to use the existing Nuffield Liberty engine, the only engine available with sufficient power to drive

Centaur

a cruiser tank. When the new Meteor engine did become available, the design was modified accordingly and given a fresh name – Cromwell (*qv*).

Leyland took up the idea and in 1942 converted their factory to tank production. The first pilot Centaur appeared in June 1942 and production began in November. The general design was of a rectangular hull and turret, with Christie suspension (Cavalier, Centaur and Cromwell are almost indistinguishable at a distance) and the main armament was a 6-pdr. gun. Later versions were armed with a British 75mm gun, and some of the earlier tanks were retrospectively re-gunned. The most important version of the Centaur was the Mark 4, which mounted a 95mm howitzer in the turret as a close-support weapon; this was issued to the Royal Marine Armoured Support Group for use in the invasion of Europe in 1944. The intention was that the tanks could fire, in support of the landings, from their stowed positions on the landing craft, after which they would go ashore and guard the beaches. In the event, the Royal Marines completed this task quite easily and then got the bit between their teeth and drove inland to fight their Centaurs as battle tanks with great success.

Other Centaur variations included the Centaur anti-aircraft tank, armed with twin 20mm cannon; the Centaur dozer, carrying a bulldozer blade and without its turret. Centaur gun tanks were solely employed as training vehicles, and were not used in action; however, a number of them were withdrawn, refitted with the new Meteor engine to become Cromwells, and in that guise were used in the battles in

CENTURION CRUISER TANK *1945–*

In 1943, after a succession of unfortunate designs, the War Office set forth a fresh specification, calling for a tank with durability, reliability, a weight of 40 tons, a width not over 3.25m (10ft 6in) (so as to negotiate the standard Bailey bridge), powerful armament, sufficient armour to shrug off the German 88mm gun, and sufficient room inside for the crew to operate in some degree of comfort. The weight restriction was later relaxed since it became obvious that the aims could not be achieved within the 40-ton limit.

In February 1944 the final specification of the A41 design was drawn up, calling for a 17-pdr. gun as the main armament, supplemented by a 20mm cannon, three machine guns, and a

Rolls-Royce Meteor engine as the power unit. By May 1944 the first mock-up had been made and approved and 20 pilot models ordered, and in May 1945 the first six production models were rushed to Germany but arrived too late to be tested in action.

The Centurion (as the A41 became known) was the first attempt to produce a 'universal' or 'capital' tank and do away with the old division between 'cruiser' and 'infantry' tanks. It featured a partly cast turret, a sloping glacis plate to deflect shot, a Horstmann suspension system to replace the Christie system previously used, and a 20mm Polsten cannon mounted in the turret alongside the main 17-pdr. gun.

Almost immediately, work began on an

improved design, the Mark 2, which appeared in 1946. This replaced the 20mm cannon with a machine gun, made the turret entirely cast, removed the machine gun from the turret rear face and substituted an escape hatch, and the main armament was fully stabilized in both azimuth and elevation. After the first 100 of these had been built, the main armament was changed to a new 3.3in 20-pdr. high velocity gun, turning the tank's designation into Mark 3.

In this form the Centurion first saw action in the Korean War in 1951 and soon proved itself to be indisputably the best tank in that theatre, notable for its astonishing cross-country ability.

In 1952 the Mark 5 version appeared, in which the American .30in Browning machine gun replaced the 7.92mm Besa; the turret was reshaped and fitted with a new cupola, and an anti-aircraft machine gun added. While this was being built, a much greater redesign was in progress, resulting in the Mark 7 version. This had a new hull with thicker armour, increased fuel capacity, better ammunition stowage and better driver's controls. The turret of the Mark 5 was used with this model, but a new turret, with better fire-control equipment and a

contra-rotating commander's cupola was then designed and this, on the improved hull, became the Mark 8.

In 1957 came a further improvement with the adoption of the 105mm high-velocity gun, leading to the Mark 9 tank. The earlier Mark 8, when fitted with the new gun, became the Mark 10. Other mark designations (there are a total of 25 different marks) refer to minor

Centurion Mark 7

changes in fire-control equipment, the fitting of infra-red driving and firing aids, and similar changes.

In addition to being used by the British Army, the Centurion has been adopted by all Commonwealth countries, and by Denmark, Egypt, India, Iraq, Israel, Jordan, Lebanon,

Libya, the Netherlands, Kuwait, Sweden and Switzerland. It has been used in combat by both India and Israel with considerable success.

Variations on the basic design include an armoured recovery vehicle, without gun but with winch, jib crane and other recovery tackle; a beach ARV, much the same but capable of operating in up to 3m (9ft 10in) of water; an AVRE (Armoured Vehicle Royal Engineers) fitted with a 165mm gun; a bridge-layer; and an ark or gap-spanning tank in which the vehicle is actually driven into the gap and forms part of the bridge. These are dealt with in more detail in the section devoted to support vehicles.

Length: 7.79m (25ft 7in). *Width:* 3.30m (10ft 10in). *Height:* 2.99m (9ft 10in). *Weight:* 51,820kg (114,245lb). *Crew:* 4. *Power:* Rolls-Royce Meteor, V–12, petrol, 27,025cc, 650bhp at 2,550rpm. *Armament:* one 105mm gun; two .30 machine guns and one .50 ranging machine gun. *Armour:* 17–152mm. *Speed:* 35km/hr (21mph). *Range:* 200km (125 miles). *Makers:* Associated Equipment Co. (AEC) Southall, Middx.; Leyland Motors Ltd., Leyland, Lancs.; Royal Ordnance Factory, Leeds; Vickers, Ltd., Elswick.

north-west Europe in 1944–5.

Length: 6.35m (20ft 10in). *Width:* 2.88m (9ft 6in). *Height:* 2.44m (8ft 0in). *Weight:* 27,942kg (61,600lb). *Crew:* 5. *Power:* Nuffield Liberty, V–12, petrol, 27,000cc, 395bhp at 1,500rpm. *Armament:* one 6-pdr. or one 75mm gun; or one 95mm howitzer and two 7.92mm Besa machine guns. *Armour:* 20–76mm. *Speed:* 43km/hr (27mph). *Range:* 300km (185 miles). *Maker:* Leyland Motors Ltd., Leyland, Lancs.

CHALLENGER CRUISER TANK
1943–1946
In 1942 the two principal complaints voiced about British tanks were their mechanical unreliability and their lack of an effective gun. With the development of the Cromwell tank (*qv*) the first problem appeared to be overcome, leaving the problem of the gun. In early 1942 the Birmingham Carriage & Wagon Company were asked to develop a tank based on the Cromwell chassis but mounting a 17-pdr. gun in the turret. The Cromwell chassis was lengthened by the addition of an extra roadwheel on each side, and a new turret, large and high in order to accommodate the gun, was placed on the hull. The result could be said to be successful insofar as it worked, but it was ungainly and the additional weight robbed it of performance. Nevertheless, it was approved for production in February 1943 and a total of 200 was built.

Due to its high silhouette, the Challenger was somewhat vulnerable when used as a battle tank, and its role came to be that of a tank killer in support of other cruisers. A typical tank troop of the 1944–5 period consisted of one Challenger backing up three Cromwells. In this role it enjoyed some success in north-west Europe in 1944–5, but it was declared obsolete soon after the end of the war.

Length: 8.02m (26ft 4in). *Width:* 2.90m (9ft 7in). *Height:* 2.66m (8ft 9in). *Weight:* 32,000kg (70,547lb). *Crew:* 5. *Power:* Rolls-Royce Meteor, V–12, petrol, 27,025cc, 570bhp at 2,500rpm. *Armament:* one 17-pdr. gun; one 7.92mm Besa machine gun. *Armour:* 20–100mm. *Speed:* 40km/hr (31mph). *Range:* 220km (135 miles). *Maker:* Birmingham Railway Carriage & Wagon Co.

Challenger

Chieftain Main Battle Tank

CHIEFTAIN MAIN BATTLE TANK *1963–*
In the early 1950s Britain began development of a new battle tank to replace the Centurion (*qv*) and a number of tentative designs were put together. In 1958 the definitive specification was issued, with priority accorded to firepower, followed by protection and finally mobility. The first prototype Chieftain was completed in September 1959, and was approved for service in May 1963. The first regiments were equipped in 1967 and a total of about 800 were eventually built for the British Army, and production has continued for export. In broad terms the Chieftain can be said to be derived from the Centurion, using the same general layout, but vastly improved in detail and with a totally new armament. The hull uses a cast front section with welded sides, and the turret is completely cast; attention has been paid to sloping the armour so as to mitigate the effects of shot and mines. The driver lies prone in the front section, part of the steps taken to achieve a low silhouette. The main armament is a 120mm gun firing a 17kg (37lb) HESH shell or one 10kg (22lb) discarding sabot shot. This calibre was selected as giving the best chance of a first-shot kill over ranges up to 4,000m (13,000ft), and an unusual feature is the use of separated bag-charge ammunition. Although this meant the difficult task of developing a sliding block breech suited to bag charges, it means that the individual items of the cartridge and shell combination are short and thus less space is required inside the turret behind the gun breech. This, in turn, allowed a heavy gun to be mounted on a relatively small turret ring.

Fire control in the early models was per-formed by a ranging machine gun mounted coaxially with the 120mm gun. The machine gun's bullet was ballistically matched to the gun projectile, the machine gun being fired until the bullet was seen to strike the target, whereupon the 120mm gun was fired with a high probability of hitting. The latest models of Chieftain incorporate an improved system which uses a laser rangefinder, laser sight, electronic fire-control computer and a variety of sensors which measure and correct for such variables as the tilt of the tank and gun, wind speed, air density and humidity and changes in muzzle velocity due to barrel wear. All these, allied to full stabilization of the gun, give a degree of accuracy which virtually guarantees first-round hits at 3,000m (9,840ft) against stationary targets and 2,000m (6,560ft) against moving ones.

Chieftain has appeared in various models; the Mark 1 is the training tank, using a 585bhp engine; Mark 2 is the service tank, with a 650bhp engine; Mark 3 is an improved Mark 2 with new auxiliary generator, cupola, etc.; Mark 3/3 is the 3 with the improved fire-control package, improved air conditioning and a 750bhp engine. Other slightly different versions have been sold to Iran.

Length: 7.51m (24ft 8in). *Width:* 3.50m (11ft 6in). *Height:* 2.89m (9ft 6in). *Weight:* 55,000kg (121,255lb). *Crew:* 4. *Power:* Leyland L–60, vertically opposed, 2-stroke multi-fuel, 750bhp at 2,100rpm. *Armament:* one 120mm gun; two 7.62mm machine guns. *Armour:* not disclosed (classified information). *Speed:* 44km/hr (27mph). *Range:* 400km (250 miles). *Maker:* Royal Ordnance Factory, Leeds; Vickers Ltd., Elswick.

CHURCHILL INFANTRY TANK
1941–1950

Upon the outbreak of war in 1939 a large body of British military opinion felt that the course of the war would be a continuation of the 1914–18 battles, and that therefore a heavily-armoured infantry tank would be needed to accompany the infantry assault across shell-torn ground. A specification was drawn up calling for 60mm of armour, a speed of no more than 16km/hr (10mph) and main armament of a 2-pdr. gun in the turret and another in the hull front. Pilot models of this A20 design were built by Harland & Wolff of Belfast, using a multi-wheel suspension said to have been inspired by a French design and powered by a Meadows 12-cyl. engine. Tests showed that the design was underpowered and overweight and it was forthwith abandoned. A new specification for Tank A22 was then given to Vauxhall Motors Ltd. in July 1940.

Vauxhall's first job was to design a suitable engine, after which they modified the A20 design to fit around the power unit. A heavier gun than the 2-pdr. was desirable but none was available, so the 2-pdr. was retained in the turret, but to augment the firepower a 3in howitzer was fitted into the front of the hull. The first production tanks were delivered in June 1941, eleven months from the issue of the specification, a remarkable feat on the part of Vauxhall who had no previous experience of tank design or manufacture.

The Churchill design was characterized by the tracks running up to hull-top height, a deep-set front plate between the tracks, and the multi-wheel suspension. Early models exhibited many mechanical faults and much reworking was necessary, but eventually it was refined into an extremely tough and reliable tank which has been described as probably the best all-round tank of its time. The armament was frequently improved; the 3in hull howitzer was removed and replaced by a machine gun, the turret gun uprated to a 6-pdr. and then a 75mm, with some close support tanks having a 95mm howitzer. The armour was also improved, first by adding plates and then by redesigning the hull and turret.

First used in action by the Canadians at Dieppe in August 1942, the Churchill continued to serve throughout the war and for some years afterwards. Numbers were sent to Russia to be used there, while in postwar years numbers were supplied to India, Jordan and Eire. As well as serving as a battle tank, the Churchill formed the basis for many of the specialized armoured vehicles used by the 79th Armoured Division.

Length: 7.44m (24ft 5in). *Width:* 3.25m (10ft 8in). *Height:* 2.48m (8ft 2in). *Weight:* 39,575kg (87,250lb). *Crew:* 5. *Power:* Bedford, 12-cyl., petrol, 21,240cc, 350bhp at 2,200rpm. *Armament:* one 2-pdr. or one 6-pdr. or one 75mm or one .95mm howitzer. Early models had one 3in howitzer in hull; two 7.92mm Besa machine guns. *Speed:* 25km/hr (16mph). *Range:* 140km (88 miles). *Maker:* Vauxhall Motors Ltd., Luton, Beds.

Comet

COMET CRUISER TANK *1944–1950*

In 1941 the British War Office asked the Tank Board for a cruiser tank mounting the heaviest possible gun; one result of this was the Challenger (*qv*) which put a 17-pdr. gun into an over-large turret on a Cromwell (*qv*) chassis. This, though, was not particularly successful and the Tank Board developed an alternative, a Cromwell chassis mounting a new gun.

The gun was one which had been privately developed by Vickers–Armstrong as a 50-calibre 75mm gun to give 808m (2,650ft) per second muzzle velocity with a 7kg (15lb) shot but take up as little room as possible inside the tank's turret. For the sake of simplicity in ammunition production, the design was changed, making the calibre 76mm so as to accept the same projectiles as the 17-pdr. gun but using the cartridge case of the 3in 20cwt (1,016kg) anti-aircraft gun. In order to avoid confusion among the innumerable 3in and 75 and 76mm guns then in service with the British Army, the new weapon was called the 77mm gun; it was, to all intents, a detuned 17-pdr., the principal advantage being in the lesser space needed in the turret and the smaller ammunition.

The Comet tank was therefore a Cromwell hull, modified to have a slightly larger turret ring, with a new turret mounting the 77mm gun. The first production models were delivered in September 1944 and, after units had been retrained, the Comet tank was first used in combat in March 1945. Apart from some disappointment over the reduced performance of the gun in comparison with the 17-pdr., the Comet was well liked, particularly for its reliability and agility. It remained in service for several years after the war.

Length: 6.55m (21ft 6in). *Width:* 3.07m (10ft 1in). *Height:* 2.67m (8ft 8in). *Weight:* 33,224kg (73,250lb). *Crew:* 5. *Power:* Rolls-Royce Meteor, V–12, petrol, 27,025cc, 600bhp at 2,550rpm. *Armament:* one 77mm gun; two 7.92mm Besa machine guns. *Armour:* 14–101mm. *Speed:* 50km/hr (31mph). *Range:* 200km (125 miles). *Maker:* Leyland Motors Ltd., Leyland, Lancs.

CONQUEROR HEAVY TANK *1956–1963*

For many years prior to and during World War II it was the practice of the British Army to have two types of tank armament; a high-velocity small-calibre gun for armour piercing, and a proportion of tanks mounting larger-calibre low-velocity guns to fire high-explosive shells for infantry support and the destruction of obstacles, but having no anti-tank capability. This idea lingered after the war, and in 1948, in order to provide a support to the Centurion (*qv*), a heavy tank known as the Conqueror was devised. This was to carry a 120mm gun derived from the American 120mm tank gun, which in turn was derived from an anti-aircraft gun. It used a brass cartridge case of enormous proportions, which demanded a large turret in order to accommodate the gun and allow room to load.

The resulting tank was a triumph of firepower over mobility, since the current state of design was incapable of devising an agile tank which would carry such a large gun. It was a massive vehicle with an all-welded hull carried on a Horstmann suspension system which used eight roadwheels on each side. The turret was cast, and the commander had his own cupola at the rear of the turret. Although the firepower was excellent, the mobility and reliability was poor and, due to its size, special transporters, bridges and servicing facilities had to be provided. Throughout its life it was plagued with electrical malfunctions and servicing the mechanical components was exceptionally difficult. The gun also gave trouble, tending to burn up the cartridge case mouth on firing. Conquerors entered service with British units in Germany in 1956 and were withdrawn seven years later.

Length: 11.58m (38ft 0in). *Width:* 3.98m (13ft 1in). *Height:* 3.35m (11ft 0in). *Weight:* 66,045kg (145,605lb). *Crew:* 4. *Power:* Rolls-Royce M–120, V–12, petrol, 27,025cc, fuel injection, 810bhp at 2,800rpm. *Armament:*

one 120mm gun L1A1; one 7.62mm machine gun. *Armour:* 25–200mm. *Speed:* 35km/hr (21mph). *Range:* 150km (95 miles). *Maker:* Royal Ordnance Factory, Leeds.

COVENANTER CRUISER TANK *1940–1944*

The Covenanter tank was a further stage in the progression of cruiser (*qv*) tank designs and was first known as the A13 Mark 3, Cruiser Mark 5. In 1937, after the failure of a design known as the A14, the London Midland Scottish Railway workshops were asked to undertake development of a cruiser tank, using as many components of the already-existing A13 Cruiser design as possible. The LMSR co-operated with the Meadows company on the development of the engine, and with Nuffield Mechanization on the development of the turret. An important innovation was the adoption of the Wilson epicyclic steering system

Covenanter

which gave more efficient and flexible control of the tank than had previously been possible.

Covenanter was a low-slung, good-looking tank on Christie suspension, and with a characteristic lozenge-shaped turret giving good deflection of shot. But in the haste to get into production, the design was cleared without waiting to test the pilot model. Deliveries

Conqueror

Cromwell with 95mm howitzer

began in mid-1940, and the tank was soon found to be seriously defective in its engine cooling arrangements. Modifications and re-design to clear up this problem resulted in Marks 1, 2, 3 and 4; eventually 1365 Covenanters were built before manufacture ceased in 1943. It was never used in battle, due to the mechanical problems and also to the excessive ground pressure of the narrow tracks, and was solely used as a training tank.

Length: 5.79m (19ft 0in). *Width:* 2.61m (8ft 7in). *Height:* 2.23m (7ft 4in). *Weight:* 18,288kg (40,320lb). *Crew:* 4. *Power:* Meadows Flat, 12-cyl., petrol, 300bhp. *Armament:* one 2-pdr. gun; one 7.92mm Besa machine gun. *Armour:* 7–40mm. *Speed:* 50km/hr (31mph). *Range:* 150km (95 miles). *Maker:* London, Midland & Scottish Railway Co., Derby.

CROMWELL CRUISER TANKS
1943–1950
By 1941 the British General Staff were forced to admit that their previously-held conception of light cruiser tanks swirling round the battle-field like a naval fleet was not being borne out by experience, and that while the agility was still desirable, so was greater firepower and more resistance to enemy shot. They therefore called for a new class of tank, a heavy cruiser, which would weigh about 25 tons, mount the 6-pdr. gun in the turret and have frontal armour of 70mm thickness. This specification produced the Cavalier (*qv*), which was not particularly good, and Leyland Motors, one of the manufacturers approached, suggested a design using a de-rated version of the Rolls-Royce Merlin aero engine, an approach which looked like providing the reliable power source which had been absent from previous British designs. Leyland's idea was taken up, but since no Merlin engines could be immediately spared for conversion, Leyland were instructed to

make do with the existing Nuffield Liberty engine. This they did, and the resulting tank became the Centaur (*qv*). However, this was only an interim stage, and as soon as the de-rated Merlin engine, known as the Meteor, was available, the design was slightly modified, the new engine fitted, and the tank thus formed became the Cromwell.

The most distinctive feature of the Cromwell was the flat-sided turret studded with prominent armour bolts and with an internal gun mantlet. The hull was rectangular with a flat front plate carrying the driver's vision port and a machine gun, while the suspension was of the Christie pattern with five roadwheels on each side.

The original armament was the 6-pdr. gun, with a 7.92mm Besa machine gun mounted coaxially; but there was sufficient space in the

turret to allow for later improvement, and later marks were armed with the British 75mm gun or, in the case of tanks used as support, the 95mm howitzer.

The Cromwell, the last and best of the cruiser series, was still under-gunned when it was used in action, in France and Germany in 1944–5, but its agility and performance were welcomed and its reliability was a considerable improvement over its forerunners. It came into its own once the German Army began falling back from France, and the battle became a matter of speed rather than slogging power. It remained in use after the war until 1950.

Length: 6.34m (20ft 10in). *Width:* 3.04m (10ft 0in). *Height:* 2.83m (9ft 4in). *Weight:* 27,945kg (61,610lb). *Crew:* 5. *Power:* Rolls-Royce Meteor, V–12, petrol, 25,025cc, 600bhp at 2,250rpm. *Armament:* one 6-pdr. gun or one 75mm gun or one 95mm howitzer; two 7.92mm Besa machine guns. *Armour:* 8–102mm. *Speed:* 65km/hr (40mph). *Range:* 275km (170 miles). *Maker:* Leyland Motors Ltd., Leyland, Lancs.

CRUISER TANKS MARKS 1–4 *1939–1943*
During the 1930s theories of armoured warfare were slowly being worked out in various armies throughout the world, and in the British Army one attractive theory was that of the cruiser tank – the name came from naval analogy – which, in formations, could sweep around an enemy's flank and strike deep into his line of communication. It was an attractive prospect, particularly when contrasted with the other official viewpoint, that of slow lumbering tanks crawling forward to support an infantry advance in World War I fashion. In 1934 Sir John Carden was asked to design a new tank to replace some of the ageing

Cruiser Mark III

Vickers Medium type (*qv*) in service; the specification given was very loose, the principal demand being that it should be cheap. Carden produced a design shortly before he was killed in an air crash late in 1935, a loss which removed one of the foremost tank brains from the scene. The prototype of his tank, the A9, appeared in April 1936; it carried only 14mm of armour, had a 2-pdr. in the turret, and thus combined speed with a good (for that time) anti-tank performance. One feature was the fitting of two small independent machine-gun turrets at the front corners of the hull, but this proved to be unsound in practice as these sub-turrets soon filled with fumes when the machine guns were fired. The suspension was bad, giving an uncomfortable ride, but as the only other designs offered were even worse, the A9 was approved for production as the Cruiser Tank Mark 1 and 125 were ordered. The first production tanks were issued in January 1939. The A9 subsequently saw combat in the Middle East and in France in 1939–40.

The specification to which Carden had worked had been sent to other designers and, also in 1936, the Vickers company produced a prototype of a heavier pattern of cruiser. This, the A10 or Cruiser Mark 2, looked very much the same as the A9 but instead of the sub-turrets mounted a single hull machine gun in a flat front plate alongside the driver. The main armament was a 2-pdr. gun in the turret, and the armour was 30mm thick, giving the tank a weight of 14 tons and proportionately less speed than the A9. One hundred and seventy of these were produced, and, like the A9, the A10 was used in France and in the Western Desert.

Unfortunately, neither the A9 nor the A10 were felt to be sufficiently fast to fill the intended cruiser role, the high-speed flanking sweep beloved of the theorists, and hopes were now pinned on a completely different design which was being undertaken by Nuffield Mechanization & Aero, Ltd. This company had been set up by Lord Nuffield as an off-shoot of Morris Motors, to build tanks and aircraft in 'shadow' factories. On the advice of the Director of Mechanization at the War Office, Lord Nuffield had bought a Christie tank from the United States and, after close examination, had adopted the suspension as a basis for a fresh design. The Christie suspension relied on a double-skin construction with large coil springs and large roadwheels, and gave a cross-country performance which was better than anything which had been seen before. In January 1937 the design was completed, and the first prototype was ready in ten months. This was the A13 or Cruiser Mark 3; it had a 2-pdr. gun, 14mm of armour, and a Nuffield version of the American Liberty aero engine.

In order to answer the requirement for a

Cruiser Tank Mark I

tank with better protection, a second version of the A13, known as the Cruiser Mark 4, was developed with 30mm of armour. Production got under way in 1938, and a total of 665 of both types was eventually built. These tanks served in France and in the Western Desert, but they were dogged with mechanical troubles throughout their lives.

Since both the Mark 3 and Mark 4 could reach speeds above 48km/hr (30mph), it seemed that the cruiser concept had at last been realized, but the War Office still thought that a more powerful tank was necessary to support them and set about developing a heavy cruiser under the titles of A14 and A16. Neither of these showed any advantages over the A13 design, so they were abandoned in 1939. But the idea persisted, and a modified heavy A13 was requested from the London Midland Scottish Railway Company; this eventually appeared as the Cruiser Mark 5 or Covenanter (*qv*).

Cruiser Mark 1 *Length:* 5.86m (19ft 3in). *Width:* 2.53m (8ft 4in). *Height:* 2.53m (8ft 4in). *Weight:* 12,190kg (26,875lb). *Crew:* 6. *Power:* AEC, 150hp, 6-cyl., petrol. *Armament:* one 2-pdr.; three machine guns. *Armour:* 6–14mm. *Speed:* 40km/hr (25mph). *Range:* 150km (95 miles).

Cruiser Mark 2 *Length:* 5.51m (18ft 1in). *Width:* 2.52m (8ft 4in). *Height:* 2.59m (8ft 6in). *Weight:* 13,970kg (30,800lb). *Crew:* 5. *Power:* AEC, 150hp, 6-cyl., petrol. *Armament:* one 2-pdr.; two machine guns. *Armour:* 10–30mm. *Speed:* 25km/hr (15mph). *Range:* 150km (95 miles).

Cruiser Mark 3 *Length:* 6.01m (19ft 9in). *Width:* 2.53m (8ft 4in). *Height:* 2.59m (8ft 6in). *Weight:* 14,225kg (31,360lb). *Crew:* 4. *Power:* Liberty, V–12, 340bhp. *Armament:* one 2-pdr.; one machine gun. *Armour:* 6–14mm. *Speed:* 50km/hr (30mph). *Range:* 175km (108 miles).

Cruiser Mark 4 *Length:* 6.01m (19ft 9in). *Width:* 2.53m (8ft 4in). *Height:* 2.59m (8ft 6in). *Weight:* 15,000kg (33,070lb). *Crew:* 4. *Power:* Liberty, V–2, 340bhp. *Armament:* one 2-pdr.; one machine gun. *Armour:* 20–30mm. *Speed:* 45km/hr (28mph). *Range:* 150km (95 miles).

Makers (all Marks): Nuffield Mechanization & Aero Ltd., Oxford; English Electric Ltd; Leyland Motors Ltd., Lancs; London, Midland & Scottish Railway, Glasgow.

Crusader Mark III

CRUSADER CRUISER TANK *1940–1943*

Crusader was the last of the pre-war cruiser designs which saw combat during the 1939–41 period, and it was developed by Nuffield as its own version of a follow-on to the previous Cruiser series (*qv*), in preference to making the Covenanter (*qv*). The new design, entitled A15, retained the basic mechanical layout of the A13 cruiser, retained the Christie suspension, adopted the lozenge-shaped turret of the Covenanter, and added an auxiliary machine-gun turret on the left front of the hull, matching a cupola for the driver on the right; this cupola also mounted a machine gun for no very good reason, since the driver was usually too busy driving to have time to fire a machine gun when action was involved. The main armament was to be the usual 2-pdr. turret gun. In order to improve the ride, and overcome the excess ground pressure problem found in the Covenanter, the track was lengthened and an extra roadwheel inserted on each side. The basic armour was to be 40mm, but even before the production had begun, more was demanded.

The first Mark 1 Crusader tanks appeared late in 1940, but they were soon supplanted by the Mark 2 which had the armour improved to

50mm thickness. The driver's machine gun was dispensed with and the removal of the auxiliary turret was also recommended, since the fumes inside affected the gunner. This was not done until some time later, and many Crusader 1 and 2 models had their auxiliary turrets removed by field workshops.

The events in France in 1940 showed the shortcomings of the 2-pdr., and these were underlined by experiences in the desert. As a result, in September 1941 Nuffield was asked for a redesign incorporating the 6-pdr. gun. This was rapidly done and the resulting Crusader Mark 3 appeared in May 1942.

In all, 4,350 Crusader gun tanks were produced, and although the design was far from perfect – it inherited troubles from both its Cruiser and Covenanter forebears – the Crusader formed the principal equipment of British armoured formations, particularly in the desert, until replaced by American M3 Grant (*qv*) and M4 Sherman (*qv*) tanks in 1942.

Length: 5.98m (19ft 8in). *Width:* 2.64m (8ft 8in). *Height:* 2.23m (7ft 4in). *Weight:* 19,300kg (42,550lb). *Crew:* 5. *Power:* Nuffield Liberty Mk 3, V–12, petrol, 27,000cc, 340bhp at 1,500rpm. *Armament:* one 2-pdr. gun; later one 6-pdr. gun; two or three 7.92mm Besa machine guns. *Armour:* 7–50mm. *Speed:* 45km/hr (28mph). *Range:* 320km (200 miles). *Maker:* Nuffield Mechanization & Aero Ltd., Oxford.

FIREFLY TANK *1944–1947*

The M4 Sherman tank (*qv*) had many good features, but the gun was not up to the standards of the opposition and, except at suicidally short ranges, the tank could be knocked

out by a German Tiger (*qv*) or Panther (*qv*) before it got close enough to do any harm. In the summer of 1943, therefore, the British Army began designing a modification which would permit their 17-pdr. anti-tank gun, a formidable weapon, to be mounted in the Sherman turret. The mock-up was completed by October 1943 and a modified tank was produced by Woolwich Arsenal on 1 January 1944. The protrusion of the gun into the turret, and the need to allow for recoil, meant that the back of the turret had to be cut away and an armoured box built up to hold the radio set and act as a counterweight to the gun's length. But the modification was a complete success and went into production forthwith, British factories converting American-supplied Shermans. The resulting tank was known as the Firefly and by the time of the Normandy invasion in June 1944 sufficient numbers had been made to allow one Firefly to each tank troop. The Germans soon realized however, that they faced a formidable weapon and Fireflys became prime targets. In an attempt to counter this, the extra length of the 17-pdr. gun was generally camouflaged by disruptive painting.

In spite of British offers to provide up to 200 17-pdr. guns a month, complete with the modification kits needed, the American Army Ground Forces Command persisted in trying to develop a 76mm gun and a 90mm gun for the Sherman. Once the United States Army was in Europe, it was equipped with Fireflys from British sources. Except for the fitting of the 17-pdr. gun into the turret and the removal of the hull-mounted machine gun (in order to provide extra ammunition stowage) the Firefly was precisely the same as the M3 Sherman. Most Fireflys were converted from the

Sherman M4A4 (known in British service as Sherman V), though small numbers were converted from other models.

HORNET MEDIUM TANK *1918–1920*
Mr. (later Sir) William Tritton was the Managing Director of Foster's of Lincoln, agricultural engineers who had built Little Willie (*qv*). A first-class engineer with an original turn of thought, he was responsible for many of the mechanical features of the first tanks and inevitably turned his mind to the question of improving them. He designed the

Hornet

Whippet (*qv*) and then, late in 1917, and after cross-questioning various officers and men with experience of tanks in France, he set out to design a new medium tank, which he called the Hornet.

The principal defects of the first tanks were that controlling the vehicle was a job divided among four men and demanding miraculous co-ordination, and the fact that the entire crew were closed inside a steel box, together with a roaring, fuming, engine. Tritton therefore designed his Hornet to do away with these problems. The adoption of a Wilson pre-selector gearbox and transmission made it possible for one man to control the tank, while the engine was isolated into a compartment of its own at the rear of the hull. Ventilation inside the tank was improved, so as to disperse the powder smoke from the guns, and the commander was given a cupola of his own and a command position from which he could oversee the entire crew.

The basic shape was still the rhomboid 'overall track' type, dictated by the need to cross wide trenches and flatten immense belts of barbed wire, but the track-top height was less and the crew were installed in a fixed superstructure which rose above track-top level. This superstructure had five ball-mountings for machine guns, though only four Hotchkiss guns were provided; the crew was expected to shift the guns around as the tactical situation required. There was also provision for opening an overhead hatch and firing one machine gun at aircraft. As with earlier tanks, two versions, a 'male', with 6-pdr. gun, and a

'female', with four machine guns, were proposed. The suspension was still unsprung, but generous mud chutes were provided which helped to keep the suspension wheels free from clogging mud.

The Hornet was demonstrated early in 1918 and was approved for service as the Tank, Medium, C. Enthusiastic plans were laid for the use of this tank in overwhelming numbers in the anticipated 1919 offensive, 200 tanks were ordered immediately after the demonstration, and in October 1918 a further 4,000 'female' and 2,000 'male' were ordered. But a month later came the Armistice and the October order was immediately cancelled. By February 1919 36 of the first 200 had been completed, and since by that time the Army was attracted by a more advanced design, the Medium D, the balance of the Medium C order was cancelled.

The Hornet was an interesting design; it saw the commencement of the gradual lowering of the track and the improvement of the superstructure which foreshadowed later design trends, and it also introduced the principle of making the sub-units in dispersed factories and assembling them at a central plant. Though few were made, it represents an important milestone in the development of the tank.

Length: 7.85m (25ft 9in). *Width:* 2.71m (8ft 11in). *Height:* 2.94m (9ft 8in). *Weight:* 19,825kg (43,706lb). *Crew:* 4. *Power:* Ricardo, 6-cyl., petrol, 150bhp at 1,200rpm. *Armament:* one 6-pdr.; three .303 machine guns (male); four .303 machine guns (female). *Armour:* 6–14mm. *Speed:* 12km/hr (7.5mph). *Range:* 120km (75 miles). *Maker:* William Foster & Co. Ltd., Lincoln.

INDEPENDENT TANK *1925–1935*
In the immediate postwar years, when armies were still evaluating tanks and their use, there tended to be an over-estimation of the value of multiple gun power, and in 1924 the British General Staff set out a specification for a fast and heavy tank with multiple armament, capable of operating independently instead of being tied to the pace of the infantry. The specification was met by Vickers-Armstrong Ltd. with their production of the A1E1 or Independent tank in 1925.

The Independent broke new ground in having its tracks less than the overall height of the tank and setting the hull in between the tracks and their suspension. The hull top was above the track level, and mounted five separate revolving turrets; mounted centrally was the main turret, carrying a 47mm gun and with

Independent

a cupola for the tank commander. In the front of the hull two machine-gun turrets at each corner flanked the driver's position, and two more machine-gun turrets were positioned at the rear of the main turret, ahead of the engine compartment. The tank commander communicated with each turret by means of a Laryngophone telephone system which picked up the voice from the larynx and thus cut out external noises from the tank and its engine. In addition, each turret was provided with a mechanical telegraph system by means of which the commander could indicate targets to the gunners.

Due to lack of funds the design was not put into production, and only the pilot was ever built. But it had great influence on later design and was widely copied in Germany and Russia.

Length: 7.74m (28ft 5in). *Width:* 3.20m (10ft 6in). *Height:* 2.69m (8ft 10in). *Weight:* 32,000kg (70,550lb). *Crew:* 8. *Power:* Armstrong-Siddeley, V–12, air-cooled, petrol, 398bhp. *Armament:* one 47mm gun; four .303 machine guns. *Armour:* 13–30mm. *Speed:* 27km/hr (17mph). *Range:* 150km (95 miles). *Maker:* Vickers-Armstrong Ltd., Elswick.

Little Willie

LITTLE WILLIE TANK *1915*

Although Little Willie was not a fighting tank, no encyclopedia of military vehicles can omit mention of him, since he was the direct forerunner of the British tanks and thus the progenitor of everything which came afterwards. In 1915 the British Landships Committee was exploring several possible solutions to the problem of crossing trenches and wire with a bulletproof machine. Among these was a suggestion from a Colonel Crompton to use the track units of two Bullock Creeping Grip tractors bought from the United States to make a long, articulated, machine which would be able to span trenches. A similar idea, using a different type of track unit, had already failed, and when the idea and the two tractors were delivered to the works of William Foster of Lincoln, their director William Tritton rapidly demonstrated that Crompton's idea was impractical. He then dismantled the two tractors and, using the track unit components, built a fresh design. This was the Bullock Track Machine which consisted of a boiler-plate rectangle with the tracks recessed beneath, surmounted by a turret carrying a 2-pdr. gun. It was propelled by a Daimler engine and steered by two wheels trailing behind and controlled by cables from within the body.

After studying the performance of this, Tritton, aided by Lieutenant Wilson, a Royal Navy armoured car commander, redesigned the machine. The tracks were now outside the body so that mud did not jam them, the turret was removed, and the trailed-wheel changed to a system of braking one track while allowing the other to drag the vehicle around. The track plates were improved and the tracks partially sprung. After tests the trailed-wheel steering was restored, since it was found to give better control for gentle curves.

Little Willie, however, could not meet the War Office specifications, since it could not cross a trench wider than 1.21m (4ft) and could not surmount an obstacle greater than 60cm (2ft) and the demand was for a 1.52m (5ft)

trench and a 1.37m (4ft 6in) vertical step. But it nevertheless gave valuable technical information, was responsible for the perfection of the track design and steering system, and thus formed an indispensable step in the development of Mother (qv), the first fighting tank.

The origin of the name Little Willie has always been a mystery. Nothing has ever been officially said about this; but in 1915 one of the most popular music-hall artists was Billy Williams, 'The Man in the Velvet Suit', singing 'Little Willie Woodbine'. It is not too much to imagine that the hit tune of the day provided inspiration when it came to naming the odd machine.

Length: 5.53m (18ft 2in). *Width:* 2.84m (9ft 4in). *Height:* 3.09m (10ft 2in). *Weight:* 18,290kg (40,320lb). *Crew:* 6. *Power:* Daimler, 6-cyl., petrol, 105bhp at 1,000rpm. *Armament:* unspecified number of light machine guns. *Armour:* not armoured; made from 6mm mild steel plate. *Speed:* 3km/hr (1.8mph). *Range:* not known. *Maker:* William Foster & Co., Lincoln.

Tank, Mark I

MARKS 1-9 COMBAT TANK SERIES
1916–1923

Under this designation, since no other is applicable, we can deal with the original tanks as developed in England in 1916–19.

The Mark 1 tank was derived directly from Mother (qv) and was of the standard rhomboidal form in order to achieve the greatest trench-crossing ability. The major difference was, of course, that the Mark 1 was made of armour plate whereas Mother had been of boiler plate. Two versions were made, the 'male' with 6-pdr. guns in side sponsons and four machine guns in ports in the tank side, and the 'female' type with the sponsons carrying two machine guns. The two designs were intended to complement each other; the 'male' could deal with German machine-gun strongpoints with the 6-pdrs., while the 'female' acted as local protection for them. Both types had a small square cupola in the front for the commander and driver.

Operation of the Mark 1 was complicated; gear changing and assistance with steering were provided by two gearsmen who sat alongside the gearbox at the rear of the tank and

Tank, Mark II

changed gear on signals from the driver. Steering was aided by a two-wheeled trailing unit controlled by wires from inside the tank.

Marks 2 and 3 were almost identical to Mark 1 but incorporated small improvements based on experience in the first tank actions. The principal alterations were improved tracks, heavier armour, and escape hatches in the roof. The wheeled steering 'tail' was abandoned, having been found unnecessary.

The Mark 4 tank appeared in March 1917; this was built of better armour in order to defeat German armour-piercing bullets, and the sponsons could be hinged into the tank to reduce the width for rail transport. On the earlier models they had to be completely removed and carried separately. The track shoes were improved by the addition of 'spuds' or cleats to give a better grip in mud, and the engine exhaust was finally provided with a silencer.

In October 1917 design work began on the Mark 5. This featured a Ricardo engine specifically designed for tank use and more powerful than the previous Daimler. A Wilson epicyclic transmission allowed one-man control of gear-changing and steering for the first time, and there was an additional rear cupola to permit better observation. The armour was thickened, and a better machine gun was placed in the rear face of the hull.

The Mark 6 tank never got beyond a wooden

mock-up. It was intended as a lighter and faster tank, though still of much the same shape, but with the principal gun, a 6-pdr., low down in the front of the hull, between the tracks. The Mark 7 reached the pilot stage; this was a lengthened Mark 5 using an hydraulic transmission system to each track to give better control, and it also featured an electric self-starter for the engine, which must have been a welcome innovation. But the transmission was too complicated and the idea was abandoned.

The Mark 8 was designed late in 1917 by the Mechanical Warfare Department and aimed at incorporating everything which had been

Tank, Mark IV

learned in combat so far. The engine was in a separate compartment; ventilating fans kept the fighting compartment free of fumes; the main turret had a commander's cupola on top; and the sponsons were hinged and mounted on roller bearings so that they could easily be swung inside the tank for rail transport. It was also known as the Liberty tank, having been adopted by the Anglo–American Tank Committee and chosen for combined production by the United States and Britain. Ambitious plans were laid for sub-contracting parts to makers in both countries and building 1,550 tanks in a French assembly plant ready for the 1919 offensive, but before this could go into effect the war ended. About 100 were actually built

Tank, Mark V

after the war, from parts which had already been made when the Armistice was declared.

The last in this numbered series was the Mark 9, intended solely as a supply tank. It was fitted with side doors and could carry either 50 men or 10 tons of stores for delivery through a bullet-swept area. Only one machine gun was fitted for local defence. This was an attempt to regularize things, since numbers of earlier marks had been converted in the field into supply vehicles. Two hundred of these were ordered, but the end of the war saw the cancellation of the contract and only 23 were ever built.

Marks 1, 2 & 3 *Length:* 9.90m (32ft 6in). *Width:* 4.19m (13ft 9in). *Height:* 2.43m (8ft 0in). *Weight:* 28,450kg (62,720lb). *Crew:* 8. *Power:* Daimler 6, petrol, 105bhp. *Armament:* two 6-pdrs.; four or six machine guns. *Armour:* 6–12mm. *Speed:* 6km/hr (3.75mph). *Range:* 36km (22 miles).

Mark 4 *Length:* 8.02m (26ft 4in). *Width:* 3.91m (12ft 10in). *Height:* 2.49m (8ft 2in). *Weight:* 28,450kg (62,720lb). *Crew:* 8. *Power:* Daimler 6, petrol, 105bhp. *Armament:* two 6-pdrs.; four or six machine guns. *Armour:* 8–15mm. *Speed:* 6km/hr (3.75mph). *Range:* 36km (22 miles).

Mark 5 *Length:* 8.04m (26ft 5in). *Width:* 4.11m (13ft 6in). *Height:* 2.64m (8ft 8in).

Tank, Mark VIII

Weight: 29,465kg (64,960lb). *Crew:* 8. *Power:* Ricardo 6, petrol, 150bhp. *Armament:* two 6-pdrs.; four or six machine guns. *Armour:* 8–15mm. *Speed:* 8km/hr (5mph). *Range:* 40km (25 miles).

Mark 7 *Length:* 8.96m (29ft 5in). *Width:* 4.11m (13ft 6in). *Height:* 2.61m (8ft 7in). *Weight:* 33,530kg (73,920lb). *Crew:* 8. *Power:* Ricardo 6, petrol, 150bhp. *Armament:* two 6-pdrs.; four machine guns. *Armour:* 8–15mm. *Speed:* 6km/hr (3.75mph). *Range:* 40km (25 miles).

Mark 8 *Length:* 10.41m (34ft 2in). *Width:* 3.75m (12ft 4in). *Height:* 3.12m (10ft 3in). *Weight:* 37,600kg (82,895lb). *Crew:* 12. *Power:* Liberty, petrol, 300bhp. *Armament:* two 6-pdrs.; seven machine guns. *Armour:* 6–16mm. *Speed:* 11km/hr (6.8mph). *Range:* 60km (37 miles).

Mark 9 *Length:* 9.73m (31ft 11 in). *Width:* 2.51m (8ft 3in). *Height:* 2.63m (8ft 8in).

Weight: 27,435kg (60,485lb). *Crew:* 4. *Power:* Ricardo, petrol, 150bhp. *Armament:* one machine gun. *Armour:* 6–10mm. *Speed:* 5.5km/hr (3.4mph). *Range:* 30km (19 miles).

Makers: William Foster, Lincoln; Metropolitan Carriage & Wagon Co. London; Brown Brothers, Edinburgh (Mark 7); North British Locomotive Co.; Armstrong Whitworth Ltd. Coventry (Mark 9).

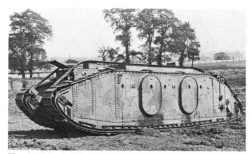

Tank, Mark IX

MATILDA INFANTRY TANKS *1936–1945*
In late 1934 General Sir Hugh Elles, recently appointed Master-General of the Ordnance, asked Vickers to design a new tank. Elles was appreciative of the need for light tanks for reconnaissance, but he was firmly convinced that the next war would be a repeat of the last and that what was most needed was a well-armoured tank capable of accompanying infantry in the assault across No Man's Land. He accordingly specified good protection, no more than a machine gun for armament, and, most important, a top price of £6,000 for the entire machine. The design was done by Sir John Carden, shortly before his death, and even within the limits imposed, it was not a good one. When the prototype was demonstrated to Elles, he observed that it waddled along like Matilda the comical duck, a contemporary strip-cartoon character; the name stuck, and the Infantry Tank A11 was Matilda thereafter.

Matilda consisted of a narrow, well-armoured body with spindly suspension at each side; on top was a one-man turret armed with a single machine gun. Carden had been forced to revert to the two-man tank idea, even though this was not liked by the military, simply because the price precluded building a big enough tank to hold three men. With a speed of only 13km/hr (8mph) it was an expensive and complex method of taking one machine gun to war.

Upon objections from the Royal Tank Corps that three men were necessary and a heavier gun was vital to protect it from other tanks, a heavier model, the A12 was put in hand, while production of Matilda was arranged.

The A12 appeared in 1938 and became known as the Matilda 2, the earlier model being now the Matilda 1. Matilda 2 was a much better design, with heavy armour, a 2-pdr. gun as the main armament, and a well-protected and much better suspension. Much of the hull was cast, and the turret was a one-piece casting. Turret rotation was hydraulic.

Both Matilda 1 and Matilda 2 went to war in 1939 and their thick armour proved invulnerable to all German anti-tank weapons, which led the Germans to a rapid improvement in their guns. Of the 136 Matilda 1s built, those which returned from France were retained as training vehicles, since their lack of effective armament told against them. The Matilda 2s, though, served well in the Western Desert until eventually replaced by M3 Grants (*qv*) and M4 Shermans (*qv*), and after that they were retained in use by the Australian Army in the Pacific theatre where their armour was proof against any Japanese anti-tank gun. After their retirement from a combat role in the Middle East they were widely adapted to specialist tasks, such as mine-clearing flails, flame-throwers and bridge carriers. In one form or another, Matilda 2 was the only British tank to serve right through the war from 1939 to 1945.

Matilda 1 *Length:* 4.85m (15ft 11in). *Width:* 2.28m (7ft 6in). *Height:* 1.86m (6ft 2in). *Weight:* 11,160kg (24,605lb). *Crew:* 2. *Power:* Ford, V–8, petrol, 70bhp at 3,500rpm. *Armament:* one .303 Vickers machine gun; later one .50 Vickers machine gun. *Armour:* 10–60mm. *Speed:* 13km/hr (8mph). *Range:* 125km (78 miles). *Maker:* Vickers Armstrong Ltd., Elswick.

Matilda 2 *Length:* 5.61m (18ft 5in). *Width:* 2.59m (8ft 6in). *Height:* 2.51m (8ft 3in). *Weight:* 26,925kg (59,360lb). *Crew:* 4. *Power:* two AEC, 6-cyl., diesel, total 174bhp; later two Leyland, 6-cyl., diesel, total 190hp. *Armament:* one 2-pdr. gun; one 7.92mm Besa machine gun or one 3in howitzer; one 7.92mm Besa machine gun. *Armour:* 14–78mm. *Speed:* 25km/hr (15.5mph). *Range:* 250km (155 miles). *Makers:* Vulcan Foundry, Warrington (design parents); William Fowler, Lincoln; Ruston & Hornsby, Grantham; London, Midland & Scottish Railway, Derby; Harland & Wolff, Belfast; North British Locomotive Works, Glasgow.

Matilda Mark I Tank

MOTHER TANK *1916*

Known also as the Wilson Machine or Big Willie, this was the first of the rhomboidal tanks which became the standard pattern during World War I.

During the manufacture of Little Willie (*qv*) Lieutenant Wilson devoted a great deal of thought to the problem of obtaining the desired trench-crossing and vertical obstacle performance demanded by the War Office. One suggestion which had been put forward was for a machine comprising a massive platform supported on 12m (45ft) diameter wheels, but while this was theoretically attractive it was totally impractical. Wilson then examined various track configurations and realized that by making the hull lozenge-shaped, and running the track completely around it, the forward lower section of the

track would then approximate to the quadrant of a 12m (45ft) wheel, achieving the same theoretical performance but in a more practical manner. The rest was a question of adapting the lessons learned from Little Willie.

Mother, as finally developed, was a steel box with all-round tracks, inside which was the engine, the crew, and the armament, all in the same compartment. Armament was provided by fitting two naval 6-pdr. guns into sponsons on the side so that they could command wide arcs of fire. Steering was accomplished by a two-wheeled trailed unit, hydraulically sprung, which guided the tank in a gentle curve; for angular turns, the tracks braked independently.

Mother was first run under her own power on 12 January 1916; on 2 January it was demonstrated at Hatfield Park to prove that it could cope with the obstacles demanded, and

on 2 February it went through its paces in front of Lloyd George, the Minister of Munitions, General Sir William Robertson, CIGS, and other distinguished figures. The demonstration was a success and the first tanks were ordered.

As a point of interest, the first tanks were classed as 'male' when they mounted two 6-pdr. guns in their sponsons, or as 'female' if they were entirely armed with machine guns. Mother, for all her title, was a male.

Length: 9.52m (31ft 3in). *Width:* 4.16m (13ft 8in). *Height:* 2.43m (8ft 1in). *Weight:* 31,500kg (69,445lb). *Crew:* 8. *Power:* Daimler, 6-cyl., petrol, 105bhp at 1,000rpm. *Armament:* two 6-pdr. guns; two machine guns. *Armour:* none; pilot model made of 6mm mild steel. *Speed:* 6km/hr (3.75mph). *Range:* 36km (22 miles). *Maker:* William Foster & Co., Lincoln.

TETRARCH LIGHT TANK *1940–1950*

After collaborating on the design of the series of British light tanks of the 1930s, Vickers-Armstrong decided that they had some better ideas and in 1937 set about developing a 'private venture' light tank. The result, known as the Light Tank Mark 7 or Tetrarch was offered to the War Office in 1938 and accepted.

Tetrarch was a very clean design, using a

Tetrarch

four-wheeled Christie-type suspension with an interesting modification; the front wheels were steerable so that the track was flexed to give the tank the necessary direction. For very tight turns a linkage engaged the track brake to add to the turning force. The turret mounted a 2-pdr. gun and a coaxial machine gun, and the vehicle was very fast and agile.

Unfortunately, just as the first production tanks were beginning to appear, in the summer of 1940, the Army was having second thoughts about light tanks. The campaign in France had shown that they were no longer viable units on the battlefield, and the General Staff was turning to the use of armoured cars for reconnaissance. Production was halted while the problem was discussed. And just at that

time a new factor appeared on the scene, the idea of airborne troops. The Tetrarch was light and compact and it was hoped that it would prove to be a viable air-portable tank. Production was restarted in 1941 and a total of 177 Tetrarchs were built. They were used in the Madagascar landings in 1942 and by the 6th Airborne Division in Normandy in 1944, having been flown in Hamilcar gliders. A small number remained in service until 1950.

Length: 4.11m (13ft 6in). *Width:* 2.31m (7ft 7in). *Height:* 2.10m (6ft 11in). *Weight:* 7,620kg (16,800lb). *Crew:* 3. *Power:* Meadows, horizontally-opposed, 12-cyl., petrol, 165bhp at 2,700rpm. *Armament:* one 2-pdr. gun; one 7.92mm Besa machine gun. *Armour:* 4–16mm. *Speed:* 65km/hr (40mph). *Range:* 225km (140 miles). *Maker:* Vickers-Armstrong, Elswick.

TOG HEAVY TANK *1940 – 1943*

At the outbreak of war in 1939 the office of Master-General of the Ordnance was abolished and munitions procurement was placed in the hands of a newly-formed Ministry of Supply. The Ministry promptly set up two committees to design tanks, though it appears to have omitted to let the Army know and therefore neither committee was briefed as to what the Army really needed – if, indeed, the Army itself really knew at that time.

One committee was headed by Sir Albert Stern, who had been one of the driving forces behind tank production during World War I, and he gathered into the committee a number of those who had worked with him then. With an eye to the well-publicized Maginot and Siegfried lines of fortifications, they decided that what was needed was a heavy assault tank based on the 1918 designs, and proceeded to design one. To commemorate its instigators, it was named TOG for 'The Old Gang'.

TOG 1 was simply an up-to-date Mark 8; it had the same all-round tracks, hull entirely between them, a 75mm howitzer in the nose

and was planned to have sponsons on each side to carry more artillery. By the time the prototype was ready, however, sufficient progress had been made on the Churchill tank (*qv*) to render TOG superfluous.

Nevertheless, work continued; TOG 1 was fitted with a Matilda 2 (*qv*) turret. Then TOG 2 appeared in March 1941, with lower tracks and a large front turret mounting a 6-pdr. gun. By this time the TOG committee had been dissolved, but the tank was kept as a test rig. It appeared again in 1943 as the TOG 2*, the turret now carrying a 17-pdr. gun in order to test various types of gun installation. After that it was finally retired; it is still in existence as a museum piece. Why effort was wasted on this device in the fraught days of 1940 is a question which has never really been answered. The main trouble with TOG was that it had been designed well, but for the wrong war.

Length: 10.13m (33ft 3in). *Width:* 3.12m (10ft 3in). *Height:* 3.04m (10ft 10in). *Weight:* 81,280kg (179,190lb). *Crew:* 6. *Power:* Ricardo, diesel, 600bhp. *Armament:* various (details in text). *Armour:* 12–62mm. *Speed:* 14km/hr (9mph). *Range:* not known. *Maker:* William Foster & Co., Lincoln.

Valentine

VALENTINE INFANTRY TANK MARK III

The government-sponsored British infantry tank of the late 1930s was the Matilda (*qv*), but the Vickers-Armstrong company were convinced that they could produce a better design, and proceeded to do so, basing it on components of the Cruiser tanks Marks I and II (*qv*). The design was submitted to the War Office on 14 February 1938 – St. Valentine's Day, from which circumstance came the tank's name. The War Office deliberated for over a year and then, in June 1939, demanded delivery in the fastest possible time. The first production tanks appeared in May 1940; by the time their crews had been trained in their use the campaign in France was over, and the Valentine first saw action in North Africa.

Tog Mark II

In June 1940 the Canadian Pacific Railway Company set up a plant for the production of Valentines in Canada; at first it was intended to build the hulls there and ship them to Britain for fitting with engines and guns, but eventually complete tanks were built, using guns and engines also made in Canada. Altogether 1,420 were built there, of which 1,390 were shipped to Russia; over 8,000 were built in Britain, about 1,300 of which also went to Russia. The Soviet Army made one of its very few acknowledgements of outside assistance when it reported that '…the Canadian-built Valentine tank [is] the best tank we have received from any of our Allies…'

The Valentine was difficult to drive, but was reliable and robust, and well-liked by its crews. The turret was somewhat cramped and deficient in vision arrangements, but this was not unusual in tanks of that period. The principal armament of the original version was the 2-pdr. gun, though few mounted a 3in howitzer for close support. Later production models carried a 6-pdr. or 75mm gun. A total of 11 different marks eventually appeared, differing in type of engine or armament.

Due to the basically sound design of the hull and running gear the Valentine was used as the basis of a number of specialist vehicles, notably the self-propelled 17-pdr. Archer (qv) and the self-propelled 25-pdr. Bishop (qv). The first DD swimming tanks were built around the Valentine, and various mine-clearing, flame-throwing and bridge-carrying versions were built, though the perfected designs was then applied to other tanks such as the Sherman or Churchill. As a fighting tank the Valentine was obsolete by 1944, but a small number of self-propelled models remained in service until the late 1940s.

Length: 5.89m (19ft 4in). *Width:* 2.63m (8ft 7½in). *Height:* 2.27m (7ft 5½in). *Weight:* 1,7272kg (3,8080lb). *Power:* GMC, 6-cyl., diesel, 165bhp. Earlier models used AEC, 6-cyl., petrol, 135bhp; or AEC 6-cyl., diesel, 131 bhp; or GMC 6-cyl., diesel of 138bhp. *Crew:* 3 or 4. *Armament:* 2-pdr. gun and 79 rounds; or 6-pdr. gun and 53 rounds; or 75mm gun and 50 rounds; 7.92mm or 7.62mm co-axial machine gun. *Armour:* 8–65mm. *Speed:* 24 km/hr (15mph); *Range:* 145km (90 miles). *Makers:* Vickers-Armstrong, Elswick, Newcastle-upon-Tyne; Canadian Pacific Railway, Montreal, Canada.

VICKERS LIGHT TANKS *1930–1941*
During the late 1920s the British Army experimented with a wide variety of light tank designs in the hope of producing a nimble vehicle for scouting and reconnaissance tasks. After trying out the Carden–Loyd (qv) designs, some of the better points of these were adopted, as well as ideas from various Vickers designs, and in 1930 the Light Tank Mark 1

Light Tank 6A

was produced in small numbers for service. This used a suspension derived from Carden's ideas and incorporating four roadwheels at each side suspended by leaf springs. A sloped superstructure on the hull housed the driver centrally and a small cylindrical turret carried a Vickers machine gun.

In 1931 the Light Tank Mark 2 was developed and 16 were built; this was an

Light Tank 2B

advance on the Mark 1 by virtue of an improved suspension on the Horstmann system, a larger rectangular turret and a Rolls-Royce engine. The crew and armament remained the same. Slightly improved versions known as the Marks 2A and 2B were later built in small numbers.

Next came the Mark 3, similar to its predecessors but with the track lengthened so as to give a more comfortable ride and better cross-country performance. Few of these were built, since a Mark 4 came along in 1933 and promised to be even better. This was the first design to use the armour structure as the chassis, instead of attaching all the mechanical components to a conventional type of chassis and then hanging the armour on afterwards. The suspension was modified, doing away with the rear, idler wheel and using the last road-wheel as an idler so as to give better track contact and less pitching.

By 1935 the difficulties inherent in a one-man turret – the occupant could either command the tank or fire the gun but not both at once – led to the Mark 5, which had a two-man turret with two machine-guns in the turret. Only 22 Mark 5s were built.

The last of the series was the Mark 6 of 1936, much the same as the Mark 5, but with the turret enlarged so as to accommodate a wireless set in the rear section. A circular cupola was added to allow the commander vision with some degree of protection. This model went into some variants; the Mark 6A improved the suspension, the 6B had a larger and more efficient cupola, while the 6C mounted a 15mm Besa machine gun and a 7.92mm Besa machine gun in the turret in place of the former Vickers guns. Numbers of Mark 6, in the various models, were used in France in 1939–40 where their performance and vulnerability was sufficient to show that the light tank no longer had much hope of surviving in a modern battlefield. Late in 1940 the light tank was dropped from British armoured divisions.

These, though, were not the last light tanks to be developed or used; the Tetrarch (*qv*) was officially known as the Light Tank Mark 7, but since it was of a totally different pattern and unrelated to the foregoing series, it is dealt with separately.

Mark 6 *Length:* 3.58m (11ft 9in). *Width:* 2.05m (6ft 9in). *Height:* 2.23m (7ft 4in). *Weight:* 5,285kg (11,650lb). *Crew:* 3. *Power:* Meadows, 6-cyl., petrol, 88bhp. *Armament:* one .5in Vickers machine gun; one .303in Vickers machine gun. *Armour:* 6–14mm. *Speed:* 55km/hr (34mph). *Range:* 200km (125 miles). *Makers:* Vickers-Armstrong Ltd., Elswick; Royal Arsenal, Woolwich.

Light Tank Mark 4

VICKERS MAIN BATTLE TANK 1963

In the late 1950s Vickers began design work on a medium tank, armed with a 105mm gun, in the hopes of interesting the British or some other army in it. At about the same time the Indian Government decided to begin manufacture of their own tank, rather than relying upon tanks bought from abroad. Indian experts visited various countries to find a suitable design and decided that the Vickers offered what they needed. In 1961 an agreement was signed between Vickers and the Indian Government; in

1963 a prototype was delivered; in 1965 the first British-built production tank arrived in India; and in 1969 the first Indian-built tank rolled from the production line of the Avadi Company of Madras. The first tanks used a large proportion of British components, but since that time more and more production has been Indianized and tanks currently being built are estimated to contain less than 10 per cent of imported components. About 1,000 Vijayanta (the Indian name for the tank) have been built.

The Vickers MBT Mark 1 was designed with a view to providing the best compromise between firepower, protection and mobility

which could be achieved within a weight limit of 38 tons. The engine and transmission were those of the Chieftain tank (*qv*), the suspension was a well-tried torsion-bar design, and the gun was the British 105mm L7, as used in the later models of Centurion (*qv*). Fire control is simple, and the main armament is ranged by using a coaxial .50 ranging machine gun. Infrared sighting and driving equipment can be fitted, as can NBC filtration equipment and a collapsible flotation screen which allows the tank to swim in any depth of water.

A Mark 2 design was projected; this was to have been armed with four Swingfire anti-tank guided missiles in launchers on each side of the turret. This project was not pursued. Instead, a Mark 3 version has recently been developed. This has a new design of turret which allows improved fire-control systems to be fitted, uses a cast armour hull front, and has the Leyland power unit replaced by a General Motors two-stroke diesel engine. An armoured recovery vehicle and a bridgelayer on the same chassis are also offered by Vickers to potential buyers. In addition to the Indian use, about 50 Vickers MBT Mark 1 were bought by Kuwait between 1970 and 1972.

Length: 7.92m (26ft 0in). *Width:* 3.16m (10ft 5in). *Height:* 2.43m (8ft 0in). *Weight:* 38,600kg (85,098lb). *Crew:* 4. *Power:* Leyland, 6-cyl., multi-fuel, 650bhp at 2,670rpm (Mark 1); General Motors, 12-cyl., diesel, 800bhp at 2,500rpm (Mark 2). *Armament:* one 105mm Gun L7; one .50 ranging machine gun; one .30 machine gun. *Armour:* 20–80mm. *Speed:* 56km/hr (35mph). *Range:* 478km (295 miles) (Mark 1); 600km (375 miles) (Mark 2). *Maker:* Vickers Ltd., Elswick; Avadi Co., Madras.

Vickers Main Battle Tank

VICKERS MEDIUM TANK MARK 2
1925–1941

In the early 1920s the official tank design department of the British Army was experimenting with some advanced designs; unfortunately, due to their advanced features they gave a good deal of trouble, and Vickers were approached to see if they could produce something simpler with which to equip the army. The Mark 1 tank they produced in 1921 did not have the performance of the experimental designs, but it was simple, reliable and cheap. Vickers were then given a contract for an improved model, the Mark 2, which became the standard British inter-war tank

The Vickers tank had a box-like hull with low tracks sprung on small bogie wheels. The driver sat at the front, alongside the engine, and the hull carried a revolving turret provided with a 3-pdr. gun. A Vickers machine gun was mounted coaxially with the main gun, and two further Vickers guns could be thrust from ports in the hull sides. Four men occupied the

fighting compartment: the commander, who also operated one machine gun; the main gunner; his loader, who operated the coaxial machine gun; and a radio-operator/gunner who looked after communications and the third machine gun.

About 160 of these were built, to form the principal equipment of the British tank forces until the late 1930s. Several were still in use at the outbreak of war; most were used for training, though a small number were still held as combat tanks in the Middle East and saw action against the Italian Army.

Length: 5.33m (17ft 6in). *Width:* 2.78m (9ft 2in). *Height:* 3.01m (9ft 11in). *Weight:* 13,665kg (30,126lb). *Crew:* 5. *Power:* Armstrong-Siddeley, air-cooled, 8-cyl., petrol, 90bhp. *Armament:* one 47mm gun; three .303 Vickers machine guns. *Armour:* 8–12mm. *Speed:* 25km/hr (15.5mph) (nominal); 48km/hr (30mph) (actual). *Range:* 200km (125 miles). *Maker:* Vickers-Armstrong Ltd., Elswick.

WHIPPET MEDIUM TANK *1917–1930*

After seeing the success of the first Mark tanks in 1916, the British Army requested lighter, faster vehicle which could take over th

Whippet

functions of the cavalry and pour through th gap made by the heavy tanks so as to pursue th enemy. Sir William Tritton, designer of th Mark 1, answered the request with his Tritto Chaser and this was accepted as the Tank Medium A or Whippet, about 200 being mad in 1917–18. They were first used on 26 Marc 1918, playing a vital part in preventing German breakthrough on the Third Arm front near Serre. They were also used in Russi in 1919, and they were copied by the German Most were withdrawn from service in the earl 1920s, a number being sold to Japan, but on or two lingered until the 1930s.

The Whippet was laid out rather like a armoured car, and was a complete break from the pattern of the Mark 1 series. The engine were in front, under a long 'bonnet', with th driver behind; two engines were used, on driving each track, and steering was done by wheel which regulated the throttles of th engines, slowing one, accelerating the other s as to change the track speed and make the tur Though attractive and efficient, it demanded highly skilled driver. The hull originally carrie a revolving turret, but this was abandoned i the production vehicles as being too compl cated, and the fighting compartment was thus simple box with ports through which the cre could fire machine guns. Due to the low pow ered engines and unsprung suspension, th Whippet could never reach the desired spee on rough country, but it was a considerabl advance for its time.

Length: 6.09m (18ft 0in). *Width:* 2.61m (8 7in). *Height:* 2.74m (9ft 0in). *Weigh* 14,225kg (31,360lb). *Crew:* 3. *Power:* tw Tylor, 6-cyl., petrol, each 45bhp. *Armamen* four .303 Hotchkiss machine guns. *Armou* 5–14mm. *Speed:* 12km/hr (8mph). *Rang* 65km (40 miles). *Maker:* William Foster Co., Lincoln.

Vickers Medium Tank Mark 2

UNITED STATES

CHRISTIE TANK DESIGNS

J. Walter Christie was an American automobile engineer who founded the Front Drive Motor Company shortly before World War I, making trucks and fire engines. During the war, as a private venture, he designed self-propelled tracked mountings for a 3in anti-aircraft gun and an 8in howitzer; the US Army bought the latter but found it to have poor performance, though it had the innovative feature of being able to have its track removed and to run on its wheels on suitable surfaces. The Army encouraged him to develop more self-propelled guns, but Christie was not amenable to direction and was now experimenting with tanks. His designs, however were not very practical and the Army ignored them. He then turned to the design of an amphibious tank in 1922, and six of these were purchased by the US Marines; one of these, in 1923, made the first recorded amphibious landing from a ship on to the shores of Puerto Rico.

Christie then designed a completely new system of suspension, using large coil springs and large-diameter rubber-tyred wheels, by which his name will always be remembered. While his prime purpose was still a convertible tank which could run on wheels or tracks, most armies lost interest in that aspect but saw great promise in his suspension which allowed far greater speeds and gave a better cross-country ride than previous types. In 1928 the US Army purchased five of the new Christie design, calling them the T3, and shortly afterwards two

Christie-type Medium Tank T3E2

were bought by Russia to form the starting point for much of their best design.

Christie tended to lose interest in a design once it had been developed and turned to something new. The US Army, on the other hand, found his designs deficient in many respects, and they could expect little co-operation from him when they returned their tanks for modifications. Eventually the two parties fell out over contractual obligations, and though Christie's patents were still used (and paid for) design was taken out of his hands. He continued to design more tanks; one was bought by Britain in 1938 to form the basis of the Cruiser designs (qv). Christie's designs, however, went more and more to extremes; he designed one tank with wings and a tail unit,

suggesting that it might fly or, alternatively, be dropped from an aircraft to glide to the ground. Another had helicopter rotors to enable it to cross obstacles. Needless to say, little interest was shown in these designs except by some of the more sensational newspapers. Christie died in January 1944, still involved in litigation with the US Government over features of wartime tanks which he claimed were taken from his designs.

Christie's strength and weakness lay in his obsession with speed to the exclusion of all else. His designs were remarkable mechanical achievements, but as practical tanks they were worthless, and in every case his basic ideas had to undergo vast modification by practical soldiers before they could be put to use.

Christie Medium Tank T4 Convertible

FORD TWO-MAN TANK *1918–1930*

In September 1917 the US Army decided to adopt two types of tank, a light, the French Renault FT–17 (*qv*), and a heavy, the British Mark V (*qv*), and contracts were drawn up for their construction. But because of production problems only a handful were built in the United States before the end of the war.

In order to fill the gap, Henry Ford proposed building a light two-man tank, using as many components of stock commercial Ford trucks and cars as could be managed. In fact what Ford envisaged was a machine-gun carrier for the infantry, but due to its shape it was inevitably called a tank. It was a tiny machine; its shape was based on that of the Renault six-ton and it was propelled by two Model T engines, one for each track – this gave good control of steering but demanded some skill in driving. A single machine gun in the front of the hull was the only armament. Another version was developed as a cargo carrier, while another was fitted with a 75mm howitzer. The pilot model was sent to France for tests and declared acceptable, after which 15,000 were ordered from Ford. By January 1919 500 were to be ready and production was to continue at a rate of 100 per day. But shortly after this decision was taken, the Armistice was declared and all tank contracts were stopped; as a result, only 15 Ford tanks were ever delivered. Nevertheless, it was a milestone in tank development insofar as it showed that automobile manufacturers could be used for tank building, a lesson which was to stand America in good stead in 1941.

Length: 4.16m (13ft 8in). *Width:* 1.67m (5ft 6in). *Height:* 1.60m (5ft 3in). *Weight:* 2,812kg (6,200lb). *Crew:* 2. *Power:* two Ford 'T', 4-cyl., petrol, each 2,900cc, 22bhp at 1,500rpm. *Armament:* one machine gun. *Armour:* 7–13mm; *Speed:* 13km/hr (8mph). *Range:* 55km (34 miles). *Maker:* Ford Motor Co., Dearborn, Mich.

M3 Medium Tank and
below the Ford Two-man

M3 MEDIUM TANK (LEE GRANT)
1941–1945

During the 1930s the Rock Island Arsenal had developed a medium tank incorporating a radial air-cooled engine and volute-spring suspension, and in the spring of 1940 this was ordered into production as the M2A1. Very shortly afterwards the US Army, having analysed reports of the campaigns in Poland and France, urged the adoption of a 75mm gun as standard tank armament; the M2A1 carried a 37mm gun. Such a large gun could not be fitted into the turret of the M2A1 and an entirely fresh one would be needed. The quickest and easiest solution was to mount the 75mm gun in a sponson at the side of the hull, such a course demanding the least modification. This idea was accepted as an interim measure, pending the production of a tank with the 75mm gun in the main turret, and this interim tank became

M3 Medium (Lee)

the Medium M3.

Production began in April 1941, at the Detroit Tank Arsenal. During the development period the British Purchasing Commission had placed orders for large numbers of M3 tanks but requested a different design of turret, one which would incorporate the radio installation as was British practice, instead of carrying it in the hull as did American tanks. These became known as the General Grant in British service, while the American models were the General Lee. Grant tanks were shipped to Egypt in 1942 and were first used in combat at Gazala in May of that year. These tanks formed an important part of British armoured strength in the Middle East and served throughout the desert campaigns. After their replacement by the General Sherman M4 (*qv*) they were sent to Australia and were used in the Pacific theatre of war until 1945.

In American service the M3 was principally a training tank, but it was used in the invasion of North Africa in 1942, continuing in use until the collapse of Tunis, and in the Pacific during the attack on the Gilbert Islands in 1943.

There were several variants of the M3:

M3	First production type; Wright Whirlwind engine and all-riveted construction. 4,924 built.
M3(D)	As M3 but with a Guiberson diesel engine.
M3A1	As for M3 but with a cast hull. 300 built.
M3A1(D)	As M3A1 but with Guiberson diesel engine. 28 built.
M3A2	As M3 but with welded hull. 12 built.
M3A3	As M3A2 but with twin GMC diesel engines. 322 built.
M3A4	As M3 but with Chrysler multi-bank engines. 109 built.
M3A5	As M3A3 but with riveted hull. 591 built.

M3 *Length:* 5.63m (18ft 6in). *Width:* 2.71m (8ft 11in). *Height:* 3.12m (10ft 3in). *Weight:* 27,215kg (60,000lb). *Crew:* 6. *Power:* Wright R975, 9-cyl., radial, air-cooled, petrol, 15,947cc, 340bhp at 2,400rpm. *Armament:* one 75mm Gun M2; one 37mm gun M5; three .30 Browning machine guns. *Armour:* 12–57mm. *Speed:* 42km/hr (26mph). *Range:* 193km (120 miles). *Makers:* Detroit Tank Arsenal (Chrysler Corp.) Detroit, Mich.; Baldwin Locomotive Co. Philadelphia, Pa.; American Locomotive Co. Schenectady, NY; Pressed Steel Corp. Pittsburgh, Pa.; Pullman–Standard Car Co. Pittsburgh, Pa.

M3/M5 LIGHT TANKS (STUART)
1940-1945

Shortly before the outbreak of war in 1939 the US Army had standardized a light tank, the M2A1, the culmination of a long process of development. But reports of the German campaign in Poland led them to consider using thicker armour, a step which required redesign of the suspension, and adding a trailing idler

M3 Light Tank

wheel. The new tank became the Light M3, standardized in July 1940.

The M3 was very much in the pre-war American idiom; high-set, with a raised rear deck to accommodate a radial air-cooled engine, volute-spring suspension, and subsidiary machine guns in side sponsons on the hull. But because of the painstaking development by Rock Island Arsenal, it was reliable and robust. Named the General Stuart by the British, the M3 went through several changes: the M3A1 improved the turret and added a turret basket and power traverse and gyrostabilization; the M3A3 made further improvements in the turret and improved the protection of the driver by a more acute type of glacis plate.

As with other American tank designs, engine production threatened to be a bottleneck, and a design was worked out in which the radial engine was replaced by twin Cadillac V–8 engines and an automatic transmission. This proved successful and was put into service as the M5; apart from the engine it was the same tank as the M3.

M3A3 *Length:* 5.02m (16ft 6in). *Width:* 2.51m (8ft 3in). *Height:* 2.28m (7ft 6in). *Weight:* 14,402kg (31,752lb). *Crew:* 4. *Power:* Continental W670–9A, 9-cyl., radial, air-cooled, petrol, 10,932cc, 250bhp at 2,400rpm. *Armament:* one 37mm gun M5 or M6; two .30 Browning machine guns. *Armour:* 12–38mm. *Speed:* 58km/hr (36mph). *Range:* 112km (70 miles). *Makers:* American Car & Foundry Co., Berwick, Pa.; Cadillac Motor Car Div. of GMC, Detroit, Mich.; Cadillac Motor Car Div. of GMC, Southgate, Cal.; Massey–Harris Corp., Racine, Wis. A total of 13,859 M3 was built.

M5 *Power:* Cadillac V–8 Series 42, each 5,670cc, 220bhp at 4,000rpm. *Range:* 160km (100 miles). Other details as for the M3A3. A total of 8,884 was built.

M5A1 Light Tank

M6 HEAVY TANK *1942*

In the summer of 1940 the Chief of Infantry, US Army, requested a design of a heavy tank to weigh about twice as much as the M3 medium (*qv*), have 7.62cm (3in) of armour, and have a main armament between 75mm and 105mm calibre. The Ordnance Department responded with a 50-ton design in two types; one with a torque converter transmission and the other with petrol-electric transmission. Main armament was a 3in gun in the turret accompanied by a coaxial 37mm gun. The hull and turret were to be cast armour and the suspension used a new design of horizontal volute spring. Power traverse elevation and full gun stabilization were also to be provided.

M4 MEDIUM TANK (SHERMAN) *1941–*
The M3 medium tank was put into production as an interim measure, pending the development of a medium tank with a turret large enough to carry a 75mm gun. Designated Medium Tank T6 the new design was to use most of the mechanical components of the M3

M4 Medium Tank

series, have a turtle-backed hull, and a central cast turret with the 75mm gun. Approval was given for this in May 1941, the prototype was ready in September, and in the following month it was standardized as the M4. It became known as the General Sherman and was produced in greater numbers than any other American tank before or since.

While the Sherman was to be the principal battle tank of both the British and US Armies throughout the war, it gradually fell behind the standards imposed by German improvements, notably in its gun power, and several variant models were devised in order to keep it battleworthy. Another source of variations was the need to use different engines, since engine production could scarcely keep pace with demand. In spite of its defects, it was, in general, a highly successful tank and, above all, was reliable and available in quantity. After the war it continued to serve the Americans through the Korean War, and several thousands were supplied to other countries in military aid programmes. Hundreds are still running, notably those with the Israeli Army which have been fitted with new engines and guns to bring them up to present-day standards.

A Medium Sherman

PRINCIPAL MODELS OF THE M4

M4	Original design with Wright engine and welded hull. 8,389 built, of which 1,641 were fitted with 105mm howitzers in the turret instead of the 75mm gun.	M4A3	Welded hull and Ford V–8 engine. 12,342 built, of which 4,542 had the 76mm gun and 3,039 had the 105mm howitzer.
M4A1	Original design with Wright engine and cast hull. 9,707 built, of which 3,426 were fitted with a new 76mm gun to replace the 75mm model.	M4A3E2	Assault tank for use in Normandy invasion; had additional armour. 254 built; originally with 75mm gun, most were converted to 76mm in the field.
M4A2	Welded hull and GMC Diesel engine. 10,968 built, of which 2,915 had the 76mm gun.	M4A4	Welded hull, Chrysler multi-bank engine. 7,499 built.

The two pilots were completed in December 1941, and in February 1942 the torque converter model was standardized as the Heavy Tank M6. A production schedule called for 500 to be built in 1942 and 5,000 in 1943. On test, however, the pilots showed defects in the braking and cooling systems, but these were corrected by April 1942.

By this time, however, the Armored Force, US Army, had decided that armour and gun power came second to mobility, and it was against the adoption of a heavy tank; it cloaked its objections by complaining that the vehicle was unreliable (though the first pilot had covered 5,630km (3,500 miles) on its original set of tracks), overweight, had poor crew conditions and obsolete fire-control equipment. Though the Ordnance Department offered to correct all these items, the Armored Force was adamant; it carried Army Ground Forces with it and production was stopped. Although the Ordnance Department continued to develop a heavy tank (which eventually became the M26 (*qv*)) it had to fight the Armored Force every inch of the way. In spite of the objections, the M6 was, in fact, a very good tank for its day. It pioneered heavy cast construction, petrol-electric and torque converter drives, power traverse mechanisms,

M6 Heavy Tank

horizontal volute-spring suspension and several other details, all of which were to be utilized in later American designs with success. Had it gone into production and been improved in the same way as the M4 (*qv*), it would probably have become one of the most useful tanks in the Allied armoury.

Length: 7.54m (24ft 9in). *Width:* 3.11m (10ft 2in). *Height:* 2.99m (9ft 10in). *Weight:* 57,380kg (126,500lb). *Crew:* 6. *Power:* Wright, 9-cyl., radial, air-cooled, petrol, 29,879cc, 800bhp at 2,300rpm. *Armament:* one 3in gun M7; one 37mm gun M6; two .50 machine guns; two .30 machine guns. *Armour:* 25–83mm. *Speed:* 35km/hr (22mph). *Range:* 160km (100 miles). *Makers:* Fisher Body Co. Detroit, Mich (12 built); Baldwin Locomotive Co., Philadelphia, Pa. (28 built).

M22 LIGHT TANK (LOCUST) *1942–1950*
In February 1941 the US Army set about the design of an airborne tank, while the Army Air Corps undertook to develop an aircraft to carry

M4A5	US designation for the Canadian Ram tank (*qv*).
M4A6	M4A4 but fitted with a Caterpillar diesel engine. 75 built.

A grand total of 49,234. Of these, 4,065 were sent to Russia and 17,181 to the British Army.

M4A3 *Length:* 6.27m (20ft 7in). *Width:* 2.66m (8ft 9in). *Height:* 2.93m (9ft 7in). *Weight:* 31,570kg (69,600lb). *Crew:* 5. *Power:* Ford GAA, V–8, petrol, 18,029cc, 450bhp at 2,600rpm. *Armament:* one 75mm gun M3; two .30 machine guns; one .50 machine gun.

Armour: 12–108mm. *Speed:* 42km/hr (26mph). *Range:* 160km (100 miles). *Makers:* Grand Blanc Tank Arsenal (Fisher Body Corp.) Grand Blanc, Mich.; Detroit Tank Arsenal (Chrysler Corp.) Detroit, Mich.; Lima Locomotive Works Lima, Ohio; Pressed Steel Car Co. Pittsburgh, Pa.; Pacific Car & Foundry Co. Renton, Wash.; Baldwin Locomotive Works Philadelphia, Pa.; American Locomotive Co. Schenectady, NY; Pullman–Standard Car Co. Pittsburgh, Pa.; Federal Machine & Welder Co. Chicago , Ill.; Ford Motor Co. Detroit, Mich.

M22 Light Tank

it. Contracts were given to various companies and a design by Marmon–Herrington was selected. After testing two pilot models, production of 500 was ordered in April 1942, followed by orders for a further 1,400. By February 1944 830 had been made and the tank standardized as the M22; production was then stopped.

The M22 resembled a miniature M4 Sherman (qv) in general form, and used a suspension akin to that of the M3 light tank (qv) with the addition of external strengthening rods between the bogies. Prime armament was the usual 37mm gun with a .30 machine gun alongside it in the turret.

The carrying aircraft was the C–54, but the tank could only be carried by slinging it beneath the fuselage, after removing the turret and stowing it inside the plane, an impractical mode of operation. As a result, although several hundred M22s were sent to England, none were ever used in the airborne role. A handful were used by the British 6th Airborne Division in the crossing of the Rhine, but they were never used by US troops in combat. The principal defects were that the armour was too thin, the gun too small, and the vehicle mechanically unreliable. Most were scrapped after the war, though a few reached the hands of the Egyptian Army in the late 1940s.
Length: 3.93m (12ft 11in). *Width:* 2.23m (7ft 4in). *Height:* 1.75m (5ft 9in). *Weight:* 7,257kg (16,000lb). *Crew:* 3. *Power:* Lycoming 0–435–T, 6-cyl., horizontally-opposed, air-cooled, petrol, 7,113cc, 162bhp at 2,800rpm. *Armament:* one 37mm gun M6; one .30 machine gun. *Armour:* 12–25mm. *Speed:* 56km/hr (35mph). *Range:* 177km (110 miles). *Maker:* Marmon–Herrington Co. Inc., Indianapolis.

M24 LIGHT TANK (CHAFFEE) 1944–
By the end of 1942 it was apparent that the M3/M5 Stuart series of light tanks (qv) had been overtaken by battlefield conditions and become obsolescent. Their principal defect was their 37mm main armament which was no longer sufficient to deal with German tanks. After some false starts, work began in April

1943 on a new light tank to carry a 75mm gun, and the pilot was ready for test in October of that year. Production began in April 1944 and the design was standardized as the Light Tank M24; it later became known as the Chaffee, to commemorate General Adna R. Chaffee, 'Father of the US Armored Force', who had died in August 1941.

The M24 was laid out in the conventional manner; driver at the front, fighting compartment behind him, and engine and transmission at the rear. The twin Cadillac engines of the M5A1 were continued in use, since they had proved extremely reliable, but the transmission was manual rather than automatic. Suspension was by torsion bars, with large rubber-tyred roadwheels. The turret carried a long 75mm gun with a coaxial machine gun, and another machine gun was mounted in the hull front, alongside the driver.

The first M24 tanks reached Europe at the end of 1944 and were used in the final advance into Germany, though they left no significant record of combat achievement. The Korean War was their first real test, and they performed there very well. Subsequently they were supplied as military aid to several countries and many are still in service, though the US Army replaced them in the early 1950s.
Length: 4.99m (16ft 4in). *Width:* 2.94m (9ft 8in). *Height:* 2.47m (8ft 2in). *Weight:* 18,370kg (40,500lb). *Crew:* 5. *Power:* twin Cadillac V–8, petrol, 5,720cc each, 110bhp at 3,400rpm each. *Armament:* one 75mm gun M6; two .30 machine guns. *Armour:* 12–38mm. *Speed:* 48km/hr (30mph). *Range:* 160km (100 miles). *Makers:* Cadillac Motor Car Div. of GMC (3,300 built); Massey–Harris Corp., Milwaukee, Wis. (770 built).

M26 HEAVY TANK (PERSHING) 1945–
When the M6 heavy tank project (qv) collapsed in late 1942, the US Ordnance Depart-

ment did not give up hope; holding out the promise of an improved M4 Sherman (qv), it obtained authority to begin developing a new series, the T20. This eventually became the T23, of which over 200 were built but which was not a success and denied standardization. The Ordnance Department then asked permission to fit a 90mm gun to the T23, but at this time the Armored Force saw the tank solely as an instrument of exploitation; fighting other tanks was the job of specialist tank destroyers,

M26 Heavy Tank (Pershing)

and therefore they saw no need for a 90mm gun. Eventually permission was obtained to develop two fresh designs, the T25 with a 90mm gun and the T26 with the same gun and with thicker armour and wider tracks; this, it was hoped, would be comparable to the German Tiger (qv).

In June 1944 the T26E3 model was demon-

M24 Light Tank

strated and it was proposed to ship the first 20 to Europe; once again, Army Ground Forces stopped the proposal, on the grounds that the design had not been sufficiently tested. But the Army Staff overruled them and in January 1945 the US Army in Europe received the first heavy tanks. In March 1945 the design was standardized as the M26 and by the end of the war there were 310 in Europe.

The M26 used torsion-bar suspension, mounted a 90mm gun and was well armoured; it was, indeed, the tank that the fighting soldiers had been demanding for a very long time, since their Shermans were no match for German armour. In post-war years it served well in Korea and was supplied to many countries as military aid.

Length: 6.80 (22ft 4in). *Width:* 3.50m (11ft 6in). *Height:* 2.76m (9ft 1in). *Weight:* 41,730kg (92,000lb). *Crew:* 5. *Power:* Ford, V–8, petrol, 16,390cc, 500bhp at 2,600rpm. *Armament:* one 90mm gun M3; two .30 Browning machine guns; one .50 Browning machine gun; *Armour:* 51–102mm (2.0–4.0in). *Speed:* 48km/hr (30mph). *Range:* 180km (110 miles). *Makers:* Detroit Tank Arsenal (Chrysler Corp.) (1,238 built); Grand Blanc Tank Arsenal Grand Blanc, Mich. (Fisher Body Corp.) (1,190 built).

M26 Heavy Tank (Pershing)

M41 LIGHT TANK (WALKER BULLDOG) 1950–

Although the M24 Chaffee tank (*qv*), with which the US Army ended the war in 1945, was a sound enough tank, no sooner had the war ended than the designers set to work to produce a better one. Indeed, a complete 'outfit' of new tanks in all weights was put under way, to incorporate all the latest developments in armament, fire control and propulsion.

The M41 was among the first tanks to be designed round a suitable engine, rather than being designed first and then an engine found which would fit. The selected engine was a horizontally-opposed six-cylinder of small size and great efficiency. The gun, a 76mm high-

velocity weapon, was fitted with a muzzle brake and, innovatively, a fume extractor which prevented the gases of combustion being drawn into the tank turret when the breech was opened. The turret was equipped with an optical rangefinder coupled to the gun stabilizer and to an electronic lead calculator which simplified aiming and increased the first-round-hit probability. All in all, the M41 was a considerable advance on its forebears.

The M41 was standardized in 1950, added urgency being give to its production by the outbreak of war in Korea. One thousand were ordered, and after this improved models, the M41A1, A2 and A3, which differed in their gun-control systems, were produced. It remained in service with the US Army until the late 1960s and several hundred have been supplied to other countries, where they are still in service. The name given to the M41 was originally Little Bulldog; this was changed to Walker Bulldog in memory of General Walton W. Walker, killed in a Jeep accident in Korea in 1951.

Length: 5.81m (19ft 1in). *Width:* 3.19m (10ft 6in). *Height:* 3.07m (10ft 1in). *Weight:* 23,495kg (51,800lb). *Crew:* 4. *Power:* Continental, 6-cyl., horizontally-opposed, petrol, 500bhp at 2,800rpm. *Armament:* one 76mm

M41 Light Tank (Walker Bulldog)

gun M32; one .30 machine gun; one .50 machine gun. *Armour:* 12–38mm. *Speed:* 72km/hr (45mph). *Range:* 160km (100 miles). *Maker:* Cleveland Tank Arsenal (Cadillac Motor Corp.), Cleveland, Ohio.

M47 MEDIUM TANK (PATTON) *1952–*

At the end of World War II the US Army started to develop a completely new series of tanks, incorporating all the latest technical improvements and based on analysis of wartime designs. In the meantime the existing M26 heavy tank (*qv*) was regraded as a medium tank and given a new engine to become the Medium M46. While the long-term development was getting under way the Korean War broke out and the political situation deteriorated, leading to demands for an improved tank at short notice. The new medium tank, the T42, had at least had its turret developed and since this was considerably better than the existing M46 design, it was joined to the M46 hull, the resulting tank being called the M47 Patton. The new turret was sharply contoured and had a pronounced bustle at the back to accommodate the radio; it mounted a 90mm high-velocity gun fitted with a fume extractor and blast deflector. An optical rangefinder was fitted in some tanks, and a ballistic computer was also used to calculate elevation and deflection. As well as being employed by the US Army, large numbers were exported.

Length: 8.00m (23ft 3in). *Width:* 3.50m (11ft 6in). *Height:* 3.32m (10ft 11in). *Weight:* 42,130kg (92,880lb). *Crew:* 5. *Power:* Continental AV–1790–5, V–12, petrol, 29,370cc, 810bhp at 2,800rpm. *Armament:* one 90mm gun M36; two .30 machine guns; one .50 machine gun. *Armour:* 25–100mm. *Speed:* 60km/hr (37mph). *Range:* 160km (100 miles). *Maker:* Detroit Tank Arsenal (Chrysler Corp.); American Locomotive Co. Schenectady, NY.

M47 Medium Tank

M60 MAIN BATTLE TANK *1959–*

In 1956 the US Army decided to improve the current M48 battle tank (*qv*); shortly after that they decided to adopt the British 105mm tank gun L7, building it in the United States and calling it the M68 gun. Adding this to the now re-engined M48 produced quite a serviceable design which was standardized as the M60 and

M48 MEDIUM TANK
1953–

The M47 (*qv*) was regarded as an interim measure, pending the development of a completely new design. And once the M47 was scheduled for production, work started on its replacement, the M48. This was to be armed with a 90mm gun, a new air-cooled diesel engine, a new transmission and the latest developments in fire-control devices. Production orders were given before the trials were completed, and deliveries began early in 1953.

The M48 was of conventional design, with torsion-bar suspension and with cast hull and turret. It was followed by several variant models: the M48A2 incorporated fuel injection for the engine, while the M48A3 changed from petrol to diesel engine; the M48A4 was to be fitted with turrets from M60 tanks (*qu* when these were refitted with Sheridan-type turrets mounting the 152mm gun/launcher, but this plan was abandoned; the M48A5, last o

the line, mounts a 105mm gun instead of the 90mm and is practically the equal of the M60. An unusual variant was the M48C which resembled the M48 in every particular, but was made of mild steel instead of armour in order to provide a cheap and effective training tank.

The M48 was widely exported, and has been used in action by Pakistan, the US Army in Vietnam, and by the Israeli Army in the 1967 Six-Day War.

Length: 6.88m (22ft 7in). *Width:* 3.63m (11ft 11in). *Height:* 3.12m (10ft 2in). *Weight:* 47,173kg (104,000lb). *Crew:* 4. *Power:* Continental 1790–2A, V–12, diesel, air-cooled, 750bhp at 2,400rpm. *Armament:* one 90mm gun M41; one .30 machine gun; one .50 machine gun. *Armour:* 12–120mm. *Speed:* 48km/hr (30mph). *Range:* 465km (290 miles). *Makers:* Ford Motor Co., Livonia; Detroit Tank Arsenal (Chrysler Corp.) Detroit, Mich.; Fisher Body Div. of GMC Detroit, Mich.; American Locomotive Co., Schenectady, NY.

The M48 Medium Tank *right* demonstrates a bridge laid by a Biber Bridgelaying Tank. *Below,* one M48 helps to pull another out of a paddy field in Vietnam.

put into production in 1959. It has stayed in more or less continuous production ever since and in addition to being used by the US Army has been exported to (among others) Austria, Italy, Iran, Israel, South Korea and Turkey. In 1975 it was reported that 3,125 had been supplied to US forces and 913 exported.

The basic M60, essentially an improved M48, was succeeded by the M60A1 with a cast hull and turret. The M60A2 had a completely new turret mounting the 152mm gun/launcher using the Shillelagh missile (*qv* M551 Sheridan). The M60A3 made improvements to the fire-control systems with a laser range-finder and electronic computer, added a new type of infra-red searchlight and night-vision equipment, and a thermal jacket for the 105mm gun. A new engine and transmission are also forecast, which will probably lead to a fresh model number. Numbers of M60A1 in the hands of the Israeli Army have proved themselves in combat and shown that they are superior to their Soviet contemporaries.

Length: 6.94m (22ft 9in). *Width:* 3.63m (11ft 11in). *Height:* 3.25m (10ft 8in). *Weight:* 48,987kg (108,000lb). *Crew:* 4. *Power:* Continental 1790–2, 12-cyl., diesel, 750bhp at 2,400rpm. *Armament:* one 105mm gun M68; one 7.62mm machine gun; one .50 machine gun. *Armour:* 12mm–120mm. *Speed:* 48km/hr (30mph). *Range:* 500km (310 miles). *Maker:* Detroit Tank Arsenal (Chrysler Corp.) Detroit, Mich.

M60 Main Battle Tank

M103 HEAVY TANK *1952–1973*
In spite of disappointment over the M6 heavy tank (*qv*), the US Ordnance Department continued to work on heavy tank designs throughout the war years. Among their efforts, the most prominent was probably the T28, a 90-ton monster with a 67-calibre 105mm gun mounted in the hull front; it was a very similar vehicle to the British Tortoise and suffered a similar fate – two were built, one of which was burned out during trials and the other was recently found rusting away in a corner of a proving ground.

Eventually, with the pressure of the Cold

War, a T43 model appeared in 1950, basically an enlarged M46 (*qv*) in appearance. When the Korean War broke out in 1950, production of the T43 was authorized and in 1952 it appeared as the M103, armed with a 120mm gun derived from an anti-aircraft gun barrel and breech. Two hundred were built, but the design had been rushed and numerous modifications had to be made before the vehicle was battleworthy; the greatest drawback was its poor performance due to being underpowered. Like the British Conqueror (*qv*) (which used almost the same gun) it served as a back-up tank destroyer for medium tank units, but once the US Army adopted the 105mm gun in the M60 tank (*qv*) the M103 was phased out, the last disappearing from service in 1973.

Length: 6.98m (22ft 11in). *Width:* 3.75m (12ft 4in). *Height:* 2.87m (9ft 5in). *Weight:* 56,700kg (125,000lb). *Crew:* 5. *Power:* Continental AV 1790–5B, V–12, diesel, air-cooled, 810bhp at 2,800rpm. *Armament:* one 120mm gun M58; one .30 machine gun; one .50 machine gun. *Armour:* 12–178mm. *Speed:* 34km/hr (21mph). *Range:* 130km (80 miles). *Maker:* Detroit Tank Arsenal (Chrysler Corp.) Detroit, Mich.

M551 LIGHT TANK (SHERIDAN) *1966–*
In 1959 the US Army decided upon a light tank with overwhelming gun power and in the following year it issued a contract for an 'Armored Reconnaissance Airborne Assault Vehicle' which would combine the hitherto separate roles of light tank and self-propelled anti-tank gun. The result, which appeared in 1966, was the M551 Sheridan, with a welded aluminium hull, torsion-bar suspension, and a turret armed with a new 152mm gun/launcher capable of firing conventional ammunition or of launching a Shillelagh guided anti-tank missile. This missile is fin stabilized and controlled

M103 (T43) Heavy Tank

by an infra-red command link; all the gunner in the tank has to do is to keep the crosswire of his sight on the target, and the missile is automatically guided in sympathy. It carries a hollow-charge warhead and is effective to a range of about 4,000m. (6,436ft).

Unfortunately the M551 suffered from a considerable number of defects; indeed, the first production was withheld from service until the vehicles could be modified. The principal problems were with the transmission, the missile and the combustible-cased conventional ammunition. After some four years of work, these problems were all overcome and Sheridan has taken its place in service with good results, notably in Vietnam. But the technical difficulties and escalation of planned cost of this tank led to a Congressional enquiry and were responsible for the extremely close watch now kept on US tank development plans and costs by Congress.

Length: 6.29m (20ft 8in). *Width:* 2.81m (9ft 3in). *Height:* 2.94m (9ft 8in). *Weight:*

15,830kg (34,829lb). *Crew:* 4. *Power:* Detroit Diesel, 6-cyl., turbocharged, 300bhp at 2,800rpm. *Armament:* one 152mm gun/launcher M81; one 7.62mm machine gun; one .50 machine gun. *Armour:* not disclosed. *Speed:* 70km/hr (45mph). *Range:* 600km (373 miles). *Maker:* Cleveland Tank-Automotive Plant, Cleveland Ohio (Allison Div. of General Motors Corp).

M551 Light Tank (Sheridan)

MARMON–HERRINGTON LIGHT TANK *1940–1946*
Between 1935 and 1941 the Marmon–Herrington Company of Indianapolis built a variety of light tanks for export to various countries. The first models, known as the CTL series, were turretless vehicles mounting machine guns in the raised superstructure. Early models used leaf-spring suspension, but in 1939 a form of volute-spring suspension, comparable to that in use on service tanks at the time, was adopted. Small numbers of CTL models in various forms were bought by the US Marine Corps from time to time for trial, but they were not adopted in quantity.

In 1940 a turreted design, the CTM, was produced to meet a Marine Corps demand; this was a three-man tank with two .50 machine guns in the turret and three .30 in the hull front. In 1941 an improved model, the CTL–4TAC, was produced for the Netherlands East Indies government. This had a smaller turret, offset to

M551 Light Tank (Sheridan)

Marmon-Herrington

the right, and was arranged for left-hand drive; a companion model, the 4TAY, had the turret on the left and right-hand drive. Before the contract could be completed, the Japanese overran the East Indies and the balance of the contract, some 240 tanks, was taken by the US Army. The 4TAC became the Light Tank T14 and the 4TAY the Light Tank T16; except for a few used in Alaska for local defence, most were employed for training.

Length: 3.50m (11ft 6in). *Width:* 2.08m (6ft 10in). *Height:* 2.10m (6ft 11in). *Weight:* 8,534kg (18,816lb). *Crew:* 3. *Power:* Hercules, 6-cyl., petrol, 124bhp at 2,200rpm. *Armament:* three .30 machine guns. *Armour:* 12–25mm. *Speed:* 48km/hr (30mph). *Range:* 100km (60 miles). *Maker:* Marmon–Herrington Co. Inc., Indianapolis.

XM-1 MAIN BATTLE TANK (ABRAMS)

In 1963 the US and German governments agreed to develop a new main battle tank between them, to be called the MBT–70 (*qv* Leopard II). The prototypes had several unusual features; the suspension could be varied in height to allow the tank to 'sit' down to make a more stable firing platform, the driver was in the turret with the rest of the crew, and a highly advanced fire-control system was postulated. But the good intentions fell apart over the question of armament; the US wanted to use the 152mm gun/launcher as

used on the Sheridan (*qv*) while the Germans refused this and wanted a conventional gun. At this point the cost of each proposed tank had exceeded $1,000,000, and in 1970 the agreement was dissolved and the two governments went their separate ways.

The Americans then started afresh, aiming at a design for the 1980s, the XM–1. In 1973 contracts were given to Chrysler and to Detroit Diesel/Allison for prototypes and in 1976 the Chrysler model was selected for development and production. It is hoped that production will commence in 1979, and some 3,312 tanks are required by the US Army.

The XM–1 will have hull and turret of British Chobham armour, claimed to be imper-

vious to most forms of attack, and first production will carry the 105mm gun; it is understood that in 1984 production will change over to mounting the 120mm smoothbore gun currently being developed in Germany, but political considerations may alter this decision.

Length: 7.79m (25ft 3in). *Width:* 3.55m (11ft 8in). *Height:* 2.36m (7ft 9in). *Weight:* 52,616kg (116,000lb). *Crew:* 4. *Power:* Lycoming AGT–T, gas, turbine, 1,500bhp. *Armament:* one 105mm M68 gun; two 7.62mm machine guns; one .50 machine gun. *Armour:* not disclosed. *Speed:* 73km/hr (45mph). *Range:* 480km (300 miles). *Maker:* Detroit Tank Arsenal (Chrysler Corp.) Detroit, Mich.

XM-1 Main Battle Tank

The Semovente 47/32 SP anti-tank gun was
outclassed shortly after entering service, but it
had to suffice for the mobile anti-tank defence
of the Italian armoured units in North Africa,
as no other vehicle was available.

SELF-PROPELLED ARTILLERY

PANZERJAGER K TANK DESTROYER
1971–
The Panzerjäger K is a development of the Saurer APC (*qv*). The hull is a complete re-design, with a French turret in the middle. This turret is an oscillating type very similar to that on the AMX–13 tank (*qv*). It is hydraulically operated with an auto-loader for the gun, which keeps the crew down to two in the turret. The gun is also French and is fed from two six-round magazines, with a total load of 43 rounds

Panzerjäger K Tank Destroyer

carried in the hull. The engine permanently drives a hydraulic pump on the differential. This allows the power to the tracks to be continuously controlled so that there is no loss when steering and the vehicle can be made to spin on its axis, if necessary. About 120 of these vehicles are in service with the Austrian Army.

Length: 5.60m (18ft 4in). *Width:* 2.50m (8ft 2in). *Height:* 2.35m (7ft 8in). *Weight:* 17,500kg (38,580lb). *Crew:* 3. *Power:* Steyr Model 6FA, 6-cyl., in-line, water-cooled, diesel, 9,980cc, 300bhp at 2,300rpm. *Armament:* one 105mm gun; one 7.62mm machine gun mounted coaxially. *Armour:* 10–40mm. *Speed:* 63km/hr (39mph). *Range:* 530km (329 miles). *Maker:* Steyr–Daimler–Puch, Steyr.

BELGIUM

JAGDPANZER KANONE JPK SELF-PROPELLED ANTI-TANK GUN *1977–*
This vehicle is a version of the German Jagd-panzer Kanone (*qv*) built in Belgium by the Henschel company and fitted with some modifications to suit the requirements of the Belgian Army. The main difference is that the wheels, brakes and transmission are taken from the Marder armoured personnel carrier (*qv*), but in addition the gun is fitted with a modern Belgian fire-control system and an improved fume-extraction arrangement. Night illumination is provided by a battery of Swedish Lyran mortars on the roof, and the machine guns are Belgian. In all other respects the vehicle is the same as the German model.

Length: 6.24m (20ft 5in). *Width:* 2.98m (9ft 9in). *Height:* 2.08m (6ft 9in). *Weight:* 25,700kg (56,642lb). *Crew:* 4. *Power:* Daimler Benz DB–837 Aa, V–8, water-cooled, diesel, 500bhp at 2,200rpm. *Armament:* one Rhein-

Jagdpanzer Kanone

metall 90/40.4 90mm gun; two 7.62mm machine guns (one coaxially mounted, one on commander's cupola). *Armour:* 12–50mm. *Speed:* 70km/hr (43mph). *Range:* 400km (248 miles). *Maker:* Henschel–Werke, Antwerp.

CZECHOSLOVAKIA

S 3 LIGHT SELF-PROPELLED GUN
1936–1939
A few of these light self-propelled guns were made in Czechoslovakia before the German invasion. They used a slightly modified chassis from an LT-35 light tank (*qv*) and put on to it a sort of truck body made of thin plate. The sides of the body could be dropped down to allow the gun to traverse, but the front plate remained in place. The gun was in a circular turret, rather like a short dustbin, with no roof and open at the back. There were three versions, one with a 37mm anti-tank gun and two machine guns. The second, with a 66m gun and two machine guns, was overloaded. The third had a Czech 37.2mm gun and an improved turret. All three were really too small and unprotected for their task and the Germans did not continue with them.

Length: 4.90m (16ft 1in). *Width:* 2.16m (7ft 1in). *Height* (third version): 2.28m (7ft 6in). *Weight:* 10,300kg (22,600lb). *Crew:* 5. *Power:* Skoda, 6-cyl., in-line, water-cooled, petrol, 120bhp at 1,800rpm. *Armament:* one 37.2mm gun; two 7.92mm machine guns. *Armour:* 12mm. *Speed:* 40km/hr (25mph). *Range:* 190km (120 miles). *Maker:* Skoda, Pilsen.

S 3

FRANCE

AMX DCA 30 SELF-PROPELLED ANTI-AIRCRAFT TANK *1962–*
The chassis of this vehicle is the AMX–13 light tank (*qv*), fitted with an S 401 A cast turret mounting two HS 831 30mm automatic guns. The guns are controlled by an 'Oeil Noir' (Black Eye) radar whose folding dish is on the

AMX-30 DCA

back of the turret. Production for the French Army was completed in 1965 and since then there have been export orders to various countries. The same turret can be mounted on the AMX–30 tank (*qv*), but this has only been supplied to Saudi Arabia.

Length: 5.15m (16ft 11in). *Width:* 2.63m (8ft 8in). *Height* (dish folded): 2.68m (8ft 10in). *Weight:* 15,000kg (33,069lb). *Crew:* 3. *Power:* SOFAM, 8-cyl., horizontally-opposed, water-cooled, petrol, 270bhp at 3,200rpm. *Armament:* two HS 831 30mm automatic guns (300 rounds each). *Armour:* 10–30mm. *Speed:* 60km/hr (37mph). *Range:* 350km (218 miles). *Maker:* Creusot–Loire, Chalon-sur-Saône.

AMX GCT 155mm SELF-PROPELLED GUN *1977–*
The GCT (Grand Cadence de Tire) is a very new design intended to replace the existing F3 155mm (*qv*). The GCT is based on an AMX–30 (*qv*) tank chassis with a large, well-armoured turret which houses the gun and crew. The turret has 360° traverse and carries 42 rounds in racks at the rear. The gun has an automatic loader and is traversed and elevated by hydraulic power. The gun can fire a burst of eight rounds in one minute at maximum rate, but the normal rate is one or two per minute. All ammunition has combustible cartridge cases and there is no need to open the turret hatches except for reloading, which takes about 30 minutes. There is full NBC protection for the crew and even a bunk so that they can rest in rotation.

Length: (gun forward): 10.42m (34ft 2in). *Width:* 3.15m (10ft 4in). *Height:* 3.00m (9ft 10in). *Weight:* 41,000kg (88,185lb). *Crew:* 4. *Power:* Hispano–Suiza HS–110, 12-cyl.,

horizontally-opposed, water-cooled, multi-fuel, 700bhp at 2,400rpm. *Armament:* one 155mm gun; one 7.62mm machine gun on anti-aircraft mounting. *Armour:* estimated at 50mm maximum. *Speed:* 60km/hr (37mph). *Range:* 450km (280 miles). *Maker:* Atelier de Construction, Roanne.

AMX GCT 155mm

AMX 105mm SELF-PROPELLED GUN
1952–
Strictly speaking, this is a self-propelled howitzer since the barrel has a maximum elevation of 70° and there are fixed increments of the charge to allow for range overlap at all angles of fire. The chassis is the AMX–13 (*qv*) and the gun is in a fixed armoured box at the rear of the hull. The box does not rotate and the gun has a traverse of 20° either side of centre; for more traverse the vehicle must be slewed. The crew compartment has an armoured roof and is reasonably spacious. There is room in it for 56 rounds of ammunition, of which six are specific

Crotale AA Vehicle

anti-tank shells. The driver and engine are in the front, the driver on the left, the engine on the right. The design has sold well and is, or has been, in service in Israel, Morocco, the Netherlands and France.

Length: 6.40m (21ft 0in). *Width:* 2.65m (8ft 8in). *Height:* 2.68m (8ft 10in). *Weight:* 16,500kg (36,367lb). *Crew:* 5. *Power:* SOFAM 8 GXB, V–8, water-cooled, petrol, 250bhp at 3,200rpm. *Armament:* one 105mm (L/23 or L/30) gun; one 7.5mm machine gun on anti-aircraft mounting on turret roof. *Armour:* 10–20mm. *Speed:* 60km/hr (37mph). *Range:* 350km (218 miles). *Maker:* originally State Factories, but any made today would be by Creusot–Loire, Chalon-sur-Saône.

AMX 105

CHAR CANON 75 LIGHT SELF-PROPELLED GUN *1918*
This interesting little vehicle was the self-propelled gun version of the original Renault FT–17 light tank (*qv*). The turret and superstructure of the tank were cut down to make as flat a platform as possible, and on to this was mounted a 75mm field gun. The gun pointed backwards, so that the vehicle had to be reversed to bring the gun into action,

Char Canon 75

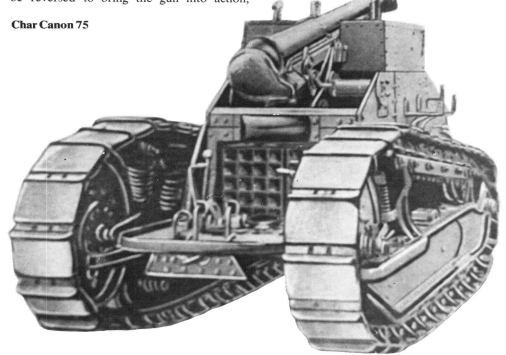

traverse was limited and very little ammunition could be carried. There was no protection for the crew, who were entirely in the open. Several prototypes were made, but the gun never entered service. A few were given a short 105mm gun, which was altogether too heavy for the chassis. Even with the 75mm the chassis was strained on firing, though much was learnt from the trials.

Length: 4.09m (13ft 5in). *Width:* 1.72m (5ft 8in). *Height:* 1.67m (5ft 6in). *Weight* (estimated): 7,300kg (16,060lb). *Crew:* 5. *Power:* Renault, 4-cyl., in-line, petrol, 35bhp at 1,500rpm. *Armament:* one 75 Modèle 1897 75mm gun. *Armour:* 8mm on hull. *Speed:* 7km/hr (4.5mph). *Range:* 35km (22 miles). *Maker:* Renault Frères, Billancourt.

CROTALE ANTI-AIRCRAFT VEHICLE SYSTEM *1971–*
The vehicles for this system were specially developed by Hotchkiss–Brandt and are now built by Creusot–Loire. Separate vehicles carry the missiles and launchers, the control data being fed by cable from the radar vehicle. Once launched, the missiles are guided by a small radar on the firing vehicle. Both vehicles are the same pattern, with the crew in the front compartment, the guidance or launch equipment in the centre, and the engine at the rear. The engine drives a generator and the motive power is provided by a DC motor at each of the four wheels. Four missiles are carried on each launch vehicle; reloading requires a further supply vehicle to come up to the fire position. Range of the CROTALE missile is 8,500m (9,290yds) and 3,000m (3,280yds) altitude. All vehicles are air-transportable.

Length: 6.20m (20ft 4in). *Width:* 2.65m (8ft 8in). *Height* (folded for air transport): 2.07m (6ft 10in). *Weight* (loaded): 14,800kg (32,620lb). *Crew* (each vehicle): 3. *Power:* Saviem HM–71 2356, 6-cyl., in-line, water-cooled, diesel, 230bhp at 2,200rpm, driving four electric motors. *Armament:* four CROTALE missiles. *Armour:* 3–5mm. *Speed:* 70km/hr (43mph). *Range:* 500km (310 miles). *Maker:* Thomson–CSF, Bagneux, in conjunction with Creusot–Loire, Chalon-sur-Saône.

F3 155mm SELF-PROPELLED HOWITZER *1965–*
The Mark F3 is the larger howitzer in service with the French Army, though it is currently being replaced by the GCT (*qv*). It uses the AMX–13 (*qv*) chassis and the howitzer is at the rear. Because of the size of the gun it is not possible to contain it within armour, and it is completely unprotected. The crew travel in a separate armoured personnel carrier together with the immediate ammunition load. To fire, the vehicle stops and lowers spades to steady

MKF3 155mm

itself against the recoil. The ammunition vehicle backs up and the crew serve the gun while standing on the ground, as if it were a towed piece. Elevation and traverse is manual and the rate of fire is normally one round per minute, with a maximum of three per minute for a short time. The vehicle has been adopted by Argentina, Chile, Ecuador, Kuwait and Venezuela.

Length (gun forward): 6.22m (20ft 5in). *Width:* 2.72m (8ft 11in). *Height:* 2.07m (6ft 10in). *Weight:* 17,400kg (38,280lb). *Crew:* 2 in vehicle, 8 in accompanying carrier. *Power:* SOFAM 8 GXb, V–8, water-cooled, petrol, 8,250cc, 250bhp at 3,200rpm. *Armament:* one 155mm Mk F3 howitzer (L/33). *Armour:* 10–20mm. *Speed:* 65km/hr (40mph). *Range:* 300km (186 miles). *Maker:* Creusot–Loire, Chalon-sur-Saône.

SAINT CHAMOND SELF–PROPELLED GUN *1918–*

In 1918 the Saint Chamond Company developed an unusual carriage upon which they mounted either a 280mm howitzer or a 194mm gun. The carriage was on a track unit derived from the usual Holt tractor, with an electric motor driving each track. The power for these motors was provided from an external

source mounted in a second vehicle. This was a tractor unit, with the same type of Holt track, which mounted a petrol engine driving a dynamo. The power from this dynamo drove the electric motors on the tracks and also, via a flexible cable, drove the motors of the gun carriage. Tractor and gun carriage were linked by a rigid drawbar for movement, and the gun unit was controlled by a steersman. The tractor driver controlled the speed of the whole equipage by either varying the speed of the petrol engine or by using a rheostat to vary the current. The tractor unit also carried ammunition, and after arrival at the gun position could be unloaded, disconnected and driven away. Less than a dozen of these vehicles were built, a few of which were used in action in the St. Mihiel sector late in 1918.

Length: 8.12m (26ft 7in). *Width:* 2.67m (8ft 9in). *Height:* 2.35m (7ft 8½in). *Weight:* 28,000kg (61,730lbs). *Crew:* 8. *Power:* Crochet–Collardeau, petrol-electric drive, propelled by Panhard 6-cyl. petrol motor, 110bhp at 1,500rpm. *Armament:* 194mm GPF gun or 280mm Schneider howitzer. *Armour:* nil. *Speed:* 10km/hr (6mph). *Range:* 50km (31 miles). *Maker:* Société des Forges et Acieries de la Marine et d'Homecourt, St. Chamond.

SCHNEIDER SELF–PROPELLED GUN *1917–1918*

The Schneider Company developed their self-propelled gun design late in 1917 after completing their contract for tanks. The carriage was completely self-contained, using a Holt track unit directly propelled by a Panhard engine via the usual gearbox arrangement. On top of this chassis a 220mm Longue Mle 1917 gun was mounted on an inclined plane, up which the gun could recoil, checked by an hydraulic buffer, and down which it ran by gravity back to the firing position. The gun was incapable of independent traverse and thus the entire mounting had to be slewed on its tracks. Unfortunately the amount of control and degree of accuracy allowed by this system was not, at that stage of tank development, sufficient to allow the gun to be laid accurately and as a result the design was not well received.

Length: 8.52m (27ft 11½in). *Width:* 2.52m (8ft 3in). *Height:* 3.04m (9ft 11½in). *Weight:* 26,000kg (57,320lb). *Crew:* 8. *Power:* Panhard, 6-cyl., petrol, 110bhp at 1,500rpm. *Armament:* one 220mm Canone Longue Mle 1917. *Armour:* nil. *Speed:* 8km/hr (5mph). *Range:* 50km (31 miles). *Makers:* Schneider et Cie, Lyon.

GERMANY

BRUMMBAR (GRUMBLER) ASSAULT GUN *1943–1945*

Brummbar, also known as the Sturmpanzer, was designed as a powerful short-range assault gun capable of dealing with almost any obstacle. The chassis and hull were those of the

Brummbar

standard PzKpfw IV tank (*qv*), and the hull was then built up into a boxy superstructure, with roof, with the special 15cm (6in) 'sturm haubitze' mounted in the front plate. The first models were produced in April 1943, and it remained in production until the end of the war, during which time 306 were built.

First used in the Kursk battles in July 1943, Brummbar was widely used on all fronts as a heavy support weapon. There were several minor changes in detail during the production run; later models had a ball-mounted machine gun in the hull front, while some had additional armour welded over the hull.

Length: 5.93m (19ft 5in). *Width:* 2.88m (9ft 5in). *Height:* 2.52m (8ft 3in). *Weight:* 28,650kg (63,165lb). *Crew:* 5. *Power:* Maybach, V–12, petrol, 11,867cc, 300bhp at 3,000rpm. *Armament:* one 15cm StuH 43 with 38 rounds. *Armour:* 10–100mm. *Speed:* 40km/hr (25mph). *Range:* 210km (130 miles). *Maker:* Deutsche Eisenwerke, Duisberg.

ELEFANT TANK DESTROYER *1943–1944*

When the Tiger tank (*qv*) was under development, the Porsche factory had, in an excess of confidence, built some 90 chassis of their own model; when the Henschel design was selected for production, these vehicles were redundant, and it was decided to turn them into heavy tank destroyers. The gun selected was the 88mm PAK 43 anti-tank gun, and in order to accommodate it, the layout of the vehicles had to be considerably altered. The driver's compartment was isolated from the rest of the vehicle and the engines were moved forward into what had originally been the turret space. The former engine space now became the fighting compartment, which had its sides, front and rear built up into a slope-walled box. In the front plate of this box went the 88mm gun; hatches in the roof gave access to the fighting compartment, and a rear port allowed ejection of spent cartridge cases. Beneath the rear of the fighting compartment was the electric transmission unit, powered by a dynamo driven by the twin engines.

Ninety Elefants were built and went into action for the first time at Kursk in July 1943.

Elefant

Due to an inexplicable oversight, no secondary armament, not even a machine gun, was fitted, and in consequence they suffered from infantry attacks in the blind zones. The survivors were withdrawn and used on other parts of the front and a few were seen in Italy. But their relative vulnerability and mechanical unreliability far outweighed the value of their gun and armour and by the end of 1944 none was left in service.

Length: 6.80m (22ft 4in). *Width:* 3.37m (11ft 1in). *Height:* 2.99m (9ft 10in). *Weight:* 66,045kg (145,600lb). *Crew:* 6. *Power:* two Maybach, V–12, petrol, each 11,867cc, 300bhp at 3,000rpm. *Armour:* 30–200mm. *Speed:* 20km/hr (12.5mph). *Range:* 150km (95 miles). *Maker:* Nibelungenwerke, Linz.

HETZER TANK DESTROYER *1943–1950*

When the German Army occupied Czechoslovakia, they took over a large number of Czech TNHP tanks and subsequently used them in operations in Europe and Russia. In early 1943 General Guderian requested a new

Hetzer

design of tank destroyer, light, well-protected and of low silhouette, and since by that time the TNHP tanks were obsolescent, they were taken as the basis of the new vehicle.

The Hetzer was a completely new design, though using components of the TNHP. The hull was wider and had well-sloped armour, and a 75mm gun was mounted in the front glacis plate. The gun was offset to the right, and the driver sat alongside it, on the left. Within the hull were the gunner and commander. The suspension was basically that of the TNHP, as were the engine and transmission. Except for being somewhat cramped internally, the Hetzer was a successful vehicle, and all production facilities for the TNHP were switched to making Hetzers in January 1944. The first vehicles were issued in July 1944, and 2,584 were built before the war ended. At the war's end the Czechs had a number left on the production line; 158 vehicles were completed and sold to Switzerland in 1946, and a further number were used for several years by the Czech Army.

Length: 4.74m (15ft 7in). *Width:* 2.18m (7ft 2in). *Height:* 1.95m (6ft 5in). *Weight:* 16,000kg (35,275lb). *Crew:* 4. *Power:* Praga AC–2, 6-cyl., petrol, 160bhp at 1,800rpm.

Armament: one 75mm PAK 39 gun with 41 rounds. *Armour:* 8–60mm. *Speed:* 42km/hr (26mph). *Range:* 175km (108 miles). *Makers:* Böhmische-Mährische Maschinenfabrik, Prague; Skodawerk, Pilsen.

HUMMEL (BUMBLEBEE) SELF-PROPELLED GUN *1944–1945*

Hummel was developed in 1942 in order to provide armoured formations with heavy artillery support, and it was the nearest thing the Germans ever built to a self-propelled artillery piece as opposed to a pure assault cannon. Unfortunately, by the time it went into service in mid-1944, sheer firepower was the prime need on the Eastern Front and most of the Hummel equipments were used in the assault gun role.

Hummel consisted of the standard 15cm Model 18 field howitzer mounted on to a chassis derived from PzKpfw III (*qv*) and IV (*qv*) components. The hull was basically a lengthened PzKpfw IV, and the suspension used PzKpfw III and IV sprockets and bogies. The engine was moved forward so as to leave the rear of the hull clear to make a working platform, on to which the gun was pedestal-mounted. The hull sides were then built up to

form an open-topped barbette structure to protect the gun and its crew. Space was restricted and it was necessary to provide each troop of four guns with an armoured ammunition carrier, which was simply a Hummel without a gun, in order to keep them supplied in action. About 660 were built before the war ended.

Length: 5.79m (19ft 0in). *Width:* 2.89m (9ft 6in). *Height:* 2.79m (9ft 2in). *Weight:* 22,860kg (50,400lb). *Crew:* 6. *Power:* Maybach, V–12, petrol, 11,860cc, 300bhp at 3,000rpm. *Armament:* one 15cm FH 18 howitzer with 18 rounds. *Armour:* 10–20mm. *Speed:* 40km/hr (25mph). *Range:* 180km (120 miles). *Makers:* Alkett, Berlin; Deutsche Eisenwerke, Duisberg.

JAGDPANTHER TANK DESTROYER *1944–1945*

In October 1942 the German Army demanded a tank destroyer mounting the powerful 88mm gun, using the chassis of the Panther tank (*qv*) as a basis. Development was slow, and a year elapsed before a wooden mock-up was seen. Production finally began in January 1944, but only 392 were built between then and the end of the war.

Hummel

Jagdpanther

The Jagdpanther adapted the Panther tank hull by extending the front glacis plate to the roof of a new armoured superstructure with well-sloped sides. Into the front plate was mounted the 88mm gun, flanked by the driver and gunner. Traverse was limited to 13° on either side of centre, but the excellent steering control of the Panther allowed the entire vehicle to be slewed rapidly. The Jagdpanther was probably the best of the assault gun/tank destroyer class, being well armoured, of low silhouette, and with a powerful gun, but by the time it was perfected, the production facilities were so disrupted by Allied bombing that there were never enough of them.

Length: 7.18m (23ft 7in). *Width:* 3.30m (10ft 10in). *Height:* 2.71m (8ft 11in). *Weight:* 46,485kg (102,480lb). *Crew:* 5. *Power:* Maybach, V–12, petrol, 23,095cc, 700bhp at 3,000rpm. *Armament:* one 8.8cm PAK 43/3 gun with 57 rounds. *Armour:* 15–80mm. *Speed:* 46km/hr (29mph). *Range:* 160km (100 miles). *Makers:* Muhlenbau Industrie AG, Brunswick; Maschinenfabrik Neidersachsen-Hannover, Hanover.

JAGDPANZER IV TANK DESTROYER
1944–1945
The Jagdpanzer was developed as an improved model of the Sturmgeschutz III (*qv*), one in which there would be better protection, more room for the crew and more ammunition stowage. Instead of simply building a superstructure on to the existing hull, as had been the previous practice, a completely new

hull outline was developed, with a sharply sloped nose in which the gun was mounted, alongside the driver. The armour was well sloped, and later production was provided with additional burster plates outside the tracks. They proved to be efficient vehicles and were specifically issued to tank-hunting detachments of Panzer divisions. Their first use was in Italy in March 1944, after which they appeared in every theatre of war. Production totalled 769 between January and November 1944.

Length: 5.93m (19ft 5in). *Width:* 3.17m (10ft 5in). *Height:* 1.85m (6ft 1in). *Weight:* 25,075kg (55,280lb). *Crew:* 4. *Power:* Maybach, V–12, petrol, 11,867cc, 300bhp at 3,000rpm. *Armament:* one 75mm PAK 40 gun with 79 rounds. *Armour:* 10–80mm. *Speed:* 40km/hr (25mph). *Range:* 210km (130 miles). *Maker:* Vomag Maschinenfabrik AG, Plauen.

Jagdpanzer IV

JAGDTIGER TANK DESTROYER
1944–1945
Limited-traverse tank destroyers are cheaper and easier to make than tanks, since they do not require the involved and expensive turret

structure, and it became common German practice to take their current tank and convert it into a tank destroyer by mounting a larger gun in the hull than could be managed in a turret. This regime was followed when the Tiger II, or King Tiger tank (*qv*) appeared, and a limited-traverse model armed with a powerful 12.8cm gun was designed. The prototype was completed in April 1944, but the Porsche-designed suspension was unsatisfactory and a fresh system had to be developed. Production finally began in July 1944, with an order for 150, but only 77 were built before the war ended.

The Jagdtiger used the Tiger II hull lengthened and built up into a fixed superstructure to house the massive gun. It was extremely well armoured and the gun could cope with anything it met, but the excessive weight meant that the engine and transmission were overloaded and prone to frequent failures. Moreover, its weight and size severely restricted its mobility, particularly where river-crossing was involved.

Length: 7.79m (25ft 7in). *Width:* 3.73m (12ft 3in). *Height:* 2.81m (9ft 3in). *Weight:* 70,000kg (154,335lb). *Crew:* 6. *Power:* Maybach, V–12, petrol, 23,095cc, 700bhp at 3,000rpm. *Armament:* one 12.8cm PAK 44 gun with 40 rounds. *Armour:* 30–250mm. *Speed:* 38km/hr (24mph). *Range:* 110km (68 miles). *Maker:* Nibelungenwerke, Linz.

Jagdtiger

KARL SELF-PROPELLED GUNS
1940–1945
Karl was the class name for the largest self-propelled guns ever built; the name was derived from General Karl Becker, then Chief of Artillery Development. Work on the design began in 1937, prompted by a demand for the heaviest siege howitzer possible, to be used in areas away from railway tracks. Six were finally built, named Adam, Eva, Thor, Odin, Loki and Ziu.

The vehicle was simply a large steel box carried on a track unit consisting of eleven roadwheels on swing arms. This box was divided into three compartments: in the front was the engine and transmission; in the centre was the gun mounting; and in the rear were the vehicle batteries and a gear mechanism which, by revolving the mountings of the roadwheel swing arms, could lower the hull so that it rested on the ground and took the weight from the suspension for firing. Welded to the bottom of the hull was a grid of steel grips which sank into the ground and kept the mounting stable during firing. The gun mount could recoil 750mm within the hull, and the weapon itself could also recoil 800mm within the mounting; this double recoil served to reduce the shock transmitted to the vehicle itself. The weapon was mounted so as to fire over the rear of the vehicle and could traverse only 2° to each side of centre.

The six vehicles were originally furnished with 60cm calibre barrels, which fired a 1,577kg (3,476lb) shell to 6,675m (7,300yd) range. After being used at Lvov in 1941, the Army requested a better range, and replace-

Karl

MARDER (MARTEN) SELF-PROPELLED GUN *1942–1945*
The title of Marder appears to have been popular with the German Army since it was applied to three distinctly different self-propelled equipments during the war. The title was later revived to designate an armoured

personnel carrier (*qv*).

Marder I appeared in 1942, a hasty conversion of the captured French Lorraine personnel carrier. The hull was built up into a high armoured box, into the front of which a 75mm anti-tank gun was mounted. One hundred and eighty-four of these were built, and while it was

workable, it was insufficiently well armoured to survive for long in combat. After losing some of the first models in Russia, the remainder were issued to occupation troops in France, and later saw action against the British and American armies in 1944.

Marder II was based on the PzKpfw II (*qv*)

ment 54cm barrels were produced which could be readily interchanged with the 60cm barrels. At 54cm calibre the shell weighed 1,247kg (2,750lb) and the maximum range was 10,515m (11,500yd).

The Karl equipments were used principally at the seige of Sebastopol in 1942; thereafter they saw little use, though one was employed to shell Warsaw during the 1944 rising.

Length: 11.22m (36ft 10in). *Width:* 3.20m (10ft 6in). *Height:* 4.47m (14ft 8in). *Weight:* 124,974kg (123 tons). *Crew:* 18. *Armament:* one 60cm howitzer Gerät 040 or one 54cm howitzer Gerät 041. *Power:* Mercedes-Benz, V–12, diesel, 44,500cc, 580bhp at 2,000rpm. *Armour:* nil. *Speed:* 10km/hr (6mph). *Maker:* Rheinmetall-Borsig AG, Dusseldorf.

MITTLERER SCHUTZENPANZER-WAGEN GERAT 909 LIGHT SUPPORT VEHICLE *1942–1945*

In 1942, with a surplus of old 75mm short tank guns acquired due to re-arming tanks with better weapons, the German Army suggested mounting them on to half-track personnel carriers to act as infantry support weapons. The armoured carrier SdKfz 251 was used, and the gun was mounted at the forward end of the crew compartment, behind a small shield. After testing the prototypes in Russia, 150 were ordered and built. Later, in 1944, the gun mounting was redesigned so that it could be inserted into any SdKfz 251 during production, so that more gun carriers could be produced whenever required.

Mittlerer Schutzenpanzerwagen Gerat 909

Length: 5.79m (19ft 0in). *Width:* 2.08m (6ft 10in). *Height:* 2.07m (6ft 9in). *Weight:* 8,670kg (19,115lb). *Crew:* 3. *Power:* Maybach, 6-cyl., petrol, 4,198cc, 100bhp at 2,800rpm. *Armament:* one 75mm KwK 37 gun with 52 rounds. *Armour:* 7–12mm. *Speed:* 50km/hr (31mph). *Range:* 320km (200 miles). *Maker:* Bussing-NAG, Leipzig.

MOBELWAGEN (FURNITURE VAN) SELF-PROPELLED ANTI-AIRCRAFT GUN *1943*

As the aerial strength of the Allies increased, the German Army demanded more self-propelled anti-aircraft guns which could accompany moving columns. Early in 1943 Möbelwagen was designed, a Panzer IV (*qv*) chassis with a wide platform on top of the hull mounting a quadruple 20mm cannon unit. The platform was surrounded by a squared-off armoured barbette, the boxy shape of which led to the nickname. These walls served to pro-

Möbelwagen

tect the gun and its crew on the move, but when action was needed, sides and ends folded down to lie flat and form an extended working platform around the gun mounting. With a rate of fire of 1,800 rounds a minute the Möbelwagen could put up a formidable curtain of fire, but by the time it was perfected it had been decided that the 20mm shell was no longer powerful enough to damage modern aircraft, nor did the weapon have sufficient range. More significant was the complete lack of protection from enemy fire while the crew were in action. As a

ull and chassis. The hull was built up into an pen-topped box, into which a 75mm anti-nk gun, complete with its own shield, was ounted. These were more efficient than arder I, even though they were high-set and ifficult to conceal, and 651 were produced etween June 1942 and June 1943. They

remained in service until the end of the war and were used on all fronts.

Marder III was the best of the group; it was based on the Czech TNHP tank chassis, mounting the same 75mm gun as the other two models, but in a more efficient manner. The tank chassis was altered by moving the engine forward so as to allow the gunners' working area to be set low at the rear of the hull. Around this area was an armoured box housing the gun. In order to improve performance, the armour thickness was reduced. Production of these began in April 1943 and 975 were built by May 1944, after which production was stopped so that the TNHP chassis could be used for the Hetzer tank destroyer (*qv*), a more efficient design.

Marder I *Length:* 5.31m (17ft 5in). *Width:* 1.83m (6ft 0in). *Height:* 2.17m (7ft 2in). *Weight:* 8,135kg (17,935lb). *Crew:* 5. *Power:* Delahaye, 6-cyl., 3,550cc, 70bhp at 2,800rpm. *Armament:* one 75mm PAK 40 gun with 30 rounds. *Armour:* 5–12mm. *Speed:* 35km/hr (21mph). *Range:* 135km (85 miles). *Maker:* Maschinenfabrik Alfred Becker, Krefeld.

Marder II *Length:* 4.93m (16ft 2in). *Width:* 2.28m (7ft 6in). *Height:* 2.20m (7ft 3in). *Weight:* 10,975kg (24,195lb). *Crew:* 3. *Power:* Maybach, 6-cyl., petrol, 6,191cc, 140bhp at 2,600rpm. *Armament:* one 75mm PAK 40 gun with 37 rounds. *Armour:* 5–30mm. *Speed:* 40km/hr (25mph). *Range:* 190km (120 miles). *Makers:* Fahrzeug und Motorenwerke, Breslau; MAN, Nuremberg; Daimler-Benz, Berlin.

Marder III *Length:* 4.95m (16ft 3in). *Width:* 2.15m (7ft 1in). *Height:* 2.48m (8ft 2in). *Weight:* 10,680kg (23,545lb). *Crew:* 4. *Power:* Praga, 6-cyl., petrol, 140bhp at 2,800rpm. *Armament:* one 75mm PAK 40 gun with 27 rounds. *Armour:* 8–15mm. *Speed:* 42km/hr (26mph). *Range:* 190km (120 miles). *Maker:* Böhmische-Mährische Maschinenfabrik, Prague.

result, the design was dropped after one prototype model had been built.

Length: 5.91m (19ft 5in). *Width:* 2.92m (9ft
7in). *Height:* 2.71m (8ft 11in). *Weight:*
22,100kg (48,722lb). *Crew:* 5. *Power:*
Maybach, V–12, petrol, 11,867cc, 272bhp at
2,800rpm. *Armament:* four 2cm Flak 38
automatic cannon with 3,600 rounds. *Armour:*
16–30mm. *Speed:* 40km/hr (25mph). *Range:*
200km (120 miles). *Maker:* Ostbau GmbH,
Sagan.

NASHORN (RHINOCEROS) TANK DESTROYER *1943–1945*

Up to mid-1942 German tank destroyers were
largely tanks with the minimum necessary
amount of alteration, but it was finally realized
that a specialist chassis would permit a better
product to be made. The necessary chassis was
therefore put together using components of
existing tanks, and it was basically a lengthened
PzKpfw IV (*qv*) hull with the chassis made up
of PzKpfw III (*qv*) and IV units. The same
chassis was later used for the Hummel self-
propelled gun (*qv*). In the case of Nashorn, the
object in view was a tank destroyer and it was
armed with an 88mm gun in a built-up, open-
topped superstructure. The engine and
transmission were moved forward to leave
room for the gun and its crew at the rear of the
hull.

Production of Nashorn began in February
1943 and continued until the end of the war, in
which time some 494 were built. In general, it
was an efficient and powerful weapon which
gave a good account of itself, though it suffered
from excessive height and insufficient armour
protection for the crew.

Nashorn

Length: 5.79m (19ft 0in). *Width:* 2.89m (9ft
6in). *Height:* 2.92m (9ft 7in). *Weight:*
24,385kg (53,760lb). *Crew:* 4. *Power:*
Maybach, V–12, petrol, 11,867cc, 300bhp at
3,000rpm. *Armament:* one 8.8cm PAK 43/1
gun with 25 rounds. *Armour:* 10–30mm.
Speed: 40km/hr (25mph). *Range:* 200km (125
miles). *Maker:* Deutsche Eisenwerke, Duisberg.

OSTWIND (EAST WIND) SELF-PROPELLED GUN *1944–1945*

When the 20mm cannon was considered no
longer effective enough to be used in self-
propelled mountings, the next gun to be
selected was the 3.7cm Flak 43. This was also
an automatic weapon, firing a heavier shell to
greater range, though at the reduced rate of
250rpm. Once the idea was approved, production of Wirbelwind (*qv*) was stopped, and a

Ostwind

fresh turret design was then inserted into the PzKpfw IV (*qv*) tank hull. Like its predecessor it was polygonal, well-sloped, and mounted the single 3.7cm gun. Production was difficult, and between July 1944 and the end of the war only 36 were converted from existing tanks while another seven were built from scratch.

Length: 5.92m (19ft 5in). *Width:* 2.92m (9ft 7in). *Height:* 3.01m (9ft 10in). *Weight:* 25,400kg (56,000lb). *Crew:* 6. *Power:* Maybach, V–12, petrol, 11,867cc, 300bhp at 3,000rpm. *Armament:* one 3.7cm Flak 43 automatic gun with 1,000 rounds. *Armour:* 16–80mm. *Speed:* 38km/hr (24mph). *Range:* 200km (125 miles). *Maker:* Ostbau GmbH, Sagan.

SIG 33

PANZERWERFER 42 SELF-PROPELLED ROCKET LAUNCHER
1943–1945

The Germans had a great deal of tactical success with their 'Nebelwerfer' field rocket launcher, using it as an artillery weapon, but its short range and field mounting left the crew very exposed to enemy fire, and in 1942 it was decided to try mounting it on an armoured half-track vehicle. The chosen vehicle was the Opel Maultier half-track cargo truck (*qv*). This was converted by armouring the body and then placing the six-barrel rocket-launcher unit on a turntable in the rear cargo space. Having been seen to work, it was then decided to improve matters by designing a new launcher with 10 barrels, and this went into production in April 1943. Three hundred Panzerwerfer vehicles, together with 289 Munitionskraftwagen or ammunition resupply vehicles, were produced before manufacture ended in March 1944.

Length: 6.15m (20ft 2in). *Width:* 2.20m (7ft 3in). *Height:* 2.50m (8ft 2in). *Weight:* 7,215kg (15,905lb). *Crew:* 3. *Power:* Opel, 6-cyl.,

petrol, 3,600cc, 68bhp at 3,000rpm. *Armament:* one 10-barrel 15cm Nebelwerfer with 20 rockets. *Armour:* 6–10mm. *Speed:* 40km/hr (25mph). *Range:* 130km (80 miles). *Maker:* Adam Opel KG, Russelsheim.

SCHWERES INFANTERIEGESCHUTZ SELF-PROPELLED GUN *1940–1945*

The heavy infantry howitzer SIG33 of 15cm was a highly valued piece of supporting artillery in the German Army, and several different self-propelled carriages were developed for it at various times. They were basically designed as indirect-fire support artillery, but as the war went on they were used more and more in assault-gun roles, for which they were not well suited since they lacked protection for the gunners. As a result, after 1943 they tended to be replaced by better-protected assault guns, though a large number were still in use when the war ended.

The first mounting was developed as a result of a pre-war request from the infantry, and consisted of a large armoured shield on top of a PzKpfw I (*qv*) chassis, with the 15cm infantry howitzer mounted in the front plate. Thirty-eight of these were built by Alkett in 1940 and were used in the Belgian and French campaigns of that year. They showed that the idea of putting the weapon on tracks was a good one, and in 1941 a more ambitious design appeared, the Sturm–Infanterie–Haubitze. This used the PzKpfw III (*qv*) chassis and mounted the howitzer in a fully armoured and closed-in superstructure. Though efficient, it was also expensive and too much of an assault gun for the infantry's requirement, and only 12 were built.

Next, late in 1941, came a version using the PzKpfw II (*qv*) chassis; the turret was removed and the hull opened out so that the gunners stood in what had previously been the fighting compartment, with the gun at the front edge. There was practically no protection for the men, but at least it was a low-set vehicle which could be easily hidden. Twelve of these were built and most appear to have been used in North Africa.

In late 1942 a fresh design was begun, using the Czech TNHP chassis as its basis. This had the hull built up into the usual open-topped superstructure with the gun frontally mounted. This gave reasonable protection, coupled with good cross-country ability and 90 of these were built in Prague between February and April 1943. It was then decided to make a thorough job of the design, and the engine was moved forward to give a clear space at the rear of the hull into which the gun was mounted with the built-up hull protecting it and the gunners. This lowered the centre of gravity and silhouette to make a very efficient vehicle, and a total of 282 were built before production ended in September 1944.

TNHP Model *Length:* 4.95m (16ft 3in). *Width:* 2.15m (7ft 1in). *Height:* 2.47m (8ft 1in). *Weight:* 12,195kg (26,885lb). *Crew:* 4. *Power:* Praga, 6-cyl., petrol, 140bhp at 2,800rpm. *Armament:* one 15cm SIG33 howitzer with 18 rounds. *Armour:* 8–15mm. *Speed:* 35km/hr (21mph). *Range:* 200km (125 miles). *Maker:* Böhmische-Mährische Maschinenfabrik, Prague.

Panzerwerfer 42

STURMGESCHUTZ III ASSAULT GUN
1940–1945

In 1936 the German Army asked for an assault gun, a tracked armoured vehicle mounting a large-calibre low-velocity gun and with a low silhouette. To achieve the desired height, it was decided to mount the gun into the hull instead of in a turret, and a short 75mm gun was developed for the task. The hull of the PzKpfw III tank (*qv*) was selected as the basis, and this was built up into an armoured superstructure, with the gun offset to the front right side, the driver sitting on the left. The first of these vehicles was issued in February 1940, and several were used in the campaign in France. After 30 had been built some design changes were introduced, in the engine and suspension, to give the

Ausf. B model, of which 320 were built.

In May 1941 the Ausf. C and D models appeared; these had various minor improvements in the armour and sighting arrangements. Fifty of the C model and 150 D were built. These were followed in September 1941 by the Ausf. E model, again with small changes in the arrangement of the armour and with the addition of a machine gun to the armament. A total of 272 Ausf. E was built.

Also in September 1941 came an instruction from Hitler that future models were to have better armour and a more powerful gun, and as a result a major redesign was done. The principal task was to fit in a new, long-barrelled gun which gave the vehicle a useful anti-tank performance, and with this some changes were

made in the superstructure. But the basic hull remained the same and the armour was not increased. This model became the Ausf. F and 359 were built.

Improvement in protection came with the Ausf. F/8 model, in September 1942. This made radical changes to the hull, lengthening it slightly, improving engine cooling, thickening the armour, and providing for an additional plate of armour external to the tracks. A total of 334 of this model was built before the end of 1942, at which time production changed to the last model of the series, the Ausf. G version. This made some changes to the superstructure, sloping the armour and improving the various vision arrangements; it also added a new gun mantlet, a coaxial machine gun and, in late

production models, a remote-controlled machine gun on the roof for local defence. Production totalled 7,893.

The StuG III was one of the most successful of all the German self-propelled guns, a fact borne out by the numbers produced. It was widely used on all fronts, and it formed the inspiration for many other designs.

Ausf. G. *Length:* 5.52m (18ft 2in). *Width:* 2.95m (9ft 8in). *Height:* 2.16m (7ft 1in). *Weight:* 24,285kg (53,540lb). *Crew:* 4. *Power:* Maybach, V–12, petrol, 11,867cc, 300bhp at 3,000rpm. *Armament:* one 75mm PAK 40 gun with 54 rounds. *Armour:* 16–80mm. *Speed:* 40km/hr (25mph). *Range:* 155km (100 miles). *Makers:* Alkett GmbH, Berlin; MIAG, Brunswick.

Sturmgeschutz IV

STURMGESCHUTZ IV ASSAULT GUN
1943–1945
The success of the StuG III self-propelled gun (*qv*) led to thoughts of using the PzKpfw IV (*qv*) chassis for a similar weapon, and in December 1943 these thoughts were translated into action after the bombing of the Alkett factory disrupted production of the StuG III. In effect, the superstructure of the existing StuG III and its long 75mm gun were grafted on to the lower hull of the PzKpfw IV tank to produce a vehicle almost the same as the StuG III and with equal performance. The design was so successful that the Krupp factory stopped making PzKpfw IV tanks at the end of 1943 and switched their production to StuG IV.

Length: 5.92m (19ft 5in). *Width:* 2.95m (9ft 8in). *Height:* 2.20m (7ft 3in). *Weight:* 23,370kg (51,522lb). *Crew:* 4. *Power:* Maybach, V–12, petrol, 11,867cc, 300bhp at 3,000rpm. *Armament:* one 75mm PAK 40 gun with 63 rounds. *Armour:* 10–80mm. *Speed:* 38km/hr (24mph). *Range:* 210km (130 miles). *Maker:* Fried. Krupp AG, Werke Gruson, Magdeburg.

STURMMORSER 38 SELF–PROPELLED ROCKET LAUNCHER *1944–1945*
In 1943 the German Army requested a well-protected tank mounting an exceptionally large howitzer so as to be able to accompany an advance and bring heavy high-angle fire to bear on any obstacle. The Tiger tank (*qv*) was taken as the basis of the design, but finding a suitable howitzer was less easy, since large-calibre howitzers tended to be very heavy weapons with more recoil than the tank could withstand. Eventually a new design of 38cm rocket launcher was developed especially for this application.

The mortar was breech-loaded with a rocket-propelled bomb; in a simple tubular barrel the rocket efflux would have caused violent recoil and would have disturbed the flight of the bomb as it left the muzzle, but in this design the blast from the rocket in the tube was deflected by a curved face on the breech block and discharged through a series of vents arranged in the double wall of the weapon's barrel. Thus the rocket blast was blown out forwards, reducing the recoil thrust.

Sturmmörser 38

The mortar was mounted in the front plate of a built-up superstructure. A prominent feature was an ammunition-handling crane at the rear of the hull, to lift the 344kg (760lb) rockets inboard.

Length: 6.28m (20ft 7in). *Width:* 3.57m (11ft 8½in). *Height:* 2.85m (9ft 4in). *Weight:* 66,045kg (145,605lb). *Crew:* 5. *Power:* Maybach, V–12, petrol, 23,095cc, 700bhp at 3,000rpm. *Armament:* one 38cm rocket launcher with 14 rounds. *Armour:* 25–150mm. *Speed:* 40km/hr (25mph). *Range:* 120km (75 miles). *Maker:* Alkett, GmbH, Berlin.

WESPE (WASP) SELF-PROPELLED GUN
1943–1945

In 1942 the German Army decided to develop a self-propelled carriage for their standard divisional fieldpiece, the 105mm leFH 18 howitzer, in support of armoured divisions. Since the PzKpfw II tank (*qv*) was by then obsolescent as a combat tank, the chassis was selected for the task and modified by placing a fixed armoured barbette on top of the hull with the howitzer in the front plate. Since the working floor of this compartment was above the engine, it meant that the vehicle had a high silhouette and was comparatively unstable when driving across rough ground. Nevertheless, it formed a workable self-propelled weapon and 676 were built between February 1943 and July 1944, together with 159 munitions carriers which were the same vehicle but without the howitzer. The equipments remained in service until the end of the war.

Length: 4.82m (15ft 10in). *Width:* 2.28m (7ft 6in). *Height:* 2.31m (7ft 7in). *Weight:* 11,176kg (24,640lb). *Crew:* 5. *Power:* Maybach, 6-cyl., petrol, 6,191cc, 140bhp at 2,600rpm. *Armament:* one 10.5cm leFH 18 howitzer with 32 rounds. *Armour:* 10–20mm. *Speed:* 40km/hr (25mph). *Range:* 140km (87 miles). *Maker:* Fahrzeug und Motorenwerke GmbH, Breslau.

Wirbelwind

WIRBELWIND (WHIRLWIND) ANTI-AIRCRAFT GUN *1944–1945*

This anti-aircraft weapon was developed in conjunction with Möbelwagen (*qv*) in order to supplement production of the latter, but since Möbelwagen was turned down, Wirbelwind became the only quadruple 20mm vehicle to go into production in any numbers. The reason for its selection was largely that it offered more protection to the gunners than had Möbelwagen, though it was still appreciated that the 20mm guns were no longer fully effective.

Wirbelwind consisted of a PzKpfw IV (*qv*)chassis and hull from which the turret had been removed and replaced by a polygonal open-topped turret in which the four guns were mounted. Within its limitations it was a successful design and could produce a useful volume of fire, but production was stopped after only 86 had been converted, so as to concentrate on designs mounting heavier guns.

Length: 5.92m (19ft 4in). *Width:* 2.92m (9ft 7in). *Height:* 2.76m (9ft 1in). *Weight:* 22,355kg (49,285lb). *Crew:* 5. *Power:* Maybach, V–12, petrol, 11,867cc, 300bhp at 3,000rpm. *Armament:* four 20mm Flak 36 automatic guns with 3,200 rounds. *Armour:* 16–80mm. *Speed:* 38km/hr (24mph). *Range:* 200km (125 miles). *Maker:* Ostbau GmbH, Sagan.

WEST GERMANY

GEPARD ANTI-AIRCRAFT TANK *1975–*

The Gepard anti-aircraft tank began development in the early 1960s, after a German Army demand for an all-weather self-propelled gun system. Of the competing designs offered, the one chosen was developed by Contraves AG of Switzerland and was based on the chassis of the German Leopard I battle tank (*qv*). In place of the normal turret is a fresh design which mounts two Oerlikon 35mm automatic cannon in 'pods'; the interior of the turret is taken up by fire-control and radar apparatus. On the rear of the turret is the elongated scanner of a search radar which sweeps through 360° and keeps continuous watch. At the front of the turret is the round antenna of the pulse-doppler tracking and fire-control radar which is 'put on' to the target electronically by the search radar. The output from this radar is fed to the computer which integrates target information with factors such as wind speed and velocity to arrive at firing data, which is then used to aim the guns. On the muzzle of each gun is a velocity analyser which constantly checks the velocity of the emerging shells and passes corrections to the data computer. The guns have a rate of fire of 550 rounds per minute each and are belt fed; the gunner can elect to fire single shots, five-shot bursts or continuous fire.

Wespe

Gepard has now entered service with the German Army and is also being adopted by the Netherlands and Belgian armies.

Length: 7.26m (23ft 10in). *Width:* 3.25m (10ft 8in). *Height:* 3.07m (10ft 1in). *Weight:* 45,000kg (99,208lb). *Crew:* 3. *Power:* Mercedes-Benz, V–10, multi-fuel, 830bhp at 2,200rpm. *Armament:* two 35mm Oerlikon cannon with 680 rounds. *Armour:* 10–70mm. *Speed:* 65km/hr (40mph). *Range:* 600km (375 miles). *Maker:* Krauss-Maffei AG, Munich.

JAGDPANZER KANONE TANK DESTROYER *1965*

When the German Army was reconstituted in the 1950s, memories of the war led them to demand a self-propelled tank destroyer, and after testing several prototypes throughout the early 1960s the Jagdpanzer Kanone (Jpz-4–5) went into production in 1965. In 1972 the Belgian Army ordered 80 vehicles, but these were considerably modified from the German design (*qv* under Belgium).

The Jpz uses a welded steel hull with well-sloped sides, carried on a torsion-bar-spring suspension. The main armament is a 90mm gun built by Rheinmetall but based on the gun used in the American M48 tank (*qv*), numbers of which are still used by the German Army. This gun is mounted in the front of the hull, slightly offset so as to leave room for the driver on its right side and the gunner on its left. The loader and commander are in the hull, behind

Gepard

the gun, and the engine and transmission occupy the rear of the vehicle.

A recent proposal is that these vehicles should be up-gunned by the adoption of the NATO standard 105mm tank gun, but no decision has yet been taken on this.

Length: 6.24m (20ft 6in). *Width:* 2.97m (9ft 9in). *Height:* 2.08m (6ft 10in). *Weight:* 27,500kg (60,627lb). *Crew:* 4. *Power:* Daimler-Benz, V–8, diesel, 500bhp at 2,200rpm. *Armament:* one 90mm gun with 51 rounds. *Armour:* 10–50mm. *Speed:* 70km/hr (44mph). *Range:* 400km (250 miles). *Maker:* Rheinstahl Sonderfertigung, Kassel.

Jagdpanzer Kanone

JAGDPANZER RAKETE TANK DESTROYER *1967–*

With the advent of anti-tank guided missiles, the German Army decided to augment its tank destroyers with missile-armed tank hunters, and this vehicle went into production in 1967.

The Jagdpanzer Rakete (RJpz–2) is based on the same hull and chassis as the Jagdpanzer Kanone (*qv*), but instead of the frontally-mounted gun, there are two launchers on the vehicle roof from which SS–11 missiles can be fired. These are wire-guided missiles made by Nord-Aviation of France; the missile controller is provided with a periscope to track the missile, and while he is so engaged, the other launcher can be reloaded. Each launcher can traverse through a 90° arc from its front, so that 180° at the front of the vehicle is completely covered.

In 1975 most of the RJpz were re-equipped with the French HOT (Haut-subsonique, Optique, Tube-launch) missile system which offered greater range and accuracy. Once re-equipped, the vehicles were known as Jaguar tank hunters. However, it has recently been announced that tests of an improved Jaguar II are in progress; this mounts a single American TOW (Tube-launch, Optical track, Wire guidance) missile plus an improved night-vision sight. The principal advantage appears to be one of cost, and it is forecast that 180 Jaguar IIs will be ordered in 1980.

L33 155mm

Armament: two SS–11 launchers with 14 missiles or two HOT launchers with 20 missiles or one TOW launcher with 15 missiles. *Weight:* 23,000kg (50,706 lb). Other details as for the Jpz-4–5.

ISRAEL

L–33 SELF-PROPELLED GUN *1973–*

The L–33 is essentially a Sherman M4A3E8 (*qv*) tank chassis fitted with a new hull and engine. The bulky superstructure is needed to accommodate the large crew and the ammunition, which is hand-loaded into the gun. The gun is made in Israel by Soltam and in this vehicle the traverse is limited by the mounting. Local defence is provided by a machine gun.

Length: 6.50m (21ft 4in). *Width:* 3.27m (10ft 9in). *Height:* 2.46m (8ft 1in). *Weight:* 41,500kg (91,466lb). *Crew:* 8. *Power:* Cummins VTA–903, V–8 water-cooled, turbocharged diesel, 450bhp at 2,600rpm. *Armament:* one Soltam M–68 155mm gun; one 7.62mm machine gun on pintle mounting. *Armour:* 12–60mm. *Speed:* 37km/hr (23mph). *Range* (estimated): 260km (160 miles). *Maker:* Soltam Ltd., Haifa.

Jagdpanzer Rakete (Jaguar)

ITALY

AUTOCANNONE 90/53 SELF-PROPELLED ANTI-AIRCRAFT GUN
1940–1945

The 90/53 was virtually identical to the German 88mm, and when on its truck mount it was much more mobile than the German method of towing on a four-wheel carriage. The Italian gun was put on to a number of commercial chassis, the most usual being the Breda 6 × 4 but the Lancia 3 RO was also used. All chassis were fitted with six outriggers which were lowered and jacked-up so as to take the loads of firing. Side plates were let down to make up a circular platform for the crew, and some guns were given an armoured shield. In all cases the gun crew had to travel in a separate vehicle, together with the ammunition.

Gun: 90mm 90/53. *Chassis:* Breda 41 6 × 4; Lancia 3 RO 4 × 2. *Maker:* Breda, Milan; Lancia, Turin.

Autocannone 90/53

AUTOCANNONE da 75 SELF–PROPELLED ANTI–AIRCRAFT GUN *1930–1943*

The Ceirano SP gun was simply a strong lorry with an anti-aircraft gun mounted on the load platform. It was unarmoured and the sides let down to allow full traverse of the mounting. The Italians made many of these guns and used them in the desert and in Italy for local anti-aircraft defence. Although not specifically used for other than aircraft defence, they would have been a most useful, though large, anti-tank gun.

Weight (estimated): 4,500kg (9,918lb). *Crew:* 4. *Chassis:* Ceirano CMA 50. *Gun:* 75mm 75/27 CK. *Maker:* Ceirano, Turin.

LANCIA IZ SELF–PROPELLED ANTI–AIRCRAFT GUN *1915–1918*

This was a truck-mounted anti-aircraft gun, using a Lancia lorry chassis. The gun was on a rotating mount which was bolted direct to the chassis frame between the rear wheels. There was no platform for the loaders to stand on,

Lancia I.Z.

although the layers were carried on saddles which rotated with the gun. It is probable that when in position a platform was carried from another vehicle and put around the mounting for the crew.

Weight: 4,000kg (8,816lb). *Crew:* 2. *Power:* Lancia, 4-cyl., petrol, 5,000cc, 70bhp at 2,200rpm. *Armament:* one 75/30 anti-aircraft gun. *Maker:* Fabbrica Automobili Lancia & Co., Turin.

SEMOVENTE 75/18 su M40, 41 and 42 SELF–PROPELLED GUN *1941–1944*

The M40 series of self-propelled guns were based on the M13/40 (*qv*), M14 and M15 tank chassis and were introduced as each of these tanks was brought into service. The conversion was a fairly straightforward matter, the turret was removed and in its place a box was bolted onto the superstructure with a simple mantlet in the front plate. Through this mantlet the gun

Autocannone da 75

Semovente 75/18

Semovente 75/18 su M 40

was swung, the top traverse being limited to 25° either side of the centre line. A light machine gun was carried for local defence and anti-aircraft protection, but it had to be mounted on an external pintle. Forty-eight rounds of ammunition for the main gun could be carried inside, but space for the crew was cramped. These self-propelled guns provided the main artillery support for the armoured divisions in North Africa and Sicily and after the Italian surrender in 1943 many were taken into German service and used in Italy.

Length: 4.92m (16ft 2in). *Width:* 2.20m (7ft 3in). *Height:* 1.92m (6ft 4in). *Weight:* 14,000kg (30,865lb). *Crew:* 4. *Power:* SPA 15 TM 41, V–8, water-cooled, diesel, 11,920cc, 145bhp at 1,900rpm. *Armament:* one Model 1935 75/18 75mm howitzer; one 6.5mm machine gun on external mounting. *Armour:*

6–30mm. *Speed:* 35km/hr (22mph). *Range:* 200km (125 miles). *Maker:* SPA–Fiat–Ansaldo, Turin.

SEMOVENTE 47/32 su L 6/40 SELF-PROPELLED ANTI-TANK GUN
1942–1943

This little self-propelled gun was derived directly from the L6/40 light tank (*qv*) and 280 were built in 1941 and 1942. The superstructure of the tank chassis was extended upwards for about an extra 30cm (11¾in), a light roof added to form the crew compartment and a 47mm anti-tank gun was fitted, pivoting in a mantlet in the front plate on the left side of the driver. Two men worked this gun while the third drove, but the available space was very cramped and vision was poor. Nevertheless, because there was none other, this vehicle had

to suffice as the mobile anti-tank defence of the armoured units in the North African campaign, though it was out classed shortly after it entered service. Eighty-nine rounds of ammunition were carried for the gun, and there was a light machine gun which could be brought into action from the roof.

Length: 3.78m (12ft 5in). *Width:* 1.92m (6ft 4in). *Height:* 1.63m (5ft 5in). *Weight:* 6,500kg (14,300lb). *Crew:* 3. *Power:* SPA 18 D, 4-cyl., in-line, water-cooled, petrol, 4,053cc, 70bhp at 2,500rpm. *Armament:* one 47/32 47mm anti-tank gun; one 6.5mm machine gun. *Armour:* 6–30mm. *Speed:* 42km/hr (26mph). *Range:* 200km (125 miles). *Maker:* SPA–Fiat–Ansaldo, Turin.

SEMOVENTE 90/53 su M41 SELF-PROPELLED GUN *1942–1944*

The 90mm Semovente M41 was introduce into the Italian Army in 1942 to provide som anti-tank fire support for the armoured forma tions. The chassis was the M13/40 tank (*q* and the gun was the 90/53 Model 39 which wa a powerful weapon and the best anti-tank gu in the Italian Army at that time. In fact it wa nearly as good as the German 88mm, but it wa almost too large for the M13/40 and had to b mounted at the extreme rear of the hull with a open mounting which left the crew exposed t HE bursts around them. Only 30 were bui and they were used in defending Sicily durin the 1943 Allied invasion. A severe drawbac was the fact that only six rounds of ammunitio could be carried on board.

Length: 5.28m (17ft 4in). *Width:* 2.26m (7 4in). *Height:* 2.15m (7ft 1in). *Weigh* 17,000kg (34,479lb). *Crew:* 4. *Power:* SPA 1 TM 41, V–8, water-cooled, diesel, 11,920c 145bhp at 1,900rpm. *Armament:* one Mod 1939 90/53 90mm gun. *Armour:* 10–40mm *Speed:* 35km/hr (22mph). *Range:* 200km (12 miles). *Makers:* SPA–Fiat–Ansaldo, Turin.

Semovente 47/32

SEMOVENTE da 149/40 SELF-PROPELLED GUN *1943*

This was a large self-propelled gun which would have gone into mass production by the end of 1943 had not political events intervened and cancelled the programme. In the event only the prototype was completed and this still exists. The chassis was a special one built by Ansaldo using suspension components from the experimental P40 heavy tank, which was also not put into production. It was intended that the 149/40 would replace the towed guns

Semovente 149/40

in the divisional artillery units, though this would have been an expensive business and difficult to complete during a war. The large 149mm gun was carried on top of the chassis and spades were lowered from the rear before firing. The crew had to ride in another vehicle and only six rounds of ammunition were on board with the gun. Top traverse was limited and the cross-country mobility of the vehicle was probably not high.

Length: 6.50m (21ft 4in). *Width:* 3.00m (9ft 8in). *Height:* 2.01m (6ft 7in). *Weight:* 24,000kg (52,896lb). *Crew:* 2 (remainder rode in another vehicle). *Power:* SPA, petrol, 240bhp. *Armament:* one 149mm gun. *Armour:* 6–25mm. *Speed:* 35km/hr (21mph). *Maker:* Ansaldo, Turin.

JAPAN

TYPE 95 HA–GO SELF-PROPELLED GUNS *1938–40*

The Type 95 (*qv*) tank chassis provided the basis for several different self-propelled guns, very few of which ever saw service in more than small numbers. The difficulty was that Japanese industry was overstretched by the war effort and could not cope. The first gun, in 1938, was a 120mm howitzer. This was altogether too much for the light chassis and no further work was done on the idea. At the same time 47mm guns were put into large turrets, which made them almost self-propelled guns since the turrets were too thinly armoured for battle as tanks; a 57mm gun was also tried. An anti-aircraft vehicle was made by lengthening the chassis and inserting another set of bogies. On top of this longer hull a twin 20mm mounting was placed and it made a reasonably successful arrangement. Very few were built and for general data on the Type 95 chassis the reader is referred to the entry for that tank.

TYPE 60 SELF-PROPELLED GUN *1960–*

The Type 60 is an unusual vehicle in that it mounts two US 106mm recoilless rifles as armament. The vehicle is a light chassis fitted with a low superstructure. The commander is in a small turret/cupola on the left side with the two guns on a cradle to his right. A loader is in the crew compartment and the driver is to the left front. The engine is at the rear driving a rear sprocket. The guns are raised hydraulically for firing, as is the commander's turret. There is then a limited amount of traverse

Type 60

available to the commander so that he can lay the guns, using the sights in his cupola. When they have been fired the loader has to get out on to the rear decking to reload, which makes it imperative that the vehicle is withdrawn into cover after every two shots. The Type 60 is now being phased out of service, but may still remain with the reserve forces.

Length: 4.32m (14ft 2in). *Width:* 2.23m (7ft 4in). *Height:* 1.38m (4ft 6in). *Weight:* 8,020kg (17,676lb). *Crew:* 3. *Power:* Komatsu T120, 6-cyl., in-line, air-cooled diesel, 120bhp at 2,400rpm. *Armament:* two 106mm recoilless rifles. *Armour:* 10–30mm. *Speed:* 48km/hr (30mph). *Range:* 130km (43 miles). *Maker:* Komatsu Manufacturing Company, Komatsu.

HSP SELF-PROPELLED GUN *1977–*

The HSP gun is a variant built on the chassis of the Type 74 STB main battle tank (*qv*) and using the same components as the tank, though the layout of the internal compartments is almost the reverse of the tank. The engine is at the front, together with the gearbox, and the large turret for the gun is at the rear so that there is easy access to the fighting compartment through the back doors. The gun is a Japanese design which is thought to have an equivalent performance to that of the long-barrelled gun on the US M109A1 (*qv*). The gun is being manufactured at the time of going to press.

Length: 6.64m (21ft 9in). *Width:* 2.25m (7ft 5in). *Height:* 3.18m (10ft 5in). *Weight:* 24,000kg (52,896lb). *Crew:* 6. *Power:* Mitsubishi, 2-stroke, diesel, 420bhp. *Armament:* one 155mm gun; one 12.7mm machine gun on external mounting. *Armour:* classified. *Speed:* 50km/hr (31mph). *Range:* 300km (186 miles). *Maker:* Mitsubishi Heavy Industries, Sagamihara.

ASU–57 AIRBORNE SELF-PROPELLED ANTI-TANK GUN *1957–*

The ASU–57 (Aiadezantnaya Samochodnaya Ustanovka) first appeared in 1957 and has remained in service ever since, though the 57mm gun is becoming less and less effective against modern armoured vehicles. The armour is thin and there is no overhead protection for the crew. Nevertheless, it is the only parachutable self-propelled anti-tank gun in the world at the moment. There are nine to each Soviet airborne regiment and all are dropped by parachute. About 40 rounds of ammunition are carried in the vehicle. For most operations the ASU–57 is backed up by the ASU–85 (*qv*).

Length (hull only): 3.73m (12ft 3in). *Width:* 2.20m (7ft 3in). *Height:* 1.42m (4ft 8in). *Weight:* 7,400kg (12,000lb). *Crew:* 3. *Power:* one ZIL–123, 6-cyl., in-line, water-cooled, petrol, 110bhp. *Armament:* one 57mm gun; one 7.62mm machine gun for local defence. *Armour:* 6–10mm. *Speed:* 64km/hr (40mph). *Range:* 320km (200 miles). *Maker:* not known.

ASU–85 SELF-PROPELLED ANTI-TANK GUN *1961–*

The ASU–85 was introduced to improve the anti-tank capability of the Soviet airborne units and it is more than just a bigger version of the ASU–57 (*qv*). It is a new design altogether and it offers much better protection for the crew though it has no amphibious ability. There are many components which are common to the PT–76 (*qv*) and it is very nearly the self-propelled gun version of that tank chassis. It is air-portable in the An–12 transport aircraft and there are some reports that it is air-dropped by parachute. The fighting compartment is in front, with the gun mounted

ASU-85

on the left side of the sloping glacis plate. There are prominent infra-red night-vision aids and full NBC protection for the crew.

Length: 6.01m (19ft 8in). *Width:* 2.80m (9ft 2in). *Height:* 2.11m (6ft 11in). *Weight:* 14,000kg (30,865lb). *Crew:* 4. *Power:* Model V–6, 6-cyl., in-line, water-cooled, diesel, 240bhp at 1,800rpm. *Armament:* one 85mm gun; one 7.62mm machine gun coaxially mounted. *Armour:* 10–40mm. *Speed:* 44km/hr (27mph). *Range:* 260km (160 miles). *Maker:* State Factories.

FROG 2, 3, 4 AND 5 ROCKETS *1957–*

The FROG missile is considered to be a tactical missile and is carried on a tracked vehicle which also acts as the launcher. The carrying rails are elevated by a hydraulic system to bring the rocket up to the firing angle. Other vehicles carry the necessary fire-control equipment and transmit the information through long cables plugged into the vehicle. The carrier is a modified PT–76 (*qv*) and not all the chassis are quite the same. In most cases the changes are minimal and are restricted to the launch gear on the top deck, but the hull is also a little longer and there is a compartment in front for the crew to ride inside. The vehicle is not amphibious and the road performance is presumably reduced by the bulk and weight of the launch gear, though there are no figures to support this.

Length: 6.94m (22ft 10in). *Width:* 3.16m (10ft 4in). *Height:* 3.08m (10ft 2in). *Crew:* 3.

Power: Model V–6, 6-cyl., in-line, water-cooled, diesel, 240bhp at 1,800rpm. *Armament:* one FROG missile. *Armour:* 11–14mm. *Speed:* 40km/hr (24mph). *Range:* 260km (160 miles). *Maker:* State Factories.

Frog 2

Frog 5

ISU–122 SELF-PROPELLED GUN *1943–*

When the IS heavy tanks (*qv*) came into service a heavy self-propelled gun was needed to give long-range support, following the Soviet doctrine of always having a larger calibre gun on the self-propelled mounting. The first models used the chassis of the KV–1 (*qv*) and had an armoured casemate on the front half carrying a 122mm gun of the same pattern as that on the towed artillery mounting. When sufficient IS chassis became available the AKV was dropped and the same gun was put on to the IS chassis. In 1944 the more powerful and lighter Model A–19S gun was fitted. By the end of the war this had been replaced by the D–25S, a gun with a long slender barrel and a prominent muzzle brake. It has remained in service ever since, though it is now in reserve in the Warsaw Pact countries. Only 30 rounds of ammunition can be carried. The secondary armament is for anti-aircraft use and ground protection has to be provided by tanks or infantry.

Length (including gun): 10.07m (33ft 1in).

ISU-122

Width: 3.07m (10ft 0in). *Height:* 2.46m (8ft 1in). *Weight:* 46,500kg (102,300lb). *Crew:* 5. *Power:* Model V–2–IS, V–12, water-cooled, diesel, 38,800cc, 520bhp at 2,100rpm. *Armament:* one Model 1944 D–25S L/43 122mm gun; one 12.7mm machine gun on anti-aircraft mounting. *Armour:* 20–110mm. *Speed:* 37km/hr (22mph). *Range:* 240km (150 miles). *Maker:* Tankograd Factory Combine, Chelyabinsk–Kirov.

ISU–152 SELF-PROPELLED GUN *1943–*

The ISU–152 is almost exactly the same vehicle as the ISU–122 (*qv*) with a larger gun. It too started in 1943 using the KV–1 (*qv*) chassis and was given the IS (*qv*) tank chassis shortly afterwards. The general layout and build are the same as for the ISU–122 and the wartime versions could interchange guns without difficulty. The later models are probably built for the one gun only. Despite the size and weight of the piece it is elevated and traversed by hand, and all loading is by hand. The rate of fire is no more than two or three rounds per minute and there is room for only 30 rounds in the casemate. Although now only in reserve in the Soviet Union and Warsaw Pact countries, the gun is still in service in other communist areas.

Length: (including gun): 9.05m (29ft 7in).

Width: 3.07m (10ft 0in). *Height:* 2.46m (8ft 1in). *Weight:* 46,500kg (102,300lb). *Crew:* 5. *Power:* Model V–2–IS, V–12, water-cooled, diesel, 38,800cc, 520bhp at 2,100rpm. *Armament:* one Model 1944 ML–20S 152mm gun; one 12.7mm machine gun on anti-aircraft mounting. *Armour:* 20–110mm. *Speed:* 37km/hr (22mph). *Range:* 240km (150 miles). *Maker:* Tankograd Factory Combine.

SA–4 GANEF SELF-PROPELLED ANTI-AIRCRAFT MISSILE LAUNCHER 1965–

This missile and its launcher are among the more mysterious of the Soviet armoury. GANEF is a long-range anti-aircraft missile of exceptional size and it is driven by ramjets. It seems only to be issued within the Soviet Union and is not used by any of the Warsaw

vehicles pass the necessary control data to the launcher vehicles.

Length: 6.80m (22ft 4in). *Width:* 3.18m (10ft 5in). *Height:* 3.45m (11ft 4in). *Weight:* 14,000kg (30,865lb). *Crew:* 3. *Power:* Model V–6, 6-cyl., in-line, water-cooled diesel, 280bhp at 2,000rpm. *Armament:* three Gainful SAM, max. range 4+ km (2½+ miles).

Scamp

SCAMP AND SCROOGE ROCKETS 1965–

SCAMP and SCROOGE are two huge intercontinental rockets which are carried on modified IS–3 (*qv*) tank chassis. SCAMP weighs 10 tonnes before launch and SCROOGE 12 tonnes. So far they have only been seen on formal parades and in all cases the actual rockets are inside large protective casings. The tank chassis both have a flat platform on the top deck on which is built the carrying and launching cradle. The hydraulic rams necessary for elevation are clearly visible, and there must be a large hydraulic pump in the engine compartment. In the case of SCAMP there is just enough room for two small cabs either side of the rocket and in these the driver and crew can squeeze. With SCROOGE there is only room for the driver in a small cockpit at the front. Both vehicles appear most unwieldy and top-heavy with their rockets on board, but this may be an illusion due to their bulk. There are no dimensions available for the vehicles, nor any performance figures, but it can be assumed that when carrying the rockets, speed is kept very low.

SA-4 Ganef AA Missile Launcher

Pact allies. The vehicle appears to be a stretched version of the PT–76 light tank (*qv*), though details are hard to obtain. The chassis has been cut down on top to give a flat superstructure and lengthened. Two large missiles are carried on rails and supported by a substantial girder at the front. The vehicle acts as the launcher, but apparently uses another radar vehicle for the guidance.

Length: 7.34m (24ft 1in). *Width:* not known. *Height* (superstructure): 1.90m (6ft 4in); (missiles) 4.73m (15ft 5in). *Weight:* not known. *Crew:* 2. *Power:* Model V–6, 6-cyl., in-line, water-cooled, diesel, 280bhp at 2,000rpm. *Armament:* two GANEF SAM, max. range 70+ km (43+ miles). This data is estimated.

SA–6 GAINFUL SELF-PROPELLED ANTI-AIRCRAFT MISSILE LAUNCHER 1967–

SA–6 Gainful is a short-range anti-aircraft missile mounted on a chassis which is yet another variant of the basic PT–76 light tank (*qv*). The crew are carried in a front compartment, in the centre is the launcher control gear, and the engine is at the rear. The three missiles stow on top of the launcher with a front support which folds down before firing. Separate radar

SA–8 SELF-PROPELLED ANTI-AIRCRAFT VEHICLE 1975–

The SA–8 does not fall into any neat classification. It is a wheeled vehicle mounting four missiles of roughly the same size as Roland. The chassis is six-wheeled and appears to be new, it may be amphibious but this is not confirmed. The missiles are carried on their launchers and it is possible that there are at least four more in the hull. There are two radars, an acquisition and a tracker, and there may be other systems also. First seen in 1975, details are still scanty and there are no dimensions yet published.

SA-6 Gainful AA Missile Launcher

Scrooge

SU–76 LIGHT SELF-PROPELLED GUN 1943–1946

The SU–76 was derived from the urgent need in 1942 to increase the firepower of the Soviet armoured formations. It used the chassis of the T–70 light tank (*qv*) which was lengthened and an extra roadwheel inserted into the suspension. An armoured box was built at the rear and armour put around the recoil gear of the gun. The gun was the 76.2mm Model 1942 and 60 rounds were carried for it, mostly anti-tank rounds. Traverse was limited and the first models proved to be unreliable in action. Later

modifications improved the performance of engine and vehicle generally, and mass production started in early 1943. By 1945 over 12,500 had been built. Attempts to fit a larger gun were not pursued. The open-topped fighting compartment was a weakness in battle and restricted tank-hunting operations.

Length: 5.00m (16ft 5in). *Width:* 2.74m (8ft 11in). *Height:* 2.20m (7ft 3in). *Weight:* 11,200kg (24,692lb). *Crew:* 4. *Power:* two GAZ–202, 6-cyl., in-line, water-cooled, petrol, 70bhp at 3,400rpm each. *Armament:* one 76.2mm Model 1942 (215–3) gun. *Armour:* 10–35mm. *Speed:* 44km/hr (28mph). *Range:* 265km (166 miles). *Maker:* Factories No. 37 and 38, GAZ Automobile Factory, Gorki.

SU-100

SU-76

SU–85 MEDIUM SELF-PROPELLED GUN *1943–1945*

When the German Panthers (*qv*) and Tigers (*qv*) appeared in 1943 they outranged the T–34/76 (*qv*) and it became imperative to pro-

SU-85

duce a Soviet answer. The gun chosen was an up-dated version of the 1939 85mm anti-aircraft gun and the chassis was that of the T–34 tank. An armoured casemate was mounted on the front with the gun on the right and the driver on the left. The crew were all in the same compartment and 48 rounds could be stowed inside with them. The vehicle was produced in a very short time and was in action well before the end of 1943. Mass production started late in the summer. The SU–85 was made redundant when the T–34 was up-gunned to take the same gun, but it served until the end of the war.

Length (with gun): 8.15m (26ft 8in). *Width:* 3.00m (9ft 10in). *Height:* 2.45m (8ft 4in). *Weight:* 29,600kg (65,256lb). *Crew:* 4. *Power:* Model V–2–34, V–12, water-cooled, diesel, 38,800cc, 500bhp at 1,800rpm. *Armament:* one Model 1943 D5-85 85mm gun. *Armour:* 20–54mm. *Speed:* 48km/hr (30mph). *Range:* 320km (200 miles). *Makers:* Uralmashzavod Tank Combine, Sverdlovsk; Kirov Factory, Chelyabinsk.

SU–100 MEDIUM SELF-PROPELLED GUN *1944–1957*

When the T–34 (*qv*) was given the 85mm gun it became necessary to build a larger self-propelled support gun and the easiest one to take was an existing ex-naval piece of 100mm. There was no time to design a new chassis and the gun was fitted into the SU–85 (*qv*), despite the fact that it was a tight fit internally. A cylindrical cupola was added for the commander and the mantlet was bigger. Otherwise there were no outward changes. The SU–100 proved to be a most effective way of destroying the large German tanks and it remained in the Soviet Army until 1957. It is still to be found in use with some Communist Armies.

Length (including gun): 9.45m (31ft 0in). *Width:* 3.00m (9ft 10in). *Height:* 2.25m (7ft 4in). *Weight:* 31,600kg (69,665lb). *Crew:* 4. *Power:* Model V–2–34, V–12, water-cooled, diesel, 38,800cc, 500bhp at 1,800rpm. *Armament:* one Model 1944 (D–10S) 100m gun. *Armour:* 20–54mm. *Speed:* 48km/hr (30mph). *Range:* 320km (200 miles). *Maker:* Uralmashzavod Tank Combine, Sverdlovsk.

KPV TWIN 14.5mm ANTI-AIRCRAFT TURRET *1965–*

This turret is fitted to both the BTR 152 and the BTR 40 (*qv*) when they are in the anti-aircraft role. The turret mounts twin guns and is elevated and traversed by hand. Maximum elevation is +80° and depression −5°; traverse is 360°. The KPV heavy machine gun has a rate of fire of 600 rounds per minute and the maximum effective range is 2,000m (6,560ft) in the ground role, and 1,400m (4,592ft) in the anti-aircraft role.

BTR 152 with 14.5mm KPV machine guns

ZSU-57-2

ZSU–57–2 SELF-PROPELLED ANTI-AIRCRAFT GUN *1956–*

This vehicle is a modified T–54 (*qv*) tank chassis with a special turret mounting two 57mm high-velocity anti-aircraft guns. There appears to be no radar and the guns are laid by optical means, perhaps supported by a separate radar vehicle to give early warning. The armour of the hull and turret is thinner than on the tank and the overall weight is lower. The suspension is slightly different from the T–54, but the engine and transmission are the same. The large turret holds five men, two of whom are loaders and one a fuse-setter. The vehicle is in service in all the Warsaw Pact countries, and several in the Middle and Far East also. The vehicle carries 316 rounds of ammunition in clips of four. These have to be hand-loaded into each gun. There is no NBC protection for the crew, nor can the vehicle swim.

Length: 6.22m (20ft 5in). *Width:* 3.27m (10ft 9in). *Height:* 2.75m (9ft 0in). *Weight:* 28,100kg (61,949lb). *Crew:* 6. *Power:* Model V–54, V–12, water-cooled, diesel, 39,000cc, 520bhp at 2,000rpm. *Armament:* two S–68 57mm guns (L/73). *Armour:* 10–15mm. *Speed:* 48km/hr (30mph). *Range:* 400km (248 miles). *Maker:* State Factories.

ZSU–23–4 SELF-PROPELLED ANTI-AIRCRAFT GUN *1964–*

The ZSU–23–4 is one of the most formidable anti-aircraft weapons in the Soviet armoury, and better than any equivalent in the world. The Zu–23 gun has a range of 3,000m (9,842ft) and the battery of four produces a combined rate of fire of almost 4,000 rounds per minute. The normal way of firing is to use bursts of not more than 50 rounds per barrel. The fire-control system is a radar carried on the back of the turret and this radar is both an acquisition set and a fire-control. The vehicle is therefore independent for all operations and it carries sufficient ammunition on board for at least 10 bursts of 50 rounds per gun. The chassis is a variant of the PT–76 (*qv*). The rectangular, flat-topped turret is over half the length of the hull, but the inside must be nearly all taken up by the guns, their ammunition chutes and the radar. The vehicle is widely used outside the USSR.

Length: 6.29m (20ft 8in). *Width:* 2.95m (9ft 8in). *Height* (radar retracted): 2.25m (7ft 5in). *Weight:* 14,000kg (30,865lb). *Crew:* 4. *Power:* Model V–6, 6-cyl., in-line, water-cooled, diesel, 240bhp at 1,800rpm. *Armament:* four Zu–23 23mm automatic guns, with 500 rounds per gun. *Armour:* 10–15mm. *Speed:* 44km/hr (27mph). *Range:* 260km (162 miles). *Maker:* State Factories.

ZSU-23-4

BANDKANON 1A 155mm SELF-PROPELLED GUN (VK–155) *1966–*

This self-propelled gun was designed and developed by Bofors in the late 1950s. The prototypes were evaluated by the Swedish Army from 1961 to 1964 and it entered service two years later. It represents one approach to the problem of mounting the largest possible gun on a tracked chassis, and it has a number of unusual features. The high-performance gun is controlled by four men and is loaded by an automatic magazine. Ammunition is picked up by the derrick on the back of the turret in clips of 14 rounds and lifted into the magazine.

From here it is fed automatically into the gun, but after 14 rounds another supply vehicle must bring up another clip, since only one can be carried in the turret. The gun has an excellent performance and can fire at 15 rounds per minute if needed. It is laid and elevated by hydraulic power, but the top traverse is limited to 15° either side of centre. The chassis is special to the weapon, but it uses a number of components from the S tank (*qv*), including the engine and transmission. The 1A self-propelled gun has apparently proved to be expensive and difficult to maintain and Sweden is contemplating moving to a less complicated design.

Length (hull): 6.55m (21ft 6in). *Width:* 3.37m (11ft 1in). *Height:* 3.35m (10ft 11in). *Weight:* 53,000kg (116,850lb). *Crew:* 6. *Power:* one Rolls-Royce K60, 6-cyl., in-line, water-cooled, diesel, opposed-piston, two-stroke, compression-ignition, multi-fuel, 240bhp at 3,750rpm; one Boeing Model 502/10MA gas turbine, developing 300 shp at 38,000rpm. *Armament:* one 155mm Bofors L/50 gun; one 7.62mm machine gun on anti-aircraft mounting. *Speed:* 28km/hr (17mph). *Range:* 230km (140 miles). *Maker:* Bofors AB, also Volvo and Landsverk AB Landskrona.

Pz Kan 68

LVKV 40mm SELF–PROPELLED ANTI–AIRCRAFT GUN *1955–1970*

This vehicle is another Swedish rebuild of an obsolete tank. Components from the pre-war m/40 light tank (*qv*) were built into a longer hull with one extra roadwheel and with the rear idler raised above ground level. A square turret was mounted in the centre of the hull and two 40mm Bofors guns fitted. The turret was open and the guns were directed by optical means. Only small numbers of these anti-aircraft vehicles were put into service, and they were employed in the mechanized units for protection.

Length: 5.79m (19ft 0in). *Width:* 2.39m (7ft 10in). *Height:* 2.39m (7ft 10in). *Weight:* 17,277kg (38,080lb). *Crew:* 4. *Power:* Scania-Vabis, 290bhp. *Armament:* two Bofors 40mm. *Armour:* 6-20mm. *Maker:* Landsverk AB, Landskrona.

LVKV 40mm SPAAG

PVKV SELF-PROPELLED ANTI-TANK GUN *1950–1970*

The PVKV was developed after the war from what was originally the m/42 tank (*qv*). Shortly

after the conversion to SP guns was started the tank was also up-gunned, so prolonging its life for at least another ten years. The PVKV was given a modern long-barrelled 75mm gun in a ball mounting. To accommodate the crew a large box superstructure had to be built on the hull, and the silhouette was fairly high and large. It was less effective than its contemporaries in other countries, and was not a great advance on those vehicles in service in 1945. However, it was cheap to produce and for the defensive type of warfare foreseen for Sweden it was adequate. Sufficient were built to equip most of the Swedish Army.

Length: 6.64m (20ft 4in). *Width:* 2.37m (7ft 10in). *Height:* 2.59m (8ft 6in). *Weight:* 23,375kg (51,520lb). *Crew:* 4. *Power:* Scania-Vabis, 370bhp. *Armament:* one 75mm gun; one 7.92mm machine gun on external mounting. *Armour:* 10-40mm. *Speed:* 45km/hr (28 mph). *Range:* 200km (124 miles). *Maker:* conversion by Landsverk AB, Landskrona.

SWITZERLAND

PANZERKANONE 68 SELF-PROPELLED GUN *1973–*

This SP gun was built on to the chassis of the Panzer 68 tank (*qv*) but so far there has been no indication of any production of the design. The gun is a development of a Swiss fortress gun, mounted in a large square turret with 360° traverse. Shortly after its inception the Swiss bought a number of US M109s (*qv*) and it seems that the PzK 68 has got no further than the prototype stage.

Length: 6.55m (21ft 5in). *Width:* 3.00m (9ft 9in). *Height:* 2.60m (8ft 6in). *Weight* (estimated): 40,000kg (88,160lb). *Crew:* 6. *Power:* one MTU MB 837, 8-cyl., horizontally-opposed, diesel, 704bhp at 2,200rpm. *Armament:* one 155mm gun; one 7.62mm machine gun on anti-aircraft mounting. *Armour* (estimated): 10–40mm. *Speed:* 50km/hr (31mph). *Range:* 300km (180 miles). *Maker:* Federal Construction Works, Thun.

TYPE 38 TANK DESTROYER *1945–1961*

The Type 38 was a World War II German vehicle which the Swiss took over at the end of the war and used with virtually no alteration apart from a new engine. In German service it was known as the PAK 39 L/48 auf. Panzerjäger 38 (t), or SdKfz 138/2. The basis of the vehicle was the Czechoslovak TNHP light tank (*qv* LT 38 light tank) and it is interesting that it survived in service in this Swiss vehicle for so long. All data are as for the SdKfz 138.

UNITED KINGDOM

ABBOT 105mm SELF-PROPELLED GUN *1964-*

In the middle 1950s the NATO members agreed upon 105mm as the close-support artillery calibre, which meant that Britain had to produce a replacement for the 25-pdr. field gun. A self-propelled design was requested, and in order to speed up development, compo-

Abbot

nents of the FV432 armoured personnel carrier (*qv*) were used, while a completely new gun was designed. The resulting vehicle, FV433, known as Abbot, entered service in 1964 and has since formed the standard divisional support artillery equipment. It has also been adopted by the Indian Army. Abbot is a full-tracked vehicle with the engine and transmission in the hull front, with the driver alongside. The 105mm gun is mounted in a fully rotating turret and has powered elevation and traverse; the barrel is fitted with a fume

ARCHER TANK DESTROYER
1943–1952

When the British Army adopted the 17-pdr. anti-tank gun in 1942 it finally had a weapon capable of punishing any tank in existence at that time; the problem lay in getting it into the battle. No British tank of the period had space for such a powerful gun in its turret, and it was thus necessary to develop an interim tank destroyer until a suitable 17-pdr. tank was produced. The solution adopted was to take the hull and chassis of the Valentine tank (qv), by

then obsolescent but available in some numbers, build on a fixed superstructure in place of the turret, and mount the gun facing backwards over the engine deck. The result was in fact quite satisfactory – a low and compact vehicle which performed well in the North-West Europe campaign. The only drawback, apart from the lack of overhead protection, was that the gun recoiled across the driving position, so that as soon as the driver had reversed the vehicle into place, he had to waste no time in getting out of his seat or be decapitated.

Archer remained in service until the early 1950s in the British Army and proved to be the last specialist tank destroyer. A total of 665 was built.

Length: 5.41m (17ft 9in). *Width:* 2.75m (9ft 0½in). *Height:* 2.23m (7ft 4in). *Weight:* 14,991kg (33,050lb). *Crew:* 4. *Power:* GMC Diesel, 6-cyl., 192bhp at 1,900rpm. *Armament:* one 17-pdr. gun Mk. 1 with 39 rounds. *Armour:* 8–60mm. *Speed:* 32km/hr (20mph). *Range:* 160km (100 miles). *Maker:* Vickers Ltd., Elswick.

---

extractor and muzzle brake, and loading is aided by a power rammer and semi-automatic breech. Access to the fighting compartment is by doors in the rear of the turret and hull. The gun fires British ammunition, but can be exchanged for a similar gun chambered to accept standard American 105mm ammunition, thus simplifying supply in areas of the world with US affiliations. A flotation screen is permanently fitted to the hull and in water the vehicle is propelled by paddle action of its tracks.

Length: 5.70m (18ft 8¾in). *Width:* 2.64m (8ft 8in). *Height:* 2.48m (8ft 2in). *Weight:* 16,556kg (36,500lb). *Crew:* 4. *Power:* Rolls-Royce K60, 6-cyl., vertically-opposed, multi-fuel, 240bhp at 2,750rpm. *Armament:* one 105mm Gun L13 with 40 rounds. *Armour:* 6–12mm. *Speed:* 48km/hr (30mph). *Range:* 390km (245 miles). *Maker:* Vickers Ltd., Elswick.

Alecto

ALECTO 95mm SELF-PROPELLED HOWITZER 1944

In 1942 the British developed a 95mm howitzer, and one of its intended roles was as a light self-propelled gun for use as direct support of infantry. Search for a suitable chassis took some time, as did the development of the howitzer, and eventually, in 1944, it was decided to adapt the chassis and hull of the Harry Hopkins light tank. This was a development of the Tetrarch (qv) of which 100 had been built but which were never issued for service. The turret was removed and the hull modified into an open-topped structure into which the howitzer was frontally mounted. The driver, unusually, sat behind the howitzer, in a slightly raised cupola on the centre line of the vehicle. The crew were somewhat cramped, and protection was minimal, but by the time the design was perfected the war in Europe had ended and Alecto was not brought into service. A second version, mounting the 25-pdr. gun, was also proposed but was never developed.

Length: 4.34m (14ft 3in). *Width:* 2.69m (8ft 10in). *Height:* 1.87m (6ft 2in). *Weight:* 8,128kg (17,920lb). *Crew:* 4. *Power:* Meadows, 12-cyl., horizontally-opposed, petrol, 165bhp at 2,700rpm. *Armament:* one 95mm Howitzer Mk 3 with 20 rounds. *Armour:* 10mm. *Speed:* 48km/hr (30mph). *Range:* 195km (120 miles). *Maker:* not known.

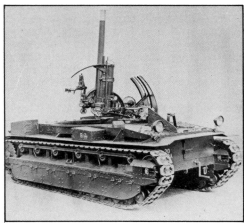

Birch Gun

BIRCH GUN 18-pdr. SELF-PROPELLED GUN 1925–1934

The Birch Gun was a self-propelled 18-pdr. field gun, developed jointly by Vickers and the Royal Arsenal between 1925 and 1928. The basic chassis was that of the Vickers Medium C tank (qv), and in place of the turret there was a special conical turret mounting an 18-pdr. gun. This configuration, however, led to an overweight vehicle and it also restricted the gun's elevation so that the full fighting range could not be reached. A second version was then developed in which the gun was pedestal-mounted in the hull and carried only a light shield to protect the crew. This was lighter, and also allowed the gun to elevate to 80° so that in addition to its field role it could function as an anti-aircraft weapon.

Eight Birch Guns were built in 1926 and issued to the Experimental Mechanized Force; the name was derived from General Sir Noel Birch, then Master-General of the Ordnance. The exercises held by the Mechanized Force led to a redesign, removing the anti-aircraft function and improving the anti-tank capability of the gun; this reached the wooden mock-up stage, but at the end of 1928 the Mechanized Force was disbanded, the Birch guns withdrawn, and they were made obsolete in 1934.

Length: 5.58m (18ft 4in). *Width:* 2.54m (8ft 4in). *Height:* 2.05m (6ft 9in). *Weight:* 9,955kg (21,947lb). *Crew:* 5. *Power:* Sunbeam, 6-cyl., petrol, 132bhp. *Armour:* 6mm. *Armament:* one 18-pdr. gun Mark 5 with 20 rounds. *Speed:* 45km/hr (28mph). *Maker:* Royal Arsenal, Woolwich.

Deacon

BISHOP 25-pdr. SELF-PROPELLED GUN
1942–1943
After experiencing the effects of German self-propelled artillery in the Western Desert, the British Army demanded a similar weapon, and as a hasty solution, Bishop was devised and issued in mid-1942. It consisted of a Valentine tank (*qv*) with the turret removed and replaced by a large armoured box, rigidly mounted, carrying the standard 25-pdr. field gun. Due to the confines of the box the gun could not achieve maximum elevation and therefore its range was restricted to 5,852m (6,400yd), less than half the range it could reach on the normal field carriage. The crew were severely hampered in their work by the space within the box, but in

spite of these drawbacks the gun proved reasonably successful and was used in North Africa, Sicily and in the first few weeks of the Italian campaign. Thereafter it was replaced by the American M7 Priest (*qv*). Perhaps the most useful function of Bishop was as an instructional vehicle to teach regiments the rudiments of self-propelled gun tactics.

Length: 5.53m (18ft 2in). *Width:* 2.62m (8ft 7½in). *Height:* 2.76m (9ft 1in). *Weight:* 17,476kg (38,528lb). *Crew:* 4. *Armament:* one 25-pdr. gun Mk 2 with 32 rounds. *Armour:* 8–60mm. *Power:* GMC Diesel, 6-cyl., 162bhp at 1,900rpm. *Speed:* 24km/hr (15mph). *Range:* 145km (90 miles). *Maker:* Vickers Ltd., Elswick.

Bishop

DEACON 6-pdr. TANK DESTROYER
1942–1944
Deacon was one of the British Army's few ventures into the tank destroyer field, and was probably inspired by similar designs appearing in the USA. It was developed in 1942 as a highly mobile anti-tank equipment for use in the Western Desert, and consisted of an AEC Matador truck chassis carrying a 6-pdr. gun on the cargo bed. The gun was protected by a squared-off shield unit covering front and sides, and the truck cab was lightly armoured.

Although serviceable enough, Deacon was high and difficult to conceal, and had a poor cross-country performance. A total of 175 were built and issued to divisional anti-tank regiments on the basis of one battery of Deacons per regiment to be used as a mobile reserve. They were used in combat throughout the latter part of the desert campaign with some success, but were thereafter withdrawn from service and were eventually sold to Turkey.

Length: 6.55m (21ft 6in). *Width:* 2.43m (8ft 0in). *Height:* 3.09m (10ft 2in). *Weight:* 12,190kg (26,875lb). *Crew:* 4. *Power:* AEC, 6-cyl., diesel, 7,580cc, 95bhp at 1,780rpm. *Armament:* one 6-pdr. gun Mk. 1 with 24 rounds. *Armour:* 10mm. *Speed:* 40km/hr (25mph). *Range:* 250km (155 miles). *Maker:* AEC, Southall.

FALCON ANTI-AIRCRAFT TANK *1976-*
Falcon is an anti-aircraft tank based on the hull of the Abbot self-propelled gun (*qv*) but carrying a turret which mounts two 30mm Hispano/Oerlikon automatic guns. The guns and their ammunition feed are in a separate compartment in the front of the turret so as to

prevent fumes entering the operating section in which the commander and gunner sit. The gunner has an optical sight and controls the elevation of the guns and traverse of the turret by a two-way joystick. A laser rangefinder feeds information to a fire-control computer which calculates aim-off and adjusts the sight accordingly. Fire-control radar information can also be fed to the computer when available. The twin guns have a rate of fire of 1,300 rounds a minute and an effective range against aircraft of about 3,000m (9,842ft). Falcon is currently being evaluated by the British and other armies.

Length: 5.33m (17ft 6in). *Width:* 2.64m (8ft 8in). *Height:* 2.51m (8ft 3in). *Weight:* 15,850kg (34,943lb). *Crew:* 3. *Power:* Rolls-Royce K60, 6-cyl., vertically-opposed, petrol, 213bhp at 3,750rpm. *Armament:* twin Hispano HSS831L 30mm cannon with 620 rounds. *Armour:* 6–12mm. *Speed:* 48km/hr (30mph). *Range:* 390km (240 miles). *Makers:* Vickers Ltd., Elswick, with British Manufacture & Research Co. Grantham.

Falcon

SEXTON 25-pdr. SELF-PROPELLED GUN *1943-*

After the US Army had developed the 105mm SP M7 (*qv*), the British Purchasing Commission in the United States requested a similar mounting for the 25-pdr. While willing to design one, the Americans would not countenance producing a weapon which they would not personally use, so the search moved to

Canada. There the facilities for making the Ram tank (*qv*) were redundant and a design was worked out using the chassis of the Ram allied to an open-topped hull, into the front face of which the 25-pdr. gun was mounted in similar manner to the Priest M7. Production began early in 1943 as the Ram carrier, but the name was soon changed to Sexton in keeping with the British tradition for ecclesiastical

nicknames for their self-propelled guns.

The first 124 made were known as Sexton I; the remainder were Sexton II, recognizable by having boxes for batteries and auxiliary generators on the rear corners of the hull. Other minor changes were made as production improvements appeared, including heavy-duty bogies, a one-piece cast hull nose and a Canadian-designed track.

Sexton became the standard equipment of artillery regiments supporting armoured divisions and first saw service in Italy. It remained in service with the British and Canadian Armies until the late 1950s. Many were sold to other countries and some are still in use with the Portuguese and South African Armies. A total of 2,150 was built.

Length: 6.12m (20ft 1in). *Width:* 2.71m (8ft 11in). *Height:* 2.43m (8ft 0in). *Weight:* 25,854kg (57,000lb). *Crew:* 6. *Power:* Continental, 9-cyl., radial, petrol, 15,847cc, 400bhp at 2,400rpm. *Armament:* one 25-pdr. gun Mk. 2C with 112 rounds. *Armour:* 12–108mm. *Speed:* 38km/hr (24mph). *Range:* 200km (125 miles). *Maker:* Montreal Locomotive Works.

SP–70 (model)

SP–70 155mm SELF-PROPELLED HOWITZER *1979–*

In the late 1960s the British and German Armies began mutual development of a 155mm howitzer under the nomenclature FH70; Italy later joined in the development, and the weapon is to enter service with the three armies in 1980. Once development of the towed howitzer was well under way, work began on a self-propelled version, known as SP–70. In this design, responsibility was apportioned between the participants as follows: Germany would deal with the engine, chassis and ordnance, Britain the turret and sights, and Italy the recoil system, loading system, elevating and balancing gear, auxiliary power units and fuel system.

At the time of writing the prototypes are still undergoing various trials and little information has been released, but photographs suggest that the chassis is based on the hull and running gear of the Leopard tank (*qv*). On the hull is a fully-rotating turret mounting the 155mm howitzer and with sufficient room to accommodate mechanized ammunition handling and loading equipment. The howitzer is fitted with fume extractor and muzzle brake and has an externally-mounted balancing gear which takes the weight of the barrel and allows it to be trunnioned well forward in the turret so as to take up the minimum space. It is anticipated that SP–70 will enter service in the early 1980s, and in British service it will replace the existing American M109 155mm self-propelled howitzer (*qv*). No specifications are yet available.

Makers: Vickers Ltd., Elswick Royal Ord-nance Factories (GB); Atlas-MaK, Kiel; Rheinmetall GmbH, Dusseldorf (Germ.); OTO–Melara, La Spezia (Italy).

UNITED STATES

M3 GUN MOTOR CARRIAGE *1941–1944*

This was the first American self-propelled weapon to be used in combat. In June 1941 the Aberdeen Proving Ground was requested to adapt the 75mm field gun to a half-track carriage in order to provide a suitable mobile weapon for the tank destroyer battalions then being contemplated. The gun was put on a pedestal mount, with a protective shield, in the cargo space, and fired forward over the cab. This was standardized as the GMC M3 in November 1941, by which time a small number had been sent to the Philippine Islands. They proved effective, shortly afterwards, in dealing with Japanese tanks during the invasion. More were sent to North Africa in the Torch landings late in 1942, where they did rather less well against German armour. The fundamental defect was that the gun dated from 1897 and was no longer sufficient to cope with modern armour. The M3 was reclassified in March 1944 and declared obsolete in September.

Length: 6.23m (20ft 5½in). *Width:* 2.15m (7ft 1in). *Height:* 2.50m (8ft 2½in). *Weight:* 9,072kg (20,000lb). *Crew:* 5. *Power:* White 160AX, 6-cyl., petrol, 6,326cc, 128bhp at 2,800rpm. *Armament:* one 75mm M1897A4 gun with 59 rounds. *Armour:* 6–12mm. *Speed:* 72km/hr (45mph). *Range:* 320km (200 miles). *Maker:* Autocar Co., Ardmore, Pa.

M6 GUN MOTOR CARRIAGE *1942-1944*

When the US Army evolved the tank destroyer philosophy, many different guns were experimentally put on many different chassis in the search for the right combination of mobility and firepower. The principal problem was production, however, and thus any idea which used a contemporary gun and a mass-produced chassis had a good chance of acceptance, irrespective of its tactical worth. Such a combination was the GMC M6, a standard 37mm anti-tank gun pedestal-mounted in the cargo bed of a Dodge ¾-ton weapons carrier (*qv*). It was standardized in February 1942 and the official description said that 'it depended

M3 GMC

M6 GMC

on its speed to travel quickly to a point of vantage, deliver firepower sufficient to knock out a light tank, and retire before heavier firepower could be concentrated against it.' This was a laudable intention, but by 1942 the 37mm was an outdated weapon, there were fewer light tanks in the enemy order of battle, and a vehicle as devoid of protection as the M6 needed very little fire to damage it. Production reached a total of 5,380, but by November 1943 all but 100 of these had been recalled and dismantled, the chassis being converted back to normal

cargo truck use. The remaining 100 were replaced by the M8 armoured car in 1944.
Length: 4.52m (14ft 10in). *Width:* 1.91m (6ft 3½in). *Height:* 2.08m (6ft 10in). *Weight:* 3,334kg (7,350lb). *Crew:* 4. *Power:* Dodge T214, 6-cyl., petrol, 3,773cc, 94bhp at 3,300rpm. *Armament:* one 37mm gun M3 with 80 rounds. *Armour:* nil. *Speed:* 88km/hr (55mph). *Range:* 385km (240 miles). *Makers:* Fargo Div., Chrysler Motor Corp. Detroit, Mich.; Dodge Div., Chrysler Motor Corp. Detroit, Mich.

M7 HOWITZER MOTOR CARRIAGE (PRIEST) *1942–1960*

In October 1941 Major-General Jacob L. Devers, Chief of the US Armored Force, recommended manufacture of two prototype SP howitzers to mount the standard 105mm weapon on the chassis of the M3 medium tank (*qv*). These were built by the Baldwin Locomotive Company and tested in February 1942. Various small modifications were agreed, including the addition of an armour-protected anti-aircraft machine gun mount at the right front of the hull, a structure which, resembling a pulpit, led to the vehicle being nicknamed Priest by the British Army. Standardized as the M7 in April 1942, it went into immediate production and a total of 3,490 was made before production ended in July 1945.

The M7 used the lower hull and running gear

of the M3 tank, to which a raised, open-topped superstructure was added. Into this went a modification of the normal split-trail carriage of the 105mm howitzer, fitted so as to allow 45° traverse and 35° elevation. In addition to the M7, an M7B1 version was built, differing only in using the M4A3 medium tank (*qv*) chassis as its basis. Like the later M7s, the M7B1 had the lower hull made of soft steel instead of armour plate as an economy measure.

During the Korean War a number of M7B1s were modified by raising the howitzer mount to allow 65° elevation; these became the M7B2. After being removed from US service, several of these were employed by the Austrian Army.
Length: 6.01m (19ft 9in). *Width:* 2.87m (9ft 5in). *Height:* 2.94m (9ft 8in). *Weight:* 22,950kg (50,600lb). *Crew:* 7. *Power:* Continental, 9-cyl., radial, petrol, 15,947cc, 400bhp

at 2,400rpm. *Armament:* one 105mm howitzer M2A1 with 69 rounds. *Armour:* 12–108mm. *Speed:* 38km/hr (24mph). *Range:* 190km (120 miles). *Makers:* American Locomotive Co. Schenectady, NY. (3,314 built); Federal Machine & Welder Co. Chicago, Ill. (176 built).

M8 HOWITZER MOTOR CARRIAGE
1942–1944

Early in 1942 the US Armored Force asked for a close support tank to work with medium tank battalions. To satisfy this demand the M5 (Stuart) light tank (*qv*) was modified to mount a 75mm field howitzer. The first attempt had an open-topped superstructure resembling a scaled-down M7 (*qv*), but this was thought to give insufficient protection to the crew and, moreover, demanded too much modification to the basic tank. Eventually a new turret, mounting the 75mm howitzer, was developed to fit into the turret ring of the M5 tank, and the resulting vehicle became the HMC M8.

Production reached 1,778 in 1942–4 and they were widely used by armoured formations in both the Pacific and European theatres until superseded in 1944. In general, the only serious defect of the M8 was its poor capacity for ammunition, for which reason it was usually fitted with a towing hook for an ammunition trailer.

Length: 4.41m (14ft 6in). *Width:* 2.24m (7ft 4½in). *Height:* 2.32m (7ft 7½in). *Weight:* 15,685kg (34,580lb). *Crew:* 4. *Power:* twin Cadillac V–8, petrol, each 5,670cc, total 220bhp at 4,000rpm. *Armament:* one 75mm howitzer M2 with 46 rounds. *Armour:* 10–28mm. *Speed:* 56km/hr (35mph). *Range:* 210km (130 miles). *Maker:* Cadillac Div. of General Motors Corp. Detroit, Mich.

M12 GUN MOTOR CARRIAGE
1943–1945

In June 1941 the US Ordnance Department announced that it had made studies of a proposal to mount a 155mm medium gun on to a tracked chassis derived from the M3 medium tank (*qv*). The US Field Artillery was not, at that time, contemplating the use of self-propelled weapons, but it agreed to the production of a pilot model. After testing, this was approved for service as the M12 and 100 vehicles were ordered, delivery being completed by March 1943.

Having got them, Army Ground Forces were unsure of what to do with them and put most in store, issuing a few as training guns. But in December 1943, when planning for the invasion of Europe was under way, a powerful self-propelled gun seemed a useful proposition, and 74 were refurbished and put into service. They subsequently proved extremely effective weapons, being able to keep medium artillery support in contact with fast-moving columns of armour.

The M12 consisted of an M3 chassis with the engine moved forward so as to leave a working space at the rear of the hull. Into this space a 155mm Gun M1917 or M1918 was mounted. The rear of the hull carried a heavy spade, resembling a bulldozer blade, which could be lowered to the ground to resist the firing shock. Six men rode on the carriage; the remainder of

M9 AND M10 GUN MOTOR CARRIAGE 1942–

In December 1941 the US Army began organizing a Tank Destroyer Force, having decided to develop specialist anti-tank troops to deal with enemy armour while the combat tanks exploited breakthroughs in support of the infantry. This doctrine demanded a mobile and powerfully armed vehicle, and the first suitable design to be standardized, in April 1942, was the GMC M9, a modification of the M3 tank (*qv*), mounting a 3in gun in an open-topped superstructure resembling the M7 Priest (*qv*). But the M9 was not mobile enough and it was belatedly discovered that there were only 27 3in gun barrels available, so in August the approval was cancelled.

Meanwhile the Tank Destroyer Board had

M8 Howitzer Motor Carriage

M12 Gun Motor Carriage

the gun squad, together with more ammunition, rode in a M30 cargo carrier, which was simply an M12 without the gun.

Length: 6.76m (22ft 2½in). *Width:* 2.67m (8ft 9in). *Height:* 2.88m (9ft 5½in). *Weight:* 26,762kg (59,000lb). *Crew:* 6. *Power:* Continental, 9-cyl., radial, petrol, 15,947cc, 400bhp at 2,400rpm. *Armament:* one 155mm Gun M1917 or M1918 with 10 rounds. *Armour:* 10–50mm. *Speed:* 38km/hr (24mph). *Range:* 225km (140 miles). *Makers:* Pressed Steel Car Co. Pittsburgh, Pa. (100); Baldwin Locomotive Co. Philadelphia, Pa. (74 refurbished).

M13–M16 MULTIPLE GUN MOTOR CARRIAGES *1942–1955*

The American Army's dedication to mechanization, taken together with reports from Europe of the effects of German aircraft in support of ground operations, led inevitably to a requirement for light, fast-firing anti-aircraft guns capable of travelling with and

M13 Multiple Gun Motor Carriage

protecting moving columns of vehicles. Various types of experimental vehicle-mounted machine guns had been tried in the 1930s, but in 1941 the standard half-track M3 (*qv*) was

M15 Al Multiple Gun Motor Carriage

asked for a vehicle with a 360° arc of fire, sloped armour to deflect shot, a low silhouette and high mobility. The resulting design, standardized in June 1942, was the GMC M10.

The M10 was based on the diesel-engined M4A2 (*qv*) tank chassis and was armed with the 3in M7 gun in an open-topped turret. The gun was balanced by adding counterweights to the rear of the turret; the shape of these varied during production, but they always formed a useful identification feature. It was a highly successful vehicle and in order to meet demands for more the M10A1 was developed, based on the Ford-engined M4A3 tank (*qv*).

The M10 was first used near Maknassy, Tunisia, in March 1943, after which it appeared in every theatre of war. A total of 1,648 were supplied to the British Army, but in early 1943 these were refitted with the British 17-pdr. gun which had a far superior performance to the 3in. As early as April 1942 this idea had been suggested to the US Army but it had turned the idea down and went on to develop a 90mm gun vehicle, the M36 (*qv*). In British service the M10 was known as the Achilles.

Length: 5.96m (19ft 7in). *Width:* 3.04m (10ft 0in). *Height:* 2.89m (9ft 6in). *Weight:* 29,575kg (65,200lb). *Crew:* 5. *Power:* GMC, 12-cyl., diesel, 13,931cc, 375bhp at 2,100rpm. *Armament:* one 3in gun M7 with 54 rounds. *Armour:* 10–57mm. *Speed:* 48km/hr (30mph). *Range:* 320km (200 miles). *Makers:* Fisher Body Div. of General Motors Corp. (4,993 M10, 675 M10A1); Ford Motor Co. Detroit, Mich. (1,038 M10A1).

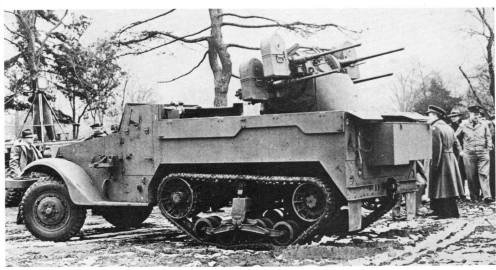

M 16 Multiple Gun Motor Carriage

settled on as the carrier, and the W. L. Maxson Company developed a power-driven mounting which carried two .50in Browning heavy machine guns. This mount was installed in the cargo space of the M3 and was provided with power from a generator driven by the vehicle engine. The complete equipment was standardized as the Multiple Gun Motor Carriage M13 in September 1942.

This design was followed by a number of improved and variant models, all based on the same combination of half-track and powered Maxson mount, differing only in the components, as follows:

M14 As for M13 but using the M5 (*qv*) half-track as its basis.

M15 An M3 half-track mounting a combination of 37mm automatic gun and two .50 machine guns, set in a rotating armoured barbette unit at the rear of the chassis.

M16 Similar to M13 but with the Maxson mount altered to take four .50 machine guns.

M17 Similar to the M16 but using the M5 half-track as its basis.

Of these vehicles, the M16 became the eventual standard model, and it remained in service for several years; numbers were used during the Korean War where they were effective as infantry ground support weapons in addition to their more normal role.

M16 *Length:* 6.50m (21ft 4in). *Width:* 1.98m (6ft 6in). *Height:* 2.23m (7ft 4in). *Weight:* 8,455kg (18,640lb). *Crew:* 5. *Power:* White 160AX, 6-cyl., petrol, 6,326cc, 128bhp at 2,800rpm. *Armament:* four .50 Browning M2HB machine guns with 5,000 rounds. *Armour:* 6–12mm. *Speed:* 72km/hr (45mph). *Range:* 338km (210 miles). *Makers:* Autocar Co., Ardmore, Pa. (M15); White Motor Co., Cleveland (M13, M16); International Harvester Co., Chicago (M14, M17).

M18 GUN MOTOR CARRIAGE (HELLCAT) 1943–

On 2 December 1941 the US General Staff recommended that a design of tank destroyer should be begun, using a Christie-type suspension and mounting a 37mm gun. By April 1942 the Ordnance Department had succeeded in persuading the Staff that the 37mm gun was obsolescent and that a 57mm should be used in its place. But after the first pilot of this design had been tested the Tank Destroyer Board demanded nothing smaller than a 75mm gun, to be fitted into an open-topped rotating turret.

By the time this had been built the Buick company had perfected a torsion-bar suspension system for tracked vehicles, and it was now recommended that a 76mm gun should be mounted on to a tracked vehicle with the Buick suspension. In January 1943 1,000 of these vehicles were ordered 'off the drawing board' without a pilot. The pilots appeared in July 1943, followed immediately by the production models. It was standardized as the M18 in November 1943 and a total of 2,507 were built.

The M18 was used in Europe in 1944–5, but its nickname Hellcat was an exaggeration, since the 76mm gun still did not have the performance to punish German heavy tanks. After the war numbers of M18s were furnished to several countries under the military aid programmes and a handful are still in service.

Length: 5.28m (17ft 4in). *Width:* 2.79m (9ft 2in). *Height:* 2.56m (8ft 5in). *Weight:* 17,032kg (37,550lb). *Crew:* 5. *Power:* Continental R975, 9-cyl., radial, petrol, 15,947cc, 460bhp at 2,400rpm. *Armament:* one 76mm gun M1A1 with 45 rounds. *Armour:* 12–25mm. *Speed:* 80km/hr (50mph). *Range:* 240km (150 miles). *Maker:* Buick Div., General Motors Corp., Flint, Mich.

M18 76mm Gun Motor Carriage

M36 Gun Motor Carriage

M19 GUN MOTOR CARRIAGE
1944–1952

Whilst the multiple gun motor carriages were eminently successful in World War II, it became apparent that an anti-aircraft weapon with greater reach and more destructive power was needed. In February 1943 Anti-Aircraft Command asked for a design based on the M5A1 light tank (*qv*) and mounting a 40mm Bofors gun, but this was refused because the M5 series was about to end production. In its place the M24 light tank (*qv*) was being developed, and work therefore began on an M24-based 40mm design; two alternatives were planned, one mounting a 40mm combined with two .50 machine guns, and one mounting twin 40mm guns. The latter design was selected and in August 1944 production of 904 was authorized, though this number was never reached.

The M19 consisted of an M24 chassis modified by moving the engine and transmission forward so as to leave room at the rear of the hull to place a rotating shielded mount carrying twin 40mm guns. The mount was power-operated and the guns could elevate to 85°. In addition to their primary role, they were provided with anti-tank ammunition and, on occasion, performed as armoured assault guns to assist infantry by shooting at ground targets.

Length: 5.46m (17ft 11in). *Width:* 2.84m (9ft 4in). *Height:* 2.98m (9ft 9½in). *Weight:* 17,463kg (38,500lb). *Crew:* 6. *Power:* twin Cadillac V–8, petrol, each 5,670cc, total of 220bhp at 3,400rpm. *Armament:* one 40mm Dual Automatic Gun M2 with 336 rounds.

Armour: 6–15mm. *Speed:* 56km/hr (35mph). *Range:* 250km (160 miles). *Makers:* Cadillac Div. of General Motors, Detroit, Mich. (125 built); Massey-Harris (Tank Div.), Racine, Wis. (160 built).

M19 Gun Motor Carriage

M36 GUN MOTOR CARRIAGE 1944–

By late 1942 the appearance of improved German tanks showed that a more powerful gun than the 3in would be required for the next generation of tank destroyers, and in October work began on modifying two 90mm anti-aircraft guns for possible use in tanks. One of these was fitted into an M10 (*qv*) tank destroyer turret and, while it worked, it was not entirely satisfactory. A new turret, better balanced and with power traverse, was designed and the Ford Motor Company built

two mild-steel pilot vehicles based on the M10A1 chassis. In December 1943 this vehicle was designated the T71 and after tests and small modifications, production of 500 was authorized. The new gun and turret were simply to be added to the chassis of existing M10A1s as they came along the production line, but it was found that only 300 M10A1s were available, the others having gone too far towards completion. To make up the required 500, 200 were withdrawn from depots and service units, returned to the factory, and converted. The 500 T71s were completed by the end of 1944 and were then standardized as the M36.

Service in Europe showed that the M36 was extremely valuable, since it was the only American armoured vehicle then capable of taking on Tiger (*qv*) or Panther (*qv*) tanks at practical fighting ranges. As a result, more were demanded and another 413 M10A1s were converted, while 187 were built by fitting the M36 turret and gun into the hull of the M4A3 medium tank (*qv*). These latter models were known as the M36B1. In 1945 another 200 M10A1s were converted in Canada, exhausting the supply, and it became necessary to convert the diesel-engined M10; these conversions became the M36B2 and 724 were built.

The M36 stayed in service for some years after the war, saw action in Korea, and was widely distributed under the Military Aid Programme.

Length: 6.14m (20ft 2in). *Width:* 3.04m (10ft 0in). *Height:* 2.71m (8ft 11in). *Weight:*

28,123kg (62,000lb). *Crew:* 5. *Power:* Ford GAA, V–8, petrol, 18,029cc, 500bhp at 2,600rpm. *Armament:* one 90mm gun M3 with 47 rounds. *Armour:* 10–50mm. *Speed:* 48km/hr (30mph). *Range:* 240km (150 miles). *Makers:* Fisher Body Div. of General Motors, Detroit, Mich. (300 M36, 187 M36B1); Massey-Harris (Tank Div.), Racine, Wis. (200 M36); American Locomotive Co. (413 M36, 672 M36B2); Montreal Locomotive Co. (200 M36, 52 M36B2).

M37 Howitzer Motor Carriage

M37 HOWITZER MOTOR CARRIAGE
1945–

Whilst the M7 105mm self-propelled howitzer (*qv*) was an effective weapon, it was thought to be overweight for the weapon it carried, and in order to develop a faster and lighter vehicle it was proposed to put the 105mm howitzer into the M24 tank (*qv*) chassis. In order to simplify construction, the M4 howitzer, which had been developed for use in the turret of the M4 tank (*qv*), was used, and this was mounted well forward so that it was unnecessary to move the engine. The general lines of the vehicle were based on the layout of the M7 (*qv*), even to the 'pulpit' for the air defence machine gun, but the vehicle was shorter and wider, allowing more working space around the gun and more ammunition stowage. The howitzer had an elevation of 45° and could therefore reach the maximum designed range of the weapon at 11,160m (12,205yd). The M37 was standardized in January 1945 and replaced the M7 in US service.

Length: 5.48m (18ft 0in). *Width:* 2.99m (9ft 10in). *Height:* 2.413m (7ft 11in). *Weight:* 20,865kg (46,000lb). *Crew:* 7. *Power:* twin

Cadillac V–8, petrol, each 5,670cc, total of 220bhp at 3,400rpm. *Armament:* one 105mm M4 howitzer with 90 rounds. *Armour:* 10–15mm. *Speed:* 48km/hr (30mph). *Range:* 160km (100 miles). *Maker:* Cadillac Div. General Motors Corp. Detroit, Mich.

M40 GUN MOTOR CARRIAGE
1945–1958

The success in combat during World War II of the 155mm SP Gun M12 (*qv*) led to a demand for more of them, but both the gun and the chassis were by then obsolescent and it was necessary to develop a fresh design, using the latest gun and chassis, a task which was begun in March 1944. Two pilot models, designated T83, were ordered, to use the latest M4 medium tank (*qv*) components – horizontal volute-spring suspension and a 58cm (23in) wide track – in building a suitable hull, and mounting the M1 155mm gun on a pedestal mount originally designed to carry the gun in a harbour defence role. The resulting vehicle was wider than the M4 tank, and had the engine moved forward with working space around the gun which was extended by a loading platform over the rear spade; as the spade was lifted for travelling, so this platform lifted and closed the rear of the working compartment.

The pilots were extensively tested and slightly modified, and production began in February 1945. It was standardized as the M40 in May, by which time two had arrived in Europe and had been proved in action. The M40 remained in service for several years after the war; a small number were used by the British Army until the late 1950s.

Length: 6.65m (21ft 10in). *Width:* 3.14m (10ft 4in). *Height:* 2.84m (9ft 4in). *Weight:* 37,195kg (82,000lb). *Crew:* 8. *Power:* Continental R975–C4, 9-cyl., radial, 15,947cc, 395bhp at 2,400rpm. *Armament:* one 155mm gun M1A1 with 20 rounds. *Armour:* 12–100mm. *Speed:* 38km/hr (24mph). *Range:* 160km (100 miles). *Maker:* Pressed Steel Car Co., Pittsburgh, Pa.

M40 Gun Motor Carriage

M41 HOWITZER MOTOR CARRIAGE
1945–1954

Although the 155mm howitzer was virtually the backbone of American medium artillery, it was not until late in 1943 that it was proposed to develop a self-propelled mounting for it. The first suggestion was to use the chassis of the M5 light tank (*qv*), but in January 1944, with the M5 production planned to end shortly, the proposal was changed in favour of a design based on the new M24 light tank (*qv*), and approval was given for the manufacture of a pilot, the T64E1. In fact the chassis design already developed for the M19 40mm self-propelled gun (*qv*) was utilized, placing the howitzer on a pedestal at the rear, surrounding it with a thinly armoured shield, and placing a heavy recoil spade at the rear. Authorization for production of 500 vehicles was given in July 1944 and the design was standardized as the M41, but in August the procurement order was cut to 250, and in the event only 60 were ever built.

The M41 was a good design, agile, and simple to operate, but it was somewhat cramped for the gunners and offered them little protection against either the elements or enemy fire. It remained in service until 1954 and saw service in Korea.

Length: 5.84m (19ft 2in). *Width:* 2.84m (9ft 4in). *Height:* 2.38m (7ft 10in). *Weight:* 18,597kg (41,000lb). *Crew:* 5. *Power:* twin Cadillac V–8, petrol, each 5,670cc, total of 220bhp at 3,400rpm. *Armament:* one 155mm howitzer M1 with 22 rounds. *Armour:* 9–12mm. *Speed:* 56km/hr (35mph). *Range:* 160km (100 miles). *Maker:* Massey-Harris (Tank Div.), Racine, Wis.

M41 Howitzer Motor Carriage

M42 40mm SELF-PROPELLED TWIN ANTI-AIRCRAFT/ARTILLERY GUN
1952–

The final stages of the war in Europe, with Allied air dominance, led most Allied soldiers to regard self-propelled anti-aircraft guns as an unnecessary luxury, and their development was largely neglected. But the Korean War showed that there was still a place for them and that they had a valuable secondary role as infantry-support assault guns, delivering a high volume of fire against field obstacles. As a result, a fresh 40mm design was begun, using the M41 Walker Bulldog light tank (*qv*) chassis as the basis. To avoid major reconstruction, the twin-gun turret was designed to fit into the hull turret ring in place of the normal tank turret. Production was begun in 1952 and continued until 1957, 3,700 being built. No longer in US first-line service, it is still used in Austria, Germany, Japan and several Middle Eastern countries.

Length: 5.81m (19ft 1in). *Width:* 3.22m (10ft 7in). *Height:* 2.84m (9ft 4in). *Weight:* 22,452kg (49,500lb). *Crew:* 6. *Power:* Lycoming, 6-cyl., horizontally-opposed, air-cooled, supercharged, petrol, 500bhp at 2,800rpm. *Armament:* twin 40mm automatic guns M2A1 with 480 rounds. *Armour:* 9–25mm. *Speed:* 72km/hr (45mph). *Range:* 160km (100 miles). *Makers:* Cadillac Div. of General Motors, Detroit, Mich.; ACF Industries Inc., Berwick, Pa.

M43 HOWITZER MOTOR CARRIAGE
1945–1955

The M1 155mm gun (towed) shared its carriage with the 8in howitzer; the different barrels could be interchanged on the same carriage comparatively easily. Therefore, when the M40 155mm self-propelled gun (*qv*) was

M43 Howitzer Motor Carriage

developed it was a logical step to mount an 8in howitzer on to the same carriage. This change was in fact done on the first pilot model of the T83 155mm gun in August 1944, and as a result the last two of the five pilot T83s were built with 8in howitzers in place and called the T89. These were completed in January 1945 and one was sent to Europe to be evaluated in combat. In November 1945 the design was standardized as the M43. A total of 576 T89s had been ordered in April 1945, but the end of the war saw this contract severely cut and only 48 were built, of which 24 were conversions from 155mm T83s by changing the barrel. They remained in service until the early 1950s, some being used in Korea.

Weight: 36,287kg (80,000lb). *Armament:* one M1 8in howitzer with 16 rounds. Other details as for GMC M40.

M44 155mm MEDIUM SELF-PROPELLED HOWITZER *1953–*

In 1947 development of a new model of self-propelled howitzer was begun in concert with work being done on a new light tank which became the M41 (*qv*). Many of the tank's suspension components were used, but a major

change placed the track idler wheel on the ground so as to provide additional support against the firing shock; the usual type of rear spade was also fitted. The chassis had the engine and transmission moved to the front of the hull, and behind this was a built-up superstructure which carried the howitzer and crew and also the driver, high up to the left of the breech. The fighting compartment was closed at the rear by swinging cartridge racks which acted as doors, and a working platform which was raised together with the spade for travelling. The howitzer was power-elevated, and had a spring-actuated shell rammer above the breech.

Manufacture began in 1952 as the T99E1, but certain modifications were made and it became the T194. In November 1953 it was standardized as the M44; a later variant, the M44A1 used a fuel-injected engine. As well as entering US service, to replace the M41, it was widely distributed under the foreign aid programmes. It was adopted by the British Army in 1956, and in 1959, after modification of the firing mechanism to suit British safety standards, it became the Howitzer 155mm L8A1. A total of 608 was built.

Length: 6.15m (20ft 2½in). *Width:* 3.23m (10ft 7½in). *Height:* 3.11m (10ft 2½in). *Weight:* 28,350kg (62,500lb). *Crew:* 5. *Power:* Continental, 6-cyl., horizontally-opposed, air-cooled, petrol, 500bhp at 2,800rpm. *Armament:* one 155mm howitzer M45 with 24 rounds. *Armour:* 12mm. *Speed:* 56km/hr (35mph). *Range:* 120km (75 miles). *Maker:* Massey-Harris (Tank Div.), Racine, Wis.

M50 106mm SELF-PROPELLED MULTIPLE RIFLE (ONTOS) *1963–1970*

Although World War II had demonstrated their limitations, there was still a weakness for

tank destroyers in some American military circles, and in 1951 work began on a new light-weight design. Once the chassis had been developed, a comparable range of armoured vehicles was proposed, but the Army lost interest; the US Marine Corps, however, could see a requirement for a light weapon capable of being landed by sea or air and this side of the project continued. To assist in reducing weight, recoilless guns were proposed, but due to the backblast from these weapons it was necessary to mount the gun outside the vehicle. Since this meant exposing the crew when reloading, multiple guns were proposed so as to allow firing several shots before the need to reload arose. Eventually, in 1963, Ontos appeared. It was a

M50 Ontos

small tracked vehicle mounting six 106mm recoilless rifles on a limited traverse turret. Two of the guns could be dismounted and fitted on tripods for ground use if required.

Ontos was used operationally by the Marine Corps in Vietnam and in the Dominican Republic, usually as a ground support weapon and rarely in the anti-tank role. The principal drawbacks were the blast, which gave away its position, and the need to reload in the open, which was more serious in the infantry support role. The vehicles were withdrawn and scrapped in 1970.

Length 3.82m (12ft 6¾in). *Width:* 2.90m (9ft 6¼in). *Height:* 2.13m (6ft 11⅜in). *Weight:* 8,641kg (19,050lb). *Crew:* 3. *Power:* Chrysler, V-8, petrol, 4,949cc, 180bhp at 3,450rpm. *Armament:* six 106mm RCL rifles M40A1C plus 18 rounds. *Armour:* 13mm. *Speed:* 48km/hr (30mph). *Range:* 240km (150 miles). *Maker:* Allis-Chalmers Mfg. Co., Milwaukee, Wis. (297 built).

M52 105mm SELF-PROPELLED LIGHT HOWITZER *1954–*

The M7 (*qv*) and M37 (*qv*) SP howitzers were both open vehicles, and in the postwar 'atomic warfare' reappraisal it was felt that all vehicles in the combat zone needed to have protection against nuclear fallout as well as against more

M44 155mm Medium Self-Propelled Howitzer

conventional missiles. In 1948 therefore, the US Army began work on a fresh series of self-propelled guns, the first of which was to fit the 105mm howitzer and equip the field artillery. This, the T98, was to use components of the M41 light tank (*qv*) then being developed. As with the concurrent M44 design (*qv*), the track idler was placed on the ground to give better resistance to the firing shock, since no recoil spade was used. The engine and transmission were in the hull front, with the rear of the hull supporting a large turret which could traverse 60° either side of centre. Into this turret went the howitzer and its crew and also the driver, his controls passing via flexible cables to the hull. Access to the turret was by doors at the rear and side, and hatches were provided in the roof for the driver, gunlayer and commander, the latter being equipped with an air-defence machine gun.

In addition to its use by the US Army, the M52, produced from 1954 onward, was also used by the German, Belgian, Greek and Japanese armies. It is no longer in first-line service with the US Army but is retained as a reserve weapon. A total of 684 was built.

Length: 5.80m (19ft 0⅜in). *Width:* 3.14m (10ft 4in). *Height:* 3.31m (10ft 10½in). *Weight:* 22,588kg (49,800lb). *Crew:* 5. *Power:* Continental, 6-cyl., supercharged, petrol, 500bhp at 2,800rpm. *Armament:* one 105mm howitzer M49 with 103 rounds. *Armour:* 12mm. *Speed:* 56km/hr (35mph). *Range:* 160km (100 miles). *Maker:* Allis-Chalmers Mfg. Co., Milwaukee, Wis.

M53 and M55

M53 155mm SELF-PROPELLED FIELD ARTILLERY GUN AND M55 8in SELF-PROPELLED HEAVY HOWITZER *1952–*
Dissatisfaction with the M40 155mm self-propelled gun (*qv*), notably in its lack of protection for the crew and lack of power assistance, led in 1946 to a demand for a new model. As with the M52 105mm, complete protection was demanded and the resulting vehicle was virtually a scaled-up M52. The engine and transmission were forward, with gun crew and driver all inside a turret capable of swinging 30° to either side of centre. Doors at the turret rear opened up and down so as to provide a working platform and a canopy, while a heavy firing spade absorbed the shock. Power ramming and shell handling were provided by an overhead runway.

As with the M40/M43 combination, it was logical to fit the 8in howitzer barrel to the same mounting, and this became the M55. Both versions went into production in 1952, but within a very short time service units were complaining of design faults and mechanical problems and almost all the vehicles had to be returned to the factory and overhauled and modified, a process completed in 1956. It was then decided to convert all the M53s to M55s by rebarrelling, a change completed by the mid-1960s. The US Marine Corps retained a number of M53s, eventually giving them up in the early 1970s. The M55 remains in service with the Belgian and Italian Armies, but has been placed in reserve by the US Army.

Length: 7.90m (25ft 11in). *Width:* 3.58m (11ft 9in). *Height:* 3.55m (11ft 8in). *Weight:* 43,545kg (96,000lb) (M53); 40,823kg (90,000lb) (M55). *Crew:* 6. *Power:* Continental, V–12, petrol, 704bhp at 2,800rpm. *Armament:* one 155mm gun M46 with 20 rounds (M53); one 8in howitzer M47 with 10 rounds (M55). *Armour:* 10–15mm. *Speed:* 48km/hr (30mph). *Range:* 258km (160 miles). *Maker:* Pacific Car & Foundry Co., Renton Wash.

M52 105mm Self-Propelled Light Howitzer

M56 90mm SELF-PROPELLED ANTI-TANK GUN (SCORPION)
1953–1971

In 1950 development of an airborne tank destroyer was begun by the US Army. Based upon the chassis of an amphibious cargo carrier, the M76 Otter, the vehicle features torsion-bar suspension allied to rubber-tyred roadwheels and a rubber track. The unarmoured hull was of aluminium and served to carry the engine, drive units and driver, while the gun was pivoted on the top of the hull. A small shield gave minimal protection to the driver and gunlayer, while the rest of the gunners stood on the ground to serve the gun. When on the move the crew appear to have hung on as best they could. As the irrefutable minimum, Scorpion could hardly be bettered. It was used by the 81st and 101st Airborne

M56 Scorpion

M107 175mm SELF-PROPELLED FIELD ARTILLERY GUN 1961–

In 1956 the US Army began development of a range of air-portable self-propelled medium artillery weapons, to include the usual 8in/155mm combination and to also include a new calibre, a 175mm gun, selected as a future replacement of the 155mm, since it offered better range and also the possibility of a nuclear projectile. This 175mm version became the M107, adopted in March 1961 and since then used by the US, British, German and other NATO and Middle East Armies.

The basic chassis and hull carries the driver, with the engine on his right front, and runs on a torsion-bar-suspended track unit. The rear of the hull mounts the 175mm gun and carries an hydraulically-operated recoil spade. The gun is power-operated in elevation and traverse, and is provided with a powered ammunition hoist/rammer unit which lifts the shell from the ground, presents it to the gun breech and then rams it.

The M107 has had a long history of malfunctions; early models were grossly unstable when fired at large traverse angles, and the ammunition gave a great deal of trouble. Much of the mechanical side had to be modified, and although it became reliable it is to be replaced in US and British service.

Length: 6.71m (22ft 0½in). *Width:* 3.14m (10ft 4in). *Height:* 3.47m (11ft 4¾in). *Weight:* 28,168kg (62,100lb). *Crew:* 5. *Power:* Detroit Diesel, V–8, turbocharged, 405bhp at 2,300rpm. *Armour:* 15mm. *Speed:* 55km/hr (34mph). *Range:* 725km (450 miles). *Makers:* FMC, San Jose, Cal.; Pacific Car & Foundry Co., Renton, Wash.; Bowen-McLaughlin-York Inc., York, Pa.

Divisions in Europe in the 1950s and 1960s and also in operations in Vietnam. It was replaced by the M551 Sheridan tank (*qv*).

Length: 5.84m (19ft 2in). *Width:* 2.57m (8ft 5½in). *Height:* 2.05m (6ft 9in). *Weight:* 5,783kg (12,750lb). *Crew:* 4. *Power:* Continental, 6-cyl., horizontally-opposed, petrol, 200bhp at 3,000rpm. *Armament:* one 90mm gun M54 with 29 rounds. *Armour:* nil. *Speed:* 45km/hr (28mph). *Range:* 225km (140 miles). *Maker:* Cadillac Motor Div. of General Motors, Detroit, Mich.

The M108 entered service in 1962 and is currently in service with the US, Belgian, Brazilian and Spanish Armies.

Length: 6.12m (20ft 1in). *Width:* 3.14m (10ft 4in). *Height:* 3.04m (10ft 0in). *Weight:* 20,965kg (46,221lb). *Crew:* 5. *Power:* Detroit Diesel, V–8, turbocharged, 405bhp at 2,300rpm. *Armament:* one 105mm howitzer M103 with 87 rounds. *Armour:* 20mm. *Speed:* 56km/hr (35mph). *Range:* 350km (220 miles). *Maker:* Cadillac Motor Car Div. of General Motors, Detroit, Mich.

itzer was being studied as a possible replacement for the existing 155mm. Moreover the current self-propelled howitzer was considered to be too heavy for air carriage and had too restricted a range of operation, so a new self-propelled mounting was also required. The 156mm proposal was abandoned, however, and the eventual result was the M109 155mm howitzer. This uses exactly the same hull, chassis and turret as the M108 105mm model, merely having modifications as necessary to accommodate the larger gun.

M108 105mm Self-Propelled Light Howitzer

M108 105mm SELF-PROPELLED LIGHT HOWITZER *1962–*

In 1953 the US Army began development of a new field-piece of 110mm calibre to replace the existing 105mm howitzer, and also began design of a self-propelled carriage for it. The 110mm, however, proved technically unsound and the 105mm remained the standard calibre. The self-propelled mounting was suitably altered and was based on components of the M113 personnel carrier (*qv*) which used aluminium armour. In general terms, the resulting vehicle resembled a tank, using a large slope-sided turret to mount the howitzer and having the driver in the hull, alongside the engine. The howitzer is provided with a fume extractor on the barrel, while all operations of elevation and traverse remain manual. Access to the turret is by rear and side doors and roof hatches, and there is also a wide door in the rear of the hull through which ammunition can be passed into the vehicle. Although not normally carried, flotation equipment is available to permit the equipment to swim rivers, propulsion being effected by paddle-action.

M109 155mm SELF-PROPELLED MEDIUM HOWITZER *1963–*

At the same time as the M108 (*qv*) began development as a 110mm gun, a 156mm how-

The M109 entered service in 1963 and has since been adopted by several countries, including Britain, Canada, Germany, Italy, Spain and Switzerland. The basic M109 had a

M109 155mm Medium Self-Propelled Howitzer

M110

prominent fume extractor and large muzzle
brake on the barrel. In 1972 the M109A1
appeared, using a longer barrel with more
slender designs of extractor and brake, a
change which gave an increase of about 20 per
cent in fighting range. Since then, most US
Army M109s have had the new barrel fitted to
become M109A1s, and the same change is currently taking place on British M109s. The
German Army, which bought 587 M109s, converted the guns by fitting a sliding-block
breech mechanism in place of the original
interrupted-thread type. The Italian Army
bought its M109s without armament and fitted
them with Italian-made guns, though these
appear to be copies of the original American
design. Swiss M109s are equipped with a
Swiss-designed automatic loader, giving a high
rate of fire.

   Length: 6.25m (20ft 6¼in). *Width:* 3.14m
(10ft 4in). *Height:* 3.04m (10ft 0in). *Weight:*
23,975kg (52,460lb). *Crew:* 6. *Power:* Detroit
Diesel, V–8, turbocharged, 405bhp at
2,300rpm. *Armament:* one 155mm gun M126
with 28 rounds. *Armour:* 20mm. *Speed:*
56km/hr (35mph). *Range:* 350km (220 miles).
Makers: Allison Div. of General Motors
Corp.; Cadillac Motor Car Div. of General
Motors Corp.; Chrysler Motor Car Corp., all in
Detroit, Mich.

M110 8in SELF-PROPELLED HEAVY HOWITZER *1962–*

This was developed at the same time as the
M107 175mm gun (*qv*) and uses the same hull
and chassis. As with the 175mm version, power
assistance is provided for elevating and traversing the weapon and a powered ammunition
hoist/rammer manipulates the shell.

   The 8in howitzer on this vehicle is virtually
unchanged from a design which originated in
1920, and although efficient and accurate in its
time, modern technology can improve on it.
This has led to the development of the
M110A1, using the M203 howitzer with a
longer barrel, and the US Army is currently
converting its M110s by installing these new
barrels, a process expected to be completed by
1980. At the same time all the 175mm M107s
will be converted, by changing barrels, into
M110A1s.

   This, though, is not thought to be sufficient,
and a completely new gun, the M110A2, is currently being developed. This has the same
length of barrel but with a muzzle brake, and is
provided with a more powerful cartridge. The
adoption of this new barrel and ammunition
will increase the weapon's range from 20.6km
to 29.1km (12½–18 miles) with the aid of a
rocket-assisted shell.

   M110 *Length:* 7.48m (24ft 6½in). *Width:*
3.14m (10ft 4in). *Height:* 2.93m (9ft 7½in).
Weight: 24,312kg (53,600lb). *Crew:* 5. *Power:*
Detroit Diesel, V–8, turbocharged, 405bhp at
2,300rpm. *Armament:* one 8in howitzer
M241E1 with 2 rounds. *Armour:* 15mm.
Speed: 56km/hr (34mph). *Range:* 725km (450
miles). *Makers:* FMC, San Jose, Cal.; Pacific
Car & Foundry Co., Renton, Wash.;
Bowen–McLaughlin–York Inc., York, Pa.

T19 Howitzer Motor Carriage

T19 HOWITZER MOTOR CARRIAGE *1942–1944*

In September 1941 the US Ordnance Department requested permission to try and develop
a self-propelled 105mm howitzer based on the
standard half-track chassis, in similar style to
the 75mm M3 (*qv*). At first refused, the
request was later approved and the project
began in October 1941. Firing trials showed
that the comparatively powerful weapon dis-

T48 Gun Motor Carriage

torted the vehicle chassis and this had to be specially reinforced. In March 1942 authority was given for the manufacture of 342 equipments, and some of these were used in the North African campaign of 1942–3. Due to the restrictions imposed by the mounting, the gun's maximum range was restricted to 10,698m (11,700yd), and the ammunition stowage space was small, but despite these drawbacks the gun performed reasonably well as a field piece, though it was less useful in the tank-destroyer role. It was eventually replaced in service by the HMC M7 (Priest) (*qv*) and declared obsolete (never having been standardized) in mid-1944.

Length: 6.03m (19ft 9½in). *Width:* 1.96m (6ft 5¼in). *Height:* 2.33m (7ft 8in). *Weight:* 9,072kg (20,000lb). *Crew:* 6. *Power:* White 160AX, 6-cyl., petrol, 6,326cc, 128bhp at 2,800rpm. *Armour:* 6–12mm. *Armament:* one 105mm howitzer M2A1 with 8 rounds. *Speed:*

72km/hr (45mph). *Range:* 320km (200 miles). *Maker:* Diamond–T Motor Co., Chicago.

T48 GUN MOTOR CARRIAGE
1942–1945
This equipment was a self-propelled anti-tank gun based on the M3 half-track weapons carrier (*qv*) and mounting the 57mm anti-tank gun, firing forward over the driver's head. Development was begun by the US Ordnance Department in April 1942 as an interim measure pending the eventual development of a full-tracked carriage, though this never appeared. The original intention was to provide the vehicle for use by both the British and US armies (since the American 57mm gun was a copy of the British 6-pdr.) but at a late stage the American Army decided against it, preferring to wait for a heavier weapon. The British agreed to take them, seeing a use for them in the Western Desert, but by the time they

eventually appeared, the desert campaign was over and the 6-pdr. had been replaced by a heavier anti-tank gun. Less than 1,000 were built; they were shipped to Britain, and almost immediately re-shipped to Russia under the Soviet Aid programme. A rare specimen survives outside the Polish Army Museum.

Length: 6.40m (21ft 0in). *Width:* 2.15m (7ft 1in). *Height:* 2.13m (7ft 0in). *Weight:* 8,618kg (19,000lb). *Crew:* 5. *Power:* White 160AX, 6-cyl., petrol, 6,326cc, 128bhp at 2,800rpm. *Armament:* one 57mm gun M1 with 99 rounds. *Armour:* 6–12mm. *Speed:* 72km/hr (45mph). *Range:* 320km (200 miles). *Maker:* Diamond–T Motor Co., Chicago.

T92 HOWITZER MOTOR CARRIAGE AND T93 GUN MOTOR CARRIAGE
The heaviest self-propelled weapons built in the United States were two 'partner pieces', the T92 240mm self-propelled howitzer and the T93 8in self-propelled gun. Development began in January 1944 using the running gear and other components of the T26 heavy tank (*qv* M26). Like the 8in howitzer/155mm gun combination, the normal towed versions of the 240mm howitzer and 8in gun shared the same design of mounting, and could therefore be similarly interchanged on a self-propelled mount. The object in view was to provide mobile heavy artillery for the invasion of Japan.

In March 1945 the designs were approved and procurement of 115 T92s and 58 T93s authorized; these figures were increased to 144 and 72 respectively in the following month. The first pilot models were completed in June and were test-fired satisfactorily, but in August, with the end of the war, the procurement contracts were cancelled and only five T92s and two T93s were built. They were used in various test programmes for about a year and then scrapped, since there was no foreseeable requirement for such weapons. No data are available.

T92 Howitzer Motor Carriage

The Belgian Minerva was one of the first
armoured cars to be produced in quantity,
commencing in August 1914. Some remained
in use until the early 1930s.

ARMOURED CARS, SCOUTING AND RECONNAISSANCE VEHICLES

AUSTRIA

ADKZ ARMOURED CAR 1938–1940

The ADKZ was an advanced design of armoured car for its day. Although it still displayed the flat armour plates of all its contemporaries and had a somewhat angular turret, it had some slope to the armour and had 6 × 6 drive with a pair of auxiliary rollers under the glacis plate to prevent it getting stuck in deep trenches. The mudguards were well rounded, though unarmoured, and the wheels carried

ADKZ

very large tyres. One particular recognition feature was a large conical ventilation dome on the forward face of the turret, between the two machine guns.

Length: 4.74m (15ft 7in). *Width:* 2.38m (7ft 10in). *Height:* 2.41m (7ft 11in). *Crew:* 4. *Armament:* one 15mm machine gun in turret; one 7.92mm machine gun coaxially mounted. *Maker:* Austro-Daimler (Österreichisches Daimler Motoren Gest.), Vienna.

AUSTRO–DAIMLER ARMOURED CAR 1904–1905

Although it was never put into production and never adopted by any army this armoured car is memorable for the fact that it was the first one to have a rotating turret and four-wheel drive. It was built as a private venture by an engineer officer of the Austro–Hungarian Army in conjunction with Paul Daimler on a special Daimler chassis. Like all the early armoured cars, it was laid out with the engine in front and the crew sitting in normal car-type seating behind. The turret was domed and mounted on a cylindrical rear portion of the body, directly over the back wheels. The original armament

was a single Maxim machine gun, but the 1905 model had two Schwarzlose guns. The Austro–Hungarian Army was not interested enough to finance the production lines, and the car disappeared.

Length: 4.86m (15ft 11in). *Width:* 1.76m (5ft 9in). *Height:* 2.74m (9ft). *Weight:* 3,000kg (6,614lb). *Crew:* 4. *Power:* Daimler, 4-cyl., petrol, 40bhp. *Armament:* one Maxim 7.92mm machine gun. Later: two Schwarzlose 8mm machine guns. *Armour:* 4mm. *Speed:* 45km/hr (28mph). *Range:* 250km (155 miles). *Maker:* Daimler Motoren, Canstatt.

BELGIUM

FN 4RM/62F AB LIGHT ARMOURED CAR 1971–

The 4RM/62F AB was specifically designed by the Fabrique Nationale for the Belgian Gendarmerie and is based on the FN 4 × 4 4RM tactical truck. It has been built in limited quantities for Belgian use, but has not so far attracted overseas buyers. It is a relatively simple and inexpensive vehicle with the minimum of sophistication and the best possible reliability. The hull is a straightforward box with the turret towards the forward end. The driver is at the extreme front, the engine and gearbox are at the rear. The turret has electric drive and there are two versions, one with twin machine guns and one with a 90mm low-velocity gun. The hull can be pressurized and is fitted with an NBC kit so that it is immune to gas attacks and Molotov Cocktails. It cannot swim, and has to carry steel channels if there is a likelihood of meeting wide ditches.

Length: 4.49m (14ft 8in). *Width:* 2.26m (7ft 5in). *Height:* 2.36m (7ft 9in). *Weight:* 8,600kg (18,954lb). *Crew:* 3. *Power:* FN Model 652, 6-

Austro-Daimler

Mors

cyl., petrol, 4,750cc, 130bhp at 3,500rpm. *Armament:* two 7.62mm machine guns in turret or one 90mm CATI gun; one 7.62mm machine gun coaxially mounted. *Armour:* 6.5–13mm. *Speed:* 110km/hr (68mph). *Range:* 600km (372 miles). *Maker:* Fabrique Nationale, Herstal.

MINERVA ARMOURED CAR *1914–1930*
During the brief period of mobile warfare in the autumn of 1914 the Belgians used motor cars to harass the German invaders. They quickly developed armour protection and the Minerva touring car formed the basis for a more or less standard pattern of armoured car. The bonnet and cab were covered with armour plate in place of the normal metal cladding, and at the back a crew compartment was constructed in the simplest manner using two straight plates and one rounded one for the back. A single Hotchkiss machine gun was mounted on a pintle. Against ordinary small-arms fire these cars were quite effective, and a few were given a 37mm Puteaux cannon instead of the machine gun. Some stayed in Belgian service until the 1930s.

Length: 4.40m (14ft 5in). *Weight:* 3,500kg (7,714lb). *Crew:* 3. *Power:* Minerva, 4-cyl., sleeve-valve, petrol, 3,600cc, 40bhp at 2,000rpm. *Armament:* one Hotchkiss 8mm machine gun. *Armour:* 5mm. *Speed:* 48km/hr (30mph). *Range:* 240km (150 miles). *Maker:* Minerva Motors SA, Mortsel.

MORS ARMOURED CAR *1915–1917*
The Mors was yet another Belgian armoured car used to harass the German advance into Belgium. It had the advantage of being of French manufacture, although it was fitted with a Belgian Minerva engine. It was a useful second string to the Minervas which had appeared first in the fighting, but the Minerva factory was overrun in October 1914 and the Mors immediately became an important asset. By 1915 the first crude attempts at armouring had been developed to a standard pattern of a high box-like structure with a single machine gun on a pintle at the rear, protected by a semi-circular shield. The driver had an armoured roof, but the remainder of the body was open. The sides were high enough for the crew to stand up in safety, but they had to climb over the top as there were no doors! Some models mounted the 37mm Puteaux gun, and at least one had a machine gun on an elementary form of coaxial mounting with the gun. Belgium sent a number of Mors cars to Russia where they operated with some success until withdrawn in 1917.

Crew: 4. *Power:* Minerva, 4-cyl., sleeve-valve, petrol, 4,392cc/3,600cc, 40bhp at 2,000rpm. *Maker:* Société. Nouvelle des Autos Mors, Paris.

SAVA ARMOURED CAR *1914–1915*
The SAVA was another of the several armoured cars that were hurriedly built in Belgium when the war started. This particular one was fairly sophisticated and certainly showed that some thought had gone into its design. SAVA built large touring cars, and they fitted the chassis of these with an armoured body mounting the conventional single Hotchkiss machine gun at the rear. Some thought was given to sloping the frontal armour and the weight was carried between the axles. After a few engagements with the German advance guards a rotating barbette was fitted for the machine guns so that the crew had some protection. Although successful, this type of armoured car did not survive the static warfare which appeared after 1915.

Crew: 4. *Armament:* one Hotchkiss 8mm machine gun. *Maker:* SAVA, Anvers.

SAVA

BRAZIL

CASCAVEL EE-9 ARMOURED CAR
1973-

The Cascavel, or EE-9, is a modern vehicle built in Brazil by the Engesa Company. It uses some of the components and techniques of the EE-11 armoured personnel carrier (*qv*) and as many commercially available parts as is possible. The result is a straightforward and reliable vehicle at a very reasonable price. The hull is made of spaced armour welded at the joints. The outer plate is harder than the inner one to improve the protection and all are sloped. The turret is French and is the same as on the AML 90 armoured car (*qv*). It also carries the same 90mm gun. In the case of Engesa it is licensed from the Belgian firm of Cockerill and made in

Engesa EE-3 Jararaca

Brazil. The suspension is unique to the Engesa range of military vehicles and includes the firm's Boomerang double-axle rear-drive which gives excellent traction and full drive to all four wheels. The hull is divided into three main sections. In the front is the driver, seated on the left with space beside him for the front-wheel drive; in the centre is the two-man turret, with access from the roof hatches; at the rear is the engine and transmission. The entire hull has an air-conditioning system which makes it impervious to the fumes of Molotov Cocktails or smoke grenades. The vehicle is in production and has been sold to Libya and Qatar.

Length: 5.15m (16ft 9in). *Width:* 2.42m (7ft 9in). *Height:* 2.3m (7ft 6in). *Weight:* 10,750kg (23,690lb). *Crew:* 3. *Power:* Mercedes Benz OM 352 A, 6-cyl., turbocharged, diesel,

5,675cc, 172bhp at 2,800rpm. *Armament:* one EC 90-1 90mm gun; one 7.62mm machine gun coaxially mounted. *Armour:* 8mm–20mm special spaced armour. *Speed:* 100km/hr (62mph). *Range:* 750km (460 miles). *Maker:* Engesa Engenheiros Especializados SA, São Paulo.

ENGESA EE-3 JARARACA LIGHT RECONNAISSANCE VEHICLE *1979–*

The Jararaca is a new venture in the Engesa range, and is the smallest so far made. It is scarcely larger than a Jeep, but carries three men with armoured protection. The hull is made from the standard Engesa double plate, welded at all joints, and has three top hatches and two side doors for the crew. All plating is sloped, and the silhouette is kept low. Although not intended as a fighting vehicle, the Jararaca can carry a variety of light weapons, including a Milan launcher or a 20mm gun, but all have to be on external mounts without the benefit of armour. The rear-mounted engine drives all four wheels, which have run-flat tyres. The speed range is impressive and cross-country mobility is said to be good. The vehicle has not so far been adopted by any country, but the prospects are encouraging.

Length: 3.88m (12ft 9in). *Width:* 2.07m (6ft 7in). *Height:* 1.28m (4ft 2in). *Weight:* 5,000kg (11,200lb). *Crew:* 3. *Power:* Mercedes-Benz, 4-cyl., supercharged, diesel, 3,874cc, 102bhp at 2,800rpm. *Armament:* various, normally one 7.62mm machine gun on external mount. *Armour:* not known. *Speed:* 110km/hr (68mph). *Range:* 600km (372 miles). *Maker:* Engesa Engenheiros Especializados SA, São Paulo.

ENGESA EE-17 SUCURI ARMOURED CAR *1977–*

The Sucuri is a large armoured car based on the experience gained with the Cascavel (*qv*) and Urutu (*qv*) vehicles. It is described by the firm as fulfilling the role of a wheeled tank, and indeed it is a large and well-armed car. The turret is the one mounted on the French AMX-13 light tank (*qv*), and it is presumed that it has the same automatic loader as is fitted to that turret. Certainly it gives the Sucuri a considerable offensive capability, to which is allied good mobility both on and off the road. An interesting point is that the Sucuri is slightly heavier than the AMX-13, though its greater hull size probably means that the car is more lightly armoured. As with all the Engesa vehicles, the Sucuri is designed to use as many commercial components as possible and has the Boomerang rear axle with an extra drive to the front wheels. The hull is divided into three compartments, the engine and driver being in the front, a middle section containing ammunition and auxiliaries, and the fighting compartment at the rear above the axle. A fairly wide range of extra items can be fitted to suit the user, and it is intended that this vehicle should be exported to those countries which need a low-cost highly-effective armoured vehicle capable of covering large distances.

Length: 6.32m (20ft 8in). *Width:* 2.49m (8ft 2in). *Height:* 2.80m (9ft 2in). *Weight:* 18,500kg (40,774lb). *Crew:* 3. *Power:* Detroit Diesel 6V 53T, V-6, supercharged diesel, 5,212cc, 300bhp at 2,800rpm. *Armament:* one 105mm gun; one 7.62mm machine gun co-

Engesa EE-17 Sucuri

axially mounted. *Armour:* not known. *Speed:* 110km/hr (68mph). *Range:* 600km (372 miles). *Maker:* Engesa Engenheiros Especializados SA, São Paulo.

CZECHOSLOVAKIA

AC30 ARMOURED CAR *1930–1937*

The AC30 does not have a clearly defined history. It apparently came into service with the Czechoslovak forces in late 1930 as a scout car and may, or may not, have survived until the German takeover in 1938. It was a long chassis with 4 × 4 drive and a sloping rear deck running back to cover the rear wheels. The stubby turret was mounted directly behind the driver and co-driver and carried two machine guns. The bonnet was heavily louvered. General mobility was bad and protection was inadequate, since the armour was hardly sloped at all. No data are available for this vehicle.

Vz30PA (TNSPE) ARMOURED CAR
1930–1940

The TNSPE was a fairly standard armoured car of conventional layout, but with good proportions and clean lines. It had the usual front bonnet, but the openings for the radiator were underneath and the air was forced in by fan. The transmission led to four back wheels and the turret was slightly forward of them so that it was nearly in the centre of the chassis. This turret was conical in shape and had a flat top. It mounted a heavy machine gun, probably a 15mm. There was a rifle-calibre machine gun in a ball mounting alongside the driver. It was fitted with particularly wide tyres for its day.

Armament: one 15mm machine gun in turret; one 7.92mm machine gun in hull.
Maker: Ceskomoravska-Kolben-Danek, Prague.

AC30

Vz30PA

FRANCE

AMX-10RC ARMOURED CAR 1978–

The AMX-10RC is the latest armoured car in France and is intended to replace the EBR series (*qv*). It is a large, heavy and sophisticated armoured car with much expensive equipment and heavy armament. The hull is all-welded and heavily sloped, particularly on the glacis plate. The driver sits alone on the left side and behind him is the fighting compartment with the large turret. The loader is on the left and the commander and gunner on the right. They

AMX-10RC

have full night-vision equipment. The engine is at the rear, together with the transmission. The six wheels do not steer, and the vehicle changes direction in the same way as a tank, i.e. each side is slowed or skidded. Each wheel can be

jacked up to alter the ground clearance, and the vehicle is fully amphibious, requiring only a trim vane to be erected by the crew before entering the water. Propulsion is effected by built-in hydro-jets. There is a tracked variant, the AMX-10C, which only differs in that it has tracks.

Length: 6.24m (20ft 6in). *Width:* 2.51m (8ft 3in). *Height:* 2.19m (7ft 2in). *Weight:* 15,000kg (33,072lb). *Crew:* 4. *Power:* Hispano-Suiza HS-115, 8-cyl., horizontally-opposed, supercharged, diesel, 280bhp at 3,000rpm. *Armament:* one 105mm gun; one 7.62mm machine gun mounted coaxially. *Armour:* not known. *Speed:* 85km/hr (53mph). *Range:* 800km (500 miles). *Maker:* Atelier de Construction, Roanne.

Charron

CHARRON ARMOURED CAR *1902–1916*
The firm of Charron built what is probably the first actual armoured car in 1902 when they put some light armour plate around the chassis of one of their touring cars and installed a machine gun. They developed this idea until, in 1904, they produced a design with a rotating turret, mounting a single machine gun. The Austrian Daimler design (*qv*) preceded the Charron, but the Charron was more successful in commercial sales and several were bought by the Russians, Turks and French. The Charron had large window openings in the hull with shields to cover them, and the generous-sized roof could be opened above the driver to give him a clear view when not in action. Like all the early armoured cars the Charron suffered from an overloaded chassis, inadequate tyres and two-wheeled drive, but it was as good as any other armoured car of the time. The French Army used some as mobile anti-aircraft guns, mounting a high-angle 75mm gun or an 11mm Hotchkiss machine gun.

Crew: 4. *Power:* Charron, 4-cyl., petrol, 30bhp. *Armament:* one Hotchkiss 8mm machine gun. *Armour:* 5mm. *Maker:* Automobiles Charron, Puteaux, Seine.

EBR-75 ARMOURED CAR *1950–*
The EBR (Engin Blindé de Reconnaissance) was designed immediately after the war, using as a basis a machine that had been conceived in 1939. The prototype appeared in 1948 and production started in 1950, a remarkable achievement in the conditions of post-war France. Manufacture ceased in 1960, by when about 1,200 had been made. It is a large vehicle with eight wheels. It normally runs on the outer four, and can steer with either two or four of them. The centre four are lowered for cross-country movement, and are driven also. They give the car excellent mobility with low ground pressure. The engine is in the centre, below the floor, and has gearing that will drive the vehicle in either direction at the same speed. There are two drivers, one at each end, and in normal running the rear driver acts as the radio operator. For an emergency withdrawal the rear driver takes over and drives the car in exactly the same way, and with identical controls, as if it was going forwards. The EBR is armed with the FL-11 turret from the AMX-

13 tank (*qv*), which is an oscillating type, but the car does not have the automatic loader. Later versions have the FL-10 turret with a 90mm gun. Both versions have a single machine gun in the floor of each driving compartment, firing forwards and controlled by the drivers. Although they are large, heavy, and fairly complicated, these armoured cars have proved to be most effective in the conflicts in which France has been engaged over the past 30 years. They are now being phased out in favour of the new AMX-10RC (*qv*).

Length: 6.15m (20ft 2in). *Width:* 2.42m (7ft 11in). *Height:* 2.34m (7ft 7in). *Weight:* 13,500kg (29,760lb). *Crew:* 4. *Power:* Panhard, 12-cyl., horizontally-opposed, air-cooled, petrol, 200bhp at 3,700rpm. *Armament:* one 75mm gun; one 7.62mm machine gun coaxially mounted; two 7.62mm machine guns, one in each driver's cockpit. *Armour:* 8–15mm. *Speed:* 105km/hr (65mph). *Range:* 650km (400 miles). *Maker:* Société Anonyme des Anciennes Établissements Panhard et Levassor, Reims.

HOTCHKISS ARMOURED CAR *1909*
The Hotchkiss was one of the many attempts by ordinary car firms to produce something that was attractive to the military authorities in

Hotchkiss Armoured Car

order to boost their sales. The Hotchkiss car was a production touring car with the back seats removed and an open-topped circular shield of armour plate mounted above the back wheels. In this shield was a machine gun on a pintle. The driver and engine were completely unarmoured and in the open. Four models were bought by Turkey, the only buyer.

Crew: 4. *Armament:* one Hotchkiss 8mm machine gun. *Maker:* Hotchkiss et Cie, Paris.

HOTCHKISS RECONNAISSANCE VEHICLE *1954–*
In the early 1950s the Hotchkiss firm developed a series of tracked vehicles to a contract from the French Army. In the event the French did not take them and they were sold to Germany, where they were in service until very recently and where some of the variants are

still running. The construction is of a fairly
normal pattern: welded hull, engine in the
front, and drive to the front sprocket. There is a
fairly high body with a small turret on top. The
suspension is by torsion bars and the track is of
alloy with rubber treads. The fittings are rather
simple by modern standards and there is
neither NBC protection nor can the vehicle
swim. In the German Army the basic vehicle
was used in several different variants, all using
the same chassis. There was an ambulance, a
mortar carrier, a command car and a cargo
carrier.

Length: 4.51m (14ft 8in). *Width:* 2.31m (7ft
6in). *Height:* 1.97m (6ft 5in). *Weight:* 8,200kg
(18,072lb). *Crew:* 5. *Power:* Hotchkiss, 6-cyl.,
petrol, 164bhp at 3,900rpm. *Armament:* one
20mm Hispano-Suiza cannon. *Armour:*
8–15mm. *Speed:* 58km/hr (36mph). *Range:*
390km (242 miles). *Maker:* Hotchkiss-Brandt,
Paris.

Hotchkiss Reconnaissance Vehicle

PANHARD AMD 178 ARMOURED CAR
1935–1960
The AMD (Automitrailleuse de Découverte)
was the successor to the wartime Laffly-White
(*qv*) which by 1930 was well out of date. The
prototype 178 appeared in 1933 and entered
service with the French Army in 1935. It was a
good design, with a simple, clean outline and
the interior divided into a fighting and an
engine compartment. The armour was reasonably sloped, though the construction used
rivets, and the performance was good. Armament consisted of a 25mm gun with a coaxial
machine gun, but some had twin machine guns.
Many of these cars were taken over by the Germans in 1940 and were used for internal security duties, but sufficient numbers survived
the war to be taken back by the French in 1945.
Production was then resumed by Panhard, so
that the 178 once again became the standard
armoured car of the French Army and
remained so until replaced by the Panhard
EBR (*qv*). One of the features of the vehicle
was that it had a rear-facing driver and could go
as fast backwards as forwards.

Length: 4.57m (15ft). *Width:* 2.23m (7ft
4in). *Height:* 2.33m (7ft 8in). *Weight:*
14,500kg (31,967lb). *Crew:* 3. *Power:* Renault,
4-cyl., petrol, 180bhp. *Armament:* one 25mm
gun and one 7.5mm machine gun mounted

AMD 178

PANHARD AML ARMOURED CAR
1960–
The AML was developed in the late 1950s to
meet a French Army requirement for a lighter
car than the EBR (*qv*). The first production
models were delivered in 1960 and since then
about 3,000 have been built and exported to
most countries in the world. It is built under
licence in South Africa and is standard equipment in armies from the Far East to South
America. One reason for its success is that it is
a relatively simple vehicle which is capable o
adaptation to many different roles. The hull is
welded steel box with the driver in front,
fighting compartment in the middle and th
engine at the rear. There are doors on each sid
for the crew, and two more in the back fo
access to the engine. The most usual version i
fitted with a 90mm gun which is housed in
large, low turret which takes up most of the to
deck, however there are many different arma
ment fits and different turrets to accommodat

coaxially or two 7.5mm machine guns or one 47mm gun and one 7.5mm machine gun mounted coaxially (this armament was included in models built in the period 1945–60). *Armour:* 6–18mm. *Speed:* 72km/hr (45mph). *Range:* 300km (146 miles). *Maker:* Société Anonyme des Anciennes Etablissements Panhard et Levassor, Reims.

PEUGEOT ARMOURED CARS
1916–1918
The Peugeot company built armoured cars from the start of the war, using the then normal techniques of mounting a machine gun on a pintle and surrounding it with an armoured shield. In 1916 they took the 18hp standard touring-car chassis and fitted twin rear wheels. On to this was built a square box-like structure

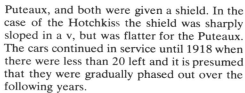
Peugeot Armoured Car

with a gun above the level of the sides. This gun was either a Hotchkiss machine gun or a 37mm

hem. It can for instance, have twin 20mm anti-aircraft cannon, a single 30mm automatic gun, single 20mm cannon and a 60mm gun-mortar, or SS-11 or SS-12 anti-tank missiles. Another option offered by Panhard is a flotation kit consisting of bolt-on boxes filled with foam plastic and a bow screen. Propellers can also be fitted and then the water speed is 7km/hr (3¾–4⅓mph). Without the propellers the speed is much slower, since the wheels are then used for propulsion.

Length: 3.79m (12ft 5in). *Width:* 1.98m (6ft 6in). *Height:* 2.07m (6ft 10in). *Weight:* 5,500kg (12,125lb). *Crew:* 3. *Power:* Panhard Model 4 HD, 4-cyl., petrol, 90bhp at 4,700rpm. *Armament:* one 90mm gun; one 7.62mm machine gun coaxially mounted; one 7.62mm machine gun on turret roof. *Armour:* 8–12mm. *Speed:* 100km/hr (62mph). *Range:* 600km (372 miles). *Maker:* Société de Constructions Mécaniques Panhard et Levassor, Paris.

Puteaux, and both were given a shield. In the case of the Hotchkiss the shield was sharply sloped in a v, but was flatter for the Puteaux. The cars continued in service until 1918 when there were less than 20 left and it is presumed that they were gradually phased out over the following years.

Crew: 4. *Power:* Peugeot, 4-cyl., petrol, 2,800cc, 30bhp. *Armament:* one Hotchkiss 8mm machine gun or one 37mm gun. *Maker:* Société Anonyme des Autos et Cycles Peugeot, Issy-les-Moulineaux.

Renault Armoured Car

RENAULT ARMOURED CAR *1914–1918*
The firm of Renault was well established before World War I and by 1914 was building about 20 per cent of all the motor vehicles in France. By November 1914 the factory at Billancourt had standardized on an armoured car, using a lorry chassis fitted with twin rear wheels. The body was built up from flat plate and was fairly simple in its construction, with an open top and a single machine gun mounted on a pintle at the rear. However, the Renault was also standardized with the 37mm gun and quite large numbers of them were turned out. The attrition rate must have been high as very few were still on charge when the war ended, and these were quickly disposed of.

Crew: 3–4. *Power:* Renault, 4-cyl., petrol, 4,600cc, 38bhp. *Armament:* one Hotchkiss 8mm machine gun or one 37mm Puteaux gun. *Maker:* Renault Frères, Billancourt.

Renault Autocanon

RENAULT 47mm AUTOCANON *1916*
The Renault autocanon is perhaps more properly a self-propelled gun rather than an armoured car, but the dividing line is fine in this case, and it was used as a support armoured car rather than a gun on wheels. It was a standard Renault lorry chassis with an armoured cab. On the load platform a 47mm gun was mounted on a naval deck mount and provided with a naval-type armoured barbette. It had no forward field of fire, therefore, but it was perfectly effective when firing broadside.

SAURER ARMOURED CAR *1930–1936*
Several of these large armoured cars were made by the Saurer company especially for the convoying of lorries across the Sahara. They were bought by the Compagnie Africaine de Transports and spent their lives driving up and down the rough tracks across the northern Sahara Desert region. The chassis was a conventional lorry with a faceted armoured box on top and a small turret above the box. There were one or two of these vehicles to each convoy and reliability was of more importance than fighting ability. The armour only needed to be sufficient to stop a rifle bullet. Crew comfort was of prime importance in the desert climate, and there was ample room in the hull and plenty of ventilation.
Length: 5.96m (19ft 7in). *Width:* 1.98m (6ft 5in). *Height:* 2.61m (8ft 7in). *Crew:* 4. *Maker:* A & E Saurer, Le Lac Constance.

Saurer

VP-90 TRACKED RECONNAISSANCE VEHICLE *1975–*
The VP-90 is an unusual little vehicle, following on in the traditions of similar ones produced in France since 1945. It is an extremely small two-man tracked vehicle, open on top,

which relies on its low silhouette for its safety and concealment. The idea is that it can move across country using the smallest bits of cover and folds in the ground to remain concealed, yet can also carry a hard-hitting gun or missile with which to strike at enemy targets. The idea is attractive, but has not yet found many takers. The VP-90 has a payload of 500kg (1,102lb) and can carry a wide range of weapons.
Length: 3.58m (11ft 9in). *Width:* 1.85m (6ft 1in). *Height:* 1.05m (3ft 5in). *Weight:* 2,700kg (5,950lb). *Crew:* 1 or 2. *Power:* Citroën CX 2000, 4-cyl., petrol, 2,000cc, 102bhp at 5,500rpm. *Armament:* none fitted, adaptable to suit role. *Armour:* none. *Speed:* 90 km/hr (56mph). *Range:* 400km (248 miles). *Maker:* Lohr SA, Hangenbieten.

VP-90

White Automitrailleuse

WHITE AUTOMITRAILLEUSE *1915–1940*
In 1915 France imported the White truck from the United States, for which an armoured body was then constructed. The resulting vehicle was fairly heavy, but quite practical and it proved to be the best and most useful of all the French cars of World War I. The layout was conventional, with a front engine driving twin rear wheels, and a turret mounted on the load-carrying platform at the rear. Driver and co-driver were in an armoured cab, and the turret was enclosed. Armament was usually a 37mm gun and a single machine gun, mounted on opposite sides of the turret, an arrangement which must have made the job of the gunner unnecessarily difficult. Some had two machine guns, mounted in the same manner. There were over 200 of these cars in service in 1918 and they remained in dwindling numbers until 1940.
Weight: 6,000kg (13,324lb). *Crew:* 4. *Power:* White, 4-cyl., petrol, 35bhp. *Armament:* one 37mm gun and one 8mm machine gun or two machine guns. *Armour:* 5mm. *Speed:* 45km/hr (28mph). *Range:* 240km (150 miles). *Maker* (chassis): White Motor Co., Cleveland, Ohio.

GERMANY

Kfz 13 ADLER LIGHT ARMOURED CAR
1932–1941

In 1932 the German Army requested a light armoured car which could be used as a reconnaissance vehicle and which would also act as an interim vehicle for armoured formations until such time as more specialized cars and tanks became available. In order to keep it as cheap and quick to produce as possible, a standard commercial car chassis, that of the Adler Standard 6, was adopted and a welded steel hull built around it. This open body carried a two-man crew and a machine gun; mechanically the vehicle was purely commercial, having a front engine driving the rear wheels only, rigid axles and semi-elliptic springs. As a result, its cross-country performance was relatively poor. The centre of gravity was high, leading to accidents, and the armour too thin to withstand even small-arms fire. Nevertheless, as training vehicles they were useful and they continued to serve, even though officially obsolete, until 1944. Some were used in the 1940 campaigns and some even saw active service in Russia in 1941.

A companion vehicle was the Adler Kfz 14, which was the same car but with provision for radio and without armament.

Length: 4.20m (13ft 9in). *Width:* 1.70m (5ft 7in). *Height:* 1.50m (4ft 11in). *Weight:* 2,200kg (4,850lb). *Crew:* 2. *Power:* Adler, 6-

Kfz 13 Adler

cyl., petrol, 2,916cc, 60bhp at 3,200rpm. *Armament:* one 7.92mm machine gun. *Armour:* 8mm. *Speed:* 60km/hr (38mph). *Range:* 230km (143 miles). *Makers:* Adlerwerke AG, Frankfurt-am-Main (chassis); Deutsche Edelstahlwerke, Linden-bei-Hannover (body).

Sd Kfz 221 AND 222 LIGHT ARMOURED CARS *1935–1945*

The smallest in the German Army series of specialized and standardized chassis was the four-wheel type developed by Auto-Union/Horch. This used a rear engine, four-wheel drive, self-locking differentials, all-

Sd Kfz 231

independent suspension, and low-range gears for cross-country work. On to this chassis an armoured car was developed, to replace the early Adler cars (*qv*). The body had well-sloped sides and carried a shallow open-topped turret mounting a 7.92mm machine gun, though some were seen with anti-tank rifles in the early days of the war. The standard car was not fitted with radio, but a special Funkwagen version was built to carry long-range radio equipment.

In 1938 the engine was improved to develop more power and the turret armed with a 2cm automatic cannon in addition to the machine gun. There were also minor changes in the hull construction, and this model became the Sd Kfz 222.

Length: 4.80m (15ft 9in). *Width:* 1.95m (6ft 5in). *Height:* 1.70m (5ft 7in). *Weight:* 4,000kg (8,818lb). *Crew:* 2. *Power:* Auto-Union/Horch, V-8, petrol, 3,517cc, 75bhp at 3,600rpm. Later models: 3,823cc, 81bhp at 3,600rpm. *Armament:* one 7.92mm machine gun. Later models: one 2cm KwK 30 gun plus machine gun. *Armour:* 5–15mm. *Speed:* 80km/hr (50mph). *Range:* 320km (200 miles). *Makers:* Auto-Union/Horch, Zwickau (engine & chassis); Eisenwerke Weserhutte AG, Bad Oyenhausen (body); F. Schichau, Elbing (assembly); Maschinenfabrik Niedersachsen, Linden-bei-Hannover (assembly).

Sd Kfz 221

Sd Kfz 231 (6 RAD) AMOURED CAR
1933–1945

In the late 1920s development of a six-wheeled armoured car was begun by three major German automobile manufacturers. The first design to be accepted for service was that by Daimler-Benz, 37 being delivered in 1932. In the following year the Bussing-NAG model appeared, and in 1934 the Magirus version. About 1,000 of the various models were built up to 1936, when manufacture was stopped in favour of an eight-wheeled car. The six-wheeled cars remained in use, numbers seeing combat in Poland and France, but thereafter they were restricted to training and internal security tasks.

Apart from differences in detail, all three versions were similar, having been built to the same specification. Structurally, they were all based on their makers' commercial truck chassis, suitably strengthened. The engines were at the front, and the transmission included a forward-reverse selector which, coupled with a secondary driving position at the rear, allowed the cars to be driven at top speed in either direction. The rear wheels were dual, and all wheels had bullet-proof tyres. The body was surmounted by a hand-operated turret which mounted either a 7.92mm machine gun or a 20mm cannon. Minor variants included a Funkwagen equipped with long-range radio and recognizable by a tubular horizontal-frame aerial above the turret and rear hull.

Length: 5.80m (19ft 0in). *Width:* 1.82m (5ft 11½in). *Height:* 2.25m (7ft 5in). *Weight:* 5,500kg (12,125lb). *Crew:* 4. *Power:* Daimler-Benz, 6-cyl., petrol, 3,460cc, 60bhp at 2,800rpm. *Armament:* one 7.92mm machine gun or one 20mm cannon. *Armour:* 8–15mm. *Speed:* 60km/hr (38mph). *Range:* 400km (250 miles). *Makers:* Daimler-Benz AG, Berlin Marienfeld; Bussing-NAG Vereinigte Nutzkraftwerk AG, Brunswick; C. D. Magirus AG (Klockner-Humboldt-Deutz), Ulm/Donau.

Sd Kfz 232

Sd Kfz 232, 233 AND 234 (8 RAD) ARMOURED CARS 1936–1945

While the six-wheeled armoured car Sd Kfz 231 (*qv*) was being developed, Bussing-NAG were asked to design an eight-wheeled chassis to be used for a cross-country truck. This vehicle never appeared, but when, shortly afterwards, a requirement for an eight-wheeled armoured car was stated, the Bussing-NAG chassis was taken as its basis. It was fitted with an armoured body with turret and, since it was to take over the functions of the six-wheeled armoured car, it was originally given the same equipment number, Sd Kfz 231. It was later followed by variant models, the first of which, with additional radio equipment, became the Sd Kfz 232. Then came a more powerfully armed model with a short 75mm gun in the turret, Sd Kfz 233; and a long-range command vehicle, Sd Kfz 263.

The basic vehicle was extremely popular and successful, though it paid the price of complex

mechanical layout. The basic chassis was relatively slender, since much of the strength of the vehicle came from the armoured body; on to

the chassis were mounted two four-whee[...] bogies, all wheels of which were driven an[...] steerable. The engine, at the 'rear' of the ve[...]

Sd Kfz 234

icle, drove through a series of transfer boxes and differentials. In normal use the front four wheels steered and the rear wheels were locked; in emergencies, the forward-reverse box was engaged, and the second driver took control to drive off backwards, in which case the former rear bogie steered and the former front bogie was locked. Originally provided with a 155bhp engine, in 1939 the cylinders were enlarged to produce 180bhp and thus give better performance.

In 1940 a fresh design was requested, to have a monocoque hull upon which the suspension was mounted, and thus doing away with the separate chassis. At the same time, tropicalization was demanded, and an air-cooled engine introduced. Development was slow, largely due to engine problems, and by the time the vehicle had been perfected, the desert campaign was over. Nevertheless, the air-cooled engine proved invaluable in Russia. Other improvements in this later design included thicker armour, more fuel capacity which, with the use of a diesel engine, increased the range of the vehicle, and air brakes. This design was allotted the model number Sd Kfz 234.

Variants of the 234 series included the Puma, armed with a short 5cm gun, and an unnamed model armed with a short 75mm gun; a few trial vehicles armed with the long, tank 75mm gun were built but were not successful.

The eight-wheeled armoured cars were among the best German military vehicles and were used to the full in every campaign.

Sd Kfz 232 *Length:* 5.85m (19ft 2in). *Width:* 2.20m (7ft 3in). *Height:* 2.34m (7ft 8in). *Weight:* 8,300kg (18,298lb). *Crew:* 4. *Power:* Bussing-NAG, V-8, petrol, 7,913cc, 155bhp at 3,000rpm. *Armament:* one 20mm automatic cannon; one 7.92mm machine gun. *Armour:* 8–15mm. *Speed:* 85km/hr (53mph). *Range:* 270km (170 miles). *Makers:* Bussing-NAG, Leipzig-Wahren (chassis); Deutsche-Werke AG, Kiel (body); F. Schichau, Elbing (assembly).

Sd Kfz 234 *Length:* 6.02m (19ft 9in). *Width:* 2.36m (7ft 9in). *Height:* 2.10m (6ft 10in). *Weight:* 10,500kg (23,148lb). *Crew:* 4. *Power:* Tatra, V-12, diesel, 14,825cc, 210bhp at 2,250rpm. *Armament:* one 20mm automatic cannon; one 7.92mm machine gun. Puma: one 50mm KwK 39 gun. Sd Kfz 234/3: one 75mm K51 gun. *Armour:* 9–30mm. *Speed:* 85km/hr (53mph). *Range:* 1,000km (625 miles). *Makers:* Bussing-NAG, Leipzig-Wahren (chassis); Deutsche Edelstahlwerke, Krefeld (body); Daimler-Benz AG, Berlin-Marienfeld (turret); F. Schichau, Elbing (turret); Ringhoffer-Tatra-Werke AG, Nesseldorf (engine).

EAST GERMANY

Sk 1

SK-1 ARMOURED CAR AND SK-2 WATER CANNON 1954–

This vehicle was developed by the East German authorities in the middle 1950s as an internal security vehicle and not as a combat vehicle. It consists of a commercial Robur 30K truck chassis with the wheelbase shortened and a steel body built on top. Dual rear wheels support the extra weight. The layout is conventional, with the engine at the front, and a hand-operated turret on top of the hull which can mount a machine gun. Vision from within is entirely by simple slits and ports, no periscopes or optical aids being provided.

The SK-1 is partnered by another vehicle, the SK-2 water cannon; this is a standard six-wheeled truck with an armoured cab surmounted by a high-pressure water cannon. The rear of the truck carries an unarmoured 4,000l (880gal) water tank.

Sk-1 *Length:* 4.00m (13ft 1in). *Width:* 2.00m (6ft 6in). *Height:* 2.80m (9ft 2in). *Weight:* 5,400kg (11,900lb). *Crew:* 5. *Power:* Robur, 4-cyl., air-cooled, diesel, 55bhp at 2,800rpm. *Armament:* one 7.92mm machine gun. *Armour:* 5–8mm. *Speed:* 80km/hr (50mph). *Range:* 350km (215 miles). *Maker:* VEB Robur-Werke, Zittau.

WEST GERMANY

RADSPAHPANZER LUCHS RECONNAISSANCE VEHICLE 1975–

In the early 1960s the German Army requested development of a new series of wheeled combat vehicles, to include a reconnaissance vehicle, troop carriers and cargo carriers. A consortium of German vehicle companies set about developing the specified range, while the Daimler-Benz company began working separately on their own designs. Prototypes were delivered for test in 1968, and in 1973 a contract was awarded for delivery of 408 Luchs (Lynx) reconnaissance vehicles, the selected design having come from the consortium.

The Luchs is an eight-wheeled car with all wheels driven and steerable, though in normal use only the front four wheels steer. The armoured steel hull is surmounted by a two-man turret carrying a 20mm cannon and a machine gun, together with infra-red sighting and vision equipment and a white-light searchlight. The driver sits at the front, while the radio operator sits at the rear where he can also drive the vehicle in reverse if needed. The interior is fully air-conditioned and protected against chemical, nuclear and biological weapons, while the fuel system is bullet-proof

Radspahpanzer Luchs

and the interior fully protected by automatic fire-fighting equipment. Provision of Luchs to the German Army has now been completed; it has not been exported.

Length: 7.74m (25ft 5in). *Width:* 2.98m (9ft 9in). *Height:* 2.84m (9ft 4in). *Weight:* 19,500kg (42,990lb). *Crew:* 4. *Power:* Daimler-Benz, 10-cyl., horizontally-opposed, turbocharged, multi-fuel, 390bhp (diesel) or 300bhp (petrol). *Armament:* one 20mm automatic cannon. *Armour:* not disclosed. *Speed:* 90km/hr (56mph). *Range:* 800km (500 miles). *Maker:* Rheinstahl AG Transporttechnik, Kassel.

HUNGARY

CSABA 39 Mpcgk ARMOURED CAR
1939–1942
This car was a last fling by the indigenous Hungarian/Czechoslovak industry to produce a native design before World War II; later models of the period were built to German design. The Csaba was a small and neat little car with simple lines and sloped armour. In many ways it resembled the British Daimler Dingo (*qv*), though it carried a rotating turret and heavier armament. The driver sat in the stubby bow with the two turret crew directly behind him. The engine was immediately behind them, housed in a compartment which sloped under at the back plate. The commander had a radio and the aeriel ran around the turret in the same way as did the Soviet designs. Only a small number of these cars was built, and they apparently never saw active service.

Length: 4.49m (14ft 9in). *Width:* 2.08m (6ft 10in). *Height:* 2.27m (7ft 5in). *Crew:* 3. *Maker:* Magyar Allani Vosopor Gepgyar.

FUG-66 AMPHIBIOUS RECONNAISSANCE VEHICLE *1966–*
The FUG-66 is a further modification of the

Csaba 39

M63 (*qv*) and, apart from mounting a turret, it seems likely that there are few differences between them. However, it is significant that this vehicle should be given another type number. The two main changes lie in the turret and the fact that it has no belly wheels. In all other respects it appears to be the same as its predecessor. An interesting and perhaps not very practical feature is that the two forward hatches over the driver and his mate have no room to open in the normal fashion and they have to be swung sideways to clear the hatch opening, and in so doing they project over the sides. It seems that few of these vehicles were made and they may now be obsolescent.

Length: 5.82m (19ft 1in). *Width:* 2.31m (7ft 6in). *Height:* 2.20m (7ft 3in). *Weight* (estimated): 6,600kg (14,546lb). *Crew:* 4. *Power:* Csepel D-414, 4-cyl., diesel, 100bhp at 2,300rpm. *Armament:* one 23mm cannon in turret (some may have 14.5mm machine gun); one 7.62mm machine gun coaxially mounted. *Armour:* 10mm. *Speed:* 67km/hr (42mph).

Range: 500km (310 miles). *Maker:* Hungarian State Factories.

FUG-70 LIGHT ARMOURED CAR *1970–*
The FUG-70 is the derivative of the FUG-66 (*qv*) which may well have been the trial version of it. It is very similar to the 66 but has a full-width superstructure, which presumably allows for greater freeboard when floating and gives more room inside. It is fully amphibious, propelled by two water jets, and at the same time is fully protected against NBC and carries infra-red driving aids. The small turret normally carries a heavy machine gun and a rifle-calibre gun. It is probably intended as a reconnaissance vehicle rather than a conventional armoured car. So far no variants or derivatives have been recognized.

Length: 5.82m (19ft 1in). *Width:* 2.31m (7ft 6in). *Height:* 2.51m (8ft 3in). *Weight:* 7,000kg (15,428lb). *Crew:* 3. *Power:* Raba-MAN D-2156, 6-cyl., diesel, 160bhp. *Armament:* one 14.5mm KPV heavy machine gun; one 7.62mm machine gun coaxially mounted. *Armour:* 10mm. *Speed:* 100km/hr (62mph). *Range:* 500km (310 miles). *Maker:* Hungarian State Factories.

FUG-M63 AMPHIBIOUS RECONNAISSANCE CAR *1963–*
The FUG (Felderito Uszo Gepkocsi) is the Hungarian equivalent of the Soviet BTR-40 (*qv*) but it has a number of differences. The hull is not the same and the engine is at the rear, but it improves on the BTR by having two belly wheels for cross-country mobility and these are powered from the engine. It is fully amphibious and NBC protected and the driver has infra-red vision for night driving. Armament is light and the vehicle is obviously not meant to fight for its information; at least three of the crew can dismount and operate on foot, though to

FUG-70

do so they have to climb through roof hatches. Space inside must be restricted. There are a few variants, at least three being in Czechoslovakia, where it is used as a small ambulance or fitted with a turret mounting a machine gun

FUG-M63

and a recoilless gun. As a pure reconnaissance vehicle it is used in Romania and Poland.

Length: 5.82m (19ft 1in). *Width:* 2.31m (7ft 6in). *Height:* 1.90m (6ft 3in). *Weight:* 6,100kg (13,444lb). *Crew:* 5. *Power:* Csepel D-414, 4-cyl., diesel, 100bhp at 2,300rpm. *Armament:* one 7.62mm machine gun on external pintle, (see text for variants). *Armour:* 10mm. *Speed:* 87km/hr (54mph). *Range:* 500km (310 miles). *Maker:* Hungarian State Factories.

ISRAEL

RBY ARMOURED RECONNAISSANCE VEHICLE *1975–*
The RBY is an interesting attempt by the Israeli Military Industries to produce a light, cheap vehicle to suit the needs of both Israel and other countries for reconnaissance and general armoured-car work. It is built from standard commercial components wherever possible and incorporates some unusual ideas. It is open-topped since the Israelis have found that it is essential to see clearly in battle, and episcopes and vision blocks are not good enough. The wheels are set well out from the body to the front and rear to minimize the

effects of blast from mines. The engine is at the back, behind the crew compartment, so that the personnel are as far away as possible from the point of a mine explosion. There is no fixed armament and the crew are meant to fire with their own weapons over the top of the fighting compartment. These arrangements may well appeal to some users, but they tend to go against the trends in most countries.

Length: 5.01m (16ft 5in). *Width:* 2.02m (6ft 7in). *Height:* 1.60m (5ft 3in). *Weight:* 3,600kg (7,934lb). *Crew:* 2 plus up to 6 infantry in fighting compartment. *Power:* Dodge Model 225, 6-cyl., petrol, 120bhp. *Armament:* see text. *Armour:* 8mm. *Speed:* 100km/hr (62mph). *Range:* 550km (340 miles). *Maker:* Ramta Structures and Systems, Beersheba.

ITALY

AB 40 ARMOURED CAR *1940–1950*
The Fiat 611 (*qv*) was not really suited to the reconnaissance role and the Italian Army called for a lighter and faster vehicle. SPA and Ansaldo co-operated in designing the AB 40 and the first prototype appeared in 1939. First issues to the army began in 1940. It was a vehicle with a number of unusual features. The four wheels were all driven and all were steered. Two spare wheels were carried on the sides on free bearings so that they assisted on rough ground to prevent bellying. There was plenty of wheel movement, with relatively soft springing. Cross-country mobility was also very good. There were two driving positions, front and rear, so that the car could get out of trouble rapidly. The small turret carried two machine guns, but there was also a third facing backwards over the engine deck and fired by the radio operator. The vehicle was a success in Italian service, and minor variants were built for the new motorized divisions. These were

AB 40

the AB 41 and 43, which only differed in detail. Altogether more than 550 were issued to service.

Length: 5.20m (17ft 1in). *Width:* 1.92m (6ft 4in). *Height:* 2.43m (8ft). *Weight:* 6,850kg (15,097lb). *Crew:* 4. *Power:* SPA, 6-cyl., petrol, 80bhp. *Armament:* three 8mm machine guns. *Armour:* 9mm. *Speed:* 76 km/hr (47mph). *Range:* 400km (250 miles). *Maker:* Ansaldo, Turin.

FIAT 611 ARMOURED CAR *1935–1945*
The Lancia IZ (*qv*) continued in service after World War I, but as it aged it became necessary to replace it. In 1934 Fiat began production of an armoured car based on a current lorry chassis, the Fiat Dovunque 6 × 4 military ver-

Fiat 611

sion. When completed, the car looked very much like a larger version of the Lancia. It had the same general shape of body, with a small turret on top mounting two machine guns firing forward, and one in the rear face. In the hull was another machine gun facing rearwards as in the Lancia. An alternative version mounted a 37mm gun in the turret. The hull was fairly large and it was only really suited to internal security duties and frontier patrolling. It was used in Ethiopia, East Africa, and in Italy by the Public Security Corps.

Length: 5.68m (18ft 7in). *Width:* 1.88m (6ft 2in). *Height:* 2.65m (8ft 8in). *Weight:* 6,900kg (15,207lb). *Crew:* 5. *Power:* Fiat, 6-cyl., petrol, 45bhp. *Armament:* four 6.5mm machine guns or one 37mm gun; two 6.5mm machine guns. *Armour:* 6–15mm. *Speed:* 28km/hr (17mph). *Range:* 560km (347 miles). *Maker:* Fiat, Turin.

RBY

Lancia

FIAT 6616M ARMOURED CAR *1976–*

The 6616M is a new venture by Fiat in conjunction with the armaments firm of Oto-Melara and the first batch will be subjected to extensive trials to validate the design. It is a light 4 × 4 vehicle intended for frontier patrols, convoy escorts, airfield security and reconnaissance. It is amphibious, propelling itself in the water by its wheels, and there is an NBC system, air-conditioning, a built-in fire-extinguishing system and a powered winch. The turret has powered traverse and it is intended that the gunner should have some capability to engage aircraft targets with his 20mm gun. If necessary a TOW or MILAN anti-tank launcher can be carried, but it has to

be mounted on top of the roof, and cannot be fired from under armour.

Length: 5.24m (17ft 2in). *Width:* 2.49m (8ft 2in). *Height:* 1.98m (6ft 6in). *Weight:* 7,400kg (16,314lb). Crew: 3. *Power:* Model 806, 6-cyl., turbocharged, diesel, 147bhp at 3,200rpm. *Armament:* one 20mm cannon; one 7.62mm machine gun coaxially mounted. *Armour:* 6–18mm. *Speed:* 95km/hr (59mph). *Range:* 750km (460 miles). *Maker:* Fiat, Turin.

LANCIA IZ ARMOURED CAR *1915–1941*

The Lancia armoured car rapidly became the standard Italian armoured car of World War I and was sufficiently successful to be still in ser-

vice in the Italian colonies when World War II started. In many ways it resembled the Rolls-Royce in that it was built on a high-class large touring car chassis, utilizing a big engine and a robust chassis frame. In fact the chassis for most of them was a Lancia truck's, but it differed little from the large cars and the conversion work was done by the Ansaldo factory in Turin, a fact which has led to some confusion over the correct name. The original turret mounted three machine guns, two in the main turret and a single one in a smaller turret on the roof of the main one. Later this was removed and the third gun placed in a ball mounting at the rear of the hull. The driver was well protected by sloped armour and there were twin wire-cutting rails running over the front. The armour plate was of good quality for the period. In addition to the turret guns the crew also carried portable light machine guns.

Length: 5.73m (18ft 9in). *Width:* 1.94m (6ft 5in). *Height:* 2.37m (7ft 10in). *Weight:* 4,190kg (9,240lb). *Crew:* 6. *Power:* Lancia, 4-cyl., petrol, 5,000cc, 70bhp at 2,200rpm. *Armament:* three 8mm St. Etienne machine guns; later; three Fiat 6.5mm machine guns. *Armour:* 6mm. *Speed:* 60km/hr (37mph). *Range:* 400km (248 miles). *Maker:* Fabbrica Automobili Lancia & Co., Turin.

Fiat 6616M

Osaka Model 2592

JAPAN

OSAKA ARMOURED CAR MODEL 2592
1932–1942

The Osaka was introduced into Japanese service in 1932, the year 2592 in the old Japanese calendar. It was a design largely based on the armoured cars current in World War I and was all but obsolete on the day it was built. The chassis was a commercial 4 × 2 truck fitted with twin rear wheels. On this was built the conventional box body of thin armour plate, fitted with a small hand-powered turret, mounting one machine gun. In the first versions the driver had another machine gun mounted so that it fired forwards on a fixed line. Although suitable for internal security duties the Osaka was of strictly limited value in proper fighting.

Length: 5.00m (16ft 4in). *Width:* 1.85m (6ft 1in). *Height:* 2.63m (8ft 7in). *Weight:* 5,805kg (12,800lb). *Crew:* 3. *Power:* Commercial, 4-cyl., petrol, 45bhp. *Armament:* one 6.5mm machine gun in turret; one 6.5mm machine gun firing forward, on some models only. *Armour:* 10mm. *Speed:* 60km/hr (37mph). *Range:* 240km (150 miles). *Maker:* not known.

SUMIDA ARMOURED CAR TYPE 2593
1933–1944

The Sumida was designed by Japanese military engineers with the particular intention that it should be equally adaptable to running on railway lines or roads. It was a 6 × 4 commercial chassis with some novel modification. The wheels could be easily removed and replaced with railway wheels, carried on the sides in special clips. There were built-in jacks to speed the wheel-changing and for different rail gauges the track could be altered. On the road the

wheels were solid-tyred, so speed and cross-country mobility were not good, but in China, where the car had most operational use, its rail-running ability was most useful and it appears that it was quite effective. The layout was the usual one for the time, a front engine and a large body with a small turret on top. Armament was one machine gun, and it is possible that the Sumida was more valuable as an armoured personnel carrier and supply vehicle.

Length: 6.55m (21ft 6in). *Width:* 1.90m (6ft 3in). *Height:* 2.97m (9ft 8in). *Weight:* 7,000kg (15,432lb). *Crew:* 6. *Power:* Commercial, 4-cyl., petrol, 45bhp. *Armament:* one 6.5mm machine gun. *Armour:* 10mm. *Speed:* 60km/hr (37mph). *Range:* 240km (150 miles). *Maker:* Ishikawajima Motor Works.

TYPE 1 HO–HA HALF-TRACK ARMOURED CAR *1938–1944*

The Type 1, or Type 98 as it is sometimes confusingly known, was the one attempt by the Japanese to produce an up-to-date armoured car before World War II started. The design was heavily influenced by the Germans and in fact the vehicle was much nearer to being a ¾-track. The basis was an Isuzu lorry fitted with suspension components and roadwheels from a light tank in place of the rear wheels. The sides were armoured, but there was an open roof and

Sumida Type 2593

protection was not really adequate. Only a few were made, since the construction was more than the over-loaded Japanese industry could manage.

Length: 6.12m (20ft 2in). *Width:* 2.09m (6ft 11in). *Height:* 1.99m (6ft 6in). *Crew:* 2 + up to 12. *Maker:* Isuzu Motor Company.

Ho Ha Type I

NETHERLANDS

M 39 PANSERWAGEN ARMOURED CAR *1939–1940*
The M 39 was based on a commercial truck chassis built by DAF. The hull was well shaped and carefully sloped, though rather bulky. The

M 39

driver had a hull-gunner sitting beside him, armed with a machine gun in a ball mounting. The small turret mounted a 37mm gun and a coaxial machine gun, but there was not much room for the two men who handled these guns. The engine was at the rear and drove the four rear wheels. Cross-country mobility was apparently quite good, and to improve the vehicle's ability to cross wide gaps there were two small idler wheels at the bottom of the glacis plate. By the time the Germans invaded in May 1940 there were only enough of these armoured cars

for one squadron and they were not used in action. They were taken over by the Wehrmacht and employed in internal security duties until the end of the war.

Length: 4.63m (15ft 2in). *Width:* 2.00m (7ft). *Height:* 2.00m (7ft). *Weight:* 6,000kg (13,220lb). *Crew:* 6. *Power:* Ford, V-8, petrol, 95bhp. *Armament:* one 37mm gun; two machine guns, one coaxially mounted, one in front hull. *Armour:* 10mm. *Speed:* 60km/hr (37mph). *Range:* 300km (180 miles). *Maker:* DAF, Eindhoven.

POLAND

URSUS Wz 29 ARMOURED CAR *1926–1940*
The Ursus was a conventional armoured car built on a lorry chassis with the usual high body, though some attempt was made to slope the armour slightly. The construction was by

the usual method of bolting plates to a frame, and the rear of the hull was made of short sections of straight plate to prevent having to roll the armour into curves. The octagonal turret carried a 37mm Puteaux gun firing in front, and a machine gun which faced to the left and could only be used at right angles to the Puteaux. There was another machine gun in the rear of the hull, but apparently none firing directly forward. These cars were under cavalry control and were used in conjunction with the horsed units, but all were swept away in 1939 and there is no record of any surviving the German invasion.

Length: 5.14m (16ft 11in). *Width:* 1.79m (5ft 11in). *Height:* 2.47m (8ft 2in). *Weight* (estimated): 6,000kg (13,224lb). *Crew:* 5 or 6. *Armament:* one 37mm Puteaux gun; one machine gun in turret; one machine gun in rear of hull; *Maker:* Fabrique d'Automobiles Ursus, Czeckowice.

SOUTH AFRICA

MARMON-HERRINGTON ARMOURED CARS *1940–1946*
During the 1930s the Marmon-Herrington Company developed a kit of parts for transforming commercial truck chassis into all-wheel-drive vehicles, on to which chassis they then built a variety of armoured bodies. Small numbers of these were bought by the US National Guard as scout cars, while others were sold to various small nations around the world as armoured cars, armed to their purchaser's choice.

In 1939 the South African government selected a Marmon-Harrington conversion as the basis for a new armoured car, the conversion being applied to a standard Ford three-ton truck chassis. The kits were supplied from the United States, the chassis from Canada, and the armoured bodies were built in South Africa. In order to speed things up, the first

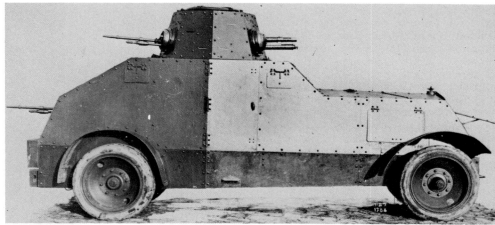

Ursus Wz 29

Marmon-Herrington Mark 3

Marmon-Herrington Mark 6

113 were actually built on to the standard chassis without the all-wheel-drive conversion. The Mark 2 cars were 4 × 4, and in their original form were provided with a hull-mounted machine gun and a second machine gun in the turret; once these cars went into action in the Western Desert this armament was considerably changed according to the fancies of the individual units, and cars were variously armed with .55in Boys anti-tank rifles, captured Italian 20mm cannon, German 37mm and Italian 47mm anti-tank guns.

The Mark 3 next appeared, using a shorter wheelbase chassis and with several improvements due to combat experience; the rear doors of the earlier model were abandoned,

the transmission and suspension strengthened and the hull machine gun omitted. This was followed, late in 1941, by the Mark 4 in which the chassis layout was radically altered by moving the engine to the rear. A much heavier turret, mounting a 2-pdr. tank gun and coaxial machine gun, was mounted. This was the most successful of the various designs.

In 1942 two further models, the Marks 5 and 6, were mooted; the 5 appears to have been an improved Mark 3, though there are few records of it, while the Mark 6 was to be a powerful eight-wheeled vehicle mounting either a 2-pdr. or 6-pdr. gun and propelled by twin Ford engines. In the event, it was appreciated that the North African campaign would be over before the Mark 6 could be put into production, and after two prototypes had been built the design was abandoned.

Length: 4.87m (16ft 0in). *Width:* 1.98m (6ft 6in). *Height:* 2.31m (7ft 7in). *Weight:* 6,290kg (13,865lb). *Crew:* 4. *Power:* Ford, V-8, petrol, 3,622cc, 85bhp at 3,000rpm. *Armament:* one 2-pdr. gun, one .303 machine gun. *Armour:* 12mm. *Speed:* 80km/hr (50mph). *Range:* 325km (200 miles). *Makers:* Marmon-Herrington Co., Indianapolis (4 × 4 kit); Ford Motor Co. of Canada (chassis); South African Iron & Steel Industrial Corp. (armoured bodies, turrets etc.); Ford Motor Co. of South Africa (assembly); Dorman, Long Steel Co. of South Africa (assembly).

SOVIET UNION

AUSTIN–PUTILOV ARMOURED CAR
1916–1920
Tsarist Russia imported a number of commercial vehicles and fitted them with armoured bodies at the Putilov Armament Works. In 1915 the works was ordered to build armoured cars using the Kegresse light track for the rear wheels, and these cars were founded on Austin chassis imported from Longbridge. Sixty were built and were successful. The layout was the familiar one for the time: a front engine, box body with vertical sides, and turret above the rear wheels. Thirty of the cars had single guns in the turret, but another 30 were given two guns, in two small turrets. The light rubber track gave these cars good mobility, and they were used well up at the front, very much in the manner of tanks. Apparently most survived the war and were employed by the Bolsheviks in their internal fighting. In winter, skis could be fitted to the front wheels and there was a rather clumsy form of extra roller that could be fitted for crossing wide trenches.

Length: 6.75m (22ft 2in). *Width:* 2.37m (7ft 10in). *Height:* 2.68m (8ft 10in). *Weight:* 5,800kg (12,787lb). *Crew:* 5. *Power:* Austin, 4-cyl., petrol, 50bhp. *Armament:* one or two Maxim 7.62mm machine guns in one or two turrets. *Armour:* 5–8mm. *Speed:* 25km/hr (18mph). *Range:* 80km (50 miles). *Makers:* Austin Motor Co., Longbridge; Putilov Factory, St. Petersburg.

Austin-Putilov

BA-10 ARMOURED CAR *1938–1943*
Throughout the 1930s the Soviet Union developed a family of armoured cars, the best ones being a series of six-wheelers starting with the BA-1 in 1932. The final one, which went into mass-production in 1938 was the BA-10 and it became the standard vehicle of reconnaissance and independent armoured units. It was not a particularly modern vehicle for its day, being a slab-sided body riveted together and built on to a military version of the truck chassis. However, it was robust and reliable and, despite the limitations of 6 × 4 drive, it served well in several different variants

BA-10

BA-27

until the German invasion. After 1941 there were few armoured cars left in service, the remainder having been lost in the first few months of the war, and such was the need for tanks that no effort was put into making more cars. One pre-war version of the BA-10 was built for railway running with flanged wheels and was used in that way in quite substantial numbers.

Length: 4.64m (15ft 3in). *Width:* 2.05m (6ft 9in). *Height:* 2.20m (7ft 3in). *Weight:* 5,140kg (11,232lb). *Crew:* 4. *Power:* GAZ-M1, 4-cyl., petrol, 50bhp at 2,800rpm. *Armament:* one 45mm gun; one 7.62mm machine gun co-axially mounted; one 7.62mm machine gun in hull beside driver. *Armour:* 6–15mm. *Speed:* 55km/hr (35mph). *Range:* 300km (190 miles). *Maker:* Izhorsk Motor Factory.

BA-27 ARMOURED CAR *1927–1936*
The BA-27 car was the first armoured car to be built since the Putilov designs of the war and the tactical thinking behind it is interesting. Finding that the new Soviet State was short of money and resources it was decided to use armoured cars in much the same way as other countries were using their light tanks. The BA series was therefore intended to provide fire support for infantry on the march as well as ranging ahead in reconnaissance. In fact, the 37mm gun in the turret was looked upon in much the same way as we should now consider a small self-propelled gun, and in the context of the time it was a perfectly fair idea. The BA cars themselves were not particularly distinguished in appearance or performance, but the 27 had the same turret as the MS light tank

(*qv*) and could be maintained much more easily than a tracked vehicle. When it was phased out of first-line service it continued in use for internal security duties, though the turret may have been changed for this. One of the drawbacks to the BA-27 was that it was only 4 × 2 drive.

Length: 4.63m (15ft 2in). *Width:* 1.81m (5ft 11in). *Height:* 2.51m (8ft 3in). *Weight:* 4,500kg (9,921lb). *Crew:* 4. *Power:* Model AMO, 4-cyl., petrol, 36bhp at 1,700rpm. *Armament:* one 37mm gun; one 7.62mm machine gun in hull. *Speed:* 45km/hr (30mph). *Range:* 400km (250 miles). *Maker:* AMO Motor Factory, Moscow.

BA-64 ARMOURED CAR *1942–1956*
The BA-64 was the exception that proved the rule, for when the war reached its most dangerous point in 1942 the Soviets turned all vehicle production to tanks and relied on US Lease-Lend trucks and Jeeps to see them through the difficult period. Armoured cars had nearly all been sacrificed in the invasion battles, and none were planned to replace them. However, the little BA-64 was put into production to fill a need for a light armoured car for commanders and their staffs, for light reconnaissance and for liaison duties. The general layout came from the GAZ-64 light cross-country car, but the angled armour was heavily influenced by contemporary German practice. The usual version carried a single machine gun in the open-topped turret, but there were innumerable variants, the most popular being a command car with radio and map boards in special fittings. One version copied the Austin-Putilov (*qv*) and had a Kegresse half-track at the rear. Others fitted 20mm cannon or anti-tank rifles, or similar rather useless additions, for the vehicle was never meant to fight. Production took second place to tanks, and was erratic until 1945 when it was stopped. Nevertheless, the little car survived in service until 1956 in the Soviet Union, and may

still be in use in some of the minor Communist armies as a police vehicle.

Length: 3.65m (12ft). *Width:* 1.52m (5ft). *Height:* 1.90m (6ft 3in). *Weight:* 2,400kg (5,290lb). *Crew:* 2. *Power:* GAZ Model MM, 4-cyl., petrol, 54bhp at 2,800rpm. *Armament:* one 7.62mm machine gun. *Armour:* 6–10mm. *Speed:* 80km/hr (50mph). *Range:* 600km (375 miles). *Maker:* GAZ Motor Factory, Moscow.

BRDM-2 AMPHIBIOUS RECONNAIS-SANCE VEHICLE 1963–

The BRDM-2 is the successor to the BRDM-1 or BTR-40P (*qv*) and it entered service with the Soviet forces within four years of the earlier one. The main differences between the two are that the later vehicle has a more powerful engine, a greater range, and a small turret, though there would also seem to be a change in the tactical use as well. The crew is reduced to four, which does not really allow for a viable group to dismount, so it must be assumed that the BRDM-2 gains its information by slightly more aggressive means than did its predecessor. The presence of a turret seems to lend some support to this idea. Like the

BTR-40P

BRDM-1 this vehicle is fitted with a single water jet for propulsion in the water, but it has an NBC outfit. For night movement there is a complete set of infra-red lights and vision equipment. There are roughly the same variants on this chassis as on the earlier one, except that it has been identified as carrying anti-aircraft missiles. It is in service in many Communist countries and is still being made in small numbers in the USSR.

Length: 5.71m (18ft 8in). *Width:* 2.28m (7ft 6in). *Height:* 2.28m (7ft 6in). *Weight:* 7,000kg (15,428lb). *Crew:* 4. *Power:* GAZ-41, V-8, petrol, 140bhp. *Armament:* one 14.5mm KPV heavy machine gun in turret; one 7.62mm machine gun coaxially mounted. *Armour:* 10mm. *Speed:* 100km/hr (62mph). *Range:* 750km (466 miles). *Maker:* Soviet State Factories.

BTR-40/BRDM-1 AMPHIBIOUS RECONNAISSANCE VEHICLE 1959–

The BTR-40P is now known also as the BRDM-1 and it followed the earlier BTR-40. Although it is now becoming fairly old, it is still in service with many Communist countries, but

BA-64

it is no longer manufactured. The crew are in the front of the hull, with the engine at the rear. There is no turret, though most vehicles carry a machine gun on an external mount, and some have two. The forward half of the roof opens to allow the crew to stand up and shoot over the sides, and there are firing ports for use when closed down. It seems that the tactical intention is that three or four of the crew should dismount to observe and gain information by stealth rather than by fighting for it. There are many variants of this little vehicle, a common one being an anti-tank version with up to six wire-guided missiles on retractable launchers

in the top of the crew compartment. These are fired by the commander from his front seat, though it is likely that he can dismount and use a remote-control box if necessary. Another version has been seen with SAM-9 anti-aircraft missiles on it, but it is not known if this is a standard variant.

Length: 5.71m (18ft 8in). *Width:* 2.20m (7ft 3in). *Height:* 1.92m (6ft 3in). *Weight:* 5,100kg (11,240lb). *Crew:* 5. *Power:* GAZ-40P, 6-cyl., petrol, 90bhp at 3,400rpm. *Armament:* see text. *Armour:* 10mm. *Speed:* 80km/hr (50mph). *Range:* 500km (310 miles). *Maker:* Soviet State Factories.

BRDM-2

M/39

SWEDEN

LANDSVERK 180 ARMOURED CAR
1935–

The Landsverk armoured cars were made in some numbers in the 1930s both for the Swedish forces and for export. The 180 is typical of the general series of large cars, though there were several in the production run from the Landsverk factory, all with minor variations but retaining the general body shape and size. The 180 was built on to a Scania-Vabis truck chassis with 6 × 4 wheel drive and twin wheels on both rear axles, making ten wheels in all. The engine was in front, with the usual armoured bonnet and louvers. The driver had a gunner sitting beside him, and the turret was forward of the rear wheels. It was fairly large for its time and carried a Madsen 20mm cannon with a coaxial machine gun. There was another machine gun in a hull mount firing over the rear decking, and this gunner had a second steering wheel so that he could drive backwards. The Landsverk 182 was a similar vehicle, but slightly smaller and with a smaller engine. All were made from flat plate riveted to a frame. Incredibly, at least three survive in reserve service in Eire, though their engines have been replaced by Leylands. Finland and Hungary have also bought this model.

Length: 5.60m (18ft 10in). *Width:* 2.18m (7ft 2in). *Height:* 2.09m (6ft 11in). *Weight:* 7,825kg (17,248lb). *Crew:* 5. *Power:* Scania-Vabis, 6-cyl., 80bhp. *Armament:* one Madsen 20mm cannon; one 7.92mm machine gun mounted coaxially; two 7.92mm machine guns in hull, firing forwards and backwards. *Armour:* 8.5mm. *Speed:* 80km/hr (50mph). *Range:* 288km (180 miles). *Maker:* Landsverk AB, Landskrona.

M/39 ARMOURED CAR *1939–1950*

The M/39 was one of many produced by the Landsverk company, but it differed from the

majority in not being just a truck chassis with a box body built on to it. The M/39 was a purpose-built armoured car with a proper 4 × 4 chassis and well-sloped armour. The turret was typical of other Landsverk products in being carefully shaped and fitted with a rounded mantlet. The first models were given solid tyres, but it was quickly found that these inhibited road speeds too much and all subsequent production used large pneumatic tyres. One feature which betrayed a lack of modern thought was the size of the crew and the fact that there was a separate machine gun to fire forwards and backwards, the rear gunner having a steering wheel for backwards driving. In Swedish service the car was known as the Lynx and it stayed in the army until the 1950s.

Length: 5.10m (16ft 9in). *Width:* 2.28m (7ft 6in). *Height:* 2.20m (7ft 3in). *Weight:* 7,800kg (17,190lb). *Crew:* 6. *Power:* Volvo, 6-cyl., petrol, 135bhp. *Armament:* one 20mm cannon; one machine gun mounted coaxially; two hull machine guns, firing forwards and backwards. *Armour:* 5–18mm. *Speed:* 70km/hr (44mph). *Range:* 250km (153 miles). *Maker:* Landsverk AB, Landskrona.

UNITED KINGDOM

AEC ARMOURED CAR *1942–1975*

In 1941 the Associated Equipment Company, makers of heavy trucks and buses, took one of

AEC

their Matador medium gun tractor chassis and built a mock-up armoured car on it, arming it with a 2-pdr. gun. It was then included in an exhibition of military vehicles, where it

Landsverk 180

attracted official attention, and an order for 150 was given.

The design was an ingenious adaptation of the original truck chassis. The engine was placed at the rear and angled so as to lie alongside the rear differential and thus reduce the height. Normally, only the front wheels were driven, the rear wheels being coupled to the drive for cross-country work. The body was of flat armour plate, tapering from the centre to each end, and surmounted with a turret. The driver relied on twin periscopes for vision when in action, but could open his hatch and raise his seat to afford fuller vision when out of danger. The basic design used a Valentine (qv) tank turret with 2-pdr. gun, though some cars were later modified to take the 6-pdr. gun. A Mark II was then devised, with a larger, three-man, turret and 6-pdr. gun, larger engine and other improvements, and finally a Mark III appeared in which the main armament was a 75mm gun. A total of 629 of all marks was built.

Length: 5.18m (17ft 0in). *Width:* 2.74m (9ft 0in). *Height:* 2.55m (8ft 4in). *Weight:* 11,175kg (24,640lb). *Crew:* 3 or 4. *Power:* AEC, 6-cyl., diesel, 105 or 158bhp at 2,000rpm. *Armament:* one 2-pdr. or one 6-pdr. or one 75mm gun. *Armour:* 7–57mm. *Speed:* 65km/hr (40mph). *Range:* 400km (250 miles). *Maker:* AEC, Southall.

THE BREN CARRIER 1934–1960

This ubiquitous vehicle began as a spin-off from the Vickers development work done on the Light Dragon gun tractor (qv). In 1934 this company developed a tracked vehicle which could double either as a gun-tower or as a machine-gun carrier; in the latter role it could mount a Vickers medium machine gun so as to fire on the move, and also carry a complete four-man gun squad and tripod so that the gun could be dismantled for action independently of the carrier. A prototype was built, and after tests a fresh version appeared in which the crew

Bren Carrier

was reduced to three men. A small number of these were built in 1936, but in the following year the Bren light machine gun was introduced and therefore the concept of the carrier was slightly changed. The Vickers gun was replaced by the Bren gun and the superstructure and interior arrangements suitably modified; some were built to carry the .55in Boys anti-tank rifle in place of the machine gun. After some improvements to the armour, this became the 'Carrier, Bren, No. 2 Mark 1' and issues began in 1938 on the scale of 10 carriers per infantry battalion.

Other units of the army saw possibilities in the carrier, and after trials some variant models were developed. The first to appear, in 1938, was the 'Carrier, Scout', intended for use by mechanized cavalry regiments. This carried a radio installation and had the ignition system suppressed. This model was followed by the 'Carrier, Cavalry', which had accommodation for six men and reduced armour, a canvas tilt cover and various racks for equipment; it was intended to carry dismounted personnel of cavalry light tank regiments.

The 'Carrier, Armoured, OP' was provided for Royal Artillery field regiments, to carry forward observation officers. It was fitted with radio and also with a telephone cable drum at the rear. The machine-gun mounting was removed and the gun port covered with a sliding shutter; this port was then available for use with observing instruments.

In addition to these official variants, the carrier was used as a basis for several experimental vehicles; these included self-propelled mountings for 2-pdr., 6-pdr. and 25-pdr. guns, mortars of various types and multiple machine gun mountings. None was acceptable for service.

Length: 3.65m (12ft 0in). *Width:* 2.05m (6ft 9in). *Height:* 1.45m (4ft 9in). *Weight:* 3,810kg (8,400lb). *Crew:* 2. *Power:* Ford, V–8, petrol, 3,923cc, 85bhp at 3,500rpm. *Payload:* 550kg (1,212lb). *Speed:* 48km/hr (30mph). *Makers:* Thornycroft Motors, Basingstoke; Morris Motors, Cowley, Oxford; Sentinel Steam Wagon Co., Shrewsbury; Aveling Barford, Ltd.; Ford Motor Co., Dagenham.

Bren Carrier

COVENTRY ARMOURED CAR
1945–1950

By the middle of the war the British Army was equipped with four marks of Humber and two of Daimler armoured cars. Both types had their advantages, and so, in order to rationalize manufacture, it was decided to combine forces and develop one car incorporating the best of both designs and then put it into production in both BSA and Rootes factories. Design work was undertaken by Humber of Coventry, from which the name of the new car was derived; Commer (a Rootes subsidiary) worked on the transmission, and Daimler developed the suspension and steering. An American engine was selected for use, and the first pilot models were put under test late in 1944.

The Coventry car was based largely on the Daimler design, but with a more roomy hull. The prototype Mark I carried a 2-pdr. gun in the turret, but a Mark II with a 75mm gun was also built. Independent suspension by swinging axles was used, with the drive taken by two shafts from a central transmission unit. About 1,600 vehicles were ordered, but the war ended and the orders were cancelled. Rela-

Coventry

tively few were produced, and most of those were sold to France shortly afterwards, to be used in Indo-China.

Length: 4.72m (15ft 6in). *Width:* 2.66m (8ft 9in). *Height:* 2.36m (7ft 9in). *Weight:* 11,685kg (25,760lb). *Crew:* 4. *Power:* Her-

cules RXLD, 6-cyl., petrol, 175bhp at 2,600rpm. *Armament:* one 2-pdr. or one 75mm gun. *Armour:* 14mm. *Speed:* 65km/h (40mph). *Range:* 400km (250 miles). *Makers:* BSA (Daimler), Coventry; Rootes (Karrier), Luton.

DAIMLER ARMOURED CAR *1941–1950*

In 1938–9 the BSA Company had developed a light scout car, later known as the Daimler Dingo, and its good results on trials led to the

suggestion that it could be scaled-up to become a full-sized armoured car. Work on this idea began in April 1939 and the prototypes were running before the end of the year. Due to in-

itial troubles with transmission and other components, it was not until April 1941 that the Daimler Armoured Car Mark I entered service.

The Daimler had many unusual technical features for its time; the vehicle used no chassis, the wheels and mechanical components being attached to the tray-like lower hull section. Drive was via a fluid flywheel torque converter and pre-selector gearbox, the first time such a system had been used on a military vehicle; disc brakes were used some 20 years before they were accepted for use in commercial vehicles, and the drive was taken from a central transmission box by four shafts, one to each wheel, which allowed a lower silhouette than the use of a central propeller shaft would have done. The turret was that of the Tetrarch light tank (*qv*) and carried a 2-pdr. gun, the first time that an armoured car was armed as well as the contemporary tanks. Duplicate steering was provided so that the vehicle could be driven backwards at speed to escape from ambush. The Daimler became the preferred armoured car of most British cavalry regiments and was used extensively in the North African and European campaigns. It remained in service for some years after the war.

Length: 3.96m (13ft 0in). *Width:* 2.43m (8ft 0in). *Height:* 2.23m (7ft 4in). *Weight:* 7,620kg (16,800lb). *Crew:* 3. *Power:* Daimler, 6-cyl., petrol, 95bhp at 3,600rpm. *Armament:* one 2-pdr. gun. *Armour:* 16mm. *Speed:* 80km/hr (50mph). *Range:* 330km (205 miles). *Maker:* BSA Ltd., Birmingham.

DAIMLER DINGO LIGHT ARMOURED SCOUT CAR *1939–1950*

In 1938 the War Office requested designs of a light armoured scout car, and competitive trials were held late in that year. Of the three competing designs, one by BSA-Daimler was selected for production. One of the unsuccessful entrants was the Alvis Dingo, and by some transposition never explained, the name Dingo came to rest on the Daimler car and stayed with it ever after.

The Dingo was a small four-wheeled car with engine at the rear and transmission by fluid torque converter and pre-selector gearbox. The two-man crew sat in an octagonal crew compartment with a folding armoured top, and the car commander had a Bren light machine gun mounted in a slot in the frontal armour. A forward-reverse transfer gearbox allowed the vehicle to be driven at speed in either direction.

The Dingo was widely used in all theatres of war and remained in British service until the middle 1950s. Many are still used by other armies throughout the world.

Length: 3.17m (10ft 5in). *Width:* 1.70m (5ft 7in). *Height:* 1.49m (4ft 11in). *Weight:* 3,050kg (6,725lb). *Crew:* 2. *Power:* Daimler, 6-cyl., petrol, 55bhp at 4,200rpm. *Armament:* one .303in Bren machine gun. *Armour:* 10–30mm. *Speed:* 88km/hr (55mph). *Range:* 320km (200 miles). *Maker:* BSA (Daimler Motors), Coventry.

FERRET ARMOURED CAR
1953–

Ferret was developed shortly after the war in order to replace the wartime Daimler Dingo scout car (*qv*). Developed by Daimler and resembling its predecessor, the Ferret is a low-set, four-wheeled car with the engine in the rear, driver at the front, and a small fighting compartment between them. An improvement is that the driver is forward of the fighting compartment, thus leaving room for a crew of two. The central compartment is somewhat higher than that of the Dingo, giving the occupants better protection, and they are provided with vision blocks and hatches.

Several variant models of Ferret have been produced; the most common change is the

Ferret

addition of a small turret to the fighting compartment, armed with a machine gun. Later marks were given larger wheels and flotation screens so that they could swim across water obstacles with minimum preparation. A version armed with Swingfire anti-tank guided missiles has also been produced. The Ferret has been bought by over 35 armies in addition to the British Army and is in widespread use throughout the world.

Length: 3.37m (11ft 1in). *Width:* 1.90m (6ft 3in). *Height:* 1.87m (6ft 2in). *Weight:* 3,483kg (7,680lb). *Crew:* 3. *Power:* Rolls-Royce, 6-cyl., petrol, 129bhp at 3,750rpm. *Armament:* one 7.62mm machine gun. *Armour:* 16mm. *Speed:* 93km/hr (58mph). *Range:* 300km (186 miles). *Maker:* Daimler Motors Ltd., Coventry.

Fox

FOX COMBAT VEHICLE, RECONNAISSANCE (WHEELED) *1973–*

Fox was developed in the late 1960s by Daimler Motors as a replacement for their Ferret armoured car, the requirement being for a vehicle capable of better firepower. In recognition of this its title was changed from scout car to Combat Vehicle, Reconnaissance, (Wheeled) or CVR(W).

In general the Fox follows the same lines as the Ferret (*qv*), but differs in mounting a much larger turret with a Rarden 30mm gun. The vehicle is entirely built from aluminium armour and mounts the engine and transmission at the rear and the driver at the front. The turret has a basket in which the commander and gunner sit. Image-intensifying sights, infra-red vision equipment and close-range surveillance radar are available as required.

In addition to being in service with the British Army, the Fox has been bought by the armies of Iran, Nigeria and Saudi Arabia. Though developed by Daimler, production is entirely by government factories.

Length: 2.24m (7ft 4½in). *Width:* 2.13m (7ft 1in). *Height:* 1.98m (6ft 6in). *Weight:* 5,386kg (11,875lb). *Crew:* 3. *Power:* Jaguar, 6-cyl., petrol, 4,235cc, 195bhp at 5,000rpm. *Armament:* one 30mm Rarden cannon with 99 rounds. *Armour:* not disclosed. *Speed:* 105km/hr (65mph). *Range:* not disclosed. *Maker:* Royal Ordnance Factory, Leeds.

GUY ARMOURED CAR *1938–1945*

In 1938 the War Office ran a long competitive trial to select a suitable armoured car, and at the end a contract was given to Guy Motors of Wolverhampton to produce what was then officially called a Light Tank (Wheeled). It was, in fact, a four-wheeled armoured car which Guy had based on components of their successful Quad Ant (*qv*) artillery tractor

chassis. The vehicle had four-wheel drive, though without independent suspension, a simple armoured body and a turret mounting the new 15mm Besa heavy machine gun. Although the pilot models used riveted construction, Guy devised a method of welding which speeded up production and was instrumental in introducing welding techniques into British armoured vehicle construction.

After building 101 Guy cars, the company became more involved in mass-production of other vehicles and had no more space to make armoured cars, but they continued to produce armoured hulls and turrets which were furnished to the Karrier company for building into the Humber armoured car (*qv*), based on the Guy design.

A small number of Guy cars were in use in France in 1940, but after that they were used exclusively as training vehicles.

Length: 4.11m (13ft 6in). *Width:* 2.05m (6ft 9in). *Height:* 2.28m (7ft 6in). *Weight:* 5,285kg (11,650lb). *Crew:* 3. *Power:* Meadows, 4-cyl., petrol, 53bhp at 2,200rpm. *Armament:* one .50 Vickers or 15mm Besa machine gun, plus one .303 Vickers or one 7.92mm Besa machine gun. *Armour:* 15mm. *Speed:* 65km/hr (40mph). *Range:* 340km (210 miles). *Maker:* Guy Motors Ltd., Wolverhampton.

HUMBER ARMOURED CAR *1941–1946*

In 1939 the existing facilities for the manufacture of armoured cars were fully committed, and yet more cars were still needed, so in October the Rootes Group of motor manufacturers were asked to undertake the design and production of a car. To save time, Rootes adopted an existing design, the Guy armoured car (*qv*) and allied it to a chassis produced by one of their subsidiaries as an artillery tractor for the Indian Army. This Karrier KT4 chassis

Guy

was modified by moving the engine to the rear and strengthening the suspension, after which a Guy-type of body was placed on top. Due to the adoption of well-tried components, the design gave little difficulty, and production began in early 1941. Although built by Karrier Ltd., the name Humber (another Rootes unit) was adopted so as to avoid confusion with the various military vehicles known as carriers.

Due to its basis in commercial vehicles, the mechanical side of the Humber was unadven-

Humber Mark IV

turous; solid axles with half-elliptic springs were used, and the engine and transmission were also ex-civil vehicle units. The turret carried a 15mm Besa heavy machine gun and a 7.92mm Besa machine gun; a later model, the Mark IV, was armed with an American 37mm gun in place of the 15mm Besa. The only defect reported in service was a short engine life, but

the Humber was liked as a command car since it had more internal room than the Daimler. Numbers are still in use around the world.

Length: 4.57m (15ft 0in). *Width:* 2.18m (7ft 2in). *Height:* 2.38m (7ft 10in). *Weight:* 6,960kg (15,345lb). *Crew:* 3. *Power:* Rootes, 6-cyl., petrol, 90bhp at 3,200rpm. *Armour:* 15mm. *Armament:* one 15mm, one 7.92mm machine gun. *Speed:* 72km/hr (45mph). *Range:* 400km (250 miles). *Maker:* Karrier Motors Ltd., Luton.

LANCHESTER ARMOURED CAR
1915–1925
The Lanchester touring car of 1914 was of advanced design and highly regarded, and it was soon adopted as a basis for an armoured car by the Royal Naval Air Service in 1915. The driver sat alongside the engine, a configuration which allowed the front of the car to be well shaped to deflect bullets, while the transmission was via a pre-selective epicyclic gearbox. The rear suspension was improved by placing dual wheels on the hubs, and the body was surmounted by a turret carrying a Vickers machine gun.

The Lanchester car was used in Belgium by the RNAS, but after the naval units were disbanded, the Army elected to standardize on Rolls-Royce and the Lanchesters were phased out. The only cars to survive for any length of time were those which accompanied No. 1 Squadron to Russia in 1916–17.

Length: 4.87m (16ft 0in). *Width:* 1.93m (6ft 4in). *Height:* 2.28m (7ft 6in). *Weight:* 4,877kg (10,752lb). *Crew:* 4. *Power:* Lanchester, 6-cyl., petrol, 60bhp. *Armament:* one Vickers .303

machine gun. *Armour:* 8mm. *Speed:* 80km/hr (50mph). *Range:* 290km (180 miles). *Maker:* Lanchester Motor Car Co., Coventry.

Oxford Carrier

THE OXFORD CARRIER *1944–1950*
Wartime experience led to a number of suggestions for improving the design of the Universal carrier (*qv*), and in 1944 work began on the 'Carrier, Tracked, CT20', which became known as the Oxford carrier. This vehicle used the same type of suspension as had its predecessors, but had a vastly improved body design incorporating a double-plate floor for protection against mines. The front was built up to give better protection and the driver was provided with vision periscope viewing. The transmission and steering arrangements were also improved, with the adoption of Hydramatic transmission and Cletrac steering. Armoured plates protected the track upper run, storage capacity was improved and seating was in a crew compartment behind the driver, with the engine at the rear.

For all its virtues the Oxford had a short run; by the time production began, the war was over

Lanchester

and the production contract severely curtailed. It functioned as a machine gun or mortar carrier and as an anti-tank gun towing vehicle with infantry battalions for some years after the war.

Length: 4.49m (14ft 9in). *Width:* 2.28m (7ft 6½in). *Height:* 1.70m (5ft 7in). *Weight:* 7,975kg (17,584lb). *Crew:* 3. *Power:* Cadillac, V–8, petrol, 5,671cc, 110bhp at 3,200rpm. *Speed:* 50km/hr (31mph). *Range:* 200km (125 miles). *Maker:* Morris Ltd., Cowley, Oxford.

SALADIN ARMOURED CAR *1959–*

The British Army used armoured cars with some success during the war, and immediately afterwards requested an improved car to incorporate all the lessons they had learned in combat. A prime requirement was better cross-country mobility, and for this the six equally-spaced wheel configuration pioneered by the American M36 car was adopted. Originally intended to have a crew of four and a 2-pdr. gun, production was delayed to allow

Saracen APCs (*qv*) to have first priority, and during this time an improved 76mm gun was developed, reducing the crew to three men.

Saladin has the driver seated centrally at the front of the hull, with the turreted fighting compartment behind him and the engine and transmission at the rear of the hull. All wheels are driven, and the front four are steered; the car can continue to function after the loss of any one wheel on a mine. The 76mm gun is provided with anti-personnel and anti-tank

ROLLS-ROYCE ARMOURED CAR
1915–1941
In 1914 the Royal Naval Air Service set up an advanced airbase in Belgium and required armoured cars in order to go forward and rescue downed aviators. After making their own vehicles from boiler-plate and miscellaneous civilian touring car chassis, an official design was produced in December 1914 which became the standard British armoured car. The Rolls-Royce Silver Ghost touring chassis was adopted, strengthened by adding leaves to the springs, and fitted with a steel body. The rear of the body was left as a load-carrying deck, and the cab position was surmounted by an open-topped turret mounting a Vickers machine gun; after some experience, these tur-

rets were given armoured tops.

In 1920 a further batch was built, much the same as the original 1914 model, but with some small improvements to the engine and with louvers on the armoured doors in front of the radiator. Finally, in 1924, a further consignment was made in which the turret was built up

and given a commander's cupola on top. In the post-war models disc wheels were used instead of the original wire-spoked pattern, and the 1924 model had wider wheels in order to withstand the weight better.

These cars were extensively used throughout the Empire between the wars and the last of them saw action in the Western Desert as late as 1940 before being replaced.

1920 Model *Length:* 5.18m (17ft 0in). *Width:* 1.90m (6ft 3in). *Height:* 2.33m (7ft 8in). *Weight:* 3,860kg (8,510lb). *Crew:* 4. *Power:* Rolls-Royce, 6-cyl., petrol, 50bhp at 2,000rpm. *Armament:* one Vickers .303 machine gun. *Armour:* 9mm. *Speed:* 80km/hr (50mph). *Range:* 240km (150 miles). *Maker:* Rolls-Royce Cars Ltd., Derby.

ammunition.

The Saladin entered service with the British Army in 1959 and numbers were subsequently purchased by other countries; they are still in wide use, though in British service they are now used only by reserve forces, having been superseded in first-line service by the Scorpion (*qv*).

Length: 4.92m (16ft 2in). *Width:* 2.53m (8ft 4in). *Height:* 2.92m (8ft 7in). *Weight:* 11,590kg (25,550lb). *Crew:* 3. *Power:* Rolls-Royce, 8-cyl., petrol, 160bhp at 3,750rpm. *Armament:* one 76mm gun with 43 rounds. *Armour:* 8–32mm. *Speed:* 72km/hr (45mph). *Range:* 400km (250 miles). *Maker:* British Leyland (Alvis Ltd.) Coventry.

SCORPION SCIMITAR AND STRIKER RECONNAISSANCE VEHICLES *1973–*

Although officially termed a Combat Vehicle, Reconnaissance, Tracked (CVR(T)), Scorpion is, by any standard, a light tank. It is a tracked vehicle using welded aluminium armour for the hull and mounting a turret which carries a 76mm gun, a lighter version of that used in the Saladin armoured car (*qv*). The engine is mounted at the right front of the hull, and the driver sits alongside on the left. The standard engine is a detuned version of the Jaguar car engine, but a GMC diesel can be fitted as an alternative. The hull carries a flotation screen and Scorpion is propelled in the water by its tracks, though an auxiliary propeller kit is available to give better speed in water.

Development of Scorpion began in the middle 1960s and first orders were placed in 1970. Since adoption by the British Army, it

Scorpion

Saladin

Scimitar

Striker

has also been taken into service by the Belgian Army, Iran and Saudi-Arabia. The Belgian vehicles are assembled in Belgium, using some Belgian-made components.

In addition to Scorpion, a family of specialist vehicles was developed around the basic chassis. Most of these are dealt with in other sections, but relevant to this section are the Scimitar and Striker. Scimitar is the same as Scorpion, except that the turret armament is the 30mm Rarden cannon. Striker is a turretless vehicle with the hull built up and mounting a launcher unit for the Swingfire anti-tank guided missile at the rear of the hull. This unit carries five missiles ready for firing, and a further five are carried inside the hull but have to be reloaded into the launcher from outside.

Scorpion *Length:* 4.38m (14ft 5in). *Width:* 2.18m (7ft 2in). *Height:* 2.09m (6ft 10½in). *Weight:* 7,960kg (17,548lb). *Crew:* 3. *Power:* Jaguar, 6-cyl., petrol, 4,225cc, 195bhp at 4,750rpm. *Armament:* one 76mm gun with 40 rounds; one 7.62mm machine gun. *Armour:* not disclosed. *Speed:* 88km/hr (55mph). *Range:* 645km (400 miles). *Maker:* British Leyland (Alvis), Coventry.

Scimitar *Weight:* 7,893kg (17,400lb). Other details as for Scorpion.

Striker *Length:* 4.75m (15ft 7in). *Width:* 2.18m (7ft 2in). *Height:* 2.21m (7ft 3in). *Weight:* 8,221kg (18,125lb). *Crew:* 3. *Power:* Jaguar, 6-cyl., petrol, 4,225cc, 195bhp at 4,750rpm. *Armament:* Swingfire missile launcher with ten missiles. *Armour:* not disclosed. Other details as for Scorpion.

SHORLAND LIGHT SCOUT CAR *1965–*

The Shorland car was originally developed as an internal security vehicle for use by the Royal Ulster Constabulary; it has since been adopted by the British Army and by several other countries as a light scout car.

Development began in 1965, using the chassis of the well-known Land-Rover as the basis. The armoured body follows the lines of the Land-Rover in severa respects, but is built up and carries a small hand-operated turret armed with a 7.62mm machine gun. Smoke or riot-gas dischargers can also be fitted. An armoured trunk at the rear holds the petrol tank and spare wheel. An experimental version mounting the Vigilant anti-tank missile has been produced but was not taken into military service.

Length: 4.59m (15ft 1in). *Width:* 1.77m. (5ft 10in). *Height:* 2.28m (7ft 6in). *Weight:* 3,360kg (7,407lb). *Crew:* 3. *Power:* Rover, 6-cyl., petrol, 91bhp at 1,750rpm. *Armament:* one 7.62mm machine gun. *Armour:* 8–11mm. *Speed:* 88km/hr (55mph). *Range:* 515km (320 miles). *Makers:* British Leyland (Rover), Solihull, Birmingham (chassis); Short Brothers & Harland Ltd., Belfast (body).

Shorland

UNIVERSAL CARRIER *1940–1960*

The popularity of the Bren carrier (*qv*) led to a number of derivatives, and it was obviously uneconomic and wasteful of effort to build several near copies in small numbers. In 1940, therefore, design of a universal carrier was begun, a basic vehicle which could, by the incorporation of small modification kits during the manufacturing stage, be adapted to almost any required role. This became the standard carrier for the rest of the war, though in spite of its official title it remained the Bren carrier to almost everybody.

The new design incorporated improved armour plating to cover all round the vehicle and the top of the engine compartment; mud deflectors over the tracks; steps for entry at the rear; and room for three men. Numbers of existing Bren carriers were modified to bring them up to 'Universal' standard, while modification kits allowed the Universal to function as an Artillery OP, mortar carrier or flamethrower. There were a number of marks and sub-marks, but the only essential differences were in the engines – some having British, some Canadian and some American engines – and in the arrangement of fittings to carry a mortar at the rear of the body. Carriers were built in Britain, Canada, Australia and New Zealand, and the US Army, considering the Universal to be overloaded and underpowered, set about improving it. They developed the 'Carrier T16', with a longer body and track and more powerful engine; over 2,600 were built, but somewhere the Americans had got the sums wrong and the T16 could not carry as much payload as the standard Universal, nor was it as reliable, so that few were put to use.

Length: 3.75m (12ft 4in). *Width:* 2.10m (6ft 11in). *Height:* 1.60m (5ft 3in). *Weight:* 4,318kg (9,520lb). *Crew:* 3. *Power:* Ford, V–8. *Makers:* As for Bren Carrier, plus: Ford Motor Co. of Canada, Windsor, Ontario; General Motors of New Zealand; New Zealand State Railways Workshop.

Universal Carrier

Boarhound T18E2

UNITED STATES

ARMOURED INFANTRY FIGHTING VEHICLE 1973–

In this vehicle the border between fighting vehicle and personnel carrier becomes somewhat blurred; we have elected to put it into this section since its function is seen as being a reconnaissance vehicle capable of carrying a file of infantry to assist in the operational role. It originated as a US Army request for an M113 APC with the additon of a turret-mounted gun and firing ports for the occupants, and two such vehicles were developed

13,470kg (29,696lb). *Crew:* 3 + 7. *Power:* Detroit Diesel, V–6, turbocharged, 264bhp at 2,800rpm. *Armament:* one 25mm cannon with 315 rounds; one 7.62mm machine gun. *Armour:* not disclosed. *Speed:* 60km/hr (37mph). *Range:* 480km (300 miles). *Maker:* FMC, San Jose, Cal.

T18E2 BOARHOUND ARMOURED CAR 1943-1945

Impressed by the German eight-wheel armoured car and its activities in the Western Desert, the British Army asked the US Armored Force to co-operate in the design of a similar vehicle early in 1942. An eight-

turret of the M3 series light tank (*qv*), complete with a 37mm gun, but the British then requested a heavier weapon and a fresh eight-wheel car mounting a 57mm gun, the T18E2, was developed.

By that time the Board of Review had ruled that no car over 6,350kg (14,000lb) weight was to be perpetuated; moreover, the US Army had produced another design which they considered superior to the T18 series. As a result, the T18 programme was closed down, but 30 T18E2 cars already under construction were completed for supply to Britain. By the time they had been shipped, the desert campaign was over and the reason for their existence had gone. Apart from being used for a variety of tests and trials in Britain the Boarhound armoured car had come to the end of its career.

Length: 6.24m (20ft 6in). *Width:* 3.07m (10ft 1in). *Height:* 2.61m (8ft 7in). *Weight:* 24,040kg (53,000lb). *Crew:* 5. *Power:* two GMC 6-cyl., petrol, each 97bhp at 3,000rpm. *Armament:* one 57mm gun M1 with 70 rounds. *Armour:* 10–30mm. *Speed:* 80km/hr (50mph). *Range:* 400km (250 miles). *Makers:* Yellow Truck & Coach Div., General Motors Corp. Pontiac, Mich.

CADILLAC GAGE COMMANDO ARMOURED CAR 1964–

The Commando armoured car was developed in 1962 by the Cadillac Gage company as a private venture. Though not developed to any US Army specification it was nevertheless accepted by them and has also been extensively

AIFV

and tested. The US Army then modified their specification and went on to promote a different vehicle, the MICV (*qv* FVS), while the FMC Corporation, who had made the two test vehicles, continued to develop the original idea to produce the AIFV. Though not adopted by the US Army, a quantity have been bought by the Netherlands government.

The vehicle body is of aluminium/steel laminated armour. The driver sits in front, the commander behind him; the gunner mans the turret gun, and the rest of the compartment can hold seven fully-equipped infantrymen. Access to the interior is by a power-activated door in the rear face of the hull. Five firing ports, each with periscope, are arranged around the hull.

The turret is armed with an Oerlikon 25mm cannon and a 7.62mm machine gun; sighting is by periscope or by an image-intensifying sight. The vehicle is fully amphibious, being propelled in the water by its tracks.

Length: 5.25m (17ft 3in). *Width:* 2.81m (9ft 3in). *Height:* 2.61m (8ft 7in). *Weight:*

wheeled car, the T18, was designed, and, as an alternative, a six-wheeled car the T18E1 was also developed. Both these vehicles used the

Cadillac

Lynx

sold overseas to some 20 countries. It is also in service in the Portuguese Army in a locally-made version known as the Chaimite.

The Commando hull is of welded construction and well-sloped, carrying a turret mounting a variety of armament. The driver is seated in the front, with the engine and transmission at the rear. All wheels are driven, but the wheels are carried on modified truck axles and are not independently sprung. The vehicle is fully amphibious, being propelled in water by the paddle-action of the wheels.

The Model V-100 was the first to appear; it was followed by the V-200, which was simply an enlarged model with more powerful engine and capable of carrying heavier armament, up to a 90mm gun. In 1971 the V-150 was produced, which is to the same dimensions as the V-100 but with better performance and various engineering improvements.

V-150 *Length:* 5.68m (18ft 8in). *Width:* 2.26m (7ft 5in). *Height:* 2.43m (8ft 0in). *Weight:* 9,550kg (21,055lb). *Crew:* 2 + 10 passengers. *Power:* Chrysler, V-8, petrol, 200bhp, or Cummins, V-6, diesel, 155bhp. *Armament:* to customer's requirements, from 7.62mm machine gun to 20mm cannon or missile launchers. *Armour:* not disclosed. *Speed:* 88km/hr (55mph). *Range:* 950km (600 miles). *Maker:* Cadillac Gage Co., Warren, Mich.

LYNX COMMAND AND RECONNAISSANCE VEHICLE *1965–*
The Lynx Command and Reconnaissance Vehicle was developed as a private venture by the Food Machinery Corporation in the early 1960s, using many components of the M113A1 APC (*qv*) which the company were then making. Development of the prototype was completed in 1963, but the US Army did

M3A1

not accept it for service and it was placed on the open market. It was subsequently adopted by the Netherlands Army (1966) and the Canadian Army (1968).

Lynx resembles the M113 APC in having a box-like body carried on full tracks; the hull is of aluminium armour, and the engine and transmission are at the rear. On top of the hull is a shallow turret carrying periscopes, on top of which is mounted a .50 Browning machine gun in a remote-control mounting which can be operated from within the vehicle. The driver is seated at the left front; the commander occupies the turret, and a third crewman sits at the rear of the crew compartment to man the radio and also a 7.62mm machine gun in his open roof hatch. The Dutch version differs slightly in seating the radio operator alongside the driver. In 1974 the Dutch Army modified 266 of their vehicles by removing the turrets and replacing them with turrets mounting 25mm Oerlikon cannon which can be used in ground or anti-aircraft roles.

Length: 4.59m (15ft 1in). *Width:* 2.41m (7ft 11in). *Height:* 2.17m (7ft 1½in). *Weight:* 8,775kg (19,345lb). *Crew:* 3. *Power:* Detroit Diesel, 6-cyl., 215bhp at 2,800rpm. *Armour:* not disclosed. *Speed:* 70km/hr (44mph). *Range:* 525km (325 miles). *Makers:* FMC, San Jose, Cal.

M3A1 WHITE SCOUT CAR *1939–*
During the 1930s the US Army experimented with a variety of armoured wheeled cars to be used by armoured cavalry for scouting missions, and in June 1939 the M3A1 scout car was standardized. It was subsequently widely used by all branches of the US Army and also by the British and other Allied Armies. In view of its makers, it was invariably known as the White scout car.

The M3A1 consisted of a specially designed and strengthened chassis with all-wheel drive, surmounted by an open-topped armoured body. Seats in the cab held the driver and vehicle commander, while seats in the rear compartment were provided for an additional six passengers. A 'skate rail' ran around the rear compartment, upon which a .50 and a .30 machine gun could be mounted, while tripods carried in the vehicle allowed the guns to be dismounted for ground action. The windscreen was of shatter-proof glass and could be further protected by a hinged steel plate with vision slots. A detachable canvas top was provided for non-combat use.

Length: 5.62m (18ft 5½in). *Width:* 2.03m (6ft 8in). *Height:* 1.99m (6ft 6½in). *Weight:* 5,625kg (12,400lb). *Crew:* 2 + 6. *Power:* Hercules JXD, 6-cyl., petrol, 5,244cc, 87bhp at 2,400rpm. *Armament:* one .50, one .30 machine gun. *Armour:* 7mm. *Speed:* 80km/hr (50mph). *Range:* 400km (250 miles). *Maker:* White Motor Co., Cleveland, Ohio.

M8 GREYHOUND ARMOURED CAR
1943–

This vehicle started life as a design for a wheeled tank destroyer mounting a 37mm gun, but early in 1942 it became apparent that there was no point in such a device and the specification was changed to an armoured car. It was standardized as the M8 in June 1942 and went into immediate production; by the end of the war some 8,523 had been built.

The M8 was a six-wheeled car with welded body, on top of which was an open-topped turret mounting a 37mm gun. Driver and bow gunner sat in the front of the hull, while the turret was occupied by the gunner and vehicle commander. The engine and transmission were at the rear of the hull.

The M8 was the most widely-used American armoured car, and it was accompanied in service by the Armoured Utility Car M20, which was simply the M8 without the turret but with a ring-mounted machine gun above the hull. This was used as a command vehicle and personnel carrier.

In post-war years the US and British Armies disposed of all their M8s, and large numbers are still in service throughout the world, notably in many African nations.

Length: 5.00m (16ft 5in). *Width:* 2.54m (8ft 4in). *Height:* 2.33m (7ft 4in). *Weight:* 7,711kg (17,000lb). *Crew:* 4. *Power:* Hercules, 6-cyl., petrol, 5,245cc, 110bhp at 3,000rpm. *Armament:* one 37mm gun M6 with 80 rounds. *Armour:* 6–20mm. *Speed:* 88km/hr (55mph). *Range:* 560km (350 miles). *Maker:* Ford Motor Co., St. Paul, Minn.

M38

M38 WOLFHOUND ARMOURED CAR
1945

While the M8 armoured car (*qv*) was an excellent road vehicle, it was less successful at cross-country work, largely because of the conventional layout of its six wheels, which prevented it crossing any sort of trench. In an endeavour to overcome this, and also produce an improved vehicle in many other respects, Chevrolet developed the M38, standardized in March 1945.

This was a six-wheeled vehicle with evenly-spaced wheels; this configuration improved the trench-crossing ability and also, since the wheels used oversize tyres and were independently suspended, improved the riding over all surfaces. The body was ballistically well-shaped, and carried a turret with a 37mm gun. All wheels were driven, and the front four pivoted for steering.

Excellent though the M38 was, it came to an abrupt end; as soon as it had been standardized, the US Army stated that they had no requirement for any further armoured cars and that the existing M8 would satisfy their immediate needs. As a result, only the prototype of the M38 was ever built.

Length: 5.10m (16ft 9in). *Width:* 2.43m (8ft 0in). *Height:* 1.98m (6ft 6in). *Weight:* 6,940kg (15,300lb). *Crew:* 4. *Power:* Cadillac, V–8, petrol, 5,671cc, 148bhp at 3,200rpm. *Armament:* one 37mm gun M6 with 93 rounds. *Armour:* 6–9mm. *Speed:* 96km/hr (60mph). *Range:* 480km (300 miles). *Maker:* Chevrolet Div., General Motors Corp., Detroit, Mich.

M114 COMMAND AND RECONNAISSANCE CARRIER *1962–*

The M114 command and reconnaissance carrier was developed in the late 1950s, the first issues taking place in 1961. It was developed to meet a US Army requirement for a protected scouting vehicle, and since its inception some 3,710 have been built. It was used in Vietnam but was found to have poor cross-country performance there and it is ,likely to be removed from service in the early 1980s in favour of a design from the XM800 development (*qv*).

The M114 has a boxy hull of aluminium armour and torsion-bar suspension of its

tracked running gear. The engine and transmission are in the right front of the hull, with the driver on the left side. The commander and radio operator occupy the crew compartment, and there is room for an additional man to serve as gunner if required. On the first M114 models the commander was provided with a .50 machine gun, and the additional crewman with a 7.62mm machine gun, both of which had to be fired from the open hatch; the M114A1 model (which appeared after the first 615 had been built) provided the commander with a rotatable cupola carrying a

M114

remote-controlled .50 machine gun. In 1969 a number were converted by fitting the cupola with a remote-controlled 20mm Hispano-Suiza cannon.

Length: 4.46m (14ft 8in). *Width:* 2.33m (7ft 8in). *Height:* 2.15m (7ft 1in). *Weight:* 6,928kg (15,275lb). *Crew:* 3 or 4. *Power:* Chevrolet, V–8, petrol, 4,638cc, 160bhp at 4,600rpm. *Armament:* one .50 machine gun and one .30 machine gun or one 20mm cannon and 7.62mm machine gun. *Armour:* not disclosed. *Speed:* 58km/hr (36mph). *Range:* 480km (300 miles). *Maker:* Cadillac Div. of General Motors Corp., Cleveland, Ohio.

T17E1 STAGHOUND ARMOURED CAR
1942–

In mid-1941 the British Army Staff in Washington and the US Armored Force combined to draw up specifications for an

Staghound

armoured car. As a result, the T17 was produced by the Chevrolet company and 3,500 were ordered. Shortly after this, the confused state of American armoured car development led to a Board of Review which first cut back the order for the T17E1 to 250 cars and then cancelled it altogether. The British, however, managed to keep it in production and eventually 2,844 were made, all of which were shipped to Britain. A further 1,000 T17E2 models were also built; these differed in being designed for anti-aircraft protection and carried a Frazer-Nash turret with twin .50 Browning machine guns.

The standard T17E1, named Staghound by the British, was a 4 × 4 car with a turret carrying a 37mm gun. Once in Britain numbers were modified by taking out the 37mm gun and substituting a 3in tank howitzer, so that the cars had a close support capability. Others were modified by removing the turret and replacing it with the turret of the Crusader tank (*qv*), complete with 6-pdr. gun.

After the war Britain disposed of these vehicles, and a number are still in service with various countries.

Length: 5.48m (18ft 0in). *Width:* 2.69m (8ft 10in). *Height:* 2.36m (7ft 9in). *Weight:* 13,925kg (30,700lb). *Crew:* 5. *Power:* two GMC 6-cyl., petrol, each 97bhp at 3,000rpm. *Armament:* one 37mm gun M6 with 103 rounds. *Armour:* 9–45mm. *Speed:* 90km/hr (56mph). *Range:* 725km (450 miles). *Maker:* Chevrolet Div. of General Motors, Detroit, Mich.

Lockheed XM800

XM800 ARMOURED RECONNAISSANCE SCOUT VEHICLE
1970–

In 1965 the United States, United Kingdom, Canada and Australia came together to develop a common scouting vehicle. This project, however, did not come to fruition and the Canadians adopted the Lynx (*qv*), the British the Scorpion (*qv*), the Australians decided to await developments, and the Americans, in 1971, canvassed a number of companies for a

XR311

suitable vehicle for their particular needs. Of the various designs submitted, two were selected and orders were given for the construction of four prototypes of each. One was by the FMC Corporation and was a tracked vehicle, the other was by the Lockheed Company and was wheeled. In 1974–5 these prototypes were extensively tested in competition with various other similar vehicles from other countries, but complaints were voiced that the vehicle had no anti-aircraft protection other than a light machine gun, could not be operated for 24 hours continuously, and could not carry the requisite amount of equipment. Modification and further tests are expected before either design is decided upon for adoption.

The FMC tracked scout resembles a light tank; it has an aluminium armour hull, and the driver is seated centrally at the front, well provided with vision blocks. The two-man turret is in the centre of the body, and mounts a 20mm cannon. Control of the turret is fully powered and the gun is stabilized; fire control is based on a complex image-intensifying sight. The vehicle is fully amphibious, being propelled in the water by the paddle-wheel action of the tracks.

The Lockheed wheeled scout resembles a conventional six-wheeled armoured car at first sight, but the two forward wheels, together with the suspension, steering, front drive and

fuel tank, are enclosed in a distinct unit which is roll-articulated to the rest of the vehicle so that the range of movement of the front wheels is far greater than possible with any normal means of suspension. The remainder of the body holds the crew, engine and turret, and is made of aluminium with an additional thickness of steel armour. The turret is of cast aluminium armour and mounts a 20mm cannon with full stabilization, power control and image-intensifying sights. The engine and transmission are at the rear of the vehicle.

FMC Tracked Scout *Length:* 4.67m (15ft 4in). *Width:* 2.43m (8ft 0in). *Height:* 2.39m (7ft 10in). *Weight:* 8,618kg (19,000lb). *Crew:* 3. *Power:* GMC Diesel, 6-cyl., 280bhp at 2,900rpm. *Armour:* not disclosed. *Armament:* one 20mm cannon, one 7.62mm machine gun. *Speed:* 88km/hr (55mph). *Range:* 725km (450 miles). *Maker:* FMC, San Jose, Cal.

Lockheed Wheeled Scout *Length:* 4.91m (16ft 1½in). *Width:* 2.43m (8ft 0in). *Height:* 2.48m (8ft 2in). *Weight:* 7,697kg (16,970lb). *Crew:* 3. *Power:* GMC Diesel, 6-cyl., 300bhp at 2,100rpm. *Armament:* one 20mm cannon; one 7.62mm machine gun. *Armour:* not disclosed. *Speed:* 105km/hr (65mph). *Range:* 725km (450 miles). *Maker:* Lockheed Missile & Space Co., Sunnyvale, Cal.

XR311 SCOUT CAR 1970–

This is officially described as a High Mobility

Wheeled Vehicle and was privately developed in 1969–70. It was intended to fill a variety of roles, including scouting, carriage of light anti-tank weapons or mortars, convoy escort and ambulance. Though extensively tested by the US Army for some years it has not yet been adopted, though a number have been sold to the Israeli Army as scouting vehicles.

The XR311 uses a sheet steel chassis, augmented by a tubular stiffening frame which passes over the passenger compartment to act as a roll bar. The engine and transmission are at the rear of the body. All wheels are independently sprung and driven, and limited-slip differentials ensure that traction is maintained under all conditions. Puncture-proof tyres are used as standard, and various optional fittings are available, including an armoured radiator, armoured fuel tank, stretcher racks, radio kits and extreme climate kits.

The standard vehicle mounts a machine gun on a ring mounting over the passenger's seat; other armament options include various types of anti-tank missile, the 106mm recoilless rifle and the 40mm grenade launcher.

Length: 4.34m (14ft 3in). *Width:* 1.93m (6ft 4in). *Height:* 1.60m (5ft 3in). *Weight:* 2,767kg (6,100lb). *Crew:* 3. *Power:* Chrysler, V–8, petrol, 187bhp at 4,000rpm. *Armament:* optional (see text). *Armour:* optional additonal kit. *Speed:* 130km/hr (80mph). *Range:* 480km (300 miles). *Maker :* FMC, San Jose, Cal.

The BTR-50 is now obsolescent but it is still in
service with many of the Soviet satellite
countries. It is fitted out for swimming with
minimal preparation, driving itself in water by
water jets.

ARMOURED PERSONNEL CARRIERS

SAURER 4K 4FA ARMOURED PERSONNEL CARRIER *1956–*

The Saurer is the standard APC of the Austrian Army and it is not in service with any other army. Development started in 1956 and there has been some modification over the years. The basic vehicle has a welded hull with the driver in front and the engine on his right. The commander is directly behind the driver, in a small turret, and he is also expected to fire the main armament. The troop compartment is at the rear and it has two rear doors and two long hatch covers in the roof, which allow the passengers to stand up and fire over the top if need be. When closed down they have no firing ports. There are many variants in service, including ambulance, command, anti-aircraft, mortar and rocket-launcher models. There is no NBC protection, nor can the vehicle swim. It has no night-driving aids as a normal fitment, though these could be added. It is now becoming fairly elderly and it must be expected that the Austrians will be looking soon for a replacement.

Length: 5.42m (17ft 8in). *Width:* 2.50m (8ft 2in). *Height:* 2.20m (7ft 2in). *Weight:* 13,500kg (29,760lb). *Crew:* 2 + 8. *Power:* Saurer, 6-cyl., diesel, 250bhp at 2,400rpm. *Armament:* one Oerlikon 204 20mm cannon in Oerlikon GAD turret. *Armour:* 8–20mm. *Speed:* 65km/hr (40mph). *Range:* 300km (190 miles). *Maker:* Saurer-Werke (now Steyr-Daimler-Puch), Steyr.

URUTU EE–11 ARMOURED PERSONNEL CARRIER *1972–*

The EE–11 is a wheeled APC which is the product of the Engesa Company and certain Brazilian government agencies. It was specially designed for the Brazilian Army and is used by them and also the Brazilian Marines, who use a slightly different version capable of swim-

EE-11

ming in the open sea. The vehicle is a 6 × 6 with the rear wheels mounted on the Engesa Boomerang suspension unit. Engine and driver are in the extreme front of the hull, and centrally behind them is the circular hatch for the commander/gunner. He can be given one of a wide variety of armament fittings up to the Swedish Hägglunds 20mm cannon turret; however, there is also a 90mm gun turret which can be squeezed in. The roof over the passenger compartment has six hatches, which

Saurer 4K 4FA

allow the occupants to fire out, but they also have eleven firing ports in the hull sides and end which allow them to use their personal weapons from under armour. The vehicle is fully amphibious and propels itself by its wheels when in the water. The Marine version has two propellers and a more powerful engine.

Length: 5.76m (18ft 9in). *Width:* 2.44m (8ft 0in). *Height:* 2.45m (8ft 1in). *Weight:* 9,000kg (19,836lb). *Crew:* 2 + 13. *Power:* Mercedes-Benz (Brazil) OM–352–A, 6-cyl., direct injection, turbocharged, diesel, 165bhp at 2,800rpm. *Armament:* see text. *Armour:* 6–12mm. *Speed:* 95km/hr (59mph). *Range:* 600km (370 miles). *Maker:* Engesa SA, São Paulo.

CHINA

TYPE 55 ARMOURED PERSONNEL CARRIER 1960–
The Type 55 is the Chinese version of the Soviet BTR–40 (*qv*) and its physical features are almost identical. The internal differences are that the Chinese version probably uses locally built engines and transmissions.

TYPE 56 ARMOURED PERSONNEL CARRIER 1958–
The Type 56 is the Chinese version of the Soviet BTR–152 (*qv*), a six-wheeled carrier which is now obsolescent in the Eastern bloc. However, it still survives in use with the Chinese reserve forces and it is suspected that there are variants in service for such tasks as light anti-aircraft self-propelled mountings, and perhaps some command vehicles. All details are as for the Soviet BTR–152.

TYPE K–63 ARMOURED PERSONNEL CARRIER 1970–
The Type K–63 is a fully tracked carrier and it is built in China, owing nothing to any foreign inspiration. It probably uses components from existing vehicles, and it seems likely that the suspension and tracks are from the T–60 light tank, which is a local variant of the Soviet PT–76 (*qv*). The engine may well come from the same source. The rather wide hull has the engine in the front with the driver and commander on either side of it, an unusual arrangement. The infantry travel in the rear half, entering and leaving by the usual rear doors. They have hatches in the roof, but no apparent firing ports. All details are scarce and none are quoted for dimensions or performance.

CZECHOSLOVAKIA

OT–62 ARMOURED PERSONNEL CARRIER 1964–
The OT–62 is the Czechoslovakian version of the Soviet BTR–50PK (*qv*), but there are some differences. The Czech vehicle is completely closed in and so resembles the command vehicle rather than the APC. It also has a more powerful engine and a better performance. In all other respects it resembles the Soviet vehicle and the details will not be repeated here. One Czech feature is the fact that it often carries an M59A recoilless anti-tank gun, which is fired from outside the armour and over the rear hatches and decking. All reloading has to be done in the open, though the actual firing trigger can be operated from inside.

Length: 7.00m (22ft 10in). *Width:* 3.20m (10ft 6in). *Height:* 2.20m (7ft 2in). *Weight:* 16,000kg (35,264lb). *Crew:* 2 + 18. *Power:* Model PV–6, 6-cyl., supercharged, diesel, 300bhp at 2,000rpm. *Armament:* according to variant. *Armour:* 6–14mm. *Speed:* 60km/hr (37mph). *Range:* 500km (310 miles). *Maker:* Czechoslovakian State Factories.

OT–64 ARMOURED PERSONNEL CARRIER SERIES 1963–
The letters OT stand for 'Obrneny Trans-porter' in Czech and there is a series of vehicles with this title. The OT–64 dates from a design study of 1959, which was undertaken jointly by Poland and Czechoslovakia, and both continue to use the vehicle together with at least eight other countries. It is large, fairly heavy and probably rather complicated. It is an 8 × 8 with semi-automatic transmission and a central air system to all wheels and tyres. The hull is built up round a tubular frame. Driver and commander are beside each other at the extreme front, with the engine between them and the infantry compartment. Over this latter compartment there are six hatches and in most models two of them are replaced with a turret, usually the one used on the Soviet BRDM–2 (*qv*). There are several variants in service and it seems unlikely that any of the purely infantry carriers are without a turret now, although they were in the first series. One variant carries Sagger ATGW on a retractable launcher over the rear and there are at least two command versions.

Length: 7.44m (24ft 5in). *Width:* 2.50m (8ft 3in). *Height:* 2.00m (6ft 6in). *Weight:* 14,300kg (31,517lb). *Crew:* 2 + 18. *Power:* Tatra Model T 928–14, V–8, air-cooled, diesel, 180bhp at 2,000rpm. *Armament:* one 7.62mm machine gun on pintle or one 14.5mm machine gun and one 7.62mm machine gun in BRDM–2 turret. *Armour:* 10mm. *Speed:* 60km/hr (37mph). *Range:* 500km (310 miles). *Maker:* Czechoslovakian State Arsenals and Factories.

OT–810 ARMOURED PERSONNEL CARRIER 1948–
The precise service status of the OT–810 is difficult to determine, but it is still seen from time to time in Czechoslovakia and in Romania, the only other country to adopt it. It is now remarkably old since it is a World War II German ¾-track, and after 1945 the Czechs took a large number of these vehicles and pressed them into service. In the 1950s they carried out a modernization programme on all of them, introducing several modifications and fitting a Tatra engine and some extra armour. The general layout is immediately recognizable as dating from before 1939. The engine is in front under a long bonnet. The driver and commander sit side by side in a cab, with a hatch for the latter. The troop compartment is above the tracked suspension with doors at the rear. There is no fixed armament, but it is usual to see these cars with a pintle-mounted machine gun on the commander's hatch. The only known variant is an anti-tank vehicle with an M59 82mm recoilless gun in the rear of the car and with the sides capable of being folded down to allow for traverse. The remaining OT–810s must be wearing out now, and are probably only used for training or border patrolling.

OT-64

OT-810

Length: 5.82m (19ft 1in). *Width:* 2.10m (6ft 9in). *Height:* 1.75m (5ft 8in). *Weight:* 8,500kg (18,734lb). *Crew:* 2 + 10. *Power:* Tatra, 6-cyl., air-cooled, diesel; 120bhp. *Armament:* none fixed, but one machine gun on pintle is usual. *Armour:* 7–12mm. *Speed:* 52km/hr (32mph). *Range:* 320km (198 miles). *Maker:* several German and Czechoslovakian companies since 1945.

EGYPT

WALID ARMOURED PERSONNEL CARRIER *1972–*

Although it has been in service for several years not much is known about this carrier. It is a 4 × 4 wheeled car very much like the Soviet BTR–40P (*qv*) in general outline, and it is very likely that it is the Egyptian version of this vehicle. There are reports that it is based on a standard commercial chassis and driven by a commercial Deutz diesel engine. It would seem to be the same size as the BRDM, but it could

be possible that the performance is less. There is no reason to suppose that the armour protection is in any way inferior to that of the Soviet car, and it would seem that the Walid is a useful, and perhaps cheaper, alternative.

Length: 5.52m (18ft 1in). *Width:* 2.20m (7ft 2in). *Height:* 1.80m (5ft 10in). *Weight:* 5,400kg (11,900lb). *Crew:* 2 + 8. *Power:* Deutz F4L, 4-cyl., air-cooled, diesel, 5,322cc, 90bhp. *Armament:* none fitted. *Armour* (estimated): 9mm. *Speed* (estimated): 75km/hr (46mph). *Range* (estimated): 280km (170 miles). *Maker:* not known.

EIRE

TIMONEY ARMOURED PERSONNEL CARRIER *1976–*

The Timoney has been built to a specification drawn up by the Irish Department of Defence for a light armoured vehicle for use both in Eire and with the United Nations Forces, of which Eire forms a part. The development of the

Timoney has taken several years, but the resulting vehicle appears to be effective and practical. The hull is a welded box, with driver and engine in front behind the rather large

Timoney

sloping front plate. The engine is the same as is used in the M113 carrier (*qv*), making the provision of spares and servicing a straightforward matter. A one-man turret is centrally mounted behind the engine and in the rear is the troop compartment. There are firing ports in the sides and hatches in the roof. All air is drawn in from the top and the exhausts run along the edge of the roof. The vehicle is amphibious and propels itself by its wheels in the water. There is comprehensive electrical equipment and the basic hull is adaptable to a number of different roles; it can also be 'stretched' to a 6 × 6 APC, which can carry up to 17 men.

Length: 4.90m (16ft 1in). *Width:* 2.40m (7ft 9in). *Height:* 2.50m (8ft 2in). *Weight:* 8,160kg (17,980lb). *Crew:* 2 + 10. *Power:* Chrysler Type 360 CID, 8-cyl., petrol, 200bhp at 4,000rpm. *Armament:* two 7.62mm machine guns in turret. *Armour* (estimated): 8mm. *Speed:* 98km/hr (60mph). *Range:* 480km (300 miles). *Maker:* Technology Investments Ltd., Dublin.

FRANCE

AMX–10P MECHANIZED INFANTRY COMBAT VEHICLE 1973–

The AMX–10P is a true MICV and is very modern in concept. The hull is made of a light alloy armour, well sloped at the front. Behind this glacis plate is the driver and the engine. The engine drives a hydraulic torque converter and preselector gearbox to the rear sprocket.

AMX 10P

Behind the driver is the fighting compartment with a powered turret mounted above it, and at the rear is the troop compartment. There are roof hatches but no firing ports, and the infantry have an electrically operated ramp at the rear instead of doors. There is a comprehensive set of vision periscopes, including six for the infantry in the rear. Night-driving equipment is fitted as standard, as is NBC protection. The tracks are carried on five roadwheels, which are sprung by torsion bars, and there are two water jets at the back for propulsion when swimming. Unusually in this type of vehicle, there is a separate commander and gunner, the commander being the infantry leader also, and he dismounts with them leaving the gunner in charge. There are at least eight variants of the AMX–10, and the design

is capable of further modification and improvement. So far it has been supplied to two foreign governments and it is in service with the French Army.

Length: 5.82m (19ft 1in). *Width:* 2.78m (9ft 2in). *Height:* 2.54m (8ft 4in). *Weight:* 13,800kg (30,410lb). *Crew:* 2 + 9. *Power:* Hispano–Suiza HS 115–2, V–8, supercharged diesel, 276bhp at 3,000rpm. *Armament:* one 20mm cannon; one 7.62mm machine gun mounted coaxially in turret. *Armour* (estimated): 6–30mm. *Speed:* 65km/hr (40mph). *Range:* 600km (372 miles). *Maker:* Atelier de Construction, Roanne (ARE).

AMX-VC1

AMX–VCI MECHANIZED INFANTRY COMBAT VEHICLE 1956–

The AMX–VCI was the first tracked APC to enter French service. It was a variant of the highly successful AMX–13 light tank (*qv*) and it uses several common components, including the engine, transmission and suspension. The front part is almost identical with the tank, the driver sitting alongside the engine and the commander and gunner behind him. The troop compartment is at the rear and the hull has had to be built up to give sufficient headroom for the infantry. They sit in the middle of the hull, facing outwards, and have firing ports in the

sides and the rear doors. Roof hatches allow them to stand up if necessary. On the original vehicle the gunner had a simple pintle mount for one machine gun, but since then the variety of armament fits has widened and now almost any weapon or missile can be put on. There are several variants, including an engineer version with lifting tackle, and an SP gun. The vehicle has been in service for over 20 years and it is still made to order. It is in service with at least eight armies outside France and complete vehicles have been assembled in Argentina. It is known by several different names in different countries, but it is still giving satisfaction and looks like doing so for some years yet.

Length: 5.54m (18ft 2in). *Width:* 2.51m (8ft 3in). *Height:* 2.32m (7ft 7in). *Weight:* 14,000kg (30,865lb). *Crew:* 1 + 12. *Power:* SOFAM 8 GXB, 8-cyl., petrol, 8,250cc, 250bhp at 3,200rpm. *Armament:* normally one 12.7mm or 7.62mm machine gun on external mount, but see text for variants. *Armour:* 10–30mm. *Speed:* 65km/hr (40mph). *Range:* 400km (250 miles). *Maker:* Creusot-Loire, Chalon-sur-Saône.

BERLIET VXB–170 ARMOURED PERSONNEL CARRIER 1971–

The Berliet is a 4 × 4 APC originally built as a private venture in the hope of capturing part of the expanding market for reasonably priced APCs. It was not taken by the French Army, but a number were bought for the police and some have been sold to African countries. An attraction of the vehicle is that it uses many commercial components from the Berliet range of heavy lorries and it also carries rather more men than do most other APCs, the extra capacity being useful for police operations. The driver and commander sit together in the front and the troop compartment is directly behind them. Unusually, the engine is at the

Berliet VXB-170

rear, on the left side, with a rear access door beside it. The main access doors are in the sides of the hull. The basic vehicle has no specific armament, but almost any combination of guns and turrets can be fitted at the user's request, and in addition there is a hydraulically operated bulldozer blade intended for the clearing of road blocks or similar obstacles. The VXB is meant to be adaptable to many different roles, and the manufacturers have designs for all foreseeable military needs. The vehicle is amphibious, using its wheels for propulsion.

Length: 6.00m (19ft 7in). *Width:* 2.52m (8ft 3in). *Height:* 2.01m (6ft 6in). *Weight:* 12,700kg (27,990lb). *Crew:* 1 + 11. *Power:* Berliet V–8, diesel, 170bhp at 3,000rpm. *Speed:* 85km/hr (53mph). *Range:* 750km (460 miles). *Maker:* Automobiles Berliet, Bourg.

EBR ETT ARMOURED PERSONNEL CARRIER 1959–
This vehicle is a variant of the Panhard EBR–75 (*qv*) and only 30 were built. They were specifically intended for the French colonies and all were sent to Africa. They have now passed into other hands. The vehicle has the same chassis as the EBR, but the rear driver's position is taken out and two rear doors put in place of it. The hull is built up into a long troop compartment in which the infantry sit back to back facing outwards. The sloping sides of the compartment lift up to give a good field of fire and also to let in cooling air. Two small turrets for machine guns are placed at each end of the troop compartment and the two centre wheels have pneumatic tyres instead of steel rims. Cross-country mobility is said to be good, but the vehicle was obviously

Panhard EBR ETT

not a success, perhaps because it was expensive.

Length: 5.56m (18ft 3in). *Width:* 2.42m (7ft 11in). *Height:* 2.32m (7ft 7in). *Weight:* 13,500kg (29,760lb). *Crew:* 1 + 14. *Power:* Panhard, 12-cyl., horizontally-opposed, air-cooled, petrol, 200bhp at 3,700rpm. *Armament:* none fitted, but turrets could take two infantry light machine guns. *Armour:* 8–15mm. *Speed:* 105km/hr (65mph). *Range:* 650km (404 miles). *Maker:* Société Anonyme des

Panhard M3

Anciennes Etablissements Panhard et Levassor, Reims.

PANHARD M3 ARMOURED PERSONNEL CARRIER 1917–
The M3 has been a most successful APC and very large numbers have been built and sold all over the world. It is in service with at least 12 armies and perhaps many more police forces and is still in production in France. It is a straightforward and relatively simple design and is capable of being adapted to many uses without great cost. The driver is in the extreme front of the welded hull with the engine and gearboxes directly behind him. The remainder of the vehicle is taken up by the rather chunky troop compartment, which has no fewer than four doors, eight firing ports and two roof hatches. A wide variety of armaments kits can be fitted to either or both of the hatches, and there are several kinds of turret which drop on. The number of variants is at least nine, and there are more if the types of armament are considered as separate models. The vehicle swims, propelling itself by its wheels, but there is no NBC protection.

Length: 4.45m (14ft 6in). *Width:* 2.40m (7ft 9in). *Height:* 2.48m (8ft 2in). *Weight:* 6,100kg (13,400lb). *Crew:* 2 + 10. *Power:* Panhard 4 HD, 4-cyl., horizontally-opposed, petrol, 90bhp at 4,700rpm. *Armament:* see text. *Armour:* 8–12mm. *Speed:* 100km/hr (62mph). *Range:* 600km (372 miles). *Maker:* Société de

Constructions Mécaniques Panhard et Levassor, Paris.

TT6

TT6 ARMOURED PERSONNEL CARRIER 1952–1965
The TT6 was the first tracked carrier for the French infantry and it was the forerunner of the Hotchkiss reconnaissance vehicle (*qv*), which the German Federal Army adopted. The TT6 was small and not very powerful, it carried only six infantrymen and there was little room for extra equipment. However, it showed the way for others to follow and later designs were far better. The later carriers all had space for more men. The driver of the TT6 sat alongside the engine in the front of the hull, and behind him the commander had a hatch on which he could mount a machine gun. The infantry sat back to back in the troop compartment and had small openings to shoot through. They entered

Saviem VAB

by two rear doors. A cargo variant had an open load bay and no roof for the driver.

Length: 3.96m (13ft 0in). *Width:* 2.28m (7ft 6in). *Height:* 1.85m (6ft 1in). *Weight:* 6,504kg (14,336lb). *Crew:* 1 + 6. *Power:* Hotchkiss, 6-cyl., petrol, 164bhp at 3,900rpm. *Armament:* none. *Armour:* 8–15mm. *Speed:* 65km/hr (40mph). *Range:* 355km (220 miles). *Maker:* Hotchkiss-Brandt, Paris.

SAVIEM VAB ARMOURED PERSONNEL CARRIER 1977–

The Saviem VAB (Véhicule de l'Avant Blindé) arose from a French Army requirement of 1969 in which an armoured carrier was called for to act as a support vehicle to the expensive mechanized infantry combat vehicle. The VAB was foreseen as ferrying troops and supplies up to the forward line and also as being used in place of the MICV, where the more expensive vehicle was not fully justified. The French Army will probably need about 4,000 of these VAB, and it can be expected that they will also be sold abroad. As far as possible commercial components have been used in the design to keep costs down. The hull is the usual welded box with driver and commander in front and the power pack behind them in one

unit. There are hatches and vision ports in the troop compartment, all of which close and seal so that the vehicle can swim without preparation apart from raising the bow vane. Water propulsion is by water jets and there is an NBC pack as a standard fitment. Armament is optional, but the basic vehicle has no turret. However the manufacturers claim that a 90mm turret, the same as on the Panhard AML–90 armoured car (*qv*) can be fitted if needed, and there is a wide range of possibilities beyond that. A prototype 6 × 6 model has been built, but the French Army is taking the 4 × 4.

Length: 5.82m (19ft 7in). *Width:* 2.50m (8ft 2in). *Height:* 2.00m (6ft 6in). *Weight:* 13,000kg (28,650lb). *Crew:* 2 + 10. *Power:* Saviem HM–71 2356, 6-cyl., diesel, 230bhp at 2,220rpm. *Armament:* see text. *Armour* (estimated): 6–15mm. *Speed:* 100km/hr (62mph). *Range:* 1,300km (800 miles). *Maker:* Société des Materiels Speciaux Saviem, Sursesnes.

WEST GERMANY

HWK–11 ARMOURED PERSONNEL CARRIER 1964–

In the late 1950s the company of Henschel-

Werke developed a light tracked chassis as a basis for a number of military vehicles, including APC, anti-tank missile carrier, anti-tank gun carrier, armoured ambulance and mortar carrier. They were primarily aimed at the export market in developing countries, but apart from selling some 40 APCs to Mexico in 1964, only two prototype reconnaissance ve-

HWK 11

hicles were built. The company then abandoned the project and have since merged to become Rheinstahl Sonderfertigung.

The HWK–11 APC is a tracked vehicle with torsion-bar suspension, and uses a boxy body with sloping front. The engine is at the right front, with the driver and vehicle commander on its left. The commander has a small hatch, which is provided with a light machine gun. The main part of the body is covered by two large hatches which can be opened to give access or partly opened to provide cover while allowing the passengers to fire their personal weapons. Two doors at the rear are normally used for passenger access. The vehicle has no amphibious capability.

Length: 5.05m (16ft 7in). *Width:* 2.53m (8ft 4in). *Height:* 1.58m (5ft 2½in). *Weight:* 11,000kg (24,250lb). *Crew:* 2 + 10. *Power:* Chrysler, V–8, petrol, 5,916cc, 211bhp at 4,000rpm. *Armament:* one 7.62mm machine gun. *Armour:* 8–15mm. *Speed:* 65km/hr (40mph). *Range:* 320km (200 miles). *Maker:* Henschel-Werke, Kassel.

MARDER MECHANIZED INFANTRY COMBAT VEHICLE *1971–*

The German Army were among the pioneers of armoured personnel carriers, and in 1959 the reconstituted Bundeswehr made such a vehicle their top priority. However, with the experience of the Russian campaign behind them, they insisted that the occupants had to be able to fight from the vehicle and not be merely passengers. Moreover it was to be well protected and carry powerful armament, all of which turned the requirement into one for a mechanized infantry combat vehicle. After long and careful development, the Marder was first issued in May 1971.

Marder has a welded steel hull capable of withstanding 20mm cannon attack at the front, and the driver and engine are side by side in the hull front. Behind this is the troop compartment in which the vehicle commander and two gunners operate and where six infantrymen can be accommodated. On the vehicle roof is a remote-controlled turret unit mounting a Rheinmetall 20mm cannon, and a smaller remote-control mount carrying a 7.62mm machine gun. At the rear of the hull a bottom-hinged door gives access and acts as a

Marder Waffenträger Roland

disembarkation ramp. Suspension is by torsion bars, and with a snorkel fitted it can wade in depths of up to 2.5m (8ft) of water. A flotation kit has been developed, but is not generally issued.

In addition to the basic MICV, variant models have been developed, of which the most important is the Waffenträger Roland. This is the Marder chassis and hull carrying a special mounting to fire the German/French 'Roland' surface-to-air missile. Two missiles are carried on the launcher, while a further eight are carried inside the hull. Issues of this

equipment began in 1978 and are expected to be completed by 1982.

Another new design, the future of which is not yet certain, is the Marder LWT3, which is fitted with a completely new type of turret which is fully stabilized and thus allows accurate fire whilst the vehicle is moving. It mounts the same Rheinmetall cannon.

Other experimental models, which have not progressed beyond prototypes, include a Marder mounting a 105mm gun in a turret, a multiple ground rocket launcher, a ground surveillance radar carrier and an anti-aircraft fire-control radar vehicle. Some of the standard models in military service have been slightly modified by their users to act as armoured ambulances or cargo vehicles.

Length: 6.79m (22ft 3in). *Width:* 3.24m (10ft 7½in). *Height:* 2.86m (9ft 4½in). *Weight:* 28,200kg (62,170lb). *Crew:* 4 + 6. *Power:* Mercedes-Benz, 6-cyl., diesel, 600bhp at 2,200rpm; *Armament:* one 20mm cannon with 1,250 rounds and one 7.62mm machine gun. *Armour:* not disclosed. *Speed:* 75km/hr (46mph). *Range:* 520km (325 miles). *Makers:* Rheinstahl Sonderfertigung, Kassel; Atlas MaK, Kiel.

Marder MICV

RHEINSTAHL UR-416 INTERNAL SECURITY VEHICLE 1965–

This is a private-venture design by Rheinstahl and consists basically of the commercial Mercedes-Benz Unimog truck chassis fitted with an armoured body. Its primary role is in internal security, though the makers have put forward a variety of suggested variants. Numbers have been bought by countries throughout the world.

The vehicle hull is of welded steel with sloped surfaces; the engine and transmission are at the front, with the driver behind them, and the remainder of the vehicle is available for the crew and passengers. Access is by doors in both sides and the rear of the hull. There are two hatches in the roof, one of which can be fitted with various armament options. Five firing ports are provided in each side of the hull and two in the rear.

The basic model is provided with a 7.62mm or similar light machine gun, protected by a small shield. Other armament packages developed include a 20mm cannon, a 90mm recoilless rifle, COBRA missiles or TOW missiles. Other versions of the basic vehicle can be adapted for use as ambulances, repair trucks, observation and command vehicles or obstacle clearing vehicles for internal security units.

Length: 4.99m (16ft 4in). *Width:* 2.26m (7ft 5in). *Height:* 2.24m (7ft 4in). *Weight:* 6,300kg (13,890lb). *Crew:* 2 + 8. *Power:* Daimler-Benz, 6-cyl., diesel, 110bhp at 2,800rpm. *Armament:* optional see text. *Armour:* 9mm. *Speed:* 80km/hr (50mph). *Range:* 700km (435 miles). *Maker:* Rheinstahl Sonderfertigung, Kassel.

UR-416

SPZ 12-3 ARMOURED PERSONNEL CARRIER 1955–

This vehicle was originally designed by Hispano-Suiza in Switzerland as one of a family of combat vehicles in 1955. At that time the Bundeswehr was re-forming, needed a tracked APC, and also wanted 'educational'

SPZ 12-3

contracts to inaugurate the building of armoured vehicles in Germany once again. As a result of all this, Hispano-Suiza were given a contract to develop the vehicle to meet the German requirement, and production contracts were placed with two German firms and, in order to speed the vehicle into service, with Leyland Motors of England. Production was completed by 1962, about 1,000 vehicles having been built, and although largely replaced by the Marder (*qv*) a number are still in service.

The SPZ 12-3 (Schutzenpanzer) is a low-set full-tracked vehicle with the engine placed at the right rear. The driver is at the left front, and alongside him is the gunner with a turret-mounted 20mm cannon. The vehicle commander has a small hatch in the crew compartment which is usually provided with a 7.62mm machine gun. Two long hatches cover the crew compartment and are thrown open to allow the passengers to dismount; the only other access is by a small door in the hull rear, alongside the engine.

Length: 5.56m (18ft 3in). *Width:* 2.54m (8ft 4in). *Height:* 1.85m (6ft 1in). *Weight:* 14,600kg (32,187lb). *Crew:* 3 + 5. *Power:* Rolls-Royce, 8-cyl., petrol, 235bhp at 3,800rpm. *Armament:* one 20mm cannon with 2,000 rounds; one 7.62mm machine gun. *Armour:* 8–30mm. *Speed:* 58km/hr (36mph). *Range:* 280km (175miles). *Makers:* Henschel-Werke, Kassel; Hanomag, Hannover-Linden; Leyland Motors, Leyland, Lancs.

ITALY

Fiat 6614

FIAT 6614 CM ARMOURED PERSONNEL CARRIER 1977–

The Fiat 6614 has yet to be accepted by the Italian Army, so it is still technically a project. It is a fairly compact wheeled vehicle with 4 × 4 drive and a useful specification. It originated from the 6614 BM, which was smaller and could carry only six infantry in the troop compartment. The CM should find a ready market among those forces needing a light and strong armoured carrier with minimum complications. It has the usual layout of driver and engine in front with turret behind them and troop compartment to the rear. There are doors in the sides and a powered ramp at the back. The body shape is good and every attempt has been made to slope the sides.

Internal space appears to be good, but the main use for a wheeled car of this size is probably more with police forces than with purely military units.

Length: 5.56m (18ft 3in). *Width:* 2.37m (7ft 8in). *Height:* 1.68m (5ft 6in). *Weight:* 7,000kg (15,248lb). *Crew:* 2 + 8. *Power:* Fiat Model 8062, 6-cyl., diesel, 128bhp at 3,200rpm. *Armour:* 6–8mm. *Speed:* 96km/hr (60mph). *Range:* 700km (434 miles). *Maker:* Fiat, Turin.

MOWAG TAIFUN MECHANIZED INFANTRY COMBAT VEHICLE 1977–

The Taifun is an experimental vehicle by Oto Melara and it is largely based on the Swiss Mowag (*qv*). It is intended to be a highly mobile MICV capable of being adapted to several different roles. The basic layout is slightly altered from that of the Mowag in that the driver has the gun turret beside him and the power pack immediately behind him, in the middle of the vehicle. This arrangement allows the gunner and driver to be close together, which is an important point when the infantry have dismounted and left the vehicle in their charge. However, it brings difficulties in servicing the engine, though it is claimed that this is easily hoisted out. The standard armament fit uses a turret of the same type as is fitted to the Fiat 6616 armoured car (*qv*) with two machine guns on Mowag remote mountings at the rear and ball joints in the sides for personal weapons. The infantry sit facing outwards and have a powered ramp at the rear instead of a door. The suspension uses six roadwheels and they are sprung by torsion bars. The drive sprocket is at the front. So far three variants have been announced, one of them having a 76mm gun in a turret the same as is on the Scorpion armoured vehicle (*qv*). It remains to be seen whether the Italian Army will take this advanced, but expensive, vehicle.

Length: 6.82m (22ft 4in). *Width:* 3.15m (10ft 4in). *Height:* 2.37m (7ft 8in). *Weight:* 22,800kg (50,250lb). *Crew:* 3 + 6. *Power:* V–8, 2-stroke, turbocharged, diesel, 530bhp. *Armament:* one 20mm cannon in turret; one 7.62mm machine gun coaxially mounted. *Armour* (estimated): 10–30mm. *Speed:* 70km/hr (43mph). *Range:* 500km (310 miles). *Maker:* Oto Melara, La Spezia.

JAPAN

TYPE 73 MECHANIZED INFANTRY COMBAT VEHICLE 1973–

The Type 73 is the successor to the SU-60 (*qv*) and the first production models were issued for service in late 1973. It is a larger and heavier vehicle than the Type 60, and more sophisticated. Once again there is a hull machine-gunner beside the driver and once again this

Type 73

forces the engine to be near the middle of the hull. It is on the left side with the main armament beside it, either mounted in a turret or on a counterbalanced external mounting. Although it is tempting to consider this as an updated Type 60, it is rather more than that, and there are few actual items that are common to both, though the crew positions are similar. The infantry have a powered ramp at the back, but in case of failure of the mechanism there is a door in the ramp which can be opened by hand. The vehicle is fully amphibious with minimal preparation and has full NBC protection. It is in production and in service with the Japanese Self Defence Forces.

Length: 5.60m (18ft 4in). *Width:* 2.80m (9ft 2in). *Height* (hull only): 1.70m (5ft 6in). *Weight:* 14,000kg (30,856lb). *Crew:* 2 + 10. *Power:* Mitsubishi, V–4, air-cooled, supercharged, diesel, 300bhp at 2,200rpm. *Armament:* one 0.5in Browning M2 machine gun on external mount or in turret; one 7.62mm machine gun in hull. *Armour:* not known. *Speed:* 60km/hr (37 mph). *Range:* not known.

Maker: Mitsubishi Heavy Industries, Sagamihara.

TYPE SU–60 ARMOURED PERSONNEL CARRIER 1960–

Development of this vehicle started in 1956 and took four years. Japan has never taken the M113 (*qv*) into service, and despite superficial likenesses, the SU-60 is different and does not apparently owe anything to the American design. The driver has a bow machine-gunner beside him, an unusual throwback to World War II armoured design, and the engine is behind him, on the left of the hull. The commander has a cupola directly behind the driver and hull machine-gunner, and an external machine gun is above a hatch to his right. There would appear to be less room than normal for the troops in the rear, and they are probably rather cramped. They enter and leave by two doors in the rear face of the hull. The tracks have five roadwheels, but there are three return rollers which distinguish the vehicle immediately from the M113. There are three variants, though one, an SP mounting, has not gone into service. The SU-60 is now being replaced with the Type 73 (*qv*), but it is likely to be seen for some years yet.

Length: 4.8m (15ft 10in). *Width:* 2.4m (7ft 9in). *Height:* 2.31m (7ft 6in). *Weight:* 11,800 kg (26,000lb). *Crew:* 2 + 8. *Power:* Mitsubishi Model HA–21 WT, V–8, turbocharged, diesel, 220bhp at 2,400rpm. *Armament:* one 0.5in Browning M2 machine gun on pintle; one .30in Browning machine gun in hull mount. *Armour* (estimated): 8–20mm. *Speed:* 45km/hr (28mph). *Range:* 230km (142 miles). *Maker:* Mitsubishi Heavy Industries, Maruko.

SU-60

YP408

NETHERLANDS

YP-408 ARMOURED PERSONNEL CARRIER 1964–

The YP-408 was designed to a specification raised by the Dutch Army and it has only been used in that Army. About 750 were built between 1964 and 1968 and production then ceased. It is a large 8 × 6 vehicle with a substantial engine compartment in front and the driver and commander seated side by side behind the engine, as if in the cab of a truck. The commander handles the main armament, which is an externally mounted heavy machine gun on a special ring mounting. Behind their seats is the troop compartment with the 10 infantry seated facing inwards. There are no firing ports in the sides, but six hatches in the roof permit them to stand up to shoot. There are two doors in the rear for entry and exit. The vehicle is made from as many commercial components in the DAF truck range as is possible, and there is a central air system for the air brakes and for tyre pumping. The two front pairs of wheels are steered, but the second pair is not driven. It is not amphibious, but can wade to a depth of 1.20m (3ft 11in) without preparation. There are at least five variants,

including one for the Brandt 120mm mortar. All the series are now becoming obsolescent and the Dutch government is reported to be considering re-equipping with one of the latest US APCs.

Length: 6.20m (20ft 4in). *Width:* 2.40m (7ft 9in). *Height* (hull): 1.55m (5ft 11in). *Weight:* 12,000kg (26,448lb). *Crew:* 2 + 10. *Power:* DAF Model DS 575, 6-cyl., direct injection, turbocharged, diesel, 165bhp at 2,400rpm. *Armament:* one 0.5in Browning M2 on DAF mounting. *Armour:* 8–15mm *Speed:* 80km/hr (50mph). *Range:* 500km (310 miles). *Maker:* DAF, Eindhoven.

ROMANIA

TAB-70 ARMOURED PERSONNEL CARRIER 1971–

Details of this carrier are scarce, but it is reported as being a copy or variant of the Soviet BTR-60 8 × 8 (*qv*), but whether it is built in Romania or is built to Romanian order in the USSR is not clear. The most likely answer would seem to be that it is made in the USSR. All dimensions and performance figures are assumed to be the same as for the Soviet model.

SOVIET UNION

BMP-1 MECHANIZED INFANTRY COMBAT VEHICLE 1967–

BMP-1 is an advanced infantry carrier and when it first appeared it caused a considerable stir in the Western World because it was well ahead of any in service with NATO Armies, and some maintain that it still is. It is a derivative of the PT-76 light tank (*qv*) and is most comprehensively equipped and heavily armed. The hull is a lightweight magnesium alloy, with the driver seated alongside the engine and transmission in the front. Immediately behind him is the commander, on the left side of the hull and well provided with periscopes and night-viewing devices. In the centre is a low turret mounting a smoothbore 73mm gun with

Sagger ATGW mounted on a rail above the barrel. The gun has an auto loader and the small turret accommodates only the gunner. To load a missile he has to open his hatch and place it on the rail, and it is presumed that only two or three missiles are carried. However, it does mean that the BMP has a considerable punch against enemy armour at all normal ranges of engagement. The eight infantrymen are carried in a cramped compartment at the rear, with a roof hatch and a firing port for each occupant. The normal entry is through two rear doors. All openings can be sealed and the vehicle will swim without preparation, propelling itself by its tracks. It is fully protected against the effects of NBC and has night-driving and sighting aids. The armour on the glacis plate is quite thick for an APC, but elsewhere it is light, and the vehicle must be vulnerable to a proper anti-armour defence. Due to the cramped space it is likely that the crew can only sustain operations for limited periods of time.

Length: 6.75m (22ft 2in). *Width:* 3.00m (9ft 9in). *Height:* 2.00m (6ft 6in). *Weight:* 12,500kg (27,550lb). *Crew:* 3 + 8. *Power:* Model V-6, 6-cyl., diesel, 280bhp at 2,000rpm. *Armament:* one 73mm smoothbore gun; one 7.62mm machine gun coaxially mounted; one launcher rail for Sagger ATGW. *Armour:* 6–14mm. *Speed:* 55km/hr (34mph). *Range:* 300km (186 miles). *Maker:* Soviet State Factories.

BTR-50 ARMOURED PERSONNEL CARRIER *1958–*

This carrier was developed directly from the PT-76 light tank (*qv*) and first appeared in the late 1950s. It is now an obsolescent design, although it is still in service with many of the satellite countries, and the Czechoslovaks build their own version of it known as the OT-62 (*qv*). The layout follows the tank fairly closely with the driver and commander side by side in front and a heavy machine gun between and behind them. Instead of the tank turret there is a large armoured box in which the troops ride in rather cramped conditions. This box projects well above the original hull top and is cut flat at the back, giving a distinctive side silhouette. The engine and transmission are at the rear and all crew members have to climb over the top to get in or out. Early versions had no roof, but most are now fitted with large hatch covers over the troop compartment. Like the PT-76 the vehicle swims with minimal preparation and drives itself by water jets. There is neither NBC protection nor are there normally any night-driving aids.

Length: 6.82m (22ft 4in). *Width:* 3.07m (10ft 1in). *Height:* 2.00m (6ft 6in). *Weight:* 14,200kg (31,300lb). *Crew:* 2 + 14. *Power:* Model V-6, 6-cyl., diesel, 240bhp at 1,800rpm. *Armament:* one 12.7mm or 14.5mm machine gun on external mount. *Armour:* 10–14mm. *Speed:* 44km/hr (27mph). *Range:* 260km (160 miles). *Maker:* Soviet State Factories.

BTR-50

BTR-60 ARMOURED PERSONNEL CARRIER *1960–*

The BTR-60 is probably the most widespread carrier in the Eastern bloc and the numbers in service must rival the M113 (*qv*). At least 18 armies have it, and that is not counting the USSR. The design is now obsolescent, but it is still a useful vehicle. All eight wheels are driven and the front four are steered by power steering gear. The driver and commander are in the extreme front with a machine-gun hatch behind them, but in the PB model there is a small turret instead of a hatch. The troop compartment is behind this turret and the engines are in the extreme rear. The troops can get in and out only by climbing over the roof and using the hatches, and this is a poor feature of the design. On the other hand it means that there are the fewest possible openings in the sides and the only preparation for swimming is to raise the bow vane. It is driven in the water by a single water jet. There are many variants of the basic APC and different users specify different fittings. Some versions have firing ports in the sides and others have extra viewing blocks. All models have a central tyre-pressure system, infra-red driving aids and NBC protection. Most have a winch and an infra-red searchlight for the commander. Although no longer in production, the BTR-60 will survive for many years yet.

Length: 7.56m (24ft 10in). *Width:* 2.85m (9ft 3in). *Height:* 2.31m (7ft 7in). *Weight:* 10,300kg (22,700lb). *Crew:* 2 + 14. *Power:* two GAZ-49B, 6-cyl., petrol, 90bhp each at 3,400rpm. *Armament:* one 7.62mm machine gun on pintle or one 14.5mm machine gun in turret; one 7.62mm machine gun coaxially mounted. *Armour:* 10–14mm. *Speed:* 80km/hr (50mph). *Range:* 500km (310 miles). *Maker:* Soviet State Factories.

BTR-152 ARMOURED PERSONNEL CARRIER 1950–

The BTR-152 was the first Soviet APC to be built after World War II and it is rather remarkable that it is still in service with many countries. The original version was based on a 6 × 6 ZIL truck, but later models used a special chassis, albeit from the same family. In design it is now obsolete as it follows the layout of pre-war armoured cars. The engine is inside a

BTR-60

prominent armoured bonnet with the driver and commander sitting side by side in an armoured cab. The troop compartment takes up the remainder of the hull, with two doors at the back for the troops to enter and leave. The seating arrangements vary; some have seats across the hull, others have them running the length of it. Some versions have no roof, others have armour with hatches. There are many variants, every user country adapting the vehicle to suit their own particular needs, and it can be seen carrying a wide variety of armament and equipment. The basic vehicle is sound and it is likely that it will continue in service outside the USSR for many years yet.

Length: 6.85m (22ft 5in). *Width:* 2.32m (7ft 7in). *Height:* 2.10m (6ft 9in). *Weight:* 8,950kg (19,370lb). *Crew:* 2 + 14. *Power:* ZIL-123, 6-cyl., petrol, 110bhp at 2,900rpm. *Armament:* see text. *Armour:* 6–12mm. *Speed:* 75km/hr (46mph). *Range:* 650km (400 miles). *Maker:* Soviet State Factories. Also built under licence in China.

M1970 ARMOURED PERSONNEL CARRIER 1976–

The M1970, or GT-T as it is also known, is the

BTR-152

M1970

latest in the series of tracked carriers derived from the PT-76 light tank (qv). It is used for many purposes of which the carriage of infantry is only one, and there is reason to believe that it is chiefly employed by the artillery. It is a fairly standard PT-76 derivative with the driver and engine in the front of the hull, behind a well-sloped glacis plate. There is a single machine gun in a turret and a commander's cupola, both well forward in the hull,

leaving the rear clear for the cargo and troop compartment. The suspension has six road-wheels and no return rollers, and it is reported that the springing is by torsion bars running across the hull floor. It is fully amphibious and propels itself in the water using two water jets at the back of the hull. The maximum stowed load is about 2,000kg (4,409lb) and it can tow a wheeled load of up to 4,000kg (8,818lb). In the APC role it carries 10 infantry.

Length: 6.35m (20ft 9in). *Width:* 2.80m (9ft 2in). *Height:* 2.25m (7ft 5in). *Weight:* 10,000kg (22,040lb). *Crew:* 3 + 10. *Power:* Model IZ-6, 6-cyl., diesel, 200bhp at 1,800rpm. *Armament:* one 7.62mm machine gun in turret. *Armour:* not known. *Speed:* 55km/hr (34mph). *Range:* 400km (248 miles). *Maker:* Soviet State Factories.

SWEDEN

M/42 SKPF ARMOURED PERSONNEL CARRIER 1954–1965

The SKPF was an interim vehicle for the Swedish Army and was scarcely a practical proposition for modern battlefields. It was in every way an armoured truck and it was built on a 4 × 4 commercial chassis with twin rear wheels. Large flat sheets of armour surrounded the front, enclosing the front wheels, and the driver and commander sat in a conventional cab behind the engine. The troop compartment had sloping sides and was open on top, though there was a canvas cover for winter. The troops entered by doors at the back, but the limitations of the vehicle were severe and its cross-country performance was very restricted. It was used in the infantry brigades only, but some are still in service with United Nations peacekeeping troops in different parts of the world.

Length: 6.78m (22ft 3in). *Width:* 2.28m (7ft 6in). *Height:* 2.26m (7ft 5in). *Weight:* 8,638kg (19,040lb). *Crew:* 2 + 13. *Power:* Scania-Vabis, petrol, 115bhp. *Armament:* none. *Armour:* 10mm. *Speed:* 45km/hr (28mph). *Maker:* Scania-Vabis, Södertälje.

Pbv 301 ARMOURED PERSONNEL CARRIER 1961–1970.

Pbv is the abbreviation for 'Panserbandvagn', or armoured tracked vehicle, and the 301 was unusual in that it was one of the very few post-war conversions of a tank to an APC. The basis was the Strm/41 light tank (qv), which was really the 1938 Czechoslovak TNHS built under licence in Sweden. These tanks were quite obsolete by the mid-1950s, but were in excellent condition and capable of running on for many more years. The firm of Hägglunds completely rebuilt the tanks into APCs, the conversion requiring a fundamental restructuring of the entire vehicle. The engine was

Pbv 301

moved from the rear to the front, a new transmission was installed and the superstructure was built up to make a suitable troop compartment. A rear door was fitted and a domed cupola put on the roof with an external machine gun on top of that. The finished APC was very good, although it only carried eight infantry. It had no swimming capability, but was otherwise fully equipped. It was replaced by the Pbv 302 (qv).

Length: 4.66m (15ft 2in). *Width:* 2.23m (7ft 4in). *Height:* 2.64m (8ft 7in). *Weight:* 11,500kg (25,346lb). *Crew:* 2 + 8. *Power:* Scania-Vabis, 6-cyl., petrol, 160bhp. *Armament:* one 7.92mm machine gun on external mounting. *Armour* (estimated): 6–12mm. *Speed:* 45km/hr (26mph). *Range:* 200km (120 miles). *Maker:* Hägglunds & Soner AB, Örnsköldsvik.

Pbv 302 ARMOURED PERSONNEL CARRIER 1966–

The Pbv 302 was introduced to give the Swedish infantry a carrier that could operate in conjunction with the S Tank (qv), and the design was completely new and owed nothing to previous vehicles in military service. The layout follows the general practice of putting the engine in front with the driver, but in this case it is under the floor and the driver sits above it. There is a turret mounting a 20mm cannon on the left side of the forward hull, and

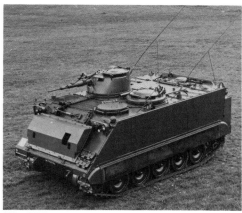

Pbv 302

the commander has a cupola on the right. From the start of the design it was intended that this vehicle should be capable of fighting and protecting itself in an armoured battle, and though the sides are flat and high, the vision is good and the infantry can open two long hatch covers and fire their weapons over the roof. There are no firing ports and the carrier is amphibious without preparation apart from raising the bow vane. The troop compartment is roomy and well heated in winter. The Swedish Army is prepared for its armoured force to have to spend a long time fully closed down in war, and the crew must have adequate room for this. There are variants on this chassis, including several command versions.

Length: 5.35m (17ft 7in). *Width:* 2.86m (9ft 5in). *Height:* 2.49m (8ft 2in). *Weight:* 13,500kg (29,760lb). *Crew:* 2 + 10. *Power:* Volvo-Penta Model THD 100B, 6-cyl., horizontal, turbocharged, diesel, 9,600cc, 280bhp at 2,200rpm. *Armament:* one HS 804 20mm cannon in turret. *Armour:* 20mm maximum. *Speed:* 66km/hr (41mph). *Range:* 300km (186 miles). *Maker:* Hägglunds & Soner AB, Örnsköldsvik.

SWITZERLAND

MOWAG GRENADIER ARMOURED PERSONNEL CARRIER *1977–*

The Grenadier is yet another of the Mowag vehicles which is offered on the open market. This one is much like the Piranha (*qv*), but it is smaller and has a better power/weight ratio. In all other respects it seems to be very similar and can be fitted with the usual range of armaments on the central roof hatch. It is fully amphibious, using a single propeller in the water.

Length: 4.84m (15ft 9in). *Width:* 2.22m (7ft 3in). *Height* (hull): 1.70m (5ft 6in). *Weight:* 4,400kg (9,700lb). *Crew:* 1 + 8. *Power:* Mowag, 8-cyl., petrol, 202bhp at 3,900rpm. *Armament:* see text. *Armour:* not known. *Speed:* 100km/hr (62mph). *Range:* 550km (341 miles). *Maker:* Mowag Motorwagenfabrik AG, Kreuzlingen.

MOWAG MR 8-01 ARMOURED PERSONNEL CARRIER *1958–*

This vehicle is a very simple police armoured carrier and it is only in service with the West German Border Police. A number of prototypes was bought from Switzerland and about 400 were then built under licence in Germany. Like the Roland it has the engine at the left rear of the hull and the remainder of the interior is free space for the crew. There are at least three variants, one of which mounts a 20mm cannon in a turret, and the other has a special bulldozer blade for clearing obstacles in streets. But the most usual version is a straightforward infantry carrier for extended

Mowag MR 8-01

border patrolling and for this there is no need for any ability to swim or to be protected from NBC.

Length: 5.30m (17ft 4in). *Width:* 2.22m (7ft 3in). *Height:* 1.92m (6ft 3in). *Weight:* 8,200kg (18,100lb). *Crew:* 3–5. *Power:* Chrysler R361, 6-cyl., petrol, 160bhp. *Armament:* normally none; variant can carry 20mm cannon in turret. *Armour:* 6–10mm. *Speed:* 80km/hr (50mph). *Range:* 400km (248 miles). *Maker:* Bussing, Brunswick and Henschel, Kassel, under licence.

MOWAG PIRANHA ARMOURED PERSONNEL CARRIER *1977–*

The Piranha is a private venture by Mowag and is intended for export. The firm has had a good

Mowag Piranha

deal of experience in producing armoured vehicles and the Piranha has features that are expected to attract foreign governments. It is supplied in three sizes, 4 × 4, 6 × 6 and 8 × 8, each carrying more than the other, but all

having almost exactly the same performance. All models have a simple welded hull with sloping sides and a sharply sloped glacis. The driver and engine are in front with a weapon installation behind him. A variety of turrets and weapons can be fitted, going up to 30mm cannon, 90mm anti-tank guns or 120mm mortars. The 8 × 8 is large enough to mount twin anti-aircraft 30mm cannon if needed, and it can also have a remotely-controlled machine gun on the rear roof. The usual hull has two firing ports in the sides and two more in the rear doors, so that the infantry can fire from under armour. The suspension is by torsion bar with special provision for long wheelbase travel, and for swimming there are two propellers under the rear doors. There is full NBC protection for all models and additional operating range can be achieved by fitting an extra external fuel tank.

4 × 4 version *Length:* 5.26m (17ft 3in). *Width:* 2.50m (8ft 2in). *Height:* 1.85m (6ft 1in). *Weight:* 7,000kg (15,430lb). *Crew:* 1 + 8. *Power:* Mowag, petrol, 190bhp at 4,000rpm. *Armament:* see text. *Armour:* 10mm maximum. *Speed:* 100km/hr (62mph). *Range:* 750km (465 miles). *Maker:* Mowag Motorwagenfabrik AG, Kreuzlingen.

MOWAG ROLAND ARMOURED PERSONNEL CARRIER *1970–*

The Roland is a simple armoured vehicle intended for use as an internal security vehicle rather than a military personnel carrier for modern battle. It is in service with several South American countries and it has been reported that in Argentina it is made under licence. The engine is at the rear on the left side, so that there is only one rear door and the troops have a door on each side under the turret. The turret can accept a variety of light armaments, but it usually mounts one machine gun only. The basic vehicle is kept simple so that the user can add the special equipment that he needs. No attempt has been made to give an amphibious capability.

Length: 4.45m (14ft 6in). *Width:* 2.01m (6ft 6in). *Height* (hull): 1.62m (5ft 4in). *Weight:* 3,900kg (8,600lb). *Crew:* 3 + 4. *Power:* Chrysler, V–8, petrol, 202bhp at 3,900rpm. *Armament:* one machine gun in turret. *Armour:* 8mm. *Speed:* 110km/hr (68mph). *Range:* 550km (340 miles). *Maker:* Mowag Motorwagenfabrik AG, Kreuzlingen.

Mowag Roland

MOWAG TORNADO MECHANIZED INFANTRY COMBAT VEHICLE 1977–

The Tornado is another of the Mowag range which is being offered to several governments, including the Swiss, who have a need for a modern MICV. The Tornado is a very sophisticated and well-equipped tracked vehicle with an impressive specification and in many ways it is not unlike the German Marder (qv). The driver and engine are beside each other in the front with the commander behind the driver. The gunner is in the middle of the vehicle in a small turret with a remotely-controlled 25mm

cannon above the turret. This unusual arrangement allows the gunner's turret to be little more than a large observation cupola and the externally mounted gun does not significantly add to the silhouette. If needed the cannon can be stabilized so that it can be fired on the move, but this is not provided for the standard version. There are two firing ports in each side of the troop compartment which allow the troops to fire sub-machine guns, and there are two more in the rear doors. The standard vehicle has two remotely-controlled external machine gun mounts on the rear roof, both of them identical to those on the Marder. There is full NBC protection, night-driving aids and an automatic fire-extinguishing system. It is not amphibious as it is too heavy, but it can wade to a depth of 1.30m (4ft 3in).

Length: 6.05m (19ft 9in). *Width:* 3.15m (10ft 4in). *Height* (hull): 1.92m (6ft 3in). *Weight:* 17,200kg (37,900lb). *Crew:* 2 + 8. *Power:* Mowag M8 DV-TLK, 8-cyl., multi-fuel, 430bhp at 2,100rpm. *Armament:* one 25mm Oerlikon B20 cannon on turret; two 7.62mm machine guns on external mountings. *Armour:* not known. *Speed:* 70km/hr (44mph). *Range:* 600km (372 miles). *Maker:* Mowag Motorwagenfabrik AG, Kreuzlingen.

UNITED KINGDOM

FV432 TROJAN ARMOURED PERSONNEL VEHICLE 1962

The development of a family of light tracked vehicles for the British Army began in the 1950s; the final design, FV432, was approved in 1962 and built from then until 1971. Originally called Trojan, this name was dropped from official use, but is still used among the troops.

The FV432 is a boxy, tracked vehicle of similar appearance to the American M113 (qv)

of the same era. The driver is at the right front, with the engine to his left. Behind the driver is the commander, with a hatch carrying a 7.62mm General Purpose Machine Gun. The remainder of the vehicle body forms the crew compartment, which can accommodate 10 fully equipped infantrymen. Over the crew compartment is a large circular hatch, and the rear of the compartment is closed by a full-width door. A flotation screen around the hull can be erected in 10 minutes and allows the vehicle to swim. Full NBC protection is given by filtering air to the interior.

In addition to the basic FV432 APC vehicle, there are a large number of variant models, some of which are given distinct identity numbers. The 432 can be modified to suit roles: as a mortar carrier, with an 81mm mortar carried inside and firing through the main hatch; as an

FV 432

ambulance, capable of lifting four stretchers; as a command vehicle with additional radios, map-boards, etc. It can also carry a Wombat 120mm recoilless anti-tank gun; be connected to a minelaying plough to mechanically lay the Barmine anti-tank mine; or be used as a surveillance vehicle, carrying the ZB298 radar or Green Archer mortar-locating radar. It is also used by artillery regiments to carry the Face fire-control computer.

More specialized variants include a version that is arranged to tow the Giant Viper minefield breaching rocket; one with a Fox armoured car turret and 30mm gun; one with twin machine guns on a high-angle mounting for use in the anti-aircraft role; and the FV434 maintenance vehicle, which carries a hydraulic crane and facilities for vehicle repair in the field. The FV438 missile carrier mounts the Swingfire guided anti-tank missile on the roof, but this version is gradually being replaced by the Striker (qv).

FV432 *Length:* 5.25m (17ft 3in). *Width:* 2.80m (9ft 2in). *Height:* 1.87m (6ft 2in). *Weight:* 15,280kg (33,686lb). *Crew:* 2 + 10. *Power:* Rolls-Royce, 6-cyl., multi-fuel, 240bhp

Mowag Tornado

AT104

at 3,750rpm. *Armament:* one 7.62mm GPMG. *Armour:* 6–12mm. *Speed:* 52km/hr (32mph). *Range:* 580km (360 miles). *Maker:* GKN-Sankey Ltd., Wellington, Salop.

GKN-SANKEY AT104 ARMOURED TRUCK *1970–*

This vehicle was developed in 1970 as a private venture by GKN-Sankey, who saw the need for a specialized internal security vehicle. It has since been purchased by Brunei and by the Dutch State Police, and a small number are in use with the British Army.

The chassis and suspension are those of the standard Bedford MK commercial truck, and the Bedford engine is retained. This is allied to an Allison automatic transmission, and the body is of welded steel construction. The driver sits in the usual position, behind the forward-mounted engine, and behind him is the crew compartment, access to which is by doors at each side of the body and twin doors at the rear. The sides and rear are also provided with firing or vision slots, and a cupola on the roof allows the commander all-round vision. This cupola can be fitted with a light machine gun or grenade discharger. A variety of equipment options is offered, including obstacle-removing blade, searchlights, smoke and tear-gas projectors and winch.

Length: 5.48m (18ft 0in). *Width:* 2.43m (8ft 0in). *Height:* 2.48m (8ft 2in). *Weight:* 8,900kg (19,620lb). *Crew:* 2 + 9. *Power:* Bedford, 6-cyl., petrol, 134bhp at 3,300rpm. *Armament:* various options (see text). *Armour:* 6–12mm. *Speed:* 80km/hr (50mph). *Range:* 640km (400 miles). *Maker:* GKN-Sankey Ltd., Wellington, Salop.

HUMBER ARMOURED TRUCK *1955–*

In the early 1950s a range of specially designed military cargo vehicles was developed, with particularly good cross-country performance. Among these was a one-ton 4 × 4 truck by Humber, and a number of these were fitted with armoured bodies in order to provide infantry with a protected vehicle as an interim

Humber Pig

measure until the Saracen APC (*qv*) was in general issue. Its increased weight, allied to the relatively soft independent suspension, led to the troops nicknaming it the Armoured Pig from the way it wallowed on rough ground. Once sufficient Saracens were provided, the Humber truck was withdrawn from service and most were either sold or scrapped. When the civil troubles broke out in Northern Ireland in the 1960s, most of the remaining vehicles were repurchased and issued as internal security trucks. They were later reworked with additional armour and stronger suspension.

The vehicle is simply an armoured box on a truck chassis; the engine is at the front, with the driver in the normal right-hand position. The remainder of the vehicle can be adapted as a cargo carrier, personnel carrier or ambulance. It is roofed, and has vision and firing slits down each side. It is not normally armed.

Length: 4.92m (16ft 2in). *Width:* 2.04m (6ft 8½in). *Height:* 2.12m (6ft 11½in). *Weight:* 6,950kg (15,325lb). *Crew:* 2 + 8. *Power:* Rolls-Royce, 6-cyl., petrol, 120bhp at 3,750rpm. *Armament:* none. *Armour:* not disclosed. *Speed:* 65km/hr (40mph). *Range:* 400km (250 miles). *Makers:* Rootes Group (Humber Motors), Ryton-on-Dunsmore (chassis); GKN-Sankey, Wellington, Salop (body).

Kangaroo

KANGAROO ARMOURED PERSONNEL CARRIER *1944–1946*

In August 1944 the 1st Canadian Army launched Operation Totalize to break out from Caen through a very strongly defended German line. Tactical surprise was virtually impossible and the Commander 2nd Canadian Corps, General Simonds, decided to drive the infantry through by placing them in armoured carriers. At the end of July the three field artillery regiments of 3rd Canadian Division had exchanged its American 105mm self-propelled howitzers M7 Priest (*qv*) for towed 25-pdr. guns, and General Simonds now obtained permission from the Americans, to whom the M7s should have been returned, to convert them into carrier vehicles for the infantry. An advanced workshop detachment, code-named Kangaroo, was given the task of conversion, which they did by removing the howitzer, seats and ammunition racks and welding a piece of armour plate over the front opening. Some of the armour, it is said, was surreptitiously removed from stranded landing craft on the Normandy beaches. When the supply of armour ran out, two sheets of steel 5cm (2in) apart, the gap packed with sand, were used. By the morning of 6 August 75 Priests had been converted, the infantry had a day in which to practise embarking and disembarking, and on the 7th the Kangaroos (the unit name now attached to the vehicles) went into action. The drivers were taken from the artillery units that had previously used the vehicles.

The Kangaroos were an unqualified success in the battle and were used on several subsequent occasions. The conversion was later applied to Sherman (qv) and Ram tanks (qv) by removing the turrets and much of the internal stowage, and Kangaroos were used by British and American units as the idea spread. These extemporized carriers undoubtedly had an effect on post-war thinking and led to the development of APCs.

SARACEN ARMOURED PERSONNEL CARRIER 1953–

The Saracen APC is basically the same vehicle as the Saladin armoured car (qv), since both were developed together. The Saladin in fact appeared first, since its presence was required in Malaya during the emergency there, and production began in 1952. After being adopted by the British Army it was widely sold overseas.

Saracen uses a welded steel hull suspended on six independently-sprung and driven wheels, the front four of which are steerable. The suspension is such that the loss of any one wheel, as, for example, by running over a mine, will not immobilize the vehicle. The engine is at the front, under an armoured bonnet, with the driver seated centrally behind it. Behind the driver are the vehicle commander and the radio operator. The crew compartment is roofed and affords seats for 10 men, and on top is a hand-operated turret mounting a machine

gun. Entry to the crew compartment is by two doors in the rear face of the body, and firing ports are provided along the sides. In addition to the turret armament, a ring mount over a hatch at the rear of the body can carry a Bren or L7 light machine gun for operation by one of the passengers.

In addition to its basic role as an APC, some have been modified to act as command vehicles, and a number were used by the Royal Artillery as Troop Command Post vehicles and carriers for the Face computer. An ambulance version was built in small numbers.

Length: 5.23m (17ft 2in). Width: 2.53m (8ft 4in). Height: 2.46m (8ft 1in). Weight: 10,170kg (22,420lb). Crew: 2 + 10. Power: Rolls-Royce, 8-cyl., petrol, 160bhp at 3,750rpm. Armament: one or two 7.62mm machine guns. Armour: 8–16mm. Speed: 72km/hr (45mph). Range: 400km (250 miles). Maker: British Leyland (Alvis), Coventry.

UNITED STATES

FIGHTING VEHICLE SYSTEM 1975–

In the 1960s the US Army began development of a 'Mechanized Infantry Fighting Vehicle' (MICV) known as the XM723. In 1972 a contract was given for the construction of 17 prototypes for rigorous testing. The development concept called for a vehicle with high mobility, protection sufficient to permit it to operate under its own artillery and be unaffected by armour-piercing ammunition of up to 20mm

calibre, fully stabilized weaponry to allow shooting on the move and room to carry an infantry squad.

The XM723, built to meet these demands, was a tracked vehicle with good protection and a turret-mounted 25mm cannon capable of high accuracy on the move. In addition to the

XM723

three-man crew, nine infantrymen could be carried, and the vehicle was fully amphibious. The extensive tests showed, however, that the commander was hampered by lack of adequate vision; that there was, in spite of the vehicle's size, no room to fit night-vision equipment; and the commander could not adequately control the gunner in his one-man turret. From considerations of these defects, a completely new concept, the Fighting Vehicle System, has been developed.

Two vehicles are postulated; the Infantry Fighting Vehicle (IFV XM2) and the Cavalry Fighting Vehicle (CFV XM3). Both are based on the original XM723 hull, but with a new two-man turret mounting the stabilized 25mm cannon, so that the commander is now in a position to oversee the battlefield and acquire targets, while the gunner's responsibility is to engage them. In addition, two TOW anti-tank missiles are fitted to the left side of the turret. Since the turret is larger, there is now room to add sophisticated night-vision and sighting equipment. The IFV carries six infantrymen in the crew compartment, each provided with a periscope and a ball-mounted automatic rifle in the hull side. The CFV carries only two men beside the normal crew, but more missiles, and is fitted with surveillance radar and other sensor devices and even carries a lightweight cross-country motorcycle for scouting or message carrying.

It is planned that about 6,500 vehicles will be procured, split about 60/40 between infantry and cavalry types. It is not anticipated that it will be in service before 1982.

XM723 Length: 6.35m (20ft 10in). Width: 3.20m (10ft 6in). Height*: 2.81m (9ft 3in). Weight*: 19,500kg (43,000lb). Crew: see text. Power: Cummins, 8-cyl., diesel, turbocharged, 450bhp at 2,600rpm. Armament: one 25mm cannon; two TOW missile launchers; one 7.62mm machine gun. Armour: not disclosed.

Saracen

M59

M75 ARMOURED PERSONNEL CARRIER *1952–*

During the last year of World War II the US Army realized the shortcomings of the M3 half-track (*qv*) as an infantry carrier, principally that it provided little or no protection for the occupants and could not keep up with the armour. So in September 1945 a specification was issued for a fully enclosed, tracked, personnel carrier. The resulting vehicle was standardized as the M75 in December 1952, and some 1,700 vehicles were built.

The hull was a steel armoured box built on to running gear built from components of the M41 light tank (*qv*). The driver sat at the front, with the engine and transmission on his right side in a package that could be removed through the hull front. The commander had a vision cupola and a .50 machine gun, while the 10 infantrymen carried could enter by twin doors in the rear of the hull. Two hatches were also provided over the passenger compartment. The vehicle was not amphibious, which proved a disadvantage, and, since it was largely built from tank components and in small numbers, was extremely expensive. It was replaced in US service by the M59 (*qv*), after which numbers of M75 were supplied to the Belgian Army, where some are still in use.

Length: 5.19m (17ft 0in). *Width:* 2.84m (9ft 4in). *Height:* 2.75m (9ft 0in). *Weight:* 18,828kg (41,510lb). *Crew:* 2 + 10. *Power:* Continental, 6-cyl., horizontally-opposed, petrol, 295bhp at 2,660rpm; *Armament:* one .50 machine gun. *Armour:* 9–25mm. *Speed:* 70km/hr (44mph). *Range:* 185km (115 miles). *Maker:* International Harvester Co., Chicago, Ill.; FMC, San Jose, Cal.

Speed: 72km/hr (45mph). *Range:* 485km (300 miles). *Maker:* FMC, San Jose, Cal. Note: Items marked * are estimates, since final vehicle configuration is not yet decided.

M59 ARMOURED PERSONNEL CARRIER *1953–*

The M75 APC (*qv*) was too expensive and lacked an amphibious capability, and so in 1953 the M59 was introduced to replace the earlier model. Whilst made to a cheaper specification it was a better vehicle, was amphibious and was less vulnerable, but it turned out to be underpowered and placed a considerable load on the maintenance services, since the engine and transmission were always being asked to do too much.

The M59 generally resembled the M75 in being a simple steel box on tracks with a sloped front, but it was a 'cleaner' design. The driver sat at the front, leaving the rest of the vehicle for the crew and passengers. Entry was by a large hydraulically operated ramp in the hull rear, and there were also two hatches over the crew compartment. The vehicle commander had a cupola with periscopes and a .50 machine gun. The engines were mounted one at each side of the crew compartment.

Variant models included an armoured ambulance version, a command vehicle, and a 4.2in mortar carrier, in which the mortar could be fired from the vehicle through the open roof or dismounted and used away from the vehicle. A limited number of the basic APC was sold abroad.

Length: 5.16m (16ft 11in). *Width:* 3.26m

M75

M113 ARMOURED PERSONNEL CARRIER *1955–*

The M59 (*qv*) and M75 APCs (*qv*) used by the US Army in the 1950s were satisfactory except that they were too heavy to be airlifted, and in 1954 a specification was drawn up for an airportable APC. This resulted in the M113, made of aluminium armour, a considerable step forward in armoured vehicle design, and manufacture commenced in 1960. The first batch was built with petrol engines, but in 1963 a fresh model, the M113A1, with a diesel engine, was standardized, and this became the production standard from then on. Well over 60,000 M113s and M113A1s had been built in

M113

the USA by the middle 1970s, as well as several thousand made in Italy under licence. It is currently in use by over 35 countries and must rank as one of the most successful armoured vehicles ever made.

The M113 is simply a box with a sloped front and tracked suspension. Driver and engine are at the front of the hull, leaving the rest clear as a crew compartment. The commander is located centrally and has a cupola with vision devices and a .50 machine gun. Ten infantrymen can sit in the hull, along the sidewalls, and entry to the compartment is by a large hydraulically operated ramp in the rear of the hull or via a hatch over the crew area. The vehicle is fully amphibious, being propelled in water by its tracks, and the only preparation required is the erection of a 'trim board' at the hull front.

There have been innumerable variants of the M113, either projected or actually produced and used. Among these the more notable are the Australian Fire Support Vehicle, an M113 with the British Saladin armoured car (*qv*) turret and 76mm gun; a bridgelayer variant used by the US Army in Vietnam; missile installations, including HOT, TOW, Dragon and SS-11; counter-mortar radar equipments; 20mm cannon turret installations by various firms; 81mm and 120mm mortar carriers; field repair vehicles with power tools and crane; recovery vehicles with winches; engineer vehicles with bulldozer blades; flamethrower ve-

hicles; and a variety of command post vehicles for artillery and infantry use. It has also been used as the platform for various anti-aircraft systems, including the Vulcan 20mm cannon, the British Rapier missile, the Italian Indigo missile and the American Hawk missile, and a highly modified version acts as the transporter and launch vehicle for the US Army's Lance ground-to-ground tactical missile.

M113A1 *Length:* 4.86m (15ft 11in). *Width:* 2.68m (8ft 10in) *Height:* 1.82m (6ft 0in). *Weight:* 11,156kg (24,595lb). *Crew:* 3 + 10. *Power:* GMC, 6-cyl., diesel, 215bhp at 2,800rpm. *Armament:* one .50 machine gun. *Armour:* 12–38mm. *Speed:* 68km/hr (42mph). *Range:* 485km (300 miles). *Makers:* FMC, San Jose, Cal.; OTO-Melara SPA, La Spezia, Italy (under licence).

M113 launching a Rapier missile

The Crab was a Sherman tank carrying a drum with steel chains attached and a rotating wire cutter at either end. During flailing the driver had to navigate with the help of a gyroscopic compass and the commander with a magnetic compass raised clear of the tank.

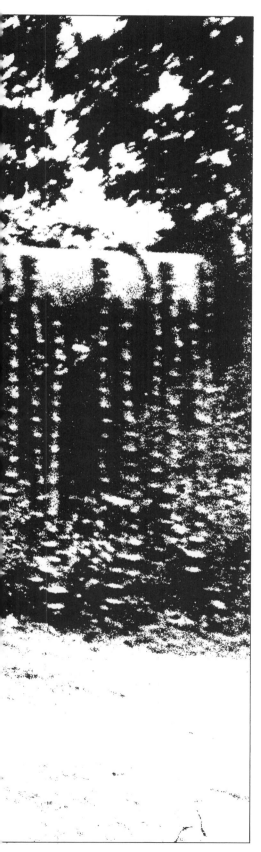

ENGINEER AND SPECIALIST VEHICLES

AUSTRALIA

MATILDA HEDGEHOG BOMBARDMENT TANK *1945*

The Matilda tank continued in service with the Australian Army till the end of the war, since it was quite adequate for fighting against the Japanese, who lacked heavy anti-tank guns. During the course of the Pacific campaign the Japanese bunker, a strongly built semi-underground strongpoint, became a major problem to the Allies since it was resistant to all but the heaviest forms of attack and usually impervious to anything the forward infantry were using.

The Hedgehog was a Naval anti-submarine spigot mortar, which fired a 28.5kg (63lb) bomb loaded with 17kg (37lb) of Torpex high explosive, and some unrecorded genius realized that such a bomb could demolish almost any bunker. The only problem was to get it into position, and from this idea the Matilda Hedgehog appeared. It was a standard Matilda II tank, with a platform of boiler-plate over the engine cover upon which seven spigots were mounted. The platform could be rotated or tilted by hydraulic rams so as to point the spigots and their bombs in the desired direction. Normal practice was to fire single bombs to adjust on to the target and then fire the

remainder as a salvo, a performance which terminated any opposition. The whole device was contrived from assorted parts designed for other purposes, but it was well engineered and most efficient. One troop of six tanks was formed in Australia and sent to Bougainville in 1945, but the war ended before they could be brought into action.

CANADA

CANADIAN RONSON FLAMETHROWER *1942–1945*

Ronson was the code name applied to a flame-thrower developed jointly by the British and Canadian armies in 1941. As with most of these devices, it relied upon compressed nitrogen to propel the flame fluid, a thickened gasolene composition, and an electric spark to ignite it as it left the gun. It had a range of 46–55m (50–60yd). In 1941 the British Army lost interest in it for various reasons and went on to produce their own variant (*qv* Wasp), but the Canadians continued development, and in 1942, when the US Marine Corps went shopping for a flamethrower, they adopted Ronson and fitted it to a number of M3 and M5 light tanks (*qv*) and LVT3 amphibians (*qv*), and used them with good results in the Pacific campaign. They were also known as Satans.

Ronson

MT-34

CZECHOSLOVAKIA

MT–34 ARMOURED BRIDGELAYER
1960–1975
The chassis of this vehicle is that of the
Czechoslovakian ARV based on the T–34 tank
(*qv*). It is one of the older types of bridgelayer
in which the unfolding process is carried out by
a mixture of hydraulic rams and winches and
cables. This takes a little longer than an all-
hydraulic operation. The bridge is 17m (55ft)
long when unfolded and will span a 15m (49ft)
gap, carrying a load of up to 50,000kg
(110,100lb). Apart from the following dimensions the vehicle is identical with the ARV.

Length (with bridge): 8.50m (27ft 9in).
Width (with bridge): 3.23m (10ft 6in). *Height*
(with bridge): 3.71m (12ft 2in). *Weight* (with
bridge): 32,000kg (70,530lb). *Maker:* State
Factories.

MT–55 ARMOURED BRIDGELAYER
1970–
The MT–55 is the replacement for the MT–34
(*qv*) bridgelayer and is based on the T–55 tank
chassis (*qv*). It has a conventional scissors
bridge folded on top of the tank and
unfolded and laid by hydraulic power gener-
ated by a pump driven off the main engine. The
surprising thing about this bridgelayer is that it
is not only used by the Czechoslovakian army
but has also been adopted by the Soviets, but in
what quantities is not known. The bridge
weighs 6,500kg (14,300lb) and opens out to
18m (59ft) long and will span a 16m (52ft 6in)
gap.

Length (with bridge): 9.81m (32ft 2in).
Width (with bridge): 3.41m (11ft 2in). *Height*
(with bridge): 3.71m (12ft 2in). *Weight* (with
bridge): 36,000kg (79,344lb). *Crew:* 2. All
other details as for the T–55 tank.

FRANCE

AMX–10 ECH ARMOURED REPAIR
VEHICLE *1977–*
The ECH is a variant of the AMX-10P
armoured personnel carrier (*qv*) and it is
intended to be the repair vehicle of the unit. It
has insufficient power to recover dead vehicles
and it is foreseen as limiting its activities to
changing engines and similar components
while in the field and without additional workshop help. In construction it is virtually an
armoured personnel carrier, with the same
turret and armament, but with a crane
mounted at the rear. This crane is operated by
a driver who has to stand with his head out of a
hatch. It is hydraulic and has an extending jib,
which will lift 6,000kg (13,200lb).

Height: 2.62m (8ft 7in). *Crew:* 5. Other
details as for the AMX–10P armoured personnel carrier.

AMX-10 ECH

AMX–13 BRIDGELAYER *1958–*
This vehicle is the standard AMX–13 Light
Tank (*qv*) with a folding Class 25 bridge on the
superstructure in place of the turret. There is a
hydraulic motor driven off the engine to provide the power for the bridgelaying operation,
and two steadying spades are driven into the
ground to support the vehicle while lowering
the bridge. The vehicle has been adopted in
several countries other than France.

Length: 7.75m (25ft 5in). *Length of bridge:*
14m (45ft 10in). *Width:* 3.05m (10ft). *Width of
bridge:* 3.05m (10ft). *Height* (with bridge):
4.3m (14ft 2in). *Weight* (with bridge):
19,700kg (43,418lb). *Armament:* none. *Speed*
(with bridge): 4km/hr (2.48mph). Other
details as for the AMX–13 light tank.

AMX–30 BRIDGELAYER *1978–*
The AMX–30 bridgelayer is only just coming
into service with the French Army, the main
reason for its delay being the expense of using a
main battle tank as the carrier vehicle. It is a
basic tank chassis with a folding bridge on top
controlled by a hydraulic motor and operating
rams to provide the power. It can be laid inside
ten minutes and when opened fully will span
22m (72ft). The tank is identical with the
AMX–30 (*qv*), the only difference being that
the turret is removed and on the flat top
decking the bridge is laid. There is an extra
hydraulic motor in the engine compartment,
but all major features are unchanged.

Length (with bridge): 11.43m (37ft 5in).
Width: 3.95m (12ft 11in). *Height* (with
bridge): 4.29m (14ft 1in). *Weight:* 43,000kg
(94,772lb). *Crew:* 3. *Power:* Hispano-Suiza
HS–110, 12-cyl., horizontally-opposed, water-
cooled, multi-fuel, 700bhp at 2,400rpm. Built
in France by Saviem. *Armament:* None.

AMX-30

Armour: Classified, estimated at 50mm thickness. *Speed:* 50km/hr (31mph). *Range:* 600km (372 miles). *Maker:* Atelier de Construction, Roanne.

FASCINE CARRIERS *1917–1918*

One of the problems which faced tanks in World War I was how to cross wide trenches. Tanks frequently became stuck when attempting to cross, and as they usually stopped with their noses in the air as they were climbing out, their thin belly plates were exposed to the enemy fire. One way of overcoming this was to fit a skid at the back, or a pair of wheels on a rigid axle, but a better way was to fill up the gap with a large bundle of brushwood tied tightly with chains. This was known as a fascine, an old name revived from seige warfare, and it was usually about 2m (7ft) in diameter. The French Renault FT 17 (*qv*) found these particularly useful and tanks were specifically set aside to carry fascines. A frame was fitted to the front of the FT 17 and a fascine winched on with chains or wire rope. On arriving at a trench the tank released the strap and dropped the fascine into the gap. Other tanks then ran over it and crossed. The fascine effectively prevented the carrying tank from engaging targets until it was dropped, but the loss of firepower was felt to be worth it.

Fascine

AMX-13

GILLOIS BRIDGE SYSTEM *1965–*

The Gillois bridge was first devised by General Gillois of the French Army and though adopted by the French the manufacture was undertaken by Eisenwerke Kaiserslautern in Germany. It is a novel idea in which the bridge structure is formed by the carrying vehicle, and the treadway runs across it. For an assault bridge or for any other short-term purpose it is ideal and must be one of the fastest bridges that it is possible to erect. However, it is obviously too expensive to leave in position for long, and it must be replaced at the first opportunity with a more long-lasting structure. Each unit is a large four-wheeled vehicle mainly consisting of a steel hull with a four-man crew compartment at the front. In the centre is an engine compartment and at the rear is the bow for moving in the water. Above the crew cab is a folded propeller, which comes down and pushes the unit when afloat. Along each side are large

GERMANY

BEFEHLSPANZER PANTHER COMMAND TANK *1943–1945*

The organization of the Panzer units of the German Army required a command tank with additional radio and fire-control equipment, which could be used to control tanks in action, keep in touch with higher formations and also act as a forward artillery observation post when required. While this could be done by virtually any vehicle capable of keeping up with the battle tanks, it was obviously better to have a vehicle based on the battle tank in order to reduce the maintenance load and also so that it could be made to look as much like the combat tank as possible and thus not be an obvious target.

The Befehlspanzer Panther was typical of

Befehlspanzer Panther

neumatic floats, which are inflated before entering the water and which provide a major portion of the buoyancy. The engine has a small compressor which inflates these and maintains their pressure. When swimming, the wheels are retracted to reduce drag and are towed in wells in the hull. The bridge works by the flotation units remaining in position and providing what is in effect a large pontoon bridge. There are two sorts of unit, a bridge vehicle, which has just been described in outline, and a ramp unit. The ramp vehicle carries shorter treadway sections, which can be raised or lowered by hydraulic power to meet the bank. Once they are in position it is possible to withdraw the vehicle, but the main flotation vehicles must stay in place and provide buoyancy. Both types carry their treadway sections on top of the hull, running lengthwise. Once in the water the treadway is swung through 90° and the hull takes position end on to the current and sideways on to the traffic. Each section is connected by hydraulic pins.

Gillois vehicles can also be joined together to make rafts. As a bridge a Gillois structure can carry up to Class 60 loads, and the rafts carry variable loads depending on the number of units used. The Gillois system is extremely versatile and mobile, but it is costly. The French Army is fully equipped with it and the British and Federal German Armies also have it, but in a slightly different form.

Length: 11.86m (38ft 11in). *Width:* 3.23m (10ft 6in). *Height:* 3.91m (12ft 9in). *Weight:* 26,950kg (59,397lb). *Crew:* 4. *Power:* Deutz, V–12, air-cooled, diesel; 220bhp at 2,000rpm. *Armament:* none. *Armour:* none. *Speed:* 64km/hr (40mph). *Range:* 780km (484 miles). *Maker:* Eisenwerke Kaiserslautern, Kaiserslautern.

---

these command tanks. It was basically the standard Panther (*qv*), but with the addition of a rear-link radio set in the hull, a fitting which displaced some of the ammunition stowage. The only outward indication of its special role was the addition of two more radio antennae

For artillery observation, a second variant known as the Beobachtungspanzer was built. This had the 75mm gun removed and replaced with a dummy; the turret was then filled with fire-control equipment, rangefinder and binocular periscope for use by the observers. The glacis plate of this model was slightly modified so as to make more room inside the hull.

Data are as for the Panther tank, except that the command tank carried only 64 rounds of ammunition and the observation tank had only two machine guns. Between May 1943 and February 1945, 329 command tanks and 41 observation tanks were built.

Borgward B IV

BORGWARD B IV DEMOLITION VEHICLE *1941–1945*

In 1939 the German Army began giving some thought to mineclearing and specified a remote-controlled vehicle of cheap construction that could tow mine-detonating rollers out into the suspected area; if it discovered a mine, then, being cheap, it was expendable. The Borgward Company developed a small tracked vehicle, radio-controlled, known as the B I, which weighed about two tonnes and some 50 were made in 1939-40. However, it turned out to be not so cheap as had been hoped and eventually it was dropped in favour of Goliath (*qv*).

Goliath, though, could not carry a sufficiently heavy charge to deal with some of the more formidable obstacles found in Russia and the B I idea was revived, using the chassis of a tracked load carrier, which the Borgward Company were then making. The B IV was basically a small tracked vehicle to the front of which a large explosive charge container was hooked. The hull hatch could be opened and a driver then got in and drove the vehicle in the normal way as far as he could safely go; he then dismounted, closed the hatch, and the remainder of the mission was completed by radio remote control. Once the vehicle arrived at the target, the charge was released and the vehicle backed away; dropping the charge activated a delay device which detonated the explosive after a short interval. This interval allowed the vehicle to be taken clear of the blast, turned and driven back to be used again. In practice, however, it was found that the

delay mechanism failed and the vehicle was destroyed by the detonation, which took place as soon as the charge was released.

There were three versions of the B IV; Ausf. A was the original; Ausf. B had the armour thickened and the radio control improved, and Ausf. C had still thicker armour and a generally simpler construction. Over 500 of all models were produced.

Ausf. B *Length:* 3.65m (12ft 0in). *Width:* 1.80m (5ft 11in). *Height:* 1.19m (3ft 10in). *Weight:* 3,660kg (8,068lb). *Crew:* 1; *Power:* Borgward, 6-cyl., 2,310cc, 49bhp at 3,300rpm. *Armament:* one 500kg (1,100lb) explosive charge. *Armour:* 10mm. *Speed:* 38km/hr (24mph). *Range:* 210km (130 miles). *Maker:* Hansa-Lloyd-Goliath Werke Carl F. W. Borgward, Bremen.

BRUCKENLEGER IV BRIDGELAYER *1940–1941*

The extensive use of ditches as anti-tank obstacles on most of the European frontiers in the 1930s led the German Army to begin experiments with armoured bridgelayers as early as 1938. Early tests with PzKpfw I and II tank (*qv*) chassis were ended because these were too small to carry a worthwhile bridge and in 1939 work was started on a design using the PzKpfw IV tank (*qv*). Two types were developed, one by Krupp, which used a pivoted A-frame to swing the bridge span from its place on top of the tank across the gap, and one by Magirus, which used hydraulic rams and a tipping frame to slide the bridge span across the gap.

Although 60 were ordered, only 20 were

built before the contract was cancelled. Four bridgelayers were attached to each of the five Panzer divisions used in France in 1940, but they saw little use, and as a result the remainder of the order was stopped. The Germans discovered that tactical surprise was worth any amount of bridgelaying tanks, and by 1941 almost all the bridgelayers had been converted back into combat tanks.

Length (with bridge): 11.00m (36ft 1in). *Width* (with bridge): 3.00m (9ft 11in). *Height* (with bridge): 3.54m (11ft 7in). *Weight* (with bridge): 28,450kg (62,720lb). *Crew:* 2. *Power:* Maybach, V–12, petrol, 11,867cc, 300bhp at 3,000rpm. *Armament:* one 7.92mm machine gun. *Bridge:* spanning 9m (30ft) and carrying 30 tonnes. *Armour:* 10–30mm. *Speed:* 40km/hr (25mph). *Range:* 200km (125 miles). *Makers:* Fried. Krupp AG, Essen; CD Magirus AG, Ulm/Donau.

Goliath

GOLIATH DEMOLITION VEHICLE
1940–1945
In 1940 the German Army requested a remote-controlled vehicle that could carry a demolition charge up to a target – e.g., a pillbox – and there be detonated; it was also to have a secondary purpose as a mine-clearance vehicle, to be driven into a minefield and there detonated so as to set off the mines by blast over-pressure. The result was Goliath, a small tracked unit propelled by electric motors and carrying a 60kg (132lb) charge of explosive. The construction was of simple pressed metal and the electric motors were powered by batteries carried in sponsons, around which ran the tracks. A drum at the rear of the vehicle carried about 1.5km (⁹/₁₀ mile) of three-core cable, two strands of which were used to transmit steering signals and the third to transmit the firing signal. The operator was provided with a small control box with switches and batteries, which controlled relays in the vehicle.

PzKpfw II

Over 2,500 of these were made and they were extensively used in both demolition and mine-clearing tasks, but it was found that the electric motors and battery power limited the range and power of the vehicles, particularly in cold weather. A second version was therefore developed, powered by a 703cc twin-cylinder motorcycle engine. The first of these carried a 75kg (165lb) charge, but it was soon replaced by a larger model carrying a 100kg (220lb) charge. Over 4,500 were built.

Goliath E (electric): *Length:* 1.50m (4ft 11in). *Width:* 0.85m (2ft 9in). *Height:* 56cm (1ft 10in). *Weight:* 375kg (828lb). *Crew:* nil. *Armament:* 60kg (132lb) explosive charge. *Armour:* 5mm. *Speed* 10km/hr (6mph). *Range:* 1.50km (⁹/₁₀ mile). *Maker:* Hansa-Lloyd-Goliath Werke Carl F. W. Borgward, Bremen.

Goliath V (petrol) *Length:* 1.63m (5ft 4in). *Width:* 0.91m (3ft 0in). *Height:* 0.62m (2ft 0in). *Weight:* 435kg (960lb). *Crew:* nil. *Power:* Zundapp, 2-cyl., 703cc, 12.5bhp at 4,500rpm. *Armament:* one 100kg (220lb) explosive charge. *Armour:* 10mm. *Speed:* 12km/hr (7.5mph). *Range:* 12km (7.5 miles). *Maker:* Zundapp GmbH, Nuremberg.

PzKpfw II (FLAMM) FLAMETHROWER
1940–1942
Early in 1939 the German Army requested a flamethrower tank with which to attack permanent fortifications such as faced them in the Maginot Line. Development began in January 1939, but progress was slow and it was not until May 1940 that production commenced, so that the French campaign was fought without them.

The basis of the design was the PzKpfw II tank (*qv*), which had its turret replaced by a smaller turret armed only with a machine gun. Two flame projectors were mounted in small housings on the front corners of the vehicle, and armour-protected lockers on the hull sides were used to stow the four nitrogen bottles providing the pressure for the flame fuel. The fuel was carried inside the tank, alongside the fighting compartment, and was piped to the projectors.

These equipments were first used in the advance into Russia in 1941 and proved to be effective, but their thin armour left them vulnerable to enemy fire and, of course, when hit they immediately exploded. They were withdrawn from service in 1942 and replaced by the PzKpfw III (Flamm) (*qv*). Most vehicles were converted into self-propelled gun chassis.

Weight: 12,190kg (26,880lb). *Height:* 1.85m (6ft 1in). *Armament:* one flamethrower with 320l (70galls) fuel; one 7.92mm machine gun. Other details as for PzKpfw II.

PzKpfw III (FLAMM)
FLAMETHROWER *1942–1945*
Combat in built-up areas in Russia led to a demand for more flamethrowing tanks, and in late 1942 a design for the PzKpfw III version was begun. The system used nitrogen pressure to deliver fuel to the projector, which was mounted in the turret in place of the normal gun. Since the maximum range of the flame projector was only 60m (196ft), additional armour was applied to the tank front so as to allow it to get close to its target. One hundred were built between February and April 1943 and they were extensively used in Russia.

Weight: 23,370kg (51,520lb). *Armament:*

PzKpfw III

Raumer-S

one flame projector with 1,000l (4,545gall) fuel; one 7.92mm machine gun. *Makers:* Muhlenbau-Industrie AG, Brunswick (chassis); Wegmann GmbH, Kassel (flame installation). Other details as for the PzKpfw III.

RAUMER–S MINE-CLEARING VEHICLE *1945–*

The German Army expended very little effort in the development of mine-clearing vehicles, probably reflecting the smaller use of mines by the Allies. In 1944, however, the problem began to increase, and Krupp were asked to develop a suitable vehicle. They elected to aim at a massive vehicle impervious to mines, which would simply roll over them and detonate them harmlessly; this approach was also

tried by the British and Americans, but without much success – manufacturing a massive and impervious vehicle is one thing, driving it another.

The Räumer-S consisted of two massive steel boxes each containing an engine and carried on two extremely heavy steel wheels about 2.75m (9ft) in diameter. These two boxes were connected together by an articulated joint, which allowed each unit to roll independently and allowed the whole machine to be steered by hydraulic rams, which 'bent' the assembly in its centre. The front of the forward unit carried the driver's cab, from which both motors were controlled. The total weight was in the region of 130 tonnes, and one vehicle had been completed and was undergoing trials at the end of the war. No further data are available.

WEST GERMANY

BIBER (BEAVER) BRIDGELAYING TANK *1973–*

Biber is a bridgelayer tank developed for the West German Army and first produced in 1973. It is based on a modified Leopard I (*qv*) tank chassis and hull, the turret being omitted and the hull completely roofed in. At the rear of the hull is the mounting for a cantilever arm, which supports the bridge unit. The bridge is in two sections, carried one above the other, and is made of aluminium alloy.

To lay the bridge the tank is driven forward to the gap and then lowers a bulldozer blade at the front to act as a support strut. The lower section of the bridge is then slid forward, beneath the upper section, until the ends align, whereupon the upper section is lowered and locked to form a solid unit. This is now extended, by means of the cantilever arm, across the gap and then lowered into place. The tank can then disconnect and retire, leaving the bridge in place, and it can return later to recover the bridge by a reversal of the laying process. The bridge will span a 20m (65ft) gap and will support a maximum weight of 60 tonnes.

Length (with bridge): 11.65m (38ft 3in). *Width* (with bridge): 4.00m (13ft 1in). *Height* (with bridge): 3.50m (11ft 6in). *Weight* (with bridge): 45,000kg (99,210lb). *Crew:* 2. *Power:* MTU, V–10, multi-fuel, 37,400cc, 830bhp at 2,200rpm. *Armament:* nil. *Armour:* 15–40mm. *Speed:* 65km/hr (40mph). *Range:* 550km (340 miles). *Maker:* Atlas-MaK Maschinenbau GmbH, Kiel.

Biber

ITALY

CV 33 BRIDGELAYER *1936–1940*

A small number of CV 33 light tanks (*qv*) were fitted with a bridge which could be laid in front of the vehicle. The bridge was in one piece and was a little longer than the CV 33 itself. It was carried on a lightweight tubular structure which winched it forward and down to the ground, motive power being provided by the crew. It seems likely that the bridge treadways were similar to the ramps that were used for running these small tanks up into their carrying trucks, and the span covered by the bridge was short. Recovering the bridge almost certainly involved the crew in having to get out and attach the lifting links by hand. There are no data for this interesting early bridgelayer.

JAPAN

TYPE 67 ARMOURED BRIDGELAYER *1971–*

The Type 67 is another variant on the basic chassis of the Type 61 tank (*qv*). The turret is removed and a flat decking substituted. On top of this is a folding bridge from the United States M48 AVLB (*qv*). This bridge folds forward to open out in front.

Length: 7.27m (23ft 9in). *Width* (with bridge): 3.53m (11ft 6in). *Height* (with bridge): 3.53m (11ft 6in). *Armament:* One 7.62mm machine gun on external mounting. Other details as for the Type 61 tank.

CV 33

TYPE 67 ARMOURED ENGINEER VEHICLE *1967–*
This vehicle is something like an ARV and is designed to carry a repair crew on the battlefield. It does not have the lifting or towing capacity of a proper ARV, but it does have a selection of special tools together with welding gear and a range of spare parts. It is a turretless Type 61 tank (*qv*) fitted with an armoured superstructure for the crew and their equipment.
Length: 7.46m (24ft 6in). *Width:* 3.23m (10ft 6in). *Height:* 2.23m (7ft 4in). *Weight:* 35,000kg (77,140lb). *Armament:* one 12.7mm machine gun on external mount; one 7.62mm machine gun. Other details as for the Type 61 tank.

Mowag Husky

SOVIET UNION

IMR COMBAT ENGINEER VEHICLE *1975–*
The IMR is a variant of the T54/55 tank (*qv*) and it appears to be specifically designed for the removal of obstacles and also the building of new ones. In place of the turret there is a small cupola in which the crane operator is seated. He has a large hydraulically operated crane with a telescopic jib and large pincer-like grabs, which can pick up trees and similar objects. There is a bulldozing blade on the front of the hull and an unditching beam at the back. The vehicle is in service in the USSR.
Length: 10.60m (34ft 8in). *Height* (top of crane): 3.37m (11ft 1in). *Crew:* 3. Other details as for the T54/55.

SWEDEN

BROBANDVAGN 941 ARMOURED BRIDGELAYER *1973–*
The Brobv 941 is another variant of the Pvb

302 (*qv*) and bears a close resemblance to the ARV (*qv*). Without its bridge the hull looks much like a Bgbv 82 without a turret. The bridge weighs seven tons and can carry vehicles up to 50 tons in weight across a 15m (49ft) gap, it is a single span and is laid by an original method devised by Hägglunds. In outline it amounts to first pushing a telescopic rail across the gap, sliding the one-piece bridge over the rail and then withdrawing the rail leaving the bridge in place. This is a much less conspicuous way of laying a bridge than the more usual 'scissor' or folding span, but it does restrict the length that can be carried on the vehicle. Recovering the bridge is the reverse of this operation, and both take no more than five minutes.
Length (with bridge): 17.00m (55ft 8in). *Width* (with bridge): 4.02m (13ft 2in). *Height* (with bridge): 3.23m (10ft 6in). *Weight* (with bridge): 29,400kg (64,797lb). *Crew:* 4. *Armament:* none. Other details as for the Bgbv 82.

SWITZERLAND

MOWAG HUSKY ARMOURED REPAIR VEHICLE *1977–*
So far this vehicle has only been taken into service in Canada and it is based on the Pirhana (*qv*). It has little extra equipment, but carries a specialist repair crew with a full range of tools and some small components. Like the Pirhana it is amphibious.

Brobandvagn 941

UNITED KINGDOM

CENTURION BRIDGELAYER *1954–*
This vehicle appeared in the early 1950s to replace the Churchill bridgelayer, which had remained in service since the war. The standard hull and chassis are used, without turret, and the single-span bridge is pivoted about a girder extension at the front of the tank so that in the travelling position it lies along the hull top, upside down. When the bridge needs to be used the vehicle is driven to the edge of the gap and, with hydraulic rams, the entire spaning unit is turned about its pivot through 180° so that it is lowered across the gap. Once the bridge is in place the tank can be unhitched and backed away. The span will bridge a 13.70m (45ft) gap and can be used immediately by

Type 67 Armoured Bridgelayer

tracked vehicles; for use by wheeled vehicles, a centre deck between the treadways has to be laid by hand. Laying the bridge takes only two minutes, and it can be recovered in four minutes by the tank reconnecting and lifting it back into the travelling position.

Length (with bridge): 16.30m (53ft 6in). *Width* (with bridge): 4.26m (14ft 0in). *Height* (with bridge): 3.88m (12ft 9in). *Weight* (with bridge): 50,485kg (111,300lb). *Crew:* 3. *Power:* Rolls-Royce, 12-cyl., petrol, 650bhp at 2,550rpm. *Armament:* one 7.62mm machine gun. *Armour, speed, range:* not disclosed. *Maker:* Royal Ordnance Factory, Leeds.

Chieftain Bridgelayer

CHIEFTAIN BRIDGELAYER 1974-

Production of this equipment began in 1974, to replace the Centurion bridgelayer (*qv*) in service. It consists of a standard Chieftain (*qv*) hull and running gear, without turret, and with a folded bridge on top, the front end of which is carried on an extended girder structure. Hydraulic pumps driven from the engine actuate five rams, which, applied to various parts of the bridge, cause it to pivot at its forward end and then unfold so as to stretch out in front of the tank and span a gap of up to 22.85m (75ft) in width. It takes between three and five minutes to unfold the bridge, after which the tank casts itself clear and backs away. When necessary, the tank can return, hook on to the bridge, and recover it in about ten minutes. The bridge span is made of light alloy and weighs only 12,200kg (26,896lb). A shorter bridge capable of carrying greater weights has been developed, but is not on general issue.

Length (with bridge): 13.74m (45ft 1in). *Width* (with bridge): 4.16m (13ft 9in). *Height* (with bridge): 3.88m (12ft 9in). *Weight* (with bridge): 53,300kg (117,505lb). *Crew:* 3. *Power:* Leyland, 12-cyl., vertically opposed, 2-stroke, multi-fuel, 720bhp at 2,250rpm. *Armament:* nil. *Armour:* not disclosed. *Speed* and *range:* not disclosed. *Maker:* Royal Ordnance Factory, Leeds.

Centurion Bridgelayer

Churchill AVRE

CHURCHILL ARMOURED VEHICLE, ROYAL ENGINEERS 1943–1955

The Dieppe Raid in 1942 indicated that a specialized armoured vehicle was needed for use by engineers clearing obstacles from beaches. After considering various tanks, the Churchill (qv) was selected since it offered maximum protection and ample space for stowage of the various items of engineer equipment. In order to provide the vehicle with the capability of smashing concrete or other obstacles, a special spigot mortar was developed by Blacker Developments and mounted on the turret. This fired a fin-stabilized bomb carrying 18kg (40lb) of high explosive, capable of breaching most types of obstacle at short range, and from its shape and low velocity it gained the nickname of the Flying Dustbin.

The interior of the tank was stripped of the usual ammunition racks and converted for engineer stores, demolition equipment, tools and similar items. After extensive trials the design was accepted and in 1943 work began on converting Churchill tanks into AVRES (Armoured Vehicle, Royal Engineers). The first 108 were converted by army workshops, the remainder by commercial firms. AVRE tanks were frequently used as a basis for attaching other special devices and could be found with a wide variety of brackets and attachments on the outside. They proved to be invaluable in the invasion of Europe and in the subsequent advance into Germany.

Length: 7.67m (15ft 2in). *Width:* 3.25m (10ft 8in). *Height:* 2.48m (8ft 2in). *Weight:* 38,610kg (85,120lb). *Crew:* 6. *Power:* Bedford, 12-cyl., horizontally opposed, petrol, 21,240cc, 350bhp at 2,200rpm. *Armament:* one 'Petard' spigot mortar with 26 bombs; one 7.92mm machine gun. *Armour:* 20–88mm. *Speed:* 24km/hr (15mph). *Range:* 200km (120 miles). *Makers:* Cockbridge & Co., Ipswich (conversion kits); MG Motors Ltd., Abingdon (actual conversion of tanks).

CHURCHILL ASSAULT BRIDGE AVRE 1944–1945

Whilst a proper bridge-carrying tank had been developed on the Churchill chassis (qv), it was designed for crossing major obstacles, and the Canadian Army, in training for the invasion of Europe, felt that something smaller was needed, to cope with anti-tank ditches, parapets and the lesser obstacles which would be met on the beachheads. Their solution was to mount a 10.40m (34ft) 'SBG' (Small Box Girder) bridge on the front of a Churchill tank. It was carried in an elevated position, the weight taken by a winch cable from the rear of the tank, and by simply releasing the winch brake the bridge could be rapidly dropped ahead of the tank across the obstacle. It could carry a weight of 40 tons, and as well as

Assault Bridge AVRE

bridging gaps it could be used to surmount walls; the bridge was dropped against the wall, after which a second AVRE could drive up the bridge and drop fascines (bundles of brushwood) over the wall so as to cushion its landing as it drove over.

CHURCHILL CARPET OBSTACLE-CROSSER 1944–1945

One of the original purposes of the tank was to break down barbed wire and leave a gap for infantry to follow through, and while tanks can certainly do this, the gap they leave is not entirely simple to negotiate, since the strands of wire tend to spring up and trip the following soldiers. During World War II, when preparing for the invasion of Europe, gapping wire was a major problem, and the gaps had to be capable of being passed not only by foot soldiers but also by wheeled vehicles. As a result, the Carpet tank was developed.

The Carpet Churchill was a standard Churchill tank (qv), complete with armament, which carried on its front two arms supporting a

drum. On this drum was wound a length of reinforced hessian matting, the free end of which was weighted. Hydraulic arms, or winches in some models, lifted the drum well into the air so that the driver could see where he was going. Once landed and approaching the wire, the drum was lowered and the weighted end of the matting allowed to fall free on the ground, where it was run over by the tank's tracks. This held the mat down, and as the tank went forward the remainder unwound from the drum. As the tank crossed the wire obstacle, so the carpet unrolled beneath it and was laid on top of the crushed wire, providing a smooth path for troops and vehicles.

Several minor variants existed, each showing some improvement on its predecessor. The first Carpet was used at Dieppe and they were extensively used in the Normandy landings in 1944.

Carpet Churchill

Onion

CHURCHILL CARROT, ONION AND GOAT DEMOLITION TANKS *1944–1945*

When contemplating the probable obstacles on the invasion beaches, the British Army concluded that there would be cases where it would be necessary to go close to an obstacle and place a substantial explosive charge on it, since no other method of breaching would suffice. Since it would be necessary to provide armoured protection for the man placing the charge, the need arose for a specialized tank capable of carrying a heavy charge and placing it with some precision.

The Churchill tank (*qv*) was selected as the carrier vehicle, and the first device, known as Carrot, was developed in July 1942. This was a simple bracket attached to the nose of the tank and carrying a maximum of 11.3kg (25lb) of high explosive. The tank drove up to the obstacle until the charge was in contact, then released the frame, starting a timing device at the same time, and backed away. The charge then detonated. Carrot worked, but the charge was too small to warrant the complication and it was dropped in favour of the Onion, which was similar but larger, a frame 2.7m (9ft) wide and 1.4m (4ft 6in) high to which charges of various sizes could be fixed. In this model the charge was electrically detonated by a wire

paid out as the tank backed from the frame.

A further development led to the Goat, a larger platform holding 816kg (1,800lb) of explosive and carried horizontally above the tank's nose. A sensing device automatically aligned and dropped the charge as soon as the tank made contact with the obstacle, after which the charge could be electrically fired. A refinement of this was the Elevatable Goat, in which the charge was carried on a long, extended frame to allow it to be placed against high obstacles.

CHURCHILL CROCODILE FLAMETHROWER *1942–1955*

The British Army had demanded a flame-throwing tank as early as 1938, and after testing several different designs of flame projector, in 1942 it was finally decided to produce one using pressurized liquid, with a minimum range of 73m (80yds) and a duration of fire of not less than one minute. Since this demanded a large quantity of fuel and pressure cylinders, it meant that the flame equipment had to be carried in a trailer rather than on board the tank. The Churchill tank (*qv*) was selected as the vehicle and development began in July 1942.

The Crocodile equipment consisted of an armoured trailer in which were five nitrogen

cylinders and 1,818l (400 galls) of flame-thrower fuel, a thickened gasoline mixture. The flame gun was mounted in the hull front in place of the usual machine gun. Connection of trailer and tank was by a special link, which could be broken by remote control from inside the tank should the trailer sustain damage or when the flame fuel was expended; afterwards the tank could revert to normal operation since it still carried its turret armament. The trailer was armoured and weighed 6½ tons when loaded.

A total of 800 Crocodile kits were built; production tanks were made with the various necessary attachment points, and any Churchill Mark 7 could be converted to a Crocodile tank in the field by fitting the components from the kit. The equipment remained in service after the war and some Crocodiles were used in Korea in 1951-2.

Data are as for Churchill Mark 7, except that the weight was 20,346kg (44,855lb).

CHURCHILL OKE FLAMETHROWER *1942*

In 1941 there was a great deal of interest in flamethrowing devices, and one which was developed by British and Canadian sources was known as Ronson (*qv* Canadian Ronson). In late 1941 a Major J. M. Oke proposed fitting

Carrot

Crocodile

this device to a Churchill tank (qv). Three were converted by the Petroleum Warfare Department in 1942. The fuel tank and pressure tank were fitted to the rear of the tank and were arranged so as to be jettisonable once their contents had been used. Pipes protected by armour ran along the side of the tank hull to the flame gun, which was mounted externally, at the front of the vehicle, inside the front track. This gun was fixed in place and could be aimed only by aiming the tank; the range was also fixed at 54.60m (50yd).

The three vehicles were taken to Dieppe in August 1942 by the Calgary Regiment, but all three were either drowned or shot up before they could be got into action. One was later retrieved by the Germans and tested, and is believed to have assisted their own development of similar devices. No more Okes were built.

Data are as for Churchill Mark II with the addition of the flame unit. It was made by Lagonda Motors, London.

Oke

COMBAT ENGINEER TRACTOR *1971–*
Whilst the AVRE tanks perform a useful role, there are times when a more versatile engineer vehicle is required in the combat zone, and for this purpose the British Army developed the 'Combat Engineer Tractor' in the early 1970s.

The CET consists of an aluminium armoured hull on a torsion-bar tracked suspension. It carries a crew of two men seated at the front, and the controls are arranged so that either can drive the vehicle. Their seats can be reversed to give them command of the rear when operating some of the equipment. At the rear end is an excavator bucket of light alloy with steel cutting edges. Hydraulically activated, this bucket can be used for digging, bulldozing or as an earth anchor when winching. A crane can be attached to the bucket and used in conjunction with the ve-

hicle winch. On top of the hull a rocket-propelled ground anchor is carried; this can be fired from the vehicle to a distance of just over 90m (100 yards), where it digs into the ground

and gives purchase to allow the winch to pull the vehicle out of soft ground, water or up otherwise insuperable obstacles. The CET can also tow a trailer with Giant Viper mine-clearing rocket equipment.

The vehicle is amphibious, being propelled in water by two jet thrust units; additional buoyancy is provided by a plastic foam block carried in the bucket when swimming. Full night-vision aids are carried and the vehicle is proofed against all forms of NBC attack.

Length: 7.50m (24ft 9in). *Width:* 2.90m (9ft 6in). *Height:* 2.60m (8ft 6in). *Weight:* 17,100kg (37,700lb). *Crew:* 2. *Power:* Rolls-Royce, 6-cyl., turbocharged, diesel, 12,200cc, 320bhp at 2,100rpm. *Armament:* one 7.62mm machine gun. *Armour:* not disclosed. *Speed:* 60km/hr (37mph). *Range:* 480km (300 miles). *Makers:* Royal Ordnance Factory, Leeds.

Grant CDL

GRANT SPECIAL-PURPOSE TANK
1942–1945

During the World War I a Commander Oscar de Thoren, RN, proposed mounting a powerful light on tanks or other vehicles so as to blind an enemy during a night attack. His idea was not pursued, and he continued to develop it in post-war years. In 1933 a syndicate was set up, and several demonstrations made, and in 1940 the War Office accepted the idea, giving orders for some 300 special turrets to be made. These turrets, designed in the first place for fitting to the Matilda II tank (*qv*), contained a 13 million candlepower arc light and a special reflector, together with a stroboscopic shutter. The effect of this was to emit a dazzling light which temporarily blinded any onlooker and allowed tanks to manoeuvre and conceal bodies of troops at night. Several demonstrations testified to its effectiveness when properly used with trained troops.

First installations were made on Matilda and Churchill tanks (*qv*), but it was then found that the turrets could be fitted to Grant tanks (*qv*), and these became the usual vehicle. The term CDL stands for Canal Defence Light, a misleading term adopted as a security measure. A similar conversion was carried out by US units, who called their versions the Shop Tractor.

In spite of its virtues, the CDL saw very little use; it was deployed at the crossing of the Rhine by both British and US forces, but functioned principally as a floodlight and not in the manner envisaged by its inventor. It is generally understood that the lack of use was due to excessive secrecy, which concealed the device's ability from commanders, and the lack of troops trained to accompany the CDL tanks in battle. In post-war years the device was refined and in its present form is known as the Xenon Searchlight.

ROYAL ENGINEER TANK *1918–1925*

One of the prime design features of the original tanks was that they had to be able to cross trenches, and even though their ability to do this was greater than most tanks designed since then, there were still some wide ditches they found impassable. In 1918 the RE Tank was designed in order to overcome this problem, and it consisted of a Mark V** battle tank with a 6m (20ft) bridge slung from the front. A jib unit on the hull top was connected by cables to the bridge and could be operated by a combination of winch and hydraulic ram to either raise the bridge to allow the tank to move forward or lower the bridge across the ditch to be crossed. Once lowered into place it could be detached from the tank, which could then either withdraw, leaving the bridge in place for other tanks to use, or cross the bridge itself.

It was intended to equip special bridging companies with these tanks towards the end of 1918, but the end of the war cancelled this plan. A small number of vehicles were built and were retained for training purposes for some years after the war.

Length (without bridge): 9.88m (32ft 5in). *Width:* 3.20m (10ft 6in). *Height* (with jib): 5.02m (16ft 6in). *Weight* (without bridge): 35,050kg (77,271lb). *Crew:* 10. *Power:* Ricardo, 6-cyl., petrol, 225bhp. *Armament:* two machine guns. *Armour:* 6–12mm. *Speed:* 6.5km/hr (4mph). *Range:* 144km (90 miles). *Maker:* Metropolitan Carriage, Wagon & Finance Co., London.

SCORPION MINEFIELD CLEARANCE TANK *1942–1943*

In the Western Desert campaign of 1941-2 the vast expanses of bare country led to an upsurge in anti-tank mine warfare, particularly by the German Army, and the British forces began seeking some method of overcoming mines which was more efficient than having a man on foot precede the armour with an electric detector or prodding the ground with a bayonet. Since anti-tank mines all depended upon pressure to set them off, it occurred to a South African engineer, Major A. S. du Toit, that beating the ground with chains might be effective, and he devised a mechanism in which a drum was suspended in front of a tank and revolved rapidly by an auxiliary engine. Attached to the drum were several lengths of

Royal Engineer Tank

Matilda Baron, a predecessor of Scorpion

chain, which, whirled by the rotating drum, flailed the ground with great force and detonated any mine which they struck. By making the drum wide enough, and providing sufficient chains, the flexibility of the chains ensured that the entire area was thoroughly beaten, leaving a safe path over which the tank could move. The detonation of a mine would merely snap the chain, whereupon a new chain could soon be fitted.

The first Scorpion was fitted to the Matilda II tank (*qv*) and had a Ford V-8 engine mounted in an armoured casing on the right side of the hull. The operator sat behind it and drove the flail, while the tank driver merely

Scorpion

drove the tank at a suitable speed. The first models used wire ropes with weighted ends to flail, but these were soon replaced with chains. Understandably, the flail operators were less than delighted with having to sit outside, and Scorpion II had some improvements to the support frame for the drum and moved the operator inside the tank, leaving the flail motor outside. As Grant M3 tanks (*qv*) became available these were also converted to Scorpions, being known as Scorpion III and IV; III had a single Bedford engine to drive the flail, but since the object was to provide a faster-moving tank than Matilda, the single engine was overstressed when flailing at full speed. Scorpion

SHERMAN CRAB MINEFIELD CLEARANCE TANK *1943–1948*

When the use of buried anti-tank mines began to increase in the Western Desert a Major A. S. du Toit of the South African Engineers suggested mounting a revolving drum on the front of a tank and hanging chains from it so that they would flail the ground in front of the tank and thus detonate the mines. This became Scorpion (*qv*). When the M4 Sherman tank became the standard Allied combat tank a flailing device called Marquis was developed for it, which used auxiliary engines to drive the flail. These engines were in a fixed housing which replaced the tank's turret and thus disarmed the tank, and for this reason it was not acceptable. The 79th Armoured Division, responsible for all specialist armoured vehicles during the World War II, then developed the Crab, which eventually became the standard Allied mine-clearing vehicle and the most effective.

Crab was a Sherman (M4) medium tank

Sherman Crab

Plough mineclearing device, a few of which were used on beaches and soft ground.

IV therefore had twin Bedford engines, mounted in an armoured shroud at the rear of the tank.

A few Sherman M4 tanks (qv) were also converted to Scorpions in the Middle East and the idea was then taken up by the Americans, who developed it as the Mine Exploder T3. This was an M4A4 tank with an auxiliary engine mounted in an armoured box on the right side of the hull, outside the tracks, driving the flail drum via a long shaft. A total of 41 of these were built and used by US troops in Italy, but they were not entirely satisfactory, and when the Crab was perfected, the Scorpion was withdrawn. The principal difference between the Scorpion and the Crab was that the latter drove its flail drum from the main engine.

It might be noted here that the name Scorpion was also applied by the Americans to an experimental Sherman tank with four flamethrowers mounted one at each corner; these were intended to protect the tank against close-in attacks particularly by Japanese suicide squads. Development of this was not completed before the war ended and was abandoned. The name was changed to Skink in 1945 to avoid confusion with the mine-clearing vehicles.

hich carried in front a hinged pair of arms ith a rotating drum between them. To this rum were attached 43 steel chains, and each nd of the drum carried a rotating wire-cutter. he whole assembly could be raised clear of e ground or lowered into the flailing position y hydraulic rams on the side of the tank. The rum was revolved at 142rpm by an auxiliary rive from the main tank engine, and the ansmission was altered so as to gear down the ack drive to a suitable flailing speed. An utomatic mechanism maintained the flail at e optimum height irrespective of the nature f the ground. The only change to the arma- ent was the removal of the bow machine gun, nce the position of the flail rotor prevented it om being used; the turret gun could be used, xcept that when the flail was raised it could ot fire directly forward.

Due to the cloud of dust and dirt thrown up y the chains when flailing, the driver was nable to see where he was going and was pro- ded with a gyroscopic compass, while the ommander had a magnetic compass which ould be raised well clear of the tank (avoiding agnetic interference) and read by an optical stem. At the rear of the tank were lights to uide following vehicles along the flailed strip, d apparatus for dropping markers and laying pe to indicate the cleared area.

Data are as for Sherman M4A3, except that e speed when flailing was 2km/hr (1.25mph). bout 600 were built.

MARK IX SUPPLY TANK 1918–1925

Soon after tank warfare began in 1916 it was appreciated that tanks were a useful way of bringing supplies up to the forward troops in an attack, particularly when they were trying to consolidate their gains, when equipment such as sandbags, extra ammunition, additional machine guns and so forth would be needed. Previously, vast carrying parties had slogged through the mud, with inevitable casualties, to deliver this equipment. As more tanks became available, the older vehicles were often con- verted into supply tanks by simply removing the main armament, but in 1918 a purpose- built supply tank, the Mark IX, was designed and built. The outline was generally as for the fighting tanks, but the hull was longer and higher so as to provide enough space to carry 30 men or 10 tons of stores. Two large doors were provided on each side, and there were a number of loopholes to allow the occupants to use their rifles. Two hundred were ordered, but with the end of the war the contract was termi- nated after only 23 had been made. Experience showed that the vehicles were underpowered and very difficult to steer due to the great length.

Length: 9.72m (31ft 11in). *Width:* 2.51m (8ft 3in). *Height:* 2.64m (8ft 8in). *Weight:* 27,435kg (60,485lb). *Crew:* 4. *Power:* Ricardo, 6-cyl., petrol, 150bhp at 1,500rpm. *Arma- ment:* nil. *Armour:* 6–12mm. *Speed:* 5.6km/hr (3½mph). *Range:* 67km (42 miles). *Maker:* Armstrong Whitworth Ltd., Coventry.

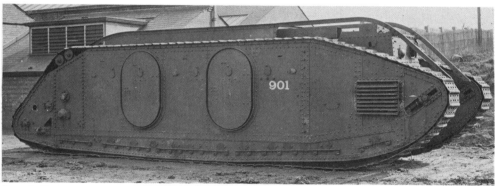

Supply Tank Mark IX

WASP FLAMETHROWER 1942–1953

Late in 1940 work began in Britain on development of a flamethrower that could be fitted into the Universal Carrier (qv). Eventu- ally the gas-pressure-operated device known as Ronson was selected, and this was fitted by mounting two tanks for fuel on the rear of the carrier hull, the nitrogen pressure cylinders inside the hull, and the flame projector on a swivel above the co-driver position. Whilst this worked it was unacceptable simply because 540l (120 galls) of flame fuel were outside the carrier, exposed to enemy fire. A fresh design was produced in which all the pressure and fuel system was inside the carrier hull, with the flame gun mounted rigidly above the co-driver. This gave a range of about 91m (100yds) and had to be aimed by pointing the whole vehicle at the target. This design was accepted for ser- vice as the Wasp Mark 1 and orders for 1,000 were given in September 1942.

While these were being built, an improved version of the flame gun was designed, which could be fitted inconspicuously into the normal machine-gun housing in front of the co-driver, thus making the vehicle less obviously a flame- thrower. This became Wasp Mark 2 and went into production late in 1943. The Mark 1 ve- hicles were relegated to training and the Mark 2 was extensively used in combat. A slight variation was the Mark 2C, built in Canada; in this model the fuel capacity was reduced to 340l (75 gall) and moved out on to the rear of the carrier so as to leave room inside for a third crew man operating a light machine gun. The Canadian contention was that once the fuel was expended their version could continue to function as a normal machine-gun carrier, and for this they were willing to accept the risks in- herent in having the flame fuel tank exposed. Experience proved them right, and by the end of the war most Wasp Mark 2s had been retired in favour of the Mark 2C.

Wasp Mark 2

UNITED STATES

M4 TANKDOZER *1943–1958*

Combat experience taught the American Army the value of having bulldozers well forward so as to deal rapidly with roadblocks, damaged roads and bridges and other routine obstacles, but heavy casualties among bulldozer operators soon led to the demand for a protected machine. The first solution was to build armoured cabs for standard machines, but this was inadequate in the face of heavy fire, and in 1942 it was decided to try mounting a bulldozer blade on to a combat tank. First attempts were unsuccessful since they used a V-shaped blade in the hope of combining bulldozing with mine clearance, but after the problem had been handed over to earthmoving engineering companies a solution was rapidly found, using a standard straight bulldozer blade, resulting in a machine equally as efficient as a standard civil engineer's bulldozer. Conversion kits were developed for fitting the blade and its controls to the M4 Sherman tank (*qv*), and in late 1943 the Tankdozer M4 was standardized. A total of 1,957 conversion kits was produced by the end of the war.

In addition to the standard model, many units in the field made up their own tankdozers by adapting standard bulldozer parts. The prime advantage of the tankdozer was that the vehicle retained its standard armament and in the event of damage to the bulldozer attachment could jettison the blade and continue to function as a combat tank. Since the war tankdozer attachment kits have been produced for later model tanks and are currently provided for the M47 (*qv*) and M48 (*qv*) tanks.

M60 AVLB

M60 ARMORED VEHICLE LAUNCHED BRIDGE *1963–*

This is basically an M60 battle tank (*qv*) with the turret removed and the hull covered over. On top is carried a scissors bridge unit, hinged to the front of the hull and extended by hydraulic rams. As the bridge is hinged forward, so the upper section unfolds, and as the bridge reaches the horizontal, so the two units lock securely to form a single rigid span. The bridge will span a gap of 18.29m (60ft) and can be emplaced in three minutes; it can be recovered in about 15 minutes.

Length (with bridge): 9.60m (31ft 6in). *Width* (with bridge): (13ft 1½in). *Height* (with bridge): 4.03m (13ft 3in). *Weight* (with bridge): 55,746kg (122,900lb). *Crew:* 2. *Power:* Continental, 12-cyl., horizontally-opposed, diesel, 750bhp at 2,400rpm. *Armament:* nil. *Armour:* not disclosed. *Speed:* 40km/hr (25mph). *Range:* 500km (310 miles). *Maker:* Chrysler Corp. Detroit.

M728 COMBAT ENGINEER VEHICLE *1968–*

This entered service in 1968 and is based on the chassis of the M60A1 battle tank (*qv*). The hull is fitted with a front-mounted bulldozer blade, hydraulically operated, and an A-Frame crane is hinged to the hull front and usually carried folded down around the turret. A two-speed winch with an 11-tonne capacity is mounted behind the turret. The turret is armed with a 165mm low-velocity demolition gun, M135, an American copy of the British AVRE gun, L9A1.

Length: 7.88m (25ft 10in). *Width:* 3.70m (12ft 2in). *Height:* 3.20m (10ft 6in). *Weight:* 52,163kg (115,000lb). *Crew:* 4. *Power:* Continental, 12-cyl., horizontally-opposed, diesel, 750bhp at 2,400rpm. *Armament:* one 165mm gun with 30 rounds; one 7.62mm machine gun; one .50in machine gun. *Armour:* not disclosed. *Speed:* 48km/hr (30mph). *Range:* 500km (310 miles). *Maker:* Chrysler Corp., Detroit.

M728 CEV

RHINOCEROS OR CULIN HEDGEROW DEVICE 1944

The Bocages country of Normandy proved to be a formidable obstacle to tank operations in 1944, due to the thick hedges planted on small banks alongside the roads. This confined the tank to the road, or else exposed its thin belly to anti-tank fire as it climbed over the hedges.

The solution was devised by Sergeant Curtis D. Culin of the 102nd Cavalry Reconnaissance Regiment, and it is pleasing to be able to record

Rhinoceros

that he was awarded the Legion of Merit for his invention. The Culin Hedgerow Device or, as it was known to British troops, the Sherman Prong, was a set of welded steel plates formed like plough shares and welded to the front plate

Tankdozer M4

T31 Demolition Tank

of the tank. There were numerous minor variations of the basic design, depending upon which advanced workshop or unit mechanic made it, but they all worked in the same way. As the tank came up to the hedge, the prongs bit into the embankment and prevented the tracks pulling the tank over the hedge. Instead, a whole section of the embankment, complete with hedge, was chopped out and pushed ahead of the tank, usually burying any enemy machine-gunners or anti-tank rocket launchers on the other side. The Culin device was used on American, British and Canadian tanks in considerable numbers, but once the Allies broke clear of Normandy there was no longer any requirement and they were removed almost as fast as they had been installed.

T1 MINE EXPLODER *1944–1945*
Whilst the British Army concentrated on developing flail devices to explode mines in the path of tanks (*qv* Sherman Crab and Scorpion), the Americans concentrated on roller devices. The first of these appeared in 1943 as the Mine Exploder T1 and consisted of two large rollers, each made of heavy steel discs 101cm (40in) in diameter, pushed ahead of the tank so that each roller cleared space for the tracks. A third set of rollers was towed behind the tank in a central position, so that the effect of the three was to clear a path as wide as the tank.

The T1 had some defects and was replaced by the T1E1, in which the third set of rollers was brought round to the front of the tank and placed ahead of the side rollers. A jib crane was mounted on the front of the tank, a Recovery Tank M32 (*qv*), to lift the rollers out of the craters resulting from the detonation of mines. Although a cumbersome device, it was accepted for use and 75 were built.

The T1E1 proved effective in the field but cumbersome to operate, and to try and make things better for the driver the T1E2 was designed. This dispensed with the central roller and widened the two outer rollers, but the principal complaint was that it was still built on to a recovery tank which carried no armament, and a mine-clearing tank usually operated in the

very front of an advance, where armament was a comforting thing to have. This led to the T1E3, a Sherman M4A1 tank (*qv*) complete with armament and twin rollers, chain-driven from the tank's front driving sprocket so as to assist manoeuvre, mounted ahead of it. In 1944 two of these were sent to Britain and two to Italy; named Aunt Jemima they were well received, and more were dispatched to Europe shortly after the June 1944 invasion.

The final roller-type exploder was the T1E5, which used serrated edges on the roller discs to provide additional traction. Each roller consisted of six discs each 63mm (2½in) thick and 1.83m (6ft) in diameter, and covered a 102cm (40in) strip with 91cm (36in) between the two rollers. A completely cleared strip was made by positioning two or more tanks so that their roller paths overlapped. The total weight of the roller unit attached to the front of the tank was 18,600kg (41,000lb).

An attempt to improve the manoeuvrability of mine-exploding devices was the T1E4, developed by the Chrysler Corporation. This used a wide sheepsfoot roller made up of 16 serrated discs of 1.2m (4ft) diameter, suspended from an A-Frame at the front of the tank. It improved mobility and cleared a 2.92m (9ft 7in) path at a speed of 8km/hr (5mph). A wider version, the T1E6 cleared a 3.49m (11ft 5½in) path and was designed to protect late-

model tanks with wider tracks.

The total production of all these various models of mine exploder was small, probably no more than 300 of all types. Their effect was good, but they were so slow and cumbersome that they were rarely used, troops preferring to push ahead and take their chances.

T31 DEMOLITION TANK *1945–*
When the British Army began developing the Churchill AVRE (*qv*) the Americans were informed and, in response to a Corps of Engineers request, development of a similar vehicle was begun in the USA. The resulting machine was the Engineer Armored Vehicle, a Sherman M4A3 (*qv*) converted by removing the gun from the turret, removing the ammunition racks from inside the hull to leave space for explosives and other engineer stores, and installing a multiple rocket launcher, with 18 7.2in rockets, above the turret. Attachments were fitted to mount a bulldozer blade on the front, and an armoured sledge was provided for carrying additional stores. Finally an 81mm mortar was issued, which could be fired from the turret to provide smoke cover.

While the EAV was a good interim solution, there was no official organization in which it would fit, and the US Army refused to adopt the British solution and assemble a specialized armour unit, with the result that only two vehicles were built and they were still awaiting shipment when the war ended.

Recognizing the defects of the EAV, in November 1944 a new proposal was put up, for a Demolition Tank T31 to replace it. This was to be a late-model Sherman with belly armour strengthened against mines, a bulldozer blade, a mine excavator, a flamethrower, two automatic 7.2in rocket launchers on the turret sides, and twin machine guns in the turret front. The vehicle was built and sent for test late in 1945; the revolver-type automatic rocket launchers failed to perform properly and rather than spend more money it was decided to abandon the whole thing and begin again with a more modern type of tank.

T1 Mine Exploder

Germany developed the 5-ton cross-country
tractor in two versions, one for engineer
troops and one for artillery. By 1942 it was
generally agreed that a lighter 3-ton model was
more suited to both these tasks.

TRACTORS AND PRIME MOVERS

CHINA

TYPE 59 TRACKED ARTILLERY TRACTOR *1960–*

The Type 59 tractor is an indigenous Chinese vehicle, specifically built to tow the larger artillery guns in the Chinese Army. It is apparently based on a Soviet design, perhaps the AT series (*qv*), but the cab is enlarged sufficiently to take all the gun detachment. There are five road-wheels with the drive sprocket at the front and the idler at the rear. It is known to be able to tow a 122mm gun, but there is little hard information beyond that. There is no dimensional data.

GERMANY

HANOMAG SS100 ROAD TRACTOR *1935–1945*

The German Army used few road tractors, since they felt that the absence of cross-country performance limited their all-round value, but a small number of these Hanomag vehicles were used for hauling heavy machinery, by the Luftwaffe for towing fuel tank trailers, and, latterly, in connection with some of the bulkier components of the A4 (V–2) guided missile system.

The Hanomag vehicle was a commercial road haulage tractor with no modification for military use. It was simply an engine and cab on four wheels, the rear wheels only being driven, and except for a small tool and store locker at the rear it had no load-carrying capacity. The double cab allowed some six men to ride in addition to the driver.

Length: 5.54m (18ft 2in). *Width:* 2.46m (8ft 1in). *Height:* 2.42m (7ft 11in). *Weight:* 6,540kg (14,418lb). *Crew:* 1. *Power:*

Hanomag, 6-cyl., diesel, 100bhp at 2,000rpm. *Towed load:* 20,000kg (44,092lb). *Speed:* 40km/hr (25mph). *Maker:* Hanomag, Hannover-Linden.

Hanomag Tractor

HK101 LIGHT MOTORCYCLE TRACTOR *1939–1945*

Late in 1939 work began on a new 'rationalized' series of semi-track vehicles for the German Army, aimed at a design simpler and quicker to produce than the existing models. It covered 1–, 3–, 6–, 9–, and 16–ton classes, but although much development work was carried out and prototypes built, only the 1-ton version, the HK101, entered service.

This remarkable vehicle was intended as a towing device for airborne artillery, and its form was due to the demand of air-portability. In essence, it was a motorcycle frame and front wheel married to a lightweight tracked suspension unit. Above the tracks was a truck-type body with lockers and rear-facing seating for two men. Though originally confined to parachute units, in accordance with the first intention, it was later widely issued to other forces and became a highly popular light supply vehicle. Its only drawback was low performance and low payload, both of which were intended

Light Motorcycle Tractor HK101

to be corrected in a slightly larger HK102, designed to carry five men; few of these were made, however.

Length: 3m (9ft 10in). *Width:* 1m (3ft 3in). *Height:* 1.20m (3ft 11in). *Weight:* 1,235kg (2,722lb). *Crew:* 1 + 2. *Power:* Opel, 4-cyl., petrol, 1,478cc, 36bhp at 3,400rpm. *Payload:* 325kg (716lb). *Towed load:* 450kg (992lb). *Speed:* 60km/hr (37mph). *Maker:* NSU-D-Rad Vereinigte Fahrzeugwerke AG, Neckarsulm.

SdKfz 101 ½-track motorcycle

SCHWERER WEHRMACHTSCHLEPPER (SWS) HEAVY MILITARY TRACTOR *1944–1945*

Development of this semi-tracked vehicle was ordered by Hitler in 1942, to be a simplified version of existing semi-tracks more suited to rapid production. Development was undertaken by Bussing-NAG and production began in 1944. The standard version was similar to earlier models, having a lorry-type cab and a cargo bed at the rear; this was later followed by an armoured-cab model in which the bonnet and cab were covered in steel plate, with vision slots for the driver and co-driver. Later still, a fully armoured version was produced as a mobile mounting for a 10-barrel rocket projector carried on top of the roofed-in cargo space.

Length: 6.67m (21ft 11in). *Width:* 2.50m (8ft 2½in). *Height:* 2.83m (9ft 4in). *Weight:* 9,500kg (20,944lb). *Crew:* 2. *Power:* Maybach HL42, 6-cyl., petrol, 4,198cc, 100bhp at 3,000rpm. *Payload:* 4,000kg (8,820lb). *Towed load:* 8,000kg (17,636lbs). *Speed:* 27km/hr (17mph). *Maker:* Bussing-NAG Vereinigte Nutzkraftwagen AG, Brunswick.

SdKfz 6 LIGHT (FIVE-TON) CROSS-COUNTRY TRACTOR *1934–1945*

Development of this vehicle (together with its companion medium and heavy versions) began

Light Cross-Country Tractor

in 1926, the object being to determine the best vehicle for use as an artillery tractor. Production began in 1934 and continued for about 10 years. Early models used a short track unit with four bogie wheels, but in later production this was increased in length and five or six wheels were used. Springing was originally by leaf springs, but torsion-bar suspension was later adopted.

Two versions were developed, one for engineer troops to tow bridging and rafting equipment, and one for artillery to tow the 105mm leFH 18 field howitzer. In both cases the vehicle body was arranged as rows of seats for the personnel with lockers at the rear end for personal equipment, ammunition and general stores. In general, it was found that the five-ton vehicle was unnecessarily large for these tasks, and a lighter three-ton model was

eventually developed, with the result that production of the five-ton was cut back after 1942.

Length: 6.02m (19ft 9in). *Width:* 2.20m (7ft 3in). *Height:* 2.48m (8ft 2in). *Weight:* 7,300kg (16,093lb). *Crew:* 1 + 10. *Power:* Maybach NL5, 6-cyl., petrol, 3,435cc, 90bhp at 3,000rpm. *Payload:* 1,500kg (3,305lb). *Towed load:* 5,000kg (11,025lb). *Winch capacity:* 2,000kg (4,410lb). *Speed:* 50km/hr (31mph). *Range:* 300km (185 miles). *Makers:* Bussing-NAG Vereinigte Nutzkraftwagen AG, Brunswick; Daimler-Benz AG, Stuttgart-Unterturkheim.

SdKfz 7 MEDIUM (EIGHT-TON) MILITARY TRACTOR *1935–1946*

This vehicle appeared in 1935 and was intended to tow medium field and anti-aircraft artillery, in particular the 15ch sFH18 field howitzer and the 8.8cm Flak 36 anti-aircraft gun. The body was arranged to provide rows of seats for the gun detatchment, plus rear lockers for personal equipment and ammunition. The suspension used six interleaved bogie wheels and leaf springs until 1937, after which torsion bars were used for springing. Military records show that at the beginning of 1943 over 3,200 of these vehicles were in use, and as well as acting as tractors large numbers were adapted to carry various light guns so as to act as improvised self-propelled weapons.

Length: 6.85m (22ft 5in). *Width:* 2.40m (7ft 10in). *Height:* 2.62m (8ft 7in). *Weight:* 9,750kg (21,495lb). *Crew:* 1 + 11. *Power:*

Heavy Military Tractor

8-ton SdKfz 7

Maybach HL62, 6-cyl., petrol, 6,200cc, 140bhp at 2,600rpm. *Payload:* 1,800kg (3,970lb). *Towed load:* 8,000kg (17,635lb). *Winch pull:* 3,000kg (6,615lb). *Speed:* 50km/hr (31mph). *Range:* 250km (155 miles). *Makers:* Krauss-Maffei AG, Munich; Carl F. W. Borgard, Bremen; Osterreichische Saurerwerk AG, Vienna.

12-ton SdKfz 8

SdKfz 8 HEAVY (12-TON) MILITARY TRACTOR *1934-1945*
In 1931 Daimler-Benz produced a semi-tracked tractor for sale to the Russian Army, and with this as a basis the company went on to develop this 12-tonner for the German Army, starting production in 1934. They were intended as towing vehicles for the 15cm K16 long-range field gun and the 21cm Lange Morser howitzer, and in later years they also towed the 17cm gun and improved 21cm howitzers in two loads, barrel and carriage. Early models used leaf springing for the track unit, but after 1938 torsion bars were adopted.

At least one of these vehicles was used as a carrier for an 8.8cm AA gun in the anti-tank role, but this does not appear to have been per-petuated in service.

Length: 7.35m (24ft 1in). *Width:* 2.50m (8ft 2½in). *Height:* 2.77m (9ft 1in). *Weight:* 12,150kg (26,786lb). *Crew:* 1 + 12. *Power:* Maybach HL85, V–12, petrol, 8,520cc, 185bhp at 2,600rpm. *Payload:* 2,550kg (5,620lb). *Towed load:* 12,000kg (26,455lb). *Winch pull:* 5,000kg (11,025lb). *Speed:* 50km/hr (31mph). *Range:* 250km (155 miles). *Makers:* Daimler-Benz AG, Marienfelde; Krupp AG, Muhlhausen; Skodawerk, Pilsen.

SdKfz 9 HEAVY (18-TON) MILITARY TRACTOR *1938–1945*
This, the heaviest semi-track in German ser-vice, was developed as an artillery tractor, a tank recovery vehicle and as a mounting for a mobile crane. The first production model appeared in 1938. For artillery use, this vehicle was generally used to tow the 24cm K3 heavy gun, which was split into five loads, the 21cm K38 gun and the 24cm H39 howitzer. They were also used by the Luftwaffe to tow their 12.8cm anti-aircraft gun.

As a recovery vehicle it sufficed until the appearance of the Tiger (*qv*) and Panther (*qv*) tanks, which were too heavy for it to handle and required the development of Bergepanzer recovery tanks (*qv*). Until these arrived in ser-vice it was the practice to couple three 18-

18-ton SdKfz 9

tonners together in order to tow one Tiger tank. Since it was still capable of handling any other armoured vehicle, it remained in service until 1945.

Length: 8.25m (27ft 1in). *Width:* 2.60m (8ft 6in). *Height:* 2.85m (9ft 4in). *Weight:* 15,130kg (33,355lb). *Crew:* 1 + 8. *Power:* Maybach HL108, V–12, petrol, 10,830cc, 250bhp at 2,600rpm. *Payload:* 2,870kg (6,327lb). *Towed load:* 18,000kg (39,683lb). *Winch pull:* 7,000kg (15,432lb). *Speed:* 50km/hr (31mph). *Range:* 260km (161 miles). *Maker.* Fahrzeug und Motorenbau GmbH, Breslau.

1-ton SdKfz 10. Rommel is shown speaking with soldiers.

SdKfz 10 LIGHT (ONE-TON) MILITARY TRACTOR *1938–1945*
In 1932, with the design of heavier semi-tracks in progress, the German Army requested a semi-track capable of towing a one-tonne load. After various development models, the Demag D7 version appeared in 1938 and became the standard pattern, some 17,000 being built. In general form it resembled the other semi-track vehicles of the tractor class, with the engine at the front, and with a tonneau body containing seats or arranged for cargo carriage. Experi-ence revealed that this size of vehicle was particularly well suited for towing the lighter anti-tank guns, and, since it formed a substan-tial platform, for mounting them on the cargo bed as a form of self-propelled weapon. It was also adopted by Army Flak troops as a carrier for the 2cm anti-aircraft gun.

Length: 4.72 (15ft 6in). *Width:* 1.82m (6ft). *Height:* 1.75m (5ft 9in). *Weight:* 3,400kg (7,495lb). *Crew:* 1 + 7. *Power:* Maybach HL42, 6 cyl., petrol, 4,199cc, 100bhp at 2,800rpm. *Payload:* 1,500kg (3,306lb). *Towed load:* 1,000kg (2,204lb). *Speed:* 65km/hr (40mph). *Range:* 350km (215 miles). *Makers:* Demag AG, Wetter/Ruhr; Mechanische Werke, Cottbus; Osterreichische Saurerwerke AG, Vienna.

SdKfz 11 LIGHT (THREE-TON) MILITARY TRACTOR 1938–1945

This vehicle was developed between 1934 and 1938 by Hansa-Loyd, after which development was taken over by Hanomag. It was of the same general pattern as the existing 5-, 8- and 12-ton series, but produced because the former vehicles were found to be too large for some applications, notably towing the 105mm field artillery howitzer. It was also used to tow various anti-tank guns, and to tow 2cm quadruple and 3.7cm anti-aircraft guns by the Luftwaffe.

The standard vehicle was provided with rows of seats and a rear locker, but variant models were produced with cargo bodies for carriage of ammunition. There were also smoke-laying vehicles, fitted with various types of smoke generator for screening targets against air attack, and decontamination vehicles on this chassis.

Length: 5.54m (18ft 2in). *Width:* 2.10m (6ft 11in). *Height:* 2m (6ft 6in). *Weight:* 4,800kg (10,582lb). *Crew:* 1 + 8. *Power:* Maybach HL45Z, 6-cyl., petrol, 4,500cc, 120bhp at 3,000rpm; *Payload:* 1,500kg (3,300lb). *Towed load:* 4,500kg (9,920lb). *Speed:* 75km/hr (46mph). *Range:* 155km (96 miles). *Makers:* Hanomag, Hannover-Linden; Borgward, Bremen; Auto-Union Adlerwerke AG, Frankfurt; Auto-Union Werke Horch, Zwickau; Skodawerk, Prague; Demag AG, Wetter/Ruhr.

RADSCHLEPPER OST CARGO TRACTOR *1942–1944*

The German Army, in its advance into Russia in 1941-2, found that while the half-track vehicles were generally satisfactory tractors, they were not at their best in deep snow or mud and, reputedly upon Hitler's orders, two specialist tractor/truck vehicles were developed, one tracked and one wheeled; the wheeled vehicle was this Radschlepper Ost. It was designed by Dr. Ferdinand Porsche and its most prominent feature was the use of large steel wheels resembling those of an agricultural tractor. Propulsion was by an air-cooled engine and all wheels were driven. It could carry four tonnes.

Unfortunately, after testing by the Artillery and other interested bodies, an adverse report was returned; the principal defect lay in the wheels, which did not provide sufficient traction, gave rise to excessive vibration, and damaged the road surfaces. As a result, no more than about 200 were made, all of which were used up on the Russian front.

Length: 5.47m (17ft 11½in). *Width:* 2.30m (7ft 6½in). *Height:* 2.78m (9ft 1in). *Weight:* 10,000kg (22,045lb). *Crew:* 2. *Power:* Steyr, 4-cyl., petrol, 80bhp at 2,200rpm. *Maker:* Porche Werke, Stuttgart.

Radschlepper Ost

RAUPENSCHLEPPER OST TRACTOR *1943–1945*

This was the tracked tractor developed at the same time as the Radschlepper Ost (*qv*) for service in the snow and mud conditions of the Eastern Front during the war. It was developed by Steyr during 1942 and used the engine and transmission of the standard Steyr 1½–tonne truck. The suspension was entirely tracked, though of crude design, which gave rise to excessive vibration in service. The suspension wheels were of steel, without rubber tyres, and springing was by quarter-elliptic leaf springs. Ground clearance was 55cm (21½in), which allowed the vehicle to keep moving in the worst conditions.

Steering was by simply braking each track, without the use of any form of controlled differential, so that fine control of steering was almost impossible. Nevertheless, with a payload of 1½ tonnes and a towed rating of two tonnes, it was produced in quantity between 1943 and 1944 and proved extremely useful in its designed role.

Length: 4.57m (15ft 0in). *Width:* 1.99m (6ft 6in). *Height:* 2.76m (9ft 1in). *Weight:* 5,000kg (11,025lb). *Crew:* 1. *Power:* Steyr, V-8, 3,500cc, air-cooled, 85bhp at 3,000rpm; later models used a Klockner-Humbolt-Deutz, 4-cyl., air-cooled, diesel. *Speed:* 18km/hr (11mph). *Range:* 250km (155 miles). *Makers:* Steyr-Daimler-Puch, Steyr; Auto-Union GmbH, Chemnitz; Gräf und Stift, Vienna; Klockner-Humboldt-Deutz, Köln-Deutz.

JAPAN

TYPE 73 TRACKED ARTILLERY TRACTOR *1974–*

The Type 73 tractor has been developed by Japan to replace the US equipment which has now become obsolete or obsolescent. The chassis has six roadwheels, with the last one acting as the idler. The drive sprocket is at the front and there are no return rollers. The body is a large box-like structure extending for the full length of the vehicle. The crew are accommodated in the front, with an anti-aircraft machine gun on the roof. The engine is in the centre and behind that is a small ammunition locker. The Type 73 is used to tow such guns as the 155mm and the bigger 175mm, and some of them have been seen with a small bulldozer blade on the front. This would be used to prepare a gun position or to remove obstacles on the route.

Length: 6.21m (20ft 4in). *Width:* 3.01m (9ft 9in). *Height:* 2.04m (6ft 7in). *Weight:* 19,800kg (43,640lb). *Crew:* 1 + 11. *Power:* 6-cyl., diesel, 450bhp at 2,200rpm. *Towed load:*

Type 73 Tractor

16,000kg (35,264lb). *Speed:* 45km/hr (28mph). *Range:* 300km (186 miles). *Maker:* not known.

POLAND

MAZUR D–350 MEDIUM TRACKED ARTILLERY TRACTOR *1956–*

The D–350 is in many ways an improved AT–S Soviet tractor (*qv*) and for carrying a gun crew it is better equipped since it has a large enough cab to take all the detachment together. It is a fully tracked vehicle with the engine in the front under a substantial square bonnet. The large square cab occupies the centre portion of the chassis, and the cargo compartment is behind that. There is a winch with a pull of 17,000kg (37,000lb) and 80m (262ft) of cable. The Polish Army uses the D–350 for towing all sizes of artillery pieces, from anti-tank guns up to 152mm howitzers. It has been supplied to Czechoslovakia, but not apparently to any other country.

Length: 5.82m (19ft 1in). *Width:* 2.92m (9ft 6in). *Height:* 2.62m (8ft 6in). *Weight:*

Raupenschlepper Ost

18,550kg (40,885lb). *Crew:* 1 + 8. *Power:*
D–350, 12–cyl., diesel, 350bhp at 1,800rpm.
Towed load: 15,000kg (33,068lb). *Speed:*
53km/hr (33mph). *Range:* 490km (304 miles).
Maker: Polish Government Factories.

Mazur 350

SOVIET UNION

AT-L AND AT-M LIGHT ARTILLERY TRACKED TRACTORS *1953–1975*

The AT series of tractors replaced the M2s (*qv*)
and became the main towing vehicles for the
Soviet artillery pieces and the large mortars.
Although still used in this role, they have to
some extent been themselves replaced by large
wheeled prime movers and are now seen in
increasing numbers in other specialized tasks.
The first version was the AT-L, but in 1956 the
tracks were modified to give it five roadwheels
and no return rollers. It was then called the
AT-M, and this is the type seen today almost
everywhere. It is used throughout the Warsaw
Pact countries and also in the Middle East and
some of the North African countries. There are
many versions, and a box-bodied type can be
used for several types of radar; others fit a
small bulldozer blade on the front and are used
for engineer tasks.

AT-M Light Tractor

AT-L Light Tractor

Length: 5.30m (17ft 4in). *Width:* 2.22m (7ft
3in). *Height:* 2.18m (7ft 2in). *Weight:* 6,300kg
(13,885lb). *Crew:* 2. *Power:* YaMZ-204Vkr,
4-cyl., diesel, 130bhp at 2,000rpm. *Speed:*
42km/hr (26mph). *Range:* 300km (186 miles).
Maker: Soviet Government Factories.

AT-S MEDIUM TRACKED ARTILLERY TRACTOR *1952-*

The AT-S was introduced to tow guns of
100mm and upwards which it has done until
very recent years when it has to some extent
been replaced in Soviet service by all-wheel-
drive trucks. But it still continues as a tractor in
other Warsaw Pact countries and is used by the
Soviets in roles other than artillery towing. For
engineer tasks it can be fitted with a bulldozer
blade, and with a large box-body it is an excellent radar vehicle. A variant has wider tracks

and pneumatic roadwheels for over-snow work. It is in general use in the Warsaw Pact countries and has been supplied to the Middle East, China, Finland and Yugoslavia. Unlike the ATS-59 which replaced it, the engine is in the front and there is a large cab in the middle of the chassis with accommodation for six men of the gun detachment.

Length: 5.87m (19ft 3in). *Width:* 2.57m (8ft 5in). *Height:* 2.53m (8ft 4in). *Weight:* 12,000kg (26,448lb). *Crew:* 2 + 6. *Power:* V-54-T, V-12, dsl; 250bhp at 1,500rpm. *Towed load:* 16,000kg (35,264lb). *Speed:* 35km/hr (22mph). *Range:* 380km (236 miles). *Maker:* Soviet Government Factories.

ATS-59 MEDIUM TRACKED ARTILLERY TRACTOR 1957–

The ATS-59 is the replacement for the AT-S (*qv*) and it is a powerful and fairly heavy vehicle. It apparently uses some components of the T-54 (*qv*) and these are probably in the suspension. It is used to tow the medium guns and howitzers of the artillery units and in this role it has seen service throughout the Warsaw Pact countries. It is made in Poland and supplements the Mazur D-350 (*qv*). Both the Soviet and the Polish versions have apparently been exported to the Middle East and some other countries, and it may be met anywhere. It is a large and impressive tractor, with a short nose caused by the fact that the engine is behind the cab in the front part of the load compartment. The tracks run on five roadwheels with no return rollers, and are driven from a sprocket at the front.

Length: 6.33m (20ft 8in). *Width:* 2.78m (9ft 2in). *Height:* 2.31m (7ft 6in). *Weight:* 13,000kg (28,652lb). *Crew:* 2. *Towed load:* 14,000kg (30,856lb). *Power:* A-650, 12-cyl., diesel, 300bhp at 1,700rpm. *Speed:* 38km/hr (23mph). *Range:* 350km (217 miles). *Maker:* Soviet Government Factories.

AT-S Tractor

AT-T HEAVY TRACKED ARTILLERY TRACTOR 1950–

The AT-T is a large and powerful version of the whole family of artillery tractors produced by the Soviet Union. It follows the usual pattern of having the engine at the front, a lorry-type cab (in this case seating four men) and an open cargo compartment behind. It is fully tracked with the track running on five large roadwheels, without return rollers, driven by a front sprocket, and it is no doubt taken from one of the medium tanks. The vehicle is used to tow the larger artillery pieces, including anti-aircraft and coast guns. There are engineer variants which fit it with a bulldozer blade or digging machines. It also has a use as a radar station. It has been supplied to the Warsaw Pact countries and to some countries in Africa.

Length: 6.99m (22ft 11in). *Width:* 3.23m (10ft 6in). *Height:* 2.58m (8ft 6in). *Weight:* 20,000kg (44,080lb). *Crew:* 4. *Power:* V-401, V-12, diesel; 415bhp at 1,500rpm. *Maker:* Soviet Government Factories.

AT-T Tractor

M2 LIGHT ARTILLERY TRACKED TRACTOR 1948–1960

The M2 was the replacement for the Ya series (*qv*), though it is already obsolescent and out of service in the USSR. However, it probably remains with other countries of the Warsaw Pact, and in Hungary it is built as a variant called the K-800. There is little to distinguish the M2 from the ones which preceded it, but internally it is said to be better designed and built and requiring less maintenance. Nevertheless, its quoted towed load is smaller.

Length: 4.90m (16ft 1in). *Width:* 2.80m (9ft 2in). *Height:* 2.35m (7ft 8in). *Weight:* 7,200kg (15,870lb). *Crew:* 2. *Power:* YaZ-204B, 4-cyl., diesel; 110bhp. *Towed load:* 6,000kg (13,227lb). *Speed:* 35km/hr (22mph). *Range:* 330km (205 miles). *Maker:* Soviet Government Factories.

Ya-12 LIGHT TRACKED ARTILLERY TRACTORS 1946–1960

The Ya series was a family of light tractors which came into service directly after World War II. They were completely conventional in appearance, having a front-mounted engine, a central cab and a crew or cargo compartment in the rear. The drive sprocket was at the rear, being driven through a normal propeller shaft, and there were five small roadwheels. The Ya-13 was identical, but had a slightly larger engine. They were taken into service in most of the Warsaw Pact countries, but are now well out of date and will only survive in reserve.

Length: 4.90m (16ft 1in). *Width:* 2.40m (7ft 9in). *Height:* 2.22m (7ft 3in). *Weight* (empty): 6,500kg (14,330lb). *Crew:* 2. *Towed load:* 8,000kg (17,636lb). *Power:* GMD 4-71, 4-cyl., diesel, 110bhp. *Speed:* 37km/hr (23mph). *Range:* 210km (180 miles). *Maker:* Soviet State Vehicle Factories.

M2 Tractor

UNITED KINGDOM

BEDFORD QLB 4 × 4 LIGHT AA TRACTOR *1941–1949*

This was a variant of the standard Bedford QL cargo and personnel carrying three-ton truck, introduced in about 1941 as a towing vehicle for the 40mm Bofors light anti-aircraft gun. The cab remained standard; behind it was a crew cab in which five members of the gun detachment rode; behind this again was a cargo section fitted with a variety of specially designed lockers, covered with a canvas tilt, and with space for two more gunners. The locker space carried four standard 40mm ammunition boxes, the spare gun barrel, one spare gun-wheel and gun tools.

Length: 5.68m (18ft 8in). *Width:* 2.28m (7ft 6in). *Height:* 2.81m (9ft 3in). *Crew:* 1 + 8. *Power:* Bedford, 6-cyl., petrol, 3,518cc, 72bhp at 3,000rpm. *Speed:* 65km/hr (35mph). *Range:* 370km (200 miles). *Maker:* Vauxhall Motors, Luton.

Bedford QLB 4 × 4 Light AA Tractor

DRAGON GUN TRACTORS *1922–1938*

After 1918, with the tank's success in overcoming bad terrain in everyone's mind, the

Dragon Medium Mark II

British Army began looking at tracked towing vehicles for artillery, and in 1922 the Royal Carriage Department at Woolwich Arsenal built the first Dragon, a word derived from a corruption of the term 'drag gun'. It used a suspension and track unit based on the current Vickers medium tank, carried 10 men in addition to the driver, and towed the 18-pdr. field gun and limber at 19 km/hr (12mph). Considered insufficiently powerful it was soon replaced by the Mark II version with a better engine, and then supplemented by the Mark II with gear ratios changed to permit towing medium guns of 5 and 6in calibre. These later models added locker space for personal equipment and gun stores and were quite successful vehicles. Finally, in 1935, the Mark IV appeared, using the suspension of the Vickers six-ton tank and driven by a diesel engine.

Whilst suitable for medium artillery, these Dragons were oversized for field-gun towing, and in 1929 a design of Light Dragon was

begun; with this, the earlier models became known as Medium Dragons. The light vehicles used a suspension system based on that of the contemporary light tanks, were simpler to build and maintain, and carried little beyond seating for the gun detachment. They were used to tow 18-pdr., 3.7in howitzers, 2-pdr. anti-tank guns and some of the first 18/25-pdr. guns. But in 1936 a policy decision was made to revert to wheeled vehicles for artillery traction, and with that the development of Dragons came to an end. Those in service were run to the end of their useful lives, and some were still operating at the outbreak of war. The Medium

Dragon Mark III

Dragon was a dead-end of development, but the Light Dragon was the precursor of the various machine gun carriers which were extensively employed by the British Army during and after World War II.

Medium Mark III *Length:* 5.00m (16ft 5in). *Width:* 2.36m (7ft 9in). *Height:* 1.87m (6ft 2in). *Weight:* 10,160kg (22,400lb). *Crew:* 1 + 10. *Power:* Armstrong-Siddeley V-8, petrol,

Dragon Light Mark II

7,800cc, air-cooled, 82bhp. *Speed* 40km/hr (25mph). *Maker:* Royal Ordnance Factory, Woolwich.

Light Mark II *Length:* 3.91m (12ft 10in). *Width:* 2.05m (6ft 9in). *Height:* 1.90m (6ft 3in). *Weight:* 4,263kg (9,400lb). *Crew:* 1 + 6. *Power:* Meadows, 6-cyl., petrol, 59bhp. *Speed:* 48km/hr (30mph). *Maker:* Royal Ordnance Factory, Woolwich.

SCAMMELL 6×4 ARTILLERY TRACTOR 1936–

The Scammell company were well known for their heavy commercial vehicles, and in the mid-1930s developed this model for military use as a tractor for heavy artillery. It became the standard towing vehicle for weapons of 6in calibre and above. Though it only had rear-wheel drive its cross-country ability was suffi-

cient for its task, and it was in fact preferred by gunners as the lack of a differential on the front axle improved the clearance and did less damage to gunpits when bringing heavy guns into position. The basic design was later adapted to a heavy wrecking vehicle, and a modernized version, with all-wheel drive, still continues in military service in this role.

Length: 6.24m (20ft 6in). *Width:* 2.51m (8ft

4×4 FIELD ARTILLERY TRACTOR 1938–1960

Although the Quad gun tractor was originally developed by Guy Motors, by far the greatest number of vehicles to this basic design came from Morris-Commercial Motors. It was the standard towing vehicle in all British field artillery regiments, towing the 25-pdr. gun; it was also widely used by Commonwealth artillery and as a towing vehicle for the 17-pdr. anti-tank gun.

The peculiar shape and metallic sheathing of the Quad led to a common belief that it was bullet-proof; this was never so, and the metal was too thin to even keep out shell splinters. The large cab held seats for the driver and the

six men of the 25-pdr. gun detachment, the gun commander sitting alongside the driver and having a hatch through which he usually stood so as to command a view of the gun and trailer behind. The remainder of the body was taken up with a winch, over the rear differential, and lockers into which the standard 25-pdr. shell and cartridge boxes fitted exactly. The spare wheel was carried on the sloping rear deck.

The four wheels were permanently driven; variant models used different sizes of wheels which varied their speed and tractive power to a small degree. The final model, the Mark 5, moved away from the characteristic Quad shape; this shape turned out to be too characteristic and too readily recognized from the air,

instantly indicating an artillery unit, and the Mark 5 was therefore given a more square body with a canvas-covered cargo space at the rear which made the vehicle resemble an ordinary cargo truck. The Morris Quad was noisy and rough-riding, but it was warm and snug and well loved by two generations of artillerymen; one is preserved by the Royal Regiment of Artillery as a memento.

Length: 4.49m (14ft 9in). *Width:* 2.28m (7ft 6in). *Height* 2.36m (7ft 9in). *Weight:* 3,302kg (7,280lb). *Crew:* 1 + 6. *Power:* Morris, 4-cyl., petrol, 70bhp at 2,500rpm. *Towed load:* 5,000kg (11,023lb). *Winch pull:* 4,000kg (8,020lb). *Speed:* 56km/hr (35mph). *Maker:* Morris-Commercial Cars Ltd., Birmingham.

3in). *Height:* 2.94m (9ft 8in). *Crew:* 1. *Power:* Gardner 6LW, 6-cyl., diesel, 8,400cc, 102bhp. *Towed load:* 15,000kg (33,070lb). *Speed:* 48km/hr (30mph). *Maker:* Scammell Lorries Ltd., Watford.

Scammel

STALWART CARGO VEHICLE *1958–*

After the Alvis company had developed the Saracen APC (*qv*), they took the basic chassis design a step further and produced a high-mobility airfield fire engine. They then went on and, as a private venture, developed a load-carrying vehicle on the same six-wheeled chassis. In addition to its ability to cross rough country, the Stalwart was made fully amphibious, merely needing to have a trim vane erected in front of the cab before taking to the water. It was adopted by the British Army in the late 1960s and is now widely used as an ammunition resupply vehicle for armoured and artillery units in armoured brigades.

Length: 6.35m (20ft 10in). *Width:* 2.61m (8ft 7in). *Height:* 2.54m (8ft 4in). *Weight:* 14,465kg (31,890lb). *Crew:* 2. *Power:* Rolls-Royce B81, 8-cyl., petrol, 220bhp at 3,750rpm. *Speed:* 56km/hr (35mph). *Range:* 400km (250 miles). *Maker:* Alvis, Coventry.

Stalwart

THORNEYCROFT HATHI GUN TRACTOR *1925–1939*

Such British guns as were mechanically towed during the World War I were towed by impressed commercial tractors, and in the 1920s the army built an experimental four-wheel-drive tractor using components taken from captured German vehicles. This was nicknamed the Hathi – the Hindustani word for elephant – in recognition of its hauling power. The War Office then drew up specifications for

Hathi

an improved version and the Thorneycroft company built about 25, known as the Hathi II.

The Hathi was of simple construction, little more than an engine and seats on top of four wheels; the wheels were permanently driven,

and there was very little storage space. Nevertheless, it proved the idea of all-wheel drive and was instrumental in paving the way for later vehicles such as the Morris Quad (*qv*) and Matador.

Length: 4.97m (16ft 4in). *Width:* 2.09m (6ft 10½in). *Height:* 2.03m (6ft 8in). *Weight:* 5,080kg (11,200lb). *Crew:* 1. *Power:* Thorneycroft GB6, 6-cyl., petrol, 11,197cc, 90bhp at 1,200rpm. *Speed:* 48km/hr (30mph). *Maker:* John I. Thorneycroft & Co., Basingstoke.

UNITED STATES

M1 MEDIUM TRACTOR *1941–1946*

In spite of the military designation, this was in fact the commercial tractor as provided by various companies for normal sale and adopted under a blanket title for military use. Although formally approved for towing 'artillery and other equipment over rough terrain' it was rarely used for artillery work and was more usually employed as a general engineer tractor. The design was straightforward; a tracked suspension with engine above and seat for one operator. In front of the engine was a winch capable of pulling 11,340kg (25,000lb), and the diesel engine was provided with the usual petrol/magneto system of starting.

IH Model TD14 *Length:* 4.21m (13ft 10in). *Width:* 2.33m (7ft 8in). *Height:* 2.31m (7ft 7in). *Weight:* 9,797kg (21,600lb). *Crew:* 1. *Power:* International Harvester TD14, 4-cyl., diesel, 7,550cc, 54bhp at 1,350rpm. *Drawbar pull:* 6,090kg (13,426lb). *Speed:* 13.6km/hr (8.5mph). *Range:* 290km (180 miles). *Makers:* International Harvester Co., Chicago (Model TD14); Allis-Chalmers Mfg. Co., Milwaukee (Model HD7W); Caterpillar Tractor Co., Peoria (Model RD6).

M2 SEVEN-TON HIGH-SPEED TRACTOR *1941–1946*

This was the first of a number of high-speed tractors designed to Ordnance specifications to combine speed with pulling power for towing artillery or other heavy loads. This version was based on commercial tractor components and was intended for towing heavy bomber aircraft to and from dispersal points on airfields; it was designed to be low enough to drive beneath the wings of major aircraft and could be used as a servicing platform.

The suspension was tracked, and specially designed to permit tight turns without undue disturbance of the airfield surface. Three men formed the operating crew, and auxiliary equipment carried included an air compressor for servicing landing gear, a three-kilowatt generator delivering 100 volts DC, and a winch capable of pulling 4,500kg (10,000lb).

Length: 4.21m (13ft 10in). *Width:* 1.77m (5ft 10in). *Height:* 1.72m (5ft 8in). *Weight:* 6,803kg (15,000lb). *Crew:* 3. *Power:* Hercules WXLC3, 6-cyl, petrol, 6,621cc, 150bhp at 3,000rpm. *Armament:* nil. *Armour:* nil. Speed 35km/hr (22mph). *Range:* 160km (100 miles). *Drawbar pull:* 4,082kg (9,000lb). *Maker:* Cleveland Tractor Co., Cleveland, Ohio.

M2 Tractor

M4 18-TON HIGH-SPEED TRACTOR *1942–1960*

Like the other high-speed tractors, the M4 was intended for towing artillery, in this case pieces ranging between 8,165 to 13,605kg (18–30,000lb). It was generally employed with the 90mm AA gun, 155mm Gun M1, 8in howitzer M1 and occasionally with the 3in AA gun and 240mm howitzer M1918. The arrangement of ammunition racks in the cargo space, and the quantity of ammunition carried, varied with the related gun, from 12 rounds with the 240mm to 54 rounds with the AA guns.

In essence it was a scaled-down model of the M6 (*qv*), with the same arrangement of crew compartment, engine room and cargo space. Ten men in addition to the driver could be carried, and a hatch above the crew compartment gave access to a ring mount upon which was a .50 machine gun for AA defence. A complete outfit of air and electric braking facilities was provided so as to be able to match any form of brakes on the towed load.

Length: 5.23m (17ft 2in). *Width:* 2.46m (8ft 1in). *Height:* 2.38m (7ft 10in). *Weight:* 14,288kg (31,500lb). *Crew:* 1 + 10. *Power:* Waukesha 145GZ, 6-cyl., petrol, 13,357cc, 210bhp at 2,100rpm. *Armament:* one .50 machine gun. *Armour:* nil. *Speed:* 56km/hr (35mph). *Range:* 290km (180 miles). *Maker:* Allis-Chalmers Mfg. Co., Milwaukee, Wis.

M1 Tractor

M4 Tractor

M5 13-TON HIGH-SPEED TRACTOR
1942–

This tractor was developed as an artillery prime mover to tow loads up to 7,000kg (16,000lb) and was generally used for towing the 105mm howitzer, 4.5in gun and 155mm howitzers. It used the track and modified suspension of the M3 light tank (*qv*), and consisted simply of a tracked suspension unit carrying a cab, engine and ammunition racks. The transmission was provided with high-and low-

M5 Tractor

speed ranges, the winch also had two speeds, and on a level road it was capable of pulling a 155mm howitzer at 56 km/hr (35mph). The ammunition racks carried from 24 to 56 rounds, depending upon the weapon being towed. In its original form, as standardized in October 1942, it carried no armament other than the personal weapons of the passengers, but in February 1944 an anti-aircraft machine gun was mounted at the rear of the cab.

Length: 4.85m (15ft 11in). *Width:* 2.54m (8ft 4in). *Height:* 2.64m (8ft 8in). *Weight:* 12,836kg (28,300lb). *Crew:* 1 + 8 passengers.

Power: Continental R6572, 6-cyl., petrol, 9,375cc; 235bhp at 2,900rpm. *Armament:* one .50 machine gun. *Armour:* nil. *Speed* 56km/hr (35mph). *Range:* 200km (125 miles). *Maker:* International Harvester Co., Chicago, Ill.

M6 38-TON HIGH-SPEED TRACTOR
1942–1960

The M6 tractor was designed as the prime mover for such heavy artillery equipments as the 240mm howitzer, the 8in gun and the 4.7in anti-aircraft gun. Development began in February 1942 of two types, the T22 with a fifth-wheel connector and the T23 in which the fifth-wheel connector was replaced by a cargo box. The T22 was intended to function with semi-trailer pattern barrel and carriage transport wagons for the two heavy field pieces, while the T23 would tow the 4.7in gun. In the event, however, the semi-trailed designs were rejected due to lack of cross-country ability and thus the T22 design was cancelled in favour of the T23, which became the M6 in June 1943.

The M6 tractor was a track-laying machine powered by two engines driving through a torque converter and two-speed constant-mesh transmission. The personnel compartment at the front could carry 11 men in two rows of seats and had an overhead hatch with anti-aircraft machine gun mount. Behind this was the engine compartment, and at the rear the cargo compartment, in which could be carried various gun stores plus 20 to 24 rounds of ammunition. It was provided with a winch, and could tow or winch loads up to 27,000kg (60,000lb) weight.

Length: 6.55m (21ft 6in). *Width:* 3.06m

(10ft 0½in). *Height:* 2.46m (8ft 1in). *Weight:* 34,019kg (75,000lb). *Crew:* 1. *Power:* two Waukesha 145GZ, 6-cyl., petrol, 13,357cc, each 191bhp at 2,100rpm. *Armament:* one .50 machine gun. *Armour:* nil. *Speed:* 33km/hr (20.5mph). *Range:* 175km (110 miles). *Maker:* Allis-Chalmers Mfg. Co., Milwaukee, Wis.

M6 Tractor

M7 SNOW TRACTOR *1943–1945*

This was a light half-track vehicle intended for carrying small loads across snow-covered terrain; the front wheels could be replaced by skis when conditions warranted it, and a ski-mounted trailer M19 was provided. When the skis of the vehicle were not in use they could be stowed alongside the bonnet to act as mud-guards. The engine, much of the transmission, and several other components were those of the 4 × 4 Willys Jeep (*qv*), and special cold-weather starting equipment was fitted. Standardized in August 1943, it was found to be in less demand than had been anticipated, and in November 1944 it was reclassified Limited Standard and was not retained after the war.

Length: 3.45m (11ft 4in). *Width:* 1.60m (5ft 3in). *Height:* 1.62m (5ft 4in). *Weight:* 1,383kg (3,049lb). *Crew:* 2. *Power:* Willys MB, 4-cyl., petrol, 2,196cc, 54bhp at 4,000rpm. *Armament:* nil. *Towed load:* 907kg (2,000lb). *Speed:* 64km/hr (40mph). *Range:* 257km (160 miles). *Maker:* Allis-Chalmers Mfg. Co., Milwaukee, Wis.

M7 Snow Tractor

M7 Snow Tractor with skis

M33, M34 AND M35 FULL-TRACK PRIME MOVERS *1944–1945*

These three vehicles were developed by modification of tanks in order to provide heavy tracked towing vehicles for heavy artillery pending the production of the M6 high-speed tractor (*qv*).

The M33 was based on the M33 tank recovery vehicle, itself a modification of the M3 medium tank (*qv*). The turret, turret ring, boom assembly and other specialist components were removed and an air compressor

M33 Full Track Prime Mover

M35 Full Track Prime Mover

fitted in order to actuate the brakes on the towed load.

The M34 was converted from the M32B1 tank recovery vehicle itself a modification of the M4 tank (*qv*) with cast hull. The M35 was a modification of the M10 tank destroyer by removal of the turret and gun. In both these cases the same air compressor modification

was provided. All vehicles held additional seats for members of the gun detachments and were fitted with heavy-duty towing attachments. They were extensively used in Italy and to a lesser extent in North-West Europe, but as soon as sufficient M6 tractors (*qv*) became available, they were all withdrawn.

M33 *Weight:* 27,215kg (60,000lb). *Speed:* 40km/hr (25mph).

M34 *Weight:* 28,576kg (63,000lb). *Speed:* 38km/hr (24mph).

M35 *Weight:* 24,947kg (55,000lb). *Speed:* 48km/hr (30mph).

M249 FRONT AND M250 REAR GUN-LIFTING TRUCKS *1950–1965*

These two highly specialized vehicles formed the support and motive power for the 280mm Gun M65 or 'Atomic Annie'. Development of this weapon as a highly mobile long-range gun began in the closing months of the war, and in order to provide it with the necessary mobility and agility it was, in effect, built like a railway gun, with supporting trucks at each end. Both vehicles are basically the same, a simple structure of engine and cab carrying a hydraulically operated cantilever arm, but the placement of these units differs. The Front Truck M249 has the cab at the front, engine behind, and the cantilever arm at the rear end, while the rear truck has the cantilever arm at its front, with the cab above and behind and the engine at the rear. To move the gun the two trucks are positioned at front and rear of the mounting and the cantilever arms lowered. They are then connected to the gun mounting and raised, lifting the mounting from the ground and suspending it between the two trucks. The arms are pivoted on the truck bodies so that the entire unit is sufficiently articulated to be able to negotiate road junctions and crossroads.

Length: 9.69m (31ft 9½in). *Width:* 3.14m (10ft 4in). *Height* (M249): 3.20m (10ft 6in). *Height* (M250): 3.492m (11ft 5½in). *Weight* (M249): 17,214kg (37,950lb). *Weight* (M250): 16,288kg (35,910lb). *Crew:* 2. *Power:* Continental A0895–4, 6-cyl., petrol, air-cooled, 295bhp at 2,660rpm. *Speed:* 40km/hr (25mph). *Range:* 265km (165 miles).

MACK 7½-TON 6×6 PRIME MOVER TRUCK *1942–1955*

Although additionally classified as being for general cargo and personnel carrying, this vehicle was almost invariably found acting as an artillery tractor, towing either the 8in howitzer M1 or the 155mm gun M1. In appearance it is of the normal cargo truck pattern, with an open-type cab and dual rear wheels. Inside the cargo space is an overhead rail with chain hoist, used to lift the gun trails and lock them to special coupling attachments when towing the weapons without limbers. This hoist could also be used for lifting ammunition in and out of the

vehicle. Air brakes were provided, with a hand controller for the towed load, and a winch capable of pulling 18,145kg (40,000lb) was fitted at the front of the vehicle. It remained in use for many years after the war and large numbers are still serving with armies other than the American to this day.

Length: 7.51m (24ft 8in). *Width:* 2.59m (8ft 6in). *Height:* 3.12m (10ft 3in). *Weight:* 19,763kg (43,570lb). *Crew:* 2. *Power:* Mack EY, 6-cyl., petrol, 11,587cc, 156bhp at 2,100rpm; *Drawbar pull:* 19,595kg (43,200lb). *Speed:* 51km/hr (32mph). *Range* (with towed load): 386km (240 miles). *Maker:* Mack Mfg. Corp., Allentown, Pa.

T36 SNOW TRACTOR *1944–1946*

This peculiar vehicle was designed for operation in deep and soft snow along the Alcan Highway and in Alaska, though it was later adopted by the US Army Air Corps for rescue work and recovery of crashed aircraft in arctic country. It consisted of a large and well-spaced track unit, designed to resist blockage by packed snow, within which lay the engine and transmission. At the rear top of this tracked unit was the cab, painted fluorescent red so as to give maximum visibility against the snow. The engine and much of the transmission were taken from the Dodge ¾-ton 4 × 4 weapons carrier (*qv*). Additional equipment included special cold-starting equipment, radio, winch and spotlights. The equipment was never standardized and was declared obsolete in post-war years.

Length: 4.36m (14ft 4in). *Width:* 1.75m (5ft 9in). *Height:* 2.08m (6ft 10in). *Weight:* 3,402kg (7,500lb). *Crew:* 2. *Power:* Dodge T-214, 6-cyl., petrol, 3,772cc; 99bhp at 3,300rpm. *Drawbar pull:* 2,268kg (5,000lb). *Speed:* 29km/hr (18mph). *Range:* 240km (150 miles). *Maker:* The Iron Fireman Mfg. Co., Chicago.

WHITE SIX-TON 6×6 PRIME MOVER AND CARGO TRUCK *1950–*

This is the post-war equivalent of the wartime Mack 7½-ton prime mover (*qv*), used for towing artillery pieces and for general cargo carriage. Though slightly smaller than the earlier model, it still has sufficient power to perform its tasks and there is, of course, less heavy artillery to be towed in the post-war US Army. The general arrangement is standard, a front-mounted engine, open-topped cab, and cargo space at the rear. Dual rear wheels are fitted, together with air brakes and a winch.

Length: 7.34m (24ft 1in). *Width:* 2.43m (8ft 0in). *Height:* 2.89m (9ft 6in). *Weight:* 10,387kg (22,900lb). *Crew:* 2. *Power:* Hercules HXD, 6-cyl., petrol, 202bhp at 2,500rpm. *Speed:* 72km/hr (45mph). *Range:* 480km (300 miles). *Maker:* White Motor Co., Cleveland, Ohio.

The Diamond T 4-ton 6 X 6 truck wrecker was
issued to all arms and services of the US forces
as a recovery unit and a mobile hoist. It was
often camouflaged to resemble an ordinary
cargo truck.

TANK TRANSPORTERS AND RECOVERY VEHICLES

AMX-13

AUSTRIA

4KH7FA-B GRIEF ARMOURED RECOVERY VEHICLE *1976–*

The Grief ARV is a variant of the Panzerjäger K tank destroyer (*qv*) and as a result it is a fairly light ARV. However, it is able to cope with both the tank destroyer and the Saurer APC (*qv*), which is all that the Austrian Army needs. It is well equipped and has a full range of tools and welding equipment as a standard load. The crane is hydraulic and has a telescoping jib with a lift of 6,500kg (14,300lb). The main winch is in the lower front hull, with the cable leading out through an opening in the front plate. There is 100m (328ft) of cable with a pull of 20,000kg (44,000lb). A small bulldozer blade on the front steadies the vehicle when it is winching or lifting. There are floodlights for night work, but no night-driving aids.

Length: 6.30m (20ft 7in). *Width:* 2.50m (8ft 2in). *Height:* 2.37m (7ft 8in). *Weight:* 19,800kg (43,640lb). *Crew:* 4. *Power:* Steyr Type 7FA, 6-cyl., diesel, 9,980cc; 320bhp at 2,300rpm. *Armament:* one 12.7mm (0.5in) machine gun on external mounting. *Armour:* 8–12mm. *Speed:* 63km/hr (38mph). *Range:* 450km (267 miles). *Maker:* Steyr-Daimler-Puch, Steyr.

Grief ARV

FRANCE

AMX-13 ARMOURED RECOVERY VEHICLE *1952–*

This vehicle is a variant of the AMX-13 tank (*qv* for full details). In place of the turret there is a small box-like structure for the commander and winch operator. An A-frame jib is carried on the rear deck and swings forward for lifting;

it can lift a maximum of 5,000kg (11,000lb). There are two winches, the main one with 50m (164ft) of cable and a pull of 16,000kg (35,273lb) and a secondary one which has 120m (393ft) of cable and can pull 2,000kg (3,500lb). Four spades steady the hull. A large number of these ARVs has been built and they are in service in several countries.

Length: 5.51m (18ft 1in). *Width:* 2.62m (8ft 6in). *Height:* 2.68m (8ft 8in). Other details as for the AMX-13 tank.

AMX-30 ARMOURED RECOVERY VEHICLE *1975–*

This vehicle is a modified AMX-30 tank (*qv*) with the turret removed and another superstructure fitted. It carries a substantial crane on the right side of this superstructure and has a large bulldozer blade on the front. When using the crane the blade is lowered to provide stability, and the lift of the crane is between four and 15 tons depending on the angle of the jib. There are two winches, a main one with 90m (295ft) of cable and a pull of 35,000kg (77,000lb) and a secondary one with 120m (393ft) of cable and a pull of 4,000kg (8,800lb). The vehicle can be used for lifting engines out of other tanks, and there is provision on the decking for carrying a spare AMX-30 engine.

Length: 7.18m (23ft 6in). *Height:* 2.65m (8ft 8in). *Weight:* 40,000kg (88,160lb). *Armament:* one 7.62mm machine gun. *Speed:* 60km/hr (37mph). *Range:* 600km (372 miles). Other details as for the AMX-30.

SAVIEM SM 340 VT TRACTOR *1976–*

The SM 340 is a civilian tractor adapted to meet a military need for a tractor which can tow a transporter trailer with a total load of 50 tons. It is a straightforward tractor with a two-man cab, which can tilt forward to expose the engine. It drives four of the six wheels and optional extras include air-conditioning and sound insulation for the crew.

Length: 7m (22ft 11in). *Width:* 2.50m (8ft 2in). *Height:* 2.80m (9ft 2in). *Weight:* 9,000kg (19,840lb). *Crew:* 1. *Power:* Saviem 2858 M4, V–8, diesel, 335bhp at 2,200rpm. *Towed load:* Up to 50,000kg (110,229lb). *Speed:* 77km/hr (48mph). *Range:* 800km (500 miles). *Maker:* Saviem, Sursesnes.

Saviem SM 340 VT

WILLEME 50-TON TANK TRANSPORTER *1946–1960*

The Willeme transporter was a creditable effort for France in the immediate post-war years. It was a straightforward design with an open cab and 6 × 4 drive. The eight-wheeled semi-trailer carried 50 tons, which was sufficient for any tanks of that time.

Length: 17.80m (58ft 4in). *Width:* 3.61m (11ft 9in). *Disposable load:* 50,000kg (110,200lb).

GERMANY

BERGEPANTHER ARMOURED RECOVERY VEHICLE *1943–1945*

The German Army had long relied on wheeled wreckers to salvage tanks in the field, but as tanks became larger and heavier these no longer sufficed, and in late 1942 development of a tracked recovery vehicle was begun. The first dozen were provided in June 1943 by simply taking a Panther (*qv*) chassis and hull, without turret, from the production line as it stood. After this, however, the basic hull was improved by the addition of a bulldozer-type spade, which could be dropped to form a ground anchor, a 40-ton winch and a 1½-ton hoist for changing engines and transmissions. The winch and hoist were in the central compartment, and the hull top was opened up and surrounded by a rectangular open-topped box for the crew. For local protection the Bergepanther was usually provided with two machine guns and some also carried a 20mm anti-aircraft cannon. A total of 447 were made, some being converted from battle-weary tanks sent in for refurbishing.

Length: 8.82m (28ft 11in). *Width:* 3.27m (10ft 9in). *Height:* 2.74m (9ft 0in). *Weight:*

AMX-30 ARV

43,000kg (94,798lb). *Crew:* 5. *Power:* Maybach V–12, petrol, 23,095cc, 700bhp at 3,000rpm. *Armament:* two 7.92mm machine guns or one 20mm automatic cannon. *Armour:* 8–80mm. *Speed:* 45km/hr (28mph). *Range:* 320km (200 miles). *Makers:* MAN, Nuremberg; Henschel GmbH, Kassel; DEMAG, Dusseldorf.

Bergepanther

BERGEPANZER III ARMOURED RECOVERY VEHICLE *1943–1945*

By late 1943 it was apparent that the PzKpfw III tank (*qv*) was obsolescent, and at the same time more recovery tanks were needed. The obvious course was followed, that of taking PzKpfw IIIs that were sent back for overhaul and converting them into Bergepanzer. The tank had its turret removed and a wooden superstructure built up on the hull. Attachment points for a jib crane were fitted at the front and rear of the hull and the crane was carried dismantled on the tank. A heavy-duty winch was fitted, driven from the main engine, and the tank was then provided with an

enormous wheeled earth anchor. This could be towed until required, whereupon the wheels were thrown out of alignment and the anchor hook dropped to the ground. The tank then pulled the hook into firm anchorage, after which it could use its winch to pull ditched vehicles out of their predicament. Special wide tracks were fitted, to improve traction in Russian snow, and some 150 were converted throughout 1944.

Height: 2.45m (8ft 0in). *Weight:* 19,300kg (42,560lb). *Armament:* two 7.92mm machine guns. Other details as for PzKpfw IV.

TANK TRANSPORTER TRAILERS *1938–1945*

The German Army of the Third Reich made comparatively little use of tank transporters, preferring to move their armour by rail. As a result, no specialist tractor-trailer units were built. Two special trailers were made and these were generally drawn by the standard 18-ton semi-tracked tractor (*qv*).

The 22-tonne trailer Sonderanhanger 116 had the platform suspended between two four-wheeled bogies. The front wheels were steered by the towing bar, while the rear wheels were

Sonderanhanger 116

steered by a wheel operated by a man in a small cab. The platform could be lowered to the ground for loading by use of winches or, on some versions, hydraulic jacks, and some models carried special ramps to allow vehicles to be off-loaded on to railway flatcars.

With the introduction of the Tiger tank (qv) a heavier trailer was needed, and the 68-ton model was produced in relatively small numbers. This ran on 24 wheels with solid tyres, which were arranged in two suspension units. All wheels took part in steering by means of a system of rods and levers connected with the trailer towing bar.

No measurements are available for either of these trailers.

WEST GERMANY

SLT-50 HEAVY TANK TRANSPORTER
1976–

After the end of the American-German MBT70 tank and its associated transporter, the German Army gave a contract for development of a tractor and semi-trailer capable of carrying the projected 'Leopard' tank (qv). This design was completed in 1975 and a total of 323 combinations have since been ordered and are under production.

The tractor unit is an 8 × 8 with glass-fibre and steel cab accommodation for a crew of four. Two hydraulic winches are fitted behind the cab, for loading purposes, and the rear of the chassis carries a fifth-wheel connector.

The semi-trailer has 12 wheels spaced over the full length of the bed, with ramps for loading at the rear end; this is rated at 56 tonnes capacity. An alternative trailer, rated at 52 tonnes, has eight wheels at the rear end. In both cases the trailer wheels have a degree of steerability to conform with the tractor's track.

SLT–50 2 Tractor *Length:* 8.83m (29ft 0in). *Width:* 3.05m (10ft 0in). *Height:* 2.98m (9ft

9in). *Weight:* 23,200kg (51,147lb). *Crew:* 4. *Power:* MTU MB–837, V–8, diesel, 29,920cc, 720bhp at 2,100rpm. *Maximum load:* 68,600kg (151,237lb). *Speed:* 65km/hr (40mph). *Range:* 500km (310 miles). *Maker:* Faun-Werke, Nuremberg.

Sattelanhanger 52t Trailer *Length:* 13.10m (43ft 0in). *Width:* 3.15m (10ft 4in). *Weight:* 16,600kg (36,600lb). *Payload:* 52,000kg (114,640lb). *Maker:* Karl Kassbohrer Fahrzeugwerken, Ulm.

Leopard ARV

LEOPARD ARMOURED RECOVERY VEHICLE *1966–*

While the Leopard battle tank (qv) was being developed, work began on an armoured recovery vehicle on the same chassis, and production of these commenced in 1966. The vehicle was designed so as to be able to perform a variety of functions: recover damaged tanks, tow disabled tanks, act as a crane in performing engine changes and, if necessary, lift

smaller vehicles; carry a spare engine so as to be able to perform an engine change at any time in the field; bulldoze; and act as a refueller.

The vehicle consists of a basic Leopard I hull and chassis without turret. The hull is extended upwards by an armoured superstructure surmounted by a commander's cupola with machine gun. At the side front, next to the driver, is a rotatable crane boom capable of lifting 20 tonnes, and on the front of the hull is a bulldozer blade which can be used for earth-moving or as a support for the tank when the crane or winch is being used. The main hauling winch is inside the hull and can provide a straight pull of 35 tonnes; this can, of course, be increased by judicious use of pulley-blocks. A platform at the rear of the hull is prepared to carry a complete Leopard engine-transmission unit, and an engine change can be performed in the field in 30 minutes.

Length: 7.56m (24ft 10in). *Width:* 3.32m (10ft 7in). *Height:* 2.69m (8ft 10in). *Weight:* 39,800kg (87,745lb). *Crew:* 4. *Power:* MTU, V–10, multi-fuel, 37,400cc, 830bhp at 2,200rpm. *Armament:* two 7.62mm machine guns. *Armour:* 15–40mm. *Speed:* 65km/hr (40mph). *Range:* 850km (525 miles). *Makers:* Atlas-MaK Maschinenbau GmbH, Kiel.

JAPAN

SE–RI ARMOURED RECOVERY VEHICLE *1939–1945*

The SE–RI was a variant of the Type 97 CHI–HA medium tank (qv) and was at the time described as an engineering vehicle. In place of the main turret was a low, conical cupola and on the back of the decking was a small A-frame crane, though some versions seem to have carried a jib crane. There were several versions of this engineering vehicle, and some were fitted with flamethrowers, though there was no apparent attempt to build a specific flamethrower tank. The main use of the SE–RI was to tow tanks that had broken down on the line of march and to effect field repairs at the first halt. Not many were made. At least one version had two cranes, mounted fore and aft with the driver in the middle. These cranes could be fitted with earth-moving buckets and they were worked by winches and drums of wire rope.

Length: 5.51m (18ft 1in). *Width:* 2.31m (7ft 6in). *Height:* 2.16m (7ft 11in). *Weight:* not known. *Crew:* 3. Other details as for Type 97 CHI-HA.

TYPE 70 ARMOURED RECOVERY VEHICLE *1971–*

This is another of the variants of the Type 61 tank (qv). It is fitted with a bulldozer blade on the front of the hull and a small flat-sided

SLT-50

superstructure replaces the turret. There is a winch on the rear of the hull and an A-frame lifting jib on the front.

Length: 8.41m (27ft 6in). *Armament:* one 12.7mm machine gun; one 7.62mm machine gun. Other details as for the Type 61.

Type 70 ARV

POLAND

WPT–TOPAS ARMOURED RECOVERY VEHICLE *1976–*

The WPT–TOPAS is a variant of the Czechoslovak OT–62A armoured personnel carrier (*qv*) used by the Polish Army. There are not many details available on this vehicle, but it would appear to be more of an engineer support vehicle than a true ARV, as, it seems, are so many of the Warsaw Pact ARVs. It has a hand-operated crane with a lift of only 1,000kg (2,200lb) and a winch with a pull of 2,500kg (5,500lb). The crew of four carries a full set of tools and welding gear for field repairs. All data are presumed to be the same as for the OT–62A since there are no apparent structural modifications.

SOVIET UNION

IS ARMOURED RECOVERY VEHICLE *1950–1975*

The IS assault gun chassis as used in the SU–122 (*qv*) and SU–152 (*qv*) is used as an ARV. Like the ones based on the T–54 (*qv*) there are several types all differing in some slight degree, and all of them more lightly equipped than would be the case in NATO. The nomenclature is confusing, but it can be assumed that all are so similar as to defy recognition except by experts. No data are quoted, but they can be taken to be almost the same as for the SU guns, the only exception being that the height of the ARV will be slightly greater due to the cranes stowed on top. The IS–2–T is simply an IS–2 tank with no

NETHERLANDS

DAF FTT 3500 TANK TRANSPORTER *1974–*

The FTT 3500 is the Dutch Army's standard tank transporter, a derivation from a civilian commercial design. It is a comprehensively equipped vehicle and it carries two winches with a pull on each of 20 tons. The tractor is optimized for use with the DAF YTS 10050

semi-trailer, which can carry a load of 55 tons, making a total vehicle weight of 100 tons on the road. Most of the payload is carried on the 16-wheel twin back axle, but up to 25 tons is transferred to the tractor via the gooseneck. There is a full dual set of air brakes and an automatic gearbox. It is in service in the Netherlands, Sweden, Denmark and Belgium.

Length: 8.01m (26ft 3in). *Width:* 3.07m (10ft 1in). *Height:* 3.25m (10ft 8in). *Weight* (Tractor): 19,000kg (41,876lb). *Power:* Detroit Diesel Model 12 V 71, V–12, 475bhp at 2,100rpm. *Towed load:* 70,000kg (154,280lb). *Speed:* 64 km/hr (40mph). *Range:* 500km (310 miles). *Maker:* DAF Trucks, Eindhoven.

turret and a small cupola. There is no special equipment at all, and all that the vehicle can do is to tow or push. The ISU–T is an SU without gun and fitted with a winch. The ISU–T Model B has the winch and a crane in addition. The lift of this crane is about 3,000kg (6,600lb). The ISU–T Model C has no crane but does have a spade at the rear for winching. The Models D and E differ only in the provision of spades and an A-frame lifting crane. All of them are in service in the Warsaw Pact countries and with their allies.

MAZ–535 AND–537 TRACTORS *1964–*

These very large 8 × 8 vehicles appear in different forms. They are cargo carriers, missile carriers and tractors towing semi-trailers. In the latter configuration they carry the largest Soviet missiles and also the whole range of armoured vehicles. Their only difference lies in the fact that the 535 series has a de-rated engine, giving 375bhp as opposed to the 537 with 525bhp. The engine is the same in both cases and is the same as is fitted to the T–55 tanks (*qv*), thereby saving in spares and simplifying maintenance. The cab is right at the front over the wheels, and the engine is in a large compartment directly behind. All eight wheels are driven and the front two pairs are steered. These tractors are in production in the USSR and are in service with the Soviet, Egyptian, Syrian and Yugoslav forces.

Length: 9.13m (29ft 11in). *Width:* 2.88m (9ft 5in). *Height:* 2.80m (9ft 2in). *Weight:* 22,500kg (49,590lb). *Crew:* 2. *Power:* D12A–525, V–12, diesel, 375 or 525bhp. *Towed load:* 50 or 75,000kg (110,200 or 165,300lb). *Speed:* 60km/hr (37mph). *Range:* 650km (403 miles). *Maker:* Minsk Motor Vehicle Plant, Minsk.

SU–85 AND SU–100 ARMOURED RECOVERY VEHICLES *1950–1975*

These two ARVs are so similar that they can be considered together. They are the SU–85 (*qv*)

and SU–100 (*qv*) chassis with the gun removed and a plate bolted over the hole in the mantlet. They had neither winch nor crane and could only push or tow stalled vehicles. The crew carried the usual range of tools to undertake field repairs, but with so little heavy gear they were handicapped and it was an expensive way to carry a repair crew on to the battlefield. They were in service throughout the Warsaw Pact countries, but are not now seen.

All data are as for the relevant SP gun.

SU–85 ARV

T–34–T ARMOURED RECOVERY VEHICLE *1948–*

There are, or have been, at least six distinct ARVs built on the T–34 (*qv*) tank chassis, the earliest ones being unsophisticated machines in which only the turret was removed and a repair crew carried. These vehicles did no more than tow a damaged tank off the battlefield and attempt to repair it with hand tools. Later versions fitted cranes, winches and the usual extras.

T–34–T: This is the earliest and simplest version in which only the turret was removed and nothing added.

T–34–T, Model B: In this version a crane and winch were fitted and a load platform was built over the engine decking.

T–34–T, Model B, East German: This was a Model B with a pushbar on the front.

WPT–34: This is the Polish version and is a much better ARV than the others. There is a large superstructure at the front of the hull for

T–34 ARV

the crew and a powerful winch in the hull. At the rear there are spades, and extra tools are carried on the outside of the hull.

SKP–5: This is another half-equipped ARV which has a crane but no winch, bulldozer blade or spades.

Czechoslovakian T–34 ARV: The designation of this vehicle is uncertain, but it is a T–34 chassis with a heavy-duty crane on top. Once again there is neither a bulldozer blade nor spades and its chief use seems to be more for lifting heavy items from tanks and in placing bridge components for the engineers rather than in actual recovery of dead vehicles.

For all the foregoing vehicles the basic data of the T–34 tank apply. The only variable dimension is the height.

MAZ-537

T–54/55 ARMOURED RECOVERY VEHICLES *1956–*

There are at least four models of the recovery version of the T–54/55 built either in the USSR or in East Germany. The first one is the T–54 ARV, which is a T–54 tank (*qv*) without a turret and the chassis fitted with a loading platform and a crane. A dozer blade is mounted at the back of the hull. There appears to be no winch and the value of the vehicle is undoubtedly limited to some extent by the light equipment. The second is an East German T–54, known as a T–54A ARV, which again has what seems to be fairly light gear. There is a pushbar instead of a winch, and a 1,000kg (2,200lb) jib crane. This vehicle can be fitted with mine-clearing ploughs. The third is the T–54B, another East German vehicle identical in all respects to the T–54A except for the addition of a generator on the back of the hull. Both of these ARVs would appear to be used more as engineer vehicles rather than ARVs in the sense that it is understood in NATO. The third model is again East German, the T–54C and it can be described as a Model A fitted with steadying spades. The crane is stronger, but there is still no winch nor is there a bulldozer blade.

Weight: 34,000kg (74,936lb). *Crew:* 3. Other details as for the T–54 tank.

T-54/55 ARV

SWEDEN

BARGNINGSBANDVAGN 82 ARMOURED RECOVERY VEHICLE *1973–*

The Bgbv 82 is a variant of the Pvb 302 armoured personnel carrier (*qv*), but it is larger, heavier and more powerful. It is one of the very few recovery vehicles not derived from a tank and the reason is that the Swedish S tank (*qv*) is comparatively light by modern standards and it was not felt necessary to use its expensive and complicated chassis for the recovery version. In fact the Bgbv 82 is a per-

Bgbv 82

fectly adequate vehicle, apart from its light armour, and it is amphibious with minimal preparation, an advantage in Sweden. It protects itself with a turret of the same type as is carried on the APC, and the crew compartment is also similar to the 302. There is a bulldozer blade on the front for moving small obstacles and steadying the vehicle when winching or using the crane. The crane will lift 5,500kg (12,000lb) and the winch will pull 20,000kg (44,000lb) on 145m (475ft) of rope. All equipment can be controlled when fully closed down.

Length: 7.23m (23ft 8in). *Width:* 3.25m (10ft 7in). *Height:* 2.45m (8ft 0in). *Weight:* 23,300kg (51,353lb). *Crew:* 4. *Power:* Volvo–Penta THD 100C, 6-cyl., turbocharged, diesel, 9,600cc, 310bhp at 2,200rpm. *Speed:* 56km/hr (35mph). *Range:* 400km (248 miles). *Maker:* Hägglund & Son, Örnsköldsrik.

SWITZERLAND

ENTPANNUNSPANZER 65 ARMOURED RECOVERY VEHICLE *1970–*

The Entp Pz 65 is the standard ARV of the Swiss Army and three of them are on the establishment of every battalion of Pz 68 tanks (*qv*). The chassis is derived from the Pz 68 and on it is built a square box-like superstructure with a small armoured cupola at the front. There is a bulldozer blade on the front and a substantial winch, which has a pull of 25,000kg (55,000lb) on 120m (400ft) of cable. The lifting gear is an A-frame swung at the front. It can pick up 15,000kg (33,000lb), which is sufficient to take a turret off one of the tanks or to replace an engine. There is also the usual range of tools and welding gear for the crew. The vehicle is in service only with the Swiss Army.

Length: 7.34m (24ft 11in). *Width:* 3.15m (10ft 5in). *Height:* 3.25m (10ft 7in). *Weight:* 39,000kg (85,960lb). *Crew:* 5. *Power:* one MTU MB 837, 8-cyl., horizontally-opposed, diesel, 704bhp at 2,200rpm. *Auxiliary engine:*

DM OM 836, 4-cyl., diesel, 35bhp at 3,500rpm. *Armament:* one 7.5mm machine gun on external mount. *Speed:* 55km/hr (34mph). *Range:* 300km (186 miles). *Maker:* Federal Engineering Works, Thun.

Entp Pz 65

UNITED KINGDOM

CENTURION ARMOURED RECOVERY VEHICLE *1947–*

The Centurion armoured recovery vehicle was developed from the Centurion battle tank (*qv*); the first version, the Mark 1, was simply a standard Centurion fitted with towing facilities, but this was soon abandoned in favour of a more purpose-built version. The Mark 2 has a superstructure of 30mm armour plate built up over the hull in place of the turret, a rear-mounted spade to act as a ground anchor, and a 30-ton winch. A jib crane capable of lifting 10 tons is carried unshipped and can be rapidly erected when required. A cupola on top of the superstructure is armed with a 7.62mm machine gun for local defence, and smoke dischargers are also fitted.

A variation of the ARV is the BARV, or Beach ARV, which is very similar to the ARV, but modified so as to be able to operate in water up to a depth of 2.89m (9ft 6in) without preparation. Its purpose is to recover tanks on landing beaches and also to push stranded landing craft off beaches into deeper water.

ARV: *Length:* 8.96m (29ft 5in). *Width:* 3.39m (11ft 1½in). *Height:* 2.89m (9ft 6in). *Weight:* 50,295kg (110,880lb). *Crew:* 4. *Power:* Rolls-Royce Meteor, 12-cyl., petrol, 650bhp at 2,550rpm. *Armament:* one 7.62mm machine gun. *Armour:* not disclosed. *Speed:* 35km/hr (21mph). *Range:* 100km (60 miles). *Maker:* Royal Ordnance Factory, Leeds.

Chieftain ARV

CHIEFTAIN ARMOURED RECOVERY VEHICLE *1974-*

Production of this vehicle, to replace the Centurion ARV, began in 1974. It uses the Chieftain Mark 5 (*qv*) hull, which is considerably modified by removing the turret and converting the interior into two compartments, one of which carries the crew and the other two independent winches, one with 30-ton and one with three-ton capacity. These winches are driven by hydraulic motors and a power take-off from the main engine. An hydraulically actuated earth spade is fitted, and also a bulldozer blade at the front of the vehicle. A cupola on top of the hull carries a machine gun for local defence.

Length: 8.25m (27ft 1in). *Width:* 3.51m (11ft 6½in). *Height:* 2.74m (9ft 0in). *Weight:* 52,000kg (114,640lb). *Crew:* 4. *Power:* Leyland, 12-cyl., vertically-opposed, 2-stroke, multi-fuel, 720bhp at 2,250rpm. *Armament:*

one 7.62mm machine gun. *Armour:* not disclosed. *Speed:* 42km/hr (26mph). *Range:* 325km (200 miles). *Maker:* Royal Ordnance Factory, Leeds.

SAMSON ARMOURED RECOVERY VEHICLE *1978–*

Samson is a light armoured recovery vehicle constructed on the chassis of the Scorpion 'Combat Vehicle, Reconnaissance, Tracked', (CVR(T)) (*qv*). It uses the same hull as the Spartan APC, a turretless box of more generous dimensions than the tank hull, and is equipped with a power winch capable of hauling 12 tonnes. At the rear of the hull are

two ground anchor spades, which can be lowered and dug in to stabilize the Samson when using the winch or when acting as a holdfast to permit another vehicle to winch itself out of difficulty by hauling against the Samson. The three-man crew have hatches with periscopes, and whilst no armament is permanently mounted, personal weapons and a light machine gun can be carried inside the vehicle.

Length: 4.93m (16ft 2in). *Width:* 2.18m (7ft 2in). *Height:* 2.02m (6ft 7in). *Weight:* 8,000kg (17,637lb). *Crew:* 3. *Power:* Jaguar, 6-cyl., petrol, 4,200cc, 195bhp at 4,750rpm. *Armament:* crew's personal weapons only. *Armour:* not disclosed. *Speed:* 87km/hr (54mph). *Range:* 645km (400 miles). *Maker:* British Leyland (Alvis Ltd.), Coventry.

SCAMMELL CONTRACTOR TANK TRANSPORTER *1969–*

The Scammell company have developed great expertise in the field of heavy transporters, and this combination tractor and semi-trailer was designed ,for the British Army in the late 1960s. The Contractor tractor is a 6 × 4 with lockable differentials and a 15-speed gearbox and is capable of moving in almost any terrain. The semi-trailer, specially built to mate with the tractor, has eight wheels and loading ramps at the rear end and can carry almost any tank in existence.

Scammel Contractor *Length:* 7.95m (26ft 1in). *Width:* 2.50m (8ft 3in). *Height:* 3.00m (9ft 10in). *Weight:* 14,200kg (31,305lb). *Crew:* 3. *Power:* Cummins NT335, 6-cyl., diesel, 14,000cc, 322bhp at 2,100rpm. *Towed load:* 74,200kg (163,582lb). *Speed:* 60km/hr (37mph). *Range:* 1,000km (620 miles). *Maker:* Scammell Motors, Watford.

Semi-trailer *Length:* 12.49m (41ft 0in). *Width:* 3.66m (12ft 0in). *Weight:* 15,850kg (34,945lb). *Payload:* 58,400kg (128,750lb). *Maker:* Crane-Freuhauf Ltd.

Samson

Scammell Contractor

THORNEYCROFT ANTAR TANK TRANSPORTER *1955–1978*

This vehicle was originally developed to haul oil field piping and machinery in the Middle East; it was then adopted by the British Army as a prime mover for tank transport and other loads, though it is now being replaced by the Scammell Contractor (*qv*). The final service version was the Mark 3, which had better accommodation in the cab and a more powerful engine than its predecessors.

The tractor unit was a 6 × 4 with lockable differential and a six-speed gearbox coupled to a six-speed transfer box. The chassis carried a fifth-wheel connector at the rear end.

The semi-trailer was of conventional type with 12 wheels at the rear and loading ramps; two spare wheels were carried at the front end, alongside the fifth-wheel unit. A later semi-trailer, rated at 60 tons, was also developed; this was of the same type but longer.

A variant model of the Antar is also in use, without the fifth-wheel connector and with couplings for towing a separate trailer. This has 32 wheels arranged in two 16-wheel bogies, the front bogie being steerable.

Antar Tractor *Length:* 8.70m (28ft 6½in). *Width:* 3.20m (10ft 6in). *Height:* 3.15m (10ft 4in). *Weight:* 21,896kg (48,272lb). *Crew:* 3. *Power:* Rolls–Royce C8 SFL–843, 8-cyl., diesel, turbocharged, 16,200cc, 333bhp at 2,100rpm. *Towed load :* 68,000kg (149,914lb). *Speed:* 32km/hr (20mph). *Range:* 700km (435 miles). *Maker:* Transport Equipment (Thornycroft) Ltd., Basingstoke.

50-ton Semi-Trailer *Length:* 11.93m (39ft 1½in). *Width:* 3.35m (11ft 0in). *Height:* 3.09m (10ft 1½in). *Weight:* 16,359kg (36,064lb). *Maker:* Taskers of Andover Ltd., Hants.

Antar Mark 2

UNITED STATES

DIAMOND-T FOUR-TON 6×6 TRUCK WRECKER *1941–1955*

This vehicle was developed for issue to all arms and services of the US forces as a recovery unit for automotive vehicles and as a general mobile hoist. Based on a four-ton truck chassis, the truck carried a frame unit behind the cab on which were mounted two boom arms, capable of swinging to their respective sides of the truck. Each arm had its own winch and cable, though both winches could be connected to one arm if required to perform a difficult lift. An additional front-mounted winch could be used to recover the vehicle if stuck or as an anchor during recovery work. Frames and canvas covers were provided so that the vehicle could be camouflaged to resemble a normal cargo truck.

Length: 6.78m (22ft 3in). *Width:* 2.43m (8ft 0in). *Height:* 2.94m (9ft 8in). *Weight:* 9,843kg (21,700lb). *Crew:* 2. *Power:* Hercules RXC, 6-cyl., petrol, 8,538cc, 131bhp at 2,300rpm. *Winch pull* (all): 6,800kg (15,000lb). *Speed:* 65km/hr (40mph). *Range:* 290km (180 miles). *Maker:* Diamond-T Motor Car Co., Chicago, Ill.

M1 AND M1A1 HEAVY WRECKING TRUCKS *1937–1960*

The US Army adopted the Heavy Wrecker M1 in 1937; this was a Marmon-Herrington 6 × 6 chassis carrying a swinging-boom crane on the rear deck and it was rated as a six-ton vehicle.

Experience proved the considerable utility of the design, but a heavier capacity was desirable, and early in the war years a more powerful model, the M1A1, was introduced and the M1 made obsolescent.

The M1A1 version was built to military specifications and had a less 'civilian' look about it than had the M1. It had an open cab and an improved crane mechanism, two winches, and carried a wide selection of welding, cutting and lifting equipment. The crane could be swung so as to act at the rear or sides of the truck; its lifting ability varied with the boom angle, but the maximum lifting capacity was 7,250kg (16,000lb). The front winch was primarily for removing the wrecker from mud if it should become stuck, while the rear winch was for recovery purposes. Hoops and canvas covers were provided so that the crane assembly could be concealed to give the vehicle the appearance of a cargo truck from the air.

Length: 7.13m (23ft 5in). *Width:* 2.56m (8ft 5in). *Height:* 3.04m (10ft 0in). *Weight:* 18,370kg (40,500lb). *Crew:* 2. *Power:* Continental 22R, 6-cyl., petrol, 8,211cc, 133bhp at 2,400rpm. *Towed load:* 27,215kg (60,000lb). *Winch pull:* front, 9,070kg (20,000lb); rear, 17,010kg (37,500lb). *Speed:* 72km/hr (45mph). *Range:* 400km (250 miles). *Makers:* Kenworth Motor Truck Corp., Kirkland, Wash; Ward LaFrance Truck Corp., Elmira, NY.

M19 45-TON TANK TRANSPORTER TRUCK-TRAILER *1942–*

This combination was originally built to a British order in Lend-Lease days; it was later adopted for service with the US Army and standardized in September 1942. In British service it was known merely as the Diamond-T, from the name of the company which made the truck.

In broad terms, the Diamond-T was more useful as a supply vehicle than as a battlefield

Diamond T/M19

recovery unit, since its cross-country ability was limited. Nevertheless, it served admirably in taking tanks from railheads to forward units, back to repair facilities and in similar tasks. The tractor was a 6 × 4 truck, and the small cargo bed above the rear axles was usually filled with concrete slabs to give more weight and grip. The crew of the vehicle normally used this as a sleeping and stowage area, covered by

a canvas tilt. The trailer was provided with ramps for loading at the rear end and with failsafe air brakes. Loading of tanks could be done either by the tank's power or by a rearmounted winch on the truck. Numbers of these combinations remain in military service with smaller countries.

M20 12-ton 6 × 4 Truck *Length:* 7.11m (23ft 3¾in). *Width:* 2.54m (8ft 4in). *Height:* 2.54m (8ft 4in). *Weight:* 12,088kg (26,650lb). *Crew:* 3. *Power:* Hercules DFXE, 6-cyl., diesel, 178bhp at 1,600rpm. *Payload:* 8,323kg (18,650lb). *Towed load:* 52,163kg (150,000lb). *Winch pull:* 18,145kg (40,000lb). *Speed:* 37km/hr (23mph). *Range:* 480km (300 miles). *Maker:* Diamond-T Motor Car Co., Chicago, Ill.

M9 45-ton 12-wheel Trailer *Length:* 9.04m (29ft 8in). *Width:* 2.89m (9ft 6in). *Height:* 1.44m (4ft 9in). *Weight:* 11,340kg (25,000lb). *Payload:* 40,823kg (90,000lb).

M19 Truck-Trailer *Length:* 16.07m (52ft 9in). *Laden weight:* 72,575kg (160,000lb). *Trailer makers:* Freuhauf Trailer Co.; Pointer Willamette Co.; Winter-Weiss Co.; Rogers Brothers.

4-Ton 6 × 6 Wrecker

M25/26 40-TON TANK TRANSPORTER TRUCK-TRAILER *1943–*

The M19 Diamond-T transporter's (qv) lack of cross-country ability and the fact that it was simply a tractor led the US Army to press for the development of a more specialized vehicle which would have improved mobility and better recovery equipment. Development was done by the Knuckey Truck Company and in June 1943 the M25 combination was standardized. It might be noted that late in 1944 the nomenclature system was changed and the units were classified separately, as detailed below.

The M26 tractor truck was a 6 × 6 armoured tractor which could operate in the combat zone. It was provided with two winches controlled from an operating platform behind the cab. The rear of the chassis carried a fifth-wheel connector for attachment of the Semi-Trailer M15. A third winch was mounted in the front of the vehicle and controlled from the cab, its primary purpose being to recover the truck-trailer should it become stuck in bad ground.

The Semi-Trailer M15 was an eight-wheeled flat-bed trailer with a front attachment to the tractor and ramps at the rear for loading tanks. The track of the rear wheels could be widened for loading vehicles of different widths.

For use in non-combat zones, a soft-skinned variant of the tractor was developed as the M26A1; this resembled the M26, but had no armour on the cab. Small improvements in post-war years resulted in the M26A2, which is still in service. In similar manner the trailer was improved; the M15A1 was given special ramps, which allowed the wider M26 series of tanks (qv) to load over the top of the trailer wheels, while the M26A2 had its payload increased from 45 tons to 50 tons.

A somewhat modified M26 tractor was developed as the towing vehicle for the 914mm (36in) mortar Little David, a weapon developed for the projected invasion of Japan but which did not enter service.

M26 Tractor *Length:* 7.72m (25ft 4in). *Width:* 3.32m (10ft 10¾in). *Height:* 3.14m (10ft 4in). *Weight:* 21,908kg (41,300lb). *Crew:* 7. *Power:* Hall-Scott 440, 6-cyl., petrol, 17,865cc, 230bhp at 2,100rpm. *Towed load:* 52,163kg (115,000lb). *Winch pull:* rear, 27,215kg each (60,000lb); front, 15,875kg (35,000lb). *Speed:* 42km/hr (26mph). *Range:* 400km (250 miles).

M26A1 similar except *Weight:* 12,519kg (27,600lb). *Maker:* Pacific Car & Foundry Co., Renton, Wash.

M15 Trailer *Length:* 11.81m (38ft 9in). *Width:* 3.81m (12ft 6½in). *Height:* 2.00m (6ft 7in). *Weight:* 15,875kg (35,000lb). *Payload:* 36,287kg (80,000lb).

M15A1 similar but *Payload:* 40,823kg (90,000lb).

M15A2 similar but *Payload:* 45,359kg (100,000lb). *Maker:* Freuhauf Trailer Co.

M31 ARV

M31 ARMORED RECOVERY VEHICLE *1942–1950*

In 1942, with heavier tanks entering service, the need for a heavier recovery vehicle than the usual wheeled wrecker became apparent, and the first US model was produced by modifying the M3 (Grant/Lee) tank (qv) chassis. All armament except the bow machine gun was removed, and the side sponson was closed by a door upon which a dummy gun was mounted. The turret was turned through 180° and a plate fitted in place of the 37mm gun mount to act as the anchorage for a crane arm, which extended over the rear of the hull. This arm was fitted with two support jacks, which could either be pinned into attachments on the vehicle hull or rested on the ground to provide support for lifting heavier loads. A winch in the crew compartment could have its cable fed beneath the hull to front or rear for direct hauling or over a pulley and to the crane arm for hoisting. Numerous stowage boxes were added to the hull in order to carry a wide variety of spare parts and tools. Just over 800 of these vehicles were built before the end of the war.

Length: 8.05m (26ft 5in). *Width:* 2.54m (8ft 4in). *Height:* 2.97m (9ft 9in). *Weight:* 27,215kg (60,000lb). *Crew:* 6. *Power:* according to original tank converted either Continental, petrol, 9-cyl., radial, 400bhp at 2,400rpm; or GMC, diesel, 12-cyl., 410bhp at 2,900rpm. *Armament:* two 7.62mm machine guns. *Armour:* 12–50mm. *Speed:* 40km/h (25mph). *Range:* 180km (110 miles). *Maker:* Baldwin Locomotive Co. Philadelphia, Pa.

M32 ARMORED RECOVERY VEHICLE *1943–1960*

As the manufacture of M3 tanks (qv) ceased, it became necessary to develop a fresh tank recovery vehicle based on the M4 Sherman (qv), and work on this began in April 1943. The turret was removed and replaced by a fixed superstructure with a rounded front made from flat plate; brackets were attached to the hull sides to which an A-Frame jib was

M25

M746/747

pivoted. This could be laid back alongside the turret when not required, or erected over the front of the vehicle to act as a crane. A winch was mounted inside the hull, behind the driver's seat, and could be used for pulling or, in conjunction with the crane, for lifting. The tank's bow machine gun was retained and augmented by a .50 machine gun on the turret top, and an 81mm mortar was carried on the left side of the hull and could be brought into action to fire screening smoke bombs to conceal a recovery from enemy observation.

Various improvements were made as production continued; the actual model number of the tank varied according to which version of the M4 was used as the starting point. Thus the M4 tank became the M32, the M4A1 the M32B1, and so on. First vehicles used the resting boom of the crane as a towbar, but a stronger towbar and hook were later fitted at the rear. The suspension was designed so as to have the springs locked out of action and thus give a more stable platform for winching and lifting. In 1945 the horizontal volute-spring suspension was adopted, adding A1 to the nomenclature, so that, for example, the M32B1 became the M32A1B1. Of the various models of M32, 1,599 were built, and they continued to serve for many years after the war.

Length: 5.82m (19ft 1in). *Width:* 2.61m (8ft 7in). *Height* 2.64m (8ft 8in). *Weight:* 28,122kg (62,000lb). *Crew:* 4. *Power:* according to M4 model converted, either Continental, 9-cyl., radial, petrol, 400bhp at 2,400rpm; or GMC, 12-cyl., diesel, 410bhp at 2,900rpm. *Armament:* one 7.62mm machine gun; one .50in machine gun; one 81mm mortar with 30 smoke bombs. *Armour:* 12–50mm. *Speed:* 38km/hr (24mph). *Range:* 195km (120 miles). *Makers:* Lima Locomotive Co., Lima, Ohio; Pressed Steel Car Co., Pittsburgh, Pa.; Baldwin Locomotive Works, Philadelphia, Pa.; Federal Machine & Welder Co.; International Harvester Co., Chicago.

M32 ARV

M74 ARMORED RECOVERY VEHICLE
1953–
With the addition of heavier tanks to the American armoury, it was apparent by the early 1950s that a more powerful recovery tank was needed, and in 1952 it was decided to see if a fresh design could be developed, but

still using the M4 tank (*qv*) as a basis – since there were still large numbers available. After some trials and modifications, the M74 was standardized in 1953 and has remained in service ever since.

M74 ARV

The M74 is basically an M4A3E8 hull and chassis, with horizontal volute springs and wide tracks. The turret is replaced by a fixed structure, which carries a winch on its front. A second winch is inside the hull, feeding its cable through a fairlead in the front glacis plate. The same type of jib crane is provided as was used on the M32 (*qv*), but it is hydraulically erected, which allows it to be used as a travelling jib. A bulldozer-type blade is added at the front of the hull for use as a stabilizer when winching or lifting, and a special towing mount and bars are provided at the rear. As with the earlier models the outline of the tank has tended to disappear under stowage bins and spare parts hung on every available surface.

Length: 7.95m (26ft 1in). *Width:* 3.09m (10ft 2in). *Height:* 3.11m (10ft 2½in). *Weight:* 42,524kg (93,750lb). *Crew:* 4. *Power:* Ford GAA, V-8 petrol, 450bhp at 2,600rpm.

Armament: one 7.62mm machine gun, one .50in machine gun; *Armour:* 12–50mm. *Speed:* 34km/hr (21mph). *Range* 160m (100 miles). *Makers:* Bowen MacLaughlin York, Inc. York, Pa.; Rock Island Arsenal, Ill.

M746 AND M747 HEAVY EQUIPMENT TRANSPORTERS *1974–*
As the M25 transporter (*qv*) grew older the US Army tried a variety of basically commercial vehicles and trailers as replacements, but had little success since most of them lacked reliability or cross-country performance. In 1965 a joint venture with the West German Army was begun with a view to developing a transporter for the proposed MBT70 tank, but when the MBT70 programme collapsed, the transporter went with it and the design was revised to meet purely American requirements. This eventually became the M746 tractor and M747 trailer, and first issues were made in 1974.

The M746 tractor is an 8 × 8 vehicle with no load-carrying capacity other than the fifth-wheel connector. It has two winches for loading purposes. The M747 semi-trailer is of conventional pattern with loading ramps at the rear; its forward end can be supported on props, so that it is possible to load the trailer in the absence of the tractor.

M746 Tractor *Length:* 8.23m (27ft 0in). *Width:* 3.05m (10ft 0in). *Height:* 3.05m (10ft 0in). *Weight:* 20,412kg (45,000lb). *Crew:* 2. *Power:* Detroit Diesel 12V71(T), V–12, 13,960cc, 608bhp at 2,500rpm. *Towed load:* 68,945kg (152,000lb). *Speed:* 62km/hr (38mph). *Range:* 320km (200 miles). *Maker:* Ward LaFrance Motor Co.

M747 Trailer *Length:* 12.21m (40ft 0in). *Width:* 3.05m (10ft 0in). *Weight:* 14,515kg (32,000lb). *Payload:* 54,430kg (120,000lb). *Maker:* Freuhauf Trailer Co.

The American ½-ton Dodge was a less
common and smaller version of the ¾-ton
weapons carrier. It was popular in the Pacific
theatre since it could easily be beach landed.

CARGO, PERSONNEL AND WEAPONS CARRIERS

AUSTRO–DAIMLER ADTK LIGHT VEHICLE 1936–1937

The ADTK was a serious attempt by Steyr to build a military vehicle for all purposes. It was in many ways the forerunner of the Jeep, though it was larger and had less power. Its failing was that it had only 4 × 2 drive and so lacked the cross-country mobility which is so necessary for a general purpose vehicle. But the general idea was right. The body was a flat topped, box-like shape with a cargo bed at the rear on which seats could be bolted. In front sat the driver and one passenger with the engine between them. Behind could be carried six more men in two rows of three. There was a tow hook and a light gun could be towed, though if the crew were in the vehicle another carrier was required for the ammunition. About 160 were built, but the idea then seems to have faded out and it is not known if the German Army took them over, but it seems likely that it did.

Length (estimated): 3.50m (11ft 6in). *Length:* 3.80m (12ft 6in). *Width:* 1.50m (4ft 11in). *Height:* 1.46m (4ft 9in). *Weight:* 1,045kg (2,303lb). *Power:* Steyr FB, 4-cyl., air-cooled, petrol, 2,312cc, 48bhp. *Maker:* Steyr-Daimler-Puch, Steyr.

GRAF UND STIFT TRUCKS 1960–

There is a range of trucks in service with the Austrian Army made by the firm of Gräf und Stift, one of the oldest manufacturers of vehicles in Europe. These trucks are all fairly large and heavy and are used mainly by the engineers for the movement of their heavy equipment. The chassis of some models are used for variants such as refuelling trucks for airfields. The data are given for one of the bigger trucks in the range, the Model ZA–200 6 × 6.

Length: 8.59m (28ft 2in). *Width:* 2.40m (7ft 9in). *Height:* 2.92m (9ft 6in). *Weight:* 10,650kg (23,470lb). *Power:* Gräf und Stift Model 6 VT-200, 6-cyl., diesel, 10,810cc, 200bhp at 2,000rpm. *Speed:* 70km/hr (44mph). *Range:* 350km (217 miles). *Maker:* Gräf und Stift AG, Vienna.

HAFLINGER 700 AP TRUCK 1960–

The Haflinger is based on a commercial vehicle of the same name and is in service with the Austrian Army as well as several overseas countries, including South Africa. It is a small 4 × 4 cargo carrier with a capacity of 400kg (881lb). The chassis is tubular with engine and transmission at the rear, and a winch can be fitted if required. There are several variants, including radio and command vehicles, weapons carriers and one which takes four

Haflinger 700 AP

Bantam ATGW. The high ground clearance and good power/weight ratio give it excellent cross-country mobility and good over-snow performance.

Length: 2.83m (9ft 3in). *Width:* 1.35m (4ft 5in). *Height:* 1.74m (5ft 8in). *Weight* (empty): 580kg (1,278lb). *Power:* Model 700 AP, 2-cyl., air-cooled, petrol, 24bhp at 4,500rpm. *Cargo load:* 570kg (1,256lb). *Speed:* 64km/hr (40mph). *Range:* 40km (248 miles). *Maker:* Steyr-Daimler-Puch AG, Graz.

PINZGAUER 710 TRUCK *1971–*

The Pinzgauer is a larger version of the Haflinger (*qv*) and is built on much the same lines. It has been in service with the Austrian Army since 1973 and is issued in either a cargo or personnel carrying form. As a personnel carrier it is fully enclosed and fitted with seating. There is also a 6 × 6 version which is still in prototype form and has yet to be given an order.

Length: 4.20m (13ft 8in). *Width:* 1.76m (5ft 8in). *Height:* 2.10m (6ft 9in). *Weight:* 1,950kg (4,297lb). *Power:* Steyr-Puch, 4-cyl., petrol, 92bhp. *Cargo load:* 1,000kg (2,204lb). *Speed:* 100km/hr (62mph). *Range:* 500km (310 miles). *Maker:* Steyr-Daimler-Puch AG, Graz.

STEYR 440 LIGHT VEHICLE *1935–1945*

The Steyr 440 is typical of a complete series of vehicles, all with similar characteristics. They were based on the Austro-Daimler ADG of 1931, which was an entirely new concept in military vehicles, and a brave venture in those times of depression and pacifism. The layout was quite complicated. There was a beam axle at the front and a front-mounted engine;

behind that was a gearbox with no fewer than seven forward speeds and three reverse. Behind the gearbox the chassis came in to form a spine, and from this spine the rear wheels were independently sprung by swinging half-axles and longitudinal half-elliptic springs freely mounted on trunnions. There was a complicated arrangement of shafting to take the drive to each of the four back wheels, but the result was that these wheels had extremely good adhesion and grip. Steyr modified this drive arrangement and used a simpler ladder-chassis with a single differential, but retained the suspension.

Spare wheels were carried on free-running bearings and projected below the body to give extra support on boggy or rough ground. This chassis carried a variety of bodies and was known by different numeral titles. There were box-bodied radio cars, command vehicles, ambulances, flat-bed trucks, personnel carriers and gun towers. The personnel versions carried between 11 and 14 men, depending on the type, and all told about 4,500 vehicles incorporating the general principles of this design were built in Austria up to 1941. Romania bought some, and in France the Laffly company bought the design and modified it to produce their own range of load carriers.

440 version *Length:* 5.24m (17ft 2in). *Width:* 1.6m (5ft 5in). *Height:* 2.3m (7ft 6in). *Weight:* 2,450kg (5,400lb). *Power:* Steyr 430, 6-cyl., petrol, 2,078cc, 45bhp at 3,800rpm. *Payload:* 1,500kg (3,306lb). *Maker:* Steyr-Daimler-Puch, Steyr.

STEYR 680 M3 TRUCK *1960–*

The M3 is a 6 × 6 cargo truck of conventional

appearance and robust construction. It can tow a trailer with 8,000kg (18,240lb) of cargo on a road and it carries a winch with a pull of 4,500kg (9,920lb) as a standard item of equipment. The suspension is well suited to cross-country movement and with its two-speed transfer gearbox it can tackle almost any slope when fully loaded.

Length: 6.73m (22ft 1in). *Width:* 2.40m (7ft 9in). *Height:* 2.85m (9ft 4in). *Weight:* 6,500kg (14,326lb). *Power:* Steyr, 6-cyl., diesel, supercharged, 165bhp at 2,800rpm. *Cargo load:* 6,700kg (14,760lb). *Speed:* 80km/hr (50mph). *Range:* 500km (310 miles). *Maker:* Steyr-Daimler-Puch AG, Graz.

Steyr 680

BELGIUM

FN AS 24 AIRBORNE VEHICLE *1959–*

This little vehicle was built by FN to an order by the Belgian Army for their airborne troops and a total of 500 were delivered. Manufacture then ceased and no more have been made since. It is a most interesting design which was specifically produced for airborne use. It has a light tubular steel chassis which collapses for parachuting and is extended before driving off the drop zone. It is normally dropped on a standard NATO pallet and can be in action within minutes of landing. The three wheels are laid out with one in front and immediately behind it is a long bench seat accommodating four men. The motorcycle engine is between the two rear wheels. There is no springing and the wheels are fitted with very wide, low-pressure tyres, which provide the suspension. There is no body, nor any load-carrying platform, but it is possible to put support weapons on the seat and still carry two men. There are limitations in the use of these light vehicles and most airborne forces prefer to use standard four-wheeled vehicles and accept the difficulties of dropping them.

Length: 1.92m (6ft 3in). *Width:* 1.64m (5ft 5in). *Height:* 85cm (2ft 8in). *Weight:* 224kg (493lb). *Power:* FN 24, 2-cyl., 2-stroke, petrol, 15bhp at 5,300rpm. *Cargo load:* 340kg (750lb). *Speed:* 57km/hr (35mph). *Range:* 200km (124 miles). *Maker:* FN Herstal, Liège.

Pinzgauer 710

FN 4RM/652 3M TRUCK *1958–*

This truck was designed to a NATO specification and production was completed in 1960. It has only been in use with the Belgian Army and is a fairly standard type of cargo vehicle which can carry up to 3,500kg (7,716lb) of cargo and tow a trailer loaded with 3,000kg (6,613lb). Alternatively, there is room for 20 fully equipped soldiers.

Length: 5.91m (19ft 4in). *Width:* 2.24m (7ft 4in). *Height:* 2.83m (9ft 3in). *Weight:* 4,450kg (9,800lb). *Power:* FN 652, 6-cyl., petrol, 130bhp at 3,500rpm. *Cargo load:* 3,150kg (6,950lb). *Speed:* 90km/hr (56mph). *Range:* 500km (310 miles). *Maker:* FN Herstal, Liège.

FN 4RM/652

FN AS 24

BRAZIL

ENGESA EE–15 TRUCK *1973–*

The Engesa EE–15 has been specially developed by the Engesa Company for military use and it has been designed with use in underdeveloped countries as a prime consideration. It is both simple and rugged and can accept a variety of power units to suit local conditions. If required it can be fitted with a winch with a pull of 7,500kg (15,356lb), which has to be positioned behind the cab, but a front-mounted winch with a pull of 3,000kg (6,613lb) can be put on the front. A variety of bodies can be fitted for whatever use the truck needs to be put to. It is reported to be in service with the Brazilian Army and has probably been bought by other countries.

Length: 5.35m (17ft 6in). *Width:* 2.10m (6ft 9in). *Height:* 2.31m (7ft 6in). *Weight:* 2,820kg (6,215lb). *Power:* Chevrolet, 6-cyl., petrol, 150bhp at 3,800rpm, or any equivalent petrol or diesel engine. *Cargo load:* 3,600kg (7,930lb). *Speed:* 90km/hr (56mph). *Range:* 600km (372 miles). *Maker:* Engesa Engenheiros Especializados SA, São Paulo.

CHINA

BJ–212 LIGHT TRUCK *1968–*

This is a light vehicle very similar to a Jeep in its general purpose, but this particular design is a derivation of the Soviet UAZ–469B (*qv*) and it carries a load of about 425kg (936lb). It is an entirely conventional vehicle with little that is unusual and it is presumed that it is entirely made inside China.

Unladen weight: 1,530kg (3,372lb). *Payload:* 425kg (936lb). Other details as for the UAZ–469B.

CZECHOSLOVAKIA

PRAGA V3S 6 × 9 TRUCK *1952–*

The V3S is a conventional truck which is widely used by both military and civilian organizations in Czechoslovakia. It has been sold to Bulgaria, China, Egypt and Romania and in some of these countries it is fitted with a multiple rocket-launching mount. The basic chassis is fitted with many bodies, including dump trucks and office bodies. A few are reported to carry twin 30mm anti-aircraft equipments. Some of the trucks have a winch on the front capable of a pull of 3,500kg (7,716lb). The quoted payload can be almost doubled on smooth roads, the figure given being for cross country only.

Length: 6.90m (22ft 7in). *Width:* 2.30m (7ft 6in). *Height:* 2.92m (9ft 6in). *Weight:* 5,350kg (11,970lb). *Power:* Tatra T–912 6-cyl., air-

Engesa EE-15

Tatra 813 8 X 8

cooled, diesel, 98bhp at 2,100rpm. *Payload:* 3,000kg (6,612lb). *Speed:* 62km/hr (38mph). *Range:* 500km (310 miles). *Maker:* Avia Zovody, Lethany.

SKODA 1100 VO LIGHT MILITARY CAR
1949–1955
The Skoda was based on the contemporary civilian car of that make and was a light military vehicle with 4 × 4 drive. It was lightly built, with independent suspension for all wheels, but was underpowered. The body was a light steel structure with four doors and a canvas top. Before full production was arranged the design was replaced by the 973P, which had a larger engine (1,221cc) and hub reduction gears. The 973 actually went into production, but before many were built the Czechoslovakian Army opted for the Soviet GAZ–69 (*qv*) and ceased to manufacture its own designs.

Length: 3.90m (12ft 8in). *Width:* 1.50m (4ft 10in). *Height:* 2.40m (5ft 2in). *Weight:* 960kg (2,115lb). *Power:* Skoda 1100, 4-cyl., petrol, 1,089cc, 32bhp at 4,200rpm. *Payload:* 400kg (880lb). *Speed:* 90km/hr (56mph). *Maker:* Skoda-Werke, Pilsen.

TATRA 4 × 4 CARS *1928–1940*
The well-known firm of Tatra produced a variety of 4 × 4 cars for military use in the 1930s.

All were based on current civilian models and differed mainly in the fact that they were fitted with open bodies and larger tyres. They all used tubular backbone chassis with independent suspension, and many had two spare wheels carried so that they provided additional 'bellying' support in the middle of the body. During World War II many of these cars were taken over by the German Army and at least one version was used in the Western Desert as a command car.

1938 T79 command car *Length:* 3.70m (12ft 2in). *Width:* 1.60m (5ft 3in). *Height:* 1.90m (6ft 3in). *Weight:* 1,480kg (3,260lb). *Power:* Tatra V799, 4-cyl., air-cooled, petrol, 2,191cc, 50bhp at 3,000rpm. *Payload:* 400kg (880lb). *Maker:* Tatra, Prague.

TATRA 6 × 4 CARS *1933–1940*
There was a series of 6 × 4 large cars from the Tatra works, all of them being based on existing truck or commercial chassis. They all featured the four swinging half axles at the rear, though there were differences in the way the power was transmitted to the wheels. No attempt was made to fit all-wheel drive, probably because it would have been too expensive. Different engines were fitted, all of them air-cooled, which was the mark of the Tatra. In general terms the power increased as the years

went by, though all of them seem to have been slightly underpowered when compared with other nationalities. Some were exported to Romania, but the majority of the production was taken by the German Army and used throughout the war.

1939 T93 Model *Power:* Tatra, V–8, air-cooled, 3,980cc, 70bhp at 3,500rpm. *Maker:* Tatra, Prague.

TATRA 813 8 × 8 TRUCK *1968–*
The 813 is a large cargo carrier closely related to the OT-64 APC (*qv*). It is the biggest of a range of three, all using similar components, and carrying progressively larger loads. The three are a 4 × 4, 6 × 6 and the 813 is 8 × 8. As a cargo carrier the 813 has a large load area behind the cab with drop sides and a drop tailboard. It can be fitted with seats and a removable canvas top. All the military versions have a central tyre pressure system and a winch with a pull of 22,000kg (48,501lb). The construction is quite massive, the engine being in the front of the cab with the transmission beneath the floor at the rear. The chassis is also used for such purposes as carrying and launching floating bridges and pontoons, or for roadway sections. However, the main purpose seems to be to tow artillery pieces and the entire gun crew can be carried also. As an ammunition

carrier the 813 would seem to offer considerable promise too, since the cross-country mobility is very good and the ground clearance high. Other versions of the vehicle are used as prime movers for specific towing use, both in the military and civilian sphere.

Length: 8.90m (29ft 2in). *Width:* 2.51m (8ft 3in). *Height:* 3.00m (9ft 7in). *Weight:* 14,420kg (31,780lb). *Power:* Tatra T–930–3, 12-cyl., air-cooled, diesel, 270bhp at 2,700rpm. *Payload:* 8,380kg (18,470lb). *Speed:* 75km/hr (46mph). *Range:* 1,000km (621 miles). *Maker:* Tatra, Narodi Podnik, Koprivnice.

FINLAND

SISU A–45 4 × 4 TRUCK *1972–*
The A-45 has been designed to carry 2,500kg (5,500lb) of cargo across country and up to 4,000kg (8,800lb) on smooth roads. It can tow the same load also. It is used by the Finnish Army in Finland and is also seen with Finnish troops on United Nations duties. It is a robust vehicle with particular application to use on poor roads and extreme climatic conditions.

Sisu A-45

Ground clearance is high and there are practically no projections below the line of the chassis. The cab is made of steel on the lower half and glass fibre for the upper part. It can be taken apart to reduce the height. The engine is in the cab at the rear and it projects backwards into the load compartment. The rear body is removable and the vehicle can be fitted with a number of different bodies and equipments. For all of them the standard features are: full cab heating; a winch; full engine cold start and oil heating gear; hydraulic power take-off for trailer wheels. The normal use of the A-45 is for the towing of artillery pieces, but it is plainly a practical vehicle, if a rather expensive one, for all general cargo use.

Length: 5.71m (18ft 8in). *Width:* 2.36m (7ft 9in). *Height:* 2.60m (8ft 6in). *Weight:* 6,250kg (13,775lb). *Power:* Valmet 411 A, 4-cyl., diesel, 90bhp; Valmet, 6-cyl., diesel, 150bhp at 2,600rpm. *Payload:* 4,150kg (9,145lb). *Speed:* 85km/hr (52mph). *Range:* 800km (500 miles). *Maker:* SISU OY, Helsinki.

FRANCE

BERLIET CBA FOUR-TON TRUCK *1914–1920*
The CBA was one of the standard load carriers of World War 1 and it followed the conventional layout of the times. The open cab was behind the engine, with a folding canvas top but no windscreen. The load compartment was covered with another canvas top and had a drop tailboard. There were twin wheels at the back, driven by chains from a counter-shaft. All tyres were solid rubber and the lorry could only be used on made-up roads. Speeds were modest, but many hundreds were in service throughout the war and apparently reliability was good.

Length: 6.10m (20ft). *Width:* 2.10m (6ft 9in). *Height:* 2.95m (9ft 7in). *Weight:* 3,250kg (7,160lb). *Power:* Berliet Model Z, 4-cyl., petrol, 5,300cc, 22CV. *Maker:* Automobiles M. Berliet SA, Lyon.

CITROEN MEHARI ARMEE MILITARY CAR *1965–*
This is a military version of the successful civilian Méhari and it is a development of the well-known Citroën 2CV light car. In the Méhari there is a steel floor-cum-chassis with a lightweight plastic body shell. There are several versions, but all feature a load-carrying area at the back and a folding windscreen. Essentially this is a light utility vehicle for such tasks as carrying radios, infantry support weapons or the smaller anti-tank guided missiles. It is

Berliet CBA

based on well-proven components and due to its light weight the cross-country mobility is good. However, it is only two-wheel drive so extremes of performance cannot be expected. It can be parachuted on a light skidboard and is in service with the French Army and Police in large numbers.

Length: 3.52m (11ft 6in). *Width:* 1.53m (5ft 1in). *Height* (top of screen): 1.61m (5ft 3in). *Weight:* 585kg (1,290lb). *Payload:* 505kg (1,113lb). *Power:* Citroën AK 2, 2-cyl., air-cooled, petrol, 26bhp at 5,500rpm. *Speed:* 100km/hr (62mph). *Range:* 300km (186 miles). *Maker:* Société Commerciale Citroën, Paris.

DELAHAYE VLR LIGHT VEHICLE *1951–54*
The VLR was an attempt to replace the wartime Jeep with a better and more versatile light vehicle. Delahaye had been making good-quality cars in France since early 1896, but with this design they unfortunately fell into the same trap as did many others who tried to

Citroën Méhari

replace the Jeep. The vehicle was too complicated and too expensive, and after a short production run it was stopped and the Willys Jeep (*qv*) brought back and built under licence by Hotchkiss. One drawback to the Delahaye was that it offered little improvement in carrying capacity over the Jeep and the additional expense went into the engine and transmission, where it was not really needed. What was wanted was better load capacity and this was provided by the Land-Rover and its derivatives when they appeared. Another complication in the Delahaye was independent suspension using torsion bars. While technically excellent, the maintenance load was too much for field workshops. It is worth mentioning that Peugeot also ventured into this field in 1955, but they too produced nothing much better than the Jeep, and since the decision had then been taken to go back to the Jeep, they withdrew before committing too much money.

Length: 3.50m (11ft 6in). *Width:* 1.58m (5ft 2in). *Weight:* 1.85m (6ft 1in). *Weight:* 1,400kg (3,085lb). *Power:* Delahaye, 4-cyl., petrol, 1,992cc, 63bhp at 3,600rpm. *Payload:* 450kg (991lb). *Maker:* Société des Automobiles Delahaye, Paris.

M201 JEEP *1953–*

Another name for this vehicle is the VLTT, 'Véhicule de Liaison Tout Terrain'. It is a World War II Jeep built in France under licence from Willys. Over 40,000 of them were built in France by Hotchkiss-Brandt, who are no longer in the vehicle business, and production ended in 1969. All details are identical with that of the Willys Jeep (*qv*) although there have been many variations on the standard chassis for the carriage of different weapons and missiles. A number of M201s were built with a longer wheelbase in order to increase the load platform.

M201

RENAULT 4 × 2 THREE-TON TRUCK *1914–1919*

Renault produced at least 1,000 of these small three-ton trucks during World War 1 and they were used for carrying searchlights, as ambulances, and in a few cases for mounting light guns. They were conventional in design, using the existing Renault engine with the radiator at the back and the familiar 'coal scuttle' bonnet. The transmission had a four-speed gearbox and shaft drive to the single rear wheels. These wheels were cast steel and had eight thin spokes each. The driver had a roof to protect him, but there was no windscreen.

Length: 5.60m (18ft 5in). *Width:* 2.10m (6ft 9in). *Height:* 2.80m (9ft 2in). *Weight:* 2,800kg (6,170lb). *Power:* Renault, 4-cyl., 29bhp. *Payload:* 3,000kg (6,612lb). *Maker:* Renault Frères, Billancourt.

SUMB 4 × 4 MH 600 BS TRUCK *1964–*

This truck, together with its bigger brother, the 3,000-kg (three-ton) model, are standard trucks in the French Army. Production was completed in the late 1960s, but spares and components are still supplied. The design is conventional with forward-mounted engine,

MH 600 BS

rear load compartment, high-set chassis and good ground clearance. The differential can be locked when the vehicle is on muddy ground. Some models have a winch on the front, but this is not a standard fitting. The driver's cab has a removable canvas top.

Length: 5.42m (17ft 1in). *Width:* 2.30m (7ft 6in). *Height:* 2.90m (9ft 6in). *Weight:* 3,670kg (8,088lb). *Power:* 8-cyl., petrol, 100bhp at 3,000rpm. *Payload:* 1,500kg (3,306lb). *Speed:* 85km/hr (53mph). *Range:* 550km (340 miles). *Maker:* FFSA, Sursesnes.

VLRA ALM

VLRA 4 × 4 ALM TYPE TPK 4-20M TRUCK *1958–*

VLRA, (Véhicule Léger de Reconnaissance et d'Appui), was developed in the late 1950s specifically for use in the Sahara and similar deserts. It has been adopted in small numbers by the French Army and several Middle Eastern countries. It has also been found useful by civilian enterprises which have an interest in desert regions, in particular oil and natural gas exploration companies. The special features of the vehicle are a powerful engine with tropical cooling, desert filters and anti-vapour lock devices. The transmission is all heavy duty and a large water tank, extra fuel tanks and sand channels are built in to the basic chassis. A winch is fitted to the front of the chassis. Military models carry mortars, machine guns or anti-tank missiles. A few trucks are used to carry CROTALE anti-aircraft missiles to the launch site. Production is now complete, but the vehicle is likely to remain in service for some years yet.

Length: 5.90m (19ft 4in). *Width:* 2.00m (6ft 6in). *Height:* 2.00m (6ft 6in). *Weight:* 4,250kg (9,367lb). *Power:* Perkins Model 6345D, 6-cyl., diesel, 125bhp at 2,800rpm. *Payload:* 2,500kg (5,510lb). *Speed:* 95km/hr (60mph). *Range:* 1,600km (994 miles). *Maker:* Ateliers de Construction Mécanique de l'Atlantique, Saint-Nazaire.

GERMANY

Kfz 1 4 × 4 LIGHT MILITARY CAR *1937–1945*

This car was developed in the middle 1930s to

Kfz 1

meet a Wehrmacht specification for a light military staff car with all-wheel drive, fully independent suspension, a self-locking differential on both axles, optional four-wheel steering, and auxiliary low gears for cross-country driving. Provided these features were incorporated the manufacturers could fit their own engines and transmissions, while the body was to be an open tourer with four doors and a collapsible canvas top.

Vehicles to this specification were produced from 1937 onward, but while they were everything the designers had hoped for – robust, with good performance over all sorts of terrain, and thoroughly reliable – they were also expensive and difficult to manufacture. As a result they were replaced by the Military Volkswagen (*qv*) in 1940 and production was closed down.

Length: 3.85m (12ft 7½in). *Width:* 1.69m (5ft 6½in). *Height:* 1.90m (6ft 3in). *Weight:* 1,700kg (3,747lbs). *Crew:* 1. *Power:* 4-cyl., petrol, 1,997cc, 50bhp. *Speed:* 80km/hr (50mph). *Range:* 400km (250 miles). *Makers:* BMW AG, Munich; Stöwer-Werke AG, Stettin; Hanomag, Hannover-Linden.

Kfz 15 4 × 4 MEDIUM MILITARY CAR
1937–1945

This was built to a similar Wehrmacht specification as the Kfz 1 light military car (*qv*) except that four-wheel steering was not incorporated, since it was thought to be too dangerous in larger and more powerful vehicles. An added feature in this model was the provision of stub axles halfway along the chassis to mount a spare wheel on each side; the wheels were free to revolve and formed a rolling surface which prevented the car 'bellying' when crossing obstacles or rough country. In all other respects it was simply an enlarged version of the light car. Production ended in 1943.

Length: 4.70m (15ft 5in). *Width:* 1.86m (6ft 1in). *Height:* 2.07m (6ft 9in). *Weight:* 2,600kg (5,732lb). *Crew:* 1. *Power:* V–8, petrol, 3,517 cc, 80bhp. *Speed:* 100km/hr (62mph). *Range:* 400km (250 miles). *Makers:* Auto-Union AG, Chemnitz; Adam Opel AG, Russelsheim.

Kfz 23 HEAVY MILITARY CAR,
1939–1945

The third of the series of Wehrmacht Standard Military Cars, the heavy model was built to a similar specification to the Kfz 15 medium car (*qv*). Some early models were fitted with four-wheel steering, but this was soon abandoned as being too dangerous in unskilled hands. As well as acting as staff cars these vehicles frequently carried radio and other communication equipment and functioned as message centres and communications vehicles with various grades of field headquarters. As with the others in this range, they were expensive and

complicated, and production was ended in 1943, their place being taken by the Steyr staff car (*qv*).

Length: 4.85m (15ft 11in). *Width:* 2.00m (6ft 7in). *Height:* 2.04m (6ft 8in). *Weight:* 3,000kg (6,615lb). *Crew:* 1. *Power:* V-8, petrol, 3,600cc, 81bhp at 3,000rpm. *Speed:* 110km/hr (70mph). *Range:* 400km (250 miles); *Makers:* Ford Motor Co. of Germany, Cologne; Auto-Union AG, Chemnitz.

MAULTIER CONVERTED TRUCKS
1942–1945

After experience of the Russian winter and spring, the German Army felt the need of a semi-tracked cargo vehicle, though one which could be built without going to the technical complexities of the standard semi-track series of tractors. The solution adopted was to take a number of standard cargo trucks and replace the rear wheels by a tracked suspension unit. Such converted trucks were known as Maultier (mule).

The vehicles selected for conversion were the Opel Blitz 36S (*qv*), the Ford Model 3000S and the Klockner-Humboldt-Deutz S3000 in the three-tonne range, and the Mercedes-Benz 4½-tonne L4500S model. The standard differential and rear axle were moved forward in the chassis and adapted to drive the track unit, and independent brakes were fitted to the track driving sprockets so that by applying them, additional steering power was available to supplement the normal front-wheel steering in difficult terrain. The track unit for the three-tonne conversions was of the Carden-Loyd pattern, with two bogies on each side. On the 4½-tonne Mercedes-Benz truck the track unit was heavier, based on that of the PzKpfw II tank (*qv*), with five roadwheels on each side.

Construction began in 1942 and continued until late 1944. The Opel Maultier was made in 1942-3, the Klockner-Humbolt-Deutz in small numbers in 1942 only, and the Ford from 1942 to 1944. The Mercedes model was built during 1943 and 1944.

The Maultier performed well, but due to the extra weight of the tracked unit and the fact that it was not well designed for load bearing, the three-tonne models were restricted to carrying only two tonnes. No restriction was placed on the 4½-tonne model, since the track unit was much more substantial. Although production ended in 1944, the Maultiers

Maultier

remained in use up to the end of the war.

Opel 36S *Length:* 6.00m (19ft 8in). *Width:* 2.28m (7ft 6in). *Height:* 2.71m (8ft 11in). *Weight:* 3,930kg (8,665lb). *Crew:* 2. *Power:* 6-cyl., petrol, 3,626cc, 68bhp at 3,000rpm. *Speed:* 38km/hr (24mph); *Range:* 300km (185 miles); *Payload:* 2,000kg (4,410lb). *Towed load:* 3,000kg (6,615 lb). *Maker:* Adam Opel AG, Russelsheim.

Mercedes-Benz L4500R *Length:* 7.90m (25ft 11in). *Width:* 2.36m (7ft 9in). *Height:* 3.00m (9ft 10in). *Weight:* 7,740kg (17,063lb). *Crew:* 2. *Power:* 6-cyl., diesel, 7,274cc, 112bhp at 2,250rpm. *Speed:* 36km/hr (22mph). *Range:* 400km (250 miles). *Payload:* 4,960kg (10,935lb). *Towed Load:* 5,000kg (11,025lb). *Maker:* Daimler-Benz AG, Berlin-Marienfelde.

Opel 36S

Opel Maultier

MERCEDES–BENZ G4 6 × 4 HEAVY CONVERTIBLE CAR *1933–1945*

This vehicle was produced in limited numbers as a prestige vehicle for high-ranking service officers and senior Nazi Party officials. Well-known from propaganda films and pictures, it is surprising to find that only 57 were ever made. A more spartan version, with all-wheel drive and slightly more powerful engine, was also produced with the intention of it being used as the Top People's front-line vehicle, but the idea failed to appeal to the Top People and very few of this 'combat' model were ever built.

Length: 5.34m (17ft 6in). *Width:* 1.87m (6ft 2in). *Height:* 1.90m (6ft 3in). *Weight:* 3,500kg (7,715lb). *Crew:* 1. *Power:* 8-cyl., petrol. 5.018cc, 100bhp. *Speed:* 130km/hr (80mph). *Range:* 320km (200 miles). *Maker:* Daimler-Benz AG, Stuttgart-Unterturkheim.

OPEL BLITZ 36S MEDIUM CARGO TRUCK *1937–1945*

The German Army's standard cargo truck throughout the war years was this Opel, a pre-war commercial design which was very slightly modified to meet military requirements. Only the twin rear wheels were driven, the cab was enclosed, and the usual body style was a flat cargo bed with canvas cover. During the period 1940–4 a limited number were built with four-

wheel drive in order to improve their off-road performance. In all, over 70,000 of these trucks were supplied to the German forces.

Length: 6.02m (19ft 9in). *Width:* 2.26m (7ft 5in). *Height:* 2.60m (8ft 6in). *Weight:* 2,500kg (5,510lb). *Crew:* 1. *Power:* 6-cyl., petrol, 3,600cc, 68bhp. *Speed:* 60km/hr (37mph). *Range:* 300km (185 miles). *Payload:* 3,000kg (6,614lb). *Towed load:* 5,000kg (11,025lb). *Maker:* Adam Opel AG, Brandenburg.

STANDARD MILITARY LIGHT TRUCK *1937–1945*

As with cars, so the German Army laid down luxurious specification for a series of military standard trucks, but of these only the light truck was ever produced. It was a complicated vehicle, with excellent cross-country ability, but it was expensive and difficult to build, and its performance was not considered to be worth the trouble; it was discontinued in 1940.

The truck used a 'backbone' chassis to which the six wheels were independently suspended by double wishbone arms and coil springs. All wheels were driven and each axle had a self-locking differential. The engine was a diesel model and an auxiliary gearbox gave a reduction ratio to the normal gearbox speeds for

cross-country working. The standard body was open-bed with a canvas tilt top, but small numbers of van bodies and closed-cab types were made.

Length: 5.35m (17ft 6in). *Width:* 2.20m (7ft 3in). *Height:* 2.35m (7ft 8½in). *Weight:* 4,200kg (9,259lb). *Crew:* 1. *Power:* 6-cyl., diesel, 6,234cc, 86bhp at 2,000rpm. *Speed:* 60km/hr (37mph). *Range:* 250km (155 miles). *Payload:* 2,500kg (5,510lb). *Towed load:* 5,000kg (11,025lb). *Makers:* Bussing–NAG, Brunswick; Henschel & Sohn AG, Kassel; C.D. Magirus AG, Ulm/Donau; MAN, Nuremberg.

STEYR STAFF CAR *1942–1945*

The Steyr Company, seeing that the standard German Army range of staff cars was proving too complicated and expensive, decided to develop one of their own. It proved to be as efficient as the standard design and considerably cheaper and easier to make, and in 1942 it was accepted for service.

In order to provide the necessary strength, the chassis was that of a production model of light truck, the Model 1500. This used a V-8 engine which provided ample power. Independent front suspension was fitted, but a normal

Mercedes-Benz Maultier

rear axle and leaf springs. All-wheel drive could be engaged if required, and a two-speed auxiliary gearbox gave a reduction gear for cross-country work. To assist traction in mud or snow, a hand-operated locking differential was fitted on the rear axle. The chassis was completed by fitting a pressed steel open-tourer body with a canvas tilt top.

Length: 5.08m (16ft 8in). *Width:* 1.85m (6ft 1in). *Height:* 2.10m (6ft 11in). *Weight:* 3,630kg (8,000lb). *Crew:* 1. *Power:* petrol, V-8, 75bhp at 2,700rpm. *Speed:* 100km/hr (62mph). *Range:* 300km (185 miles). *Makers:* Steyr-Daimler-Puch, Vienna; Auto-Union AG, Chemnitz.

VOLKSWAGEN LIGHT CAR *1940–*

The Volkswagen, originally designed as a light civilian car, was brought into German military service in 1940 as a means of providing a cheaper and less complicated light staff car and to replace the Standard Light Military Car (*qv*). The chassis and suspension of the military Volkswagen were to the same pattern as those of the civil model, though somewhat stronger, but the bodywork was in military style, and a self-locking differential was fitted on the rear drive together with reduction gears, these features giving the car a better cross-country performance. The chassis was a tubular 'back-bone' made up from metal pressings, and on to this the engine and torsion-bar suspension were assembled. This gave a very robust foundation to the vehicle which, with the light weight and flexible suspension, made for excellent off-the-road performance. The body was also made up from metal pressings in a severely rectangular shape; a four-seater, it was provided with a canvas top and removable side-screens for weather protection.

Length: 3.74m (12ft 3in). *Width:* 1.60m (5ft 3in). *Height:* 1.65m (5ft 5in). *Weight:* 685kg (1,510lb). *Crew:* 1. *Power:* 4-cyl., horizontally-opposed, air-cooled, petrol, 986cc, 24bhp at 3,000rpm (later 1,100cc, 25bhp at 3,000rpm). *Speed:* 100km/hr (62mph). *Range:* 350km (215 miles). *Makers:* Volkswagenwerke GmbH, Wolfsburg.

WEST GERMANY

MAN 630 TRUCK *1970–*

The MAN five-ton 4 × 4 truck is one of the standard German Army vehicles and is also used by the armies of Belgium and India (where it is known as the Shaktiman). It is extremely robust but of generally conventional form having a cargo bed and open cab, both of which can be covered by canvas hoods. Some models can be found with dual rear wheels, others with winches mounted ahead of the engine. The transmission uses a reduction gearbox to provide low ratios for cross-country

Unimog 421

work, and the all-wheel drive can be brought into or out of play as required. In addition to the cargo vehicle, the German Army has a number of variant models including an ambulance, a field kitchen, a radar vehicle, a fuel tanker and a carrier and launch vehicle for the CL809 remote-piloted, reconnaissance drone aircraft.

Length: 7.9m (25ft 11in). *Width:* 2.5m (8ft 2½in). *Height:* 2.85m (9ft 4in). *Weight* 7,515kg (16,567lb). *Crew:* 2. *Power:* MAN D1246, 6-cyl., multi-fuel, 130bhp at 2,000rpm. *Speed:* 66km/hr (41mph); *Range:* 440km (273 miles). *Payload:* 5,500kg (12,125lb). *Makers:* MAN, Nuremburg.

UNIMOG 421 TRUCK *1970–*

The Unimog (Universal Motor Gerat) series of light trucks was developed by Mercedes-Benz in the late 1940s and several minor variations have since been built for both civil and military applications. The Model 421 is currently in use with the German Army, as well as in many other armies in Europe, India, Turkey and the USA. It is a 4 × 4 cross-country vehicle with

Man 630

cargo body and is used as a basic cargo truck, an artillery towing vehicle, a command post, radio vehicle or stores truck. A similar model, though with longer wheelbase, is the Model 416.

Length: 4.55m (14ft 11in). *Width:* 1.80m (5ft 11in). *Height:* 2.20m (7ft 2½in). *Weight:* 2,500kg (5,511lb). *Crew:* 1. *Power:* 4-cyl., diesel, 66bhp at 3,500rpm. *Speed:* 80km/hr (50mph). *Range:* 500km (310 miles). *Payload:* 1,500kg (3,306lbs). *Towed load:* 1,500kg (3,306lbs). *Makers:* Mercedes Benz, Stuttgart.

VOLKSWAGEN 181 LIGHT CAR *1969–*

This is the general utility and staff car of the Federal German Army and is essentially the civilian Volkswagen 1500 car in military form. It uses the same chassis, engine, front seats and

Volkswagen 181

steering as the VW 1500 and is fitted with an all-steel open tourer body with a PVC top and sidescreens for weather protection. The rear seats can be folded flat to give more cargo space and when a radio is fitted the engine is provided with an additional generator. Two thousand were issued to the German Army in 1969/70, and others have since been bought by the armies of Denmark and the Netherlands. It is also available on the civilian market.

Length: 3.78m (12ft 5in). *Width:* 1.64m (5ft

4½in). *Height:* 1.62m (5ft 3¾in). *Weight:* 900kg (1,984lb). *Crew:* 1. *Power:* 4-cyl., horizontally-opposed, petrol, 1,584cc, 53bhp at 4,200rpm. *Speed:* 115km/hr (71mph). *Range:* 230km (143 miles). *Payload:* 440kg (970lb). *Maker:* Volkswagen GmbH, Wolfsburg.

VOLKSGAGEN ILTIS LIGHT CAR *1979–*
This vehicle was developed by Volkswagen to meet a German Army requirement for a light-weight Jeep-type vehicle. This requirement had first been stated in the 1960s and included an amphibian capability but this was found to be too expensive and impractical a demand and was dropped.

The Iltis is an all-wheel drive, cross-country vehicle which uses components from the current VW–Audi commercial car range as much as possible in order to keep development and production costs down. The body is of pressed steel and seats four persons; the two rear seats can be removed to give a cargo space, or, alternatively, two extra seats can be fitted. A roll bar can also be fitted, to which seat-belts for driver and front passenger are connected, and this bar can also be used to mount a machine gun or a Milan anti-tank missile launcher. The engine is that of the Volkswagen Passat car and is mounted ahead of the front wheels; drive is normally to the rear wheels, but all-wheel drive can be connected at will. There is no auxiliary reduction gearbox, but the normal five-speed box has a very low first gear.

It is understood that the German Army will purchase some 8,800 Iltis vehicles; first deliveries were made in 1979.
Length: 3.88m (12ft 9in). *Width:* 1.52m (5ft 0in). *Height:* 1.83m (6ft 0½in). *Weight:* 1,550 kg (3,417lb). *Crew:* 1. *Power:* 4-cyl., petrol, 1,714cc, 75bhp at 5,500rpm. *Speed:* 130km/hr (80mph). *Range:* not announced. *Payload:* 500kg (1,100lb). *Makers:* Volkswagen GmbH, Wolfsburg.

HUNGARY

CSEPEL D-344 TRUCK *1966–*
The Csepel factory turns out large numbers of trucks of different sizes and for different purposes. The D-344 has been chosen as a representative of the entire range, and it is the latest from a line of development going back to the early 1950s. It is a robust vehicle of conventional layout, a fully-enclosed one-piece cab and a flat load-bed behind fitted with drop sides and rear. It comes in the middle of the Csepel range, with 4 × 2 versions on one side and 6 × 6 and 8 × 8 among the larger sizes. The D-344 is one of the 4 × 4 trucks and it is in service with the Hungarian Army and many of the state civilian enterprises. It has been used by Romania, and there has always been an

Volkswagen Iltis

interchange of manufactured goods between these two countries. There are no particular outstanding features of the series. They are good, simple and apparently reliable vehicles.
Length: 6.70m (21ft 10in). *Width:* 2.50m (8ft 3in). *Height:* 2.40m (7ft 9in). *Weight:* 5,400kg (11,900lb). *Power:* D-414H, 4-cyl., diesel, 100bhp. *Payload:* 3,500kg (7,700lb). *Speed:* 82km/hr (51mph). *Range:* 530km (330 miles). *Maker:* Csepel, Budapest.

Csepel D-344

ITALY

CL 51 1,800kg TRUCK *1952–*
The CL 51 was in production until 1970 and it is in service with the Italian army in some numbers. Production was spread between three different factories and so there are some differences in the various models despite the fact that they were built to the same specification. In general terms the CL 51 is a forward-control light truck of conventional design, having a good cross-country performance and versatility. There are no particular special features.
Length: 4.50m (14ft 8in). *Width:* 2.00m (6ft 6in). *Height:* 2.26m (7ft 5in). *Weight:* 2,830kg (6,238lb). *Power:* OM Model 20.005, 4-cyl., petrol, 2,545cc, 63bhp. *Payload:* 1,800kg (3,967lb). *Maker:* Bianchi, OM and Lancia, Turin.

FIAT 38R 2,500kg TRUCK *1936–1944*
The Fiat 38 is typical of the many makes of trucks that were in service in the Italian Army throughout World War II. They were nearly all derived directly from civilian versions and

many were 4 × 2. The Fiat 38R was a 4 × 2 of no particular distinction, but it was used in large numbers in many different variants and became the workhorse of the Army. They were built in conjunction with SPA which in 1948 became a division of the Fiat concern. The 38 had a steel cab with a wooden-sided load bed behind. In the larger models the rear axle was doubled and the vehicle became a 6 × 4. A few were built as 4 × 4, but the Italians do not seem to have had many all-wheel drive trucks and relied on such as the 38R for most tasks.
Length: 5.80m (19ft 1in). *Width:* 2.10m (6ft 9in). *Weight:* 2.60m (8ft 6in). *Weight:* 3,360kg (7,405lb). *Power:* Fiat SPA 18R, 4-cyl., petrol, 4,053cc, 55bhp at 2,000rpm. *Payload:* 2,500kg (5,510lb). *Maker:* Fiat, Turin.

FIAT 75 2,000kg TRUCK *1975–*
The Fiat 75 has been produced for both civil and military use and is one of a family of trucks of different sizes. They all follow the same general pattern in that they have the engine inside the cab with the transmission below floor level and between the cab and the load compartment. Among the optional extra equipment is a lockable front differential, an extra gearbox and a winch. All vehicles of the family are in production and some are in service with armies outside Italy.
Length: 5.10m (16ft 8in). *Width:* 2.30m (7ft 6in). *Height:* 2.50m (8ft 2in). *Weight:* 4,770kg (10,510lb). *Power:* Fiat Model 8060.04, 6-cyl., diesel, 122bhp at 3,200rpm. *Payload:* 2,000kg (4,400lb). *Speed:* 80km/hr (50mph). *Range:* 800km (500 miles). *Maker:* Fiat, Turin.

Fiat 75

FIAT 508 C LIGHT DELIVERY TRUCK
1937–1942
The 508 was the famous Ballila Fiat car and the light delivery truck was derived from it. This was taken for military service almost without modification and used in some numbers in the early stages of the war. Apart from use as a light utility carrier it was also fitted with twin Breda machine guns and provided low-level anti-aircraft defence for convoys.
Length: 3.07m (10ft 10in). *Weight* (loaded): 1,520kg (3,350lb). *Payload:* 350kg (770lb). *Power:* Fiat, 4-cyl., petrol, 1089cc, 28bhp. *Maker:* Fiat, Turin.

FIAT 1107 AD JEEP *1974–*
The 1107 is the latest replacement for the AR series (*qv*) and the main differences are a more powerful engine, a better load-carrying capacity and the option of the hard top if needed. The body style has been modified and

Fiat 1107 AD

the separate front wings have been merged into the body, but in all general respects it is much the same as its predecessor. It is possible that this vehicle will also be built under licence in Yugoslavia to replace their ageing versions of the AR–51.

Length: 3.81m (12ft 5in). *Width:* 1.58m (5ft 2in). *Height:* 1.85m (6ft 0in). *Weight:* 1,727kg (3,806lb). *Power:* Fiat, 4-cyl., 80bhp at 4,600rpm. *Payload:* 610kg (1,344lb). *Speed:* 110km/hr (68mph). *Range:* 400km (248 miles). *Maker:* Fiat, Turin.

FIAT 6602 CM 5,000kg TRUCK *1970–*
The 6602 is one of the largest cargo carriers in service with the Italian Army today. It carries 5,000 kg (11,020lb) of cargo on either roads or cross country and though it is listed as a 4 × 4 it is always fitted with twin rear wheels so that there is extra traction. It follows the layout of the other Fiat military cargo carriers in that it has a forward control cab with the engine and transmission largely under the floor and plenty of ground clearance. It is strongly built of steel with wood sides to the load compartment, and obviously the design owed much to current civilian practice.

Length: 6.50m (21ft 4in). Width: 2.50m (8ft 2in). *Height:* 2.70m (8ft 9in). *Weight;* 7,500kg (16,530lb). *Power:* Fiat model 8202.02, 6-cyl., diesel, 193bhp at 2,500rpm. *Payload:* 5,000kg (11,020lb). *Speed:* 74km/hr (46mph). *Range:* 700km (430 miles). *Maker:* Fiat, Turin.

Fiat 6602

FIAT AR JEEP SERIES *1951–*
Directly after World War II the Fiat company set about designing a general utility vehicle for the Italian Army. This was adopted in 1951 as the AR–51, AR standing for 'Autovettura da Ricognizione', or Reconnaissance Vehicle. In 1955 the AR–51 was replaced by the AR–55, which had a more powerful engine, and in 1959 this was replaced by the AR–59, or model 1101B. This vehicle has been in service ever since, though it is now being phased out in favour of the 1107 AD (*qv*). The AR series was plainly inspired originally by the Willys Jeep (*qv*), but over the years several improvements were incorporated and the final versions are little different in specification from any typical light military vehicle, such as the Land-Rover (*qv*). Despite the light weight of the ARs, the Italian Army uses them to tow the 105mm Pack howitzer, which weighs 1,300kg (2,866lb) and is well above the recommended towing limit. This same vehicle is also made in Yugoslavia under licence, where it is known as the AR–51 Zastava.

Length: 3.62m (11ft 9in). *Width:* 1.57m (5ft 2in). *Height:* 1.55m (5ft 10in). *Power:* AR–59. Fiat Model 105B.017, 4-cyl., petrol, 56bhp at 4,000rpm. *Payload:* 480kg (1,057lb). *Speed:* 110km/hr (68mph). *Range:* 450km (280 miles). *Maker:* Fiat, Turin.

Fiat AR-59

FIAT MODEL 18 TRUCK *1914–1920*
Nearly 5,000 of these trucks were built for military service in World War I and they were used extensively on the mountainous Northern Front where the Italian Army was fighting the Austrians. Because the roads were so narrow and winding it was not possible to tow trailers, which complicated the movement of supplies. The Fiat 18P was a slightly more powerful version of the 18BL, which had appeared a little earlier. Both were of the same general pattern, a front engine mounted behind the front axle, a small open cab and a flat load bed behind. Both used chain drive to the rear wheels, but the chains were enclosed in a casing which must have increased their life. The 18 BL carried 3,500kg (7,712lb) while the 18P, which was meant for the mountain roads, 2,500kg (5,510lb). Both had solid tyres and spoked cast-steel wheels with brakes on the rear ones only.

Model 18P *Length:* 5.50m (18ft 1in). *Width:* 1.85m (6ft 1in). *Weight:* 2,300kg (5,070lb). *Power:* Fiat Model 53A, 4-cyl., petrol, 4,398cc, 40bhp at 1,800rpm. *Payload:* 2,500kg (5,510lb). *Speed:* 30km/hr (18mph). *Maker:* Fiat, Turin.

MOTO GUZZI MULO MECCANICO CARGO TRUCK *1959–1968*
The Mulo Meccanico was an unusual light cargo carrier designed for the Alpini to carry their support weapons and ammunition in different or mountainous country. It was a three-wheeler with one wheel in front and two driven ones behind. The driver sat astride the frame and engine, much like he would with a motorcycle, steering by a wheel. Behind him, and between the rear wheels, was a small load bed capable of carrying 500kg (1,102lb). All three wheels were driven, the front one requiring an expensive train of gears to take the power from a torque-dividing differential, which sent 1/5 of the power forwards, and 4/5 behind to the back wheels. Two small idler wheels were permanently carried off the ground behind the back wheels and these could be brought down so that a small track could be laid round them and each back wheel, so improving the grip and traction of soft ground. Although the Mulo Meccanico was most ingenious and a triumph of engineering, it was expensive and complicated to maintain.

Weight: 1,000kg (2,204lb). *Power:* Moto Guzzi, V–2, air-cooled, 20bhp. *Payload:* 500kg (1,102lb). *Maker:* Moto Guzzi SPA, Como.

SPA DOVUNQUE 35 TRUCK *1936–1948*
The SPA firm had been producing automobiles since the early years of the century and in the mid-thirties it was given a contract for its 6 × 4 load carrier for the Italian Army. It was a compact and robust vehicle with the ability to traverse rough going. The engine was inside the cab and the rear overhang was kept short in order not to catch on steep declines. Two spare wheels were carried on stub axles beneath the cab and prevented the chassis from 'bellying'. The transmission was strong and it was normal to fit twin wheels to each of the rear axles, making a total of 10 tyres in contact with the ground.

Length: 5.00m (16ft 5in). *Width:* 2.00m (6ft 6in). *Height:* 2.90m (9ft 6in). *Weight:* 4,000kg (8,810lb). *Power:* SPA Model 18D, 4-cyl., petrol, 4,053cc, 60bhp. *Payload:* 3,000kg (6,610lb). *Maker:* SPA, Turin.

JAPAN

HINO 4,000kg 6 × 6 TRUCKS *1968–*
Hino has produced a series of trucks, mainly of 6 × 6 layout and the one described here is a

Hino 6 X 6

typical example. All have a conventional layout with the engine in the front, the cab behind that, and the load compartment at the rear. They are large, strong, and rather heavy vehicles which are adaptable to a wide variety of roles. They are, for example, used as a load carrier, a dump truck, rocket launcher, resupply ammunition carrier, snow plough, tractor and breakdown recovery vehicle. Most have a winch on the front and all have tow hooks front and rear.

Length: 7.77m (25ft 6in). *Width:* 2.40m (7ft 9in). *Height:* 2.90m (9ft 6in). *Weight:* 12,200kg (26,890lb). *Power:* Hino, 6-cyl., diesel, 160bhp at 2,400rpm. *Payload:* 4,000kg (8,816lb). *Speed:* 78km/hr (48mph). *Maker:* Hino Motors, Tokyo.

ISUZU 2,500kg 6 × 6 TRUCK 1953–

The Isuzu was the first post-war Japanese truck design and it was closely based on the United States 2½-tonner. Many versions of the original have been built since 1953 and the truck is in service with several armies in the Far East. It is, like its originator, a robust and tough vehicle with few frills but plenty of power. It is still in

Isuzu 6 X 6

production and is used by both military and civil services.

Length: 6.75m (22ft 1in). *Width:* 2.28m (7ft 6in). *Height:* 2.90m (9ft 6in). *Weight:* 10,615kg (23,395lb). *Power:* Isuzu, 6-cyl., diesel, 130bhp at 2,600rpm. *Payload:* 2,500kg (5,510lb). *Maker:* Isuzu Motors, Tokyo.

TOYOTA LAND CRUISER 1958–

The Land Cruiser was developed in the 1950s

for the civilian market. However, it has now been adopted by several of the smaller armies in the Middle East and in South America. It is a vehicle with very similar characteristics to those of the Land-Rover (*qv*), which it rivals in the markets of the world. For the military users there are few changes in the specification and one of the attractions is that all spares and servicing are available in the agencies established by Toyota. There is a diesel version, a long-wheelbase model and several types of hard-top. It is built under licence in Brazil.

Length: 3.90m (12ft 8in). *Width:* 1.70m (5ft 6in). *Height:* 1.95m (6ft 4in). *Weight:* 1,585kg (3,943lb). *Power:* Toyota 6-cyl., petrol, 135bhp at 3,600rpm. *Payload:* 710kg (1,564lb). *Speed:* 100km/hr (62mph). *Maker:* Toyota Motor Company, Aichi-ken.

Toyota Land Cruiser

TYPE 1 THREE-WHEELED MOTORTRICYCLE 1937–1945

The Type 1 was an attempt to produce a light battlefield weapon and ammunition carrier based on the civilian light delivery tricycles. The front part was that of a large motorcycle, and behind the saddle it became a two-wheeled box load-carrier truck. The drive from the gearbox went through a shaft to a car-type differential and there was a light chassis running between the rear axle and the steering head. A tail gate hinged down at the back for easier loading and on reasonably good ground the vehicle performed well. It was not good at cross-country motoring and it was tempting to overload it.

Weight: 540kg (1,190lb). *Power:* Kurogane 2-cyl., vee, 21bhp. *Maker:* Nippon Nainenki Seiko Co., Tokyo.

TYPE 73 JEEP 1973–

The Type 73 is a derivation from the Willys Jeep (*qv*). The original licence to make this was obtained in 1953 and since then the Mitsubishi company has steadily manufactured it in slightly different forms, but all recognizably jeeps. They now make a wide range of Jeep-type vehicles with different wheelbases and different body fittings. There are both diesel and petrol engines, though they are roughly the same in performance. The Type 73 is used extensively by the Japanese Self Defence Forces and there have been some sales to other Far Eastern countries.

Length: 3.41m (11ft 2in). *Width:* 1.64m (5ft 4in). *Height:* 1.92m (6ft 3in). *Weight:* 1,080kg (2,380lb). *Power:* Mitsubishi, 4-cyl., petrol, 110bhp at 5,000rpm. *Payload:* 550kg (1,212lb). *Speed:* 100km/hr (62mph). *Range:* 400km (248 miles). *Maker:* Mitsubishi Motors, Tokyo.

TYPE 95 SCOUT CAR 1934–1945

The Type 95 was a small scout car designed to provide a fast vehicle for use on the edges of the battlefield. It was almost too light to be able to stand up to active service use and for the most part it was operated in the home islands or in rear areas of the overseas theatres. It was fairly typical of pre-war Japanese car manufacture, being light and rather under-powered. However, it had some good features. The front suspension was independent, using coil springs. The four-wheel drive was adventurous for a car of that size, and the economy of fuel was impressive. The brakes were on the rear wheels only. The first bodies were two-seaters, but it was realized that this was not enough, and the later bodies had a third seat in the back. About 4,800 were built.

Length: 3.50m (11ft 5in). *Width:* 1.50m (4ft 11in). *Height:* 1.60m (5ft 3in). *Weight* (approx): 1,000kg (2,204lb). *Power:* Kurogane, 2-cyl. vee, air-cooled, petrol, 33bhp. *Payload:* 300kg (660lb). *Maker:* Nippon Nainenki Seiko Co., Tokyo.

NETHERLANDS

Daf MC 139

DAF MC 139 COMMAND CAR 1939–1940

The MC 139 was an ambitious venture by the firm of DAF to produce a command car that could go anywhere. It had 4 × 4 drive and was amphibious. The driver had a choice of two-or four-wheel steering and he also had two driving positions, front and rear. All of this mechanical complication undoubtedly interfered with the primary purpose of the vehicle and left it with little enough space in which the military crew could find a seat or do their job. However, it was an interesting experiment.

The suspension was independent all round and the engine was amidships, placed transversely, driving the front and rear propeller shafts directly from a transverse gearbox. For swimming there was a water propeller, driven by another shaft. There were seats for four men, and virtually no room for equipment nor radios. Only one was built, and though its performance was impressive, so too was the price and the maintenance problem.

Length: 3.50m (11ft 6in). *Width:* 1.70m (5ft 6in). *Height:* 1.60m (5ft 3in). *Weight:* 1,260kg (2,777lb). *Power:* Citroën, 4-cyl., petrol, 48bhp. *Maker:* DAF, Eindhoven.

Daf 66 YA

DAF 66 YA MILITARY CAR *1973–*
The 66 YA is a military utility version of the well-known DAF light car and it has the same infinitely variable gearing using belts. The 66 YA is a well-equipped light Jeep-type vehicle, which sits rather lower to the ground than do most of the others in this class, largely due to the fact that it has smaller wheels. It can be adapted to many roles, including a radio station and an ambulance. It is in service with the Dutch Army, for which 1,200 were built starting in 1973.

Length: 3.75m (12ft 4in). *Width:* 1.52m (4ft 10in). *Height:* 1.59m (5ft 2in). *Weight:* 860kg (1,895lb). *Power:* DAF B11OE, 4-cyl., petrol, 47bhp at 5,000rpm. *Payload:* 435kg (958lb). *Speed:* 115km/hr (71mph). *Range:* 500km (310 miles). *Maker:* DAF BV, Eindhoven.

DAF YA 126 WEAPON CARRIER *1952–*
The 126 is a vehicle which can be conveniently classed as a weapon carrier. It has a useful payload of up to 1,000kg (2,204lb) or a total of 10 men, or it can tow a wheeled load of 2,500kg (5,511lb). This gives it considerable flexibility in use and it is very like the better-known Dodge weapon carrier (*qv*) of World War II brought up to date. The steel body is comparatively low and all the weather protection is capable of being folded flat to reduce the silhouette. The suspension is novel in that it is independent to all four wheels, taking the drive through a complicated arrangement of drive shafts. However, reliability is good. The two spare wheels are carried on the sides and free wheel to improve cross-country mobility and

prevent bellying on soft ground or hummocks. The vehicle can tow a field gun and there are variants which act as ambulances, radio stations and workshop trucks. Production is now complete, but the truck is likely to stay in service for some years yet.

Length: 4.51m (14ft 8in). *Width:* 2.10m (6ft 9in). *Height:* 1.55m (5ft 10in). *Weight:* 3,230kg (7,118lb). *Power:* DAF Hercules JXC, 6-cyl., petrol, 102bhp at 3,200rpm. *Payload:* 1,000kg (2,204lb). *Speed:* 84km/hr (52mph). *Range:* 330km (205 miles). *Maker:* DAF Trucks, Eindhoven.

DAF YA 314 3,000kg TRUCK *1955–*
The 314 is the standard load carrier of the Dutch Army and although production has been finished since 1965 it seems likely that it will be in service for some years yet. It is a conventional vehicle, owing much to civilian design, but essentially robust and resistant to tough use. It has been adapted to almost every military task and is to be found with a wide variety of bodies and accessories. The vehicle has also been built under licence in Spain as the Pegaso 3045. Later version of the home-produced model were known as the 324, but there were few differences.

Length: 6.00m (19ft 7in). *Width:* 2.50m (8ft 2in). *Height:* 2.80m (9ft 2in). *Weight:* 4,500kg (9,920lb). *Power:* Hercules JXC, 6-cyl., petrol, 102bhp at 3,200rpm. *Payload:* 3,000kg (6,612lb). *Speed:* 76km/hr (47mph). *Range:* 630km (391 miles). *Maker:* DAF Trucks, Eindhoven.

Star 66

majority were light cars and small delivery trucks which became command and liaison vehicles and small gun tractors and reconnaissance cars. The most successful was the 508 series which were most useful two-litre cars with a good chassis and straightforward, robust components. Several variants were built on this chassis and it was used in some numbers at the time of the German invasion. None survived.

STAR 66 2,500kg TRUCK *1958–*
The Star is one of the widest used native designs in Poland. It is a large and strong vehicle which was originaly designed to meet the requirements of the Army. Over the years there has been steady development, but the present vehicle bears a strong resemblance to its predecessors. The main changes have been in the power unit and the accessories. The Star is a forward-control vehicle with the engine in the cab and the transmission between cab and load compartment. It is very widely used and is adapted to practically every military and civil

Daf YA 314

POLAND

POLSKI FIAT 4 × 2 CARS *1930-1939*
The Fiat combine established a factory in Poland in the 1920s and soon started to convert the civilian designs to military use. The

purpose. It has also been supplied to Czechoslovakia and Vietnam, who use it in both civil and military roles. There are many different body styles and most military versions have a front-mounted winch with a pull of 6,000kg (13,227lb).

Length: 6.50m (21ft 4in). *Width:* 2.40m (7ft

9in). *Height:* 2.50m (8ft 3in). *Weight:* 5,700kg (12,562lb). *Power:* S-47, 6-cyl., petrol, 105bhp. *Speed:* 74km/hr (46mph). *Range:* 650km (403 miles). *Maker:* Polish State Factories.

ROMANIA

ARO 240 JEEP *1970–*
The ARO is the standard Romanian Army Jeep-type light vehicle. It has been in production since 1970 and has been offered for export since 1972. It is a version of the Soviet UAZ–69 (*qv*), but has a more powerful engine, which is one bank of the SR–113 heavy truck motor. There are several minor variants of the ARO, one of which has a permanently attached box body.

Length: 3.97m (13ft 1in). *Width:* 1.78m (5ft 9in). *Height:* 1.94m (6ft 4in). *Weight:* 1,500kg (3,305lb). *Power:* L 25, 4-cyl., petrol, 80bhp at 4,200rpm. *Speed:* 100km/hr (62mph). *Range:* 500km (310 miles). *Maker:* Romanian State Factories.

SOVIET UNION

GAZ TRUCKS *1930–*
Until 1930 the production of home-built vehicles in the Soviet Union was small. There was an AMO 1½-tonner from 1924 which was a Fiat design built under licence and with a good deal of Italian help. One year later a three-tonner was built, but the output was far too small for the domestic market of the time, and most vehicles were imported. In 1930 a factory was built to produce the American Model A Ford truck. At that time it was the most successful general cargo carrier in the world and it is said that the Soviet plant used a great deal of machinery and equipment from the German factory that had to move to new premises. This factory was set up in Gorky and became one of the largest in the world. It is the GAZ factory, the letters standing for 'Gorky Automobilova Zavod', the last word meaning factory. Another factory set up soon afterwards was the ZIL in Moscow. GAZ became known also as ZIM, or 'Zavod Industrial Molotova' in deference to Molotov, the Foreign Minister. Confusingly, the two names are used for the same model at times, and matters are not helped by the fact that name is not used now. Furthermore, the ZIL plant was for some years renamed ZIS in honour of Stalin. That name fell into disuse in 1957. However, all this is largely irrelevant to the Western observer since the vehicles were all close copies of the Ford Model A, AA and AAA trucks.

These trucks were the workhorses of the Soviet Union until after World War II and they were fitted with every conceivable kind of body

and modification. When fuel was short in the war they were given producer-gas plants or cylinders of compressed town gas. They were given twin axles and became 6 × 4s. They mounted rocket launchers and light guns and they towed artillery pieces and ammunition trailers. Even so there were never enough of them and it is worth mentioning that the Soviet forces which swept into Berlin in 1945 were using at least 50% Lease-Lend American vehicles in the supply lines, and many German ones also.

GAZ–AA0 Length: 5.30m (17ft 5in). *Width:* 2.04m (6ft 6in). *Height:* 1.90m (6ft 3in). *Weight:* 1,810kg (3,990lb). *Power:* GAZ, 4-cyl., petrol, 40bhp. *Payload:* 1,500kg (3,310lb). *Speed:* 70km/hr (43mph). *Maker:* Gorky Automobile Factory, Gorky.

Gaz-63

GAZ–51 AND GAZ–63 TRUCKS *1946–*
The GAZ–51 is a modernized truck produced after World War II when it was imperative to introduce new, standard vehicles to replace the worn-out heterogeneous fleet that had seen the Red Army through its campaigns. The GAZ–51 and its later version, the 51A, are very representative of the straightforward cargo trucks of their era and were designed with the virtues of simplicity, reliability and robustness in mind. Production continued until the late 1960s, by which time enormous numbers had been turned out. A 4 × 4 version was also introduced in 1946 and it was made with a few improvements, until 1968. There are so many variants of these basic trucks that it is quite impracticable to list them, but they are used for every conceivable task all over the Warsaw Pact countries, the Middle East, Africa and parts of the Far East. Spares are still available and it can be expected that they will continue in service for many years yet.

Length: 5.70m (18ft 8in). *Width:* 2.30m (7ft 6in). *Height:* 2.30m (7ft 6in). *Weight:* 2,710kg (5,972lb). *Power:* GAZ–51A, 6-cyl., petrol, 70bhp at 2,800rpm. *Payload:* 2,500kg (5,510lb). *Speed:* 70km/hr (43mph). *Range:* 450km (280 miles). *Maker:* Gorky Automobile Factory, Gorky.

GAZ–66 TRUCK *1964–*
The GAZ–66 is the replacement for the

GAZ–69 AND 69A TRUCKS *1952–*
Although production of the GAZ–69 series was completed some years ago the family of vehicles based on the original GAZ–69 of 1952 is still in service in the USSR and in all countries of the Warsaw Pact as well as the great majority of those which have received Soviet aid during the past 30 years. The GAZ–69 was designed to replace the war-time Willys Jeep (*qv*) supplied under Lease-Lend, and it incorporated a number of improvements, including the fact that it was larger and carried more cargo. It was also more powerful and was specifically intended to be able to tow light field guns, though it was only provided with a three-speed gearbox. The 69 has two doors and seating in the rear of the body for four men. The 69A has four doors and can lift five men as well as 100kg (220lb) of cargo. Both models have canvas tops and the bodies

can be stripped down until they are about half their normal height. Both have four-wheel drive to rigid axles and semi-elliptic cart springing. There are numerous variants for different jobs, and the vehicle has been built under licence in several Communist countries, each one adding their own alterations. In Romania it is known as the M–461 and has a four-speed gearbox. Although now being replaced by the UAZ–469B (qv) the old GAZ–69 is going to be in evidence for many more years yet before it fades away.

Length: 3.85m (12ft 7in). *Width:* 1.85m (6ft 1in). *Height:* 2.10m (6ft 9in). *Weight:* 1,525kg (3,361lb). *Power:* M–20, 4-cyl., petrol, 55bhp at 600rpm. *Payload:* 500kg (1,102lb). *Speed:* 90km/hr (56mph). *Range:* 530km (330 miles). *Makers:* 1952–56, Gorky Motor Plant, Gorky; 1956–65, Ulyanovsk Motor Vehicle Plant, Ulyanovsk.

GAZ–63 (qv) and is a more modern and perhaps more versatile vehicle. It has a forward control cab, four-wheel drive and many vehicles have a winch. It is in wide use with the Soviet armed forces and with many civilian organizations within the Soviet Union. It has also been supplied to the members of the Warsaw Pact and may have been given to some other countries.

Length: 5.60m (18ft 4in). *Width:* 2.30m (7ft 6in). *Height:* 2.40m (7ft 9in). *Weight:* 3,470kg (7,650lb). *Power:* ZMZ–66, V–8, petrol, 115bhp at 3,200rpm. *Payload:* 2,000kg (4,408lb). *Speed:* 95km/hr (60mph). *Range:* 525km (325 miles). *Maker:* Gorky Automobile Factory, Gorky.

Kraz 255B

KrAZ–255 HEAVY TRUCK 1967–
The KrAZ is one of several heavy trucks of a similar layout which are in service with the Soviet and Warsaw Pact Armies. It is largely used for the carrying of engineer stores, such as pontoon bridges, or possibly for ammunition. It has all the usual features of such large vehicles, including full winter heating and starting equipment.

Length: 8.60m (28ft 2in). *Width:* 2.70m (8ft 9in). *Height:* 2.90m (9ft 6in). *Weight:* 11,950kg (26,337lb). *Power:* YaMZ–238, V–8, diesel, 240bhp at 2,100rpm. *Payload:* 7,500kg (16,530lb). *Speed:* 71km/hr (44mph). *Range:* 650km (400 miles). *Maker:* Kremenchug Motor Vehicle Plant, Ukraine.

LuAZ–969 LIGHT TRUCK 1966–
The LuAZ 969 (it does not seem to have any other name) is a very light vehicle which was first produced in 1965 for the civilian market. Although still classified as a civilian vehicle it has an obvious military application and could be expected to be brought into service if required. It is an all-steel one-piece body with independent suspension using torsion bars. The engine is a new departure in Soviet design and appears to give adequate power with good fuel consumption. It is in production now, though does not so far seem to have been exported to any other countries.

Length: 3.20m (10ft 6in). *Width:* 1.60m (5ft 3in). *Height:* 1.80m (5ft 11in). *Weight:* 820kg

(1,807lb). *Power:* MeMZ–966, V–4, petrol, air-cooled, 27bhp. *Payload:* 400kg (881lb). *Speed:* 75km/hr (46mph). *Range:* 400km (250 miles). *Maker:* Lutsk Motor Vehicle Plant, Ukraine.

UAZ–469B TRUCK 1972–
The UAZ–469B is the successor to the famous GAZ–69 (qv) and it is a slightly larger, more powerful and roomier vehicle incorporating a number of modern ideas. The general layout is with the engine in the front in the normal position and a four-door crew compartment behind that. The top is normally of canvas, but there is a hard-top version. The standard model with the canvas roof is meant to be used with the roof erected, and the doors are full-height, though the upper halves can be removed if necessary. In general this is a robust vehicle designed to withstand the rigours of the Russian weather with reasonable comfort for the crew and the best possible cross-country performance. Up to seven men can be carried, and with four or five it would seem to make a useful command car, carrying the radios in the cargo area behind the back seat. It is in production and in service with the Red Army.

Length: 4.05m (13ft 3in). *Width:* 1.80m (5ft 10in). *Height:* 2.00m (6ft 6in). *Weight:* 1,800kg (3,967lb). *Power:* UMZ–451M, 4-cyl., petrol, 75bhp. *Payload:* 600kg (1,322lb). *Speed:* 100km/hr (62mph). *Range:* 750km (466 miles). *Maker:* Ulyanosvk Motor Vehicle Plant, Ulyanovsk.

URAL 375 HEAVY TRUCK 1961–
The Ural 375 is a large multi-purpose truck which seems to be used mainly for engineer tasks in the Soviet Army. It is an extremely strong six-wheeler capable of carrying dense, compact loads or mounting such items as cranes, winches, rocket launchers or fuel tanks. It is also used in a modified form as a tractor for large trailers and perhaps large guns too. It is in extensive service with the Soviet Army and has been supplied to the Warsaw Pact countries and some of their allies in the Middle East. It has 6 × 6 drive.

Length: 7.35m (24ft 1in). *Width:* 2.70m (8ft 9in). *Height:* 2.70m (8ft 9in). *Weight:* 8,400kg (18,513lb). *Power:* ZIL–375, V–8, petrol, 180bhp at 3,200rpm. *Payload:* 4,500kg (9,918lb). *Speed:* 75km/hr (46mph). *Range:* 650km (400 miles). *Maker:* Ural Motor Plant, Miass.

ZIL–131 HEAVY TRUCK. 1966–
The 131 is the replacement for the earlier 157 truck, which is very similar. The 131 is mainly used for carrying heavy cargo, such as ammunition, and towing medium artillery pieces. It is a large and strong vehicle, built entirely of steel and carrying a winch with a pull of 4,500kg (9,918lb). It is also made as a prime mover and

Zil-131

tows large semi-trailers. There are many variants and it has been supplied to the Warsaw Pact countries.

Length: 6.90m (22ft 7in). *Width:* 2.50m (8ft 3in). *Height:* 2.50m (8ft 3in). *Weight:* 6,700 kg (14,766lb). *Power:* ZIL–131, V–8, petrol, 150bhp at 3,200rpm. *Payload:* 3,500kg (7,714lb). *Speed:* 80km/hr (50mph). *Range:* 525km (325 miles). *Maker:* Likachev Motor Vehicle Plant, Moscow.

ZIS TRUCKS *1934–*

In general terms, the ZIS trucks were heavier than the GAZ and carried about twice the load. There were two versions, a 4 × 2 which carried three tons, and a 6 × 4 with a payload of up to four tons. Both were fitted with twin wheels on each axle to improve mobility on the many dirt roads in the Soviet Union, and both were adapted to a multitude of different tasks. The standard body was simple cargo vehicle with drop sides and tailboard, but this was frequently modified locally to suit the requirements. During the war all models were likely to be adapted to take gas fuel.

ZIS-5 4×4 Length: 6.10m (20ft 0in). *Width:* 2.20m (7ft 3in). *Height:* 2.10m (6ft 9in). *Weight:* 3,100kg (6,830lb). *Power:* ZIS–5, 6-cyl., petrol, 5,550cc, 73bhp at 2,300rpm. *Payload:* ZIS-5, 3,000kg (6,612lb); ZIS–6, 4,000kg (8,816lb). *Maker:* ZIS, Moscow.

SPAIN

BARREIROS KA–90 COMMANDO CARGO TRUCK *1963–*

Only 25 of these interesting vehicles were built for the Spanish Army and none have been made since 1963. They were probably expensive, but they were also novel. The general layout was that of a high-chassis 4 × 4 load-carrier with a forward-control cab and short overhangs at both ends. Cross-country mobility was good and on made-up roads the load could be doubled to three tons. The engine was the intriguing part of the design, since it was designed to be adaptable to either petrol or diesel within one hour. All that was necessary, or so it was claimed, was that the

fuel in the tank was drained off and replaced, the coil ignition was taken out and an injector pump bolted in place, and the cylinder head replaced. This, the factory claimed, could be done by the driver and a mechanic in one hour. The reverse process took the same time. The gearbox had five forward and two reverse gears, and there was a two-speed transfer box for four-wheel drive. There were two large sizes of Barreiros truck, in 2½ and five tons, and both were only built in small numbers. They are still in service in the Spanish Army and some of them are used as weapons carriers.

Length: 4.80m (15ft 8in). *Width:* 2.25m (7ft 4in). *Height:* 2.42m (7ft 10in). *Weight:* 4,430kg (9,763lb). *Power:* Barreiros A-90, 6-cyl., alternative diesel/petrol, 5,010cc, 90bhp at 2,400rpm. *Payload:* 1,500 or 3,000kg (3,306 or 6,612lb). *Maker:* Barreiros Group of companies. Now Chrysler España SA.

SWEDEN

SAAB–SCANIA SBA SERIES OF HEAVY TRUCKS *1968–*

The Swedish Army decided some years ago that the lighter vehicles would be built by Volvo, while the heavier trucks would come from Saab-Scania, the descendants of the original Scania-Vabis firm. The SBA trucks are the result of this decision and are built with the intention of using the maximum number of civilian components while retaining the military requirements for strength, simplicity of maintenance and overall reliability. The basic model is the SBA 4 × 4 with a capacity of

4,500 kg (9,920lb). It appears in a number of variants with different equipment mounted on it. It is also used for such tasks as mounting radar sets or towing guns. The SBAT is the 6 × 6 version of the same vehicle. It is longer, but in most other respects is very similar and about 90% of the components are said to be interchangeable. The engines are the same, the 6 × 6 having a turbosupercharger which gives an extra 100bhp. This larger truck is used for towing medium guns and carrying the crew and some ammunition at the same time. In both trucks the drivers cab is very fully equipped and there is cold weather starting and engine heating gear on all models. All have a winch with a pull of 8,000kg (17,636lb).

SBA: 4 × 4 Length: 6.75m (22ft 2in). *Width:* 2.50m (8ft 1in). *Height:* 2.90m (9ft 6in). *Weight:* 9,150kg (20,166lb). *Power:* Saab-Scania, 6-cyl., diesel, 202bhp at 2,200rpm. *Speed:* 90km/hr (56mph). *Range:* 600km (37 miles). *Maker:* Saab-Scania, Södertälje.

SCANIA–VABIS 2,000kg TRUCK *1920–1935*

Lorry production and design in Sweden has been in the hands of both Volvo and Scania-Vabis since the first ones were built. The 2,000-kg (2-ton) truck is a typical example of Scania output after World War I. It was very similar to all other trucks of its type at that time, having cast spoked wheels with solid tyres, enclosed chain drive, an open cab and a 4-cyl. engine. A slight change from the more normal European design was the fact that the radiator had shutters and the air vents in the

Saab-Scania SBAT

Volvo Laplander

bonnet were also fitted with doors so that the engine ventilation could be cut off in the severe Swedish winter.

Power: Scania Model 1545, 4-cyl., 45bhp. *Payload:* 2,000kg (4,408lb). *Maker:* Scania Maskinfabrik, Södertälje.

VOLVO L2204 1,500kg TRUCK 1955–

The 2204 was designed in the late 1940s for the Swedish Army and production started some years later. Manufacture finished in 1959, but the vehicle is still reported in service. It is a very strong truck with a comprehensive specification. The chassis is robust and carries the 6 × 6 gearboxes and drive shafts. Each differential can be locked independently and the gearbox has a power take-off leading to a winch. This can be led to either end of the chassis and has a pull of 4,000 kg (8,800lb) and 75m (246ft) of cable. All body parts are of steel, and the cab has a solid roof which cannot be removed. There are at least two variants in service, though by now the entire range must be ready for replacement.

Length: 5.80m (19ft 1in). *Width:* 1.90m (6ft 3in). *Height:* 2.15m (7ft 1in). *Weight:* 4,200kg (9,250lb). *Power:* Volvo A6, 6-cyl., petrol, 115bhp at 3,000rpm. *Payload:* 2,250kg (4,950lb). *Speed:* 80km/hr (50mph). *Range:* 300km (186 miles). *Maker:* Volvo AB, Göteborg.

VOLVO LAPLANDER LIGHT CARGO VEHICLE 1962–

The Laplander has been a remarkably successful light cargo vehicle and since the first one was built there have been more than 10,000 produced and sold to more than 40 countries all over the world. The original Laplander was intended for use in Sweden in all weathers and over all terrain. There were two versions, a pick-up and a hard-top. The hard-top is primarily for carrying men and it has a steel body with adequate heating for the Swedish winter. The pick-up has a flat load-bed behind the all-enclosed cab. The chassis of both is a steel box-frame with tubular and box support members. The engine is inside the cab, driving to a central gearbox from which shafts take the drive to all four wheels. Ground clearance is excellent and an optional extra is a forward-mounted winch for pulling out of soft ground.

Volvo L 2204

Although no longer made in Sweden, a later version of the Laplander, the C202 is still made under licence in Hungary by Csepel, using a Volvo engine also made under licence.

Length: 3.90m (12ft 8in). *Width:* 1.66m (5ft 5in). *Height:* 2.10m (6ft 9in). *Weight:* 1,502kg (3,350lb). *Power:* Volvo B 18A, 4-cyl., petrol, 75bhp at 4,500rpm. *Payload:* 900kg (1,983lb). *Speed:* 90km/hr (56mph). *Range:* 330km (205 miles). *Maker:* Volvo AB, Göteborg.

Volvo TP L2104

VOLVO TP L2104 COMMAND VEHICLE
1956–
The TP L2104 is a command vehicle designed for use throughout the year in Sweden and capable of good cross-country performance and offering reasonable weather protection. It is not unlike a large four-door saloon car, but it is strongly built and has a powerful engine with good pulling characteristics. It has the same chassis as one of the Volvo light trucks, with two rigid axles with four-wheel drive and a differential lock operated by vacuum. It normally carries a maximum of five passengers, one of these being the driver. There is room for two radio sets and their batteries and the back-seat passengers have small folding map boards. Production ceased some years ago but the vehicle is still in service with the Swedish Army.

Length: 4.60m (15ft 1in). *Width:* 1.90m (6ft 3in). *Height:* 1.92m (6ft 4in). *Weight:* 2,850kg (6,281lb). *Power:* Volvo, 6-cyl., model ED, petrol, 90bhp at 3,600rpm. *Payload:* 350kg (771lb). *Speed:* 105km/hr (65mph). *Range:* 300km (186 miles). *Maker:* AB Volvo, Göteborg.

SWITZERLAND

SAURER TRUCKS *1949–*
Saurer trucks have been made for the Swiss Army in several sizes since the end of World War II and are also built by the firm of Berna to the same design. There is a series of these vehicles, going up in size from 3,500 kg to 5,000 kg (3½–5 ton). All are fairly standard 4 × 4 though the layout differs with size. The 3,500

kg (3½-ton) all have forward control cabs, as do the 5,000kg (5-ton). But the intermediate size, the 4,500 kg (4½-ton) has a conventional cab and this model had eight forward gears, against the five for the others. All are diesel powered and all carry a winch of at least 6,000kg (1,300lb) pull. There is a good deal of commonality of components between the models in the range and this may explain why it has not been thought necessary to introduce a 6 × 4. The 5,000 kg (5-ton) model does have twin rear wheels, however.

3,500 kg Saurer Truck *Length:* 5.90m (19ft 5in). *Width:* 2.20m (7ft 3in). *Height:* 3.10m (10ft 2in). *Weight:* 5,500kg (12,122lb). *Power:* Saurer Model CR2D, 4-cyl., diesel, 75bhp. *Payload:* 3,500kg (7,710lb). *Speed:* 57km/hr (35mph). *Maker:* Adolph Saurer, Arbon.

Saurer 5-ton

SAURER AND BERNA TRUCKS *1903–*
The two firms of Saurer and Berna built trucks of various sizes from 1903 onwards. Both used conventional designs of their day, though Berna were quick to turn to shaft drive. The Berna Model C2 was introduced in 1917, and

despite its modest power output it continued to be built until 1928. It was adopted by the Swiss, French and British armies during World War I when transport was short and may have survived in Swiss service well into the 1930s. The Saurer model of the same vintage was the A, also first built in 1917 and that too continued in use for many years. Both of these trucks had a carrying capacity of about four tons, the Saurer actually claiming five tons. There were other vehicles in the range, but these two were the biggest at that time. Both firms continued to build trucks throughout the 1930s and 40s, following the pattern of the time. Saurer had a strong civilian market in long-distance trucks for the European continental routes and the two firms combined after World War II. The two factories continue to exist, but build the same models designed in a combined drawing office.

SWISS MILITARY LIGHT VEHICLES
1920–1940
The Swiss authorities used mostly civilian vehicles for the lighter end of the load-carrying requirement, and did not specifically order military types. As a result there is no real series of vehicles to report on until after 1945. In 1940 machine-gun squads were still carried in ordinary saloon cars, often American. Motorcycles and sidecars were often used in conjunction with a small trailer to act as repair teams. The two men in the machine were competent mechanics and drove their combination at the rear of a mobile column, where they were best placed to help breakdowns. Most of these machines were Motosacoche, bought from France.

Saurer 4½-ton

Swiss Military Light Vehicle

UNITED KINGDOM

AEC MILITANT 10-TON CARGO TRUCK
1962–
This was first developed in the early 1960s by AEC to meet a military specification for a 10-ton 6 × 6 general service truck, largely based on commercial components. In addition, a wide range of variants was produced, including an artillery tractor, bridging crane, tanker, excavator carrier and tractor for semi-trailed loads. Various improvements were tested, and in 1966 the Mark 3 version appeared, which has since become the standard 10-ton vehicle. All-wheel drive is provided, with a fully articulated rear bogie giving good cross-country performance. Six forward and one reverse gear, plus a two-speed transfer box, give an ample range of speeds, and power-assisted steering and brakes are standard.

Length: 9.06m (29ft 9in). *Width:* 2.48m (8ft 2in). *Height:* 3.50m (11ft 6in). *Weight:* 11,850kg (26,125lb). *Crew:* 1. *Power:* AEC AV760, 6-cyl., diesel, 12,473cc, 226bhp at 2,200rpm. *Payload:* 10,150kg (22,377lb). *Speed:* 53km/hr (33mph). *Range:* 480km (300 miles). *Maker:* AEC (British Leyland), Southall, Middlesex.

Austin K2 Ambulance

AUSTIN K2 4 × 2 HEAVY AMBULANCE
1940–1970
This was the standard ambulance used by British forces from 1940 until the early 1970s, and over 13,000 were built. The ventilated and heated body carried four stretchers or up to 10 sitting casualties, while the attendant and driver rode on the cab; an intercommunicating

door between cab and body allowed the attendant access to the patients in transit. Loading was done via double doors at the rear.

Length: 5.48m (18ft 0in). *Width:* 2.21m (7ft 3in). *Height:* 2.79m (9ft 2in). *Weight:* 3,124kg (6,888lb). *Crew:* 2. *Power:* Austin, 6-cyl., petrol, 3,460cc, 60bhp at 3,000rpm. *Payload:* 940kg (2,072lb). *Speed:* 72km/hr (45mph). *Range:* 400km (250 miles). *Maker:* Austin Motor Co., Longbridge, Birmingham.

AEC Militant

Austin K3 GS Truck

AUSTIN K3 THREE-TON 4 × 2 GENERAL SERVICE TRUCK *1942–1955*
Over 17,000 of these cargo trucks were produced during World War II and many remained in use until the middle 1950s. First models, produced in 1942, used an open cab with canvas roof and side-screens, but these were later superseded by a version with a steel cab having an anti-aircraft machine-gun hatch over the passenger's seat in the cab. The cargo body was made of wood or steel.

Length: 6.37m (20ft 11in). *Width* 2.28m (7ft 6in). *Height:* 3.09m (10ft 2in). *Weight:* 2,895kg (6,384lb). *Crew:* 1. *Power:* Austin, 6-cyl., petrol, 3,460cc, 63bhp at 3,000rpm. *Payload:* 3,720kg (8,200lb). *Speed:* 72km/hr (45mph). *Range:* 450km (280 miles). *Maker:*

Austin Motor Co., Longbridge, Birmingham.

BEDFORD MK FOUR-TON 4×4 CARGO TRUCK *1965–*
Though three imperial tons had always been the British Army's standard medium-sized general-purpose truck, conformity with NATO standards led to the adoption of four tonnes as the new standard in the 1960s, and this was among the first vehicles to be made to this standard. It is a derivative of the commercial Bedford TK series and was originally designed with an aluminium body, which allowed a five-ton payload. This proved too expensive and production models use a steel body. A variant model is fitted with a winch, while specialist versions for RAF use include refuellers and bomb-carriers.

Length: 6.58m (21ft 7in). *Width:* 2.48m (8ft 2in). *Height:* 3.40m (11ft 2in). *Weight:* 5,910kg (13,030lb). *Crew:* 1. *Power:* Bedford,

Bedford 4-ton MK

6-cyl., multi-fuel, compression-ignition, 5,418cc, 102bhp at 2,800rpm. *Payload:* 3,560kg (7,858lb). *Speed:* 75km/hr (45mph). *Range:* 560km (350 miles). *Maker:* Vauxhall Motors, Luton (chassis); Marshall of Cambridge (Engineering) Ltd. (body).

BEDFORD MWD 4×2 GENERAL SERVICE TRUCK *1938–1952*

Introduced shortly before the war, the Bedford 15-cwt (762kg) truck became the backbone of the British Army's transportation throughout the war years and well into the 1950s. Simple to maintain and robust, it was used by every arm of the service as a general cargo and personnel carrier and it was also the vehicle on which thousands of military drivers learned to drive. The first version had canvas 'doors' and small windscreens and was universally known as the 'pneumonia wagon'; later, metal doors and a full-width windscreen were fitted.

Length: 4.38m (14ft 4½in). *Width:* 1.99m (6ft 6½in). *Height:* 1.93m (6ft 4in). *Weight:* 2,134kg (4,704lb). *Crew:* 1. *Power:* Bedford, 6-cyl., petrol, 3,500cc, 72bhp at 3,000rpm; *Payload:* 1,247kg (2,750lb). *Speed:* 72km/hr (45mph). *Range:* 280km (175 miles). *Maker:* Vauxhall Motors, Luton.

BEDFORD QL THREE-TON 4×4 TROOP-CARRIER TRUCK *1940–1960*

Known to the soldiers as the TCV (for Troop Carrying Vehicle), this was designed to lift an infantry platoon, and thus had seating for 36 men, arranged in bench seats down the sides and a central, back-to-back, seat in the centre. Doors at the forward end of each side gave access, as did double doors at the rear. A canvas tilt covered the personnel compartment, with flaps at the front to allow a through passage of air to prevent exhaust fumes being sucked in at the rear. With all-wheel drive the cross-country ability was good, and these vehicles provided the mobility for lorried infantry regiments, as well as being used as buses in training establishments. A notable characteristic was the whining spiral bevel rear axle.

Length: 5.94m (19ft 6in). *Width:* 2.55m (18ft 4½in). *Height:* 3.11m (10ft 2½in). *Crew:* 1. *Power:* Bedford, 6-cyl., petrol, 3,518cc 72bhp at 3,000rpm; *Payload:* 3,050kg (6,700lb). *Speed:* 80km/hr (50mph). *Range:* 440km (275 miles). *Maker:* Vauxhall Motors, Ltd., Luton.

Bedford 3-ton QL

CHEVROLET 4×4 GENERAL SERVICE TRUCK *1941–1955*

This was also called the Canadian Military Pattern or, more familiarly, the Canadian Chev. and was the Canadian Army's standard load carrier. It was also built in a number of variants, including workshop, crane, office, bridge-carrying and water-tank types. It was unusual because of the odd reverse slope to the windscreen, claimed to reduce the chance of reflection revealing the truck to aerial reconnaissance. Similar vehicles were built in the 15-cwt (726kg) and 30-cwt (1,524kg) range, and a 4 × 4 gun tractor on the 15-cwt (762kg) chassis.

Length: 5.56m (18ft 3in). *Width:* 2.13m (7ft 0in). *Height:* 2.97m (9ft 9in). *Crew:* 1. *Power:* Chevrolet, 6-cyl., petrol, 3,540cc, 78bhp at 3,200rpm. *Payload:* 3,050kg (6,700lb). *Speed:* 80km/hr (50mph). *Range:* 400km (250 miles). *Maker:* General Motors of Canada, Oshawa, Ontario.

COMMER Q4 THREE-TON 4×4 GENERAL SERVICE TRUCK *1952–1968*

This was one of the post-war range of vehicles introduced into the British Army in the early 1950s. Whilst designed to a Ministry of Defence specification, they used many components of standard commercial vehicles in order to keep development costs down. This is the basic vehicle of the group, being a cargo truck with folding bench seats for 20 men; in addition to this, there were some 10 other variant models, covering workshop trucks, office trucks, wireless and tipping trucks. Most were superseded in the late 1960s.

Length: 6.98m (22ft 11in). *Width:* 2.41m (7ft 11in). *Height:* 3.09m (10ft 2in). *Weight:* 5,920kg (13,050lb). *Crew:* 1. *Power:* Commer,

6-cyl., petrol, 4,750cc, 95bhp at 3,000rpm. *Payload:* 3,625kg (8,000lb). *Speed:* 72km/hr (45mph). *Range:* 400km (250 miles). *Maker:* Commer Cars Ltd., Luton.

FODEN 8×4 LOW-MOBILITY CARGO TRUCK *1970–*

This was developed by Foden in order to meet a military demand for a vehicle capable of carrying 20 tons on surfaced or unsurfaced roads. It was based on commercial components modified to service standards. The cab can be reduced in height to permit loading into aircraft and can also be tipped forward to give access to the engine and transmission. Suspension is by semi-elliptic springs all round, and only the rear wheels are driven. Variant models include a tanker, a tipper and a recovery vehicle, the latter not yet accepted for service.

Length: 10.27m (33ft 8½in). *Width:* 2.49m (8ft 2in). *Height:* 3.31m (10ft 10½in). *Weight:* 9,553kg (21,060lb). *Crew:* 1. *Power:* Rolls-Royce 222, 8-cyl., diesel, 220bhp at 2,100rpm. *Payload:* 20,000kg (44,095lb). *Speed:* 72km/hr (45mph). *Range:* 400km (250 miles). *Maker:* Foden Ltd., Sandbach, Cheshire.

Foden 16-tonne truck

FORD 30-CWT 4×2 GENERAL SERVICE TRUCK *1939–1950*

This was a universal load-carrying vehicle, principally used by the British Air Force, though numbers were employed during the war by the other services. As well as being found as a cargo truck, variants were made to accommodate a number of different workshop assemblies for Light Aid Detachments and mobile repair facilities. They remained in use

Ford 30-cwt 4 X 2

Chevrolet GS 4 X 4

until the middle 1950s.

Length: 5.79m (19ft 0in). *Width:* 2.21m (7ft 3in). *Height:* 2.89m (9ft 6in). *Weight:* 1,525kg (3,360lb). *Crew:* 1. *Power:* Ford, V–8, petrol, 3,620cc, 85bhp at 3,800rpm. *Payload:* 1,525kg (3,360lb). *Speed:* 72km/hr (45mph). *Range:* 480km (300 miles). *Maker:* Ford Motor Co., Dagenham.

FORD 4×2 HEAVY UTILITY CAR *1941–1948*

These vehicles were adapted from Canadian Ford/Mercury civilian shooting brakes and used as general utility vehicles, particularly in the Middle Eastern theatre. Modifications from the civil pattern included radio supression, fitting combat tyres, weapons racks and tool racks, and the addition of blackout to the windows. The standard version seated five passengers on bench seats and had a cargo space at the rear, with access through a double, horizontal, rear door, which was split so that the lower half could be extended as a tailboard to carry long loads. A second version had an additional seat for two extra passengers in place of the cargo space.

Length: 4.9m (16ft 2in). *Width:* 2.0m (6ft 7in). *Height:* 1.82m (6ft 0in). *Crew:* 1. *Power:* Ford Mercury, V–8, petrol, 3,910cc, 95bhp at 3,600rpm. *Payload:* 680kg (1,500lb). *Speed:* 88km/hr (55mph). *Range:* 300km (185 miles). *Maker:* Ford Motor Co. of Canada, Windsor, Ontario.

LAND-ROVER ¾-TON 4×4 GENERAL SERVICE TRUCK *1950–*

This is based on the commercial long wheelbase Land-Rover, with some modification to better fit it for military use. These changes include reinforcing the frame, fitting divided wheels, twin fuel tanks, radio-mounting points and a reinforced front bumper to allow one vehicle to push another. The springs are specially fitted on deeper hangers so that large sand tyres can be fitted if required, and a two-

stretcher conversion kit is available to permit the vehicle to be used as a forward-area ambulance.

Length: 4.64m (15ft 3in). *Width:* 1.68m (5ft 6½in). *Height:* 2.05m (6ft 9in). *Weight:* 1,680kg (3,686lb). *Crew:* 1. *Power:* Rover, 4-cyl., petrol, 2,286cc, 77bhp at 4,250rpm. *Payload:* 940kg (2,072lb). *Speed:* 72km/hr (45mph). *Range:* 450km (280 miles). *Makers:* Rover Co. Ltd., Solihull.

MORRIS 4×2 LIGHT UTILITY CAR *1939–1948*

This vehicle, together with similar models based on Austin, Hillman and Standard chassis, was derived from the basic chassis of pre-war family saloon cars and was designed to be used as a light pick-up truck, a runabout, and in place of staff cars for lower-grade officers. Two passengers were carried in the

Morris 8-cwt Light Utility

cargo space on fold-away seats, while the cab held two seats; the cab passenger's seat could fold forward to give access to the rear seats. For cargo use a tailboard could be lowered, and the canvas tilt cover could be used to close the rear. The spare wheel was generally on the cab roof.

Length: 4.11m (13ft 6in). *Width:* 1.52m (5ft 0in). *Height:* 1.93m (6ft 4in). *Weight:* 1,105kg (2,436lb). *Crew:* 1. *Power:* Morris, 4-cyl., petrol, 1,140cc, 37bhp at 3,600rpm. *Payload:* 510kg (1,125lb). *Speed:* 96km/hr (60mph). *Range:* 400km (250 miles). *Maker:* Morris Motors, Cowley, Oxford.

Morris C8 15-cwt Truck

MORRIS C8 15-CWT 4×4 GENERAL SERVICE TRUCK *1944–1955*

Introduced in 1944 this vehicle used the basic chassis components of the Morris Quad artillery tractor (*qv*) to produce an all-wheel-drive truck. It was followed by radio, office, water-tank and other variant models. The cargo truck could be found with either wood or steel body, and remained in service until the middle 1950s.

Length: 4.62m (15ft 2in). *Width:* 2.08m (6ft 10in). *Height:* 2.13m (7ft 0in). *Weight:* 2,591kg (5,712lb). *Crew:* 1. *Power:* Morris, 4-cyl., petrol, 3,500cc, 70bhp at 3,000rpm. *Payload:* 1,422kg (3,135lb). *Speed:* 88km/hr (55mph). *Range:* 390km (240 miles). *Maker:* Morris-Commercial Motors, Adderly Park, Birmingham.

ROVER ¾-ton 4 × 4 AMBULANCE *1963–*

The system of evacuating front-line casualties by stretchers carried on ¼-ton Jeep-type trucks is not without its drawbacks, particularly to the welfare of the patients, and this vehicle was designed in order to provide a more comfortable method of casualty evacuation. It is based on the long-wheelbase Land-Rover (*qv*) chassis and carries an aluminium panelled ambulance body with thermal insulation offering accommodation for a medical orderly and two or four stretcher cases, or, alternatively, various combinations of stretcher and sitting cases. Ventilation and heating are provided.

Length: 4.82m (15ft 10in). *Width:* 1.90m (6ft 3in). *Height:* 2.13m (7ft 0½in). *Weight:* 1,930kg (4,256lb). *Crew:* 2. *Power:* Rover, 4-cyl., petrol, 2,286cc, 77bhp at 4,250rpm. *Payload:* 740kg (1,630lb). *Speed:* 72km/hr (45mph). *Range:* 450km (280 miles). *Maker:* Rover Co. Ltd., Solihull.

ROVER ONE-TON FORWARD-CONTROL CARGO TRUCK *1966*

This vehicle was developed jointly by Rover and the British Army in order to provide a vehicle capable of carrying one tonne, towing a powered-axle trailer and acting as a tractor for the 105mm light gun. The cab-over-engine chassis uses the Rover V-8 engine, detuned to operate with low-octane fuel, and carries an aluminium body capable of carrying 1,000kg (2,204lb) of cargo or eight fully equipped troops. A power take-off from the engine can be used to drive either a winch or a powered-axle trailer; such a trailer, capable of carrying another 1,000kg (2,204lb), has been developed, but has not been accepted for service. The upperworks of the vehicle can be readily removed and in this stripped-down condition it can be air-lifted by larger helicopters.

Length: 4.12m (13ft 6½in). *Width:* 1.84m (6ft 0½in). *Height:* 2.28m (7ft 6in). *Weight:* 1,924kg (4,241lb). *Crew:* 2. *Power:* Rover, V-8, petrol, 3,528cc, 156bhp at 5,000rpm. *Payload:* 1,220kg (2,690lb). *Speed:* 120km/hr (75mph). *Range:* 560km (350 miles). *Maker:* Rover Co. Ltd., Solihull.

ROVER LIGHTWEIGHT GENERAL SERVICE TRUCK *1965–*

Whilst the Land-Rover was a satisfactory general-purpose vehicle for the British Army, there was a requirement for a lighter version capable of being helicopter-lifted but with a useful payload and capable of towing light support weapons. Work began in 1965 and resulted in this lightweight version, generally known as the APGP for Air-Portable, General Purpose . Two versions are produced, one for general service and one specially fitted for radio installation.

Length: 3.73m (12ft 3in). *Width:* 1.61m (5ft 3¾in). *Height:* 1.95m (6ft 5in). *Weight:* 1,593kg (3,514lb). *Crew:* 1. *Power:* Rover, 4-cyl., 2,286cc, petrol, 77bhp at 4,250rpm. *Payload:* 395kg (870lb). *Speed:* 72km/hr (45mph). *Range:* 560km (350 miles). *Maker:* Rover Co. Ltd., Solihull.

UNITED STATES

Dodge 1½-ton 6 X 6

DODGE 1½-TON 6×6 CARGO TRUCK *1942–1945*

This vehicle was designed as a substitute for the standard 2½-ton truck, since the demand for the latter could not be met by the available manufacturing facilities. It was constructed, as far as possible, by using components of the ¾-ton 6 × 6, which were already in volume production. The principal changes lay in the

Dodge ¾-ton 4 X 4

addition of an extra bogie axle and the lengthening of the chassis and body so as to accommodate greater cargo. Models with or without a winch were built and, as with the ¾-ton model, a desert equipment kit was provided. Some vehicles were fitted with a machine-gun pedestal or ring mounting on top of the cab structure.

Length: 5.70m (18ft 8½in). *Width:* 2.10m (6ft 10¾in). *Height:* 2.15m (7ft 0¾in). *Weight:* 4,774kg (10,525lb). *Crew:* 1. *Power:* Dodge T-214, 6-cyl., petrol, 3,772cc, 76bhp at 3,200rpm. *Payload:* 1,497kg (3,300lb). *Towed load:* 1,587kg (3,500lb). *Winch pull:* 3,401kg (7,500lb). *Speed:* 80km/hr (50mph). *Range:* 385km (240 miles). *Maker:* Dodge Brothers Corp., Fargo Motor Div. of Chrysler Corp., Detroit, Mich.

DODGE ¾-TON 4×4 WEAPONS-CARRIER TRUCK *1941–1960*

Widely used by all arms of the US forces, the

widely used, so much so that it went back into production from 1950 to 1955 to meet the demands of the Korean War. By that time it was a perpetuation of an obsolete design and Dodge were asked to produce a more modern version. This appeared as the M37 in 1958 and was in production in the USA and Canada until 1964.

In appearance its ancestry can be easily seen; the same hood and fenders, folded windshield and open cab as the wartime vehicle, with slight differences in contour. The cargo body is deeper, and some were built with steel doors to the cab. Ambulance, telephone maintenance and missile-carrying trucks have been built on the same chassis, and the basic cargo truck has been supplied to many countries under the Military Aid Program.

Length: 4.81m (15ft 9in). *Width:* 1.78m (5ft 10in). *Height:* 2.27m (7ft 6in). *Weight:* 2,585kg (5,700lb). *Crew:* 1. *Power:* Dodge, 4-cyl., petrol, 78bhp at 3,200rpm. *Payload:* 907kg (2,000lb). *Towed load:* 2,722kg (6,000lb). *Speed:* 88km/hr (55mph). *Range:* 360km (255 miles). *Maker:* Dodge Div. of Chrysler Motor Corp., Detroit, Mich.

M38 4 X 4

Dodge weapons carrier was originally developed as an infantry vehicle to carry the heavier weapons of the company, but later became universal as a cargo and general-purpose truck with good cross-country ability. Versions with and without the front-mounted winch were produced. A special desert conversion was also available, which added an expansion tank to the radiator system, and an engine-driven air compressor so that the tyres could be readily deflated or inflated to cope with sand conditions.

Length: 4.48m (14ft 8½in). *Width:* 2.10m (6ft 10¾in). *Height:* 2.07m (6ft 10in). *Weight:* 3,334kg (7,350lb). *Crew:* 1. *Power:* Dodge T-214, 6-cyl., petrol, 3,772cc, 76bhp at 3,200rpm. *Payload:* 680kg (1,500lb). *Towed load:* 453kg (1,000lb). *Winch pull:* 2,267kg (5,000lb). *Speed:* 87km/hr (54mph). *Range:* 390km (240 miles). *Maker:* Dodge Brothers Corp., Fargo Motor Div. of Chrysler Corp., Detroit, Mich.

M37 DODGE ¾-TON 4 × 4 CARGO TRUCK *1958–*
The Dodge ¾-ton weapons carrier (*qv*) of the wartime years was extremely popular and

M37 ¾-ton 4 X 4

M38 4 × 4 UTILITY TRUCK *1955–*
The original Jeep caught the public's fancy during the war, and immediately afterwards the Willys Company began development of a civilian counterpart, the CJ-3. This was simply the military pattern vehicle with its contours made more acceptable and fashionable and the interior rather more comfortable. As the wartime military Jeeps began to thin out due to wear, the US Army decided to purchase a number of CJ-3 models to replace them until a more purpose-built vehicle could be developed. The M38 was a militarized version of the CJ-3, with the suspension strengthened and a 24-volt electrical system fitted. After adoption by the US forces the Willys company sold the M38 to numerous armies throughout the world and also concluded licensing agreements whereby the vehicle was built in several other countries.

Length: 3.37m (11ft 1in). *Width:* 1.57m (5ft

2in). *Height:* 1.87m (6ft 2in). *Weight:* 1,247kg (2,750lb). *Crew:* 1. *Power:* Willys, 4-cyl., petrol, 60bhp at 4,000rpm. *Payload:* 500kg (1,100lb). *Towed load:* 900kg (1,985lb). *Speed:* 88km/hr (55mph). *Range:* 360km (225 miles). *Maker:* AM General Corp., Wayne, Mich.

M151 ¼-TON 4 × 4 UTILITY TRUCK *1960–*

In 1951 the original Jeeps were reaching the end of their useful lives and the Ford Motor Company were invited to develop a suitable replacement. After several trial models, the M151 was put into production in 1960. In broad terms it is the wartime Jeep with such developments in design as have appeared since 1940 – coil-spring suspension, an overhead-valve engine of more power, a better transmission and better performance. Various conversion kits permit the carriage of heavy weapons, generators, xenon searchlights, radio equipment, the fitting of heaters and deep-fording

M151 ¼-ton 4 X 4

kits, while variant models include the M718 ambulance and the M825 106mm recoilless rifle carrier. In addition to serving with the US Army, M151s are also used by Israel and the Netherlands.

Length: 3.35m (11ft 0in). *Width:* 1.58m (5ft 2in). *Height:* 1.80m (5ft 11in). *Weight:* 1,012kg (2,231lb). *Crew:* 1. *Power:* Ford, 4-cyl., petrol, 71bhp at 4,000rpm. *Payload:* 550kg (1,212lb). *Speed:* 106km/hr (65mph). *Range:* 480km (160 miles). *Makers:* Ford Motor Co., Highland Park, Mich.; AM General Corp., Wayne, Mich.

M274 MECHANICAL MULE CROSS-COUNTRY TRUCK *1955–*

This was developed in the early 1950s as a low-profile cross-country vehicle in which every unnecessary item had been stripped away to leave the most basic load carrier. It is no more than a platform with four wheels, an engine and the basic driving controls. These controls can be swivelled forward and down so that, under fire, the driver can walk or crouch behind the vehicle and control it. Basically a cargo vehicle, for transport of ammunition and

M274

stores, it can also be used as a mobile mounting for a recoilless gun or machine gun.

The Mule consists of an aluminium platform mounted on a simple chassis; the wheels are rigidly fixed without any suspension system, the low-pressure tyres serving to absorb shocks and irregularities. The engine is at the rear end; various engines have been fitted, ranging from 4-cyl. water-cooled to 2-cyl. air-cooled. It has been proved in action in Vietnam and is in extensive use with the US Army and Marine Corps.

Length: 2.98m (9ft 9in). *Width:* 1.17m (3ft 10in). *Height:* 0.68m (2ft 3in). *Weight:* 376kg (828lb). *Crew:* 1. *Power:* Willys, 4-cyl., air-cooled, petrol, 25bhp at 4,500rpm. *Payload:* 450kg (991lb). *Speed:* 40km/hr (25mph). *Range:* 190km (120 miles). *Makers:* (Willys) Jeep Corp., Mich.; Baifield Industries, Carrollton, Texas; Brunswick Corp.

M520 GOER EIGHT-TON 4 × 4 CARGO TRUCK *1963–*

This is a borderline case between a truck and an amphibian; it was developed by the Caterpillar Corporation in the late 1950s as an all-terrain, go-anywhere vehicle, and it was doubtless influenced by some of that company's earth-moving equipment. It consists of two two-wheeled units, a tractor and trailer, joined by a flexible connector giving considerable articulation. It is fully amphibious, being propelled in water by its wheels, and the forward section carries a winch. It was extensively tested in Germany in the early 1960s and was afterwards used with great success in Vietnam. Some 800 cargo trucks were built, plus 117 modified to act as recovery vehicles and 371 tankers, which have the cargo body modified to take a 93,751 (2,500 US gall.) tank and hose reels.

Length: 9.75m (32ft 0in). *Width:* 2.74m (9ft 0in). *Height:* 3.39m (11ft 2in). *Weight:* 10,240kg (22,575lb). *Crew:* 2. *Power:* Caterpillar D333, 6-cyl., turbocharged diesel, 213bhp at 2,200rpm. *Payload:* 8,260kg (18,200lb). *Winch pull:* 4,535kg (10,000lb). *Speed:* 48km/hr (30mph). *Makers:* Caterpillar Tractor Co., Peoria, Ill.

M561 GAMA GOAT 1½-TON 6 × 6 TRUCK *1971–*

This vehicle gets its name from Mr. R. L. Gamaunt, the inventor, and its goat-like ability to negotiate rough country. The M561 consists of two light alloy bodies joined by a roll-articulated joint, which allows the two units to pitch and roll with respect to each other. The joint carries a transmission shaft which passes drive to the wheels in the rear unit, so that the vehicle can be used as a 6 × 4, with the two rear sets of wheels driven, or as a 6 × 6 with all wheels driven. Front and rear axles have

M561 Gamma Goat

WILLYS ⅟₄-TON 4 × 4 JEEP 1940–1955

In June 1940 the US Army issued a specification calling for a ¼-ton combat truck with all-wheel drive to carry a 272kg (600lb) payload and weigh no more than 590kg (1,300lb). Of the 135 manufacturers invited to compete and to provide specimens within 75 days, only two firms took up the challenge, American Bantam of Butler, Pa., and Willys-Overland of Toledo, Ohio, but only Bantam managed to produce a vehicle within the specification and inside the time limit. As a result they were given the initial contract, but experience soon showed that the Bantam car, good as it was, was underpowered and insufficiently robust. Willys chief engineer considered the Army specification too stringent and refused to compromise; instead he set about developing his idea of what the army needed, a stronger vehicle with a more powerful engine. After argument and

test, he was proved right and his design became the Willys Model combat car.

The Ford Motor Company had by this time become interested in the specification and had

put up their own model, known as the GP (for General Purpose), but since its engine was less powerful the Army decided to standardize on the Willys design and have it built by both firms; when built by Ford it became the Model GPW. Produced by the tens of thousands, the Jeep was to be found in every theatre of war and was used by every Allied army. It remained in service unchanged until the middle 1950s, after which it was replaced by improved models.

Length: 3.35m (11ft 0½in). *Width:* 1.57m (5ft 2in). *Height:* 1.77m (5ft 9¾in). *Weight:* 1,112kg (2,453lb). *Crew:* 1. *Power:* Willys MB, 4-cyl., petrol, 2,199cc, 60bhp at 4,000rpm. *Payload:* 362kg (800lb). *Towed load:* 454kg (1,000lb). *Speed:* 105km/hr (65mph). *Range:* 480km (300 miles). *Maker:* Willys-Overland Motor Co., Toledo, Ohio; Ford Motor Co., Detroit, Mich.

---

independent suspension, while the centre axle is a beam axle with transverse springing. The vehicle is fully amphibious, being propelled in water by paddle-action of its wheels. The rear section of the body is entirely devoted to cargo space, while the front section carries the engine, transmission and driver's controls; there is a winch at the front end. As well as a cargo version, specialist versions with TOW missiles, radar, radio equipment or a recoilless gun have also been used.

Length: 5.75m (18ft 11in). *Width:* 2.13m (7ft 0in). *Height:* 2.31m (7ft 7in). *Weight:* 3,175kg (7,000lb). *Crew:* 1. *Power:* GMC 3–53, 3-cyl., diesel, 103bhp at 2,800rpm. *Payload:* 1,134kg (2,500lb). *Towed load:* 2,721kg (6,000lb). *Winch pull:* 3,628kg (8,000lb). *Speed:* 88km/hr (55mph). *Range:* 835km (450 miles). *Makers:* Ling-Temco-Vought (Design & development), Anaheim, Calif.; CONDEC Corp. (Production), Old Greenwich, Conn.

YUGOSLAVIA

Fap

FAP SERIES OF TRUCKS.

Until recent years Yugoslavia relied on imported vehicles of all kinds, but there is now a flourishing modern plant building all sizes of commercial vehicle including trucks of up to 11,000kg (24,244lb) capacity. Most of these are multi-purpose trucks for both civil and military use, and they range from a 4 × 2 with a 5,000kg (11,020lb) load to the 11,000kg

(24,244lb) in 4 × 4. Some of the range are Saurer designs, built under licence, but the latest ones are original designs and at least two are specifically for the Yugoslav Army and not for civil use. These are the 2220 BDS and 2020. These are used for the carriage of heavy items and engineer equipments such as bridging. They have forward-control cabs and full drive to all wheels.

Length: 7.70m (25ft 4in). *Width:* 2.50m (8ft 3in). *Height:* 2.90m (9ft 6in). *Weight:* 8,600kg (18,950lb). *Power:* 2F/002A, 6-cyl., diesel, 200bhp (licenced from British Leyland). *Payload:* 11,000kg (24,244lb). *Speed:* 60km/hr (37mph). *Range:* 800km (500 miles). *Maker:* Yugoslav Motor Vehicle Plant, Pribos.

ZASTAVA AR–51 LIGHT VEHICLE 1972–

The Zastava is in fact the Italian Fiat AR–59 built under licence, and reference should be made to that for all details.

These motorcycle scouts with Harley
Davidson 45 WLAs and poised submachine
guns were a dashing part of the Armoured
Divisions during World War II.

MOTORCYCLES

AUSTRIA

PUCH 800 MOTORCYCLE *1936–1945*
The Puch 800 is a typical machine of its day. It was a civilian design which was bought for military service direct from the factory and some were in use with their civilian paint and finish. The engine was unusual in that it was a shallow vee set across the frame. Almost all of these bikes were fitted with sidecars.
Weight: 290kg (640lb). *Payload:* 250kg (550lb). *Power:* Puch, 4-cyl., V–4, air-cooled, petrol, 792cc, 20bhp at 4,000rpm. *Maker:* Steyr-Daimler-Puch, Steyr.

PUCH MCH 175 MOTORCYCLE *1958–1970*
The MCH 175 is a light one-man machine which was intended for short-range dispatch and message carrying. Like so many of these smaller machines it was not a great success and it has now all but faded out from Austrian military service.
Weight: 120kg (264lb). *Payload:* 150kg (330lb). *Power:* Puch, 2-stroke, 2-cyl., petrol, 172cc, 10bhp at 4,000rpm. *Maker:* Steyr-Daimler-Puch, Steyr.

BELGIUM

FN M12 MOTORCYCLE *1937–1940*
The M12 was a better machine than the M86 (*qv*) and was specifically built with the military in mind. It had a larger and more powerful engine and drove to the rear wheel by shaft and to the sidecar wheel through a differential and shaft. A reverse gear enabled the crew to manoeuvre in small spaces. The sidecar was a box-like structure fitted with machine-gun mounting fore and aft.
Weight: 240kg (530lb). *Power:* FN, 2-cyl., flat twin, 1,000cc, 22bhp. *Speed:* 100km/hr (62mph). *Maker:* FN, Herstal, Liège.

FN M12

FN M86 MOTORCYCLE *1936–1940*
The FN Company in Liège had been producing civilian motorcycles since 1902, and some of these were impressed into military service during World War I. In 1936 the company sold a number of the M86 civilian sidecar machines to the Belgian Army. It was used with and without a sidecar, but with the car it could carry a Browning BAR light machine gun or a small load of cargo. Cross-country mobility was limited by the fact that only the bike wheel was driven. A few were produced with an armoured sidecar, a rare example of this type of vehicle, and with a light armoured shield for the driver. Argentina bought some, but they must have been much too heavy for their engine and suspension.
Power: FN, 1-cyl., air-cooled, petrol, 600cc. *Maker:* FN, Herstal, Liège.

CZECHOSLOVAKIA

CZ 175 MOTORCYCLE *1935–1941*
The CZ 175 was one of several similar types used by the Czechoslovakian Army in the 1930s and it is included here to show the general design of all of them. It was a light single-seater of limited performance and power, but capable of being easily manhandled on rough country. As with many other mid-European models of that time it had a pressed-steel frame and limited suspension on the front wheel only.
Weight: 120kg (264lb). *Power:* CZ, 1-cyl., air-cooled, petrol, 2-stroke, 172cc, 5.5bhp. *Maker:* Ceska Zbrojovka, Narodni Podnik, Strakonice.

FRANCE

PRE-WAR FRENCH MOTORCYCLES
The French Army used a number of different types of motorcycle in the 1930s, and it is not practical to list them individually and describe their characteristics. The following list covers the majority that were used up to 1940.
Monet-Goyon 1935–1940: 500cc solos.
Motobecane 1930–1940: various sizes.
Peugeot 1934–: light solo.
René Gillet: 1928–1940: up to 750cc sidecar models.
Terrot: 1938–1940: up to 750cc sidecar models.

GNOME-RHONE 750 ARMEE MOTORCYCLE *1938–1940*
The Armée model was largely based on contemporary civilian design, but it was both heavier and stronger. It was almost always used with a sidecar, and the French Army displayed some ingenuity in the uses to which sidecars were put. However, the main purpose of the

Gnome was to act as a light communications vehicle, carrying one passenger. It had a robust flat-twin engine with shaft drive to the rear wheel, but not to the sidecar wheel. A later model, the AX2, drove the car wheel, and after 1945 a slightly up-dated version was put into production again for a few years. The AX2 had an engine of 804cc and much better traction on poor ground.

Weight: 320kg (705lb). *Power:* Gnome Rhône, 2-cyl., flat twin, 750cc. *Speed:* 80km/hr (50mph). *Maker:* Société des Moteurs Gnome, Paris.

GERMANY

BMW R75 MOTORCYCLE *1938–1945*
The R75 was one of the heavy German motorcycles specially built for sidecar work. It was meant to be a light weapon carrier for the battlefield and the sidecar was fitted with racks to carry either a machine gun or a mortar. It was not intended that the machine should be ridden as a solo, though it is reported that this was done on occasions. The construction was relatively massive and the rear and sidecar wheels were joined by a lockable differential and braked hydraulically. These large combinations were used in special Kradschutzen units and were also issued to the parachute troops who brought them to the battle inside the cargo hold of the Junkers 52.

Length: 2.40m (7ft 9in). *Width:* 1.73m (5ft 7in). *Height:* 1.00m (3ft 3in). *Weight:* 400kg (881lb). *Power:* BMW, 2-cyl., horizontally-opposed, twin, 750cc, 26bhp at 4,400rpm. *Maker:* BMW AG, Munich.

ZUNDAPP KS750 MOTORCYCLE *1940–1944*
The Zundapp was the counterpart of the large BMW (*qv*) and fulfilled the same function. It was a large and heavy machine with a frame of pressed steel in the usual Zundapp fashion. It pulled the standardized sidecar, which could accept the usual loads of a machine gun or a mortar. Apart from the frame, there was little in the Zundapp that was different from the BMW for even the engine was the same size and layout.

Zundapp

Length: 2.38m (7ft 10in). *Width:* 1.65m (5ft 5in). *Height:* 1.01m (3ft 4in). *Weight:* 400kg (881lb). *Power:* Zundapp, 2-cyl., horizontally-opposed, 750cc, 25bhp. *Maker:* Zundapp-werke, Munich.

ITALY

MOTO GUZZI MOTORCYCLE *1946–1950*
The Moto Guzzi was one of the more famous names in post-war motorcycling, and the racing models made a reputation for the firm within a few years of the end of the war. The 1946 500cc solo machine was ahead of its time and it had a sprung back wheel, using an advanced arrangement of parallel swinging links. The engine lay horizontally with the cylinder head facing forwards, and the centre of gravity was low. Stability was good and cross-country mobility better than average.

Weight: 200kg (440lb). *Power:* Moto Guzzi, 1-cyl., air-cooled, petrol, 500cc, 18.5bhp. *Speed:* 110km/hr (68mph). *Maker:* Moto Guzzi SPA, Como.

JAPAN

TYPE 97 MOTORCYCLE *1937–1945*
The Type 97 was closely patterned on the US Harley-Davidson and it was generally used with a light sidecar. Some sidecars were given machine guns, though this does not seem to

BMW R75

Moto Guzzi

have been a normal use for these vehicles. Many were ridden as solos. The main use of them was in Japan itself, though a few were taken overseas as the war progressed.

Weight: 500kg (1,102lb). *Power:* Sankyo, 2-cyl., V–2, air-cooled, petrol, 24bhp. *Speed:* 70km/hr (43mph).

POLAND

CWS–M111 MOTORCYCLE *1932–1938*
There were several attempts to make indigenous equipment and vehicles in Poland during the inter-war years, but a combination of pressure from foreign firms, local indifference to things military and chronic lack of finance usually ensured that all that appeared was too small and too little to be of much use. The CWS firm tried hard and produced this motorcycle with a sidecar. It took its general layout from other designs, but a useful feature was the loop frame, which ensured reasonable strength. The sidecar often carried a machine gun. Not many were built, and those that remained in 1939 were destroyed in the German invasion.

Power: V–2, air-cooled, petrol, 21bhp at 3,500rpm. *Maker:* CWS, Warsaw.

SWITZERLAND

CONDOR A–580–1 MOTORCYCLE *1948–1960*
The Condor 580 was the larger of the two Condors and closely resembled the German BMW (*qv*) in layout. It was a twin-cylinder shaft-drive machine of robust build and good power output. It was derived directly from a civilian

model, but despite its virtues it was phased out in the late 1950s as motorcycles went out of favour with armies.

Weight: 195kg (430lb). *Power:* Condor, 2-cyl., horizontally-opposed, air-cooled, petrol, 680cc, 20bhp. *Maker:* Condor Works AG, Jura.

UNITED KINGDOM

BSA MOTORCYCLES *1938–1945*
The BSA firm produced 126,334 motorcycles from 1939–45. The vast majority were either 350cc or 500cc 1-cyl. models of great reliability but considerable weight and strength. The 350 was used as a solo machine and gained some respect for its ability to take rough treatment, though its performance was not exciting. The 500cc model was often fitted with a sidecar, which overloaded it, but as a solo it had some reserve of power. Both models survived the war in large numbers to become civilian transport for many years.

350 Model *Length:* 2.02m (6ft 9in). *Width:* 68cm (2ft 3in). *Height:* 99cm (3ft 3in). *Weight:* 158kg (350lb). *Power:* BSA, 1-cyl., overhead valve, 348cc, 15bhp, *Maker:* BSA Cycles Ltd., Birmingham.

EXCELSIOR WELBIKE MOTORCYCLE *1942–1945*
The Welbike was an attempt to improve the mobility of airborne forces by providing them with a motorcycle which could be parachuted in a container. As the dimensions of a container were very restricted the size of the bike was necessarily small. It turned out to be a 98cc machine with tiny wheels and a folding saddle pillar and handlebar pillar. The riding position was not very comfortable for a man of more than average height and no equipment could be carried at all. Indeed, one man overloaded it. Although several thousand were made and issued, it was quickly found that the small wheels made the vehicle virtually useless away from a made-up road, and the additional mobility provided was not enough to warrant the manufacturing effort. The design was revived after the war when it achieved some success as an economical and easily-stowed means of civilian transport.

Condor

The motorcycle section of the Czech Army train in England on BSAs

Length: 1.34m (4ft 4in). *Width:* 56cm (1ft 10in). *Height* (stowed): 38cm (1ft 3in). *Weight:* 31.7kg (70lb). *Power:* 1-cyl., 98cc, 2-stroke. *Maker:* Excelsior Motor Co., Birmingham.

NORTON 16H MOTORCYCLE *1938–1945*
The well-known Norton 16H side-valve machine was brought in quite large numbers for use by the Army just before the war started. The RAF also took it and usually fitted it with a single-seater sidecar. The sidecars were less often used by the Army who preferred the solo machine for despatch riding and convoy marshalling work. The 16H was a dependable and rugged machine of modest performance but considerable charm and popularity. It was supplied to Canada and used by the Canadian Army for despatch riding. After the war many

Excelsior Welbike

survived in civilian use for upwards of twenty years.
Power: 1-cyl., 490cc, side-valve, 12bhp.
Maker: Norton Motors Ltd., Birmingham.

NORTON 633 MOTORCYCLE *1937–1945*

The 633 was a bigger version of the more usual 16H (*qv*) and it was specifically intended to pull a sidecar. A few were used as solos, but the weight and bulk counted against it on rough country. As a sidecar combination the 633 was both practical and useful, carrying two men and their kit with the same reliability as the 16H. The sidecar was sometimes used as a machine-gun carrier, and all standard versions were in any case fitted with a rack for a Bren LMG. This machine was the only British machine to have an optional drive to the sidecar wheel. All others only drove the bike back wheel. The sidecar on the 633 was not a civilian type, but a functional open box with virtually no weather protection at all.
Length: 2.16m (7ft 2in). *Width:* 1.70m (5ft 6in). *Height:* 1.17m (3ft 10in). *Weight:* 308kg (679lb). *Power:* Norton, 1-cyl., side-valve, 14.5bhp at 4,000rpm. *Maker:* Norton Motors Ltd., Birmingham.

UNITED STATES

CUSHMAN AIRBORNE MOTOR SCOOTER *1944–1945*

This was developed for airborne troop use and was the civilian Cushman scooter with slight modification. The Cushman had been adopted for military use by messengers and employees in large depots early in the war, usually with a small sidecar attached for delivery purposes,

Airborne Scooter

Harley-Davidson 45 WLAs

but the airborne version was adopted in March 1944. Controls and accessories were minimal; the four-stroke engine was under the seat, a foot pedal selected the two speeds and another applied the rear brake. No lights were fitted, nor any instrumentation. Dropped by parachute in a suitable container, or simply suspended from parachute rings, the scooter was widely used by airborne troops for assembling after a drop and as a reconnaissance machine.
Length: 1.90m (6ft 3in). *Width:* 0.58m (1ft 11in). *Height:* 0.96m (3ft 2in). *Weight:* 226kg (499lb). *Crew:* 1. *Power:* Cushman, 1-cyl., 4bhp at 3,500rpm. *Speed:* 65km/hr (40mph). *Range:* 169km (100miles). *Maker:* Cushman Motor Works.

HARLEY-DAVIDSON MODEL WLA MOTORCYCLE *1941–1946*

This was basically a civil machine slightly adapted for military purposes; it was officially described as being for 'reconnaissance, messenger service and police operations'. It was fitted with brackets for carrying a submachine gun and an ammunition box, and the lighting was altered to conform with military combat zone requirements. For operation in desert conditions the standard 4.00 × 18 tyres could be replaced by 5.50 × 16 sand tyres. Drive was by conventional chain and the gearbox was hand operated.
Length: 2.23m (7ft 4in). *Width:* 0.92m (3ft 0½in). *Height:* 1.04m (3ft 5in). *Weight:* 261kg (576lb). *Crew:* 1. *Power:* Harley-Davidson WLA, V–2, petrol, 740cc, 23bhp at 3,000rpm. *Speed:* 105km/hr (65mph). *Range:* 200km (125 miles). *Maker:* Harley-Davidson Motor Co., Milwaukee, Wis.

M1 EXTRA LIGHT SOLO MOTORCYCLE *1944-1945*

This machine was developed especially for airborne troops and was standardized in December 1944. However, it was later

authorized for other formations and services and became a general-purpose machine for messengers. With a weight of less than half the standard Harley-Davidson machine, the M1 proved to be equally rugged and reliable and with a better cross-country performance. It was provided with attachment points for parachute dropping and a 'paracrate' was also produced in order to protect the wheels when dropped. The battery and oil-bath air cleaner were designed so as to be unaffected by dropping, and magneto ignition allowed the machine to operate without the battery if necessary. A towing hook at the rear allowed a light utility cart to be pulled. In spite of its several advantages over the heavier standard machine, the M1 did not survive for long after the war.
Length: 1.96m (6ft 5½in). *Width:* 0.71m (2ft 4in). *Height:* 0.92m (3ft 0½in). *Weight:* 109kg (241lb). *Crew:* 1. *Power:* Indian Model 144, 1-cyl., petrol, 221cc, 6.2bhp at 4,700rpm. *Speed:* 72km/hr (45mph). *Range:* 400km (250 miles). *Maker:* Indian Motorcycle Co., Springfield, Mass.

SIMPLEX MOTOR-DRIVEN BICYCLE *1943–1945*

This unusual machine was procured in limited numbers in 1943 for airborne troop use. It was, in effect, an extra-heavy bicycle, complete with pedals, with the addition of a two-stroke engine driving the rear wheels through a vee-belt and pulley arrangement. High and low-ratio gearing was obtained by a foot which tensioned the belt and moved it from one pulley groove into another. The engine was started by either pedalling or pushing. It was replaced by the light M1 motorcycle (*qv*).
Length: 1.77m (5ft 10in). *Width:* 0.72m (2ft 4½in). *Height:* 0.96m (3ft 2in). *Weight:* 165kg (365lb). *Crew:* 1. *Power:* Servi-Cycle, 1-cyl., 2-stroke, 1.6bhp at 2,000rpm. *Speed:* 48km/hr (30mph). *Maker:* Simplex Manufacturing Co., Richmond, Cal.

The Landwasserschlepper was an unusual
amphibian, being designed as a boat with the
ability to move on land, rather than as a
vehicle capable of swimming.

AMPHIBIOUS AND LANDING VEHICLES

GERMANY

VOLKSWAGEN AMPHIBIOUS CAR
1942–1945

This vehicle was introduced in 1942 to meet a need for a light reconnaissance vehicle capable of overcoming the many streams and rivers confronting the German troops in Russia. Although nominally a Volkswagen there were a number of mechanical differences from the standard car. The body was constructed of metal pressing welded together to form a watertight hull, and the transmission was altered to give optional four-wheel drive and an auxiliary low gear which came into operation whenever four-wheel drive was selected. To propel the car in water there was a propeller unit which hinged up, over the rear of the car, when not in use. When lowered into operating position it was automatically engaged with an extension from the engine crankshaft and the drive went via chain and sprocket gearing to the propeller. It was a successful and popular vehicle, but in 1944, when the tactical situation changed, there was less need for it and production was dropped.

Length: 3.82m (12ft 6½in). *Width:* 1.48m (4ft 10in). *Height:* 1.61m (5ft 3½in). *Weight:* 910kg (2,006lb). *Crew:* 1. *Power:* Volkswagen, 4-cyl., petrol, 25bhp. *Speed:* land, 80km/hr (50mph); water, 10km/hr (6mph). *Maker:* Volkswagenwerke GmbH, Wolfsburg.

LANDWASSERSCHLEPPER LIGHT RIVER TUG *1935–1945*

This German Army equipment was somewhat different from the usual run of amphibians; most amphibians are land vehicles designed to operate in water, but the Landwasserschlepper was a light river tug designed to operate on land. It was ordered by the engineer branch of the Army Weapons Office in 1935 and designed by Rheinmetall. The development took some considerable time and it did not enter service until 1942 and then only in small numbers. The object was to provide the engineers with a suitable equipment to assist in bridging and river-crossing operations, and in this it was successful.

The hull resembled a boat, but was recessed at each side to accommodate the tracked suspension. The upperworks were on the lines of a motor-launch, with a fully-enclosed cabin and a form of conning-tower on top. Winches were provided on the after deck. Water propulsion was by two propellers at the rear.

Weight: 34,000kg (74,957lb). *Crew:* 2 + 20. *Power:* Maybach HL120, V-12, petrol, 11,867cc, 300bhp at 300rpm. *Speed:* land, 35km/hr (21mph); water, 12km/hr (7½mph). *Maker:* Rheinmetall-Borsig, Dusseldorf.

TAUCHPANZER III AMPHIBIOUS TANK *1940–1943*

When planning for Operation Sealion, the projected invasion of England in 1940, the Ger-

Amphibious Volkswagen

Amphibious Volkswagen

FIAT 6640A AMPHIBIOUS CARGO TRUCK *1973–*

The 6640A has been designed to meet a number of different requirements, both civil and military. It is produced as required, and is in service with the Italian Fire and Civil Defence departments. The hull is built up with welded aluminium in the shape of a pontoon, and in this is the engine and load compartment. The engine is at the front with the driver separated by a fire-proof bulkhead. Behind him is the load compartment, and as with all amphibians the cargo had to be lifted in and out over the sides since there are no doors or hatches. The four wheels are independently sprung and all can be driven. The transfer box also allows a power take-off to the propeller for swimming. A winch in the front can be used to pull the vehicle out over a difficult bank.

Length: 7.30m (23ft 10in). *Width:* 2.50m (8ft 3in). *Height:* 2.28m (7ft 6in). *Weight:* 4,810kg (10,601lb). *Power:* Fiat Model 8060, diesel, 6-cyl., 117bhp at 3,200rpm. *Payload:* 2,140kg (4,720lb). *Speed:* 90km/hr (56mph). *Range:* 750km (465 miles). *Maker:* Fiat, Turin.

mans were confronted with much the same problem as the British were in 1944 – namely, landing tanks on to a hostile beach. Their solution was similar to that of the British, to release the tanks into the sea well clear of the beach so that they arrived on shore in immediate fighting order, but instead of floating the tanks ashore, the Germans chose to make them com-

Tauchpanzer III

pletely submersible and drive them ashore on the sea bed.

The PzKpfw III tank (*qv*) was selected as the basis of the idea. All air intakes were fitted with water-tight covers and the exhausts with a non-return valve. Gun ports and mantlets were sealed with waterproof covers and the turret ring joint was closed by an inflatable rubber ring. The air intake for the engine was diverted to the interior of the tank, and a special breathing tube extended from the tank and carried a float, a flap valve and radio antenna. In operation the tank drove off the landing craft

at a suitable distance from the shore so that it landed in no more than 15m (50ft) of water; the float then held the air tube on the surface and all air for the engine and the crew came via this tube. Once ashore the air tube was dropped, the waterproof covers removed and the tank was fully operational.

Extensive tests of this device were carried out on the island of Sylt in the late summer of 1940 and 168 PzKpfw III were converted. When Operation Sealion was eventually abandoned the tanks were withdrawn and most were modified by having the air tube removed and replaced with a short, fixed tube to allow them to run submerged across rivers. In this guise several were used in the invasion of Russia in 1941-2.

BAV 485 AMPHIBIOUS TRUCK *1952–*

This vehicle was produced to complement the smaller GAZ–46 (*qv*) and it is much more a copy of the DUKW (*qv*), to the extent that it carries roughly the same load and has roughly the same performance. The basis was the ZIL–151 truck and later models used improved versions of the truck chassis as these came out. The hull closely resembles that of the

Fiat 6640

BAV 485

DUKW with the exception that there is a drop tail-gate, a major improvement which allows vehicles to be driven straight into the cargo compartment, though suitable ramps have to be used to get over the sill. However, it is much better than the DUKW loading arrangements where everything had to go over the side. There is a canvas cover for the cargo area and a canvas dodger for the bows. Water propulsion is by a propeller. Although an elderly design the BAV is still in service with several of the Communist countries and the Red Army. It has been seen in the Middle East.

Length: 9.54m (31ft 4in). *Width:* 2.80m (9ft 2in). *Height* (with hood): 2.66m (8ft 8in). *Weight:* 7,150kg (15,760lb). *Power:* ZIL–123, 6-cyl., petrol, 110bhp at 2,900rpm. *Payload:* 2,500kg (5,510lb). *Speed:* 60km/hr (37mph). *Range:* 480km (298 miles). *Maker:* Likachev Motor Plant, Moscow.

GAZ–46 *1952–*

The GAZ–46 probably had its origins in the US amphibious vehicles supplied to the Soviet Union during World War II. In many ways it resembles a smaller version of the DUKW (*qv*), and the layout is very similar. It is a four-wheeled vehicle with the engine conventionally mounted in the front and the crew/cargo compartment behind the centre line of the hull. The hull is a watertight box with a sloping bow and stern and a trim vane is erected on the forward deck before entering the water. This allows the vehicle to run down a steep bank into the water and also prevents flooding by high waves or wash. Water propulsion is by a small propeller but the whole design is now old and is being slowly replaced with more modern vehicles such as the BTR-40 (*qv*). Production is thought to have ended some years ago but it is still in use with the Soviet and other Armies.

Length: 5.12m (16ft 8in). *Width:* 1.74m (5ft 8in). *Height* (with hood): 2.10m (6ft 9in). *Power:* M–20, 4-cyl., petrol, 55bhp. *Payload:* 500kg (1,102lb). *Speed:* 90km/hr (56mph). *Range:* 500km (310 miles). *Maker:* Gorky Automobile Factory, Gorky.

PTS

PTS TRACKED AMPHIBIAN *1965–*

The PTS is the latest tracked amphibian in service with the Red Army and with the Warsaw Pact allies. It has also been supplied to Egypt and may have been taken by some other Middle East countries, though the sightings have been few. It is a very large vehicle with a good load-carrying capacity both on land and in the water. It is used not only for the carriage of vehicles and men, which is the usual task, but also for engineer equipment and in particular, bridging gear. The hull is a large watertight box with the tracks running in recesses along each side. A strong tail-gate lets down at the rear to form a ramp so that vehicles can be driven straight in. The crew are seated in the extreme bow and so as not to impede the cargo compartment the engine is under the floor. In the water the propulsion is by twin propellers fitted inside tunnels to prevent damage when on land. Unusually, there is an amphibious trailer for this vehicle. It is a two-wheeled vehicle with a boat-shaped hull and it has two extra sponsons which swing down over the sides to give extra stability in the water. On land they are carried on top of the sides to reduce the width. This trailer can carry a medium artillery-piece while the PTS lifts the towing vehicle, crew, and some ammunition.

Length: 11.52m (37ft 8in). *Width:* 3.32m (10ft 9in). *Height:* 2.65m (8ft 8in). *Weight:* 17,700kg (39,000lb). *Power:* A–712P, V–12, diesel, 250bhp. *Payload:* land, 5,000kg (11,020lb); water, 10,000kg (22,040lb). *Speed:* 40km/hr (25mph). *Range:* 300km (186 miles). *Maker:* Soviet State Factories.

DUPLEX DRIVE (DD) AMPHIBIOUS TANK

When planning for the invasion of Europe got under way, one of the greatest problems was the question of putting tanks ashore. The Dieppe raid had shown that tanks delivered to the beach in landing craft were highly vulnerable since they were unable to fight until they were clear of the craft. The solution was found by Mr. Nicholas Straussler, a mechanical engineer who had designed various armoured cars and other fighting vehicles in pre-war days. His design involved fitting each tank with a deep canvas screen, which could be carried collapsed around the track guard and erected by inflating high-pressure air tubes running vertically inside the screen. With these inflated, steel struts were locked in place so as to retain the screen should the 36 air columns be punctured. The erection of the screen gave the tank additional displacement and thus sufficient buoyancy to float. For propulsion auxiliary propellers were fitted at the rear, geared to the tank's drive sprockets; these revolved in contra-direction and could be swivelled for steering. Maximum speed in water was about 10km/hr (6mph), and the DD tank could swim in up to Force 5 wind conditions.

The first DD tanks to be built were based on the Valentine tank (*qv*), and the design was submitted to the 79th Armoured Division (the British unit responsible for all the specialized armour to be used in the invasion) in April 1943. General P. C. S. Hobart, Division Commander, objected that the Valentine was by then obsolescent, and he insisted that the Sherman tank (*qv*) was the only tank to which it was worth applying the idea.

With the screen erected, none of the occupants of the tank had any vision, nor could any of the weapons be used. In order to operate in

DD Tank

water the tank periscopes were extended so as to see over the screen, and a 'steering platform' at the rear of the turret top allowed the tank commander to stand so as to see across the screen and steer the tank with a hand-operated tiller. A compass was provided for the steersman, and also a gyroscopic compass for the driver.

In operation the DD tanks were loaded into landing craft with the screens down. During the approach to the landing area the screens were erected by inflating the columns from air bottles carried on each tank and the locking struts secured. At a suitable distance – anything from 1–5km (³/₅–3 miles) from the beach, depending upon the sea and other conditions – the landing craft opened its doors and the tanks drove into the water and swam to the beach. As soon as the tracks gripped and the hull level was clear of the water, the tubes were instantly deflated and the locking struts collapsed by hydraulic rams, so that the tank's armament and normal vision devices were immediately available for use. Thereafter the tank drove and operated as a normal land vehicle, the propellers being swung up and locked out of the way as opportunity offered.

The use of DD tanks in the Normandy invasion was of undoubted benefit, even though weather conditions were adverse.

UNITED STATES

DUKW 2½-TON 6×6 AMPHIBIOUS TRUCK *1942–*

This vehicle was developed by the US National Defense Research Council to a military specification and was standardized in October 1942. It was based on the mechanical components of the standard 2½-ton 6 × 6 truck fitted into the watertight hull. For land operation it used the usual six-wheel drive; for water operation it was driven by propeller and steered by a combination of the front wheels and a rear rudder. The driver's cab was separate from the cargo compartment, which could carry 25 men or up to 2½ tons of cargo. Hatches in the deck gave access to storage compartments, to the engine, and to the rear-mounted winch. Two mechanical pumps and one hand pump were provided to clear water from the hull should it be necessary.

Large numbers of these vehicles performed invaluable service in amphibious landings and river crossing operations during the war and a surprising number are still in use today.
Length: 9.44m (31ft 0in). *Width:* 2.54m (8ft 3in). *Height:* 2.66m (8ft 9in). *Weight:* 8,876kg (19,570lb). *Crew:* 1. *Power:* GMC 270, 6-cyl., petrol, 4,417cc, 104bhp at 2,750rpm. *Payload:*

2,426kg (5,350lb). *Winch pull:* 4,535kg (10,000lb). *Speed:* land, 72km/hr (45mph); water, 10km/hr (6.3mph). *Range:* land, 350km (220 miles); water, 80km (50 miles). *Maker:* Yellow Truck & Coach Mfg. Co., Pontiac, Mich.

FORD AMPHIBIOUS JEEP *1943–1945*

This vehicle was standardized in February 1943 and comprised the principal mechanical components of the ¼-ton Jeep (*qv*) in a watertight hull. For movement in water a propeller and rudder were fitted at the rear of the hull. A folding windscreen and canvas hood were provided, and a spray screen at the front could be folded into place to prevent water entering the engine compartment when afloat. It was provided with a towing attachment and could tow a ¼-ton trailer, which would also float when carrying its rated payload.
Length: 4.61m (15ft 1¾in). *Width:* 1.62m (5ft 4in). *Height:* 1.72m (5ft 8in). *Weight:* 1,950kg (4,350 lb). *Crew:* 4. *Power:* Ford, 4-cyl., petrol, 2,199cc, 54bhp at 4,000rpm. *Towed load:* 453kg (1,000lb). *Payload:* 362kg (800lb). *Speed:* land, 88km/hr (55mph); water, 8.8km/hr (5½mph). *Range:* land, 400km (250 miles); water, 56km (35 miles). *Maker:* Ford.

Amphibious Jeep

LARC-5

LARC-5 FIVE-TON LIGHTER, AMPHIBIOUS, RESUPPLY, CARGO, VEHICLE *1960–*

This was developed in the late 1950s as a replacement for the amphibious DUKW cargo truck (*qv*). It consists of a welded aluminium hull with a control cabin at the front, engine room at the rear and cargo space in the middle. Propulsion on land is by four-wheel drive, while in water it is provided by a propeller at the rear. It is far more seaworthy than the DUKW and can carry more cargo or, alternatively, 20 fully-equipped soldiers.

Length: 10.66m (35ft 0in). *Width:* 3.14m (10ft 4in). *Height:* 3.03m (9ft 11in). *Weight:* 9,502kg (20,950lb). *Crew:* 3. *Power:* Cummins, V-8, diesel, 300bhp at 2,400rpm. *Payload:* 4,536kg (10,000lb). *Speed:* land, 48km/hr (30mph); water, 16km/hr (10mph). *Range:* land, 400km (250 miles); water, 60km (37 miles). *Makers:* Le Tourneau Westinghouse; Consolidated Diesel Corp.

LVT-2

LVT-1

LVT-1 LANDING VEHICLE TRACKED MARK 1 *1940-1945*

In the 1930s a Mr. Donald Roebling, a retired engineer, occupied himself in designing an amphibious vehicle to operate in the flooded Florida Everglades. By 1940 he had perfected his Alligator; it was featured in a magazine article and thus the attention of the US Marines was drawn to it. The Marines had been looking for a suitable vehicle to carry troops ashore and then operate on land with them and after examining Roebling's design asked for some modifications and placed an order for 300 late in 1940. This became the LVT-1; made of steel, it was not armoured, and was intended solely as a supply vehicle to back up a landing.

The LTV-1 had a driver's compartment at the forward end; the remainder of the body was used for cargo space except for a small engine room at the rear. The tracks had oblique shoes, which were Roebling's patented method of water propulsion as well as giving the vehicle good grip on land. The rest of the hull was divided into watertight compartments and provided with a bilge pump. The cargo compartment was encircled by a skate rail upon which machine guns could be mounted.

Length: 6.55m (21ft 6in). *Width:* 2.99m (9ft 10in). *Height:* 2.46m (8ft 1in). *Weight:* 9,888kg (21,800lb). *Crew:* 3. *Power:* Hercules WXLC3, 6-cyl., petrol, 6,621cc, 146bhp at 2,400rpm. *Payload:* 2,040kg (4,500lb). *Speed:* land, 19km/hr (12mph); water, 9.8km/hr (6.1mph). *Range:* land, 240km (210 miles); water, 96km (60 miles). *Makers:* FMC, Lake-

land, Fla. and Riverside, Cal.; Donald Roebling Co., Clearwater, Fla; Graham-Paige Motor Corp., Detroit, Mich.; Ingersoll Div., Borg-Warner Corp, Kalamazoo, Mich.; St. Louis Car Co., St. Louis, Mo.

LVT(A)1 LANDING VEHICLE TRACKED, ARMORED MARK 1 *1942-1945*

In spite of the nomenclature this is not a modified LVT-1 (*qv*) but a totally different model. It was, in strict fact, an amphibious tank based on the LVT-2 (*qv*) hull. This was armoured to the same standard as the LVT(A)-2 (*qv*), but had the addition of an M3 light tank (*qv*) turret and gun behind the driver's cab. The cargo compartment was covered in armour so as to approximate to a tank hull, and there was sufficient space for a reduced amount of cargo to be carried if needed.

Length: 7.95m (26ft 1in). *Width:* 3.25m (10ft 8in). *Height* 3.07m (10ft 1in). *Weight:* 14,877kg (32,800lb). *Crew:* 6. *Power:* Continental W670-9A, 7-cyl., radial, air-cooled, petrol, 10,932cc, 262bhp at 2,400rpm. *Armament:* one 37mm gun, three .30 machine guns. *Armour* 6-12mm. *Payload:* 453kg (1,000lb). *Speed:* land, 40km/hr (25mph); water,

LVT(A)1

10.5km/hr (6.5mph). *Range:* land, 200km (125 miles); water, 120km (75 miles). *Maker:* Donald Roebling, Clearwater, Fla; FMC, Riverside, Cal.

LVT(A)2

LVT-2 AND LVT(A)-2 LANDING VEHICLE TRACKED MARK 2 *1943-1945*

After experience with the LVT-1 (*qv*) the US Marines set about designing an improved model. The primary defect with the LVT-1 had been the rigid suspension and track system, which led to frequent breakdowns and poor riding on land. The LVT-2 used an improved track with W-shaped shoes, which could be quickly replaced when they wore down. It also featured a form of sprung suspension which improved the riding quality. To save time and simplify production the engine and major transmission components of the M3 light tank (*qv*) were incorporated in the design. Apart from these mechanical changes the general layout of the craft was the same as that of the LVT-1.

Total production of the LVT-2 amounted to some 2,600, and they were extensively used in the South Pacific. It became obvious that more protection was needed and this gave rise to the LVT(A)-2, the (A) indicating it was armoured. The cab of this pattern was protected with 1.25cm (½-in) armour plate and the rest of the hull with 64mm (¼-in) armour plate. The added weight meant that the craft afloat drew some 5cm (2in) more water, but apart

LVT-3

from that its dimensions and performance were the same as the LVT-2.

LVT-2 *Length:* 7.95m (26ft 1in). *Width:* 3.25m (10ft 8in). *Height:* 2.46m (8ft 1in). *Weight:* LVT-2, 11,000kg (24,250lb); LVT(A)-2, 12,245kg (27,000lb). *Crew:* LVT-2, 6; LVT(A)-2, 4. *Power:* Continental W-670-9A, 7-cyl., radial, air-cooled, petrol, 10,932cc, 262bhp at 2,400rpm. *Payload:* 3,152kg (6,950lb). *Speed:* land, 32km/hr (20mph); water, 12km/hr (7.5mph). *Range:* land, 240km (150 miles); water, 80km (50 miles). *Makers:* FMC, San Jose, Cal; Graham-Paige Motor Corp., Detroit, Mich.; Ingersoll Div., Borg-Warner Corp., Kalamazoo, Mich.; St. Louis Car Co., St. Louis, Mo.

LVT-3 LANDING VEHICLE TRACKED MARK 3 *1945-1955*
One of the drawbacks of the LVT-1 (*qv*) and LVT-2 (*qv*) was that the cargo had to be lifted in and out over the side. The Borg-Warner Corporation set about improving matters by moving the engine forward and placing a bottom-hinged door at the rear of the hull which acted as a loading and unloading ramp. This became the LVT-3; it was made slightly wider than earlier models so that a standard Jeep could be driven up the ramp and carried in the cargo space, and it could be used to carry 30 men. Some 3,000 or so were built, and it was first used at Okinawa in 1945. This model used the engine and transmission of the obsolescent M5 series of light tanks (*qv*), and it continued in use in the post-war years.

Length: 7.46m (24ft 6in). *Width:* 3.40m (11ft 2in). *Height:* 3.02m (9ft 11in). *Weight:* 12,065kg (26,600lb). *Crew:* 3. *Power:* Twin Cadillac, each V-8, petrol, 5,670cc, 148bhp at 3,200rpm. *Payload:* 4,082kg (9,000lb). *Speed:* land, 27km/hr (17mph); water, 9.6km/hr (6mph). *Range:* land, 240km (150 miles); water, 120km (75 miles). *Makers:* Graham-Paige Motor Corp., Detroit, Mich.; Ingersoll Div., Borg-Warner Corp., Kalamazoo, Mich.

LVT-4 LANDING VEHICLE TRACKED MARK 4 *1944-1955*
This was developed by FMC in the same manner as the LVT-3 (*qv*), by moving the engine forward so as to allow for a ramp door at the rear of the hull. Since no major changes of engine were made, the design was faster to

completion and the first LVT-4 were in action at Saipan in June 1944. Its superiority over the earlier models, due to it being easier and quicker to load and unload, led to it being produced in greater numbers; over 8,300 were built.

A slightly modified version was the LVT(A)-4, which, like the LVT(A)-1, was virtually an amphibious tank. The cargo compartment was covered, the entire vehicle armoured, and the turret of the Howitzer Motor Carriage M8, with 75mm howitzer, was installed. This vehicle was then used as a close-support equipment for US Marine landings and proved highly effective. This also had its debut at Saipan; after the war a number had the turrets removed and replaced by those of

LVT-4

the M24 light tank, complete with 75mm gun.
Length: 7.95m (26ft 1in). *Width:* 3.25m (10ft 8in). *Height:* 2.46m (8ft 1in). *Weight:* LVT-4, 12,428kg (27,400lb); LVT(A)-4, 17,898kg (39,460lb). *Crew:* 6. *Power:* Continental W670-9A, 7-cyl., radial, petrol, air-cooled, 10,932cc, 262bhp at 2,400rpm. *Payload:* 4,082kg (9,000lb). *Speed:* land, 32km/hr (20mph); water, 12km/hr (7½mph). *Range:* land, 240km (150 miles); water, 120km (75 miles). *Makers:* FMC, San Jose, Cal., Riverside, Cal, and Lakeland, Fla.; Graham-Paige Motor Corp., Detroit, Mich.; St. Louis Car Co., St. Louis, Mo.

LVTP-5 LANDING VEHICLE TRACKED, PERSONNEL, MARK 5 *1955-1970*
LVTH-6 LANDING VEHICLE TRACKED, HOWITZER, MARK 6 *1955-1970*
Once the war ended the US Marines drew up a specification for a fully armoured and more powerful landing vehicle and these came into service in the middle 1950s.

The LVTP-5 and LVTH-6 were basically similar. They both had: a squared-off armoured body with the tracks set low in the sides and with a ramp door at the forward end; roof hatches to give additional means of entry

to the cargo space; and the driver in a slightly raised cab with cupola at the forward end of the hull. The engine compartment was at the rear. The LVTH-6 used the same hull and track unit, but had a turret with a 105mm howitzer mounted centrally, slightly behind the driver.

In spite of (or perhaps because of) their advanced design these vehicles proved unsuccessful, due to heavy maintenance demands and frequent breakdowns. They were eventually replaced by the LVTP-7 series (*qv*).
Length: 9.04m (29ft 8in). *Width:* 3.55m (11ft 8in). *Height:* 3.06m (10ft 0in). *Weight:* 31,650kg (69,790lb). *Crew:* 3 + 25 passengers. *Power:* Continental, V-12, petrol, 810bhp at 2,400rpm. *Payload:* 8,164kg

Troops prepare to board LVT-4s

(18,000lb). *Speed:* land, 48km/hr (30mph); water, 11km/hr (7mph). *Range:* land, 300km (190 miles); water, 90km (57 miles). *Maker:* Borg-Warner Corp., Kalamazoo, Mich.

LVTP-7 LANDING VEHICLE TRACKED PERSONNEL MARK 7 *1964–*

In 1964 the US Marines laid down a specification for a new LVT to replace the unsuccessful LVTP–5 series (*qv*). The resulting LVTP–7 appeared in service in August 1971 and a total of 942 were built, the last being delivered in 1974.

The hull is of welded aluminium armour and is ballistically shaped to some extent. The driver is at the front, alongside the engine and transmission; at the right side of the hull is a turret mounting a .50 machine gun; and the rear of the hull is taken up by a cargo and passenger compartment which can carry 25 troops. The suspension and track unit resembles that of contemporary tanks and uses large roadwheels held on torsion bars. Water propulsion is by two water-jet units at the rear, with deflectors for steering; in emergency the vehicle can also propel itself in water by its tracks.

Minor variations of this design are the LVTR–7, a recovery vehicle with winch and repair equipment; the LVTC–7, a command vehicle with additional communications equipment; and the LVTE–7, an engineer vehicle with bulldozer blade and minefield clearing equipment. The latter has not been cleared for production. An LVTH–7 with 105mm how-

LVTP-7

itzer was also designed, but this was not taken into service.

Length: 7.94m (26ft 1in). *Width:* 3.27m (10ft 9in). *Height:* 3.26m (10ft 8in). *Weight:* 18,257kg (40,250lb). *Crew:* 3 + 25. *Power:* Detroit Diesel 8V53T, V–8, turbocharged, diesel, 400bhp at 2,800rpm. *Payload:* 4,990kg (11,000lb). *Armour:* 6–35mm. *Speed:* land, 64km/hr (40mph); water, 13.5km/hr (8.5mph). *Range:* land, 480km (300 miles); water, 100km (60 miles). *Maker:* FMC, San Jose, Cal.

M29 Cargo Carrier

M28 Cargo Carrier

M28 AND M29 (WEASEL) CARGO CARRIERS *1948–*

Operations in Alaska, the Aleutians and other arctic areas showed the US Army the need for a specialist vehicle to move in snow, and in 1943 the Cargo Carrier M28 was introduced. This was a lightweight tracked vehicle with 46cm-wide (18in) tracks for good flotation over soft snow and with a limited cargo-carrying capacity. The engine was at the rear and the drive sprockets at the front in accordance with current tank practice.

This was followed quickly by the M29 model, in which the positions of engine and drive were reversed; this gave better distribu-

tion of weight and improved the space available inside the vehicle so that more cargo or passengers could be carried. The suspension arrangements were also improved, and the tracks widened to 50cm (20in).

Finally came the M29C version, which made the vehicle fully amphibious. Buoyancy chambers were added at front and rear, a spray guard on the bow, twin rudders coupled to the steering controls, and a small centrally mounted capstan. Propulsion in water was done by track action. These modifications were so designed that a standard M29 could be converted into an M29C in the field if required. Both the M29 and M29C remained in US service into the late 1960s and several are still in use in other countries.

Length: 4.87m (16ft 0in). *Width:* 1.70m (5ft 7½in). *Height:* 1.80m (5ft 11in). *Weight:* 2,721kg (6,000lb). *Crew:* 2–4. *Power:* Studebaker 6–170, 6-cyl., petrol, 2,779cc, 65bhp at 3,600rpm. *Payload:* 544kg (1,200lb). *Towed load:* 1,905kg (4,200lb). *Speed:* land, 58km/hr (36mph); water, 6.5km/hr (4mph). *Range:* land, 280km (175 miles); water, 40km (25 miles). *Maker:* Studebaker Corp., South Bend, Ind.

GLOSSARY

M3 75mm Gun Motor Carriage

AP Armour Piercing. Ammunition which is designed to penetrate armour plate. Also used to describe a simple type of armour-piercing shell of solid construction.

APC Armoured Personnel Carrier. A vehicle, either wheeled or tracked, for carrying men under protective armour.

APCBC: Armour-Piercing Capped, Ballistic Cap. An AP shell fitted with a soft cap to reduce the tendency to ricochet when it hits hard armour. This cap is blunt in shape and so a ballistic cap is added to streamline the nose and improve the flight. The ballistic cap is very light and makes no difference to the penetration.

ARV Armoured Recovery Vehicle. A vehicle intended for retrieving damaged tanks on the battlefield. Often based on a current tank.

ANTENNA Radio Aerial.

ARMOUR A generic term for all armoured vehicles. Also, the protective plate used in

these vehicles. Originally all armour was homogenous, or of one material throughout. Though still used, much modern armour is made in several layers, either separated, or rolled together, or spaced by other materials.

ARMOURED CAR Wheeled vehicle protected by armour. Usually taken to mean that the vehicle is armed with one or more guns. The oldest form of armoured vehicle.

AUTOMATIC GUN A gun which, once the first shot has been fired by the gunner, will continue to load and fire itself until the trigger is released or the ammunition expended.

AUXILIARY GENERATOR A small engine used in large vehicles to supply electricity and any other necessary service. It is quieter and cheaper to run than starting the main engines.

BARV Beach Armoured Recovery Vehicle. A specialized vehicle for use in amphibious landings.

BARBETTE An open gun mounting, generally with protection to the front and sides, but not the back or top. Naval term.

BASKET In an armoured vehicle, the framework suspended below the turret which carries the turret crew and certain equipment. It rotates with the turret.

BOGIE A combination of wheels in a track-laying system. Usually taken to mean any two wheels joined by a common axle and acting as roadwheels. Ex-railway expression.

CARGO CARRIER Vehicle for the carriage of supplies and ammunition.

CHAR French expression for tank.

CHASSIS The section of a vehicle which contains the engine, transmission and suspension.

COAXIAL Guns which are mounted in the same turret or mantlet and which rotate together. They need not elevate together.

COMBAT VEHICLE American term for any vehicle which is intended for fighting.

DECKING Usually taken to mean the upper surface of the superstructure, often that part above the engine.

GROUSER An extension added to the track of a vehicle to reduce the ground pressure and enable it to cross soft surfaces.

HOLLOW CHARGE also SHAPED CHARGE or HEAT. A means of defeating armour by concentrating the power of an explosive charge into a jet of extremely high-velocity gas. This then burns its way through the armour to make a small but deep hole. The jet can cause damage on the other side of the armour. Frequently used in man-carried weapons, but less often in tank guns.

HOWITZER An artillery piece with a short barrel and capable of high-angle fire.

HULL That portion of an armoured vehicle which contains the crew, engine, transmission and all associated equipment. The turret and/or superstructure are mounted on the hull and the suspension supports it.

IDLER The end wheel of a track which is not driven. The idler is usually mounted so that it may be moved to adjust track tension.

LANDING VEHICLE TRACKED A light tracked amphibian propelled in water by its tracks.

MANTLET A piece of armour which protects the hole in the vehicle through which a gun is mounted. The mantlet is usually attached to the gun, but it is often a large casting rotating with the gun trunnions.

MOBILITY A measure of ability of a vehicle to move.

MUZZLE BRAKE An attachment on the muzzle of a gun which reduces the recoil force.

PERISCOPE An optical device which enables a viewer to see over obstacles by the use of mirrors or prisms. Used in armoured vehicles to enable the crew to look out through the top while remaining under cover.

PRIME MOVER A vehicle intended to tow trailers or similar loads.

RECONNAISSANCE VEHICLE or RECCE VEHICLE A vehicle specifically intended for the gathering of information on the battlefield. Generally small and light and only armed with light weapons. Sometimes carrying a few infantry for foot patrolling.

ROADWHEEL In a tracked vehicle, one of the wheels which runs on that part of the track which is in contact with the ground.

ROUND A complete unit of ammunition comprising projectile, propellant and ignition.

RUNNING GEAR Another name for suspension.

SEMI–AUTOMATIC A gun in which each shot is fired by the firer pulling the trigger. All loading actions are automatic.

SHAPED CHARGE See Hollow Charge.

SHELL A hollow munition fired from a gun and invariably rifled. Inside the shell may carry a variety of fillings, including high explosive, chemicals, smoke etc. A solid shell is generally referred to as shot.

SHOT A solid shell, usually used for armour penetration.

SLOPED ARMOUR Protective armour so angled that the majority of projectiles will strike it acutely. They will then either ricochet or be forced to penetrate diagonally through the armour and thus have more to overcome.

SNORKEL A long breather-pipe which can be swung up to the vertical so allowing the vehicle to run along the bottom of a water obstacle, partially or fully submerged. It is an alternative to swimming, and somewhat easier for tanks.

SP or SELF–PROPELLED. A term applied to guns which can move under their own power. The great majority of self-propelled guns utilize a tank chassis with the gun mounted in the superstructure. The traverse is generally limited, but the gun is invariably larger than that mounted in the same tank. Exceptions are AA self-propelled guns, which are often a smaller calibre, and a few modern self-propelled guns where the gun is inside a large turret permitting all-round traverse.

SPONSON A gun mounting which projects from the side of the hull of an armoured vehicle. The gun is limited in its arc, and usually can only traverse up to 90°.

SPRING That part of the suspension of a vehicle which absorbs the vertical accelerations caused by uneven ground, and which also enables the driven parts of the suspension to remain in contact with the ground. There are several types of spring:
  Belleville Washers: Heavily dished washers which flatten under load.
  Leaf Springs: Also known as Cart Springs. Made of long thin leaves placed together. Supported at each end and the load applied on the centre.
  Helical or **Coil Spring:** A bar wound in the form of a helix or coil and used in compression.
  Torsion Bar: A bar anchored at one end and attached to an axle at the other. It acts by being rotated by the axle. Often used in tanks where the bars can be located conveniently beneath the floor.
  Volute Spring: A conical spring made from a strip of metal wound so that each coil overlaps the next. Used in compression.
  Rubber: Occasionally used in light vehicles. Usually in compression or torsion.

SPROCKET A toothed wheel which transmits the power to a track.

SPUD Another name for a Grouser.

SUPERSTRUCTURE The upper part of the hull of an armoured vehicle. It may be put to a variety of different uses.

SUPPORT ROLLER also RETURN ROLLER. A small wheel or roller which carries the track on its upper return run between the idler and the sprocket. Where there is no return roller the track runs back on the top of the roadwheels.

SUSPENSION That part of the vehicle comprising the wheels, tracks and their associated springing.

TANK A primary fighting vehicle combining the qualities of firepower, protection and mobility. Almost invariably tracked, but wheeled tanks do exist.

TRACK An endless belt circling the sprocket, idler, roadwheels and return rollers of a tracked suspension and providing the surface for the wheels to run on. Tracks vary in complexity from simple rubber-based bands to complex linkages of metal castings joined by pins and hinges.

TRANSMISSION The system for varying the speed and power of the drive between the engine and the driven wheels or tracks. It is usually a mechanical arrangement but it is possible to use electric transmission, in which case the engine drives a dynamo and each wheel is driven by an electric motor. Speed and power is determined by varying the electric current.

TURRET A revolving armoured box mounting one or more guns and carrying the crew needed to man these guns.

INDEX